LEARNING CIVIL PROCEDURE

SECOND EDITION

By

Jeffrey W. Stempel

Doris S. & Theodore B. Lee Professor of Law
William S. Boyd School of Law
University of Nevada Las Vegas

Steven Baicker-McKee

Assistant Professor of Law
Duquesne University School of Law

Brooke D. Coleman

Associate Professor of Law
Seattle University School of Law

David F. Herr, Esq.

Maslon Edelman Borman & Brand, LLP
Adjunct Professor of Law
William Mitchell College of Law

Michael J. Kaufman

Associate Dean for Academic Affairs and Professor of Law
Director, Education Law and Policy Institute
Loyola University Chicago School of Law

LEARNING SERIES

WEST
ACADEMIC
PUBLISHING

© 2013 LEG, Inc. d/b/a/ West Academic Publishing
© 2015 LEG, Inc. d/b/a West Academic
444 Cedar Street, Suite 700
St. Paul, MN 55101
1-877-888-1330

Printed in the United States of America
ISBN: 978-1-62810-269-7

DEDICATION

For Ann, Ryan, Shanen and Reed

To Carol, Karen, and Kelsey for their cheerful and enthusiastic support and assistance

To Mark, Dad, Mom, Cole, Ardon and Ezra, with boundless gratitude and love

To My Loving Family

For Gagas

ACKNOWLEDGMENTS

This book reflects not only the collaboration of its five authors but also the influence and support of family, friends, and colleagues. Including the names of everyone who has touched our group in some way concerning our involvement with civil litigation would produce a list resembling a phone book that could not realistically be used here. But we wish to give particular mention to those who have been particularly important in the development of this coursebook.

Jeff thanks Mayara Cueto-Diaz, Elizabeth Ellison, Steve Gensler, Dan Hamilton, Doris and Ted Lee, Mary Langsner, Jenapher Lin, Thom Main, Suzette Malveaux, Annette Mann, David McClure, Ann McGinley, Dick Morgan, Linda Mullenix, Emily Navasca, Ashley Newton, Russ Pearce, Ngai Pindell, Jeanne Price, Nancy Rapaport, Sandra Rodriguez, the late Jim Rogers, Mike and Sonya Saltman, Liz Schneider, Steve Subrin, Jean Sternlight, Suja Thomas, Spencer Waller, and John White.

Steve extends his heartfelt thanks to Dean Ken Gormley and the faculty at Duquesne Law School for giving him the chance to pursue his passion. Thanks also to Dean Dan Steinbock, Ken Kilbert, and the rest of the faculty at the University of Toledo for the opportunity to dip his toe into the academic waters. Thanks to Bill Janssen and Bernie Corr for their patience and counsel as he wrestled with whether to dive in. And thanks to his coauthors on this project for their support and friendship.

Brooke thanks Professors Arthur Miller, Jeff Stempel, and Suja Thomas for inspiring and sustaining her dedication to Civil Procedure. Thanks also to Professors Dan Capra, Robert Chang, Julie Shapiro, Norman Spaulding, Adam Steinman, Hon. David F. Levi and Hon. Lee H. Rosenthal for their encouragement and support. This book would not have been possible without the research and editorial assistance of Brett Carnahan, Evelyn Emanuel, Brian Fisher, Jack Guthrie, Albert Kang, Erin Lecocq, Matt Link, Constance Locklear, Kaya Lurie, Crystal Maria, and Joseph Thomas.

David thanks his colleagues at Maslon LLP, for their support and the many members of the bench and bar who have taught so much. Lynette Shanahan deserves boundless thanks for assistance and advice. Finally, he hastens to note that this book would not be the resource it is without the great insights into civil procedure, and civil practice and how to teach them shared so generously by his co-authors.

Mike thanks Professors Zelda Harris, Cynthia Ho, Richard Michael, Alex Tsesis and Spencer Waller for their incredible insight, wisdom, and support. Thanks are also due to Meghan Helder, Sarah Kaufman, Lorena Galvez, Zachary Kaufman, Elaine Gist and Ashley Heard for their outstanding research and editorial assistance.

We also thank West Academic Publishing for its confidence in us and support of the project. Special thanks are due to Executive Acquisitions Editor Louis Higgins for his steadfast and capable support and to Laura Kruse and Megan Anderson of Red Line Editorial. Thanks also to Deborah Jones Merritt, for helping to launch us toward this book and for generous comments on a draft manuscript.

PREFACE

In a world of scarce resources, there seems nonetheless to be no shortage of civil procedure books, many of them quite good. But in our years of teaching the course, we had yet to find the optimal coursebook and found ourselves supplementing the other casebooks we have used with additional reading and lectures designed to fill the gaps of other books. At the same time, we grew disenchanted with the constant parade of case after case after case as an effective or efficient method of illustrating a particular procedural point. Although the traditional Langdellian case method can be a powerful tool for learning, we do not believe it should be the nearly exclusive tool for teaching civil procedure. Most civil procedure books include 60 or more excerpted cases, some as many as 80 or 90. As some point, a civil procedure book can begin to look merely like a set of bound cases with some connecting transitions.

And what transitions—often notes between the excerpted cases that refer to other cases (often without much or any explanation) under the assumption that busy first-year law students will actually find the time to examine these additional cases in addition to keeping up with the assigned reading, doing legal writing assignments, and grabbing a few hours of sleep while attempting to maintain some semblance of a normal life during law school. These notes often include relatively esoteric procedural questions that, although occasionally fascinating to the law professoriate, are not particularly germane to mainstream civil litigation and almost never come up for the average practitioner. *Learning Civil Procedure* eliminates these "How Many Angels Can Dance on the Head of a Pin?" questions that are a staple following case excerpts in many traditional casebooks and replaces them with examples, exercises, and problems designed to build student mastery of the discipline.

At the same time that some books fall prey to esoteric doctrine, they also often provide students with little or no history or background regarding the discipline. Other books have so much historical or political background that the student may think there has been a registration mistake and the law school has been overrun by the political science department. *Learning Civil Procedure*, although practical in orientation, understands that the civil rules and attendant doctrine did not develop in a vacuum. Good lawyers need to know some of the history and institutions responsible for the current state of civil litigation – and this is provided in this coursebook.

Despite scores of cases, most books provide relatively little opportunity for students to test their knowledge with problems of the type they will encounter in final examinations or in practice. Most civil procedure books also skimp on the building practical litigation and lawyering skills and assessment of dispute resolution realities.

Thus, despite the crowded market of civil procedure books we concluded that there was room for one more—if it was sufficiently different from and an improvement upon the status quo. At the same time we were planning such a book, Thomson/West published *Learning Evidence* by Deborah Jones Merritt and Ric Simmons. This text was a dramatic departure from the traditional evidence casebook in terms of organization, format, presentation, reinforcement, and the use of explanatory scenarios and problems as teaching tools rather than excerpted court cases. In fact, *Learning Evidence* is a coursebook without a single case excerpted at any length. It instead focuses on the Rules of Evidence as the core of the subject and upon the application of those rules to frequently encountered litigation matters.

Learning Evidence was a watershed in law school casebooks and has come close to revolutionizing the field with its success as a widely adopted book that has changed the way the course is taught in many law schools. It inspired West Academic Publishing to create a series of books using this type of approach and solidified our desire to create a civil procedure text in the same vein. We were thrilled to be able to become a part of this emerging new series of coursebooks with *Learning Civil Procedure*.

Learning Civil Procedure follows the popular approach of *Learning Evidence*. In particular *Learning Civil Procedure* is presented in an attractive, readable visual format like all books in West's *Learning* series. As detailed in the Study Guide at the outset of the book, each chapter begins with a list of **Key Concepts** to orient the student and provide a road map for the chapter. Icons, text boxes, and other visual aids differentiate material and help guide the reader. Material that is somewhat tangential but nonetheless important or useful is set of in colored text box bubbles to differentiate it from core material. Excerpted cases are distinctly set off, as are the book's **Examples & Analysis** feature and more extensive **Additional Exercises** that can be used for class discussion. Also unique as compared to other civil procedure casebooks is the **In Practice** feature (marked by the Esq. icon), providing practical litigation knowledge and advice to students, the sort of thing lawyers usually learn only after being in the field.

We also adapt *Learning Evidence* as necessary to the differences between civil procedure and other first-year courses and evidence or other upper-division courses. Particularly for a first-year course, part of the educational goal is to create culturally literate lawyers who not only know doctrinal and practical substance but also appreciate the history and of the field and key developments in the field.

For civil procedure and other courses, some of the key developments are cases – and we have therefore not completely eliminated the study of cases from our approach to studying civil litigation. In particularly, iconic cases such as *Louisville & Nashville Railroad v. Mottley* (Ch. 1), *International Shoe v. Washington* (Ch. 2), *Hickman v. Taylor* (Ch. 12), and *Erie v. Tompkins* (Ch. 4) have been included, as have current applications of difficult areas of law such as *Teamsters v. Terry* (Ch. 16), *Shady Grove Orthopedic v. Allstate Insurance* (Ch. 4), and *Taylor v. Sturgell* (Ch. 20). But despite including these cases, *Learning Civil Procedure* includes only 15 excerpted cases along with some occasionally extensive quotation of a few other important cases – a far cry from other civil procedure books.[1] Each of these cases is excerpted in sufficient length and detail that students gain the advantages of analyzing a case that has not been unduly condensed and edited. The case excerpts permit a close reading of precedent and extensive discussion of judicial analysis to the extent desired by the instructor.

Rather than cases alone, this book focuses on the on the nature of civil litigation as a whole, in particular the Rules of Civil Procedure, statutes, and constitutional provisions most often operative in civil litigation. Important provisions are excerpted in the book itself so that students need not be constantly flipping back and forth between the casebook and a rules-and- statutes supplement. After the introduction of a concept, the applicable rule or

---

1   On a website supporting use of this book, we are providing edited versions of many of the important, classic, or iconic cases that of necessity had to be left out in order to create the slimmer, more problem-oriented book published. But if an instructor wishes to add additional cases or substitute one important case (*e.g.*, *Gasperini v. Center for the Humanities* instead of *Shady Grove v. Allstate* when studying the *Erie* doctrine in Ch. 4), this can easily be done.

statutory provision is quoted, followed by examples and analyses that help flesh out the concept and emphasize the provision. Students engage in application of new concepts and develop basic understanding before moving on to new topics. This approach is more consistent with current learning theory than the traditional pure case method.

Learning Civil Procedure is also distinguished from other books in the field by its practice-based orientation. It is the only civil procedure coursebook by a major publisher with authors who have more than 60 years of collective full-time litigation experience as well as more than 50 years of full-time law teaching experience. *Learning Civil Procedure* focuses on the civil procedure issues that arise with frequency in real world litigation and addresses them in a practical manner, without sacrificing material and opportunity to explore more complex, less frequent problems that may be of pedagogical value.

Learning Civil Procedure is a broad but succinct coursebook easily adapted to a four-credit, five-credit, or six–credit format. More time can be taken with the material in the book itself and it can be supplemented with additional cases and materials for discussion available in the book's Teacher's Manual or website. *Learning Civil Procedure* is adaptable to suit the instructor's discretion and is also well-supported. The Teacher's Manual contains extensive analyses of the more involved and complex **Additional Exercises** at the end of each Chapter as well as supplementary analyses of the **Examples and Explanations** in each chapter so that the instructor can go beyond the answers provided in text. Similarly, the Teacher's Manual provides analysis of questions posed in the book and provides material for further discussion at the discretion of the instructor.

In addition to edited versions of additional cases for possible use and Westlaw links to full versions of many cases found in traditional civil procedure casebooks that do not appear in *Learning Civil Procedure*, the book's website also provides a "Comprehensive Study Guide" that instructors may provide to students in order to provide them with additional grounding in legal concepts useful in studying civil procedure and other law school course. The website also provides PowerPoint slides that the instructor may use in class if desired to assist in covering the assigned material.

Learning Civil Procedure can stand on its own but most instructors will probably assign a supplementary book containing the entire Federal Rules of Civil Procedure and important statutes and constitutional provisions.

In addition, as noted in the Comprehensive Study Guide available on the website, there are a number of useful treatises that can further flesh out the student's understanding of the civil litigation issues addressed in this book.

We have endeavored to make *Learning Civil Procedure* a fun and effective part of legal education and hope students and faculty will agree. Questions or comments can be addressed to the authors according to the contact information listed below. We hope users of this book come to understand and appreciate the civil litigation process, succeed as litigators and lawyers, and work during their careers to maintain and improve our system of civil dispute resolution.

April 2015

Jeffrey W. Stempel
Doris S. & Theodore B. Lee Professor of Law
William S. Boyd School of Law
University of Nevada Las Vegas
4505 Maryland Parkway – Box 451003
Las Vegas, Nevada 89154-1003
702-895-2361
jeff.stempel@unlv.edu

Steven Baicker-McKee
Assistant Professor of Law
Duquesne University School of Law
600 Forbes Ave.
Pittsburgh, PA 15282
(412) 396-2258
baickermckees@duq.edu

Brooke Coleman
Associate Professor of Law
Seattle University School of Law
901 12th Avenue
Seattle, WA 98122
206-398-4987
colemanb@seattleu.edu

David F. Herr, Esq.
Maslon Edelman Borman & Brand LLP
3300 Wells Fargo Center
90 South Seventh Street
Minneapolis, MN 55402-4140
612-672-8350
david.herr@maslon.com

Michael J. Kaufman
Associate Dean for Academic Affairs and Professor of Law
Director, Education Law and Policy Institute
Loyola University Chicago School of Law
25 East Pearson Street
Chicago, IL 60611
312-915-7143
mkaufma@luc.edu

TABLE OF CONTENTS

Chapter 9: Complex Joinder and Class Actions 397
Key Concepts 397
Introduction 397
A. Intervention 398
Rule 24 399
B. Indispensable Parties 404
Rule 19(a)-(c) 405
C. Interpleader 410
Rule 22 412
28 U.S.C. § 1335 414
28 U.S.C. § 2361 415
D. Multiparty, Multiforum Jurisdiction Act 417
E. Class Actions 417
1. The Constitutional Requirements for Class Actions 420
Hansberry v. Lee 311 U.S. 32 (1940) 424
2. Class Actions in Practice 428
Rule 23(a) & (b) 428
Rule 23(c) 432
Rule 23(d) 435
Rule 23(e) 436
Quick Summary 439

Chapter 10: Rule 15: Amended and Supplemental Pleadings 441
Key Concepts 441
Introduction 441
A. The Rule 442
B. Rule 15(a): Amendments Before Trial 442
Rule 15(a) 442
1. Rule 15(a)(1) Amendments as a Matter of Course 443
2. Rule 15(a)(2) Amendments by Party Consent or Court Approval 445
C. Rule 15(b): Amendments During and After Trial 448
Rule 15(b) 448
D. Rule 15(c): Relation Back of Amendments 450
Rule 15(c)(1)(A) 451
1. Relation Back Under the Applicable Law's Statute of Limitations 451
2. Relation Back When Adding a Claim 452
Rule 15(c)(1)(B) 452
3. Relation Back When Adding a Party 453
Rule 15(c)(1)(C) 453
E. Rule 15(d): Supplemental Pleadings 457
Rule 15(d) 458
Quick Summary 465

TABLE OF CASES

The principal cases are in bold type. Cases cited or discussed in the text are in roman type. References are to pages. Cases cited in principal cases and within other quoted materials are not included.

STUDY GUIDE

If you are taking this course in your first year of law school, you will be developing study techniques that are likely different from those you used in previous educational settings. Moreover, even within law school, different courses may require different approaches.

One learning technique that has traditionally been fundamental to law school is applying the "Socratic method" to judicial opinions. Under this methodology, students read cases, usually appellate cases, with the professor then asking questions about the cases. The questions are designed to draw out the important principles and the underlying policies and tensions. Although learning to read cases is an extremely important, if not essential, skill to acquire in your first year of law school, it can also be an inefficient way to learn the substantive concepts embedded in the cases.

Civil Procedure is different from most first year classes, in that substantial portions of the class are based on codified rules, not just case law. Accordingly, this book takes a different approach. As part of the LEARNING SERIES, this book de-emphasizes cases and focuses more on explanation and short hypotheticals, illustrations, or problems. The vision behind *Learning Civil Procedure* is that because Civil Procedure is in significant measure based on codified rules, it is preferable to teach it by explaining the concepts, then allowing students to explore the contours and parameters of those concepts through studying the rules and illustrative examples, rather than distilling the concepts from cases. Notwithstanding the de-emphasis of cases, there are times when the study of cases may be the optimal learning tool. In addition, there are some classic, key, or famous cases that a literate lawyer should know. Consequently, this book at times includes case excerpts for study.

Civil Procedure is also an opportunity to focus on how to read and construe statutory language, another critical skill for lawyers in almost every discipline. Accordingly, rather than refer you to a supplement, this book sets forth the key language of major Federal Civil Rules and important procedural statutes in text. So while you try to develop and hone your skills in reading cases in your other classes, you can focus on reading statutory language in this class. As you analyze the cases, statutes and rules presented throughout this book, you also should begin to assess the overall fairness and efficiency of the American civil justice system.

1. Organization of This Book

Learning Civil Procedure starts with some general concepts that apply to civil litigation, then proceeds through the stages of a lawsuit. Look at the table of contents to see the progression through this material in detail, and also at the flowchart at the end of the book, which depicts the generalized flow of a civil dispute through its various stages.

The initial concepts include:

- **subject matter jurisdiction** (the types of cases that courts—and particularly federal courts of limited jurisdiction—are permitted to handle);

- **personal jurisdiction** (the ability of a court in one state to force a defendant to participate in the proceedings);

- **notice** (the manner in which a defendant must be served with the papers commencing litigation);

- **venue** (the rules controlling which courts are appropriate and convenient for handling a lawsuit, and for transferring a lawsuit to more convenient courts); and

- **the *Erie* Doctrine** (which determines whether federal or state law applies to cases proceeding in federal court).

The book then proceeds to cover:

- the commencement of a lawsuit and framing of the issues through the complaint and answer;

- early motions to dispose of a case;

- rules controlling which claims and parties may be joined in a single lawsuit;

- amending pleadings;

- the discovery process (where the parties can seek information and evidence relating to the claims and defenses);

- motions to dispose of a case after discovery;

- trials, including the right to a jury;

- post-trial motions;

- appeals; and

- the effects of the results of the case on future cases involving related issues and parties.

Each chapter addressing these topics follows the same organizational structure.

The chapters start with a list of the **Key Concepts**. This list identifies the important concepts contained in the chapter. As you read the chapter, make sure you are understanding these key concepts.

The chapters next contain an **Introduction**, which provides an overview of the concepts covered in the chapter and puts those concepts in context.

The Rule. Periodically, important portions of the rules and statutes are reprinted in colored boxes. Key language in the rules and statutes is set forth in bolded text. Be sure to look carefully at this bolded language to see the role it plays in the rule or statute and in the explanation that follows.

THE RULE   Rule 20(a)(2)

Defendants

Persons . . . may be joined in one action as defendant if:

(A) any right to relief is asserted against them jointly, severally, or in the alternative with respect to or **arising out of the same transaction or occurrence**, or series of transactions or occurrences; and

(B) any **question of law or fact common to all defendants** will arise in the action.

Examples and Analysis. One of the fundamental aspects of the approach in *Learning Civil Procedure* is the many problems found throughout the text. Some of these problems are followed by the answers, in the Examples and Analysis sections. These problems or "hypos" are designed to illustrate how the concepts in question apply in different contexts or situations. Look at the example, conduct your own analysis and reach your own conclusions, then look at the analysis.[1]

> **EXAMPLE:** Parker sells his house to Dan for $100,000. Dan pays by check, and the check bounces. Parker sues Dan in federal court. Two months after Dan is properly served, he still has not answered the complaint or filed any papers. Can Parker take advantage of Rule 55 default, and if so how?

Text Boxes. When words or concepts are discussed in the text that might be unfamiliar, or that warrant some "sidebar" discussion, look to the text boxes nearby for that additional content. Typically, the words tied to the text box will be printed in the same color as the text box background.

> *Sua sponte* means that the court did something on its own. It did not respond to a party's motion or request, but instead spotted an issue and requested the parties to respond.

From the Court. Although *Learning Civil Procedure* de-emphasizes cases, judicially-created doctrines and interpretation form an important part of the law governing civil litigation. We have excerpted portions of cases that are particularly defining or otherwise important in the evolution this area of the law. Those cases are set out in boxes and contain the caption or "style" of the case at the beginning. Other cases that are important but do not warrant reprinting are described in the text.

IN PRACTICE

This content gives you a window into how the rules and concepts in civil procedure work in practice, in the real world. Often, lawyers and judges routinely handle procedures in a manner that is not necessarily intuitive from the text of the rules themselves. Learning Civil Procedure includes authors with extensive experience in civil litigation who can tell you how things really work.

Additional Exercises. Near the end of each chapter, we list additional questions. In this section, the answers are not provided. You should test your understanding of the material by attempting to analyze and answer these questions, and you should be prepared to discuss them in class.

 **Quick Summary**. Finally, each chapter ends with a quick summary of the important principles from the chapter. This section will not contain everything you need to know from the chapter, but you should make sure you have mastered these concepts.

2. How to Prepare for Class

The key to picking up the concepts in *Learning Civil Procedure* lies in the hypotheticals presented in the Examples and Exercises. The explanation of the concepts in the text is quite important, of course, but the essence of legal thinking is applying legal principles to different fact patterns. So it is through the Examples and Exercises that you can test your ability to apply the principles explained in the text.

Study after study has shown that active learning is more effective than passive learning. In other words, if you simply read the material in the book and listen in class, you may have a difficult time comprehending and recalling the material. In contrast, if you process the information actively, by preparing outlines, participating in study groups where you discuss the concepts, and by working through sample problems, you are much more likely to be successful.

Accordingly, when preparing for class, do not just passively read the text and the Examples and Exercises. Rather, test yourself with the Examples and Exercises. In the Examples and Analysis section, cover the provided Analysis and conduct your own, then review the analysis to check your understanding. With the Additional Exercises, conduct your analysis and be prepared to present it in class.

These Exercises will help you develop a fuller understanding of the material, prepare for your exams, and ultimately become a better lawyer.

3. How to Prepare for Exams

Both for your exam in civil procedure and eventually for the bar exam, proper preparation and strategy are instrumental in your success.

Law school exams typically measure your knowledge of the various rules and doctrines that you learn in class and in the class text, and your ability to apply those rules and doctrines to fact patterns, some of which may be close calls or in the "gray area."

The Key Concepts and **Quick Summary** sections should give you a big picture summary of the concepts for which you will be responsible. Make sure you understand these issues and the underlying analysis that is discussed in this book and during class. If you create an outline, which many students find helpful, the issues identified in these sections are a good starting point. Also, pay attention to the language that is bolded in the text of the rules— these are key phrases that you should be familiar with and that you may want to use in your answers.

Your outline and the Key Concepts and **Quick Summary** will help you to get prepared to discuss the rules and doctrines, but how do you prepare to apply those rules and doctrines to the hypotheticals in your exam questions? That is where the Examples and Exercises come in. If you can absorb how the rules apply in the different contexts presented in the Examples and Exercises, you will be well on your way to understanding how the rules work in practice in different contexts. There are also many good sources of additional questions and answers if you want additional practice.

The way that you present your knowledge is also important. A logical presentation of the information, following the IRAC (Issue, Rule, Analysis, Conclusion) approach (or whatever legal writing approach your law school teaches) can make a big difference in how your exam answers are received and graded.

Finally, be sure to follow general test taking advice: take a deep breath and relax at the outset of the exam; read the instructions carefully and make sure you follow them; read the questions carefully and make sure you answer the actual question; review the issues presented in class and make sure you address all issues raised by the questions; consider all the facts in the question, and make sure to address the facts that work against your conclusion as well as those that favor it; and budget your time.

Enjoy your study of Civil Procedure. It can be fascinating and rewarding, even if you are not headed to a career in the courtroom.

LEARNING CIVIL PROCEDURE
SECOND EDITION

I

The Rules of Civil Procedure provide the infrastructure for resolution of civil disputes. This text studies the Rules as they are applied in litigation and some of the cases applying them. The study of procedure is necessarily a study of practice. There is certainly theory involved, but the Rules and the procedures they create are fundamentally practical in nature.

The Rules don't actually resolve the disputes, nor do they create substantive rules of law. They facilitate and structure the process whereby disputes can be resolved fairly and efficiently. Indeed, the hallmark of procedural rules is that they are transubstantive—they apply across types of disputes. The rules for pleading, discovery, trial, and appeal generally apply with equal force to tort and contract cases, to product liability, securities, and antitrust matters. How they are applied may vary depending on the needs of particular cases, but the rules apply across the board.

The twenty chapters in this book follow a fairly typical model of how cases progress through the system. The chapters take up the issues in the order in which they are most commonly encountered, starting in Unit I (Forum Selection Issues) with threshold questions about where a dispute may be resolved and progressing through Unit II (Commencement of the Case), which deals with some of the structural rules governing lawsuits—how a claim is pled, how a party may respond to the complaint, how various claims and parties may be joined in a single action, and how pleadings may be amended. Unit III addresses Development of the Case, which focuses primarily on discovery—the collection of procedures whereby parties learn the details of claims and evidence that bear on the issues. These procedures are important in virtually every case, and consume the majority of the time and effort expended in most cases. Unit IV, examining the adjudication

process itself, discusses the right to a jury trial and the procedures governing decision short of trial (dismissal and summary judgment), as well as
trial itself. This final unit also discusses post-trial motions and appeals and
ultimately the reduction of the dispute to a judgment.

Unit I addresses several related areas, all of which must be considered before an informed decision can be made about how and where to resolve
a dispute. These four chapters—Chapter 1 (Subject Matter Jurisdiction),
Chapter 2 (Personal Jurisdiction), Chapter 3 (Venue), and Chapter 4 (Applicable Law)—are generally thought of as threshold issues. They are different from many other procedural topics because they may include questions
of constitutional law.

Subject matter jurisdiction of the federal courts (Ch. 1), for example, is
defined in large part by the fundamental structure of our federal system
of government defined in the United States Constitution. Specific statutes
implement the constitutional mandates of Article III, Section 1 of the Constitution, calling for the establishment of "inferior" courts. The study of the
complex—and some would say arcane—interaction of the constitution, the
various Congressional acts that implement the constitutional mandate over
the years, as well as a robust common law make jurisdiction a favorite topic
of civil procedure professors and textbook authors. This book addresses
the most important of the cases as well as the constitutional and statutory
provisions providing firm grounding in this fundamental area.

Chapter 2 covers personal jurisdiction. Subject matter jurisdiction asks
which courts, or whether a particular court or courts, have legal authority
to address a dispute of the type raised in a particular case. Personal jurisdiction asks a similar question, but it focuses not on the nature of the dispute
but whether the parties are properly entitled to avail themselves of that
court's authority and whether the court can impose a judgment against the
party sued. At its simplest, personal jurisdiction will answer whether an
Arkansas court can resolve a dispute between an Arkansas consumer and,
for example, a California manufacturer. Personal jurisdiction is also subject
to constitutional constraints, but typically the concerns arise not under the
provisions establishing the courts, but the due process clauses which limit
how the courts can assert authority over an individual or corporate person.

Chapter 3 addresses venue, studying where a case can properly be brought.
Although sometimes related to personal jurisdiction or subject matter ju-

risdiction, venue is fundamentally different and more practical, and asks where a dispute can be heard. It focuses on the location with respect to the particular dispute and particular parties involved, and not the broader questions of whether the court can properly hear that category of case. Venue also examines the ability of courts to transfer cases to other courts when the convenience of the parties and witnesses would be served by doing so.

Chapter 4 discusses choice of law. This topic is largely a common law subject, and addresses what body of law—typically what states' law applies when there are connections in the case across state lines, or whether state or federal law applies. Occasionally truly foreign law—the law of another nation—is at issue and may affect the outcome of a case. This discussion of choice of law is important and is particularly important to address before a lawsuit is filed. In many instances, the court is prone to follow its own law—a Nevada court has some tendency to favor the application of Nevada law to disputes before it, even in a case between two Texas companies undertaking a joint venture in Nevada or a tort claim brought by a Florida consumer against a New York drugstore chain that just happened to cause injury in Nevada. The rules for deciding what law applies are complex and consider many variables. The answer to these questions may be outcome-determinative. How that decision is made is the subject of the discussion in Chapter 4. A very important case in Chapter 4 is *Erie Railroad Co. v. Tompkins*, which deals with the source of law applied in federal court cases based on diversity of jurisdiction. *Erie* is a time-honored decision more than 75 years old that continues to impact court decisions rendered every day by federal courts throughout the United States.

These subjects are all important to deciding whether to commence litigation and in determining where to bring a case if litigation is appropriate. They are threshold issues because failure to address them in advance frequently results in dismissal or transfer of the case, added expense for the parties, or simply failure to pursue the best litigation strategy for the client.

1

Subject Matter Jurisdiction

Key Concepts

- The power—or subject matter jurisdiction—of federal and state courts to adjudicate particular kinds of claims
- The limited nature of federal subject matter jurisdiction
- The constitutional and statutory structure of federal subject matter jurisdiction
- The primary grants of subject matter jurisdiction to the federal courts: (1) cases that arise under federal law; and (2) controversies in which there is a diversity of citizenship
- Supplemental jurisdiction
- Removal jurisdiction

Introduction

Subject matter jurisdiction is the power of a state or federal court over the subject matter of a case or controversy.

Each state has its own judicial system. Most states have created a three-level court system: (1) the courts of original jurisdiction, where complaints are filed to initiate lawsuits and trials are conducted; (2) the courts of appeals, which typically only have jurisdiction to review orders and judgments entered by the courts of original jurisdiction; and (3) the supreme court of the state, which has the ultimate jurisdiction to review important rulings made by the state's lower courts.

The states have given to their courts of original jurisdiction a variety of labels, including circuit courts, district courts or superior courts. Most of these state courts in America are courts of **general** subject matter jurisdiction. As a rule, these courts have the power to adjudicate all kinds of civil actions. The only exception to that rule is if there is **exclusive** jurisdiction granted to a different court. Many states have granted exclusive jurisdiction to special courts within the state, which have the sole power to hear specific kinds of cases such as domestic relations matters or small claims matters. Moreover, the federal courts have exclusive jurisdiction to adjudicate some kinds of special cases, such as those involving admiralty. 28 U.S.C. § 1333.

In the absence of an explicit grant of exclusive jurisdiction to the federal courts, however the state courts have subject matter jurisdiction even over claims which can be filed in federal court. The state courts and the federal courts have **concurrent** jurisdiction over those claims, which means that the claims can be adjudicated in either federal or state court. In those situations in which the federal and state courts have concurrent jurisdiction over a claim, the plaintiff can choose to file the claim in either state court or federal court.

The **federal** courts are courts of **limited** jurisdiction. The United States Constitution must delegate the power to adjudicate a particular kind of case to the federal judiciary, and Congress must grant that power to the lower federal courts.

The relationship between the subject matter jurisdiction of the federal and state courts can be displayed as follows:

As this diagram suggests, the vast majority of all civil actions in America are litigated in state court rather than federal court. Because state courts have virtually unlimited subject matter jurisdiction, the issue of whether a state court has subject matter jurisdiction over a particular claim is rarely litigated.

The limited jurisdiction delegated to the federal courts, on the other hand, gives rise to a great deal of litigation about whether the federal courts have subject matter jurisdiction over a particular claim. Attorneys who represent plaintiffs therefore must have a comprehensive and deep understanding of federal jurisdiction in assessing their ability to file a civil action in federal court. Defense counsel as well must appreciate the nuances of federal jurisdiction in deciding whether to move to dismiss an action for the lack of jurisdiction or to attempt to remove an action filed in state court to federal court. The important practical issue of whether the federal courts have subject matter jurisdiction over a civil action requires a careful analysis of the constitutional structure of the federal courts.

THE CONSTITUTIONAL STRUCTURE OF THE FEDERAL COURTS

THE CONSTITUTION Art. III

Article III, Section 1. The **judicial Power** of the United States shall be vested in one **Supreme Court**, and in such **inferior Courts** as the **Congress may** from time to time ordain and **establish**.

Article III, Section 2. The judicial Power shall extend to all Cases, in Law and Equity:

arising under this Constitution, the Laws of the United States, and Treaties made, or which shall be made, under their Authority;

to all Cases affecting Ambassadors, other public Ministers and Consuls;

to all Cases of admiralty and maritime Jurisdiction;

to Controversies to which the United States shall be a Party;

to Controversies between two or more States;

between Citizens of the same State claiming Lands under Grants of different States; and between a State and Citizens of another State;

between Citizens of different States;

between a State, or the Citizens thereof, and foreign states, Citizens or Subjects.

* * *

The 10th Amendment to the Constitution provides: The powers not delegated to the United States by the Constitution, nor prohibited by it to the States, are reserved to the States respectively or the people.

EXPLANATION

 In Article III, the United States Constitution establishes the federal judiciary. Article III, Section 1 expressly creates only one federal court: the United States Supreme Court. That Section, however, also delegates to Congress the power to establish the "inferior" federal courts. Congress' power to create the lower federal courts is also granted in Article I, which enables it to establish courts that are inferior to the Supreme Court.

Article III, Section 2 of the Constitution delineates the "judicial power" that is given to the federal courts. That power is given directly to the United States Supreme Court. The same power also is granted to Congress, which in turn can extend that power to any lower federal courts it decides to create.

The Tenth Amendment to the Constitution makes clear that the judicial power of the federal courts is limited to the express grants of power in Article III. The powers that are not explicitly delegated in Article III to the federal courts must be reserved to the states.

In light of the constitutional structure of the federal judiciary, the issue whether the federal district courts have subject matter jurisdiction requires a two-step analysis. First, the Constitution must delegate the power to the federal judiciary in Article III. Second, Congress through its legislation must supply the power to its lower, federal district courts.

The Constitution grants to the Supreme Court the power to adjudicate cases "arising under" federal law, and controversies between citizens of different states. Congress has also delegated to its lower federal courts these two primary jurisdictional bases: 28 U.S.C. § 1331 (Federal Question Jurisdiction) and 28 U.S.C. § 1332 (Diversity Jurisdiction). Most of the claims filed in federal court acquire subject matter jurisdiction from one of these jurisdictional bases. *See* Administrative Office of the United States Courts Annual Report of the Director (2012) (84% of all civil actions filed in federal court are based on either federal question (49%) or diversity jurisdiction (35%)). These two primary jurisdictional categories will be explored in greater detail in this chapter.

 EXAMPLES & ANALYSIS

Based on the fundamental constitutional structure of the judicial branch, consider the following questions:

EXAMPLE: Does Congress have the power to create the lower federal courts?

Analysis: Yes. The Constitution expressly delegates to Congress the power to create the lower federal courts. Congress has in fact used that power and has created the federal district courts and the federal appellate courts. The federal judicial system currently is divided into 94 federal judicial districts. The federal district courts are courts of original jurisdiction; they are the trial courts in the federal system, where complaints are filed to initiate civil lawsuits. The districts are organized into 12 regional circuits.

Each of those circuits has a United States Court of Appeals. The appellate courts have been granted appellate jurisdiction, and thus have the power only to hear appeals from orders and judgments entered by the federal district courts in their region. A map of the federal circuit courts is included in the Appendix.

EXAMPLE: Can Congress abolish the lower federal courts?

Analysis: Yes. The Constitution allows, but does not require, Congress to create the lower federal courts. Accordingly, Congress has the power to eliminate those courts. If it ever decided to eliminate those courts, however,

Congress would likely have to provide some mechanism for managing any pending litigation.

EXAMPLE: Can Congress give its lower federal courts more power than granted to the federal judiciary in Article III of the United States Constitution?

Analysis: No. The judicial power of the Supreme Court, and of the lower federal courts created by Congress, is limited to the express grants of judicial power in Article III of the Constitution. By virtue of the Tenth Amendment, any power not expressly delegated to the federal government in Article III must be reserved to the states. Congress cannot grant to its lower federal courts more power than is delegated to the federal judiciary in Article III of the United States Constitution.

EXAMPLE: Can Congress give to its lower federal courts less power than allowed in Article III? For example, could Congress grant subject matter jurisdiction to the lower federal courts to adjudicate all cases arising under federal law, except those involving the right to privacy?

Analysis: Yes. Although Congress cannot give to its lower federal courts **more** power than allotted in the Constitution, it can give to its lower federal courts **less** power than allotted. Congress need not exercise the full extent of the constitutional power that it has been given. Accordingly, Congress need not grant original jurisdiction to the federal district courts over any cases arising under federal law. In fact, Congress did not grant to its lower federal courts the power to adjudicate cases arising under federal law in any systematic way until it passed the Judiciary Act of 1875.

Nor must Congress grant to its lower federal courts the power to adjudicate any cases between citizens of different states. In fact, Congress has often debated whether to eliminate such "diversity jurisdiction" from its lower federal courts. Rather than eliminating diversity jurisdiction entirely, Congress thus far has made the political judgment to **limit** the kind of diversity cases that can be adjudicated in its lower federal courts.

FEDERAL QUESTION JURISDICTION: CASES ARISING UNDER FEDERAL LAW

Key Concepts

• The constitutional grant of federal question jurisdiction

• The separate and narrower congressional grant of federal question jurisdiction to the lower federal courts

Introduction

The Framers of the Constitution gave to the federal judiciary the power to resolve cases arising under federal law because they wanted to foster a uniform, national interpretation of federal law. Congress, as well, recognized "the importance, and even necessity of **uniformity** of decisions throughout the whole United States, upon all subjects within the purview of the constitution." *Martin v. Hunter's Lessee*, 1 Wheat. 304, 347-48 (1816) (Story, J.) (emphasis in original).

In addition, the Framers and Congress empowered the federal courts to resolve cases arising under federal law because they believed a federal judiciary that specializes in federal law would develop expertise in the adjudication of federal issues and be more likely to apply federal law correctly. Because federal-question cases are litigated often in federal court, those courts, "have acquired a considerable expertness in the interpretation and application of federal law. . . . As a result, the federal courts are comparatively more skilled at interpreting and

> This citation to the Supreme Court's opinion refers to Henry Wheaton, who served as the official Reporter of Supreme Court Decisions from 1816-1827. The Reporter of Decisions was responsible for compiling, editing and publishing the Supreme Court's opinions. This case appeared in the first volume prepared by Wheaton, at page 304. The specific quotation appears on pages 347-48. The Supreme Court's opinions now are published by the government printing office and are compiled in numbered volumes referenced by "U.S." The *Osborn* case has both notations. The opinions issued by the federal appellate courts are compiled in the "Federal" ("F.") reporter while those issued by the federal district courts appear in the "Federal Supplement." ("F. Supp.")

applying federal law, and are much more likely correctly to divine Congress' intent in enacting legislation." *See Merrell Dow Pharmaceuticals, Inc. v. Thompson*, 478 U.S. 804, 827 (1986) (Brennan, J. dissenting). Remember, however, that state courts have concurrent jurisdiction over cases arising under federal law. This concurrent jurisdiction is sometimes in tension with the goals of uniformity and expertise.

A. The Constitutional Grant of Federal-Question Jurisdiction

In *Osborn v. Bank of the United States*, 22 U.S. (9 Wheat.) 738 (1824), the Bank of the United States brought suit in federal court against the state auditor of Ohio. The Bank wanted to enjoin the state auditor from collecting from it a tax the Bank alleged to be unconstitutional. The congressional statute chartering the bank authorized it "to sue and be sued in any Circuit Court of the United States." The Supreme Court, in an opinion written by Chief Justice John Marshall, concluded that Congress had the constitutional power to confer jurisdiction over these cases pursuant to the "arising under" language of Article III § 2. In particular, the Court found that the constitutional grant of arising-under jurisdiction was broad enough to include any case in which a federal question could be raised, even in a case in which the Bank brought a breach of contract claim created by state law:

> When a party seeks an **injunction**, the party is asking the court to force the opposing party to do something (or to stop them from doing something). This is different from a remedy seeking monetary damages. An injunction is an equitable remedy. The remedy of monetary damages by contrast is a remedy available at law.
>
> *See* Chapters 15 and 20.

. . . But the question respecting the right to make a particular contract, or to acquire a particular property, or to sue on account of a particular injury, belongs to every particular case, and may be renewed in every case. The question forms an original ingredient in every cause. Whether it be in fact relied on or not in the defense, it is still a part of the cause, and may be relied on. The questions which the case involves, then, must determine its character, whether those questions be made in the cause or not.

> The appellants say that the case arises on the contract but the validity of the contract depends on a law of the United States, and the plaintiff is compelled, in every case, to show its validity. The case arises emphatically under the [federal] law. . . 22 U.S. (9 Wheat.) at 825.

The Court in *Osborn* concluded that the constitutional grant of arising under jurisdiction extends to cases in which federal law is an essential ingredient of a claim.

The *Osborn* case has since been interpreted, however, to extend the **constitutional** grant of arising under jurisdiction to virtually all cases which raise **any federal question**. *See, e.g., Textile Workers Union of America v. Lincoln Mills of Alabama*, 353 U.S. 448, 471 (1957).

B. The Congressional Grant of Federal-Question Jurisdiction to the Lower Federal Courts

THE STATUTE 28 U.S.C. § 1331

Federal Question Jurisdiction

The district courts shall have original jurisdiction of all civil actions **arising under** the Constitution, laws, or treaties of the United States.

EXPLANATION

In this statute, Congress gives to its federal district courts original jurisdiction to adjudicate civil actions that arise under federal law. The congressional grant of arising-under jurisdiction has been interpreted in a series of important Supreme Court cases.

As will be explored later in this Chapter, and detailed in Chapter 7, objections to the court's lack of subject matter jurisdiction can be raised by the parties at any time during the case, including for the very first time during the appeal. Even if the parties fail to raise an objection to the court's lack of subject matter jurisdiction, the court on its own must dismiss an action that lacks subject matter jurisdiction.

Those decisions have limited the scope of arising under jurisdiction granted to the lower federal courts. In other words, the congressional grant of power is more narrow than the constitutional power found in *Osborn*. One of the most significant limitations on the reach of federal question jurisdiction in the lower courts is the well-pleaded complaint rule.

1. The Well-Pleaded Complaint Rule

FROM THE COURT

Louisville & Nashville Railroad Co. v. Mottley
211 U.S. 149 (1908)

Supreme Court of the United States

Appeal from the Circuit Court of the United States for the Western District of Kentucky. . . .

The appellees (husband and wife), being residents and citizens of Kentucky, brought this suit in equity in the circuit court of the United States for the western district of Kentucky against the appellant, a railroad company and a citizen of the same state. The bill alleged that in September, 1871, plaintiffs, while passengers upon the defendant railroad, were injured by defendant's negligence, and released their respective claims for damages in consideration of the agreement for transportation during their lives, expressed in the contract. It is alleged that the contract was performed by the defendant up to January 1, 1907, when the defendant declined to renew the passes. The bill then alleges that the refusal to comply with the contract was based solely upon that part of the act of Congress of June 29, 1906 . . . which forbids the giving of free passes or free transportation. The bill further alleges: First, that the act of Congress referred to does not prohibit the giving of passes under the circumstances of this case; and, second, that, if the law is to be construed as prohibiting such passes, it is in conflict with the 5th Amendment of the Constitution, because it deprives the plaintiffs of their property without due process of law. The defendants demurred to the bill. The judge of the circuit court overruled the demurrer, entered a decree for the relief prayed for, and the defendant appealed directly to this court.

MR. JUSTICE MOODY, after making the foregoing statement, delivered the opinion of the court.

Two questions of law were raised by the demurrer to the bill, were brought here by appeal, and have been argued before us. They are, first, whether the act of Congress of June 29, 1906 makes it unlawful to perform a contract for transportation of persons who, in good faith, before the passage of the act, had accepted such contract in satisfaction of a valid cause of action against the railroad; and, second, whether the statute, if it should be construed to render such a contract unlawful, is in violation of the 5th Amendment of the Constitution of the United States. We do not deem it necessary, however, to consider either of these questions, because, in our opinion, the court below was without jurisdiction of the cause. Neither party has questioned that jurisdiction, but it is the duty of this court to see to it that the jurisdiction of the circuit court, which is defined and limited by statute, is not exceeded.

There was no diversity of citizenship, and it is not and cannot be suggested that there was any ground of jurisdiction, except that the case was a "suit arising under the Constitution or laws of the United States." 25 Stat. at L. 434, chap. 866, U.S. Comp. Stat. 1901, p. 509. It is the settled interpretation of these words, as used in this statute, conferring jurisdiction, that a suit arises under the Constitution and laws of the United States only when the plaintiff's statement of his own cause of action shows that it is based upon those laws or that Constitution. It is not enough that the plaintiff alleges some anticipated defense to his cause of action, and asserts that the defense is invalidated by some provision of the Constitution of the United States. Although such allegations show that very likely, in the course of the litigation, a question under the Constitution would arise, they do not show that the suit, that is, the plaintiff's original cause of action, arises under the Constitution. In *Tennessee v. Union & Planters' Bank*, 152 U.S. 454, 38 L.Ed. 511, 14 S.Ct. Rep. 654, the plaintiff, the state of Tennessee, brought suit in the circuit court of the United States to recover from the defendant certain taxes alleged to be due under the laws of the state. The plaintiff alleged that the defendant claimed an immunity from the taxation by virtue of its charter, and that therefore the tax was void, because in violation of the provision of the Constitution of the United

States, which forbids any state from passing a law impairing the obligation of contracts. The cause was held to be beyond the jurisdiction of the circuit court, the court saying, by Mr. Justice Gray (p. 464): "A suggestion of one party, that the other will or may set up a claim under the Constitution or laws of the United States, does not make the suit one arising under that Constitution or those laws." Again, in *Boston & M. Consol. Copper & S. Min. Co. v. Montana Ore Purchasing Co.*, 188 U.S. 632, 47 L.Ed. 626, 23 S.Ct.Rep. 434, the plaintiff brought suit in the circuit court of the United States for the conversion of copper ore and for an injunction against its continuance. The plaintiff then alleged, for the purpose of showing jurisdiction, in substance, that the defendant would set up in defense certain laws of the United States. The cause was held to be beyond the jurisdiction of the circuit court, the court saying, by Mr. Justice Peckham (pp. 638, 639):

> It would be wholly unnecessary and improper, in order to prove complainant's cause of action, to go into any matters of defense which the defendants might possibly set up, and then attempt to reply to such defense, and thus, if possible, to show that a Federal question might or probably would arise in the course of the trial of the case. To allege such defense and then make an answer to it before the defendant has the opportunity to itself plead or prove its own defense is inconsistent with any known rule of pleading, so far as we are aware, and is improper.

> The rule is a reasonable and just one that the complainant in the first instance shall be confined to a statement of its cause of action, leaving to the defendant to set up in his answer what his defense is, and, if anything more than a denial of complainant's cause of action, imposing upon the defendant the burden of proving such defense.

Conforming itself to that rule, the complainant would not, in the assertion or proof of its cause of action, bring up a single Federal question. The presentation of its cause of action would not show that it was one arising under the Constitution or laws of the United States.

The application of this rule to the case at bar is decisive against the jurisdiction of the circuit court. It is ordered that the judgment be reversed and the case be remitted to the circuit court with instructions to dismiss the suit for want of jurisdiction.

CASE ANALYSIS & QUESTIONS

1. In *Mottley*, the plaintiffs filed their **bill** in federal court in the circuit court for the western district of Kentucky. At the time, that inferior federal court had been established by Congress, and had been given the congressional power to adjudicate cases arising under federal law.

> A **bill** was the label given to the document filed by the plaintiffs to commence the litigation, to present their causes of action and to submit their requests for equitable relief. In federal court and in most state courts, a bill is now called a complaint.

2. The Mottleys' bill included: (1) allegations that the railroad had breached its contract with them by denying them free passage; (2) allegations that the railroad would raise a defense to their breach of contract claim based upon the federal law; and (3) allegations that the railroad's defense based on federal law was unavailing because: (a) the federal law should not be interpreted retroactively, and (b) if the federal law were interpreted retroactively, it would be a violation of the United States Constitution's Due Process Clause.

3. The bill certainly included federal issues. In fact, the defendant filed a **demurrer** to the bill. In many jurisdictions at the time, the filing of a demurrer to a complaint constituted a waiver of a defendant's right to challenge the factual allegations in that complaint. The defendants were required to admit the factual allegations as true. As a consequence, if the defendants were wrong about the law, their admission of the facts would result in losing the case. In virtually all jurisdictions, defendants may now file

> A "**demurrer**" is a response to the complaint by which the defendant asserts that even if all the allegations in the complaint were true, the complaint nonetheless fails to state any cause of action for which the law provides relief. In other words, the plaintiff's claim must be rejected as a matter of law. The demurrer is the modern-day motion to dismiss. (*See* Chapter 7).

a motion to dismiss without waiving their right to challenge the factual allegations in the complaint.

4. When the railroad filed its demurrer to the Mottleys' complaint, which **factual** allegations was it willing to admit as true? What **legal** arguments did the railroad make to the lower federal court to support its assertion that the Mottleys' claim should be dismissed?

5. Did the lower federal court judge accept or reject the railroad's argument that the Mottleys' claim should be dismissed?

6. In determining whether to accept or reject the railroad's demurrer, which legal questions did the lower federal court have to address and resolve? Were the legal questions about state or federal law?

7. In the United States Supreme Court, which precise legal questions did the railroad raise in its appeal from the lower court's order? Why did the United States Supreme Court decide not to resolve those questions?

8. What did the United States Supreme Court mean when it declared that "the court below was without jurisdiction of the cause?" Who argued to the Supreme Court that the court lacked jurisdiction over the cause? When was the issue of whether the court below had jurisdiction first raised? By whom?

9. Were there "federal questions" that had to be answered in order to resolve the Mottleys' claim? If so, why was the existence of those federal questions in this case not sufficient to confer jurisdiction, as it was in *Osborn*?

10. What is the "rule of pleading" alluded to by the *Mottley* court?

11. How does *Mottley* define federal-question jurisdiction?

12. After the Supreme Court concluded that the federal court lacked jurisdiction over the Mottleys' claim, they then re-filed their claim in Kentucky state court. Eventually, the action was appealed again to the United States Supreme Court, this time from the Supreme Court of Kentucky. The United States Supreme Court took the appeal and ruled for the railroad. How did the United States Supreme Court have subject matter jurisdiction over that appeal?

EXAMPLE: Paula, a citizen of New York, files a complaint in federal district court against Donald, also a citizen of New York. In her complaint, Paula alleges both that Donald breached his contract with her for the supply of goods, and that Donald's defense that the contract cannot be enforced because it violates the federal antitrust laws is not valid. Donald moves to dismiss Paula's complaint for lack of subject matter jurisdiction. How should the federal district judge rule?

Analysis: The federal judge should grant Donald's motion to dismiss for lack of subject matter jurisdiction. The issue is whether the federal district court has subject matter jurisdiction over Paula's claim. Federal courts are courts of limited jurisdiction. Therefore, the United States Constitution must grant the power to the federal judiciary and Congress must supply the power to its lower federal courts. There are two primary alternative jurisdictional bases: claims that arise under federal law, and actions in which there are diverse parties.

In order for a claim to arise under federal law in the congressional grant of power to the federal district court, a federal issue must appear on the face of the plaintiff's well-pleaded complaint, and not merely by way of an anticipated defense. In this case, the plaintiff's well-pleaded complaint would have alleged only a state law contract action. Although the defense to that claim might be federal, *Mottley* instructs that the federal issue must appear on the face of the well-pleaded complaint, or part of the plaintiff's own claim, and not merely—as was true here—as a defense. Therefore, Paula's **claim** does not arise under any federal law, and the motion to dismiss should be granted.

a. The Plaintiff as Master of the Complaint

As a rule, the plaintiff is in control of the claims pled and filed. The plaintiff generally may choose to avoid pleading federal claims in order to bar their **removal** to federal court. Under the "artful pleading doctrine," however, the plaintiff may not avoid federal jurisdiction by pleading state law claims that are completely **pre-**

> **Removal**, which will be discussed later in this chapter, is the act of a defendant in removing an action from state court where it was filed to federal court. *See generally* 28 U.S.C. § 1441 et seq.

empted by federal law. Moreover, federal-question jurisdiction will exist over **declaratory judgment** actions only if the underlying claim itself would have raised a federal question on the face of the well-pleaded complaint. *See Skelly Oil Co. v. Phillips Petroleum Co.*, 339 U.S. 667 (1950). In many cases, however, a party who is threatened with a lawsuit will come to court proactively as a plaintiff and seek a declaratory judgment. In *Medtronic, Inc. v. Mirowski Family Ventures, LLC*, 134 S. Ct. 843 (2014), the

> Under Article VI, Paragraph 2, of the United States Constitution, which is often called the Supremacy Clause, federal law "shall be the supreme law of the land." Accordingly, if federal law and state law are in conflict, the federal law **preempts**, or displaces, the state law.

> A **declaratory judgment** is a judgment entered by a court in a civil action in which the court will declare the rights and obligations of the parties with regard to a case or controversy between them. When a plaintiff files a declaratory judgment, the plaintiff is asking the court for a declaration of rights and obligations among the parties.

Supreme Court concluded that in determining whether a declaratory judgment claim arises under federal law, the court must look to the "character of the threatened action" that provoked the claim for declaratory relief. If a claim arising under federal law would have been asserted in the absence of the request for declaratory relief, then a declaratory judgment action, which attempts to preclude a threatened claim that "arises under" federal law, would also arise under federal law.

b. Counterclaims

The fact that a defendant's counterclaim may arise under federal law will not provide subject matter jurisdiction over the plaintiff's claims. *See, e.g., Holmes Group, Inc. v. Vornado Air Circulation Systems, Inc.*, 535 U.S. 826 (2002).

2. Federal Questions Appearing on the Face of a Well-Pleaded Complaint

As *Mottley* indicates, the lower federal courts do not have arising-under jurisdiction over cases in which the federal issue appears merely by way of a defense—even one that is anticipated by the plaintiffs in their complaint. How might a federal issue appear on the face of a plaintiff's well-pleaded complaint? First, the plaintiff's claim itself could be **created by** a federal law.

Second, the plaintiff's claim might be created by state law, but that state law claim might itself raise federal questions.

a. Federal Jurisdiction Over Claims That Are Created by Federal Law

Federal law includes the United States Constitution, treaties and statutes passed by Congress. The Constitution generally does not create any right for private individuals to sue for monetary damages if they are the victim of a constitutional violation. Treaties also do not generally contain language from which a private right of action can be created. Statutes passed by Congress, by contrast, often contain language that expressly or impliedly authorizes a private individual to bring a civil action for monetary damages caused by a violation of the statute. If a federal law expressly or through un-mistakable inference creates a right for private individuals to bring a claim, that claim clearly does "arise under" federal law.

In *American Well Works Co. v. Layne & Bowler Co.*, 241 U.S. 257, 260 (1916), the United States Supreme Court in an opinion written by Justice Holmes, declared: "[a] suit arises under the law that creates the cause of action." Under Holmes' test, a claim arises under federal law if, but only if, that claim is created by federal law. That test would preclude the assertion of federal jurisdiction over claims that are created by state law, but which depend upon a substantial federal question or federal ingredient. As we will discover, the viability of Holmes' narrow test for federal-question jurisdiction is debatable.

EXAMPLES & ANALYSIS

EXAMPLE: Suppose Congress passes a law—The Interstate Food Transportation Safety Act—that has the following provisions:

i. It shall be unlawful to injure any person as a result of the inter-state transportation of food.

ii. The Federal Food Commission shall have the power to enforce this statute.

      iii. Any civil action shall be filed within 2 years of the discovery of the action.

      iv. Any person injured as the result of the interstate transportation of food shall be able to bring a private action to recover damages.

      v. The federal district courts shall have subject matter jurisdiction over all actions brought to redress violations of this statute.

Would a claim by an individual seeking damages for a violation of this statute "arise under" federal law?

Analysis: Yes. In its fourth provision, this federal statute expressly **creates** a private right of action for individuals to sue for damages. As such, the plaintiff's claim would be "created by" federal law. For good measure, the fifth provision makes clear that the federal courts have subject matter jurisdiction over this particular claim.

> **EXAMPLE:** If the fifth provision were deleted, would there still be federal-question jurisdiction over a claim brought by a person injured from a violation of this statute?

Analysis: Yes. The fifth provision makes clear that this statute grants subject matter jurisdiction. But, even in the absence of that sentence, 28 U.S.C. § 1331 itself confers federal jurisdiction over claims that arise under any federal law, including this one. The fourth sentence expressly creates a private right of action, and its existence makes absolutely clear that a claim alleging a violation of this federal statute is created by federal law, and thus does arise under federal law.

> **EXAMPLE:** Would there still be federal-question jurisdiction even if the fourth and fifth provisions were deleted from this federal statute?

Analysis: Probably yes. The deletion of the fourth provision removes language that expressly creates a private right of action. Yet, the third provision contains language from which there is an unmistakable inference that Congress intended there to be a private right of action for viola-

The **statute of limitations** is the amount of time in which a particular cause of action can be brought. It varies depending on the cause of action asserted. The statute generally begins to run from the time of known injury but its running may be "tolled" or suspended in cases where the victim did not know and could not have reasonably known that the defendant had caused injury. It is also tolled when the victim is underage or incapacitated, but when the victim reaches the age of majority (generally 18 years of age) or regains capacity, the limitations period begins running again. The running of the limitations period may also be tolled by fraudulent concealment by a defendant, but only until such time as a reasonable person in the victim's position would have discovered the concealment.

tions of the statute. The language alludes to a civil action and provides a **statute of limitations** period. The private right of action is "implied" by this language. Accordingly, the federal law implicitly creates the claim, and therefore the claim would likely arise under federal law.

EXAMPLE: Would there still be federal-question jurisdiction if the fifth, fourth and third provisions were deleted from this federal statute?

Analysis: In this situation, the federal law would not create a private cause of action, but it would create a **duty** not to injure persons through the interstate transportation of food. Any claim brought by a plaintiff for a violation of that duty would be created by state law, but it would perhaps require the resolution of a federal question. Whether the existence of such a federal question on the face of a plaintiff's complaint is sufficient to establish federal-question jurisdiction is addressed in the following line of Supreme Court cases.

b. Federal Jurisdiction over Claims That Are Created by State Law Rather than Federal Law, but Which Necessarily Depend on a Substantial Federal Question

In *Smith v. Kansas City Title & Trust Co.*, 255 U.S. 180 (1921), a shareholder sued to enjoin a Missouri Trust Company from investing in federal bonds, claiming the Act of Congress authorizing their issuance was unconstitutional. The plaintiff alleged that under Missouri law the company's investment in securities was beyond the lawful power granted by state law and should be enjoined. The cause of action was created by Missouri state law, but the

SUBSTANTIAL
B/C ESSENTIAL
TO SOLVING CASE

claim necessarily depended on the resolution of an interpretation of the Constitution. The Supreme Court held that the action arose under federal law:

> The general rule is that where it appears from the bill or statement of the plaintiff that the right to relief depends upon the construction or application of the Constitution or laws of the United States, and that such federal claim is not merely colorable, and rests upon a reasonable foundation, the District Court has jurisdiction. . . .

255 U.S. at 199.

In *Moore v. Chesapeake & Ohio Railway Co.*, 291 U.S. 205 (1934), however, the plaintiff brought an action under Kentucky's Employer Liability Act, which provided that a defendant who violated a federal employee safety law could not raise a defense of contributory negligence or assumption of risk. The plaintiff alleged that the defendant violated the Federal Safety Appliance Act. Although the cause of action was created by the state, the case depended on a question of federal law. The Supreme Court, however, found that federal-question jurisdiction did not exist, holding that:

> [A] suit brought under the state statute which defines liability to employees who are injured while engaged in intrastate commerce, and brings within the purview of the statute a breach of the duty imposed by the federal statute, should [not] be regarded as a suit arising under the laws of the United States and cognizable in the federal court in the absence of diversity of citizenship.

291 U.S. at 214–15.

In both *Smith* and *Moore*, the plaintiff's claim was created by state law, but depended on the resolution of a federal question. Yet, the Supreme Court found federal-question jurisdiction in *Smith* and not in *Moore*. In *Merrell Dow*, the Supreme Court attempted to clarify whether the existence of a federal issue as part of a claim created by state law is sufficient to confer federal-question jurisdiction.

FROM THE COURT

Merrell Dow Pharmaceuticals Inc. v. Thompson
478 U.S. 804 (1986)
Supreme Court of the United States

Certiorari to the United States Court of Appeals for the Sixth Circuit.

Justice Stevens delivered the opinion of the court.

The question presented is whether the incorporation of a federal standard in a state-law private action, when Congress has intended that there not be a federal private action for violations of that federal standard, makes the action one "arising under the Constitution, laws, or treaties of the United States." 28 U.S. C. § 1331.

NOT ESSENTIAL TO SOLVING CASE

I

The Thompson respondents are residents of Canada and the Mac-Tavishes reside in Scotland. They filed virtually identical complaints against petitioner, a corporation, that manufacturers and distributes the drug Bendectin in the Court of Common Pleas in Hamilton County, Ohio. Each complaint alleged that a child was born with multiple deformities as a result of the mother's ingestion of Bendectin during pregnancy. In five of the six counts, the recovery of substantial damages was requested on common-law theories of negligence, breach of warranty, strict liability, fraud, and gross negligence. In Count IV, respondents alleged that the drug Bendectin was "misbranded" in violation of the Federal Food, Drug, and Cosmetic Act (FDCA), . . . because its labeling did not provide adequate warning that its use was potentially dangerous. Paragraph 26 alleged that the violation of the FDCA "in the promotion" of Bendectin "constitutes a rebuttable presumption of negligence." Paragraph 27 alleged that the "violation of said federal statutes directly and proximately caused the injuries suffered" by the two infants . . . .

Petitioner filed a timely petition for removal . . . alleging that the action was "founded, in part, on an alleged claim arising under the laws of the United States." . . . Respondents filed a motion to remand to the state forum on the ground that the federal court lacked subject matter jurisdiction. Relying on our decision in *Smith v. Kansas City Title & Trust*

Co., . . . the District Court held that Count IV of the complaint alleged a cause of action arising under federal law and denied the motion to remand. It then granted petitioner's motion to dismiss on *forum non conveniens* grounds.

The Court of Appeals for the Sixth Circuit reversed. . . . [N]oting "that the FDCA does not create or imply a private right of action for individuals injured as a result of violations of the act," it explained:

> *Forum non conveniens* will be discussed in Chapter 3. The basic concept is that a court has discretion to dismiss a case filed in a proper forum if the court concludes that the forum is grossly inconvenient and that the case should be adjudicated in a different forum.

> "Federal question jurisdiction would, thus, exist only if plaintiffs' right to relief *depended necessarily* on a substantial question of federal law. Plaintiffs' causes of action referred to the FDCA merely as one available criterion for determining whether Merrell Dow was negligent. Because the jury could find negligence on the part of Merrell Dow without finding a violation of the FDCA, the plaintiffs' causes of action did not depend necessarily upon a question of federal law. Consequently, the causes of action did not arise under federal law and, therefore, were improperly removed to federal court."

We granted Certiorari, and we now affirm.

* * *

[T]he propriety of the removal in this case turns on whether the case falls within the original "federal question" jurisdiction of the federal courts. There is no "single, precise definition" of that concept . . . . This much, however, is clear. The "vast majority" of cases that come within this grant of jurisdiction are covered by Justice Holmes' statement that a " 'suit arises under the law that creates the cause of action.' " . . . *American Well Works Co. v. Layne & Bowler Co.* Thus, the vast majority of cases brought under the general federal question jurisdiction of the federal courts are those in which federal law creates the cause of action. . . . We have, however, also noted that a case may arise under federal law "where the vindication of a right under state law necessarily turned on some construction of federal law."

This case does not pose a federal question of the first kind; respondents do not allege that federal law creates any of the causes of action that they have asserted. This case thus poses what Justice Frankfurter called the "litigation-provoking problem,"—the presence of a federal issue in a state-created cause of action.

* * *

In this case, both parties agree with the Court of Appeals' conclusion that there is no federal cause of action for FDCA violations. For purposes of our decision, we assume that this is a correct interpretation of the FDCA. . . . In short, Congress did not intend a private federal remedy for violations of the statute that it enacted.

* * *

The significance of the necessary assumption that there is no federal private cause of action cannot be overstated. For the ultimate import of such a conclusion, as we have repeatedly emphasized, is that it would flout congressional intent to provide a private federal remedy for the violation of the federal statute. We think it would similarly flout, or at least undermine, congressional intent to conclude that the federal courts might nevertheless exercise federal-question jurisdiction and provide remedies for violations of that federal statute solely because the violation of the federal statute is said to be a "rebuttable presumption" or a "proximate cause" under state law, rather than a federal action under federal law.

. . . Given the significance of the assumed congressional determination to preclude federal private remedies, the presence of the federal issue as an element of the state tort is not the kind of adjudication for which jurisdiction would serve congressional purposes and the federal system.

. . . We simply conclude that the congressional determination that there should be no federal remedy for the violation of this federal statute is tantamount to a congressional conclusion that the presence of a claimed violation of the statute as an element of a state cause of action is insufficiently "substantial" to confer federal-question jurisdiction.

* * *

IV

We conclude that a complaint alleging a violation of a federal statute as an element of a state cause of action, when Congress has determined that there should be no private, federal cause of action for the violation, does not state a claim "arising under the Constitution, laws or treaties of the United States." 28 U.S.C. § 1331.

The judgment of the Court of Appeals is affirmed.

It is so ordered.

CASE ANALYSIS & QUESTIONS

1. In *Merrell Dow*, the Court considered and rejected three arguments that the plaintiff's claim arose under federal law: (1) under *Smith*, federal question jurisdiction is present if a "substantial, disputed question of federal law is a necessary element of one of the well-pleaded state claims"; (2) a federal forum is warranted to ensure uniform interpretation of the federal statute; and (3) "special circumstances" relating to the extraterritorial effect of the statute warrant affording a federal forum.

    The dissent written by Justice Brennan argued that this case was governed by *Smith*, which held that a state law claim **does** arise under federal law if that claim **necessarily depends on a substantial federal question**. The majority responded by contending that even if the plaintiff's claim in *Merrell Dow* necessarily depended on a federal question, that federal question was not "substantial." Why not?

2. Since *Merrell Dow*, the Supreme Court has reaffirmed that a claim created by state law can arise under federal law, but only if that claim necessarily depends on a substantial (*i.e.*, constitutional) question.

    (a) In *Grable & Sons Metal Products, Inc. v. Darue Engineering & Manufacturing*, 545 U.S. 308 (2005), the Court considered whether a case concerning a federal tax law should be heard in federal court. Grable had property seized by the IRS and was then served with notice via certified mail before the IRS sold the seized property to Darue. Grable sued Darue, alleging that federal law required the IRS to serve Grable with personal service, not certified mail, and thus Darue's title was invalid.

The Supreme Court held that this particular claim did involve a substantial federal question, reasoning narrowly that "the national interest in providing a federal forum for federal tax litigation is sufficiently substantial to support the exercise of federal question jurisdiction over the disputed issue . . . [and that accepting federal court jurisdiction] would not distort any division of labor between the state and federal courts."

(b) In *Empire Healthchoice Assurance, Inc. v. McVeigh*, 547 U.S. 677 (2006), however, the Court made clear that, absent the "slim" exceptional circumstances present in *Grable*, a claim created by state law which necessarily depends on the resolution of a federal **statute**, does not raise a substantial enough federal question to establish federal-question jurisdiction. After McVeigh's personal injury action was settled in state court, Empire filed suit in federal court under the Federal Employees' Health Benefits Act of 1959, seeking reimbursement for amounts it had paid for McVeigh's medical care. The federal statute sets up a regime for governmental payments of medical expenses to federal employees like McVeigh, but it does not contain any right of action on behalf of insurance companies like Empire to sue federal employees to recoup the amounts they had paid. Empire's claim therefore was created entirely by state law. While that claim may have involved a federal statutory structure, it did not necessarily depend on any **substantial** federal question. In the wake of *Empire*, *Grable*, and *Merrell Dow*, which federal questions are sufficiently "substantial" to provide federal-question jurisdiction?

(c) In *Gunn v. Minton*, 133 S. Ct. 1059 (2013), the Supreme Court unanimously held that a legal malpractice claim that necessarily depended on a question of federal patent law did not "arise under" federal law for subject matter jurisdiction purposes. Refining its analysis in *Empire Healthchoice* and *Grable*, the Court declared: "federal jurisdiction over a state law claim will lie [only] if a federal issue is: (1) necessarily raised, (2) actually disputed, (3) substantial, and (4) capable of resolution in federal court without upsetting the federal-state-balance approved by Congress." 133 S. Ct. at 1065.

In the case, Minton's legal malpractice claim "necessarily raised" an "actually disputed" federal question regarding the underlying merits of his federal patent infringement case because his claim required a showing that he would have prevailed in the absence of the defendant's malpractice. Nonetheless, the Court concluded that the federal question was not "substantial" because, although it was important to the litigants, it was not important to the "federal system as a whole." 133 S. Ct. at 1066.

Unlike the strong federal interest in the recovery of delinquent taxes at issue in *Grable* or the constitutional issue at stake in *Smith*, the federal question raised by Minton's claim was unique to the merits of his particular action and the state court resolution of that question would not undermine the development of a uniform body of federal law or upset the "balance of federal and state judicial responsibilities." 133 S.Ct. at 1068.

EXAMPLES & ANALYSIS

EXAMPLE: Paula files a complaint against Debra in federal district court, alleging that Debra committed fraud in connection with Paula's purchase of securities in violation of the federal statute that authorizes a private action for damages caused by such fraud. Does Paula's claim arise under federal law?

Analysis: Yes. In this case, the federal issue appears on the face of the plaintiff Paula's well-pleaded complaint—not a defense. Moreover, Paula's claim is **created by** federal law. Congress passed a federal statute that **creates** a private remedy for individuals like Paula who suffer losses caused by this fraud.

EXAMPLE: Paula files a complaint against Debra in federal district court, alleging that Debra's violation of the federal Leadtoy Safety Act caused her injuries. The Leadtoy Safety Act provides that: "It shall be unlawful to manufacture and distribute toys with lead in them. . . Service of process in any civil action to redress violations of this statute may be effectuated through first-class mail." Does Paula's claim arise under federal law?

Analysis: Probably yes. This federal statute does not **expressly** create a private right of action for damages, but it **impliedly** does so because it indicates a method of service of process for civil actions.

EXAMPLE: Paula files a complaint against Dexter Pharmaceuticals, Inc. in federal district court, alleging that it violated the federal Food Drug and Cosmetic Act by failing to warn her of the harmful side-effects of medicine she purchased from the corporation. Does Paula's claim arise under federal law?

Analysis: No. As the United States Supreme Court held in *Merrell Dow*, this claim is not **created by** the federal Food Drug and Cosmetic Act because that statute neither expressly nor impliedly creates a private right of action for damages. It is a classic tort claim, created by state law. Moreover, although the claim may necessarily depend on a question of that federal law, that federal question is not **substantial** enough to satisfy the test for arising-under jurisdiction. The federal question involves only the interpretation of a federal statute, not the federal Constitution. Moreover, the federal provision at issue is not central to a national scheme of federal taxation, as was true in the *Grable* case. As the Supreme Court indicated in *Gunn*, the federal question must be important to the federal system as a whole or to the uniform development of federal law. Accordingly, this claim does not—as it must—**necessarily depend** on a **substantial** federal question.

> **EXAMPLE:** Pam files a complaint in federal district court alleging that agents of the FBI searched her and seized her property in violation of the Fourth Amendment to the United States Constitution's prohibition on unreasonable searches and seizures. Congress has passed a statute expressly allowing individuals who have been injured as a result of violations of their constitutional rights by **state** agents to sue those state agents for damages. *See* 42 U.S.C. § 1983. But Congress has created no such right to sue federal agents. Does Pam's claim arise under federal law?

Analysis: Probably yes. Pam's claim is not expressly created by federal law because the Fourth Amendment to the United States Constitution does not explicitly create any private right of action. In *Bivens v. Six Unknown Named Agents of the Federal Bureau of Narcotics*, 403 US. 388 (1971), however, the United States Supreme Court recognized an implied private right of action against federal officials who violate constitutional rights. Alternatively, Paula's claim here could be viewed as a state law tort claim in which the "duty" breached is supplied by the United States Constitution. As such, her claim would be created by state law, but would necessarily depend on a substantial (*i.e.* constitutional) federal question.

DIVERSITY JURISDICTION

Key Concepts

- The basic requirements for diversity jurisdiction, including complete diversity and the amount in controversy
- The citizenship of individuals, corporations and unincorporated associations for diversity purposes
- Alienage jurisdiction

Introduction

The Framers granted to the federal judiciary the power to adjudicate claims between citizens of different states because they were concerned about the perception that state courts might be biased against out of state citizens.

The Constitution also grants to the federal judiciary the power to resolve controversies involving citizens of the United States and foreign citizens. This grant of power is often labeled "alienage jurisdiction."

THE CONSTITUTION Art. III, § 2

Article III, Section 2 of the United States Constitution extends the judicial power of the United States to controversies *"between citizens of different states . . . and between a State, or the Citizens thereof, and foreign States, Citizens or Subjects."*

A. The Constitutional Grant of Diversity Jurisdiction

By its plain language, the constitutional grant of diversity empowers the federal judiciary to adjudicate any controversy that is "between citizens of different states." That grant of power is broad enough to include the power to resolve cases in which any single plaintiff is from a different state than any single defendant. Accordingly, Congress could legislate that its lower federal courts have broad power over cases in which there is only the slightest diversity. But Congress has given to its lower federal courts less power than allowed by the Constitution.

B. The Limited Congressional Grant of Diversity Jurisdiction

THE STATUTE 28 U.S.C. § 1332

Diversity of citizenship; amount in controversy

Section 1332 provides that the district courts shall have original jurisdiction of all civil actions where **the matter in controversy exceeds the sum or value of $75,000,** exclusive of interest and costs, and is between (1) **citizens of different States** ***.

EXPLANATION

 The congressional statute granting diversity jurisdiction to the lower federal courts limits the constitutional grant of diversity jurisdiction in two key respects: (1) there must be complete diversity; and (2) the amount in controversy must exceed $75,000 without counting any interest due or costs that may be awarded in the litigation.

1. The Rule of Complete Diversity of Citizenship

Chief Justice John Marshall in *Strawbridge v. Curtiss*, 7 U.S. 267 (1806), declared that the congressional grant of diversity jurisdiction to the lower federal courts requires complete diversity of citizenship. In *State Farm Fire & Casualty Co. v. Tashire*, 386 U.S. 523, 531 (1967), the Court confirmed that the rule of complete diversity is a congressional limitation, rather than a constitutional one.

The rule of complete diversity means that no single plaintiff may be a citizen of the same state as any single defendant. The rule precludes the lower federal courts from adjudicating an action in which any plaintiff is a citizen of the same state as any defendant. As such, the lower federal courts will not have jurisdiction over some controversies that are "between citizens of different states."

 EXAMPLES & ANALYSIS

Would there be complete diversity in the following situations?

1. Missouri v. Illinois, Wisconsin

> P (MO) v. D1 (IL); D2 (WI)

> When determining whether there is complete diversity, it is very helpful to diagram the problems, aligning each party and its state of citizenship. Once the plaintiffs are assigned their states of citizenship on one side of the "v." and the defendants are lined up on the other side, it will be apparent that any match of citizenship that crosses the "v." will destroy complete diversity.

Analysis: Yes. No single plaintiff is a citizen of the same state as any single defendant.

2. Missouri v. Illinois, Missouri

> P (MO) v. D1 (IL); D2 (MO)

Analysis: No. This case lacks complete diversity because there is a Missouri plaintiff against a Missouri defendant.

3. Missouri v. Illinois, Illinois

> P (MO) v. D1 (IL); D2 (IL)

Analysis: Yes. In this case, although both defendants are citizens of Illinois, there is still complete diversity because no single **plaintiff** is a citizen of the same state as any single **defendant**.

The rule of complete diversity serves the objective of the congressional grant of diversity jurisdiction to the federal district courts, which is to lessen the apprehension of bias by state courts against out of state parties.

In the second example, an Illinois state court would likely not be biased against a particular "side" of the litigation because there are Missouri parties on both sides. There is no need to go to federal court to avoid bias.

By contrast, in the third example, an Illinois state court judge could be biased against the Missouri plaintiff and in favor of the defendants, both of whom are from Illinois. Accordingly, that action should go to federal court.

In order to decide whether there is complete diversity, the court must determine the citizenship of the parties.

The courts and Congress have created various rules to determine the citizenship of different kinds of parties, including individuals, corporations, and unincorporated associations.

a. The Citizenship of Individuals

FROM THE COURT

Mas v. Perry

489 F.2d 1396 (5th Cir.), *cert. denied,* 419 U.S. 842 (1974)
United States Court of Appeals, Fifth Circuit

Ainsworth, Circuit Judge

* * *

Appellees Jean Paul Mas, a citizen of France, and Judy Mas were married at her home in Jackson, Mississippi. Prior to their marriage, Mr. and Mrs. Mas were graduate assistants, pursuing coursework as well as performing teaching duties for approximately nine months and one year, respectively, at Louisiana State University in Baton Rouge, Louisiana. Shortly after their marriage, they returned to Baton Rouge to resume their duties as graduate assistants at LSU. They remained in Baton Rouge for approximately two more years, after which they moved to Park Ridge, Illinois. At the time of the trial in this case, it was their intention to return to Baton Rouge while Mr. Mas finished his studies for the degree of Doctor of Philosophy. Mr. and Mrs. Mas were undecided as to where they would reside after that.

Upon their return to Baton Rouge after their marriage, appellees rented an apartment from appellant Oliver H. Perry, a citizen of Louisiana. This appeal arises from a final judgment entered on a jury verdict awarding $5,000 to Mr. Mas and $15,000 to Mrs. Mas for damages incurred by them as a result of the discovery that their bedroom and bathroom contained "two-way" mirrors and that they had been watched through them by the appellant during three of the first four months of their marriage.

At the close of the appellees' case at trial, appellant made an oral motion to dismiss for lack of jurisdiction. The motion was denied by the district court. Before this Court, appellant challenges the final judgment below solely on jurisdictional grounds, contending that appellees failed to prove diversity of citizenship among the parties and that the requisite jurisdictional amount is lacking with respect to Mr. Mas. Finding no merit to these contentions, we affirm. Under section 1332(a)(2), the federal judicial power extends to the claim of Mr. Mas, a citizen of France, against the appellant, a citizen of Louisiana. Since we conclude that Mrs. Mas is a citizen of Mississippi for diversity purposes, the district court also properly had jurisdiction under section 1332(a)(1) of her claim.

> When the *Mas* case was filed, the congressional statute granting diversity jurisdiction to the lower federal courts required that the amount in controversy exceed only $10,000. Congress has subsequently increased the amount requirement—first to an amount exceeding $50,000, and now to an amount exceeding $75,000.

It has long been the general rule that complete diversity of parties is required in order that diversity jurisdiction obtain; that is, no party on one side may be a citizen of the same State as any party on the other side. Strawbridge v. Curtiss . . . . This determination of one's State citizenship for diversity purposes is controlled by federal law, not by the law of any State. . . . As is the case in other areas of federal jurisdiction, the diverse citizenship among adverse parties must be present at the time the complaint is filed. . . . Jurisdiction is unaffected by subsequent changes in the citizenship of the parties. . . . The burden of pleading the diverse citizenship is upon the party invoking federal jurisdiction . . . and if the diversity jurisdiction is properly challenged, that party also bears the burden of proof.

To be a citizen of a State within the meaning of section 1332, a natural person must be both a citizen of the United States . . . and a domiciliary of that State. . . . For diversity purposes, citizenship means domicile; mere residence in the State is not sufficient.

* * *

A person's domicile is the place of "his true, fixed and permanent home and a principal establishment, and to which he has the intention of returning whenever he is absent therefrom . . . ." A change of domicile may be effected only by a combination of two elements: (a) taking up residence in a different domicile with (b) the intention to remain there. . . .

It is clear that at the time of her marriage, Mrs. Mas was a domiciliary of the State of Mississippi. While it is generally the case that the domicile of the wife—and, consequently, her State citizenship for purposes of diversity jurisdiction—is deemed to be that of her husband, . . . we find no precedent for extending this concept to the situation here, in which the husband is a citizen of a foreign state but resides in the United States. Indeed, such a fiction would work absurd results on the facts before us. If Mr. Mas were considered a domiciliary of France—as he would be since he had lived in Louisiana as a student-teaching assistant prior to filing this suit . . .—then Mrs. Mas would also be deemed a domiciliary, and thus, fictionally at least, a citizen of France. She would not be a citizen of any State and could not sue in a federal court on that basis; nor could she invoke the alienage jurisdiction to bring her claim in federal court, since she is not an alien. . . . On the other hand, if Mrs. Mas's domicile were Louisiana, she would become a Louisiana citizen for diversity purposes and could not bring suit with her husband against appellant, also a Louisiana citizen, on the basis of diversity jurisdiction. These are curious results under a rule arising from the theoretical identity of person and interest of the married couple. . . . An American woman is not deemed to have lost her United States citizenship solely by reason of her marriage to an alien. 8 U.S.C. § 1489. Similarly, we conclude that for diversity purposes a woman does not have her domicile or State citizenship changed solely by reason of her marriage to an alien.

Mrs. Mas's Mississippi citizenship was disturbed neither by her year in Louisiana prior to her marriage nor as a result of the time she and her husband spent at LSU after their marriage, since for both periods she was a graduate assistant at LSU. . . . Though she testified that after her marriage she had no intention of returning to her parents' home in Mississippi, Mrs. Mas did not affect a change of domicile since she and Mr. Mas were in Louisiana only as students and lacked the requisite intention to remain there. Until she acquires a new domicile, she remains a domiciliary, and thus a citizen of Mississippi. . . .

[The court's discussion of the jurisdictional amount is omitted.] Affirmed.

CASE ANALYSIS & QUESTIONS

1. The *Mas v. Perry* case articulates a number of interpretive rules and presumptions for the application of the diversity statute. The court begins by articulating **the rule of complete diversity** that no single plaintiff may be a citizen of the same state as any single defendant.

2. The court in *Mas v. Perry* also states that diversity must exist when the lawsuit is filed. That rule enables the federal district court to determine whether there is diversity from the face of the plaintiff's complaint, as soon as it is filed. *See Grupo Dataflux v. Atlas Global Group, L.P.*, 541 U.S. 567, 569-72 (2004). The date of filing therefore is the only relevant date for determining citizenship. Subsequent changes in the citizenship of the parties are irrelevant. What is the rationale for this rule?

3. The court declares that a person is presumed to maintain his existing domicile until there is affirmative evidence of a change in domicile. Why?

> Affirmative evidence of a change in domicile would require evidence of a new, true, permanent home **and** a new intent to remain there indefinitely.

4. The court reiterates what was then the "general" rule that a woman takes on a man's domicile upon marriage, until divorce—unless the woman marries an alien. This general rule has since been rejected by some courts. *See e.g., Samuel v. University of Pittsburgh*, 375 F. Supp. 1119, 1134 (W.D. Pa. 1974), *decision to decertify class vacated*, 538 F.2d 991 (3d Cir. 1976). What are the arguments supporting and opposing this seemingly archaic rule?

EXAMPLES & ANALYSIS

EXAMPLE: Portia was born and raised in Wyoming. She currently resides in Boulder, Colorado, where she is a freshman at the University of Colorado. Is there diversity between Portia and Donald, who is a domicile of Wyoming?

Analysis: No. In the absence of affirmative evidence of a change in her domicile, Portia's domicile is still Wyoming. Her residence in Colorado as a student alone is not sufficient to change her domicile to Colorado for diversity purposes. Accordingly, there is no diversity between Portia (a citizen of Wyoming) and Donald (also a citizen of Wyoming).

EXAMPLE: Peter was born and raised in Virginia. After attending college in Virginia, he accepts a full-time job in Maryland, buys a house in Maryland and obtains a Maryland driver's license. He loves Maryland and intends to remain there for a long time. Is there diversity between Peter and Desiree, who is a domicile of Virginia?

Analysis: Yes. Peter has become a citizen of Maryland. Although he is presumed to retain his original domicile of Virginia, there is affirmative evidence here that he has changed his domicile to Maryland: (1) he has established a new permanent home, and (2) intends to remain there indefinitely. Therefore, there would be diversity between Peter (a Maryland citizen) and Desiree (a Virginia citizen).

EXAMPLE: Suppose in that prior example, Peter filed his complaint against Desiree on May 1, and graduated college two weeks later. Would there be diversity?

Analysis: No. In this case, Peter's domicile would have been Virginia because that was his domicile when his lawsuit was filed. Domicile is fixed for diversity purposes when the lawsuit is filed and is not altered by subsequent changes. Therefore, there would be no diversity between Peter (a Virginia citizen) and Desiree (a Virginia citizen).

b. The Citizenship of Corporations

THE STATUTE 28 U.S.C. § 1332(c)(1)

a corporation shall be deemed to be a citizen of every State *** by which it has been **incorporated** and of the State *** where it has its **principal place of business** ***.

A corporation has two separate states of citizenship for diversity purposes. The first is any state in which the corporation is incorporated. The second is where the corporation has its principal place of business, which is typically where its headquarters is located.

EXPLANATION

 A corporation is a distinct legal entity. For diversity purposes, it is deemed to be a citizen of the state or states of its incorporation and the state where its principal place of business is located. Unlike individuals who only have one place of citizenship, corporations have dual citizenship. Both states count when determining whether there is complete diversity. For a long time, the lower federal courts disagreed about the best way to determine where a corporation's principal place of business is located. In *Hertz Corp. v. Friend*, 559 U.S. 77, 92-93 (2010), the Supreme Court settled the issue, holding that a corporation's principal place of business is where, "the corporation's high level officers direct, control, and coordinate the corporation's activities—[which] will typically be found at a corporation's headquarters."

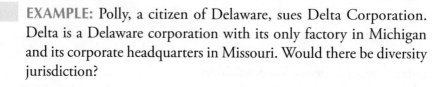

EXAMPLES & ANALYSIS

EXAMPLE: Polly, a citizen of Delaware, sues Delta Corporation. Delta is a Delaware corporation with its only factory in Michigan and its corporate headquarters in Missouri. Would there be diversity jurisdiction?

Analysis: No. Because Delta Corporation is considered to be both a citizen of Delaware and Missouri, there would be no diversity in an action brought against Delta Corporation by Polly, a Delaware Citizen.

EXAMPLE: Would there be diversity in an action against Delta Corporation by a Paul, a Michigan Plaintiff?

Analysis: Yes. Delta Corporation is a citizen of Delaware and Missouri. Therefore, there would be diversity in an action brought by any plaintiff who is not a citizen of Delaware or Missouri.

EXAMPLE: Patricia, a domicile of California, sues Dexter Rental Car Corporation, which is incorporated in Virginia. Dexter Rental's corporate headquarters is located in New Jersey, where it conducts its administrative and executive functions. But all of its manufacturing occurs in California. Should the court dismiss for lack of diversity jurisdiction?

Analysis: No. Dexter Corporation is a citizen of both Virginia and New Jersey, where its headquarters is located. Therefore, there would be complete diversity in an action between Patricia from California and Dexter Corporation from Virginia and New Jersey. The fact that a large amount of business or manufacturing is conducted in a particular state is not a controlling factor when determining the citizenship of a corporation. Only the state of incorporation and principal place of business matter. As the Supreme Court held in *Hertz Corp. v. Friend,* 559 U.S. 77, 92-93 (2010), a corporation's principal place of business typically is where its headquarters is located, not where the bulk of its physical activities take place.

c. The Citizenship of Unincorporated Associations

For diversity purposes, an unincorporated association such as a union, a partnership, a limited partnership, a limited liability company or a political party is deemed to be a citizen of every state in which any one of its members or owners is a citizen. *Lincoln Property Co. v. Roche,* 546 U.S. 81, 89 (2005); *Carden v. Arkoma Assocs.,* 494 U.S. 185, 189 (1990).

EXAMPLES & ANALYSIS

EXAMPLE: The Midwest Wheatgrowers, Ltd. is a limited partnership with limited partners domiciled in Iowa, Nebraska and Missouri. Would there be diversity in an action brought by the Midwest Wheatgrowers Ltd., against Diggers, Corp., a Missouri defendant?

Analysis: No. As an unincorporated association, the Midwest Wheatgrowers, Ltd. is deemed to be a citizen of every state in which any one of its limited partners is domiciled, including Iowa, Nebraska and Missouri. Therefore, there would be no complete diversity in an action against Diggers Corp., a Missouri defendant.

IN PRACTICE

The fact that an unincorporated association is deemed to be a citizen of every state in which any one of its owners or members is domiciled creates significant practical challenges in alleging and satisfying complete diversity. It is extremely difficult to establish complete diversity in an action involving an unincorporated association because it is very likely that a plaintiff will be a citizen of the same state as at least one of the owners or members of the association. Moreover, the plaintiff's attorney often will be unable to determine the citizenship of all of the owners or members of an unincorporated association before filing a lawsuit, making it very hard to acquire sufficient information to allege in good faith the existence of diversity jurisdiction.

d. The Citizenship of Aliens and Related Issues

THE STATUTE 28 USC § 1332(a)

The district courts shall have original jurisdiction of all civil actions where the matter in controversy exceeds the sum or value of $75,000, exclusive of interest and costs, and is between * * *

    (2) citizens of a State and **citizens** or subjects of a **foreign state**; * * *

    (3) citizens of **different States** and in which citizens or subjects of a **foreign state** are **additional parties**; * * *.

EXPLANATION

 In Article III, Section 2, the United States Constitution empowers the federal judiciary to adjudicate actions between citizens of the United States and citizens of a foreign country. Congress as well has given to its district courts subject matter jurisdiction over some cases and controversies that involve aliens.

The constitutional and congressional grant of alienage jurisdiction, however, is precise.

First, a citizen of a foreign country may not sue another citizen of a foreign country in federal court based on diversity. They may sue each other in state court, or in federal court based on another jurisdictional grant of power, such as federal-question jurisdiction.

Second, an American citizen generally may sue or be sued by a citizen of a foreign country based on diversity.

Third, an American citizen domiciled in a particular state may not sue a citizen of a foreign country who has been admitted to the United States as a permanent resident and is domiciled in that same state.

Fourth, a citizen of a foreign country may generally join an action in which an American citizen sues another American citizen from a different state.

Fifth, an American citizen who is domiciled outside America cannot sue or be sued in federal court based on diversity. That party is an American citizen, and therefore cannot go to federal court based on alienage jurisdiction. Moreover, an American citizen who is domiciled outside America is not a citizen of any state in the United States, and therefore cannot establish that its action is between citizens of different states.

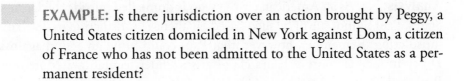
EXAMPLES & ANALYSIS

EXAMPLE: Is there jurisdiction over an action brought by Peggy, a United States citizen domiciled in New York against Dom, a citizen of France who has not been admitted to the United States as a permanent resident?

Analysis: Yes. This action is brought by a citizen of a state against a citizen of a foreign state.

EXAMPLE: Is there jurisdiction over an action by Pamela, a United States citizen domiciled in Florida, against Des, a permanent resident alien from Spain who is domiciled in Wyoming?

Analysis: Yes. This action is between a citizen of a state (Florida) and a citizen of a foreign state (Spain).

EXAMPLE: Is there jurisdiction over an action brought by Pamela, a United States citizen domiciled in Florida against Desiree, a citizen of Spain who has been admitted to the United States as a permanent resident, domiciled in Florida?

Analysis: No. This is the exception. In this case, a citizen of a state (Florida) is bringing an action against a citizen of a foreign state (Spain) who is a permanent resident domiciled in the same state as the plaintiff (Florida).

EXAMPLE: Is there jurisdiction over an action brought by Pamela, a United States citizen domiciled in Florida against Dale, a United States citizen domiciled in New York, and Demitri, a foreign citizen from France?

Analysis: Yes. In this case, a citizen of a state (Florida) is suing a citizen of a different state (New York) and there is an additional party who is a citizen of a foreign state (France).

EXAMPLE: Is there jurisdiction over an action brought by Paul, a United States citizen who has been domiciled in Canada for the past 30 years and Dusty, a United States citizen domiciled in California?

Analysis: No. As an American citizen who is domiciled outside the United States, Paul cannot sue or be sued based on alienage jurisdiction or diversity jurisdiction. Remember, however, that Paul could bring an action against Dusty in federal court if Paul's claim arises under federal law. Moreover, Paul could bring the action against Dusty in state court.

2. The Amount in Controversy Requirement

In order for there to be diversity jurisdiction, the amount in controversy must exceed $75,000 not including interest and costs. In order to determine whether the amount in controversy exceeds $75,000, the courts have created a number of guidelines.

a. The Plaintiff's Viewpoint Rule

Most courts have held that only the value to the **plaintiff** may be used to determine the jurisdictional amount.

b. Non-Monetary Relief

In *Glenwood Light & Water Co. v. Mutual Light, Heat & Power Co.*, 239 U.S. 121 (1915), the Supreme Court recognized that a claim for non-monetary relief such as an injunction could meet the amount in controversy requirement if the **value** of the relief sought by the plaintiff exceeds the jurisdictional amount requirement.

c. Aggregation

A single plaintiff generally may aggregate its claims together against a single defendant to exceed the jurisdictional amount requirement, even if those claims are not related to each other. Two or more plaintiffs, however, generally may not add together their claims to do so. In other words, the value of the relief sought by a single plaintiff must fully exceed $75,000.

d. Amount Alleged or Recovered?

The amount alleged in the complaint is sufficient to satisfy the jurisdictional requirement, even if a lesser amount is obtained at trial or through a settlement. The amount alleged in the complaint, however, will not suffice if it appears to a "legal certainty" that the plaintiff could not recover an amount in excess of $75,000. The amount alleged must exceed the sum or value of $75,000, without regard to interest or costs.

e. Recovery of $75,000 or Less

Although the ultimate amount recovered by the Plaintiff is irrelevant to whether the court has jurisdiction over the action, 28 U.S.C. § 1332(b) authorizes the federal court in its discretion to assess costs (but not attorney fees) against a plaintiff who fails to recover an amount exceeding the sum or value of $75,000. This discretion to award costs, however, is rarely exercised.

EXAMPLES & ANALYSIS

EXAMPLE: Paul, a citizen of California, sues Don, a citizen of New York, seeking $75,000. Is there diversity jurisdiction?

Analysis: No. Although there is complete diversity, the amount in controversy is only $75,000 and thus does not **exceed** $75,000.

EXAMPLE: Paula, a citizen of California, files two claims in the same action against Donna, a citizen of New York. The first claim seeks $40,000 and alleges that Donna breached her contract with Paula. The second unrelated claim alleges that Donna breached an unrelated contract and seeks $50,000. Is there diversity jurisdiction?

Analysis: Yes. A single plaintiff like Paula may aggregate her claims together, even if they are unrelated, to **exceed** $75,000.

EXAMPLE: Paula, a citizen of California, files a claim against Donald, a citizen of New York for $45,000. Peter, a citizen of California, files a related claim in the same action against Donald for $45,000. Is there diversity jurisdiction?

Analysis: No. Neither claim separately exceeds the $75,000 jurisdictional requirement. Moreover, two or more plaintiffs may not aggregate their claims to exceed $75,000, even if those claims are related.

EXAMPLE: Paula, a citizen of California, sues Denise, a citizen of Michigan, for $100,000. Peter, a citizen of California, also sues Denise in the same action, but for only $10,000. Is there diversity jurisdiction?

Analysis: No. There would be diversity jurisdiction over Paula's claim, which exceeds $75,000. But there is no diversity over Peter's claim for only $10,000. Nor can Peter aggregate his claim with that of Paula to exceed $75,000. As we will discover, however, the federal court may nonetheless have **supplemental** jurisdiction over Peter's claim, if it derives from a common nucleus of operative fact with Paula's claim.

EXAMPLE: Portnoy, a citizen of Indiana, owns lakefront property. Dumping Group, Inc., a Delaware Corporation with its headquarters in California, has been dumping toxic waste in the lake. Portnoy files an action against Dumping Group, Inc., requesting only that the court enjoin the defendant from dumping waste in the lake. Is there diversity jurisdiction?

Analysis: Probably. Although Portnoy does not seek any monetary damages, the amount in controversy requirement would still be satisfied if he alleges that the **value** to him of the injunctive relief he seeks would exceed $75,000.

C. Judicially-Created Exceptions to Diversity Jurisdiction

The federal courts have developed judicially-created exceptions to diversity jurisdiction: domestic relations matters, probate cases, and disputes involving real property. These controversies involve local matters of state law on which state court judges have developed a unique expertise. Accordingly, even if the requirements of diversity jurisdiction are met, a federal court will dismiss these particular actions for lack of subject matter jurisdiction.

1. Domestic Relations Matters

In *Ankenbrandt v. Richards*, 504 U.S. 689 (1992), Plaintiff sought diversity jurisdiction over her claims of physical and sexual abuse on behalf of her daughters against the children's father and his companion. The Supreme Court reaffirmed that a domestic-relations exception to diversity does exist, reasoning that Congress' failure to amend its diversity statute to reject the federal courts' long-standing domestic relations exception could be interpreted as congressional acquiescence in that exception.

The *Ankenbrandt* Court also declared that the domestic-relations exception is supported by principles of judicial economy and expertise:

> As a matter of judicial economy, state courts are eminently more suited to work of this type than are federal courts, which lack the close association with state and local government organizations dedicated to handling issues that arise out of conflicts over divorce, alimony, and child custody decrees. Moreover, as a matter of judicial expertise, it makes far more sense to retain the rule that federal courts lack power to issue these types of decrees because of the special proficiency developed by state tribunals over the past century and a half in handling issues that arise in the granting of such decrees.

504 U.S. at 704.

Nevertheless, the Supreme Court concluded that the domestic-relations exception should be limited to claims involving **divorce**, **alimony** or **child custody**. The tort claims for child abuse at issue in *Ankenbrandt* were outside the ambit of those core domestic relations matters. Accordingly, the Supreme Court held that the domestic relations exception did not preclude the assertion of diversity jurisdictions over those tort claims.

2. Probate Matters

The Supreme Court delineated the probate exception in *Marshall v. Marshall*, 547 U.S. 293 (2006). In that case, J. Howard Marshall died, leaving his entire estate to a son and nothing to his widow. Two years later, the widow, the late Vickie Marshall, better known as model Anna Nicole Smith, filed for bankruptcy in the Federal Bankruptcy Court of Central California. In that bankruptcy action, the son filed a claim, asserting the widow had defamed him. The widow counter-claimed, alleging that the son had tortiously interfered to prevent her husband from making her a promised gift of money. The bankruptcy judge dismissed the son's claim and found for the widow, awarding her nearly $500 million. The son filed a post-trial motion, arguing that under the probate exception to federal court jurisdiction, the federal court could not assert subject matter jurisdiction over claims that involve the validity of a decedent's estate planning instrument.

The Supreme Court, however, held that the widow's claim, seeking damages for a widely recognized tort, did not interfere with state probate proceedings and was within the subject matter jurisdiction of the federal courts. According to the Court, the probate exception is limited to actions that involve the **administration of a decendent's estate or the validity or interpretation of a decedent's estate planning document**. 547 U.S. at 311–12.

3. Real Property Disputes

The federal courts also have declined to adjudicate disputes involving **real property**, even if they would otherwise have jurisdiction to do so. Controversies involving land depend on peculiarly local issues such as boundaries, water rights, adverse possession and easements. The federal courts therefore have deferred to the particular expertise of state courts in resolving these matters. *See* Herr, Haydock, & Stempel, MOTION PRACTICE (5th ed.) § 10.03[F] 10-14 (2012) (the federal courts have "long been loath" to adjudicate local property disputes even if there is jurisdiction); John D. Echeverria, Note, *Land Use Regulation, the Federal Courts, and the Abstention Doctrine*, 89 YALE L.J. 1134 (1980) (observing that the federal courts have refrained from adjudicating local controversies, such as disputes over real property, out of comity or deference to state court power).

D. Congressional Exceptions to the General Diversity Rules

Congress has enacted several statutes that alter the complete diversity and amount in controversy requirements of Section 1332 in specific kinds of cases. These cases include some relatively large class actions, interpleader actions in which the holder of a common fund brings a lawsuit against all rival claimants to its own fund, and multi-party, multi-forum cases involving multiple victims of a disaster. These exceptional situations will be addressed in Chapter 9.

SUPPLEMENTAL JURISDICTION

Key Concepts

- The supplemental jurisdiction of the federal courts to assert subject matter jurisdiction over some claims that have no primary jurisdictional basis
- The limits of supplemental jurisdiction

Introduction

We have discussed the two primary bases for subject matter jurisdiction in federal court: (1) cases that arise under federal law; and (2) controversies in which there is complete diversity and in which the amount exceeds $75,000. If any such primary jurisdictional basis exists for each of the claims filed in federal court, then the federal court has subject matter jurisdiction over those claims. Suppose, however, a plaintiff files two claims in federal court and there is a primary jurisdictional basis for the first claim, but no such primary jurisdictional basis for the second claim. The federal court would certainly have subject matter jurisdiction over the first claim. But could the federal court also assert subject matter jurisdiction over the second claim—even though that claim has no primary jurisdictional basis? It certainly would be efficient to allow the federal court to adjudicate both claims together in a single action, particularly when the claims derive from a common core of facts. Yet, the jurisdiction granted to the federal courts is limited to the power granted in the Constitution and from Congress. That limited jurisdiction cannot be expanded for the sake of efficiency or convenience.

Nonetheless, through a series of critical Supreme Court cases, the federal courts were given the power to adjudicate some claims for which there is no primary jurisdictional basis—if those claims derive from a common nucleus of operative fact with a claim for which there is a primary jurisdictional basis. The Supreme Court initially identified this power as "pendant claim jurisdiction," "pendant party jurisdiction," and "ancillary jurisdiction." In 1990, all of these concepts were brought together by Congress in one statute, under the label "supplemental jurisdiction." 28 U.S.C. § 1367.

A. Pendent Claim Jurisdiction

For a long time, the term "pendent jurisdiction" was used when the plaintiff, in the complaint, appended a claim lacking an independent basis for federal jurisdiction to a claim possessing such a basis.

In *United Mine Workers of America v. Gibbs,* 383 U.S. 715 (1966), Paul Gibbs was awarded compensatory and punitive damages in his action against the United Mine Workers of America for alleged violations of § 303 of the federal Labor Management Relations Act, and of the common law of Tennessee. The Supreme Court held that the federal courts have the power to assert subject matter jurisdiction over Gibb's state common law claim, even though there was no independent jurisdictional basis for that claim. The Court reasoned that Article III, Section 2 of the Constitution extends the judicial **power** of the United States to **cases** "arising under [the] Constitution, the Laws of the United States, and Treaties made, or which shall be made, under their Authority . . . ." A "case" could arise under federal law if just one of the claims arises under federal law and the other claims comprise one constitutional "case." Two or more claims can comprise one case that arises under federal law if the federal claim has:

> substance sufficient to confer subject matter jurisdiction on the court. . . . The state and federal claims must derive from a common nucleus of operative fact. But if, considered without regard for their federal or state character, a plaintiff's claims are such that he would ordinarily be expected to try them all in one judicial proceeding, then, assuming substantiality of the federal issues, there is *power* in federal courts to hear the whole.

383 U.S. at 725 (emphasis in original).

The *Gibbs* opinion also made clear, however, that the power:

> need not be exercised in every case in which it is found to exist. . . . [P]endent jurisdiction is a doctrine of discretion. Its justification lies in considerations of judicial economy, convenience and fairness to litigants; if these are not present a federal court should hesitate to exercise jurisdiction over state claims. . . . Needless decisions of state law should be avoided both as a matter of comity and to promote justice between the

parties, by procuring for them a surer-footed reading of applicable law. Certainly, if the federal claims are dismissed before trial, even though not insubstantial in a jurisdictional sense, the state claims should be dismissed as well. Similarly, if it appears that the state issues substantially predominate, whether, in terms of proof, of the scope of the issues raised, or of the comprehensiveness of the remedy sought, the state claims may be dismissed without prejudice and left for resolution to state tribunals. There may, on the other hand, be situations in which the state claim is so closely tied to questions of federal policy that the argument for exercise of pendent jurisdiction is particularly strong. . . . Finally, there may be reasons independent of jurisdictional considerations, such as the likelihood of jury confusion in treating divergent legal theories of relief, that would justify separating state and federal claims for trial. . . . If so, jurisdiction should ordinarily be refused. . . . Once it appears that a state claim constitutes the real body of a case, to which the federal claim is only an appendage, the state claim may fairly be dismissed.

383 U.S. at 726–27.

B. Pendent Party Jurisdiction

In *Finley v. United States*, 490 U.S. 545 (1989), however, the Supreme Court rejected the assertion of pendent jurisdiction where the plaintiff seeks to bring a non-federal, non-diverse claim against an additional **party**. Plaintiff's husband and two of her children were killed when their plane struck electric power lines on its approach to a city-run airfield in San Diego, California. Plaintiff alleged that the Federal Aviation Administration had been negligent in its operation and maintenance of the runway lights and in its performance of air traffic control functions, and invoked jurisdiction under the Federal Tort Claims Act, 28 U.S.C. § 1346(b). Later, plaintiff amended her complaint to include state-law tort claims against both the city of San Diego and the utility company that maintained the power lines. In deciding that the federal courts lacked jurisdiction over the non-diverse state law claim, the Supreme Court declared:

It remains rudimentary law that "[a]s regards all courts of the United States inferior to this tribunal, two things are necessary to create jurisdiction, whether original or appellate. The Constitution must have given to the court the capacity to take it, *and an act of Congress must have supplied it* . . . . To the extent that such action is not taken, the power lies dormant." *The Mayor v. Cooper*, 73 U.S. (6 Wall.) 247, 252, 18 L.Ed. 851 (1868) (emphasis added) . . . . Analytically, petitioner's case is fundamentally different from *Gibbs* in that it brings into question what has become known as pendent-party jurisdiction, that is, jurisdiction over parties not named in any claim that is independently cognizable by the federal court. We may assume, without deciding, that the constitutional criterion for pendent-party jurisdiction is analogous to the constitutional criterion for pendent-claim jurisdiction, and that petitioner's state-law claims pass that test. Our cases show, however, that with respect to the addition of parties, as opposed to the addition of only claims, we will not assume that the full constitutional power has been congressionally authorized, and will not read jurisdictional statutes broadly. . . .

The FTCA, § 1346(b), confers jurisdiction over "civil actions on claims against the United States." It does not say "civil actions on claims that include requested relief against the United States," nor "civil actions in which there is a claim against the United States"—formulations one might expect if the presence of a claim against the United States constituted merely a minimum jurisdiction requirement, rather than a definition of the permissible scope of FTCA actions. Just as the statutory provision "between . . . citizens of different States" has been held to mean citizens of different States and no one else, . . . so also here we conclude that "against the United States" means against the United States and no one else. . . .

> Congress immediately responded to the Supreme Court's invitation by passing 28 U.S.C. § 1367, which grants supplemental jurisdiction over claims that involve different parties.

Whatever we say regarding the scope of jurisdiction conferred by a particular statute can of course be changed by **Congress**. What is of paramount importance is that Congress be able to legislate against a background of clear interpretive rules, so that it may know the effect of the language it adopts. All our cases . . . have held that a grant of jurisdiction over claims involving particular parties does not itself confer jurisdiction over additional claims by or against different parties. so also here we conclude that "against the United States" means against the United States and no one else. . . .

Whatever we say regarding the scope of jurisdiction conferred by a particular statute can of course be changed by **Congress**. What is of paramount importance is that Congress be able to legislate against a background of clear interpretive rules, so that it may know the effect of the language it adopts. All our cases . . . have held that a grant of jurisdiction over claims involving particular parties does not itself confer jurisdiction over additional claims by or against different parties.

490 U.S. at 548–556.

C. Ancillary Jurisdiction

The term "ancillary jurisdiction" was used when a party injected a claim lacking an independent jurisdictional basis by way of a counterclaim, cross-claim, or third-party claim.

In *Owen Equipment & Erection Co v. Kroger*, 437 U.S. 365 (1978), Kroger, a citizen of Iowa, sued Omaha Public Power District (OPPD), a Nebraska corporation, for the wrongful death of her husband, who had been tragically electrocuted. Kroger brought the action in federal district court in Nebraska based on diversity of citizenship, alleging that OPPD's negligent operation of the power line had caused her husband's death. OPPD then filed a **third-party complaint** pursuant to Federal Rule 14(a) against Owen Equipment & Erection Company ("Owen"), alleging that the crane was owned and operated by Owen, and that it was Owen's negligence that had been the proximate cause of Kroger's husband's death.

Kroger was allowed to amend her complaint to name Owen as a defendant, which she alleged was a Nebraska corporation with its principal place of business in Nebraska. OPPD requested, and was

> A **third-party complaint** is a complaint filed by a defendant against a new party that asserts that the new party may be liable for all or part of the defendant's same liability to the plaintiff. Third-party complaints are governed by Federal Rule of Civil Procedure 14 and discussed in Chapter 8.

granted, summary judgment, leaving Owen as the sole defendant. During the course of the trial, it was discovered that Owen's principal place of business was actually in Iowa. As a result, Owen moved to dismiss the case based on a lack of subject matter jurisdiction. The Supreme Court concluded that the federal court lacked subject matter jurisdiction over Kroger's claim against Owen:

It is apparent that *Gibbs* delineated the constitutional limits of judicial power. . . . Constitutional power [, however,] is merely the first hurdle that must be overcome in determining that a federal court has jurisdiction over a particular controversy. For the jurisdiction of the federal courts is limited not only by the provisions of Art. III of the Constitution, but also by Acts of Congress. . . . [A] finding that federal and nonfederal claims arise from a "common nucleus of operative fact," the test of *Gibbs*, does not end the inquiry into whether a federal court has power to hear the nonfederal claims along with the federal ones. Beyond this constitutional minimum, there must be an examination of the posture in which the nonfederal claim is asserted and of the specific statute that confers jurisdiction over the federal claim, in order to determine whether "Congress in [that statute] has . . . expressly or by implication negated" the exercise of jurisdiction over the particular nonfederal claim. . . . The relevant statute in this case, 28 U.S.C. § 1332(a)(1), . . . and its predecessors have consistently been held to require complete diversity of citizenship. . . . Over the years Congress has repeatedly re-enacted or amended the statute conferring diversity jurisdiction, leaving intact this rule of complete diversity. Whatever may have been the original purposes of diversity-of-citizenship jurisdiction, this subsequent history clearly demonstrates a congressional mandate that diversity jurisdiction is not to be available when any plaintiff is a citizen of the same state as any defendant. . . .

Thus it is clear that the respondent could not originally have brought suit in federal court naming Owen and OPPD as codefendants, since citizens of Iowa would have been on both sides of the litigation. Yet the identical lawsuit resulted when she amended her complaint. Complete diversity was destroyed just as surely as if she had sued Owen initially. . . . [U]nder the [contrary] reasoning of the Court of Appeals in this case, a plaintiff could defeat the statutory requirement of complete diversity by the simple expedient of suing only defendants who were of diverse citizenship and waiting for them to implead nondiverse defendants. . . .

It is not unreasonable to assume that, in generally requiring complete diversity, Congress did not intend to confine the jurisdiction of federal courts so inflexibly that they are unable to protect legal rights or effectively to resolve an entire, logically entwined lawsuit. Those practical needs are the basis of the doctrine of ancillary jurisdiction. But neither the convenience of litigants nor considerations of judicial economy can suffice to justify extension of the doctrine of ancillary jurisdiction to a plaintiff's cause of action against a citizen of the same State in a diversity case. Congress has established the basic rule that diversity jurisdiction exists . . . only when there is complete diversity of citizenship. . . . To allow the requirement of complete diversity to be circumvented as it was in this case would simply flout the congressional command.

437 U.S. at 371–77.

In 1990, Congress responded to this line of Supreme Court cases by enacting 28 U.S.C. § 1367, and re-naming these concepts **supplemental jurisdiction**. As you analyze this statute, consider whether Congress has codified, overruled, or modified the Supreme Court's decisions in *Gibbs*, *Finley* and *Kroger*.

D. The Supplemental Jurisdiction General Rule: Section 1367(a) and (c)

THE STATUTE   28 U.S.C. § 1367(a) & (c)

Supplemental Jurisdiction

(a) Except as provided in subsections (b) and (c) or as expressly provided otherwise by Federal statute, in any civil action of which the district courts have **original jurisdiction**, the district courts shall have **supplemental jurisdiction** over all other claims that are **so related** to claims in the action within such original jurisdiction that they form part of the **same case or controversy** under Article III of the United States Constitution. Such supplemental jurisdiction **shall include** claims that involve the joinder or intervention of **additional parties**.

* * *

(c) The district courts **may decline** to exercise supplemental jurisdiction over a claim under subsection (a) if:

(1) the claim raises a novel or complex issue of State law,

(2) the claim substantially predominates over the claim or claims over which the district court has original jurisdiction,

(3) the district court has dismissed all claims over which it has original jurisdiction, or

(4) in exceptional circumstances, there are other compelling reasons for declining jurisdiction.

EXPLANATION

In order for this supplemental jurisdiction statute to apply, a civil action filed in federal court must:

(1) have at least two claims, and

(2) at least one of the claims filed in federal court must have a primary jurisdictional basis.

If so, the federal court has discretion to assert supplemental jurisdiction over additional claims, even if those claims lack a primary jurisdictional basis if the claims are so related to each other as to be part of the same "case." They are part of the same case if they derive from a common nucleus of operative fact. The federal court, however, may decide in its discretion to decline to exercise supplemental jurisdiction.

The statute uses the clause "same case or controversy," which has been read to be the same as "common nucleus of operative fact" from *Gibbs*.

EXAMPLES & ANALYSIS

EXAMPLE: Paula, from Illinois, files two claims in federal court against Development Corp., an Illinois 1 corporation with its principal place of business in Illinois. The first claim alleges a violation of the federal securities laws. The second claim alleges a state-law-created common law fraud claim. The claims stem from the same purchase of stock. Development Corp. moves to dismiss for lack of supplemental jurisdiction. How should the court rule?

Analysis: The motion should be denied. Although Paula's common law fraud claim has no primary jurisdictional basis (it is neither arising under federal law nor diverse), the federal court nonetheless has **discretion** to assert supplemental jurisdiction over that claim because it derives from a common nucleus of operative fact with Paula's federal securities fraud claim. As such, 28 U.S.C. § 1367(a) codifies the result and reasoning in the *Gibbs* case. Notice that 28 U.S.C. § 1367(c) also codifies the factors discussed in *Gibbs* that would guide the federal court's discretion in deciding whether to exercise supplemental jurisdiction over a non-diverse state law claim, including the novelty and complexity of the state law at issue, the predominance of the state law claim, the dismissal of claims over which there is primary jurisdiction, and any other exceptional circumstances.

EXAMPLE: Suppose Paula filed her first claim under the federal securities laws against Development Corp., but filed her second claim for common law fraud against Donald, who is Development Corp.'s CEO from Illinois?

Analysis: The court would still have discretion to assert supplemental jurisdiction. As long as there is a primary jurisdictional basis for one claim, the federal court **generally** has discretion to assert supplemental jurisdiction over additional claims—even if they involve additional parties like Donald. As such, 28 U.S.C. § 1367(a) overturns the result in *Finley*.

EXAMPLE: Suppose Paula filed her first claim under the federal securities laws against Development Corp., but her second claim against Donald was an **unrelated** defamation claim?

Analysis: The court would not have supplemental jurisdiction because the claim for which there is a primary jurisdictional basis does **not** derive from a common nucleus of operative fact with the claim for which there is no such primary jurisdictional basis.

E. The Supplemental Jurisdiction Exception: Section 1367(b)

THE STATUTE   § 1367(b)

Supplemental Jurisdiction

(b) In any civil action of which the district courts have original jurisdiction founded solely on section 1332 of this title, the district courts shall not have supplemental jurisdiction under subsection (a) over claims by plaintiffs against persons made parties under Rule 14, 19, 20, or 24 of the Federal Rules of Civil Procedure, or over claims by persons proposed to be joined as plaintiffs under Rule 19 of such rules, or seeking to intervene as plaintiffs under Rule 24 of such rules, when exercising supplemental jurisdiction over such claims would be inconsistent with the jurisdictional requirements of section 1332.

1. The Section 1367(b) Bar

EXPLANATION

 This statutory exception to Congress' general grant of supplemental jurisdiction is very narrow. The exception only applies when:

(1) the only primary jurisdictional basis in the action is **diversity**;

(2) the **plaintiff** (or a person proposed to intervene or be joined as a plaintiff) brings additional claims;

(3) the plaintiff's additional claims are **against persons** who are, or who are proposed to be, joined to the lawsuit under precisely **enumerated joinder rules**; and

(4) the additional claims **do not otherwise satisfy** the requirements of **diversity** jurisdiction.

Accordingly, the 28 U.S.C. § 1367(b) bar to supplemental jurisdiction does not preclude supplemental jurisdiction if: (1) there is any claim in the action that has a jurisdictional basis other than diversity (*i.e.*, any claim arising under federal law); or (2) a party other than the plaintiff (*i.e.*, defendant) asserts supplemental jurisdiction.

Moreover, the exception to supplemental jurisdiction only applies where the plaintiff attempts to assert claims against persons made parties pursuant to the following specifically enumerated federal joinder rules: 14, 19, 20, and 24. Each of these joinder rules also will be discussed in Chapters 8 and 9.

- Rule 14 generally allows defendants to implead into the lawsuit a brand new claim against a brand new third party defendant, if the new party may be liable to the defendant for "all or part" of the defendant's same liability to the plaintiff.

EXAMPLES & ANALYSIS

EXAMPLE: Paula (a New York citizen) sues Donald (a Wisconsin citizen) in federal court for $100,000, stemming from an auto accident. Donald impleads a new claim against a new party, Tony (a New York citizen). Paula then brings a claim against Tony. Would there be supplemental jurisdiction?

Analysis: No. Here, the only jurisdictional basis is diversity, and Paula (the plaintiff) is bringing an additional claim against a nondiverse party (Tony) joined under Rule 14. This was the situation in *Kroger*, in which the Supreme Court also rejected the assertion of jurisdiction.

- Rule 19 allows and sometimes requires the joinder of additional parties who are necessary for the full and fair adjudication of a civil action. Rule 19 allows the joinder of additional parties on either the plaintiff's or the defendant's side.

EXAMPLE: Paula (from New York) sues Donald (from Wisconsin) for $100,000 arising out of an auto accident that also injures Petra (from Wisconsin). The court decides that Petra must be joined as an additional Plaintiff in order for a full and fair adjudication, and the court wants to use its power under Rule 19 to compel the joinder of Petra. Would there be supplemental jurisdiction over Petra's claim against Donald?

Analysis: No. Here, the only jurisdictional basis is diversity, and Petra (from Wisconsin), who is proposed to be joined as a plaintiff under Rule 19, would be asserting a non-diverse claim against Donald (also from Wisconsin).

- Rule 20 generally allows for the joinder of parties to a single lawsuit so long as the claims against those parties derive from the same transaction or occurrence or at least the same series of transactions or occurrences.

EXAMPLE: Paula (from New York) brings a state law tort claim against Donald (from Wisconsin) for $100,000. Paula attempts to bring an additional claim against Tony (from New York) stemming from the same accident. May Paula use supplemental jurisdiction to do so?

Analysis: No. In this case, the only jurisdictional basis is diversity, and Paula (the plaintiff) is asserting a non-diverse claim against an additional party (Tony from New York) who was joined pursuant to Rule 20.

- Rule 24 allows the intervention of non-parties into an ongoing lawsuit where the non-parties show that they have an interest which as a practical matter will be adversely affected by the lawsuit, or where there are common issues of fact or law between the ongoing litigation and those affecting the intervenor. The intervenor may join the lawsuit as either a plaintiff or a defendant.

EXAMPLES & ANALYSIS

EXAMPLE: Paula (from New York) brings a state law tort claim against Donald (from Wisconsin) for $100,000. Tony (from New York) is concerned that, as a practical matter, his interests will be harmed by the lawsuit and intervenes as a defendant. Paula files a claim against Tony. Would there be supplemental jurisdiction?

Analysis: No. Section 1367(b) explicitly bars the assertion of supplemental jurisdiction over claims brought by or against parties who intervene under Rule 24.

EXAMPLE: Paula (from New York) brings a state law claim against Donald (from Wisconsin) for $100,000. Portia (from Wisconsin) was injured in the same accident, and moves to intervene in the lawsuit to file a claim against Donald. Would there be supplemental jurisdiction?

Analysis: No. Section 1367(b) specifically bars such claims brought by plaintiffs who are proposed to be joined under Rule 24's intervention rule. The same result would follow if Portia were proposed to be joined as a plaintiff because she was an indispensable party under Rule 19.

2. The Section 1367(b) Bar and the Amount-in-Controversy Requirement

Section 1367(b), which applies when the district court exercises original jurisdiction solely under the diversity jurisdiction statute, 28 U.S.C. § 1332, has generated a number of questions involving the application of the amount-in-controversy requirement to supplemental claims and parties.

EXAMPLES & ANALYSIS

EXAMPLE: Pedro (from New York) sues Don (from New Jersey) for a tort claim arising out of a car accident and seeks $80,000 in damages. Paula (from New York) was in the same car crash and wants to sue Don as well, but her damages were only $35,000. Can the court assert supplemental jurisdiction over Paula's claim against Don?

Analysis: Yes. In *Exxon Mobil Corp v. Allapattah Services, Inc.*, 545 U.S. 546 (2005), the Supreme Court held that a federal court in a diversity action may exercise supplemental jurisdiction over additional plaintiffs whose claims do not satisfy the amount-in-controversy requirement.

In particular, the Court declared:

> where the other elements of jurisdiction are present and at least one named plaintiff in the action satisfies the amount-in-controversy requirement, § 1367 does authorize supplemental jurisdiction over the claims of other plaintiffs in the same Article III case or controversy, even if those claims are for less than the jurisdictional amount specified in the statute setting forth the requirements for diversity jurisdiction.

545 U.S. at 549.

The Court reasoned:

> [W]hen the well-pleaded complaint contains at least one claim that satisfies the amount-in-controversy requirement, and there are no other relevant jurisdictional defects, the district court, beyond all question, has original jurisdiction over that claim. The presence of other claims in the complaint, over which the district court may lack original jurisdiction, is of no moment.
>
>   * * *
>
> While § 1367(b) qualifies the broad rule of § 1367(a), it does not withdraw supplemental jurisdiction over the claims of the additional parties at issue here. . . . The natural, indeed the necessary, inference is that § 1367

confers supplemental jurisdiction over claims by Rule 20 and Rule 23 plaintiffs. This inference, at least with respect to Rule 20 plaintiffs, is strengthened by the fact that § 1367(b) explicitly excludes supplemental jurisdiction over claims against defendants joined under Rule 20.

The contamination theory [that the inclusion of a claim falling outside of the court's original jurisdiction contaminates every other claim in the complaint] can make some sense in the special context of the complete diversity requirement because the presence of nondiverse parties on both sides of a lawsuit eliminates the justification for providing a federal forum. The theory, however, makes little sense with respect to the amount-in-controversy requirement, which is meant to ensure that a dispute is sufficiently important to warrant federal-court attention. The presence of a single nondiverse party may eliminate the fear of bias with respect to all claims, but the presence of a claim that falls short of the minimum amount in controversy does nothing to reduce the importance of the claims that do meet this requirement.

545 U.S. at 559–62.

Accordingly, in *Exxon*, the Supreme Court concluded that even if the only primary jurisdictional basis is diversity, a court can assert supplemental jurisdiction over additional claims that do not themselves exceed $75,000.

LITIGATING SUBJECT MATTER JURISDICTION

A. Litigating Subject Matter Jurisdiction: Objections and Waiver

Subject matter jurisdiction is a limited grant of power to the courts. The federal courts acquire subject matter jurisdiction only from the United States Constitution and from Congress. The state courts acquire their subject matter jurisdiction from their state constitution and their state legislature. This particular jurisdictional concept, therefore, involves a delicate balance of power between the judicial branch and the legislative branch. The subject matter jurisdiction granted to the federal courts also implicates **federalism**—the careful interplay between the power of the states and the power of the federal government. The constitutional underpinnings of subject matter jurisdiction shape the practice of litigation.

First, a judgment entered by any court that lacked subject matter jurisdiction is void. The court never had the authority to adjudicate the matter, and thus its judgments are a nullity.

Second, the parties to a litigation cannot consent to litigating their dispute in a court that lacks subject matter jurisdiction. The individual litigants are powerless to give to the courts authority that the courts do not otherwise have from the Constitution and the legislature. The balance of power struck by subject matter jurisdiction involves state and federal relations, and judicial and legislative relations. Subject matter jurisdiction does not directly involve the power of the government relative to the **individual**. As we will see, personal jurisdiction—which is the power of the state or federal government over the **person** of the defendant—does directly implicate the power of the government relative to the individual. As such, individual defendants may **consent** to personal jurisdiction. But individual parties may not consent to subject matter jurisdiction.

Third, because the parties cannot consent to litigating in a court that lacks subject matter jurisdiction, objections to a court's lack of subject matter jurisdiction cannot be waived. In other words, there is no definitive time-frame in which a party must make its objection to the court's lack of subject matter jurisdiction.

Fourth, a court on its own has an obligation to dismiss an action for a lack of subject matter jurisdiction. Even if no party challenged subject matter jurisdiction, the court must act *sua sponte* to dismiss the action if it determines that it lacks jurisdiction.

Federal Rule 12(h)(3) codifies this concept by making clear that: "If the court determines at **any time** that it lacks subject-matter jurisdiction, the court **must** dismiss the action." This rule is in stark contrast to those governing other motions to dismiss, which are waivable if not made in a proper and timely manner. The rule also clearly requires the court to dismiss an action for lack of subject matter jurisdiction—regardless of whether any party has made a motion. Responsive pleadings and motions are discussed in more detail in Chapter 7.

Fifth, the fact that objections to the lack of subject matter jurisdiction cannot be waived has given rise to some apparently anomalous results.

In *Capron v. Van Noorden*, 6 U.S. 126 (1804), the Supreme Court made abundantly clear that the concept of subject matter jurisdiction is critically important. In that case, George Capron sued Hadrianus Van Noorden for trespass on the case in federal court. Capron lost a jury verdict. Nonetheless, Capron argued to the Supreme Court that the judgment against him should be vacated because the court that entered that judgment lacked subject matter jurisdiction. In particular, Capron claimed that his own complaint failed to allege that he was from a different state than Van Noorden, which would have given the court diversity jurisdiction. The Supreme Court agreed, and vacated the judgment for lack of subject matter jurisdiction. The court was willing to do so despite the fact that Capron had chosen the wrong forum, had failed to allege the basis for jurisdiction in his own complaint, had lost a judgment on the merits, and had failed to raise any objection to subject matter jurisdiction until after he lost that judgment.

Recall, also, that in *Mottley*, the Supreme Court initially took the case to review the merits of the lower federal court's interpretation of federal law, and the parties briefed those federal issues and engaged in oral arguments in front of the Supreme Court on those questions. The Supreme Court then refused to reach the merits of the federal issues, concluding for the first time—on its own, and without any briefing—that the lower court lacked subject matter jurisdiction.

Similarly, in *Mas v. Perry*, the defendant made its objection to the lack of subject matter jurisdiction only after the presentation of evidence at trial. The defendant waited to make its objection until after it was pretty clear that the trial was not going well.

B. Litigating Subject Matter Jurisdiction: the Choice to File in Federal Court

If the federal courts have "exclusive" jurisdiction over a particular claim, the plaintiff must file that claim in federal court. If the federal courts lack subject matter jurisdiction over the claim, the plaintiff must file that claim in state court.

Yet, where the federal courts have subject matter jurisdiction over a claim and federal jurisdiction is not exclusive, the federal and state courts have "concurrent jurisdiction." In situations where there is concurrent jurisdiction, the plaintiffs have an initial choice to make: file in federal or state court. That choice is a multi-factoral strategic decision made by the plaintiffs' attorneys, based on their judgment and experience. What factors should a plaintiff's attorney consider in deciding whether to file a civil action in state or federal court?

Even if the plaintiff chooses to file an action in state court, however, the defendant may be able to **remove** the action to federal court.

REMOVAL AND REMAND

Key Concepts

- How claims filed in state court can be removed to federal court
- The power of the federal court to remand cases back to state court

Introduction

Removal is the process by which a defendant removes an action from state court, where it was filed by the plaintiff, to federal district court. In order to remove an action from state court to federal court, however, the defendant must follow statutory removal procedures, and the federal court must have subject matter jurisdiction over the removed claims. An action that has been improperly removed to federal court will be remanded to state court.

THE STATUTE 28 U.S.C. § 1441(a)-(c)

Removal of Civil Actions

(a) Generally.—Except as otherwise expressly provided by Act of Congress, any civil action brought in a State court of which the district courts of the United States have **original jurisdiction**, may be **removed** by the defendant or the **defendants**, to the district court of the United States for the district and division **embracing the place** where such action is pending. ***

(b) Removal Based on Diversity of Citizenship.—

(1) *** in determining whether a civil action is removable on the basis of the jurisdiction under section 1332(a) of this title, the citizenship of defendants sued under fictitious names shall be disregarded.

(2) A civil action otherwise removable solely on the basis of the jurisdiction under section 1332(a) of this title may not be removed if any of the parties in interest properly joined and served as defendants is a citizen of the State in which such action is brought.

(c) Joinder of Federal Law Claims and State Law Claims.—

(1) If a civil action includes—

(A) a claim arising under the Constitution, laws, or treaties of the United States (within the meaning of section 1331 of this title), and

(B) a claim not within the original or supplemental jurisdiction of the district court or a claim that has been made nonremovable by statute,

the entire action may be removed if the action would be removable without the inclusion of the claim described in subparagraph (B).

(2) Upon removal of an action described in paragraph (1), the district court shall sever from the action all claims described in paragraph (1)(B) and shall **remand** the severed claims to the State court from which the action was removed. Only defendants against whom a claim described in paragraph (1)(A) has been asserted are required to join in or consent to the removal under paragraph (1).

EXPLANATION

The removal statute provides that defendants may remove a civil action filed in state court to federal court as long as the federal court would have original jurisdiction over the action. Accordingly, the statute authorizes the removal of any civil action if at least one claim filed by the plaintiff is within the original subject matter jurisdiction of the federal court.

The action must be removed only to that particular federal district that geographically embraces the state court. As such, an action filed in state court in Cook County Illinois can be removed only to the federal district court for the Northern District of Illinois because that district encompasses the location where the state court sits.

The statute also makes clear that only defendants may remove an action from state court to federal court. In fact, all of the defendants in the action must "join in or consent to" the removal of the action. 28 U.S.C. § 1446(b)(2)(A). Plaintiffs have no right to remove even if they are served with a counterclaim that provides a basis for federal jurisdiction.

The federal courts have subject matter jurisdiction over removed claims so long as the claims are within their original or supplemental jurisdiction. The issue of whether claims are removable therefore begins with a familiar analysis. Those claims are removable if the federal court would have subject matter jurisdiction over them. Because federal courts are courts of limited jurisdiction, there must be a primary or supplemental jurisdictional basis for the removed claims.

The removal statute, 28 U.S.C. § 1441(c), also makes clear that an entire action may be removed if it includes at least one claim arising under federal law, even if additional claims would have no primary or supplemental jurisdictional basis. In that situation, however, the federal court must sever those additional claims and remand them back to state court. The court then may adjudicate the remaining claims over which it has jurisdiction.

A. Exceptions to Removal Where the Only Jurisdictional Basis Is Diversity

A defendant may generally remove an action filed against it in state court if there is complete diversity and if the amount in controversy exceeds $75,000. Congress, however, has created two exceptions to the removal of claims where the only jurisdictional basis is diversity.

1. If Any Defendant Is a Citizen of the Forum State

An action otherwise removable based on diversity may not be removed if any single defendant is a citizen of the state where the action was filed.

EXAMPLES & ANALYSIS

EXAMPLE: Paula (from New Jersey) files a state law trespass claim against Dan (from Connecticut) for $100,000 in Connecticut state court. Is this action removable to federal court?

Analysis: No. Although there is complete diversity and the amount exceeds $75,000, this action nonetheless may not be removed because the defendant (Dan) is a citizen of the state where the action was filed (Connecticut).

The rationale for this particular removal bar derives from the underlying rationale for diversity jurisdiction itself. The Framers and Congress have given to federal judges the power to adjudicate diversity actions to prevent the appearance of bias by state court judges against out of state parties. When the action is filed in the state where the defendant is domiciled, that defendant would not be subjected to bias by the state court judge from the defendant's home state. Accordingly, there is no need to provide a federal forum for a diversity case against that defendant, or for any defendants, who have been sued in one of their own state's courts.

In determining whether this bar applies, however, only those defendants who are real "parties in interest" and are "properly joined" are considered. Plaintiffs who file claims in state court typically have a strategic interest in maintaining the action in that forum, and in precluding removal. Plaintiffs therefore have an incentive to add a defendant to a state court action who is a citizen of the forum state merely to prevent removal to federal court. The removal statute prevents this tactic by requiring the court to disregard any defendant who was not properly joined or is not a real party in interest.

Similarly, because plaintiffs may have an incentive to allege that the amount in controversy does not exceed $75,000 to block removal, the statute requires that the plaintiff allege the sum in "good faith," and allows the defendant to assert the requisite amount in controversy in the notice of removal and prove up that amount by a preponderance of the evidence. 28 U.S.C. § 1446(c)(2).

2. The One-Year Bar to Removal of Diversity Cases

In its removal provisions, Congress also generally bars the removal of an action based solely on diversity, if the notice of removal is filed more than one year after the original action was filed. 28 U.S.C. § 1446(c)(1).

As a general rule, defendants must file a notice of removal within 30 days of the service of a pleading from which it may "first be ascertained" that the case is removable. 28 U.S.C. § 1446(b)(3). Yet, if the only jurisdictional basis is diversity, a defendant generally may not remove the action more than one year after the initial action was filed, regardless of when that defendant first ascertained that removal was possible. The only exception to this one year bar is if the plaintiff has acted in "bad faith" to prevent removal.

B. The Process of Removal and Remand

1. Removal

In order to remove an action from state to federal court, the defendants must:

- File a "notice of removal" in the federal court that geographically embraces the state court in which the action was filed;

- Sign the notice of removal pursuant to Federal Rule of Civil Procedure 11, which generally requires that the notice is filed for a proper purpose, warranted by law and supported by evidence (See Chapter 5 regarding Rule 11);

- Include in the notice of removal a short and plain statement of the grounds for removal, including the basis for the court's jurisdiction;

- Include in the filing copies of all of the pleadings and orders entered thus far in the state court; and

- Promptly after filing the notice of removal, provide written notice to all adverse parties and file a copy of the notice in the state court where the action was filed.

As soon as a copy of the notice of removal is filed in the state court, the action is automatically removed to federal court, and the state court may do nothing else in the action unless the action is remanded back to that state court.

2. Remand

After the action is removed to federal court, the real issue becomes whether the federal court should retain the removed claims or instead should remand some or all of those claims back to state court. The federal judge, rather than the state judge, decides whether removal to federal court was proper, and whether to remand the action back to state court.

The federal judge may remand the action back to state court if there was a defect in the removal process, but only if the plaintiff has filed a motion to remand the action back to state court based on such a defect within 30 days of the filing of the notice of removal.

But, in any event, the federal judge must remand the action back to state court at any time before the judgment, if the court finds that it lacks subject matter jurisdiction. Once again, the federal court must act on its own to remand the action for a lack of subject matter jurisdiction, even if no party has objected on that basis.

3. Severing and Remanding Specific Claims

In an action removed to federal court with multiple claims, the federal court will retain jurisdiction over all of the claims if it finds that it has primary or supplemental jurisdiction over those claims. Suppose however that two claims are removed to federal court, one of which arises under federal law and the other of which is an unrelated non-diverse state law tort claim. Although there would be a primary jurisdictional basis for the first claim (arising under), there would be no primary or even supplemental jurisdictional basis for the second unrelated claim. In that situation, the entire action may still be removed to federal court, but the federal court must "sever" and "remand" the unrelated non-federal and non-diverse tort claim. 28 U.S.C. § 1441 (c). As a result, the claims that arise under federal law will be litigated in federal court, while the unrelated state law claims will be litigated in state court.

ADDITIONAL EXERCISES

1. Peter, a domicile of Maine, files a state law tort claim in federal court against Demo L.L.C. and Dennis. Demo L.L.C. is a limited liability company whose members are domiciled entirely on the west coast. Dennis is a citizen of Canada, who has been admitted to the United States as a permanent resident, domiciled in Maine. The defendants move to dismiss the action for lack of subject matter jurisdiction. **How should the court rule?**

2. Paula was born and raised in California, where she attended UCLA. After graduation, Paula decides to settle down and start a family with Donald in New York, where she moves after they get married. After having their first child (Ruby), Paula and Donald purchase a new, fancy crib at the popular furniture store, Desks & Doors, Inc. Desks & Doors is a Delaware corporation with headquarters in Houston, Texas. When Ruby is one month old, she develops a severe allergic reaction, and her parents discover that the cause is the lead-based paint used on the crib. After doing some research, Paula comes across the recently enacted, "Safe Furniture Act," which says, "No furniture provider may make available for purchase any piece of furniture that contains lead paint." The Act later says, "Any customer who has suffered physical injury as a result of

lead paint on furniture may seek to recover damages up to the amount of health care costs. Service of process may only be made via certified mail or in-hand delivery of the complaint and summons to the defendant." Paula comes to you as her attorney, seeking to file a claim under the federal "Safe Furniture Act," as well as a garden-variety negligence claim against Desks & Doors. **May Paula file in federal court?**

3. Paula (from New York) and Portia (from Wisconsin) file a law suit in which each one asserts a single state law tort claim for $100,000 against Donald (from Wisconsin) arising out of the same auto accident. Donald moves to dismiss for the lack of federal subject matter jurisdiction. **How should the court rule?**

4. Pam, a citizen of Illinois, is suing David, a citizen of Wisconsin, for breach of contract in federal court based on diversity jurisdiction. Pam's claim seeks $100,000. Pam and David get into an automobile accident while leaving a deposition. Pam wants to add another claim for $50,000 against David for her personal injuries. Pam also wants to sue David for $75,000 for intentional infliction of emotional distress. **May Pam join these claims?**

5. Pascal, a Hawaii citizen, sues Denise, a citizen of Tennessee, for her injuries arising out of an automobile accident. The action is filed in federal court based on diversity. Pascal also wishes to sue Tom, her primary care physician, whose office is located in Hawaii, for medical malpractice. **May Pascal sue both Denise and Tom in the same federal court action?**

6. Paula, a citizen of Illinois, is hit by David, a citizen of Wisconsin, who was driving a large truck. Paula sues David in federal court based on diversity. David wants to sue the car manufacturer, claiming that he hit Paula because his brakes suddenly gave out. The car manufacturer is incorporated in Delaware and has its headquarters in Wisconsin. **May David sue the car manufacturer in this action?**

7. Peter is a citizen of Illinois who wishes to sue three doctors who operated on him at a hospital in Wisconsin. One of the doctors, however, lives in Illinois. Because Peter wants to sue the doctors in federal court based on diversity jurisdiction, he only names 2 of the 3 doctors, both of whom are Wisconsin citizens. **May Peter continue with the case without naming the third doctor?**

8. Paula, a citizen of Wyoming, brings a civil action against Debra and Demolition Partners in state court in Wyoming. Paula asserts one claim against Demolition Partners that is created by the federal labor laws and another related claim against Demolition Partners created by the state tort law of Wyoming. Demolition Partners is a Delaware Corporation with its headquarters in Wyoming. Paula also asserts a state law tort claim against Debra, who is a domicile of Wyoming. Two months after being served with the state court complaint, Debra and Demolition Partners file a notice of removal to federal court. Two months after the notice of removal was filed, Paula moves to remand the action back to state court, arguing that the process of removal was defective and that the court lacks subject matter jurisdiction. ***How should the court rule?***

9. Paula and Peter went canoeing in the Boundary Waters between the United States and Canada. Paula was born in Illinois, but has been a student at the University of Michigan for the past three years. Peter is a citizen of Norway, who has been admitted to the United States as a permanent resident of Illinois. While on their canoe trip, Paula and Peter each suffered serious injuries, caused by their exposure to toxic waste that had been dumped into the Boundary Waters by Dexter International Corporation ("Dexter"). Dexter is a Delaware Corporation with its only factory in Illinois, and its headquarters in Michigan.

On January 10, Paula and Peter filed a civil action against Dexter in Illinois state court in Chicago, Illinois. They asserted two claims in their complaint: (1) a tort claim for negligence; and (2) a claim alleging that Dexter's violation of the Boundary Waters Treaty caused them injuries. The Boundary Waters Treaty has been signed by the United States and Canada and provides only the following:

> "It shall be unlawful for any corporation incorporated within the United States or Canada to dump toxic waste in the Boundary Waters."

The complaint was properly served upon Dexter on February 1. On May 1, Dexter filed a notice of removal in the federal district court for the Northern District of Illinois. On May 15, Paula and Peter filed a motion to remand the action back to state court. ***Should the federal judge grant or deny that motion to remand?***

Quick Summary

- The state courts are courts of general subject matter jurisdiction. They have the power to adjudicate all kinds of civil actions, unless there is exclusive jurisdiction assigned to a different forum.

- The federal courts, by contrast, are courts of limited jurisdiction. The Constitution must delegate to the federal judiciary the power to resolve a certain kind of case, and Congress must grant that power to its lower federal courts.

- Congress has given to its federal district courts two primary alternative grants of original jurisdiction: (1) federal-question jurisdiction; and (2) diversity jurisdiction.

- Congress has given to federal judges discretion to assert supplemental jurisdiction over some non-federal and non-diverse claims that derive from the same case or controversy as a federal or a diverse claim.

- Even if the plaintiff decides to file a civil action in state court, defendants may be able to remove the action to federal court if the federal court would have subject matter jurisdiction over the removed claims.

- The concept of subject matter jurisdiction is so important that any judgment entered by a court that lacked subject matter jurisdiction is void. The parties cannot consent to the court's lack of subject matter jurisdiction or waive their objections to the lack of jurisdiction. In fact, the court on its own has a duty to dismiss an action if there is no subject matter jurisdiction.

2

Due Process: Personal Jurisdiction, Notice, and Opportunity to Be Heard

PERSONAL JURISDICTION

Key Concepts

- The power of the court to assert authority over a party—personal jurisdiction
- The statutory and constitutional requirements for personal jurisdiction in state and federal court

Introduction

Personal jurisdiction is the power of a state or federal court over the person or property of the defendant. It is the power that a court has to compel a defendant to appear in court to defend a lawsuit, adjudicated by that court.

A. The Historic Basis for Personal Jurisdiction

In order to be valid, a judicial proceeding must be presided over by a judge with lawful authority to render and to execute a judgment. *See Burnham v. Superior Court*, 495 U.S. 604, 608 (1990). Any judgment entered without personal jurisdiction, therefore, is entered without lawful judicial authority and is void and unenforceable.

In order to determine when a federal or state court could lawfully assert power over the person or the property of a defendant in a lawsuit, the Supreme Court initially relied upon traditional notions of sovereignty adopted from international law. The states were treated like countries, each with exclusive sovereignty over its own persons or property within its own territory. As such, a state or federal court could assert personal jurisdiction over any defendant who **consented** to be subjected to the power of the sovereign or over any defendant whose person or property was physically **present** in the forum state.

The courts have traditionally distinguished between three different kinds of jurisdiction over a defendant's person or property.

First, an **in personam** action is one in which the court asserts power over the person of a defendant who is present in the forum state. The court has power to enter and execute the full judgment against that present defendant.

Second, in an **in rem** action, the defendant's property is located in the forum state, and that property is at issue in the litigation. The court has the power to adjudicate all aspects of that property itself.

Finally, in a **quasi in rem** action, the defendant has property in the forum state which is brought under the control of the court, but the property is used to satisfy an unrelated judgment against the defendant. Accordingly, a court's power to effectuate any judgment is limited to the property itself.

As commerce, transportation and communication advanced, however, the courts expanded the bases of power beyond consent and presence.

B. Personal Jurisdiction and Due Process

1. The Relevance of Due Process

The traditional conceptions of personal jurisdiction are now incorporated within the Constitution's Due Process Clauses. The Fifth Amendment precludes a federal court from depriving persons of their liberty or property without due process, and the Fourteenth Amendment prohibits the state courts from doing so. Whenever a civil action is filed, the state or federal government through its court system will inevitably deprive one or both of the parties of their liberty or their property. For example, if a lawsuit is filed in Arizona state court, the state of Arizona through its court system will serve upon the defendant a "summons" to appear in its courts. The summons is a deprivation of liberty; it requires the defendant to do something it would not otherwise want to do. Yet, if the defendant refuses to appear, the state will enter a default judgment against that defendant, enabling the state to begin the process of taking the defendant's property to satisfy that judgment. In every lawsuit, therefore, a state or federal court threatens defendants with a deprivation of their liberty or their property.

Under what circumstances may a state or federal court deprive persons of their liberty or property? The Constitution allows such a deprivation, but only if that state or federal court affords the defendant "due process." The court must insure that its assertions of power over a defendant satisfy the constitutional requirements of due process because a judgment entered without due process is void and cannot be enforced.

2. The Fundamental Requirements of Due Process

At a minimum, the Due Process Clause requires that a court has proper subject matter jurisdiction over the matter, has proper personal jurisdiction over the defendant, has afforded the defendant appropriate notice of the action, and has given the defendant an opportunity to be heard. We have already discussed the critical concept of subject matter jurisdiction. In this chapter, we address the due process requirements of personal jurisdiction, notice and opportunity to be heard.

C. The Analytical Structure of Personal Jurisdiction

The language of the Due Process Clause establishes the structure for any analysis of personal jurisdiction. That clause states that if the state or federal government through its courts wishes to deprive persons of their liberty or their property, it must afford due process.

The first question to ask in any analysis of due process is whether the state or federal court is even attempting to assert its power to deprive persons of their liberty or property. If the state or federal court is not asserting such power, then the Due Process Clause is not triggered.

If, however, a state or federal court **does** wish to assert power over the defendant, then the question is whether that power is compatible with due process. Therefore, a state or federal court may assert personal jurisdiction over a defendant only if **two** things are both true:

(1) The law of the forum itself grants the power to assert personal jurisdiction over the defendant; and

(2) The application of that power over the defendant also is constitutional under the Due Process Clause.

1. The Forum's Law

Traditionally, the courts have asserted power over defendants who have **consented** to the assertion of a court's power or who are **present** in the territory of the state where the court sits.

In addition, states have expanded their assertion of power over out-of-state defendants through long-arm statutes. Accordingly, under the law of virtually every state, there are three alternative bases for personal jurisdiction: (1) consent; (2) presence; and (3) the **long-arm statute** of the state.

> A **long-arm statute** is a statute that empowers the state to reach outside its territory to compel the appearance of non-resident defendants who perform a particular act in the state.

2. Constitutionality

Even if the forum's own law grants personal jurisdiction, that law must also be constitutional. As we will discover, the Supreme Court has declared that a forum's assertion of personal jurisdiction is constitutional if the defendant engaged in such minimum contacts with the forum that it would not offend traditional notions of fair play and substantial justice to assert power over that defendant. The constitutional test now involves a case-by-case analysis of the nature and quality of the defendant's **contacts** with the forum, as well as the relative **fairness** of conducting litigation in that court.

D. The Personal Jurisdiction Law of the Forum

1. Consent

EXAMPLES & ANALYSIS

EXAMPLE: Donald negligently injured Paula in New York. Paula and Donald were both born and raised in New York, and neither has ever traveled outside the state. Nonetheless, Paula and her attorney decide to sue Donald in Hawaii state court, hoping to take advantage of that state's beautiful climate during the litigation. Donald, who has no connection whatsoever with the state of Hawaii, could object to being sued in that state on the ground that the court lacks personal jurisdiction over him. Yet, Donald also would prefer to litigate in Hawaii state court because of Hawaii's climate. Donald instructs his lawyer not to object to the Hawaii court's personal jurisdiction over him. Donald's lawyer informs Paula's lawyer that Donald has chosen to **consent** to the Hawaii court's assertion of personal jurisdiction over him, and will **waive** any such objection that he could have been able to raise. Does the court in Hawaii have personal jurisdiction over Donald?

Analysis: The issue presented by this scenario is whether **consent** by the defendant is a valid basis for personal jurisdiction. We have already seen that **consent** is not a valid basis for subject matter jurisdiction. The parties cannot agree to litigate in a court that lacks subject matter jurisdiction, and cannot waive any objections that can be made to the lack of subject matter jurisdiction. In fact, the court has a duty to act on its own (**sua sponte**) to dismiss an action that lacks subject matter jurisdiction.

But is **consent** a valid basis for personal jurisdiction? Can defendants waive their objections to the court's personal jurisdiction over them? The answer is yes. Subject matter jurisdiction involves the balance of power between the federal and state sovereigns. That balance does not directly involve individual rights. Personal jurisdiction, by contrast, involves personal rights, and a balance of power between the individual and the government.

The Due Process Clauses of the Fifth and Fourteenth Amendments protect **persons** from deprivations of their "life, liberty or property by the government without due process."

Accordingly, the right of any person to be free from such a deprivation can be waived by that person. Personal jurisdiction, thus, can be waived by the defendant. Put another way, consent by the defendant is a valid basis for personal jurisdiction. Indeed, the law in virtually every state allows for the assertion of personal jurisdiction over defendants who consent to that jurisdiction.

But how is consent demonstrated? There are two kinds of consent: express and implied.

a. Express Consent

Express consent can take several forms. First, as in Paula's case against Donald, the defendant, either in person or through his lawyer, can simply consent to personal jurisdiction in a statement in writing or in court.

Alternatively, a defendant may express consent in a contract with another party. The contract to supply goods, for instance, may have a clause by which the parties to that contract agree to litigate any claims arising out of the contract in a particular state court. Such a contractual provision is recognized as an expression of consent to personal jurisdiction in that state's courts. *See, e.g., Carnival Cruise Lines, Inc. v. Shute*, 499 U.S. 585, 595 (1991) (contractual clause agreeing that "all disputes and matters . . . shall be litigated . . . in and before a court located in the State of Florida" constituted an express consent to personal jurisdiction in Florida courts.)

Most states also infer express consent to personal jurisdiction from the fact that the defendant has expressly appointed an agent in the state to accept service of process on its behalf in a lawsuit initiated in that state.

b. Implied Consent

Even if the defendant has not expressly consented to personal jurisdiction, he may nonetheless have impliedly done so. Implied consent can take two forms.

First, the state may have enacted a statute which requires non-residents who perform certain activities in the state to appoint a state official to accept service of process in the state on their behalf, thereby constructively consenting to being sued in that state. In *Hess v. Pawloski*, 274 U.S. 352, 357 (1927), for example, the Supreme Court upheld such statutes that employ implied consent to subject non–resident drivers to personal jurisdiction over them in any state in which they allegedly cause an accident. There, Hess, a resident of Pennsylvania, negligently struck Pawloski while driving through Massachusetts. Under Massachusetts law, non-resident motorists such as Hess are deemed to consent to the appointment of the Massachusetts Registrar of Vehicles as their agent to accept process in the state. The Supreme Court concluded that states have the constitutional power to assert personal jurisdiction over non-residents who impliedly consent to personal jurisdiction through the statutorily-required appointment of an agent in the state.

Second, implied consent will be found if a defendant fails to object to personal jurisdiction in a proper and timely manner. Every state court in its rules of civil procedure establishes requirements for preserving objections to personal jurisdiction.

Some states still require that such objections be made by a **special appearance**. A special appearance is an appearance in court solely to contest personal jurisdiction or service of process. In those states which require a special appearance, any appearance in court for any reason other than one solely to challenge personal jurisdiction or process constitutes a **general appearance** and is a waiver of any objections to personal jurisdiction or process. For example, if a defendant files a special appearance to contest personal jurisdiction, but also moves to dismiss the action for failure to state a meritorious cause of action, the defendant has thereby converted the special appearance into a general appearance and in so doing has waived its objection to personal jurisdiction. The rationale of this relatively harsh waiver rule is that a defendant who challenges the merits of a case against him effectively accedes to the court's power and hence cannot also challenge that court's power.

The federal courts and most state courts, however, have abandoned this rigid special appearance regime. Under the federal rules of civil procedure, and under the rules of civil procedure in most states, there is no longer any special appearance required or even recognized. Instead, defendants may combine objections to the court's lack of personal jurisdiction with other defenses. Chapter 7 will explore the technical ways in which these objections can be made.

2. Presence

a. The Judicial Foundations of Presence

Even if a defendant has neither expressly nor impliedly consented to personal jurisdiction, a state may assert personal jurisdiction over him if he is **present** in that state.

In *Pennoyer v. Neff,* 95 U.S. 714 (1877), the Supreme Court declared that a state may acquire jurisdiction over a defendant's property located within the state if the state attaches the property or otherwise brings it within the state's control when the lawsuit is commenced.

Sylvester Pennoyer claimed to have acquired land in Oregon under a sheriff's deed, made upon a sale of the property to execute a prior judgment entered against Marcus Neff in Oregon state court. The case turned upon the validity of this judgment. Neff claimed the previous judgment against him was invalid because the Oregon court lacked personal jurisdiction. Pennoyer argued that Oregon had personal jurisdiction because Neff's property was located in Oregon.

Although the Supreme Court found that the Oregon court lacked personal jurisdiction in the case because it failed to attach Neff's property when the lawsuit began, it articulated the "general, if not universal, law" that: "The authority of every tribunal is necessarily restricted by the territorial limits of the State in which it is established." 95 U.S. at 720. According to the Court:

> the several States of the Union are not, it is true, in every respect independent, many of the rights and powers which originally belonged to them being now vested in the government created by the Constitution. But, except as restrained and limited by that instrument, they possess and exercise the authority of independent States.

95 U.S. at 722.

The Court relied upon: "two well-established principles of public law respecting the jurisdiction of an independent State over persons and property." *Id.* One of these principles is that every state possesses exclusive jurisdiction and sovereignty over persons and property within its territory. The other principle of public law is that no state can exercise direct jurisdiction and authority over persons or property outside of its territory. The several states are of equal dignity and authority, and the independence of one implies the exclusion of power from all others." *Id.*

The Supreme Court then found that the same traditional, public law concept of presence exists within the Constitution's Full Faith and Credit Clause, and the Fourteenth Amendment's Due Process Clause. The Full Faith and Credit Clause requires each federal or state court to recognize and enforce a judgment entered by another court, but only if that judgment was entered by a court with proper subject matter jurisdiction and proper personal jurisdiction. 95 U.S. at 729.

The Due Process Clause allows a defendant to challenge a judgment entered by a court without personal jurisdiction as a deprivation of property without due process. According to the Supreme Court, the Due Process Clause requires that, in order to be valid, a judgment must be entered by:

> a tribunal competent by its constitution—that is, by the law of its creation—to pass upon the subject-matter of the suit; and, if that involves merely a determination of the personal liability of the defendant, he must be brought within its jurisdiction by service of process within the State, or his voluntary appearance.

95 U.S. at 733.

Accordingly, the Supreme Court indicated that the Due Process Clause permits a court to enter and to execute a judgment if the defendant voluntarily **consented** to the court's power or if the defendant's person or property was **present** in the state, and brought under control of the court when the lawsuit began.

In *Burnham v. Superior Court*, 495 U.S. 604 (1990), the Supreme Court unanimously re-affirmed that the Constitution generally permits a state to assert personal jurisdiction over a defendant who is actually physically present in the forum state while served with process—even if the lawsuit is unrelated to the defendant's presence.

Dennis Burnham married Francie Burnham in 1976 in West Virginia. In 1977 the couple moved to New Jersey, where their two children were born. In July 1987 the Burnhams decided to separate. They agreed that Mrs. Burnham, who intended to move to California, would take custody of the children. Mrs. Burnham brought suit for divorce in California state court in early January 1988.

In late January, Dennis Burnham visited southern California on business, after which he went north to visit his children in the San Francisco Bay area, where his wife resided. He took the older child to San Francisco for the weekend. Upon returning the child to Mrs. Burnham's home, Dennis was served with a California court summons and a copy of Mrs. Burnham's divorce petition.

Later that year, Dennis Burnham made a special appearance in the California Superior Court, moving to quash the service of process on the ground that the court lacked personal jurisdiction over him because his only contacts with California were a few short visits to the state for the purposes of conducting business and visiting his children.

In his opinion for the Supreme Court, Justice Scalia wrote that: "The short of the matter is that jurisdiction based on physical presence alone constitutes due process because it is one of the continuing traditions of our legal system that define the due process standard of 'traditional notions of fair play and substantial justice'." 495 U.S. at 619.

Justice Scalia's opinion, however, did not attract five votes. Indeed, Justice Brennan wrote separately for four members of the Court to make clear that although the Due Process Clause of the Fourteenth Amendment generally permits a state court to exercise jurisdiction over a defendant if he is served with process while voluntarily present in the forum state, that court nonetheless must conduct a case-by-case analysis of the defendant's contacts with the forum state and the fairness of compelling the defendant to return to defend a lawsuit. 495 U.S. at 629 (Brennan, J. concurring).

Justice White also refused to accept Justice Scalia's approach, and concurred separately to declare: "The rule allowing jurisdiction to be obtained over a nonresident by personal service in the forum state, without more, has been, and is, so widely accepted throughout this country that I could not possibly strike it down . . . ." 495 U.S. at 628 (White, J. concurring).

Justice Stevens supplied the final vote, writing separately to reject any broad rule and to observe that the historical evidence and consensus identified by Justice Scalia, and considerations of fairness and common sense all combine to demonstrate that this is a "very easy case" for the constitutionality of the assertion of personal jurisdiction. 495 U.S. at 640 (Stevens, J. concurring).

The Supreme Court's opinions therefore establish that a state's assertion of personal jurisdiction over a defendant who is voluntarily **present** in the state while served with process will generally pass constitutional muster. The courts have had to decide, however, what constitutes sufficient presence by the defendant in the forum state to confer personal jurisdiction.

b. Three Kinds of Presence

1. The Actual Voluntary Physical Presence of the Defendant in the State While Served with Process

The principle that a state may assert personal jurisdiction over a defendant who is present while served with process in that state gives rise to some questions regarding the length and nature of the defendant's presence.

EXAMPLES & ANALYSIS

EXAMPLE: Dancing Defendants (How long must the defendant be present in the state?)

Suppose defendant Donald Dancer, a ballroom-dancing instructor who owns a studio located on the border between California and Oregon, is sued in a state court in California. The defendant is giving waltz lessons in his ballroom-dancing studio while an authorized process-server attempts to serve him with the complaint and summons in the lawsuit. The defendant and his students waltz back and forth between California and Oregon in the course of the lesson in the studio. The authorized process-server is able to serve the dancing defendant with the process while his left foot is squarely planted in California before he waltzes back into Oregon. May the state of California assert personal jurisdiction over him?

Analysis: Yes. A state generally may assert personal jurisdiction over a defendant who is actually physically present in the state as long as the defendant is present while served with process. The concept of presence is rooted in the principle that the state may assert power over persons who are physically located in that state. Accordingly, so long as the state's assertion of power through service of process takes place while that person is located within the state, the state usually may compel that person to defend a lawsuit in that state. In *Burnham v. Superior Court*, 495 U.S. 604 (1990), however, a majority of the Supreme Court left open the possibility that the assertion of personal jurisdiction based solely on fleeting presence might be so unfair in some circumstances as to raise constitutional concerns.

EXAMPLE: Involuntary Defendants (Must the defendant's actual presence in the state be "voluntary"?)

Suppose that our dancing defendant is dragged into California against his will, and then served with process? Or suppose that the defendant is enticed to enter California by a fraudulent misrepresentation.

Analysis: The logic of the doctrine of presence derived from *Pennoyer* may still allow the assertion of personal jurisdiction in these situations because the state could assert power over the defendant while he is present in the state, no matter how or why he became present there. Nonetheless, the states have uniformly precluded the assertion of personal jurisdiction over defendants who are involuntarily present in the state through force or fraud. In a similar vein, the states also have barred the assertion of personal jurisdiction over defendants who are in the state because they have been compelled by subpoena to take part in judicial proceedings.

EXAMPLE: Flying Defendants (Must the defendant's presence be on the ground within the state?)

Suppose the dancing defendant is returning to his home in Oregon from a trip to Hawaii. As it approaches Oregon, his airplane passes through northern California, at which point an authorized process-server sitting next to him on the plane serves him with process—while in the airspace over California. May the California court assert personal jurisdiction? Was the defendant actually physically present while served?

Analysis: Yes. A defendant who is within the airspace of a state is nonetheless actually physically present in the state for personal jurisdiction purposes. *See, e.g., Grace v. MacArthur*, 170 F. Supp. 442 (E.D. Ark. 1959).

2. Domicile

Can a defendant who is not actually physically present in a state (or even in its airspace) still be considered to be present in that state for personal jurisdiction purposes?

As interstate travel became easier and more common, the states were forced to confront this question. Suppose a defendant born and raised in California exits the state as soon as a California lawsuit is filed against him. That defendant would not be actually physically present in the state and could not be subject to personal jurisdiction under the literal doctrine of presence.

Nonetheless, the states began to extend the doctrine of presence by construing defendants to be present in the state if their **domicile** is in that state. As we learned from our discussion of subject matter jurisdiction in Chapter 1, a person's domicile is: (1) their true, fixed and permanent home; and (2) where they intend to return, even if they are not physically present there. By virtue of this form of constructive presence, states commonly assert personal jurisdiction over defendants who are not served with process in the state, as long as their domicile is in that state.

3. Doing Business

Where is an organization such as a corporation present?

As artificial entities, organizations do not have an actual physical presence. The states readily employed the concept of domicile to find that an organization is present in the state or states where it is domiciled. For example, a corporation is domiciled in the state of its incorporation and also in the state where its principal place of business is located. As such, that corporation would also be present in those states for personal jurisdiction.

Yet, could a corporation be present in other states as well? Suppose a Delaware corporation with its principal place of business (its corporate headquarters) in Texas, does regular, systematic, and continuous business within the state of Wisconsin. Could the state of Wisconsin assert personal jurisdiction over that corporation on the grounds that the corporation is present in Wisconsin?

Virtually every state attempted to do so. They argued that a corporation that is **doing business** in a state was constructively present in that state for personal jurisdiction purposes. The Supreme Court recognized that presence could be construed from a corporation that is doing business in a state. *See, e.g., Philadelphia & Reading Railway Co. v. McKibbin*, 243 U.S. 264, 265 (1917).

The courts have defined doing business as the regular, systematic, continuous, and ongoing in-state business. An organization that merely solicits business in the state does not engage in this level of in-state business. Nor does a corporation that has sporadic or casual or occasional business in a state reach the level of instate business necessary to be doing business within the state.

As we will see, the Supreme Court in *International Shoe* confronted the constitutionality of the assertion of personal jurisdiction over a corporation that is doing business in a state, and more recently in *Daimler AG v. Baumann et al*, narrowed the scope of the doing business doctrine.

E. The Constitutionality of the Assertion of Personal Jurisdiction

The assertion of personal jurisdiction over a defendant by a state or federal court must be constitutional under the Due Process Clause. The constitutionality of personal jurisdiction evolved from a fairly clear bright line test involving **consent** or **presence**, to a more nuanced standard requiring a case-by-case analysis of the defendant's **contacts** with the forum and the **fairness** of litigating in that forum. In *International Shoe*, the Supreme Court established the framework for the current analysis of the constitutionality of the assertion of personal jurisdiction. The Court allows the assertion of personal jurisdiction beyond consent and presence, if the defendant engaged in such minimum **contacts** with the forum that it would not offend traditional notions of fair play and substantial justice to compel the defendant to litigate there. Since *International Shoe*, the courts have tried to add definition to the requirements of **minimum contacts** and **fairness**.

1. Contemporary Due Process and *International Shoe*

FROM THE COURT

International Shoe Co. v. State of Washington
326 U.S. 310 (1945)
Supreme Court of the United States

Appeal from the Supreme Court of the State of Washington.

Mr. Chief Justice Stone delivered the opinion of the Court.

The questions for decision are (1) whether, within the limitations of the due process clause of the Fourteenth Amendment, appellant, a Delaware corporation, has by its activities in the State of Washington rendered itself amenable to proceedings in the courts of that state to recover unpaid contributions to the state unemployment compensation fund exacted by state statutes, . . . and (2) whether the state can exact those contributions consistently with the due process clause of the Fourteenth Amendment.

The statutes in question set up a comprehensive scheme of unemployment compensation, the costs of which are defrayed by contributions required to be made by employers to a state unemployment compensation fund. The contributions are a specified percentage of the wages payable annually by each employer for his employees' services in the state. The assessment and collection of the contributions and the fund are administered by respondents. Section 14(c) of the Act, Wash.Rev.Stat. 1941 Supp., § 9998-114c, authorizes respondent Commissioner to issue an order and notice of assessment of delinquent contributions upon prescribed personal service of the notice upon the employer if found within the state, or, if not so found, by mailing the notice to the employer by registered mail at his last known address. That section also authorizes the Commissioner to collect the assessment by distraint if it is not paid within ten days after the service of the notice. . . .

In this case notice of assessment for the years in question was personally served upon a sales solicitor employed by appellant in the State of Washington, and a copy of the notice was mailed by registered mail to appellant at its address in St. Louis, Missouri. Appellant appeared specially before the office of unemployment and moved to set aside the order and notice of assessment on the ground that the service upon appellant's salesman was not proper service upon appellant; that appellant was not a corporation of the State of Washington and was not doing business within the state; that it had no agent within the state upon whom service could be made; and that appellant is not an employer and does not furnish employment within the meaning of the statute.

The motion was heard on evidence and a stipulation of facts by the appeal tribunal which denied the motion and ruled that respondent Commissioner was entitled to recover the unpaid contributions. That action was affirmed by the Commissioner; both the Superior Court and the Supreme Court affirmed. . . . Appellant in each of these courts assailed the statute as applied, as a violation of the due process clause of the Fourteenth Amendment, and as imposing a constitutionally prohibited burden on interstate commerce.

* * *

Appellant is a Delaware corporation, having its principal place of business in St. Louis, Missouri, and is engaged in the manufacture and sale of shoes and other footwear. It maintains places of business in several states, other than Washington, at which its manufacturing is carried on and from which its merchandise is distributed interstate through several sales units or branches located outside the state of Washington.

Appellant has no office in Washington and makes no contracts either for sale or purchase of merchandise there. It maintains no stock of merchandise in that state and makes there no deliveries of goods in intrastate commerce. During the years from 1937 to 1940, now in question, appellant employed eleven to thirteen salesmen under direct supervision and control of sales managers located in St. Louis. These salesmen resided in Washington; their principal activities were confined to that state; and they were compensated by commissions based upon the amount of their sales. The commissions for each year totaled more than $31,000. Appellant supplies its salesmen with a line of samples, each consisting of one shoe of a pair, which they display to prospective purchasers. On occasion they rent permanent sample rooms, for exhibiting samples, in business buildings, or rent rooms in hotels or business buildings temporarily for that purpose. The cost of such rentals is reimbursed by appellant.

The authority of the salesmen is limited to exhibiting their samples and soliciting orders from prospective buyers, at prices and on terms fixed by appellant. The salesmen transmit the orders to appellant's office in St. Louis for acceptance or rejection, and when accepted the merchandise for filling the orders is shipped f.o.b. from points outside Washington to the purchasers within the state. All the merchandise shipped into Washington is invoiced at the place of shipment from which collections are made. No salesman has authority to enter into contracts or to make collections.

The Supreme Court of Washington was of opinion that the regular and systematic solicitation of orders in the state by appellant's salesmen, resulting in a continuous flow of appellant's product into the state, was sufficient to constitute doing business in the state so as to make appellant amenable to suit in its courts. But it was also of opinion that there were sufficient additional activities shown to bring the case within the rule frequently stated that solicitation within a state by the agents of a foreign corporation plus some additional activities there are sufficient to render the corporation amenable to suit brought in the courts of the state to enforce an obligation arising out of its activities there. . . . The court found such additional activities in the salesmen's display of samples sometimes in permanent display rooms, and the salesmen's residence within the state, continued over a period of years, all resulting in a substantial volume of merchandise regularly shipped by appellant to purchasers within the state. . . .

Appellant . . . insists that its activities within the state were not sufficient to manifest its "presence" there and that in its absence the state courts were without jurisdiction, that consequently it was a denial of due process for the state to subject appellant to suit. It refers to those cases in which it was said that the mere solicitation of orders for the purchase of goods within a state, to be accepted without the state and filled by shipment of the purchased goods interstate, does not render the corporation seller amenable to suit within the state. . . . . And appellant further argues that since it was not present within the state, it is a denial of due process to subject it to taxation or other money exaction. It thus denies the power of the state to lay the tax or to subject appellant to a suit for its collection.

Historically the jurisdiction of courts to render judgment *in personam* is grounded on their de facto power over the defendant's person. Hence his presence within the territorial jurisdiction of a court was prerequisite to its rendition of a judgment personally binding him. *Pennoyer v. Neff* . . . . But now that the capias ad respondendum has given way to personal service of summons or other form of notice, **due process requires only that in order to subject a defendant to a judgment in personam, if he be not present within the territory of the forum, he have certain minimum contacts with it such that the maintenance of the suit does not offend "traditional notions of fair play and substantial justice."** ***

> The Latin phrase **capias ad respondendum** refers to a writ issued by a court commanding the sheriff or other officer to seize the body of a defendant and take him into custody to ensure that he will will appear in court to answer the claims against him.

Since the corporate personality is a fiction, although a fiction intended to be acted upon as though it were a fact . . . , it is clear that unlike an individual its "presence" without, as well as within, the state of its origin can be manifested only by activities carried on in its behalf by those who are authorized to act for it. To say that the corporation is so far "present" there as to satisfy due process requirements, for purposes of taxation or the maintenance of suits against it in the courts of the state, is to beg the question to be decided. For the terms "present" or "presence" are used merely to symbolize those activities of the corporation's agent within the state which courts will deem to be sufficient to satisfy the demands of due process. . . . Those demands may be met by such contacts of the corporation with the state of the forum as make it reasonable, in the context of our federal system of government, to require the corporation to defend the particular suit which is brought there. An "estimate of the inconveniences" which would result to the corporation from a trial away from its "home" or principal place of business is relevant in this connection. . . .

"Presence" in the state in this sense has never been doubted when the activities of the corporation there have not only been continuous and systematic, but also give rise to the liabilities sued on, even though no consent to be sued or authorization to an agent to accept service of process has been given. . . . Conversely it has been generally recognized that the casual presence of the corporate agent or even his conduct of single or isolated items of activities in a state in the corporation's behalf are not enough to subject it to suit on causes of action unconnected with the activities there. . . . To require the corporation in such circumstances to defend the suit away from its home or other jurisdiction where it carries on more substantial activities has been thought to lay too great and unreasonable a burden on the corporation to comport with due process.

While it has been held in cases on which appellant relies that continuous activity of some sorts within a state is not enough to support the demand that the corporation be amenable to suits unrelated to that activity . . ., there have been instances in which the continuous corporate operations within a state were thought so substantial and of such a nature as to justify suit against it on causes of action arising from dealings entirely distinct from those activities. . . .

Finally, although the commission of some single or occasional acts of the corporate agent in a state sufficient to impose an obligation or liability on the corporation has not been thought to confer upon the state authority to enforce it, . . . other such acts, because of their nature and quality and the circumstances of their commission, may be deemed sufficient to render the corporation liable to suit. . . . True, some of the decisions holding the corporation amenable to suit have been supported by resort to the legal fiction that it has given its consent to service and suit, consent being implied from its presence in the state through the acts of its authorized agents. . . . But more realistically it may be said that those authorized acts were of such a nature as to justify the fiction.

* * *

It is evident that the criteria by which we mark the boundary line between those activities which justify the subjection of a corporation to suit, and those which do not, cannot be simply mechanical or quantitative. The test is not merely, as has sometimes been suggested, whether the activity, which the corporation has seen fit to procure through its agents in another state, is a little more or a little less. . . . Whether due process is satisfied must depend rather upon the quality and nature of the activity in relation to the fair and orderly administration of the laws which it was the purpose of the due process clause to insure. That clause does not contemplate that a state may make binding a judgment *in personam* against an individual or corporate defendant with which the state has no contacts, ties, or relations. . . .

But to the extent that a corporation exercises the privilege of conducting activities within a state, it enjoys the benefits and protection of the laws of that state. The exercise of that privilege may give rise to obligations; and, so far as those obligations arise out of or are connected with the activities within the state, a procedure which requires the corporation to respond to a suit brought to enforce them can, in most instances, hardly be said to be undue. . . .

Applying these standards, the activities carried on in behalf of appellant in the State of Washington were neither irregular nor casual. They were systematic and continuous throughout the years in question. They resulted in a large volume of interstate business, in the course of which appellant received the benefits and protection of the laws of the state, including the right to resort to the courts for the enforcement of its rights. The obligation which is here sued upon arose out of those very activities. It is evident that these operations establish sufficient contacts or ties with the state of the forum to make it reasonable and just according to our traditional conception of fair play and substantial justice to permit the state to enforce the obligations which appellant has incurred there. Hence we cannot say that the maintenance of the present suit in the State of Washington involves an unreasonable or undue procedure.

CASE ANALYSIS & QUESTIONS

 1. The Fourteenth Amendment's Due Process Clause sets the outer boundaries of a state tribunal's authority to proceed against a defendant. The path-breaking decision of *International Shoe* provides that state courts may exercise personal jurisdiction over an out-of-state defendant who has "certain minimum contacts with [the State] such that the maintenance of the suit does not offend 'traditional notions of fair play and substantial justice.'" 326 U.S. at 316.

2. The Court in *International Shoe* stressed the relevance of two factors in determining the constitutionality of personal jurisdiction: (1) the degree of contacts with the state; and (2) the relationship between those contacts and the lawsuit filed. From those two factors, the court then delineated four different kinds of cases that can be charted as follows:

	Regular, systematic and continuous contact in the state	**Isolated**, casual and sporadic contacts with the state
Contacts **unrelated** to the lawsuit	**General** personal jurisdiction will exist if the contacts are substantial, continuous, and systematic ("at home")	Personal jurisdiction will **not** exist.
Contacts **related** to the lawsuit.	Personal jurisdiction **will** exist as was the case in *International Shoe*	Some isolated contacts by virtue of their nature, quality and circumstances are sufficient to confer **specific** personal jurisdiction on a **related** lawsuit.

3. Specific Jurisdiction: The Court recognized that jurisdiction could be asserted where the corporation's in-state activity was both "continuous and systematic" and gave rise to the lawsuit filed. *International Shoe*, 326 U.S. at 317. It also observed that the commission of "single or occasional acts" in a state may be sufficient to render a corporation answerable in that state with respect to those acts, if there is a specific connection between those

acts and the lawsuit filed. 326 U.S. at 318. This type of jurisdiction is often termed "specific jurisdiction," because jurisdiction is based on a **specific connection** between the defendant's **specific** activity in the state and the resulting lawsuit.

4. General Jurisdiction: *International Shoe* distinguished "specific jurisdiction" from "instances in which the continuous corporate operations within a state [are] so substantial and of such a nature as to justify suit against a defendant on causes of action arising from dealings entirely distinct from those activities." 326 U.S. at 318. Adjudicatory authority so grounded is called "general jurisdiction." *See Helicopteros Nacioneles de Columbia, S.A. v. Hall*, 466 U.S. 408, 414, n.9 (1984).

Since *International Shoe*, the Supreme Court's decisions primarily have involved circumstances that warrant the exercise of specific jurisdiction. In only four decisions postdating *International Shoe*, the Court has considered whether an out-of-state corporate defendant's in-state contacts were sufficiently "continuous and systematic" to justify the exercise of general jurisdiction over claims unrelated to those contacts: *Daimler AG v. Bauman et al.*, 134 S. Ct. 746 (2014); *Goodyear Dunlop Tires Operations, S.A. v. Brown*, 131 S.Ct. 2846 (2011); *Perkins v. Benguet Consolidated Mining Co.*, 342 U.S. 437 (1952); and *Helicopteros*, 466 U.S. at 408.

In *Daimler*, the Supreme Court held that the constitution's due process clause prevented California from asserting "general" personal jurisdiction over Daimler for injuries allegedly caused by the conduct of one of its subsidiaries that took place outside the state. The Court limited general jurisdiction to those situations in which a corporation is incorporated in the state, its principal place of business is within the state, or it has "continuous and systematic" operations in the state that are so substantial as to render it essentially "**at home**" in the state. 134 S. Ct. at 761. Although one of Daimler's subsidiaries distributed its vehicles to dealers in the state of California, the Court concluded that general jurisdiction was not proper because Daimler was not "at home" in California and none of the claims involved any conduct or impact that occurred in that state.

Similarly, in *Goodyear*, the Supreme Court held that defendants were not amenable to suit in North Carolina on claims **unrelated** to their activities in the forum state. North Carolina residents whose sons died in a bus accident outside Paris, France, filed a wrongful-death action in North

Carolina state court. Alleging that the accident was caused by tire failure, they named as defendants Goodyear USA, an Ohio corporation, and three Goodyear USA subsidiaries, organized and operating in Luxembourg, Turkey, and France. The foreign subsidiaries' tires were manufactured primarily for European and Asian markets and differed in size and construction from tires ordinarily sold in the United States. The subsidiaries were not registered to do business in North Carolina; had no place of business, employees, or bank accounts in the state; did not design, manufacture, or advertise their products in the state; and did not solicit business in the state or sell or ship tires to North Carolina customers. A small percentage of their tires were distributed in North Carolina by other Goodyear USA affiliates. The Court concluded that defendants lacked the kind of continuous and systematic general business contacts necessary to allow North Carolina to entertain a suit against them unrelated to anything that connects them to the State.

The Court distinguished cases in which general jurisdiction might be appropriate.

In *Perkins*, general jurisdiction was properly exercised over a Philippine corporation sued in Ohio, because the company's systematic and continuous affairs were overseen in that state. The company had moved its management to Ohio because the Philippines had been invaded by Japan. The corporation was effectively "at home" in the state of Ohio.

The sporadic state activities by the tire subsidiaries in *Goodyear* were more akin to those found insufficient to establish general jurisdiction in *Helicopteros*. There, representatives of U.S. citizens, who were killed when a helicopter owned by a Colombian corporation crashed in Peru, could not maintain wrongful-death actions against that corporation in Texas. The company's contacts "consisted of sending its chief executive officer to Houston for a contract-negotiation session; accepting into its New York bank account checks drawn on a Houston bank; purchasing helicopters, equipment and training service from [a Texas enterprise] for substantial sums; and sending personnel to [Texas] for training." 466 U.S. at 416. According to the Supreme Court, these links to Texas did not constitute the kind of continuous and systematic general business contacts found to exist in *Perkins*, and were insufficient to support the exercise of jurisdiction over a claim that neither arose out of nor related to the defendant's activities in Texas. 466 U.S. at 415–16.

2. *International Shoe* and the Development of Long-Arm Statutes

The Supreme Court in *International Shoe* signaled that a state could constitutionally assert specific personal jurisdiction over a defendant who performs even a single act in the state so long as that single act: (1) is significant to the state by virtue of its nature, quality or circumstance; and (2) gives rise to the lawsuit filed in that state.

The Court's opinion thus invited the states to assert their power over defendants who perform a single act in that state if the act has a specific connection to the lawsuit. The states accepted the invitation, and enacted **long-arm statutes** by which they reached outside their territory to compel out-of-state defendants to defend a lawsuit in the state's courts. These long-arm statutes take three basic forms.

a. To the Maximum Extent Allowed by the Constitution

Some states, like California, enacted long-arm statutes that simply asserted personal jurisdiction to the maximum extent permitted by the federal constitution: "A court of this state may exercise jurisdiction on any basis not inconsistent with the Constitution of this state or of the United States." See California Long Arm Statute (Cal. Code Civ. Proc § 410.10).

b. Specific Activities, Related to a Lawsuit

Some states enacted long-arm statutes that explicitly identified those kinds of activities that are so important to the state that if the defendant performs any such activity in the state which gives rise to a lawsuit, that conduct is sufficient to confer specific personal jurisdiction. The statutes generally identify five kinds of conduct:

1. **Land**—the ownership, use or possession of land by the defendant in the state, from which the lawsuit derives.

2. **Injury from tort**—injury in the state from a tort or breach of duty committed by the defendant, from which the lawsuit derives.

3. **Matrimony**—a matrimonial relationship in the state, or the performance of an act in the state that gives rise to a claim for separation, annulment, or divorce.

4. Insurance Contracts—the defendant enters an insurance contract for a risk located in the state, from which the lawsuit derives.

5. Transaction of Business—the defendant enters into a transaction in the state, from which the lawsuit derives.

See, e.g., New York Long Arm Statute, N.Y.C.P.L.R., 302 (2003); Oregon Long Arm Statute, Or. R. Civ. P. 4.

c. Hybrid Statutes

Some states have enacted long-arm statutes that contain both specific jurisdictional bases and a catch-all clause that asserts power to the maximum extent permitted by the Constitution. Illinois § 2-209 is an excellent example:

THE STATUTE   735 ILCS 5/2-209

Act submitting to jurisdiction—Process

(a) Any person, whether or not a citizen or resident of this State, who in person or through an agent does any of the acts hereinafter enumerated, thereby submits such person, and, if an individual, his or her personal representative, to the jurisdiction of the courts of this State as to any cause of action arising from the doing of any of such acts:

(1) The transaction of any business within this State;

(2) The commission of a tortious act within this State;

(3) The ownership, use, or possession of any real estate situated in this State;

(4) Contracting to insure any person, property or risk located within this State at the time of contracting;

(5) With respect to actions of dissolution of marriage, declaration of invalidity of marriage and legal separation, the maintenance in this State of a matrimonial domicile at the time this cause of action arose or the commission in this State of any act giving rise to the cause of action;

(b) A court may exercise jurisdiction in any action arising within or without this State against any person who:

(1) Is a natural person present within this State when served;

(2) Is a natural person domiciled or resident within this State when the cause of action arose, the action was commenced, or process was served;

(3) Is a corporation organized under the laws of this State; or

(4) Is a natural person or corporation doing business within this State.

(c) A court may also exercise jurisdiction on any other basis now or hereafter permitted by the Illinois Constitution and the Constitution of the United States.

This long-arm statute is extremely aggressive. It enumerates specific activities which will confer personal jurisdiction in a related lawsuit. But the statute also codifies the traditional, common law, general jurisdictional bases of consent and presence. Moreover, the statute contains a catch-all clause that ensures that Illinois law grants to Illinois courts personal jurisdiction to the maximum extent allowed by the state and federal constitution.

EXAMPLES & ANALYSIS

EXAMPLE: Debra, a domiciliary of Vermont, rented an apartment in Chicago, Illinois for 6 months. With two months remaining on her lease, Debra returned to Vermont, and has refused to pay the rent due for the remaining two months. The Landlord brings a lawsuit in Illinois State Court against Debra for back rent. Debra files a timely motion to dismiss for lack of personal jurisdiction. How should the court rule?

Analysis: The court should deny the motion. Although Debra has not consented to personal jurisdiction, and is not present in Illinois, nonetheless the Illinois long-arm statute grants specific personal jurisdiction here because Debra has possessed real estate situated in Illinois, from which this lawsuit is derived.

EXAMPLE: Phyllis was severely injured when a water heater exploded in her home in Illinois. Phyllis sues Dexter Valves Inc. in Illinois State Court, alleging that this Ohio corporation's negligent installation of a defective valve in her water heater at its Ohio factory caused her injuries. Dexter Valves Inc. moves to dismiss for lack of personal jurisdiction. How should the court rule?

Analysis: The motion should be denied. Even if Dexter Valves Inc. has not consented to personal jurisdiction and is not present in Illinois, the Illinois long-arm statute nonetheless provides for personal jurisdiction because the defendant committed a tortious act in Illinois—where the injury from its alleged negligence occurred. *See Gray v. American Radiator & Standard Sanitary Corp.* 22 Ill. 2d 432, 176 N.E.2d 761 (1961).

In Practice

This state statute's grant of personal jurisdiction to the extent permitted by the constitution means that the issue of whether Illinois law grants personal jurisdiction and the issue of the constitutionality of Illinois law become logically the same. Nonetheless, courts and litigants in this situation typically try to find a specifically-enumerated basis for the assertion of personal jurisdiction rather than resorting to the catch-all clause.

3. The Application and Evolution of *International Shoe* and Due Process

In the years following *International Shoe*, the courts generally expanded the constitutional power to compel out-of-state defendants to appear in distant jurisdictions.

In *McGee v. International Life Insurance Co.*, 355 U.S. 220 (1957), McGee was the beneficiary of a life insurance policy issued by the Empire Mutual Insurance Co., an Arizona corporation, to Lowell Franklin, a resident of California. In 1948, the defendant, International Life Insurance Co., assumed Empire Mutual's insurance obligations. Franklin and International Life transacted business by mail until Franklin's death in 1950. Neither Empire Mutual nor International Life ever had any office or agent in California, and International Life had never solicited or done any insurance business in California other than the policy with Franklin. When International Life refused to pay McGee upon Franklin's death, she sued in a California state court. The Supreme Court held that the exercise of jurisdiction by California was proper.

The Court noted that, with increased "nationalization of commerce," the tremendous growth "in the amount of business conducted by mail across state lines" and the frequency with which "commercial transactions touch two or more States," there had developed "a trend [that] is clearly discernible toward expanding the permissible scope of state jurisdiction over foreign corporations and other nonresidents." 355 U.S. at 222. The Court reasoned:

> . . . [W]e think it apparent that the Due Process Clause did not preclude the California court from entering a judgment binding on respondent. It is sufficient . . . that the suit was based on a contract which had substantial connection with that State. . . . The contract was delivered in California, the premiums were mailed from there and the insured was a resident of that State when he died. . . . California has a manifest interest in providing effective means of redress for its residents when their insurers refuse to pay claims. These residents would be at a severe disadvantage if they were forced to follow the insurance company to a distant State in order to hold it legally accountable. When claims were small or moderate individual claimants frequently could not afford the cost of bringing an action in a foreign forum- thus in effect making the company judgment proof. Often the crucial witnesses- as here on the company's defense of suicide- will be found in the insured's locality. Of course there may be inconvenience to the insurer if it is held amenable to suit in California where it had this contract but certainly nothing which amounts to a denial of due process.

355 U.S. at 223-24.

In *World-Wide Volkswagen Corp. v. Woodson*, 444 U.S. 286 (1980), however, the Supreme Court limited the expansion of personal jurisdiction, and created a more exacting template for the assertion of personal jurisdiction.

FROM THE COURT

World-Wide Volkswagen Corp. v. Woodson
444 U.S. 286 (1980)
Supreme Court of the United States

Certiorari to the Supreme Court of Oklahoma

Mr. Justice White delivered the opinion of the Court.

The issue before us is whether, consistently with the Due Process Clause of the Fourteenth Amendment, an Oklahoma court may exercise *in personam* jurisdiction over a nonresident automobile retailer and its wholesale distributor in a products liability action, when the defendants' only connection to Oklahoma is the fact that an automobile sold in New York to New York residents became involved in an accident in Oklahoma.

I.

Respondents Harry and Kay Robinson purchased a new Audi automobile from petitioner Seaway Volkswagen, Inc. (Seaway) in Massena, N.Y., in 1976. The following year the Robinson family, who resided in New York, left that State for a new home in Arizona. As they passed through the state of Oklahoma, another car struck their Audi in the rear, causing a fire which severely burned Kay Robinson and her two children.

The Robinsons subsequently brought a products liability action in the District Court for Creek County, Okla., claiming that their injuries resulted from defective design and placement of the Audi's gas tank and fuel system. They joined as defendants the automobile's manufacturer, NSU Auto Union Aktiengesellschaft (Audi); its importer, Volkswagen of America, Inc. (Volkswagen); its regional distributor, petitioner World-Wide Volkswagen Corporation (World-Wide); and its retail dealer, petitioner Seaway. Seaway and World-Wide entered special appearances, claiming that Oklahoma's exercise of jurisdiction over them would offend the limitations on the State's jurisdiction imposed by the Due Process clause of the Fourteenth Amendment.

The facts presented to the District Court showed that World-Wide is incorporated and has its business office in New York. It distributes vehicles, parts, and accessories, under contract with Volkswagen, to retail dealers in New York, New Jersey, and Connecticut. Seaway, one of these retail dealers, is incorporated and has its place of business in New York. Insofar as the record reveals, Seaway and World-Wide are fully independent corporations whose relations with each other and with Volkswagen and Audi are contractual only. Respondents adduced no evidence that either World-Wide or Seaway does any business in Oklahoma, ships or sells any products to or in that State, has an agent to receive process there, or purchases advertisements in any media calculated to reach Oklahoma. In fact, . . . there was no showing that any automobile sold by World-Wide or Seaway has ever entered Oklahoma with the single exception of the vehicle involved in the present case.

Despite the apparent paucity of contacts between petitioners and Oklahoma, the District Court rejected their constitutional claim and reaffirmed that ruling in denying petitioners' motion for reconsideration. Petitioners then sought a writ of prohibition in the Supreme Court of Oklahoma to restrain the District Judge, respondent Charles S. Woodson, from exercising *in personam* jurisdiction over them. They renewed their contention that, because they had no "minimal contacts" . . . with the State of Oklahoma, the actions of the District Judge were in violation of their rights under the Due Process Clause.

The Supreme Court of Oklahoma denied the writ, . . . holding that personal jurisdiction over petitioners was authorized by Oklahoma's "long-arm" statute, Okla.Stat., Tit. 12, § 1702.03(a)(4)(1971). Although the court noted that the proper approach was to test jurisdiction against both statutory and constitutional standards, its analysis did not distinguish these questions, probably because § 1701.03(a)(4) has been interpreted as conferring jurisdiction to the limits permitted by the United States Constitution. The court's rationale was contained in the following paragraph . . .:

> In the case before us, the product being sold and distributed by the petitioners is by its very design and purpose so mobile that petitioners can foresee its possible use in Oklahoma. This is especially true of the distributor, who has the exclusive right to

distribute such automobile in New York, New Jersey and Connecticut. The evidence presented below demonstrated that goods sold and distributed by the petitioners were used in the State of Oklahoma, and under the facts we believe it reasonable to infer, given the retail value of the automobile, that the petitioners derive substantial income from automobiles which from time to time are used in the State of Oklahoma. This being the case, we hold that under the facts presented, the trial court was justified in concluding that the petitioners derive substantial revenue from goods used or consumed in this State.

We granted certiorari . . . to consider an important constitutional question with respect to state-court jurisdiction and to resolve a conflict between the Supreme Court of Oklahoma and the highest courts of at least four other States. We reverse.

II

* * *

As has long been settled, and as we affirm today, a state court may exercise personal jurisdiction over a nonresident defendant only so long as there exist "minimum contacts" between the defendant and the forum State. *International Shoe Co. v. Washington* . . . . The concept of minimum contacts, in turn, can be seen to perform two related, but distinguishable, functions. It protects the defendant against the burdens of litigating in a distant or inconvenient forum. And it acts to ensure that the States, through their courts, do not reach out beyond the limits imposed on them by their status as coequal sovereigns in a federal system.

The protection against inconvenient litigation is typically described in terms of "reasonableness" or "fairness." We have said that the defendant's contacts with the forum State must be such that maintenance of the suit "does not offend 'traditional notions of fair play and substantial justice.'" . . . The relationship between the defendant and the forum must be such that it is "reasonable . . . to require the corporation to defend the particular suit which is brought there." . . . Implicit in this emphasis on reasonableness is the understanding that the burden on the defendant, while always a primary concern, will in an appropriate case be considered in light of other relevant factors, including the forum

State's interest in adjudicating the dispute . . .; the plaintiff's interest in obtaining convenient and effective relief, . . . at least when that interest is not adequately protected by the plaintiff's power to choose the forum . . .; the interstate judicial system's interest in obtaining the most efficient resolution of controversies; and the shared interest of the several States in furthering fundamental substantive social policies . . . .

III

Applying these principles to the case at hand, we find in the record before us a total absence of those affiliating circumstances that are a necessary predicate to any exercise of state-court jurisdiction. Petitioners carry on no activity whatsoever in Oklahoma. They close no sales and perform no services there. They avail themselves of none of the privileges and benefits of Oklahoma law. They solicit no business there either through salespersons or through advertising reasonably calculated to reach the State. Nor does the record show that they regularly sell cars at wholesale or retail to Oklahoma customers or residents or that they indirectly, through others, serve or seek to serve the Oklahoma market. In short, respondents seek to base jurisdiction on one, isolated occurrence and whatever inferences can be drawn therefrom: the fortuitous circumstance that a single Audi automobile, sold in New York to New York residents, happened to suffer an accident while passing through Oklahoma.

It is argued, however, that because an automobile is mobile by its very design and purpose it was "foreseeable" that the Robinsons' Audi would cause injury in Oklahoma. Yet "foreseeability" alone has never been a sufficient benchmark for personal jurisdiction under the Due Process Clause. In *Hanson v. Denckla*, 357 U.S. 235 (1958) . . . it was no doubt foreseeable that the settlor of a Delaware trust would subsequently move to Florida and seek to exercise a power of appointment there; yet we held that Florida courts could not constitutionally exercise jurisdiction over a Delaware trustee that had no other contacts with the forum State. . . .

If foreseeability were the criterion, a local California tire retailer could be forced to defend in Pennsylvania when a blowout occurs there, . . . a Wisconsin seller of a defective automobile jack could be haled before a distant court for damage caused in New Jersey, . . . or a Florida soft-drink concessionaire could be summoned to Alaska to account for injuries happening there . . . . Every seller of chattels would in effect appoint the chattel his agent for service of process. His amenability to suit would travel with the chattel. . . .

This is not to say, of course, that foreseeability is wholly irrelevant. But the foreseeability that is critical to due process analysis is not the mere likelihood that a product will find its way into the forum State. Rather, it is that the defendant's conduct and connection with the forum State are such that he should reasonably anticipate being haled into court there. . . . The Due Process Clause, by ensuring the "orderly administration of the laws," . . . gives a degree of predictability to the legal system that allows potential defendants to structure their primary conduct with some minimum assurance as to where that conduct will and will not render them liable to suit.

When a corporation "purposefully avails itself of the privilege of conducting activities within the forum State," . . . it has clear notice that it is subject to suit there, and can act to alleviate the risk of burdensome litigation by procuring insurance, passing the expected costs on to customers, or, if the risks are too great, severing its connection with the State. Hence if the sale of a product of a manufacturer or distributor such as Audi or Volkswagen is not simply an isolated occurrence, but arises from the efforts of the manufacturer or distributor to serve, directly or indirectly, the market for its product in other States, it is not unreasonable to subject it to suit in one of those States if its allegedly defective merchandise has there been the source of injury to its owner or to others. The forum State does not exceed its powers under the Due Process Clause if it asserts personal jurisdiction over a corporation that delivers its products into the stream of commerce with the expectation that they will be purchased by consumers in the forum State. Cf. *Gray v. American Radiator & Standard Sanitary Corp.* . . .

But there is no such or similar basis for Oklahoma jurisdiction over World-Wide or Seaway in this case. Seaway's sales are made in Massena, N.Y. World-Wide's market, although substantially larger, is limited to dealers in New York, New Jersey, and Connecticut. There is no evidence of record that any automobiles distributed by World-Wide are sold to retail customers outside this tri-state area. It is foreseeable that the purchasers of automobiles sold by World-Wide and Seaway may take them to Oklahoma. But the mere "unilateral activity of those who claim some relationship with a nonresident defendant cannot satisfy the requirement of contact with the forum State." . . .

In a variant on the previous argument, it is contended that jurisdiction can be supported by the fact that petitioners earn substantial revenue from goods used in Oklahoma. . . . While this inference seems less than compelling on the facts of the instant case, we need not question the court's factual findings in order to reject its reasoning.

This argument seems to make the point that the purchase of automobiles in New York, from which the petitioners earn substantial revenue, would not occur but for the fact that the automobiles are capable of use in distant States like Oklahoma. Respondents observe that the very purpose of an automobile is to travel, and that travel of automobiles sold by petitioners is facilitated by an extensive chain of Volkswagen service centers throughout the country, including some in Oklahoma. However, financial benefits accruing to the defendant from a collateral relation to the forum State will not support jurisdiction if they do not stem from a constitutionally cognizable contact with that State. . . . In our view, whatever marginal revenues petitioners may receive by virtue of the fact that their products are capable of use in Oklahoma is far too attenuated a contact to justify that State's exercise of *in personam* jurisdiction over them.

Because we find that petitioners have no "contacts, ties, or relations" with the State of Oklahoma, *International Shoe Co. v. Washington*, . . . the judgment of the Supreme Court of Oklahoma is

Reversed.

CASE ANALYSIS & QUESTIONS

1. The *World-Wide* Template

The Supreme Court in *World-Wide* crafted a template for the constitutional analysis of personal jurisdiction that is still controlling law. According to the Court's reasoning, the *International Shoe* standard actually created two related, but distinct steps in the Analysis: (1) minimum contacts, and (2) fairness.

First, as a threshold matter, the defendant must have minimum contacts with the forum state. In determining whether there are minimum contacts, the court will consider whether the defendant **purposefully availed** itself of the benefits and protections of the forum state's laws and consumers. If there are no such minimum contacts, the assertion of personal jurisdiction would be unconstitutional—regardless of the fairness of the assertion of that jurisdiction.

Second, if there are minimum contacts, then the defendant can avoid personal jurisdiction by showing that it would be unfair to litigate the matter in the forum state. In considering whether it would be unfair, the courts will weigh five fairness factors:

  a. The defendant's burden in litigating in the forum court;

  b. The forum state's interest in having the litigation in its own courts;

  c. The plaintiff's interest in litigating in its chosen forum;

  d. The interstate judicial system's interest in the most efficient resolution of the entire litigation; and

  e. The shared several states' interest in furthering substantive social policies.

2. The Application of the *World-Wide* Template

In *Burger King Corp. v. Rudzewicz*, 471 U.S. 462 (1985), Burger King, a Florida corporation whose principal offices are in Miami, Florida, brought an action in federal court in Florida based on diversity jurisdiction against Michigan residents John Rudzewicz and Brian MacShara, alleging that they breached their twenty-year franchise contract by failing to make the required monthly payments. The franchisees claimed that, because they were

Michigan residents and because Burger King's claim did not arise within Florida, the District Court lacked personal jurisdiction over them.

But the Supreme Court held that the assertion of personal jurisdiction was constitutional because the franchisees had purposefully availed themselves of the benefits of Florida, and they could not establish that it would be unfair to require them to litigate in Florida. The Court began by determining that the defendants had purposefully availed themselves of Florida, because they entered into a twenty-year franchise contract with Burger King, "which had a substantial connection with that State." 471 U.S. at 479-80. In particular, the franchise agreement stated:

> This Agreement shall become valid when executed and accepted by BKC at Miami, Florida; it shall be deemed made and entered into in the State of Florida and shall be governed and construed under and in accordance with the laws of the State of Florida.

471 U.S. at 481.

The Court declared that if there is evidence of purposeful availment, the burden then transfers to the defendant to present a compelling case of unfairness. In *Burger King*, the defendants failed to meet their burden of showing that the assertion of jurisdiction over them would be unfair under the five fairness factors articulated in *World-Wide*.

3. Flexibility in the Due Process Clause?

The Supreme Court in *Burger King* indicated that where the burden on a party to litigate in a particular forum is so grave as to deprive that party of its day in court, it would be a violation of due process for the court to reach a judgment. The court declared:

> Just as the Due Process Clause allows flexibility in ensuring that commercial actors are not effectively "judgment proof" for the consequences of obligations they voluntarily assume in other States, McGee v. International Life Insurance Co., . . . so too does it prevent rules that would unfairly enable them to obtain default judgments against unwitting customers. . . .

471 U.S. at 486.

What does the Court mean by this statement regarding the flexibility of the Due Process Clause?

In *Asahi Metal Industry Co., Ltd. v. Superior Court of California*, 480 U.S. 102 (1987), the Supreme Court addressed the question whether the mere awareness on the part of a foreign defendant that the component it manufactured, sold, and delivered outside the United States would reach the forum state in the stream of commerce constitutes minimum contacts between the defendant and the forum state such that the exercise of jurisdiction does not offend traditional notions of fair play and substantial justice.

Gary Zurcher lost control of his motorcycle and collided with a tractor in California. Zurcher was severely injured, and his passenger and wife, was killed. Zurcher filed a product liability action in California state court, alleging that the accident was caused by defects in the motorcycle's tire, tube and sealant. Zurcher's complaint named, *inter alia*, Cheng Shin Rubber Industrial Co., Ltd. (Cheng Shin), the Taiwanese manufacturer of the tube. Cheng Shin in turn filed a cross-complaint seeking indemnification from Asahi Metal Industry Co., Ltd. (Asahi), the manufacturer of the tube's valve assembly. Zurcher's claims against Cheng Shin and the other defendants were settled and dismissed, however, leaving only Cheng Shin's indemnity action against Asahi.

> The Latin phrase, "**inter alia**," means *among others*.

The Supreme Court of California found the exercise of jurisdiction over Asahi to be consistent with the Due Process Clause. It concluded that Asahi knew that some of the valve assemblies sold to Cheng Shin would be incorporated into tire tubes sold in California, and that Asahi benefited indirectly from the sale in California of products incorporating its components. The California Supreme Court considered Asahi's intentional act of placing its components into the stream of commerce—that is, by delivering the components to Cheng Shin in Taiwan—coupled with Asahi's awareness that some of the components would eventually find their way into California, sufficient to form the basis for state court jurisdiction under the Due Process Clause. But the Supreme Court of the United States reversed.

Writing for four justices, Justice O'Connor declared:

> The "substantial connection" . . . between the defendant and the forum
> State necessary for a finding of minimum contacts must come about
> by an action of the defendant purposefully directed toward the forum
> State. . . . The placement of a product into the stream of commerce,
> without more, is not an act of the defendant purposefully directed to-
> ward the forum State. **Additional conduct of the defendant may indi-
> cate an intent or purpose to serve the market in the forum State, for
> example, designing the product for the market in the forum State,
> advertising in the forum State, establishing channels for providing
> regular advice to customers in the forum State, or marketing the prod-
> uct through a distributor who has agreed to serve as the sales agent
> in the forum State. But a defendant's awareness that the stream of
> commerce may or will sweep the product into the forum State does
> not convert the mere act of placing the product into the stream into
> an act purposefully directed toward the forum State.**
>
> Assuming, arguendo, that respondents have established Asahi's aware-
> ness that some of the valves sold to Cheng Shin would be incorporated
> into tire tubes sold in California, respondents have not demonstrated
> any action by Asahi to **purposefully avail** itself of the California mar-
> ket. Asahi does not do business in California. It has no office, agents,
> employees, or property in California. It does not advertise or otherwise
> solicit business in California. It did not create, control, or employ the
> distribution system that brought its valves to California. . . . There is
> no evidence that Asahi designed its product in anticipation of sales in
> California. . . . On the basis of these facts, the exertion of personal
> jurisdiction over Asahi by the Superior Court of California exceeds the
> limits of due process.

480 U.S. at 112-13.

Although Justice O'Connor's discussion of minimum contacts and purposeful availment garnered only four votes, eight Justices agreed that even
if Asahi had purposefully availed itself of California, personal jurisdiction
would nonetheless still be unconstitutional because of the extreme unfairness of the forum. The burden on the defendant Asahi to litigate in another
country's courts was substantial; the plaintiff Cheng Shin's interest in liti-

gating its lingering indemnity action in that forum was modest; the state of California's interest in the indemnity action governed by foreign law was slight, and the interests of the judicial system and of the states favored litigation in another country's judicial system.

Justice Stevens also wrote separately to declare:

> [w]hether or not this conduct rises to the level of purposeful availment requires a constitutional determination that is affected by the volume, the value, and the hazardous character of the components. In most circumstances I would be inclined to conclude that a regular course of dealing that results in deliveries of over 100,000 units annually over a period of several years would constitute "purposeful availment" even though the item delivered to the forum State was a standard product marketed throughout the world.

480 U.S. at 122. (Stevens, J., concurring).

In *J. McIntyre Machinery, Ltd. v. Nicastro*, 131 S.Ct. 2780 (2011), the Supreme Court suggested that the purposeful availment requirement could only be met if the defendant intended to invoke or benefit from the forum state's laws by specifically targeting consumers in that particular state. Nicastro injured his hand while using a metal-shearing machine that J. McIntyre Machinery, Ltd. (J. McIntyre), manufactured in England, where the company is incorporated and operates. Nicastro filed a products-liability suit in a state court in New Jersey, where the accident occurred, but J.McIntyre sought to dismiss the suit for lack of personal jurisdiction.

Nicastro's jurisdictional claim was based on three primary facts: (1) a United States distributor agreed to sell J. McIntyre's machines in the United States; (2) J. McIntyre officials attended trade shows in several states, albeit not in New Jersey; and (3) up to four J.McIntyre machines, including the one at issue, ended up in New Jersey.

The State Supreme Court held that New Jersey's courts can exercise jurisdiction over a foreign manufacturer without contravening the Fourteenth Amendment's Due Process Clause so long as the manufacturer knew or reasonably should have known that its products are distributed through a nationwide distribution system that might lead to sales in any of the states. Invoking this stream-of-commerce doctrine of jurisdiction, the court concluded that J. McIntyre was subject to jurisdiction in New Jersey, even though at no time had it advertised in, sent goods to, or in any relevant sense targeted the state.

The United States Supreme Court, however, reversed. Writing for four justices, Justice Kennedy concluded that because J. McIntyre never engaged in any activities in New Jersey that revealed an intent to benefit from the protection of the state's laws, or an intent to target the state's consumers, New Jersey was without power to adjudge the company's rights and liabilities, and its exercise of jurisdiction would violate due process. In his opinion, Justice Kennedy reasoned:

(a) First,

> [a] court may subject a defendant to judgment only when the defendant has sufficient contacts with the sovereign ... As a general rule, the sovereign's exercise of power requires some act by which the defendant "purposefully avails itself of the privilege of conducting activities within the forum State, thus invoking the benefits and protections of its laws."

131 S. Ct. at 2787.

(b) Second,

> [t]he rules and standards for determining when a state does or does not have jurisdiction over an absent party have been unclear because of decades-old questions left open in *Asahi* ... The imprecision arising from *Asahi*, for the most part, results from its statement of the relation between jurisdiction and the "stream of commerce." ... [A] defendant's placement of goods into commerce "with the expectation that they will be purchased by consumers within the forum State" may indicate purposeful availment. ... But that statement does not amend the general rule of personal jurisdiction. **The principal inquiry in cases of this sort is whether the defendant's activities manifest an intention to submit to the power of a sovereign.**

131 S.Ct. at 2785-88.

(c) Third, Nicastro

> has not established that J. McIntyre engaged in conduct purposefully
> directed at New Jersey. ... [The company] had no office in New Jersey;
> it neither paid taxes nor owned property there; and it neither advertised
> in, nor sent any employees to, the State. Indeed, the trial court found
> that the 'defendant does not have a single contact with New Jersey short
> of the machine in question ended up in [the] state.' *** These facts may
> reveal an intent to serve the U.S. market, but they do not show that J.
> McIntyre purposefully availed itself of the New Jersey market.

131 S.Ct. at 2790.

In *Nicastro*, Justice Breyer, joined by Justice Alito, agreed that the New
Jersey Supreme Court's judgment must be reversed, but concluded that
because this case does not present issues arising from recent changes in
commerce and communication, it is unwise to announce a rule of broad
applicability without fully considering modern-day consequences. Rather,
Justices Breyer and Alito believe that the outcome of the case can be determined by the Supreme Court's precedents. According to these Justices,
none of the Court's precedents finds that a single isolated sale, even if accompanied by the kind of sales effort indicated here, is sufficient. Here, the
relevant facts showed no regular flow or course of sales in New Jersey. None
of the additional evidence of purposeful availment mentioned in *Asahi* existed, such as special state-related design, advertising, advice, or marketing
that would warrant the assertion of jurisdiction. *Nicastro* demonstrated no
specific effort by the British Manufacturer to sell in New Jersey. And he did
not otherwise show that the British Manufacturer "purposefully avail[ed]
itself of the privilege of conducting activities" within New Jersey, or that it
delivered its goods in the stream of commerce "with the expectation that
they will be purchased" by New Jersey consumers. 131 S.Ct. at 2791-2794
(Breyer, J., concurring).

In light of the various opinions in *Nicastro* and *Asahi*, therefore, minimum
contacts with a forum state will be found only if the defendant has purposefully availed itself of the **particular** forum state's laws or has specifically
targeted the forum state's consumers.

In *Walden v. Fiore*, 134 S. Ct. 1115 (2014), the Supreme Court further
clarified that a state may not assert personal jurisdiction unless the defendant has purposefully created contact with the forum state. There, Ne-

vada attempted to assert specific personal jurisdiction over a police officer who allegedly improperly seized the plaintiffs' cash at the Atlanta airport and then filed a false affidavit attempting to support a forfeiture action designed to prevent the plaintiffs from recovering their seized funds. Although the defendant was fully aware that his conduct would impact the plaintiffs who had strong connections to Nevada, the Court declared that the mere fact that the defendant's conduct "affected plaintiffs with connections to the forum State does not suffice to authorize jurisdiction." 134 S. Ct. at 1136. Rather, "it is the defendant, not the plaintiff or third parties, who must create contact in the forum state." *Id.* As in *McIntyre*, the Court in *Walden* indicated that the constitutional assertion of personal jurisdiction requires a showing that the defendant purposefully directed its activities toward the forum State, not just toward individuals who happen to have a connection to that state.

4. Personal Jurisdiction and the Internet

In applying the evolving test for the constitutionality of the assertion of personal jurisdiction, the courts have grappled with analyzing the extent to which a defendant's internet presence constitutes minimum contacts with a forum state. A defendant who operates a website reaches out to the world and therefore arguably purposefully avails itself of the benefits and protections of every state.

Nonetheless, the courts are now virtually uniform in their judgment that a defendant's use of the internet to support its business operations **alone** will not establish sufficient contacts with a particular forum state to support the constitutional assertion of personal jurisdiction. *See, e.g., Pebble Beach, Co. v. Caddy*, 453 F.3d 1151 (9th Cir. 2006)(bed and breakfast owner in England did not purposefully avail itself of California for personal jurisdiction purposes merely by advertising its services over its website). Rather, the courts are "careful in resolving questions about personal jurisdiction involving online contacts to ensure that a defendant is not haled into court simply because the defendant owns or operates a website that is accessible in the forum state, even if that site is 'interactive.' " *BE2LLC and be2 Holding, A-G v. Ivanov*, 642 F.3d 555, 558 (7th Cir. 2011), citing *Illinois v. Hemi Group*, LLC, 622 F.3d 754, 760 (7th Cir. 2010) (defendant's operation of an interactive website that had attracted some in-state responses not sufficient to establish personal jurisdiction absent additional evidence of targeting the state).

In *Zippo Manufacturing Co. v. Zippo Dot Com, Inc.* 952 F. Supp. 1119, 1124 (W.D. Pa. 1997), the district court established a sliding-scale approach under which a defendant's web presence is placed on a spectrum. On one end of the spectrum are defendants who, because they employ active web sites to effectuate their transactions with customers, are subject to personal jurisdiction. On the other end of the spectrum, defendants who keep passive websites are not subject to personal jurisdiction. For defendants in the middle, who operate interactive websites for the exchange of information with customers, additional commercial activity must be weighed.

Most courts, however, have discarded the Zippo sliding-scale test. Beyond simply operating an interactive website that is accessible from the forum state, a defendant must in some way target the forum state's market. *See Chloé v. Queen Bee of Beverly Hills*, LLC, 616 F. 3d 158, 171 (2d Cir. 2010) (operation of a website over which counterfeit handbags were sold, combined with shipment into the state and other substantial business activity sufficient to confer personal jurisdiction); *Snowney v. Harrah's Entertainment, Inc.*, 35 Cal. 4th 1054, 112 P. 3d 28(2005) (Nevada casino hotel's marketing efforts directed toward California customers allow assertion of personal jurisdiction by California courts); *Rio Properties, Inc. v. Rio International Interlink*, 284 F. 3d 1007, 1020 (9th Cir. 2002) (personal jurisdiction proper over operator of internet gambling site who also specifically targeted in-state customers).

If the defendant merely operates a highly interactive website that is accessible from, but does not target, the forum state, then the defendant may not be haled into court in that state without offending the Constitution. *See Carefirst of Maryland, Inc. v. Carefirst Pregnancy Centers, Inc.*, 334 F. 3d 390, 394-95, 401 (4th Cir. 2003) (operation of semi-interactive website without "something more" evidencing an intent to target the state not sufficient); *GTE New Media Services Inc. v. BellSouth Corp.*, 199 F. 3d 1343, 1349-50 (D.C. Cir. 2000) (mere operation of highly interactive website accessible to in-state consumers not sufficient to establish purposeful availment).

5. In Rem and Quasi-in-Rem Jurisdiction

Recall that in the aftermath of *Pennoyer*, there was **in personem** jurisdiction (judicial power over the defendant's person), **in rem jurisdiction** (judicial power over a thing located in the forum state), and **quasi-in rem jurisdiction** (judicial power over defendant's property located in the forum state which, if properly brought within the control of the court, could be used to satisfy an unrelated judgment against a defendant not personally present in the state).

In rem jurisdiction remains a basis for exercising judicial power over property located in the forum state. It continues to be used to address issues involving real property, including title, boundaries, and easements.

Although quasi-in-rem jurisdiction has not been abolished, its utility was greatly reduced by the Supreme Court's decision in *Shaffer v. Heitner*, 433 U.S. 186 (1977), in which the Court held that "all" exercises of personal jurisdiction must be assessed according to the minimum contacts template of International Shoe.

In *Shaffer*, the Court declared unconstitutional the seizure of defendants' stock, which was constructively present in Delaware, to acquire personal jurisdiction over defendants who were sued on claims unrelated to the property and had no other significant contacts with the state. After *Shaffer*, the constitutionality of the assertion of personal jurisdiction in a quasi in rem situation must be analyzed on a case by case basis in light of the minimum contacts and fairness standards established in *International Shoe*.

But also recall that despite *Shaffer*, four Justices in *Burnham v. Superior Court* clearly found that "tag" personal jurisdiction established by serving a defendant in transit through the forum state did not need to meet the International Shoe minimum contacts test. The views of the other five members of the *Burnham* Court are less clear. Nonetheless Burnham and continued use of tag jurisdiction without a minimum contacts inquiry is in tension with *Shaffer v. Heitner*.

PERSONAL JURISDICTION IN FEDERAL COURT

Introduction

Although personal jurisdiction usually involves the power of a state court over the person or property of a defendant, that power also is implicated when a lawsuit is filed in federal court. When a federal court adjudicates a civil action, it threatens the parties with a deprivation of their liberty and property. The Fifth Amendment's Due Process Clause prohibits the federal courts from depriving persons of their liberty or property without due process. Because personal jurisdiction is a fundamental ingredient of due process, a federal court may not enter a binding and enforceable judgment unless it has proper personal jurisdiction over the defendant.

The issue whether a federal court has personal jurisdiction requires a familiar two-step analysis. First, the forum's own law must grant personal jurisdiction. Second, if the forum's law grants personal jurisdiction, the next issue is whether the application of that law would be constitutional. In federal court, the forum's law derives from the federal rules of civil procedure, particularly Rule 4.

A. The Federal Rule

THE RULE   Rule 4(k)

Territorial Limits of Effective Service

(1) ***In General.*** Serving a summons or filing a waiver of service establishes **personal jurisdiction** over a defendant:

    (A) **who is subject to the jurisdiction of a court of general jurisdiction in the state** where the district court is located;

    (B) who is a party joined under Rule 14 or 19 and is served within a judicial district of the United States and not more than 100 miles from where the summons was issued; or

    (C) when authorized by a federal statute.

(2) ***Federal Claim Outside State-Court Jurisdiction.*** For a claim that arises under federal law, serving a summons or filing a waiver of service establishes personal jurisdiction over a defendant if:

    (A) the defendant is not subject to jurisdiction in any state's courts of general jurisdiction; and

    (B) exercising jurisdiction is consistent with the United States Constitution and laws.

EXPLANATION

1. Primary Grants of Personal Jurisdiction

 This rule grants to the federal courts personal jurisdiction over defendants in two basic ways: (1) if a federal statute governing the claim expressly authorizes personal jurisdiction, or (2) if the law of the state where the federal court sits would grant personal jurisdiction.

a. Federal Statutory Authority

In some exceptional cases, Congress has authorized the assertion of personal jurisdiction as an explicit part of a statute creating a private right of action. For instance, in its federal securities laws and federal antitrust laws, Congress has explicitly granted to the federal courts the power to exercise personal jurisdiction over defendants served anywhere in the United States. *See, e.g.,* 15 U.S.C. §§ 77v(a), 78aa; 15 U.S.C. §§ 5, 22, 25.

b. The Personal Jurisdiction Law of the State Where the Federal Court Sits

Because Congress' explicit statutory authorization of personal jurisdiction is rare, a federal court typically will rely upon the law of the state where it sits to exercise personal jurisdiction. Rule 4(k)(1)(A) enables a federal court simply to borrow the same personal jurisdiction law of the state where it is located. A federal court sitting in Wyoming, for example, acts just like a Wyoming state court for personal jurisdiction purposes, and adopts that state's local personal jurisdiction law as its own.

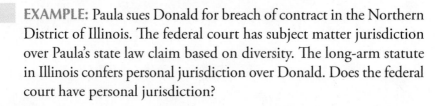

EXAMPLES & ANALYSIS

EXAMPLE: Paula sues Donald for breach of contract in the Northern District of Illinois. The federal court has subject matter jurisdiction over Paula's state law claim based on diversity. The long-arm statute in Illinois confers personal jurisdiction over Donald. Does the federal court have personal jurisdiction?

Analysis: Yes, as long as the federal court's assertion of the Illinois long-arm statute would be constitutional. A federal court has personal jurisdiction if: (1) the law of the forum grants personal jurisdiction; and (2) if the application of the forum law is constitutional. In this diversity action where the claim is created by state law, there can be no federal statute that grants personal jurisdiction. In the absence of such a statute, the federal court borrows the personal jurisdiction law of the state where it sits. The federal court in Illinois thus may employ the Illinois long-arm statute as the law of the forum. Because that Illinois law grants personal jurisdiction, the federal court's forum law grants personal jurisdiction as well. Even if that forum law grants personal jurisdiction, however, the assertion of that law must still be constitutional.

2. Exceptional Grants of Personal Jurisdiction

Federal Rule 4 also authorizes the assertion of personal jurisdiction in two other exceptional circumstances.

a. The 100-Mile Rule

First, a federal court may assert personal jurisdiction over additional parties who are impleaded under Rule 14 or who are joined as indispensable parties under Rule 19. In these precise joinder situations, a federal court may assert personal jurisdiction over the joined parties, if they are served with process within 100 miles—measured as a straight line in any direction— from the federal court. This 100-mile authorization does not apply to plaintiffs initiating an action against defendants; it only applies to parties joined under Rule 14 or 19.

The 100-mile zone may extend beyond state borders, but not beyond national borders.

EXAMPLES & ANALYSIS

EXAMPLE: Paula files a state law tort claim against Donald in federal court in the Northern District of Illinois based on diversity. Donald impleads Teresa, alleging that Teresa is liable for part of any liability to Paula. Donald arranges for an authorized process-server to serve Teresa personally in Centuryville, Indiana, which is 65 miles from the federal courthouse. Do the federal rules authorize the assertion of personal jurisdiction over Teresa?

Analysis: Yes. Rule 4(k)(1)(B) authorizes the assertion of personal jurisdiction over Teresa because she was joined as a third-party defendant, impled under Rule 14, and was served within 100 miles of the federal courthouse.

b. Contacts with the United States

Federal Rule 4(k)(2) grants personal jurisdiction over some defendants who have sufficient minimum contacts with the United States as a whole, even if they would not otherwise be subject to personal jurisdiction in a particular state. This exercise of personal jurisdiction, however, only works if the claim arises under federal law and the exercise of personal jurisdiction would be constitutional.

ADDITIONAL EXERCISES

1. The Oregon Automobile Insurance Company sends its President to solicit the purchase of Auto Insurance policies from Chicago citizens. Paula, from Chicago, purchases a policy covering her car, which is garaged in Chicago. After Paula enters into the contract of insurance, her car is negligently destroyed, in an Illinois collision. When Paula attempts to collect from the Oregon Auto Insurance Company, they deny coverage. Paula files a lawsuit for breach of the insurance contract in Illinois State Court. The Oregon Insurance Company files a timely **Motion to Dismiss for Lack of Personal Jurisdiction**. How should the Court rule?

2. Pretty Matchmakers, Inc. operates a match-making service over the internet at pm.com. Dale, a citizen of New Jersey, is the CEO of Dale, Inc., a competing internet match-making site. Dale decided to move his existing match-making site to pm.net. Pretty Matchmakers, Inc., filed a lawsuit in the federal district court for the Northern District of Illinois against Dale and Dale, Inc., alleging that they deliberately misappropriated Petty Matchmakers, Inc's existing domain address with the intent to mislead customers in violation of a federal statute. That federal law, which prohibits the conduct allegedly performed by defendants Dale and his corporation, does not contain any provision expressly granting personal jurisdiction. Defendants moved to dismiss the complaint for the lack of personal jurisdiction, arguing that the only contact between them and the forum state was the fact that twenty residents of Illinois had registered their personal information on pm.net. How should the court rule?

3. Would it make a difference in your analysis if the defendants had heavily marketed their website in the Midwest through billboards and at local restaurants and bars?

4. Would it change the analysis if Dale had traveled to Illinois often to attend trade shows and seminars designed to educate the audience about the unique nature of the Illinois market for dating services?

DUE PROCESS: NOTICE

Key Concepts

- The mechanics of serving the opposing party with a summons and a copy of the complaint
- The proper methods of providing notice through service of process
- The constitutionality of the various methods of service of process

Introduction

The Due Process Clause of the United States Constitution requires that a defendant receive proper notice of a lawsuit. The notice must be sufficient to afford the defendant an opportunity to be heard in the action.

At a minimum, proper notice requires that the defendant be served with a copy of the complaint and summons by an authorized process server. The authorized process server must serve the defendant within a reasonable time after the complaint is filed.

The issue of whether the method of service of process is proper requires a two-step analysis. First, the method of process must be allowed under the **forum's own rules**. Second, the method employed must be **constitutional** under the Due Process Clause.

> A **summons** is a paper issued by a court. It informs a person that a suit has been filed against him. The summons is also the way the court asserts its authority over the defendant. It is the official document that requires the opposing party to respond to the complaint.

A. The Mechanics of Service of Process

The mechanics of process begin when the complaint is filed. At the time of filing, the plaintiff's attorney typically completes a summons and presents it to the clerk of courts. The clerk then signs, seals and issues the summons for service on each defendant.

> A party uses **Rule 4** only for the complaint that commences the lawsuit. For all other documents that the parties may exchange, Rule 5 governs. Rule 5 allows for more convenient service of documents, including delivery via e-mail.

Federal Rule of Civil Procedure 4 governs two critical components of the mechanics of serving process in federal court. The first is what information must be included in the documentation. This is the "process" itself, meaning what the papers look like and what information they contain. Two sections of Rule 4 describe what is required in a summons. Rule 4(a) mandates what information must be included in the summons itself, while Rule 4(c) describes what must accompany that summons (namely, the complaint) as well as who can deliver the documents to the opposing party.

The second critical feature of Rule 4 is that it describes how that documentation must be delivered to the defendant. This is the service of process—how the papers should be delivered to the opposing party. Rules 4(d), 4(e), 4(f), 4(g), 4(h), 4(i), and 4(j) describe how the documents are delivered to particular categories of defendants.

> **Personal jurisdiction and service of process** are separate doctrines. In other words, there can be effective service of process, but not personal jurisdiction and vice versa. Be sure to analyze the two concepts separately. Also, note that the objections to be made under Rule 12 are separate as well. (See Chapter 7 for discussion of Rule 12). Rule 12(b)(2) is an objection on the basis of personal jurisdiction, Rule 12(b)(4) is an objection to the process papers, and Rule 12(b)(5) is an objection to the method of service.

1. The Summons

THE RULE	Rule 4(a)(1)

Summons

A summons must:

(A) name the court and the parties;

(B) be directed to the defendant; (C) state the name and address of the plaintiff's attorney or—if unrepresented—of the plaintiff;

(D) state the time within which the defendant must appear and defend;

(E) notify the defendant that a failure to appear and defend will result in a default judgment against the defendant for the relief demanded in the complaint;

(F) be signed by the clerk; and

(G) bear the court's seal.

After the summons is issued by the clerk, the plaintiff is responsible for its proper service on each defendant in the case. A summons must be served with a copy of the complaint. The plaintiff is responsible for having the summons and complaint served in a timely manner.

EXAMPLE: Paulina's counsel went to court to file a complaint against Dexter. Immediately after filing the complaint, Paulina's counsel saw Dexter entering the courthouse. Paulina's counsel handed Dexter a copy of the original summons that did not bear the name of the court. After Dexter accepted the summons, Paulina's counsel said: "Sorry about the poor quality of the copy. The name of the court didn't properly show up. I just filed it at this court. I'll see you in court at the appointed time." Does the summons meet the requirements of Rule 4(a)?

Analysis: No, it does not. However, because Dexter is aware of the missing information, a court is unlikely to find this defect fatal. In most cases, courts will overlook technical errors in the summons unless the error is prejudicial to the opposing party. In this case, the court would likely allow Paulina's counsel to amend the summons to include the name of court. However, some defects, such as the lack of a clerk's signature on the summons, are not curable, and the party will be forced to re-serve the summons and complaint.

2. Service

> ### THE RULE   Rule 4(c)
>
> ### Service
>
> (1) **In General.** A **summons must be served with a copy of the complaint.** The plaintiff is responsible for having the summons and complaint served **within the time allowed by Rule 4(m)** and must furnish the necessary copies to the person who makes service.
>
> (2) **By Whom.** Any person who is **at least 18 years old and not a party** may serve a summons and complaint.
>
> (3) **By a Marshal or Someone Specially Appointed.** At the plaintiff's request, the **court may order** that service be made by a United States Marshal * * *.

Rule 4(c) explains that when the summons is served on the opposing party, a copy of the complaint must also be served. This puts the opposing party on sufficient notice of the litigation (through the summons itself) as well as the content of the litigation (through the complaint, which will be explored further in Chapter 6). Rule 4(c) also explains who can serve these documents on the opposing party.

a. Who Is an Authorized Process Server?

Federal Rule 4(c) provides that any person who is at least 18 years old and not a party may serve a summons and complaint.

Moreover, at the plaintiff's request, the court may order that service be made by a United States marshal or deputy marshal or by a person specially appointed by the court.

b. What is the Time Frame for Effective Service?

> Rule 4(m) is also critical in determining whether an amendment to a pleading that adds a claim against a new party after the statute of limitations period will relate back to the date of an earlier timely-filed complaint to conform to the statute of limitations period under Rule 15.

State and federal rules require that service be effectuated within a reasonable time after a complaint is filed. Some state courts do not establish a fixed deadline for service, but require that reasonable diligence be used by the process-server in attempting to provide service.

The federal rule sets a deadline. Federal Rule 4(c) requires that service be accomplished within the time allowed by Rule 4(m). Under Federal Rule 4(m), a complaint generally must be served within 120 days of its filing. If a defendant is not served within 120 days after filing, the court—on motion or on its own after notice to the plaintiff—must dismiss the action **without prejudice** against that defendant or order that service be made within a specified time. But if the plaintiff shows good cause for the failure, the court must extend the time for service for an appropriate period.

> The phrase **without prejudice** is a term of art which in this context means that the plaintiff generally may re-file the action.

c. What Must Be Provided as Evidence of Effective Service?

Unless service is waived, proof of service must be made to the court. Proof of service generally requires the authorized process server to file an affidavit attesting that service was performed. In some jurisdictions, the process server's affidavit that service was made properly takes the form of a "return of service."

EXAMPLES & ANALYSIS

EXAMPLE: Peggy's Counsel and Draper work on the same floor of a small office building. Leading up to the filing of the complaint, Peggy's Counsel has sent Draper many pieces of correspondence, including a politely-worded demand letter. The day before Peggy's Counsel filed his complaint, he walked next door and let Draper know that the complaint would be filed the next day. The following day, Peggy's Counsel filed the complaint and had Draper served with only the summons. Was service proper under Rule 4(c)?

Analysis: No. Strict adherence to Rule 4 is generally required when serving opposing parties in litigation. This avoids default judgments and facilitates the parties litigating the matter at issue on its merits. Here, Draper anticipated the filing of the complaint. Judging by the correspondence that occurred between Peggy's Counsel and Draper, Draper likely knew what would be pled in the complaint. Nonetheless, the Rule requires proper service of the complaint in order to provide the parties with ample notice of the allegations being made against them. This avoids the distasteful elements of surprise and brinksmanship that courts disfavor. Peggy's Counsel should have ensured that Draper was properly served with both the summons and complaint.

EXAMPLE: Peter and Donald live on the same street in the same neighborhood. Last week, they were in a car accident. Donald hit Peter's car as Donald was backing out of his driveway and into the street. Peter has decided to sue Donald for the damages to his car. Peter went to their mutual neighbor, Michael, to help him serve the summons and complaint. However, Michael was not home, so Peter asked Michael's son to serve the documents. Peter mistakenly believes that Michael's son is 18 years old. Michael's son served the documents to Donald personally at his home. Was service proper under Rule 4(c)?

Analysis: No. Because Michael's son is not yet 18 years old, the service is not proper. Peter's mistaken belief that Michael's son was 18 does not excuse him from executing proper service. Peter did not fulfill the strict requirements of Rule 4(c).

EXAMPLE: Paige and Derrick were once business partners in an internet dot.com venture. Paige sued Derrick for damages based on Derrick's failure to perform promises in their business contract. Derrick has a habit of moving around and changing his address repeatedly, making him very difficult to find. Paige has been unable to find Derrick in order to serve him. The court has appointed a United States Marshal to perform service on behalf of Paige. The United

States Marshal happened to see Derrick in his neighborhood; Derrick was coincidentally moving in next door to the Marshal's house. The Marshal took the summons and complaint over to Derrick along with a cup of sugar. The Marshal handed Derrick the documents and sugar. Derrick slammed the door in the Marshal's face. Was service proper under Rule 4(c)?

Analysis: Yes. The United States Marshal is authorized to serve the defendant on behalf of the plaintiff when ordered to do so by the court. In most cases, the United States Marshal will not be used. The plaintiff will hire a private process-server to effectuate service or the defendant will waive service under Rule 4(d). However, when the plaintiff has attempted to serve the defendant, and the defendant has eluded service, the court can step in and require the United States Marshal to make the service. In this case, the Marshal was acting according to the court order, and he properly served Derrick. That Derrick refused to accept the papers does not change the fact he was properly served.

B. The Proper Methods of Service of Process Under Federal and State Rules

Introduction

With rare exception, the rules of civil procedure governing a particular jurisdiction delineate the proper methods of service of process in that jurisdiction. State and federal rules authorize a variety of process methods. The methods range from in-hand, personal service on the defendant, to publishing notice in a newspaper. In order to effectuate proper service in a particular forum, the plaintiff must satisfy the requirements of a precise method of process allowed in that particular jurisdiction.

Federal Rule 4 authorizes the use of five basic methods of process in civil actions filed in federal court:

- Waiver

- Personal Service

- Abode Service

- Agent Service

- State Methods

1. Waiver

THE RULE	Rule 4(d)

Waiving Service

(1) **Requesting a Waiver.** An individual, corporation, or association * * * has a duty to avoid unnecessary expenses of serving the summons. The plaintiff may notify such a defendant that an action has been commenced and request that the defendant waive service of a summons. The notice and request must:

(A) be in writing and be addressed:

    (i) to the individual defendant; or

    (ii) for [an entity] to an officer, a managing or general agent, or any other agent authorized by appointment or by law to receive service of process;

(B) name the court where the complaint was filed;

(C) be accompanied by a copy of the complaint, two copies of a waiver form, and a prepaid means for returning the form;

(D) inform the defendant, using text prescribed in Form 5, of the consequences of waiving and not waiving service;

(E) state the date when the request is sent;

(F) give the defendant a reasonable time of at least 30 days after the request was sent—or at least 60 days if sent to the defendant outside any judicial district of the United States- to return the waiver; and

(G) be sent by first-class mail or other reliable means.

(2) **Failure to Waive.** If a defendant located within the United States fails, without good cause, to sign and return a waiver requested by a plaintiff located within the United States, the court must impose on the defendant:

(A) the expenses later incurred in making service; and

(B) the reasonable expenses, including attorney's fees, of any motion required to collect those service expenses.

(3) **Time to Answer After a Waiver.** A defendant who, before being served with process, timely returns a waiver need not serve an answer to the complaint until 60 days after the request was sent

* * *

(5) **Jurisdiction and Venue Not Waived.** Waiving service of a summons does not waive any objection to personal jurisdiction or to venue.

EXPLANATION

 The federal rules, and those in some states, establish a procedure that encourages the defendant to waive formal methods of process. In federal court, the plaintiff may mail to the defendant a formal request that the defendant waive formal process, together with a copy of the complaint.

Why, in an adversary system, would a defendant waive formal process? The waiver regime creates two incentives for waiver.

First, if the defendant waives formal process, the defendant is granted more time in which to respond to the complaint. Typically, the defendant must file its response within 21 days of service of process. But if the defendant waives formal process, the defendant receives 60 days from the date the request for waiver was sent in which to respond to the complaint.

Second, if the defendant refuses to waive process without good cause, the defendant must pay the costs of making formal service, as well as the reasonable expenses incurred by the plaintiff in having to make a motion to recover those costs.

Does the fact that the defendant waives service of process constitute a waiver of the defendant's right to object to jurisdiction or venue? The federal rules make clear that no such waiver results.

2. Personal Service

THE RULE   **Rule 4(e)(2)(A)**

Serving An Individual Within a Judicial District of the United States

Unless federal law provides otherwise, an individual—other than a minor, an incompetent person, or a person whose waiver has been filed—may be served in a judicial district of the United States by * * * delivering a copy of the summons and of the complaint to the individual personally.

The most effective method of service of process is **personal service**—by which an authorized process-server makes in-hand delivery of the process directly to the person of the defendant. The process-server must deliver the complaint and summons directly to the defendant. The process-server cannot give the process to someone else to be redirected to the defendant.

Personal service, however, does not always require in-hand delivery. Suppose a defendant, upon making eye contact with an approaching process-server, begins to flee in the opposite direction. May the authorized process-server leave the complaint and summons at the feet of the fleeing defendant?

The courts have answered "yes." If the defendant evidences reluctance to accept service, the authorized process server may then leave the process in the "vicinity" of that reluctant defendant. *See e.g., Travelers Casualty & Surety Co. of America v. Brenneke*, 551 F.3d 1132, 1136 (9th Cir. 2009) (service proper in the proximity of an evasive defendant).

3. Abode Service

THE RULE	Rule 4(e)(2)(B)

**Serving An Individual Within a Judicial District
of the United States**

[A]n individual * * * may be served * * * by * * * leaving a copy at the individual's dwelling or usual place of abode with someone of suitable age and discretion who resides there.

EXPLANATION

In order to effectuate proper **abode** service, an authorized process server must:

- leave the complaint and summons;

- at the defendant's "dwelling" or "usual place of abode";

- with someone;

- who resides there;

- who has suitable age; and

- discretion.

EXAMPLES & ANALYSIS

EXAMPLE: An authorized process-server attempts to serve the process through in-hand delivery on a prominent executive. When the executive flees from service, the process-server leaves the process with the executive's body guard. The body guard gives the process to the executive shortly thereafter. Was process proper in federal court?

Analysis: No. Personal service was not proper because the process-server did not serve the defendant directly through in-hand delivery. Nor was the process left in the vicinity of the reluctant executive. The fact that the executive actually received the process through redelivery to him by the body guard cannot render the method of process valid. *See, e.g., Sikhs for Justice v. Nath*, 850 F. Supp. 2d 435 (S.D. N.Y. 2012).

EXAMPLE: An authorized process-server leaves the complaint and summons in the defendant's mailbox. Was process proper in federal court?

Analysis: No. There is no federal rule that authorizes this method. Personal service was not effectuated. Nor was abode service properly made because the process was not left with anyone.

EXAMPLE: An authorized process-server leaves the complaint and summons with the defendant's spouse in a hotel room where the defendant has been staying for 10 days. Was process proper in federal court?

Analysis: No. A hotel room is generally not an abode, unless that room has been the defendant's dwelling place for a long, continuous period of time. *Howard Johnson International, Inc. v. Wang*, 7 F.Supp. 2d 336, 340 (S.D.N.Y. 1998), aff'd, 181 F.3d 82 (2d Cir. 1999).

EXAMPLE: An authorized process-server leaves the complaint and summons with the defendant's babysitter at the defendant's usual abode. Was process proper in federal court?

Analysis: Generally no. A babysitter typically does not reside in the defendant's dwelling. If, however, the sitter were a live-in nanny, then the courts may approve of the service.

EXAMPLE: An authorized process-server leaves the complaint and summons at the defendant's usual abode with the defendant's 13-year-old daughter. Was process proper in federal court?

Analysis: Generally yes. In addressing the issue whether the recipient is of "suitable age and discretion," the federal courts generally have held that teenagers are qualified to accept abode service, although some state courts require the recipient to be older than 13.

4. Agent Service

THE RULE	Rule 4(e)(2)(c) & 4(h)

Serving An Individual Within a Judicial District of the United States

[A]n individual * * * may be served * * * by * * * delivering a copy to an agent authorized by appointment or by law to receive service of process.

Serving a Corporation, Partnership, or Association

Unless federal law provides otherwise or the defendant's waiver has been filed, a domestic or foreign corporation, or a partnership or other unincorporated association that is subject to suit under a common name, must be served:

(1) in a judicial district of the United States:

(A) in the manner prescribed by Rule 4(e)(1) for serving an individual; or

(B) by delivering a copy of the summons and of the complaint to an officer, a managing or general agent, or any other agent authorized by appointment or by law to receive service of process and—if the agent is one authorized by statute and the statute so requires—by also mailing a copy of each to the defendant . . . .

EXPLANATION

An authorized process-server may serve an individual defendant in the United States by serving an agent of that defendant who is appointed by that defendant to receive service, or who is authorized by law to receive service.

The concept of agent service, however, is most often used in effectuating process on an entity, such as a corporation, a partnership, or a limited liability company. The authorized process-server must effectuate personal service on, or mail a proper request to waive formal process to, an authorized or a managing agent of the defendant. A managing agent is an agent who exercises executive responsibility over the organization. The federal rules do not generally allow service of an agent at that agent's abode. Nor do they permit service of an organization by leaving the process at the defendant's office or even headquarters.

The federal rules do, however, require an agent of the defendant to waive formal process under the same regime governing individual defendants themselves. Accordingly, a managing agent of a corporation who fails to waive formal process without "good cause" will be sanctioned. See Federal Rule 4(d)(2).

EXAMPLE: In a civil action filed in federal court against Durigibles, Inc., an authorized process-server leaves the complaint and summons with the spouse of Durigibles, Inc.'s Chief Executive Officer at the CEO's abode. Was process proper?

Analysis: No. Although Durigibles Inc's Chief Executive Officer is a managing agent qualified to accept process on behalf of the corporation, the **abode** service method used here was not a proper method of service on the agent.

5. State Methods

THE RULE	Rule 4(e)(1); 4(g) & 4(n)

Serving An Individual Within a Judicial District of the United States

[A] person * * * may be served * * * by following state law for serving a summons in an action brought in courts of general jurisdiction in the state where the district court is located or where service is made

* * *

Serving a Minor or an Incompetent Person

A minor or an incompetent person in a judicial district of the United States must be served by following state law for serving a summons or like process on such a defendant in an action brought in the courts of general jurisdiction of the state where service is made. A minor or an incompetent person who is not within any judicial district of the United States must be served in the manner prescribed by Rule 4(f)(2)(A), (f)(2)(B), or (f)(3).

* * *

Asserting Jurisdiction over Property or Assets

(1) **Federal Law.** the court may assert jurisdiction over property if authorized by a federal statute. Notice to claimants of the property must be given as provided in the statute or by serving a summons under this rule.

(2) **State Law.** On a showing that personal jurisdiction over a defendant cannot be obtained in the district where the action is brought by reasonable efforts to serve a summons under this rule, the court may assert jurisdiction over the defendant's assets found in the district. Jurisdiction is acquired by seizing the assets under the circumstances and in the manner provided by state law in that district.

EXPLANATION

Federal Rule of Civil Procedure 4 also empowers the federal courts to employ methods of service of process and notice authorized by state rules of procedure in three situations.

First, Rule 4(e)(1) permits service of process on individuals within the United States by any method allowed by the rules of process either in the state where the federal court sits or in the state where service is to be effectuated.

This provision permits service in federal court by methods that are not specifically allowed under the federal rules themselves. For example, the federal rules do not directly authorize service by leaving the process at the defendant's office or place of business. Yet, a federal court located in a state where such service is permitted may borrow that method. In addition, although the federal rules do not explicitly allow publication notice, that method of notice is allowed in a federal court sitting in a state that authorizes publication. Because virtually every state permits publication notice in certain situations, publication is thereby available in federal court on those same terms as well.

Second, under Federal Rule 4(g), a minor or incompetent defendant in the United States must be served in compliance with the rules for serving such defendants that exist in the state where the service is attempted.

> **EXAMPLE:** In a federal court action in the Northern District of Indiana, an authorized process-server mails the complaint and summons to the defendant's last place of residence. The defendant is a minor. Under Indiana law, mailing the process to a defendant is generally proper, except where the defendant is a minor, in which case both the minor and the minor's custodial parent must be properly served. Was process proper?

Analysis: No. In federal court, service of process on a minor must satisfy the requirements of Indiana law for such service because that is the state where the process was attempted. Because the process here failed to satisfy Indiana's requirement that the custodial parent be properly served, the method of process was improper in this federal court action. *See, e.g., Seibels, Bruce & Co. v. Nicke*, 168 F.R.D. 542, 545 (M.D.N.C. 1996).

Third, Federal Rule 4(n)(2) allows a federal district court to assert jurisdiction over a defendant's assets located in that district by satisfying the requirements for seizing those assets under the law of the state in which the district sits. This rule enables a federal court to seize a defendant's assets in accordance with state law, but only if, despite "reasonable efforts," the defendant cannot otherwise be properly served with process. The rule typically works in tandem with state court publication regimes, which authorize notice by publication if coupled with: (1) the attachment of the defendant's property in the state when the action is commenced; and/or (2) a showing that despite reasonable efforts or diligence, the defendant could not otherwise be notified. In the next section, we will discover that by requiring both the seizure of assets in a district and a showing of reasonable efforts to provide proper service, Rule 4(n) complies with the constitutional notice standards for publication.

EXAMPLE: Patricia and Don have a contract dispute. Patricia hired Don to paint a portrait of her son. She paid Don for the portrait, but he has not delivered it yet. Patricia and Don both live in San Francisco, California. However, for the past several months Don has been living in Chicago painting portraits for other customers there. Don has worked so much in Chicago that he rented an apartment to stay in when he is in town. Patricia filed her action in federal court in California and mailed a copy of the summons and complaint to Don's apartment in Chicago via certified mail. She knew that Don was currently living there, and she received a return receipt. Ten days later, when Don returned from Chicago, Patricia also asked his adult friend, Lara, to personally serve him when she picked him up at the airport. Lara did so. California state procedural rules allow service of process on a person located outside the state by certified mail if there is a return receipt. Did Patricia properly serve Don when she mailed the summons and complaint to his Chicago apartment? Did she properly serve Don by asking Lara to serve him personally at the airport?

Analysis: Yes on both accounts. The service via certified mail was proper under Rule 4(e)(1) because Patricia used applicable state law to effect service. According to that rule, a plaintiff can use the rules regarding service of process in either the state where the case is filed or in the state where service is made. Here, the state where the case was filed—California—allows for service via certified mail. (Note that Patricia will still have to meet the other requirements of Rule 4, including Rule 4(a). The applicable state law provision only applies to the method of service of process.) Had the California rules been different, however, this mode of service would be ineffective under the federal rules. The federal rules generally do not allow for service via the mail. Finally, even if the mailed service were not sufficient, the personal service at the airport was also proper. Under Rule 4(e)(2)(A), Don was personally served by a non-party over the age of 18. Thus, he was properly served.

EXAMPLE: Petra and Diane were involved in a car accident in Boston, Massachusetts, where they both lived at the time. After the accident, Diane obtained a job that required her to move to New York City, New York. Diane moved out of her old apartment in Boston, Massachusetts and rented an apartment in New York. But, Diane kept her Boston driver's license with her old apartment address on it. She also kept her voter registration in Massachusetts, and the address listed on that registration is her parents' home address. Petra asked a friend to go to Diane's parents' home to serve the summons and complaint. Because Diane was not there, Petra's friend left the documents with Diane's younger brother, who was wearing his high school letterman jacket at the time. Was service on Diane at her parents' home proper?

Analysis: Probably not. This is an example of abode service. Most circuit courts define dwelling or usual place of abode as the place where the defendant lives when service is made. This is not to say that a person cannot have more than one place of dwelling or usual place of abode. To the contrary, many circuits have found that a person can have multiple places of abode, including places that the person may only use occasionally. However, even in these cases, the individual has to have lived in the dwelling, meaning that he must have spent time in the home, made home improvements, listed it on official documents, and/or regularly gone to that home.

Diane's parents' home probably does not meet these requirements. There is no evidence that she has recently lived there, and the only official document listing her parents' home is her voter registration card, which she probably procured while living at home years ago. Without more evidence that she lives in her parents' home with some regularity, it is unlikely that a court would find that Diane's parents' home is her dwelling or usual place of abode. *See, e.g., Cox v. Quigley*, 141 F.R.D. 222 (D. Me. 1992) (defendant's parents' home was not his "dwelling house or usual place of abode," even though defendant used his parents' address for some purposes, including his driver's license, receipt of financial mail, and real estate transactions, because defendant had recently graduated from college, left home, found a job, obtained a new tax residence, voted in a different state, and maintained employment records with a new address); *Thanco Products and Imports, Inc. v. Kontos*, 72 Fed. R. Serv. 3d 1201 (S.D. Tex. 2009) (where defendant is a dual citizen of the U.S. and Greece, but claimed his dwelling or usual place of abode was in Greece, service was proper at his mother's United States address because he used that address for his voter registration and shipping).

Finally, even if the court found Diane's parents' home to be her dwelling or usual place of abode, it might question whether her brother is of "suitable age" to accept service under Rule 4(e). Suitable age is not defined in the rule, and there is some variation among circuits. The general approach is to determine whether the individual is old enough to know that he or she needs to pass the papers on to the defendant—generally at least 13 years of age. In this case, a high school student would know to ask his sister about the papers. If a court determined that this was her dwelling or usual place of abode, it would probably find that her brother was of suitable age.

EXAMPLE: Plowing, Inc., a Delaware corporation, rented farm equipment to Diet Farmers LLC, a Michigan limited liability company doing business in New York. Plowing Inc. sued Diet Farmers for defaulting on its payments under the parties' rental contract. The contract designates Dave Davies as Diet Farmers' agent in New York for the purpose of accepting service. Plowing, Inc. served a copy of the summons and complaint on Dave Davies at his New York location. When he received it, Dave forwarded the summons and complaint to Diet Farmers. Was service proper under Rule 4?

Analysis: Yes. Service was proper under Rule 4(e)(2)(C) because the contract authorized Dave Davies to accept service on behalf of Diet Farmers. To meet the requirements of Rule 4(e)(2)(C), the agent must be specifically authorized to receive service of process. Either a contract or the operation of state or federal law can create an agent for this purpose. The agent must be appointed for the purpose of receiving service and cannot just be an agent in the general sense. Here, Dave Davies was appointed for service of process, meeting the requirements of Rule 4(e)(2)(C).

IN PRACTICE

In federal court cases involving questions of substantive federal law, the statute of limitations will stop running once the complaint is filed. Whether service is made before or after the statute of limitations has run is of no consequence, as long as the complaint was filed in time. This can vary under state law, however. Some states will not stop the statute of limitations from running until service is made. Careful attorneys always make sure to check state law governing when the statute of limitations runs before filing and serving a complaint in state court. Under the *Erie* doctrine (discussed in Chapter 4) the state rule on running the statute of limitations may apply where the case is in federal court based only on diversity of citizenship.

C. The Constitutionality of Methods of Notice

In *Mullane v. Central Hanover Bank & Trust Co.*, 339 U.S. 306 (1950), the United States Supreme Court established the standard for the constitutionality of notice under the Due Process Clause. In that case, Central Hanover Bank & Trust Co. established a trust fund and petitioned the New York Court for settlement of its first account as common trustee. During the accounting period the bank managed a substantial amount of funds which had been pooled together by more than one hundred smaller trusts. Many of the beneficiaries of the trusts lived outside of New York, and some of their names and addresses were unknown.

The only notice given the beneficiaries was by publication in a local newspaper for four successive weeks in compliance with the requirements of the New York Banking Law. The notice included the name and address of the trust company, the name and the date of the establishment of the common trust fund, and a list of all participating estates, trusts or funds. The Supreme Court began its analysis of the constitutionality of this type of publication notice by articulating the fundamental requirements of due process.

FROM THE COURT

Mullane v. Central Hanover Bank & Trust Co.
339 U.S. 306 (1950)
Supreme Court of the United States

. . . Many controversies have raged about the cryptic and abstract words of the Due Process Clause but there can be no doubt that at a minimum they require that deprivation of life, liberty or property by adjudication be preceded by notice and opportunity for hearing appropriate to the nature of the case. . . .

Personal service of written notice within the jurisdiction is the classic form of notice always adequate in any type of proceeding. But the vital interest of the state in bringing any issues as to its fiduciaries to a final settlement can be served only if interests or claims of individuals who are outside of the State can somehow be determined. A construction of the Due Process Clause which would place impossible or impractical obstacles in the way could not be justified.

Against this interest of the State we must balance the individual interest sought to be protected by the Fourteenth Amendment. This is defined by our holding that "The fundamental requisite of due process of law is the opportunity to be heard." *Grannis v. Ordean*, 234 U.S. 385, 394 [(1914)]. This right to be heard has little reality or worth unless one is informed that the matter is pending and can choose for himself whether to appear or default, acquiesce or contest.

The Court has not committed itself to any formula achieving a balance between these interests in a particular proceeding or determining when constructive notice may be utilized or what test it must meet. Personal service has not in all circumstances been regarded as indispensable to the process due to residents, and it has more often been held unnecessary as to nonresidents . . . .

An elementary and fundamental requirement of due process in any proceeding which is to be accorded finality is **notice reasonably calculated, under all the circumstances, to apprise interested parties of the pendency of the action and afford them an opportunity to present their objections**. . . . The notice must be of such nature as reasonably to convey the required information . . . and it must afford a reasonable time for those interested to make their appearance . . . But if with due regard for the practicalities and peculiarities of the case these conditions are reasonably met the constitutional requirements are satisfied. . . .

But when notice is a person's due, process which is a mere gesture is not due process. The means employed must be such as one desirous of actually informing the absentee might reasonably adopt to accomplish it. The reasonableness and hence the constitutional validity of any chosen method may be defended on the ground that it is in itself reasonably certain to inform those affected . . . , or, where conditions do not reasonably permit such notice, that the form chosen is not substantially less likely to bring home notice than other of the feasible and customary substitutes.

339 U.S. at 313-14.

The *Mullane* Court then turned to the particular method of publication notice at issue in the case. Although the Court recognized that publication is not likely to produce actual notice to defendants, it nonetheless indicated that publication can be constitutional in either of two situations. First, publication can be constitutional if coupled with other means of notifying the defendant, including seizing or attaching the defendant's property in the jurisdiction when the lawsuit begins. Second, where persons interested in the litigation cannot, despite reasonable diligence be served any more effective way, then publication can be constitutional as a last resort. 339 U.S. at 315–18. The Court stated that:

. . . it has been recognized that, in the case of persons missing or unknown, employment of an indirect and even a probably futile means of notification is all that the situation permits and creates no constitutional bar to a final decree foreclosing their rights. . . .

Those beneficiaries represented by appellant whose interests or whereabouts could not with due diligence be ascertained come clearly within this category. As to them the statutory notice is sufficient. However great the odds that publication will never reach the eyes of such unknown parties, it is not in the typical case much more likely to fail than any of the choices open to legislators endeavoring to prescribe the best notice practicable.

> . . . As to known present beneficiaries of known place and residence,
> however, notice by publication stands on a different footing. Exceptions
> in the name of necessity do not sweep away the rule that within the
> limits of practicability notice must be such as is reasonably calculated
> to reach interested parties. Where the names and post office addresses
> of those affected by a proceeding are at hand, the reasons disappear for
> resort to means less likely than the mails to apprise them of its pen-
> dency. . . .

339 U.S. at 317–18.

CASE ANALYSIS & QUESTIONS

1. The *Mullane* case provides the key test for the constitutionality of notice:

   Notice is constitutional if it is reasonably calculated, under all the circumstances, to apprise interested parties of the pendency of the action
   and afford them an opportunity to present their objections.

2. The particular form of notice at issue was publication in a newspaper circulating once a week for four weeks in a row where the action was pending. The Supreme Court declared that it would be "idle to pretend that
   publication alone" is a reliable method of notice. 339 U.S. at 315. The
   Court also recognizes that publication may be used where, despite reasonable efforts, it is not reasonably possible or practical to give more adequate notice. In that situation, publication is constitutional not because
   it is reasonably calculated to apprise interested parties of the litigation;
   rather, it is constitutional because "the form chosen is not substantially
   less likely to bring home notice than other of the feasible and customary
   substitutes." 339 U.S. at 315. In other words, publication becomes no
   worse than other—attempted but unsuccessful—forms of notice.

3. Does the *Mullane* standard require "actual" notice? Notice is constitutional if it is reasonably calculated to apprise defendants of litigation—not if it actually apprises defendants of litigation. Moreover, in
   the case itself, the Court upholds the constitutionality of notice to some
   beneficiaries even though it concedes that publication will never afford

them actual notice of the litigation. As such, does *Mullane* allow a court to enter a binding, enforceable judgment against some defendants who would have no notice of the litigation, and no opportunity to be heard? If so, the court would thereby be empowered to deprive defendants of their property without notice and a hearing. How can the Due Process Clause of the Constitution allow that deprivation?

4. If, as the Supreme Court states, publication alone is not a reliable method of notice, what must be coupled with publication to render it constitutional? The Court observes that publication used as a supplement to the attachment of the defendant's property or assets within the jurisdiction has "traditionally" been accepted as a valid form of notice. 339 U.S. at 316. Recall that in *Pennoyer v. Neff*, the Supreme Court indicated that publication plus attachment of Marcus Neff's property in Oregon would have sufficed if the attachment had occurred in conjunction with the commencement of the action.

5. Under the *Mullane* standard, the publication notice in the case was found constitutional as to some claims involving some beneficiaries, but unconstitutional as to the other claims against other beneficiaries. How does the Court draw that distinction?

6. According to the *Mullane* test, are the following commonly used methods of notice constitutional: (1) personal service; (2) abode service; (3) agent service; (4) service by mail; (5) service by leaving the process at the defendant's business office; and (6) the federal court waiver regime?

7. Would a federal or state rule allowing for service of process through electronic means such as email or facebook be constitutional? *See, Rio Properties, Inc. v. Rio International Interlink*, 284 F. 3d 1007, 1017 (9th Cir. 2002) (finding the use of email service to be constitutional because it is reasonably calculated to apprise parties of litigation and is "zealously embraced" by the business community).

EXAMPLES & ANALYSIS

EXAMPLE: Is the following publication regime constitutional under the *Mullane* standard:

"Whenever, in any action affecting property or status within the jurisdiction of the court . . . plaintiff or his or her attorney shall file . . . an affidavit showing the defendant resides or has gone out of this state, or on due inquiry cannot be found, or is concealed within that state, so that process cannot be served upon him or her . . . , the clerk shall cause publication to be made [in a newspaper circulating where the action is pending once a week for three weeks in a row]". *See* Illinois Code of Civil Procedure, 735 ILCS 5/2-206.

Analysis: Yes. Publication becomes constitutional if coupled with **either** attachment of property at issue in the jurisdiction or a showing that despite due inquiry, the defendant could not otherwise be served. This statute seems to require **both** as a condition to publication.

EXAMPLE: Suppose in that same publication statute, there is an additional requirement that the clerk mail a copy of the process to the defendant's last known address, but only if that address can be ascertained by the plaintiff with reasonable diligence. Would the statute be constitutional?

Analysis: Yes. This additional requirement only enhances the case that publication here is accompanied by other devices designed to apprise parties of litigation.

EXAMPLE: Dean was serving a prison term that resulted from a federal drug conviction. While in prison, the FBI sought to forfeit cash officers seized when they searched his residence at the time of his arrest pursuant to a search warrant. The FBI provided notice to Dean of its intended forfeiture by certified mail. Did that notice satisfy due process?

Analysis: Yes. The Supreme Court found that it did, holding the Due Process Clause "requires only that the Government's effort be 'reasonably calculated' to apprise a party of the pendency of the action... ." *Dusenbery v. United States*, 534 U.S. 161, 170 (2002).

EXAMPLE: Don moved out of his house and into an apartment, but failed to notify the state of his new address. Eventually, the state tax authority sent a letter by certified mail to the house notifying Don that there were years of unpaid property taxes and that the house would be sold if the taxes remained unpaid. The letter was returned undelivered and the property was sold. Was the notice here constitutional?

Analysis: No. This method of notice in this case violated the Due Process Clause. The Supreme Court held: "additional reasonable steps" are required when such a letter is returned undelivered to the state. In so holding, the Court reiterated the due process requirement that notice be reasonably calculated to apprise interested parties of litigation and to give them an opportunity to be heard. *Jones v. Flowers*, 547 U.S. 220, 225 (2006).

DUE PROCESS: OPPORTUNITY TO BE HEARD

Key Concepts

- The constitutional requirement of an opportunity to be heard
- Exceptions to the constitutional requirement of an opportunity to be heard

Introduction

As the Supreme Court declared in *Mullane*, the fundamental requisite of due process of law is the opportunity to be heard. As such, the Constitution generally forbids a state or federal court from depriving a party of its property without affording that party an opportunity to be heard. Yet, when must that opportunity to be heard be given? What kind of hearing must be afforded to satisfy the standards of due process? And what are the exceptional circumstances that justify deprivations of property by the government without a hearing?

A. The Right to a Hearing—At a Meaningful Time

In *Fuentes v. Shevin*, 407 U.S. 67 (1972), the Supreme Court declared that, as a rule, the Due Process Clause prohibits a state from depriving persons of their property unless they afford those persons a hearing **before** the property is taken.

Margarita Fuentes, a resident of Florida, purchased a gas stove and service policy from the Firestone Tire and Rubber Company ("Firestone") under a conditional sales contract calling for monthly payments over a period of time. A few months later, she purchased a stereo from the same company under the same kind of contract. The total cost of the stove and stereo was about $500, plus an additional financing charge of over $100. Under the contracts, Firestone retained title to the merchandise, but Mrs. Fuentes was entitled to possession unless and until she defaulted on her installment payments.

For more than a year, Mrs. Fuentes made her installation payments. But then, with only about $200 remaining to be paid, a dispute developed between her and Firestone over the servicing of the stove. Firestone instituted an action in a small claims court for repossession of both the stove and the stereo, claiming that Mrs. Fuentes had refused to make her remaining payments. Simultaneously with the filing of that action and before Mrs. Fuentes had even received a summons to answer its complaint, Firestone obtained a writ of replevin ordering a sheriff to seize the disputed goods at once. *Fuentes*, 407 U.S. at 70-71.

Under the Florida statute at issue, "[a]ny person whose goods or chattels are wrongfully detained by any other person . . . may have a writ of replevin to recover them . . . ." *Fuentes*, 407 U.S. at 73, citing Fla. Stat. Ann. § 78.01, F.S.A. There was no requirement that the applicant make a convincing showing before the seizure that the goods were, in fact, wrongfully detained. Rather, Florida law required only that the applicant file a security **bond** and complaint, reciting in conclusory fashion that he is lawfully entitled to the possession of the property. On the sole basis of the complaint and bond, a writ issued "command[ing] the officer to whom it may be directed to re-

> A **bond** is a written promise to pay money upon the occurrence or non-occurence of a specific act. In a civil case like this one, a bond is posted by one party to guarantee that the other party will be protected from the risk that property at issue in the lawsuit will be depleted before the lawsuit is resolved. The obligor on a bond is called a "surety," and is often an insurance company or similar financial institution.

plevy the goods and chattels in possession of the defendant . . . and to summon the defendant to answer the complaint." 407 U.S. at 75, citing Fla. Stat. Ann. § 78.08. If the goods were "in any dwelling house or other building or enclosure," the officer was required to demand their delivery; but if they are not delivered, "he shall cause such house, building or enclosure to be broken open and shall make replevin according to the writ . . . ." *Id.*, citing Fla. Stat. Ann. § 78.10.

The Supreme Court declared this Florida process unconstitutional because it failed to provide for a hearing at a meaningful time:

> . . . at the same moment that the defendant receives the complaint seeking repossession of property through court action, the property is seized from him. He is provided no prior notice and allowed no opportunity whatever to challenge the issuance of the writ. After the property has been seized, he will have an opportunity for a hearing, as the defendant in the trial of the court action for repossession, which the plaintiff is required to pursue. In addition, under the Florida statute, the officer who seizes the property must keep it for three days, and during that period the defendant may reclaim possession of the property by posting his own security bond in double its value. But if the defendant does not post such a bond, the property is transferred to the party who sought the writ, pending a final judgment in the underlying action for repossession.
>
> The constitutional right to be heard is a basic aspect of the duty of government to follow a fair process of decision making when it acts to deprive a person of his possessions. The purpose of this requirement is not only to ensure abstract fair play to the individual. Its purpose, more particularly, is to protect his use and possession of property from arbitrary encroachment—to minimize substantively unfair or mistaken deprivations of property, . . . The prohibition against the deprivation of property without due process of law reflects the high value, embedded in our constitutional and political history, that we place on a person's right to enjoy what is his, free of governmental interference. . . .
>
> The requirement of notice and an opportunity to be heard raises no impenetrable barrier to the taking of a person's possessions. But the fair process of decision-making that it guarantees works, by itself, to protect against arbitrary deprivation of property. For when a person has an opportunity to speak up in his own defense, and when the State must listen to what he has to say, substantively unfair and simply mistaken deprivations of property interests can be prevented. It has long been

recognized that "fairness can rarely be obtained by secret, one-sided determination of facts decisive of rights. . . . [And n]o better instrument has been devised for arriving at truth than to give a person in jeopardy of serious loss notice of the case against him and opportunity to meet it." *Joint Anti-Fascist Refugee Committee v. McGrath*, 341 U.S. 123, 170-172 [1951] (Frankfurter, J., concurring).

If the right to notice and a hearing is to serve its full purpose, then, it is clear that it must be granted at a time when the deprivation can still be prevented. At a later hearing, an individual's possessions can be returned to him if they were unfairly or mistakenly taken in the first place. Damages may even be awarded to him for the wrongful deprivation. But no later hearing and no damage award can undo the fact that the arbitrary taking that was subject to the right of procedural due process has already occurred. . . .

This is no new principle of constitutional law. The right to a prior hearing has long been recognized by this Court under the Fourteenth and Fifth Amendments. . . .

This is no new principle of constitutional law. The right to a prior hearing has long been recognized by this Court under the Fourteenth and Fifth Amendments. . . .

[The state] requirements [of filing conclusory allegations and posting a bond] are hardly a substitute for a prior hearing, for they test no more than the strength of the applicant's own belief in his rights. Since his private gain is at stake, the danger is all too great that his confidence in his cause will be misplaced. . . .

The minimal deterrent effect of a bond requirement is, in a practical sense, no substitute for an informed evaluation by a neutral official. More specifically, as a matter of constitutional principle, it is no replacement for the right to a prior hearing that is the only truly effective safeguard against arbitrary deprivation of property. While the existence of these other, less effective, safeguards may be among the considerations that affect the form of hearing demanded by due process, they are far from enough by themselves to obviate the right to a prior hearing of some kind.

Fuentes, 407 U.S. at 75–84.

B. Exceptions to the Right to a Pre-Deprivation Hearing

The *Fuentes* Court, however, addressed two exceptions to its rule that a hearing must be afforded before deprivation.

First, according to the court, there are "extraordinary situations" that justify postponing notice and opportunity for a hearing. *Fuentes*, 407 U.S. at 90. In these situations, the seizure must be directly necessary to secure an important governmental or general public interest, there must be a special need for very prompt action, and the state must keep strict control over its use of legitimate force. Thus, the Court has allowed summary seizure of property to collect the internal revenue of the United States, to meet the needs of a national war effort, to protect against the economic disaster of a bank failure, and to protect the public from misbranded drugs and contaminated food.

Second, the Court considered whether a party's right to a pre-deprivation hearing can be waived. The contract signed by Mrs. Fuentes provided in small print that "in the event of default of any payment or payments, Seller at its option may take back the merchandise ...." *Fuentes*, 407 U.S. at 94.

The Court concluded, however, that this language did not **clearly** waive the right to a hearing:

> The contracts included nothing about the waiver of a prior hearing. They did not indicate how or through what process—a final judgment, self-help, prejudgment replevin with a prior hearing—the seller could take back the goods. Rather, the purported waiver provisions were no more than a statement of the seller's right to repossession upon the occurrence of certain events.

Fuentes, 407 U.S. at 95–96.

Accordingly, the *Fuentes* Court held "that the prejudgment replevin provisions work a deprivation of property without due process of law insofar as they deny the right to a prior opportunity to be heard before chattels are taken away from their possessor." 407 U.S. at 96. The Court stressed that its holding, however, was a narrow one. The Court did not question the power of a state to seize goods before a final judgment in order to protect the security interests of creditors. Moreover, the Court stressed that the nature and form of any required hearing is open to "many potential variations." 407 U.S. at 96–97.

EXAMPLES & ANALYSIS

EXAMPLE: Pam's property was taken pursuant to a Virginia state law that affords defendants the right to be heard, but only if they respond to the complaint within five days of service. Pam was provided with a complaint, but she missed the five-day deadline for responding to the complaint. Her property was taken without a hearing. She later challenges the taking of her property. What will the court decide?

Analysis: Because Pam only had five days to prepare for her hearing, the court would likely determine that she had inadequate time to prepare and that her due process rights were violated when her property was taken. *See Roller v. Holly* 176 U.S. 398, 413 (1900).

EXAMPLE: A Wisconsin statute allows that state to garnish a defendant's wages before a hearing on the underlying merits of a claim against that defendant. Does that statute satisfy due process?

Garnishment typically involves state action to take or hold a portion of a defendant's wages or bank accounts.
Replevin is a procedure by which a seller of goods enlists the help of the state in executing an order that seizes goods which have not been fully paid for by the buyer.

Analysis: No. In *Sniadach v. Family Finance Corp.*, 395 U.S. 337, 340 (1969), the Supreme Court held that the statute violated the Due Process Clause. The Court particularly stressed the "tremendous hardship" that the statute imposed upon wage earners who support their families.

EXAMPLE: A Louisiana procedure allows a court, through a neutral judicial officer, to seize a defendant's property without a hearing where the plaintiff establishes that the defendant may remove or deplete the property before a hearing can take place. The plaintiff also must show that it has a **lien** on the property, is required to post a bond, and must allege the reasons necessitating pre-hearing seizure under oath and with particularity. Louisiana also enables the defendant to reclaim its property, and provides a prompt post-deprivation hearing. Does this procedure satisfy due process?

Analysis: Yes. In *Mitchell v. W.T. Grant, Co.*, 416 U.S. 600, 605 (1974), the Supreme Court upheld this Louisiana procedure. Moreover, in *Mathews v. Eldridge*, 424 U.S. 319, 335, 349 (1976), the Court concluded that the government may terminate Social Security disability benefits without first holding a hearing. The Court balanced three factors in determining that a post-deprivation hearing was constitutionally adequate: (1) the private interest affected by the government action; (2) the risk

> A **lien** is a claim that one party has on another party's property interest. The lien places a legal encumbrance or cloud upon the property. The seller of goods for example may retain a "lien" on the goods sold to the buyer, which enables the seller to repossess those goods if the buyer fails to meet certain contractual obligations.

of erroneous deprivation and the probable value of additional procedural safeguards; and (3) the governmental interest, including the administrative and financial burden created by additional procedures. In *North Georgia Finishing, Inc. v. Di-Chem*, 419 U.S. 601 (1975), by contrast, the Court declared unconstitutional a Georgia law that allowed the seizure of property without a hearing based only on the **conclusory** sworn statements by the plaintiff. Finally, in *Connecticut v. Doehr*, 501 U.S. 1 (1991), the Supreme Court struck down a Connecticut statute that allowed plaintiffs to seize a defendant's property without a hearing, in order to secure sufficient assets to satisfy an unrelated judgment. Unlike the statute upheld in Mitchell, the Connecticut procedure did not require the plaintiff to post a bond, to have a lien on the property, or to allege under oath that the defendant was going to remove or deplete the seized assets. 501 U.S. at 14-15. Moreover, the plaintiff suing Doehr had no financial interest or claim to Doehr's house; rather that house was simply used as an asset that the plaintiff wished to reach if the plaintiff prevailed on his unrelated tort claims arising out of an altercation at a public park. 501 U.S. at 16.

C. The Nature of the Hearing

Assuming that the Constitution mandates a pre-deprivation hearing, what kind of hearing is required?

In *Goldberg v. Kelly*, 397 U.S. 254 (1970), the Supreme Court held that the Due Process Clause requires that the beneficiary of public assistance receive a hearing before public benefits are terminated. The Court recognized that the hearing need not be a full-blown trial on the merits; rather, the nature of the hearing "must be tailored to the capacities and circumstances of those who are to be heard." 397 U.S. at 269.

ADDITIONAL EXERCISES

1. Is there a clear test for the constitutionality of procedures that allow the deprivation of property without a hearing? *Which of the following procedural safeguards are or should be constitutionally required?*

    a. The plaintiff must post a bond;

    b. A neutral judicial officer must be involved in the decision whether to allow seizure;

    c. The plaintiff must allege under oath and with particularity that prompt seizure is necessary to prevent the defendant from depleting the seized assets; and/or

    d. The defendants must be given a reasonable opportunity to reclaim the seized property before the trial on the merits?

2. Products Inc. sold and delivered commercial painting supplies to Donaldson Ltd. When Donaldson Ltd. failed to pay for the goods, Products Inc. filed a lawsuit in state court for breach of contract and simultaneously followed the state's procedure for garnishing Donaldson Ltd.'s bank account. Under that procedure, Products Inc. was required to post a bond in a sum double the amount claimed due, and to file an affidavit before a clerk of court containing conclusory allegations about the merits of the claim and the possibility that the defendant would lack sufficient assets to satisfy the judgment in the absence of garnishment. Donaldson, Inc. challenges the state procedure as a violation of due process. *How should the court rule?* See, e.g., *North Georgia Finishing, Inc. v. Di-Chem, Inc.*, 419 U.S. 601 (1975).

3. Suppose, in the prior exercise, the state's garnishment procedure also required a prompt post-deprivation hearing. *Would the statute pass constitutional muster?*

4. Paula received seven parking tickets placed on her windshield for illegally parking her car. The city then immobilized her car by placing

a "boot" on the back left tire. Paula argues that the deprivation of her use of her car without a hearing constitutes an unconstitutional denial of due process. **What result?** *See, e.g., Patterson v. Cronin,* 650 P.2d 531 (Colo. 1982).

5. Federal Rule 12(a) generally requires that defendants respond to the complaint within 21 days of service. A defendant's failure to respond in that timely manner could result in a default judgment, by which the court would deprive the defendant of its property. *Is that time frame sufficient to satisfy due process?*

6. The Federal Rules of Civil Procedure, and the rules of civil procedure in virtually every state, authorize a court to issue temporary or provisional remedies. For example, the Federal Rules allow a federal court to enter a temporary restraining order (TRO), which may well result in the seizure of property before a hearing can take place. *If you were asked to draft the federal TRO rule to ensure that it satisfied due process requirements, what procedural steps and protections would you insist upon?* *See* Fed. R. Civ. P. 65(b)(1).

7. In *Fuentes*, the Court specifically warned against the risk of arbitrary and mistaken deprivation of property that can result from the absence of an adversarial process, and in Mitchell the Court emphasized the critical role of a neutral judicial officer. *Based on this limited guidance, which of the following procedural protections must be built into a "hearing" before the government deprives a person of his or her property?*

    a. the right to appear before a neutral arbiter;

    b. the right to counsel;

    c. the right to have written notice of the adversary's claims;

    d. the right to discover and examine evidence presented by the adversary;

    e. the right to discover and examine witnesses; and/or

    f. the right to trial by jury?

Quick Summary

• Under the Constitution's Due Process Clause, a judgment entered by a court in a civil action will not be valid and enforceable unless all of the following are true:(1) the court must have proper subject matter jurisdiction;(2) the court must have proper personal jurisdiction;(3) the court must afford the parties proper notice of the lawsuit, and (4) the court must afford the parties an appropriate opportunity to be heard.

• A court does have proper personal jurisdiction if the law of the forum state grants power over the defendant's person or property, and if the assertion of that power is constitutional.

• The law of the forum state generally grants personal jurisdiction over defendants who consent to that jurisdiction or who are present in the forum state. In addition, most states have long-arm statutes that extend personal jurisdiction to out-of-state defendants who do specific kinds of activities in the state that give rise to a lawsuit.

• Even if the forum law grants personal jurisdiction, the assertion of that jurisdiction may be unconstitutional unless the defendant had such minimum contacts with the state that it would not be unfair to compel it to defend a lawsuit in that state. The constitutional test requires that the defendant purposefully avail itself of the forum state's laws or target its consumers.

• A court provides proper notice of a civil action only if it adheres to a method of service of process authorized by the forum's own rules of procedure, and if that method would be constitutional. Process is constitutional under the Due Process Clause as long as it is reasonably calculated to apprise interested parties of litigation.

- The Due Process Clause also requires that a party must generally be afforded an opportunity to be heard before its property is taken in a court proceeding. Yet, a pre-deprivation hearing is not required if there are compelling governmental interests that necessitate a deprivation of property before a hearing can place, or if the party has properly waived its right to such a hearing.

3

Venue and Related Issues

Key Concepts

- The statutory venue requirement
- Determining proper venue
- The court's discretion to transfer venue
- Forum non conveniens
- Multi-district litigation transfers

Introduction

Venue is not a jurisdictional concept. Rather, the concept of venue is about which location within a federal or state court judicial system is an appropriate and convenient place for the litigation.

In state courts, the issue of venue typically depends on a legislative judgment about which **counties** in a state court system are the most convenient locations for a lawsuit. States commonly have general rules for venue which declare that venue is proper in a county where any defendant resides, or where any part of the cause of action arose. The focus on the defendant's residence stems from the presumption that litigation in that county would be convenient for the defendant. The focus on the county where the claim arose stems from the presumption that most of the evidence and witnesses are likely to be located there. The plaintiff's residence is not usually a proper venue. Yet, plaintiffs have the initial choice of forum and will likely select the available venue option most convenient to them.

State courts also commonly create exceptions to their general venue rules. For instance, many states declare that actions involving land may only be filed in the county where the land is located. They also tend to make venue proper in "any county" if no defendant resides in the state.

The federal court system is divided into 94 federal districts. There are 89 districts in the 50 states, and district courts also exist in Puerto Rico, the Virgin

Islands, the District of Columbia, Guam and the Northern Mariana Islands. Some states, like Alaska, have a single judicial district. Other states, such as New York and California, are divided into multiple regional districts.

In federal court, therefore, the venue question is about which of the federal districts is a proper and convenient district in which to adjudicate a civil action. Congress has enacted a general venue statute which provides the rules for proper venue in all federal court civil actions. Those provisions generally focus upon where defendants reside and where the claim arose. In addition, Congress has established ground rules for allowing a federal court to transfer an action from one federal district to another federal district.

The requirement of venue is separate from the requirement of jurisdiction. An action may be dismissed for improper venue, even if it is filed in a forum with proper subject matter jurisdiction and personal jurisdiction.

A. Proper Venue in Federal Court

THE STATUTE   **28 U.S.C. § 1391(b)**

Venue Generally

(b) Venue in general.—A civil action may be brought in—

(1) a judicial district in which **any defendant resides, if all defendants are residents of the State** in which the district is located;

(2) a judicial district in which a substantial part of the events or omissions **giving rise to the claim occurred**, or a substantial part of **property** that is the subject of the action is situated; or

(3) if there is no district in which an action may otherwise be brought as provided in this section, any judicial district in which any defendant is subject to the court's **personal jurisdiction** with respect to such action.

EXPLANATION

The federal venue statute—Section 1391—applies to virtually all kinds of civil actions in federal court, regardless of the basis for subject matter jurisdiction. Under that statute, venue is generally proper in a particular federal district if any of the following is true of that district:

(1) **any** defendant resides in that **district**—so long as **all defendants** are residents of the **state** in which the district is located; or

(2) a substantial part of the events or omissions giving rise to the **claim arose** in that district, or a substantial part of the **property** that is the subject of the action is located in that district.

1. A District Where Any Defendant Resides, if All Defendants Reside in That Same State

The first venue basis, which focuses on the defendants' residences, requires a two-step analysis. First, **all** of the defendants must reside in the **state** where the district is located. If not all of the defendants reside in that state, then venue cannot be proper in a district on this basis.

Second, if all defendants do reside in that state, then at least one defendant must reside in the particular district.

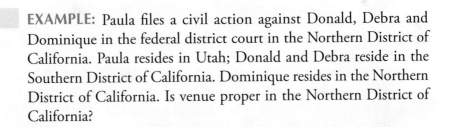

EXAMPLES & ANALYSIS

EXAMPLE: Paula files a civil action against Donald, Debra and Dominique in the federal district court in the Northern District of California. Paula resides in Utah; Donald and Debra reside in the Southern District of California. Dominique resides in the Northern District of California. Is venue proper in the Northern District of California?

Analysis: Yes. Venue is proper in a federal district where any defendant resides, so long as all defendants reside in the state in which the district is located. Dominique resides in the Northern District of California, and the other two defendants reside in the state of California. It does not matter that those other two defendants do not reside in the Northern District of California. As long as one defendant (Dominique) resides in that district, it is sufficient that the other defendants reside somewhere in the state of California. Nor is it relevant that the plaintiff Paula does not reside in the state of California. The plaintiff's residence is irrelevant to this statutory basis for venue.

EXAMPLE: Paula brings a civil action against Dustin and Dante in the Southern District of New York. Dustin resides in the Southern District of New York. Dante resides in Connecticut. Is venue proper in the Southern District of New York?

Analysis: No. Although Dustin resides in the district in which the action was filed, the fact that another defendant (Dante) resides in Connecticut rather than in the state in which the district sits (New York) renders venue improper.

These examples assume that the court has determined the residence of the various parties. How is residence established for venue purposes? Congress supplies some statutory guidance.

THE STATUTE   28 U.S.C. § 1391(c) & (d)

§ 1391(c) Residency—For all venue purposes—

(1) a natural person, including an alien lawfully admitted for permanent residence in the United States, shall be deemed to reside in the judicial district in which that person is **domiciled**;

(2) an entity with the capacity to sue and be sued in its common name under applicable law, whether or not incorporated, shall be deemed to reside, if a defendant, in any judicial district in which such defendant is subject to the court's **personal jurisdiction** with respect to the civil action in question and, if a plaintiff, only in the judicial district in which it maintains its principal place of business; and

(3) a defendant not resident in the United States may be sued in any judicial district, and the joinder of such a defendant shall be disregarded in determining where the action may be brought with respect to other defendants.

(d) Residency of corporations in States with multiple districts.— For purposes of venue under this chapter, in a State which has more than one judicial district and in which a defendant that is a corporation is subject to personal jurisdiction at the time an action is commenced, such corporation shall be deemed to reside in any district in that State within which its contacts would be sufficient to subject it to personal jurisdiction if that district were a separate State, and, if there is no such district, the corporation shall be deemed to reside in the district within which it has the most significant contacts.

EXPLANATION

Congress expressly defines the residence of individuals and entities. For venue purposes, individuals reside where they are domiciled. A person's domicile is not

> This definition of **domicile** is the same as in the context of diversity jurisdiction, discussed in Chapter 1.

necessarily their current residence; rather, it is their true and permanent home and where they intend to remain if they are living there or to return if they are not currently living there.

An entity's residence is dependent upon the law governing personal jurisdiction. In this context, entities include corporations as well as unincorporated associations like partnerships and limited liability companies. *See, e.g., The Denver and Rio Grande Western Railroad Co. v. Brotherhood of Railroad Trainmen*, 387 U.S. 556, 559-62 (1967) ("We think it most nearly approximates the intent of Congress to recognize the reality of the multi-state, unincorporated association such as a labor union and to permit suit against that entity, like the analogous corporate entity, wherever it is 'doing business.'").

If the action is filed in a state with only one federal district court, an entity resides in that district if the state would have personal jurisdiction over that entity.

If the action is filed in a federal district within a state that has multiple districts, and the state itself would have personal jurisdiction over the entity, the entity resides in any district in the state that would have personal jurisdiction over that entity—as if the district were a state for personal jurisdiction purposes. In other words, under this provision of the venue statute, imagine that the districts are different states. Then, determine which of those "states" would have personal jurisdiction over the defendant.

If the action is filed in a district within a state that has multiple districts, and that state would have personal jurisdiction over the entity, but no particular district would have personal jurisdiction over the entity, then the entity is deemed to reside in that particular district with which it has the most significant contacts.

EXAMPLES & ANALYSIS

EXAMPLE: Petra files a civil action against Diane and Duke in the federal court for the District of South Carolina. Duke was born and raised in North Carolina, but attends college in South Carolina. Diane was born and raised in South Carolina, and has never left that state. Is venue proper in the District of South Carolina based on the defendants' residence?

Analysis: No. Venue would be proper in the District of South Carolina only if all defendants "reside" in the State of South Carolina, which requires that all defendants be "domiciled" there. In this case, although Duke may reside temporarily in South Carolina, he is domiciled in North Carolina, where his true home is located and where he intends to return. Therefore, venue is not proper in the District of South Carolina.

EXAMPLE: Portia files a civil action against Delta Corporation in the District of Nebraska. Delta Corporation is a Delaware Corporation with its principal place of business in Wyoming. But Delta Corporation engages in regular and systematic business activities in Nebraska, and purposefully avails itself of Nebraska consumers by targeting them for sales. Is venue proper in the District of Nebraska based on the defendant's residence?

Analysis: Yes. As an entity, Delta Corporation "resides" in the District of Nebraska because it would be subject to the Nebraska court's personal jurisdiction, given its level of contacts with that state.

EXAMPLE: Peter brings a civil action against Delta Corporation in the Southern District of Texas. Delta Corporation engages in significant business relations with suppliers in Dallas, Texas, which is located in the Northern District of Texas, but Delta has no contacts within the Southern District of Texas. The Northern District of Texas encompasses Abilene, Amarillo, Dallas, Fort Worth, and Lubbock. The Southern District of Texas includes Houston, Galveston, Corpus Christi, and Brownsville. Would venue be proper in the Southern District of Texas based on the defendant's residence?

Analysis: No. In this case, although the state of Texas may have personal jurisdiction over Delta Corporation, that corporation resides only in the Northern District of Texas for venue purposes because Texas has more than one district, and only the Northern District of Texas would have personal jurisdiction over Delta—as if that particular district were a state.

EXAMPLE: Paula files a civil action against Delta Corporation in the Middle District of Alabama. Because Delta Corporation has significant contacts with consumers throughout the state, Alabama may assert personal jurisdiction over the corporation. Yet, Delta Corporation's contacts are scattered such that no particular district within Alabama would have personal jurisdiction over Delta Corporation, assuming each of those districts were a state. Is venue proper in the Middle District of Alabama?

Analysis: Yes, so long as that district is the one in Alabama with which Delta Corporation has the "most significant contacts." When, as here, the state of Alabama has multiple districts and the state as a whole would have personal jurisdiction over the corporation, but no individual district would, then the corporation is deemed to reside in the district with which it has the most significant contacts.

2. A District Where the Claim Arose or the Property at Issue Is Located

The federal venue statute provides that venue is also proper in a federal district where a "substantial part" of the claim arose or where a "substantial part" of the property at issue is located. In applying this statute to the facts, the most difficult issue is determining what "a substantial part" means.

- Does the statute render venue proper in a district where "any" part of the claim arose, or "any" part the property is located?

- Does the statute render venue proper in a district where the "most" substantial part of the claim arose?

The plain language of the statute provides some guidance. By restricting venue to districts in which a "substantial" part of the claim arose, Congress intended that that connection between the lawsuit and the district be more than casual. *See, e.g., Gulf Insurance Co. v. Glasbrenner*, 417 F.3d 353, 357 (2d Cir. 2005) (defining "substantial" to require that "significant events material to the plaintiff's claim" occurred in the district). Yet, "a" substantial part of the claim could well arise in more than one district. Accordingly, courts have recognized that a substantial part of a claim arises in any federal district in which an essential element of that claim occurred. *See e.g., Bates v. C. & S. Adjusters, Inc.*, 980 F. 2d 865, 868 (2d Cir. 1992) (a substantial part of Fair Debt Collection Practices Act claim arose in district where notice of demand for payment was received because receipt of notice is an essential element of the claim).

EXAMPLES & ANALYSIS

EXAMPLE: Paul brings a civil action against Danielle in the Northern District of Illinois, alleging that Danielle breached a contract entered in Wisconsin by failing to complete the construction of a building located in northern Illinois. Is venue proper in the Northern District of Illinois?

Analysis: Yes. Venue is proper in the Northern District of Illinois because a substantial part of the events giving rise to the breach of contract claim arose in that district. An essential element of a breach of contract claim occurred in the Northern District of Illinois because that is where the contract to construct the building was to be performed.

EXAMPLE: Petra brings a products liability tort claim against Donald's Supply Corporation in the Southern District of Florida, alleging that the defendant manufactured a defective product at its plant in northern Texas which resulted in serious injury to Petra within the Southern District of Florida. Is venue proper in the Southern District of Florida?

Analysis: Yes. A substantial part of the events that gave rise to Petra's tort claim occurred in the Southern District of Florida because that is where the injury occurred, and injury is an essential element of the tort claim.

3. Exceptional Venue Provisions

a. The Venue Gap Filler

Suppose that there is no federal district court in which venue would be proper. Section 1391 contains a gap-filling venue rule for that situation. If, but only if, there is no district which would otherwise have proper venue, then venue becomes proper in any district in which any defendant would be subject to the court's personal jurisdiction.

EXAMPLE: Portia files a civil action against Demetri and Daniel in the Northern District of Texas. Daniel is domiciled in the Northern District of Texas, and Demetri is domiciled in Oklahoma. The property in dispute is located entirely in Mexico. Is venue proper in the Northern District of Texas?

Analysis: Yes. In this case, neither of the two principal venue options provided by § 1391(b) would render venue proper in the Northern District of Texas. First, although one defendant (Daniel) resides (is domiciled) in northern Texas, the two defendants do not both reside in that same state because Demetri is a domicile of Oklahoma. Second, a substantial part of the property at issue is located in Mexico.

Yet, this result would be anomalous if the Northern District of Texas would otherwise be a proper forum in that it would have subject matter and personal jurisdiction over the action and the defendants. Accordingly, § 1391(b) provides a gap-filler that renders venue proper in the Northern District of Texas because one defendant (certainly Daniel) would be subject to personal jurisdiction in that court.

b. Aliens

Section 1391(c)(3) provides that a defendant who does not reside in the United States may be sued in any district. This provision governs lawsuits against aliens who have not been admitted as permanent residents; aliens who have been admitted as permanent residents are treated like American citizens for venue purposes. Venue in an action against a non-resident alien is proper in any judicial district, and a non-resident alien's presence in a lawsuit with other defendants will be disregarded for purposes of determining the propriety of venue.

c. Actions Against the United States, or Its Agencies, Officers, or Employees

Section 1391(e) involves lawsuits against:

- The United States;

- An agency of the United States; or

- An officer or employee of the United States acting in his official capacity or under the color of legal authority.

In such an action, Congress has expanded the venue options such that venue is proper in a federal district in which:

- any one of the defendants resides; or

- a substantial part of the claim arose or the property at issue is located; or

- the plaintiff resides (but only if the action does not involve real property).

B. Transferring Venue

As will be discussed in Chapter 7, federal judges have the power to dismiss an action for improper venue. *See* Rule 12(b)(3).

Under 28 U.S.C. § 1406(a), however, the court also has discretion to transfer the action to a proper venue rather than to dismiss the action. Section 1406(a) provides that if an action is filed in an improper venue, the court "shall dismiss, **or** if it be in the interest of justice, transfer." Rather than dismiss, the judge may decide to **transfer** from an improper venue to a proper venue in the "interest of justice." In practice, federal courts rarely dismiss for improper venue when transferring is an option.

Federal courts also have the power to transfer an action from one **proper** venue to another **equally proper** venue. Why would a court transfer a lawsuit from one proper "transferor" venue to another equally proper "transferee" venue? The judge may decide that the new transferee forum is more convenient for parties and witnesses than the original transferor forum.

> Where, as is common, the statute of limitations has run in the period between filing the original action and dismissal for improper venue, the plaintiff will be unable to refile the action in a proper venue because it will be time-barred. Transferring the action allows the plaintiff to maintain the original filing date (and thus avoid a statute of limitations problem).

In state court systems, the state court judge typically will transfer an action from a court sitting within one county in the state to a court sitting in another county in that state. A state court judge, however, has no power to transfer an action to a court in a different state. A court has no power to transfer an action to a different judicial system.

> Transferring an action is different from remanding the action. As discussed in Chapter 1, a federal court may remand an action to state court if the action was improperly removed to federal court. But a federal court may only transfer an action from one federal court to another federal court.

In federal court, the judge may transfer an action from one federal district court to another federal district court. The federal judge, however, may not transfer an action from federal court to state court, or from federal court to a court in a different country's judicial system.

Because the federal court system is not bound by state borders and is national in scope, a federal court's power to transfer an action from one federal district court to another federal district court is quite significant. The federal court, for example, may transfer an action from northern California to southern New York. The court has the power to transfer the action to the Southern District of New York even if the Northern District of California is a proper venue.

> A **motion to transfer** is a vehicle by which defendants can relocate the action from the plaintiff's chosen district to a forum that is more convenient for the defendants. As such, defendants often consider filing motions to transfer venue in federal cases.

THE STATUTE   28 U.S.C. § 1404(a)

Change of Venue

(a) For the convenience of parties and witnesses, in the interest of justice, a district court may transfer any civil action to any other district or division where it **might have been brought** or to any district or division to which all parties have consented.

EXPLANATION

The plain language of this congressional statute establishes the structure of any analysis of a motion to transfer venue.

1. Authority to Transfer Only to a Proper Venue

First, the court has authority to transfer an action only to a federal district where either:

- it might have been brought, or

- all parties consent.

a. Might Have Been Brought

According to the Supreme Court, a transferee district is one where the action "might have been brought" only if that district would have had proper subject matter jurisdiction, proper personal jurisdiction and proper venue if the plaintiff had filed the action there in the first place. *See Hoffman v. Blaski*, 363 U.S. 335, 343 (1960). In *Hoffman*, the Court reasoned in part that the phrase "might have" is subjunctive and thus requires an analysis of the propriety of venue in a hypothetical situation—as if the plaintiff had originally filed the action in the new forum when the lawsuit began.

EXAMPLE: Peter brings a civil action against Dennis in the Eastern District of Wisconsin. Dennis files a motion to transfer to the Northern District of Illinois. The parties agree that there is no personal jurisdiction over Dennis in the Northern District of Illinois and that venue would be improper in that district. But Dennis waives his objections to improper personal jurisdiction and venue and consents to both in the new forum. After all, it is Dennis who has moved to transfer the action there. May the court transfer the action to the Northern District of Illinois?

Analysis: No. The federal court may only transfer an action to a district where the action might have been brought by the plaintiff in the first place. The plaintiff could not have initially filed the action in the Northern District of Illinois because that forum would not have had proper personal jurisdiction or venue. Therefore, the court has no power to transfer the action to that district. This result seems anomalous because the defendant has consented to the transfer, and the defendant's consent typically is a valid basis for personal jurisdiction and venue. Nonetheless, consent by the defendant alone cannot be used in the context of transferring venue to convert an otherwise improper venue into a proper one. If **all** parties had consented to the transfer, then transfer would have been proper.

b. All Parties Consent

Congress attempted to modify the result in the *Hoffman* case to some extent. Section 1404(a) now also gives federal judges the power to transfer a lawsuit to an improper venue if **all** the parties consent to the transfer. This provision, however, does not permit defendants to transfer a lawsuit to an improper venue based solely on defendants' consent. Rather, "all" parties, including the plaintiff, must agree to the transfer. Because the plaintiff has chosen the original venue, it is unlikely that the plaintiff would "consent" to the transfer of venue to a different district. The plaintiff, however, may "consent" to the transfer by entering a contract with the defendant in which there is a clause that consents to the selection of the transferee forum.

The first step in analyzing whether a court should transfer a lawsuit usually is determining whether the new, transferee district is one in which the action could originally have been filed by the plaintiff. That inquiry, in turn, requires an analysis of whether the transferee district has proper subject matter jurisdiction, personal jurisdiction and venue. In performing that analysis, the defendant's consent to the transfer should be disregarded unless all parties, including the plaintiff, consent to the transfer. If the transferee district is an improper venue, then the court has no discretion to transfer the action to that district.

2. Discretion to Transfer to a Proper Venue

If, but only if, the transferee district is proper, then the federal judge "may" transfer the action to that district. In deciding whether to transfer the action to a new proper venue, the court has wide discretion to weigh the following factors on a case-by-case basis:

- Convenience to the plaintiff;

- Convenience to the defendant;

- Convenience to the witnesses;

- The interest of justice; and

- A forum selection clause.

The relative convenience of the transferor and transferee districts to the parties may turn on the financial burden placed on each to travel to the court. In particular, one party or another may be significantly disadvantaged by litigation in a distant forum because of the burden on it to produce evidence and to call witnesses in a distant forum. Similarly, witnesses may be inconvenienced in having to travel to attend court sessions or trial. The "interest of justice" factor encompasses a wide range of considerations including the proximity of the forum to the litigation, and the interests of the locality in having its own residents serve as jurors for an action that has arisen in the district. Some courts also are influenced by the volume of litigation in a particular district. If the action can be transferred to a district with less docket-congestion, it is likely that the litigation will proceed at a faster pace.

Finally, some contracts contain clauses by which the contracting parties agree to litigate their disputes in a particular federal district court. These clauses cannot provide any basis for subject matter jurisdiction, which can never be waived or consented to by the parties. Yet, a forum selection clause is a critically important factor to be considered by a federal court in deciding whether to transfer an action to a proper federal district, as part of the court's weighing of convenience and the interests of justice. *See Stewart Organization, Inc. v. Ricoh Corp.*, 487 U.S. 22, 29-32 (1988).

In *Atlantic Marine Construction, Inc. v. District Court*, 134 S. Ct. 568 (2013), the Supreme Court unanimously made clear that a federal court under 28 U.S.C. §1404(a) has the authority to transfer an action to any district where the action might have been brought or to any district where the parties have consented to litigate in a contract or stipulation. In circumstances in which the parties have entered into a contract with a valid forum-selection clause, the district court should transfer the action to the parties' chosen forum unless extraordinary circumstances unrelated to the parties' convenience disfavor the transfer.

> EXAMPLE: Pascal files a tort action based on diversity jurisdiction against Dante Corporation in federal court in the Northern District of Illinois. Pascal's complaint alleges that Dante Corporation manufactured a defective product in its only factory in eastern Wisconsin, which caused Pascal serious injuries when he used the product in northern Illinois. Dante files a timely motion to dismiss the action for improper venue, and in the alternative to transfer the action to the Eastern District of Wisconsin. How should the court rule?

Analysis: The court should deny the motion to dismiss, but may use its discretion to grant the motion to transfer. The first issue is whether the court should dismiss for improper venue. In this case, the action was filed in a proper venue. A substantial part of this tort claim arose in the Northern District of Illinois because that is where the allegedly defective product was used and caused injury to the plaintiff.

The court, however, has discretion to transfer the action, provided that the transferee district is one in which the plaintiff might originally have filed the action. Here, the Eastern District of Wisconsin would have had personal jurisdiction over Dante Corporation because that is where its factory is located. Therefore, venue would have been proper there because Dante Corporation "resides" in that district. Accordingly, the transferee district is a proper venue and the court may use its discretion to send the action there weighing the relative convenience of the parties and witnesses and the interest of justice.

3. Which Law Applies?

In an action in federal court that is governed by state law, the federal court must often decide which state's law to apply. For example, in a breach of contract claim alleging that the contract was formed in Wyoming but breached in Texas, which state's substantive contract law will govern the dispute? Each state has developed an entire body of choice-of-law rules which answer that question. Those choice-of-law rules may direct a state court to apply the law of a different state. In an action filed in Wyoming, the state of Wyoming's choice-of-law rules actually may dictate that the Wyoming court apply Texas contract law to resolve a dispute involving a contract with a substantial relationship to Texas.

In deciding which state's substantive law will govern an action, a federal court usually applies the choice-of-law rules from the state where the federal court is located. *Klaxon Co. v. Stentor Electric Manufacturing Co.*, 313 U.S. 487, 496 (1941). That state's choice-of-law rules might direct the federal court to apply the substantive law of a different state.

This choice-of-law issue is raised in the context of transferring venue in federal court. When a federal court action is transferred from a federal court in one state to a federal court in a different state, which state's choice-of-law rules should the court apply? The Supreme Court has concluded that where a federal court transfers an action from a **proper** venue to another venue under 28 U.S.C. § 1404(a), the court must apply the choice-of-law rules of the state from which the case was transferred. By contrast, when the court transfers an action from an **improper** venue to a proper one under 28 U.S.C. § 1406(a), the court must apply the choice-of-law rules of the state where the new, transferee court is located. In other words, the state law of the state court located in the **first proper** federal court venue usually must be applied. *Van Dusen v. Barrack*, 376 U.S. 612, 615 (1964). The only exception to this general rule is when a party bound by a forum-selection clause flouts its contractual obligation and files suit in a different forum. Even if the plaintiff files suit in an otherwise proper venue, that venue's choice of law rules will not govern the action. Rather, once the action is transferred to the forum selected by the parties in their contract, that transferee forum's choice of law rules will be applied.

EXAMPLE: Portia sues Debra in federal district court in Pennsylvania. Although venue was proper in that district, the federal court transferred the action to the federal court in Massachusetts. Which state's choice-of-law rules must the federal court in Massachusetts apply?

Analysis: The federal court in Massachusetts must apply Pennsylvania's choice-of-law rules because the federal court in Pennsylvania was the first proper venue.

EXAMPLE: Penny sues David in federal court in Maryland. The federal court in Maryland concludes that venue is improper in that district, and transfers the action to the federal court in Maine. Which state's choice-of-law rules will govern the action in federal court in Maine?

Analysis: The federal court in Maine must apply Maine's choice-of-law rules. The original venue in the federal court in Maryland was improper, and therefore the first proper venue would be the federal court in Maine. Accordingly, Maine's choice-of-law rules would govern.

C. Forum Non Conveniens

Under the doctrine of **forum non conveniens**, a court has discretion to dismiss a lawsuit for inconvenience, even if that lawsuit was filed in a forum with proper jurisdiction and venue.

The doctrine typically applies when the court determines that the action has been filed in an inappropriate judicial system. In state court, for instance, the judge may determine that the action belongs in a different state. Because a state court judge has no power to **transfer** an action to a different state, the remedy is dismissal for **forum non conveniens**. Similarly, in federal court, the judge might decide that the action belongs in a different country's judicial system. Because a federal court has no power to transfer an action outside of the United States, the remedy is dismissal for **forum non conveniens**.

The doctrine can be particularly prejudicial to plaintiffs. After all, the plaintiff has filed an action in a forum that has proper subject matter jurisdiction, proper personal jurisdiction and proper venue. Nonetheless, the court still has discretion to dismiss the action and require the plaintiff to refile the action in a different judicial system.

In exercising their discretion, therefore, the courts adhere to a presumption favoring the plaintiff's choice of a proper forum, unless that plaintiff is a foreign citizen who has chosen a United States forum. The presumption generally favoring the plaintiff's chosen forum will be overcome only if the defendant can show that the following public and private factors weigh in favor of dismissal:

1. Public Factors

- Administrative difficulties from docket congestion in the chosen forum;

- Jury duty should be imposed only on those in a community connected to the litigation;

- The proximity of the trial to those affected by it;

- Local controversies should be resolved locally; and

- The connection between the forum and the substantive law to be applied.

2. Private Factors

- Relative ease of access to sources of proof;

- Burdens on obtaining the presence of witnesses;

- Possibility of viewing the premises at issue;

- Enforceability of the judgment; and

- Relative advantages and obstacles to a fair trial.

Unless the balance of these factors is in favor of the defendant, the plaintiff's choice of a proper forum will rarely be disturbed. *Gulf Oil Corp. v. Gilbert*, 330 U.S. 501, 512 (1947). *See also Piper Aircraft Co. v. Reyno*, 454 U.S. 235, 238 (1981) (district court did not abuse discretion under forum non conveniens in dismissing suit from the Middle District of Pennsylvania where public and private interest factors dictated that it should have been brought in Scotland where the accident occurred, even though the law to be applied in Scotland would be less advantageous to the plaintiff).

In light of the exceptional nature of a forum non conveniens dismissal, some states require that dismissal be "conditional" upon the availability to the plaintiff of an alternative forum. For example, the judge may require the defendants to waive their objections to the running of the statute of limitations or to personal jurisdiction and process, if the plaintiff refiles in a more appropriate forum within a reasonable time.

D. Multidistrict Litigation Transfers

Congress has authorized the creation of the Judicial Panel on Multidistrict Litigation, which is a panel of judges who facilitate and oversee litigation that traverses many federal districts. The panel consists of seven federal appellate and district court judges designated by the Chief Justice of the United States. That panel has the power to transfer multiple civil actions pending in multiple federal districts to a single federal district, and to consolidate those actions for efficient and coordinated pre-trial proceedings. After coordinated proceedings in the transferee court, the case (if it has not been resolved by motion or settlement), must be transferred back to the district where it was initially filed, and the trial will take place in that original district. The panel may act upon a motion by any of the parties litigating in any of the pending actions, or on its own. The standards for determining whether to transfer the actions for multidistrict treatment are articulated by Congress in its enabling statute.

THE STATUTE   28 U.S.C. § 1407(a)

Multidistrict Litigation

(a) When civil actions involving one or more **common questions of fact** are pending in different districts, such actions may be transferred to **any district** for coordinated or consolidated pretrial proceedings. Such transfers shall be made by the Judicial Panel on Multidistrict Litigation authorized by this section upon its determination that transfers for such proceedings will be for the convenience of parties and witnesses and will promote the just and efficient conduct of such actions. Each action so transferred shall be remanded by the panel at or before the conclusion of such pretrial proceedings to the district from which it was transferred unless it shall have been previously terminated; *Provided, however*, That the panel may separate any claim, cross-claim, counter-claim, or third-party claim and remand any of such claims before the remainder of the action is remanded.

EXPLANATION

 This statute gives to the Judicial Panel on Multidistrict Litigation discretion to transfer multiple pending actions which have common factual issues to a single district for pretrial proceedings. Unlike the general venue statute, the multidistrict litigation transfer provision authorizes the transfer of many separate actions to "any" federal district court. In determining whether to transfer and consolidate the actions, the panel must consider the convenience of the parties and witnesses, and the interest of justice. The panel also has the power to assign the consolidated cases to any district court judge within the transferee district who is authorized to conduct pretrial proceedings.

The statute also indicates that the actions should be returned to their original districts as soon as pretrial proceedings have been completed. The transferee judge therefore has no statutory power to conduct a trial of the actions. Rather, the statute contemplates that each of the actions must be sent back ("remanded") to their original districts for trial.

Nonetheless, the statute does provide that the panel need not remand an action back to its original district if that action has "been previously terminated." This language suggests that the transferee district judge has the power to resolve dispositive motions as part of conducting pretrial proceedings.

ADDITIONAL EXERCISES

1. Patricia, who is domiciled in Arizona, files a civil action for breach of contract against Daniel in federal court for the District of Arizona. The contract was entered in France, and allegedly required Daniel to perform advertising services in Paris. Daniel, a citizen of France, makes a timely (1) motion to dismiss the lawsuit for improper venue, and (2) an alternative motion to transfer the lawsuit to the Southern District of New York where Daniel's summer home and local counsel are located, and (3) an alternative motion to dismiss on the grounds of forum non conveniens. Patricia responds to the motion by asserting that she filed the lawsuit in a proper and convenient forum, and that Arizona law would be much more favorable to her than the law of France. *How should the court resolve each of the three motions?*

2. Penelope drove from her home in Minneapolis to visit her brother, Ilia, an attorney living in Chicago, Illinois. On the way, Penelope stopped to get her brakes tightened at Don's Tune-ups, Inc., which is a Delaware corporation with its headquarters and only shop in eastern Wisconsin. After Don's Tune-Ups, Inc. finished its work on her car, Penelope continued driving towards Chicago. After she passed into northern Illinois, however, Penelope was seriously injured in a crash resulting from the failure of her brakes. Penelope files a tort claim in the Northern District of Illinois against Don's Tune-Ups Inc. The defendant files the following motions: (1) a motion to dismiss for lack of subject matter jurisdiction; (2) a motion to dismiss for lack of personal jurisdiction; (3) a motion to dismiss for improper venue; and (4) an alternative motion to transfer venue to the Eastern District of Wisconsin. *How should the court rule on each of these four motions?*

Quick Summary

• Venue is not a jurisdictional concept.

• Venue rules in state and federal court direct litigation to a convenient county within the state or a convenient district within the federal system.

• Venue is generally proper where defendants reside or where the claim arose.

• Federal and state court judges have broad discretion to transfer an action from where it was filed to a new proper venue for the convenience of parties and witnesses and in the interest of justice.

• Under the doctrine of forum non conveniens, those judges also have discretion to dismiss an action that has been filed in a proper forum, if that forum would be grossly inconvenient and if the lawsuit would be more properly litigated in a different judicial system.

• The Judicial Panel on Multidistrict Litigation may transfer multiple pending lawsuits with common factual questions to any single district for consolidated pretrial proceedings.

4

Applicable Law in Civil Litigation:
The *Erie* Doctrine and Choice of Law

Key Concepts

- Determination of the law applicable to disputes
- "Vertical" (choice between federal and state law) and "horizontal" (choice between the laws of different states) choice of law
- The difference between "substantive" law and "procedural" law
- *Erie v. Tompkins* and the "*Erie* Doctrine" today
- Overview of conflict of laws and choice of law

Introduction

The *Erie* doctrine in essence mandates application of state substantive law in federal court cases where the basis of subject matter jurisdiction is not a federal question. This doctrine and much choice of law doctrine selecting among competing state law grows out of the nature and structure of the United States itself. The United States, as contrasted with the more "unitary" systems of Europe and most nations, is a system in which states retain substantial authority and state law is accommodated unless there is controlling federal substantive law or a need for procedural uniformity in the federal courts.

> **The Doctrine.** The *Erie* Doctrine is the product of case law construing the Rules of Decision Act in light of the Supreme Court's view of the Constitution and equitable and efficient jurisprudence generally.

Under the *Erie* doctrine, where there is on-point federal law (from the Constitution, a treaty, or federal legislation) this law governs the dispute. But in the absence of such federal law, the federal courts must apply state law. Where a case is in federal court on the basis of diversity jurisdiction

(28 U.S.C. § 1332, discussed in Ch. 2) or where a claim is in federal court based on supplemental jurisdiction (28 U.S.C. § 1367, discussed in Ch. 1), the case will be one in which state law provides the substantive rule of decision.

THE STATUTE   **28 U.S.C. § 1652**

State Laws as Rules of Decision

[T]he laws of the several states, except where the Constitution or treaties of the United States or Acts of Congress otherwise require or provide, shall be regarded as rules of decision in civil actions in the courts of the United States, in cases where they apply.

A. The Pre-*Erie* World

The Rules of Decision Act has been in effect since it was enacted as part of the Judiciary Act of 1789. Its seemingly straightforward text leaves many questions unanswered. For example, does "laws of the several states" mean state constitutional provisions? What about: state statutes? state administrative regulations? interpretative rulings of states agencies? state supreme court precedent? all state court precedent? opinions of the state attorney general? Does "laws" mean all of these—or only some portions of these?

In *Swift v. Tyson*, 41 U.S. 1 (1842), the Supreme Court set down an authoritative construction of § 1652 that would stand for nearly a century. According to the *Swift* Court, "laws" as used in the Act meant only state statutory law or law linked to local matters. In *Swift*, the Court took the position that its precedents clearly supported its holding but cited no cases. *See* 41 U.S. at 18-19. Federal courts were not required to follow state judicial precedent but only state statutory commands—unless the matter was sufficiently local, such as where the case involved "rights and titles to things having a permanent locality, such as the rights and title to real estate, and other matter immovable and intra-territorial in their nature and character." In these local matters, state judicial precedents fell within § 1652 and were controlling law in the case. But where a matter was sufficiently non-local, general rules of law as articulated by federal court precedent (federal common law) were controlling. So, for example, if there were a contract dispute in a diversity action, the dispute would not necessarily be governed by either citizen's state law, but instead by federal common law.

B. The *Tompkins-Erie Railroad* Litigation

Harry Tompkins was walking home from his mother-in-law's home along the path parallel to the railroad when he was struck, allegedly by something protruding from a passing railroad car. Tompkins lost an arm. He sued the Railroad, which defended vigorously. In addition to arguing that the accident happened through no fault of the company, the Railroad had an even better defense under the law—the argument that it owed Tompkins no duty of care. Recall that under the negligence law of most states, a plaintiff must prove (1) duty owed by defendant, (2) breach of duty, (3) that proximately causes (4) injury and damages to plaintiff.

Under Pennsylvania law Tompkins was a mere trespasser rather than an "invitee" of the Railroad or someone tacitly permitted to use the footpath along the tracks. But, pursuant to *Swift v. Tyson*, Tompkins (or rather his New York-based attorney) appeared to have thwarted the Railroad's defense based on Pennsylvania tort law by filing in federal court in the Southern District of New York. This could be done because Tompkins (a Pennsylvanian) and the Railroad (incorporated in Delaware and having a principle place of business in New York) were citizens of different states and the matter was sufficiently serious to meet the jurisdictional minimum under 28 U.S.C. § 1332 ($10,000 at the time). This established subject matter jurisdiction in the federal courts, with proper venue in New York because the Railroad had its home offices in Manhattan. Personal jurisdiction was satisfied as well because the Railroad was in New York.

By getting to federal court, Tompkins became the beneficiary of federal common law per *Swift v. Tyson*. Under federal common law, Tompkins was not considered a trespasser but a de facto licensee, provided that the Railroad was aware that townsfolk used the footpath near the tracks and failed to take reasonable steps to stop them. Under this law, the railroad had to defend on the merits. A jury hearing the case awarded Tompkins $30,000 (more than $500,000 in 2014 dollars) after finding the railroad negligent. Tompkins, through forum shopping, had won a great victory.

The Railroad appealed but lost before the U.S. Court of Appeals for the Second Circuit, which affirmed because of the *Swift v. Tyson* precedent, finding that the standard of care for railroads regarding those walking alongside the tracks was a matter of general law, which was governed by federal common law—and not the type of local law for which the Rules of Decision Act required deference to the most applicable state law. *See Tompkins v. Erie Railroad Co.*, 90 F.2d 603 (2d Cir. 1937). The Railroad petitioned for certiorari.

FROM THE COURT

Erie Railroad Co. v. Tompkins

304 U.S. 64 (1938)

Supreme Court of the United States

MR. JUSTICE BRANDEIS delivered the opinion of the Court.

The question for decision is whether the oft-challenged doctrine of *Swift v. Tyson* shall now be disapproved. . . .

First. Swift v. *Tyson*, 16 Pet. 1, 18, held that federal courts exercising jurisdiction on the ground of diversity of citizenship need not, in matters of general jurisprudence, apply the unwritten law of the State as declared by its highest court; that they are free to exercise an independent judgment as to what the common law of the State is—or should be. . . .

Doubt was repeatedly expressed as to the correctness of the construction given the [the rules of the decision in *Swift]*, and as to the soundness of the rule which it introduced. But it was the more recent research of a competent scholar [citing Charles Warren, *New Light on the History of the Federal Judiciary Act of 1789*, 37 HARV. L. REV. 49, 51-52, 81-88, 108 (1923)], who examined the original document, which established that the construction given to it by the Court was erroneous; and that the purpose of the section was merely to make certain that, in all matters except those in which some federal law is controlling, the federal courts exercising jurisdiction in diversity of citizenship cases would apply as their rules of decision the law of the State, unwritten as well as written.

Criticism of the doctrine became widespread after the decision of *Black & White Taxicab Co.* v. *Brown & Yellow Taxicab Co.* There, Brown and Yellow, a Kentucky corporation owned by Kentuckians, and the Louisville and Nashville Railroad, also a Kentucky corporation, wished that the former should have the exclusive privilege of soliciting passenger and baggage transportation at the Bowling Green, Kentucky, railroad station; and that the Black and White, a competing Kentucky corporation, should be prevented from interfering with that privilege. Knowing that such a contract would be void under the common law of Kentucky, it was arranged that Brown and Yellow reincorporate under the law of Tennessee, and that the contract with the railroad should be executed there. The suit was then brought by the Tennessee corporation in the federal court for western Kentucky to enjoin competition by the Black and White; an injunction issued by the District Court was sustained by the Court of Appeals; and this Court, citing many decisions in which the doctrine of *Swift* v. *Tyson* had been applied, affirmed the decree.

Second. Experience in applying the doctrine of *Swift* v. *Tyson* had revealed its defects, political and social; and the benefits expected to flow from the rule did not accrue. Persistence of state courts in their own opinions on questions of common law prevented uniformity; and the impossibility of discovering a satisfactory line of demarcation between the province of general law and that of local law developed a new well of uncertainties. . . .

On the other hand, the mischievous results of the doctrine had become apparent. Diversity of citizenship jurisdiction was conferred in order to prevent apprehended discrimination in state courts against those not citizens of the State. *Swift* v. *Tyson* introduced grave discrimination by non-citizens against citizens. It made rights enjoyed under the unwritten "general law" vary according to whether enforcement was sought in the state or in the federal court; and the privilege of selecting the court in which the right should be determined was conferred upon the non-citizen. Thus, the doctrine rendered impossible equal protection of the law. In attempting to promote uniformity of law throughout the United States, the doctrine had prevented uniformity in the administration of the law of the State. . . .

The discrimination resulting became in practice far-reaching. This resulted in part from the broad province accorded to the so-called "general law" as to which federal courts exercised an independent judgment. In addition to questions of purely commercial law, "general law" was held to include the obligations under contracts entered into and to be performed within the State, [the validity of exculpatory clauses,] the liability for torts committed within the State upon persons resident or property located there, even where the question of liability depended upon the scope of a property right conferred by the State; and the right to exemplary or punitive damages. Furthermore, state decisions construing local deeds, mineral conveyances, and even devises of real estate were disregarded.

In part the discrimination resulted from the wide range of persons held entitled to avail themselves of the federal rule by resort to the diversity of citizenship jurisdiction. [I]individual citizens willing to remove from their own State and become citizens of another might avail themselves of the federal rule. And, without even change of residence, a corporate citizen of the State could avail itself of the federal rule by re-incorporating under the laws of another State, as was done in the *Taxicab* case.

The injustice and confusion incident to the doctrine of *Swift* v. *Tyson* have been repeatedly urged as reasons for abolishing or limiting diversity of citizenship jurisdiction. Other legislative relief has been proposed. If only a question of statutory construction were involved, we should not be prepared to abandon a doctrine so widely applied throughout nearly a century. But the unconstitutionality of the course pursued has now been made clear and compels us to do so.

Third. Except in matters governed by the Federal Constitution or by Acts of Congress, the law to be applied in any case is the law of the State. And whether the law of the State shall be declared by its Legislature in a statute or by its highest court in a decision is not a matter of federal concern. There is no federal general common law. Congress has no power to declare substantive rules of common law applicable in a State whether they be local in their nature or "general," be they commercial law or a part of the law of torts. And no clause in the Constitution purports to confer such a power upon the federal courts. . . .

Thus the doctrine of *Swift* v. *Tyson* is, as Mr. Justice Holmes said [in his dissent in *Black & White Taxicab Co.* v. *Brown & Yellow Taxicab Co.*], "an unconstitutional assumption of powers by courts of the United States which no lapse of time or respectable array of opinion should make us hesitate to correct." In disapproving that doctrine we do not hold unconstitutional § 34 of the Federal Judiciary Act of 1789 or any other Act of Congress. We merely declare that in applying the doctrine this Court and the lower courts have invaded rights which in our opinion are reserved by the Constitution to the several States.

MR. JUSTICE BUTLER, dissenting, joined by Justice McReynolds.

The laws of a state are more usually understood to mean the rules and enactments promulgated by the legislative authority thereof, or long established local customs having the force of laws. *In all the various cases, which have hitherto come before us for decision,* [the Court has uniformly ruled] that the true interpretation of [the Rules of Decision Act] limited its application to state laws strictly local, that is to say, to the positive statutes of the state, and the construction thereof adopted by the local tribunals, and to rights and titles to things having a permanent locality, such as the rights and titles to real estate, and other matters immovable and intraterritorial in their nature and character.

> The Brandeis majority opinion and the Butler dissenting opinion present rather different characterizations of the judiciary's historical attitude toward *Swift v. Tyson*. Brandeis paints *Swift* as long unpopular with many jurists, including icons like Chief Justice Stephen Field and Justice Oliver Wendell Holmes while Butler suggests that there had not been widespread dissatisfaction with *Swift*.

It never has been supposed by us, that the section did apply, or was designed to apply, to questions of a more general nature. . . . The doctrine [of *Swift v. Tyson*] has been followed by this Court in an unbroken line of decisions. So far as appears, it was not questioned until more than 50 years later, and then by a single judge. *Baltimore & Ohio R. Co.* v. *Baugh*, 149 U.S. 368, 390 (1893). In that case, Mr. Justice Brewer, speaking for the Court [reaffirmed *Swift*].

While amendments to [28 U.S.C. § 1652] have from time to time been suggested, the section stands as originally enacted. Evidently Congress has intended throughout the years that the rule of decision as construed should continue to govern federal courts in trials at common law. The opinion just announced suggests that Mr. Warren's research has established that from the beginning this Court has erroneously construed § 34. But that author's "New Light on the History of the Federal Judiciary Act of 1789" does not purport to be authoritative and was intended to be no more than suggestive. The weight to be given to his discovery has never been discussed at this bar. Nor does the opinion indicate the ground disclosed by the research.

* * *

It is hard to foresee the consequences of the radical change so made. . . . This Court has often emphasized its reluctance to consider constitutional questions, and that legislation will not be held invalid as repugnant to the fundamental law if the case may be decided upon any other ground. In view of grave consequences liable to result from erroneous exertion of its power to set aside legislation, the Court should move cautiously, seek assistance of counsel, act only after ample deliberation . . . .[Justice Butler also cited to a statute requiring notice to the Attorney General when the constitutionality of a statute was called into question and observed that this had not been done in the *Erie* litigation.]

> Here, Justice Butler is arguing that there has been legislative acquiescence that effectively makes *Swift v. Tyson* the correct construction of the statute. But does that follow? Can a subsequent Congress determine (or even influence) the meaning of a statute drafted by an earlier Congress without actually re-enacting the law? What if a later Congress amends the statute but does nothing to legislatively overrule *Swift*? Would that make Justice Butler's argument more persuasive?

* * *

I am of opinion that the constitutional validity of the rule need not be considered, because under the law, as found by the courts of Pennsylvania and generally throughout the country, it is plain that the evidence required a finding that plaintiff was guilty of negligence that contributed to cause his injuries and that the judgment below should be reversed upon that ground.

MR. JUSTICE REED, concurring.

The "unconstitutional" course referred to in the majority opinion is apparently the ruling in *Swift* v. *Tyson* that the supposed omission of Congress to legislate as to the effect of decisions leaves federal courts free to interpret general law for themselves. I am not at all sure whether, in the absence of federal statutory direction, federal courts would be compelled to follow state decisions. There was sufficient doubt about the matter in 1789 to induce the first Congress to legislate. No former opinions of this Court have passed upon it. . . .If the opinion commits this Court to the position that the Congress is without power to declare what rules of substantive law shall govern the federal courts, that conclusion also seems questionable.

The line between procedural and substantive law is hazy but no one doubts federal power over procedure. The Judiciary Article and the "necessary and proper" clause of Article One may fully authorize legislation, such as this section of the Judiciary Act.

In this Court, *stare decisis*, in statutory construction, is a useful rule, not an inexorable command. It seems preferable to overturn an established construction of an Act of Congress, rather than, in the circumstances of this case, to interpret the Constitution. There is no occasion to discuss further the range or soundness of these few phrases of the opinion. It is sufficient now to call attention to them and express my own non-acquiescence.

I concur in the conclusion reached in this case, in the disapproval of the doctrine of *Swift* v. *Tyson*, and in the reasoning of the majority opinion except in so far as it relies upon the unconstitutionality of the "course pursued" by the federal courts. . . .

EXPLANATION

1. The Wake of *Erie*

 After the Court's decision, the case was remanded to the Second Circuit for decision pursuant to applicable state law. The panel applied Pennsylvania law under which Tompkins was a trespasser, found no evidence that the Railroad had acted recklessly or maliciously, and entered judgment for the Railroad. *See Tompkins v. Erie Railroad Co.*, 98 F.2d 49 (2d Cir.), *cert. denied*, 305 U.S. 637 (1938). Tompkins was left with nothing. Ironically, prior to the Supreme Court decision, the railroad had hinted to Tompkins that it would be willing to settle the case for $7,500 (more than $125,000 in 2014 dollars) a result far better than Tompkins ultimately achieved. With only one arm and little education, he found it difficult to get work as a laborer and died in 1961 at age 54. For fascinating background about the case, *see* Edward A. Purcell, Jr., *The Story of* Erie: *How Litigants, Lawyers, Judges, Politics, and Social Change Reshape the Law*, in KEVIN M. CLERMONT (ED.), CIVIL PROCEDURE STORIES 21 (2d ed. 2007)(describing in detail the socio-political forces at work on American law during the era and their impact in bringing about the *Erie* decision) and Irving Younger, *What Happened in* Erie, 56 TEX. L. REV. 1011 (1978). Although largely invisible to the general public, the decision quickly attracted attention in legal circles, where observers noted the sea change it brought about in civil litigation.

2. Equal Protection or Not

Some have argued that the *Erie* Court was too quick to constitutionalize its holding by suggesting that the *Swift* rule violated the Equal Protection Clause of the Constitution by giving rise to different results depending on the citizenship of the parties and the court in which the dispute was adjudicated. Yet, cases come out differently or "unfairly" all the time based on a number of factors: assigned judge; jury composition; respective quality of counsel; litigants' availability of information and resources; and current events that shape juror attitudes. The legal system treats this type of variance as acceptable (that's why "forum shopping," despite its negative connotation, is permitted if done within the rules of the dispute resolution game and why a case once decided cannot be retried even if the result is considered unwise so long as there was no legal error). Lawyers know full well that the venue of a case, the assignment of a judge, or a key evidence ruling can have a dramatic outcome on a dispute.

Why is this type of case-to-case variance acceptable while *Swift* is not? What's different about the posited inequality of outcomes? And does it really rise to a constitutional level? What if Congress disagreed with the *Erie* decision? Could Congress revise the Rules of Decision Act (28 U.S.C.§ 1652) to state:

> the statutes of the states, and only the statutes, shall be controlling law in federal court cases where jurisdiction is founded upon diversity of citizenship. State court decisions, administrative rulings, and opinions of the attorneys general may be considered in a

federal court's determination of state law but are not binding upon any federal court.

Would this hypothetical revised § 1652 be unconstitutional?

CODIFYING SWIFT V. TYSON

Indeed, Justice Butler noted that it might have been a good idea (and an exercise in judicial respect for the Executive Branch) to have invited the Attorney General to provide the Government's view on the issue of whether *Swift* should be overruled and whether § 1652 as construed by *Swift* was unconstitutional.

3. The Reed Concurrence

Justice Reed's concurrence is important in that it makes clear that the majority's decision does not require federal courts to defer to state procedural rules. His view has become part of the legal landscape in that we now often summarize *Erie* as a rule that states that in federal court, federal procedural rules are always applied, even when jurisdiction is founded on diversity of citizenship, but that state substantive law applies in diversity cases with federal law governing in federal question cases or where federal law otherwise provides the "rule of decision."

4. *Erie*'s Immediate Aftermath

With the *Erie* decision and the promulgation of the Federal Rules of Civil Procedure (and with it the demise of the Conformity Act), 1938 proved a pivotal year in civil litigation. The Conformity Act (28 U.S.C. § 724) had required that federal courts use the procedure of the state in which the federal court was located. Thus, in 1938 there was a complete "flip" in the law in that by 1939, federal courts in diversity cases applied federal procedure (because of the 1938 Federal Rules) and state substantive law (because of *Erie*) although the exact opposite had been the case a year before.

The cases that followed defined the outline of this "flip." In *Cities Service Oil Co. v. Dunlap*, 308 U.S. 208 (1939), the Court applied state law regarding the burden of proof required under Texas law for a claimant attacking another's legal title to property, ruling that this was substantive law under *Erie*. In *Sibbach v. Wilson & Co.*, 312 U.S. 1 (1941), the Court applied Fed. R. Civ. P. 35 regarding medical exams (*see* Chapter 13)—which the Court regarded as procedural—in an action in federal district court in Illinois despite an objection arguing that such exams were not permitted in

Illinois state courts. (In *Schlagenhauf v. Holder*, 379 U.S. 104 (1964), the Court extended the *Sibbach* analysis to a plaintiff's request for a Rule 35 examination of a defendant, again holding that the Rule was sufficiently procedural to withstand an *Erie* attack.) In *Palmer v. Hoffman*, 318 U.S. 109 (1943), the Court applied Massachusetts tort law placing the burden of establishing lack of contributory negligence on a tort plaintiff, ruling that this was substantive state law that was not altered by Fed. R. Civ. P. 8(c), which treats contributory negligence as an affirmative defense to be pled and proved by defendants.

C. Applying *Erie*

EXAMPLES & ANALYSIS

EXAMPLE: Pia Pedestrian, a tourist from North Dakota, is cutting through the grounds at Dino's Diner in South Dakota and steps in a pothole, breaking her ankle. Pia sues Dino in federal court in South Dakota. Does federal or state law apply to this tort claim?

Analysis: Pia is a less dramatically injured version of Harry Tompkins. Because the lawsuit is in federal court only on the basis of diversity jurisdiction, there is no federal question and no applicability of federal common law. Accordingly, the substantive tort law of South Dakota applies and Pia may or may not prevail depending on the standard of care applied to Dino and whether his maintenance of the parking lot constitutes negligence.

EXAMPLE: Pat purchases pickled peppers from Don through Don's internet website. Pat lives in Minnesota and Don's headquarters and warehouse are in Pittsburgh. Pat finds the merchandise unacceptable and sues Don in federal court in Minneapolis for a refund. What law applies?

Analysis: Although this is a breach of contract claim rather than a negligence claim as in the prior example and the *Erie* case, the same ground rules apply. If the case is in federal court only on the basis of diversity jurisdiction, there is no constitutional provision or federal statute to construe and no general federal common law to apply. Rather, the most applicable state contract law will apply. The selection of state law depends on the methodology prevailing in the state in which the court sits. Normally, the place where the contract is "made" or finalized is determinative and that may depend on how Don's website structures the transaction in terms of offer, acceptance, payment, and completion of the transaction.

Under *Erie*, as emphasized in Justice Reed's concurrence, the sufficiency of a Rule 12(b)(1) motion alleging lack of subject matter jurisdiction, a Rule 12(b)(2) motion alleging lack of personal jurisdiction, or a Rule 12(b)(3) motion alleging improper venue would be assessed according to the federal procedural law of Rule 12, the federal rule governing motions to dismiss. A motion to transfer to a more convenient venue would be governed by 28 U.S.C. § 1404, discussed in Chapter 3. Federal procedural law controls in federal court even where the *Erie* doctrine mandates application of state substantive law.

EXAMPLE: Paul (a citizen of New Mexico) files a complaint on letter size paper against Deirdre (a citizen of Colorado) in federal court in Colorado. Deirdre moves to dismiss on the ground Colorado Rev. Stat. § XYZ requires that all pleadings be on legal size paper. What ruling will the court make? What if there is undisputed evidence from the legislative history of the law that it was passed at the behest of the Legal Size File Folders Guild, a special interest group? What if it was enacted at the behest of the Green Guerillas, an environmental group that had irrefutable evidence that use of legal size paper has substantial environmental benefits?

Analysis: In this and most other cases, courts will not look beneath the face and function of a statute and allow the motives of the legislature to affect application of the statute. Thus, whether the legal size paper requirement is a special interest boondoggle or a valid environmental regulation has no bearing here. What is important is that the statute does not create or affect substantive legal rights. Equally or more important is that federal rules regarding paper size are also procedural rather than substantive. Rules impacting the presentation of court papers are governed by the rules of the court in which the action is proceeding.

EXAMPLE: Piper (a citizen of Connecticut) sues Drummer (a citizen of Massachusetts) in Connecticut state court alleging breach of contract in connection with purchase of expensive jewelry that she alleges is fake. Drummer removes the action to federal district court in Connecticut. After discovery is completed six months later (see Chs. 12-14), Piper seeks to amend her complaint to add a fraud claim. Drummer opposes on the basis of Connecticut Rev. Stat. § 123, which permits amendment of pleadings only if sought within 90 days of the filing of the original pleading. Piper contends that the motion instead should be controlled by Fed. R. Civ. P. 15, which essentially permits amendment whenever it is in the interests of justice so long as the opposition is not unduly prejudiced (*see* Ch. 10). Which law applies?

Analysis: Any motion to amend would be governed by Fed. R. Civ. P. 15, the federal rule governing amendments to pleadings because the case is in federal court and Rule 15 is a procedural rule—not a substantive rule—although it in this case has the important result of permitting Piper to make a fraud claim that would apparently have been foreclosed to her in Connecticut state court, where she originally filed suit. Ironically, by removing to federal court, Drummer ended up worse off than if he had allowed the case to stay in state court, at least regarding this aspect of the case.

EXAMPLE: Per (a citizen of Virginia) sues Dagmar (a citizen of North Carolina) in federal court in North Carolina for injuries after being struck by her car at an intersection in North Carolina while on an over-the-border shopping trip. Convinced Per is exaggerating his injuries, Dagmar seeks an independent medical examination pursuant to Fed. R. Civ. P. 35. Per protests, noting that the North Carolina Bodily Privacy Act grants "every person" an "absolute right to refuse medical examination." How will the court rule?

Analysis: Although the state's Bodily Privacy Act reflects an important state policy, Rule 35 is a procedural rule designed to foster development of information so that federal courts can render a more accurate adjudication of disputes—and the case is in federal court. This is just like *Sibbach v. Wilson*, 312 U.S. 1 (1941), discussed earlier in this chapter. As with the previous example, there is some irony here. Per chose to sue in federal court when he could have sued in North Carolina state court, where he would have been able to avoid a medical examination (but probably not production of his medical records), making it harder for Dagmar to question the bona fides of his alleged injuries.

D. Federal Common Law

Federal tort law exists only in particular circumstances such as when the defendants are federal entities or when allegedly tortuous conduct occurred on federal property. This is what Justice Brandeis meant in *Erie* by stating that there is no general federal common law. Because of the state-centered federalism of American government, politics, and law, the federal government generally does not reach out to federalize any more tort law than is necessary. For example, the Federal Tort Claims Act, 28 U.S.C. § 1346(b), permits U.S. government liability for tortious injury—but only to the extent a private person would be similarly liable under controlling applicable state law.

After *Erie*, there is no general federal common law that applies in diversity jurisdiction cases across the board. But there may be instances that call for the application of "specific" federal common law such as when litigation involves federal officers, property, or important interests. Federal common law is also often used to flesh out application of a federal statute or program because it promotes greater uniformity than would borrowing from different states in different cases involving the federal statute or program.

For example, the Employee Retirement Income Security Act, 29 U.S.C. § 1002, et seq., governs employee benefit plans provided by businesses to their workers. Benefit plans such as a 401(k) retirement plan or a group health insurance policy create contractual rights for the parties. When disputes arose regarding denials of benefits under such plans/contracts, issues arose as to what law should be applied. The federal courts concluded that contract rights involving ERISA plans would be assessed according to federal common law of contract rather than state contract law.

There are other situations involving disputes where it would seem completely incorrect to look to state law for the rule of decision even if there is not a controlling federal statute on point. For example, states may sue one another over boundaries or water rights (Arizona and California have done so with some frequency regarding use of Colorado River water). Such disputes are usually governed by federal common law rather than any given state law. *See also United States v. Standard Oil Co.*, 332 U.S. 301 (1947)(federal common law governs whether U.S. government can obtain reimbursement from tortfeasor driver who injured pedestrian soldier at intersection in Los Angeles); *Clearfield Trust Co. v. United States*, 318 U.S. 363, 367 (1943) (federal common law governs liabilities arising out of forged endorsement on check issued by U.S. government).

On the same day that *Erie* was decided, the Court in *Hinderlider v. La Plata River & Cherry Creek Ditch Co.*, 304 U.S. 92, 110 (1938) stated that "whether the water of an interstate stream mouth be apportioned between the two States is a question of 'federal common law' upon which neither the states nor the decision of either State can be conclusive." Who was the author of this *Hinderlider* opinion embracing federal common law regarding interstate water rights? The same Justice Brandeis who said in *Erie* that there was no general federal common law.

Federal common law may not be all that different from the state law that would otherwise apply to a dispute. Consider, for example, cases involving ERISA plans. The federal common law of contract that governs these disputes generally looks like the majority of state contract law. Indeed, federal common law typically derives from the national court system's assessment of the better decisions of state court systems, which usually comprise the majority rule on an issue. Courts crafting federal common law will also consider matters of public policy, equity, fairness, scholarly assessment, existing state legislation on the topic, and other factors. In some cases, the federal judiciary will actually adopt state law of which it approves as federal common law. *See, e.g., Kamen v. Kemper Financial Services, Inc.*, 500 U.S. 90 (1991)(adopting state law regarding permissibility of shareholder derivative lawsuit); *Board of Regents v. Tomanio*, 446 U.S. 478 (1980)(applying state statute of limitations to federal statutory claim where Congress did not specify a limitations period for the federal cause of action in question).

1. *York*—And its Wake

In *Guaranty Trust Co. v. York*, 326 U.S. 99 (1945), the Court faced the question of whether a federal court hearing a class action suit based on diversity jurisdiction was required to apply the forum state's statute of limitations. The Second Circuit had ruled that statutes of limitations were sufficiently procedural and non-substantive (in that they did not speak to the merits of the claim) that application of the state limitations period was not required under *Erie*. Instead, the Second Circuit applied the federal common law of **laches.**

The Supreme Court in *York* held that the lower courts should have dismissed the action as untimely if it would have been barred by the state limitations period. The rationale is pretty straightforward. *Erie* stands for the proposition that a dispute not expressly governed by federal law should be subject to the same substantive law regardless of whether the action qualifies for diversity jurisdiction and thus becomes a federal case. The suit against the trust company would be time-barred if brought in state court. If it is not time-barred when brought instead in federal court, we have the same problems of undue forum shopping and divergent outcomes which existed under the *Swift* regime and that were supposed to be eliminated by *Erie*.

> **Laches** is the concept of barring an action because so much time has passed since the date of the wrong that it would be inequitable to sue the defendant so long after the alleged wrong. Laches doctrine is flexible and has a certain "rough justice in the eye of the beholder" character as well as being unburdened by any particular deadline (e.g., three years from the date of the infraction) as is the case with statutes of limitation. With this greater flexibility, the Second Circuit was willing to permit the case alleging misconduct by the trust company to proceed even though it would have been barred by the statute of limitations had the action been in New York state court.

Another rationale is that the time limit allowed by the state for bringing suit over an alleged wrong is part of the substantive right itself. New York may, for example, provide a cause of action for plaintiffs who are defrauded, negligently injured, or who suffer contract breach—but to pursue the remedy, the plaintiff must sue before the relevant statute of limitations expires. Because this limitations period is part of the substantive right, it is substantive law that must, pursuant to *Erie*, apply to an action based on diversity jurisdiction, just as the tort rights of Harry Tompkins under Pennsylvania law hinged in part on his status relative to the property on which the injury occurred.

2. The "Outcome Determinative" Test of *York*— And its Progeny

The holding in *York* (that the state statute of limitations, rather than the federal doctrine of laches, applied) is perfectly consistent with these rationales—but the test emanating from *York* came to be seen as problematic. The *York* Court stated that the means for determining whether a legal rule was one of substance or procedure hinged on whether application of the rule would change the outcome of the case. In *York* itself, application of the test was fairly easy: if the stricter state statute of limitations was applied rather than the more relaxed laches standard, the case would be dismissed. Thus, application of the state law was "outcome determinative" and therefore must be substantive rather than procedural.

The "outcome determinative" test for which *York* is best known has a beguiling simplicity but raised concerns in that it could be applied so broadly as to sweep away federal law altogether in diversity cases. Even a rule that seems completely "procedural," such as the time limit for amending a complaint or the requirement that motions be printed on paper of a particular color would be viewed as substantive under a strong version of the *York* test. Thus, if a motion is printed on the wrong color paper, it could be denied. Consequently, compliance with a hypothetical state court rule about paper color or typeface could be viewed as sufficiently outcome determinative to merit enforcement under *York*. If outcome determinative, the rule would then be substantive and a federal court would be forced to apply it in a diversity case even if the federal court's own rules on the topic were to the contrary.

Clearly, a strong version of the *York* outcome determinative test could lead to problems. But during the first decade after *York*, the outcome determinative test continued to hold sway without much reservation, although the Court continued to uphold application of some Federal Rules based on the substance/procedure distinction and did not take *York* to the limits of overturning federal court rules on paper size, color, and the like.

In *Mississippi Publishing Corp. v. Murphree*, 326 U.S. 438 (1946), the Court upheld application of Fed. R. Civ. P. 4 regarding service of process over an objection that service in a federal court action must comport with a state statute to be valid.

In *Ragan v. Merchants Transfer & Warehouse Co.*, 337 U.S. 530 (1949), the Court ruled that the federal practice of deeming a case commenced for statute of limitations purposes upon filing of the complaint was displaced by Kansas law providing that only in hand service of the summons and complaint commences an action and beats the statute of limitations. Rule 3 stated that an action in federal court is commenced by filing but was viewed as merely establishing federal procedural time frames and not acting as the measuring stick for state statutes of limitation.

In *Woods v. Interstate Realty Co.*, 337 U.S. 535 (1949), the Court refused to apply a Mississippi statute requiring that corporations be in good regulatory standing as a condition for bringing lawsuits. The *Woods* majority reasoned that although the statute might bind state courts, it could not restrict access to the federal courts, which were entitled to set their own rules regarding access. Three Justices dissented, contending that the state law was substantive under *Erie* and violated no federal policy so long as it did not discriminate between state and federal courts (which it did not as the requirement, if applied, would prevent bringing suit in both state and federal courts). *See* 337 U.S. at 538 (Jackson, J., dissenting)("the Court's action in refusing to accept the state court's determination of the effect of its own status is a perversion" of *Erie*).

In *Cohen v. Beneficial Industrial Loan Corp.*, 337 U.S. 541 (1949), the Court required application of a New Jersey statute requiring plaintiffs in shareholder derivative actions to post security for expenses that can be used to indemnify defendants for costs and counsel fees if the defendant prevails. Lack of compliance with the requirement required dismissal of the federal lawsuit.

In *Bernhardt v. Polygraphic Co. of America*, 350 U.S. 198 (1956), the Court ruled that a Vermont state law deeming an arbitration clause unenforceable in employment agreements applied in a federal court diversity action by an employee, forcing denial of the employer's motion to compel arbitration.[1]

While these decisions did not seem to take *York*'s outcome determination too far, with the increasing march of *York*'s influence, prominent commentators became concerned. For example, Second Circuit Judge Charles Clark

---

1   *Bernhardt* was constructively overruled by *Southland Corp. v. Keating*, 452 U.S. 1 (1984), in which the Court held that the Federal Arbitration Act, 9 U.S.C. § 1, et. seq., creates controlling federal substantive law regarding the enforceability of arbitration agreements and is not merely a procedural statute governing federal litigation.

(who as Yale Law Dean had been the Reporter of the 1938 Civil Rules), worried that under a strong version of *York*'s outcome determinative test, federal judges were becoming mere "ventriloquists' dummies" required to mouth state law, even where it arguably intruded on federal procedural prerogatives and important federal policies.

3. *Byrd v. Blue Ridge*

This concern found voice and a counter-attack of sorts in *Byrd v. Blue Ridge Rural Elec. Coop., Inc.*, 356 U.S. 525 (1958). The issue was whether the Seventh Amendment's right to jury trial (*see* Chapter 16) applied in an action brought by an injured power line worker against the electric cooperative.

In a familiar scenario, the worker sought to recover in tort while the defendant sought to characterize him as an employee. The accident and injury took place in South Carolina, which like most states since the early 20th Century has had in place a workers' compensation law. Worker suits against employers were only sporadically successful prior to these laws because employers could invoke defenses such as assumption of the risk, the fellow servant rule, and strict contributory negligence as a bar to all recovery. Subsequently, tort law largely moved away from upholding these defenses, resulting in a situation in which workers' compensation claims were less attractive to the injured because they provided less advantage over tort law regarding liability but contained caps on recovery. As a result, those injured on the job—such as Byrd—often sought to avoid the workers compensation statutes by being characterized as independent contractors rather than employees.

Under South Carolina law, the question of an injured worker's status (employee vs. independent contractor) was to be determined by the judge presiding over the case rather than a jury as this was the established practice in state court. Because Byrd could sue in federal court pursuant to diversity jurisdiction, he sought a jury trial, which was the norm in federal court on legal issues, rather than a bench determination of his stature. The federal trial court agreed and permitted jury consideration, which was favorable to plaintiff Byrd, who obtained a tort award for his injuries. The Fourth Circuit reversed on the jury trial issue and also found Byrd to be an employee who could not sue in tort and was relegated to workers' comp remedies. The Supreme Court effectively reinstated the verdict favoring Byrd by ruling that he was entitled to a jury trial on the question of his employment status because of the strong federal policy in favor of jury trial of legal issues in federal courts.

Byrd is regarded as a resounding blow in favor of permitting federal courts to run their trials their way without bowing to state court procedural norms. But the *Byrd v. Blue Ridge* Court could perhaps have gone farther and produced a simpler opinion by simply stating that the Seventh Amendment was not merely evidence of a strong federal policy but was controlling substantive federal law (the Constitution) in federal court, just as a federal statute would apply to federal proceedings. In addition, Federal Rule 38 provides for a right to jury trial to the extent of the Seventh Amendment. In short, there were countervailing federal interests in preserving the right to jury trial in federal court that overcame the state interests protected by the *Erie* Doctrine.

EXAMPLES & ANALYSIS

EXAMPLE: A South Carolina statute caps damages for workplace injury, regardless of the worker's status as employee or independent contractor. Must federal courts apply this statute under *Erie*?

Analysis: This type of damages cap would almost certainly be deemed substantive law under *Erie* as it sets forth the legal rights of a claimant. It is not a procedural provision governing the manner and conduct of litigation.

EXAMPLE: Patience sues Dr. Daryl in federal court in New Jersey alleging injury from medical malpractice. New Jersey has no caps on medical malpractice damages but provides that trials are to be bifurcated (with a jury first deciding fault and the judge then determining damages). Must the federal court bifurcate in this manner? May Patience obtain a jury determination of damages if she prevails on the question of Dr. Daryl's liability?

Analysis: Pursuant to *Erie*, the conduct of the trial would appear to be a procedural matter governed by the Federal Rules and the judge's discretion. However, if the state legislature has expressed the view that bifurcation is necessary to reduce the incidence of "sympathy" verdicts (where jurors are tempted to find fault with even good medical care because they are aware of the plaintiff's severe injuries), this could be characterized as substantive state law applicable under *Erie*. Pursuant to *Byrd v. Blue Ridge Electric*, Patience would almost surely be entitled to a jury determination of damages because of the strong federal policy in favor of jury trials in matters "at law" seeking monetary damages. But depending on the legislative history and state court precedent, Dr. Daryl may be able to craft a winning argument that the judicial determination of damages was intended to be substantive state law applied to all medical malpractice claims brought pursuant to New Jersey law.

E. *Hanna v. Plumer*

More important even than *Byrd v. Blue Ridge* for constraining *York* was *Hanna v. Plumer*, 380 U.S. 460 (1965). The case began with an auto accident-related tort claim made in federal district court against the estate of the alleged tortfeasor. A Massachusetts statute (Mass. Gen. Laws Ann., c. 197, § 9) required service "in hand" upon the executor within one year of the decedent's death. In contrast to Fed. R. Civ. P. 4, substituted service, such as leaving a copy of the summons and complaint with the executor's spouse or adult children, was not sufficient, nor were other methods that might be available pursuant to the Federal Rules. The executor received the summons and complaint within the one-year statute of limitations but the service was effected pursuant to Rule 4 (the papers were left with his wife) rather than the Massachusetts statute.

The executor brought a Rule 12 motion seeking dismissal—and was successful at trial and before the First Circuit. The Supreme Court reversed, holding that Rule 4 was a procedural rule applicable in federal court and that its reach did not exceed the permissible scope of the Rules Enabling Act. In other words, the alternative methods of service provided by Rule 4 did not improperly strip the defendant of substantive rights enjoyed under Massachusetts law.

Hanna, written by Chief Justice Earl Warren, is considered important in that it shifted the *Erie* analysis to a degree and established what many see as a two-track approach to *Erie* problems. In cases like *Erie* itself, there is no Federal Rule of Civil Procedure at issue but merely the question of whether there exists applicable federal substantive law that can displace otherwise applicable state law. In cases like *Hanna* (and its predecessors such as *Muphree*, *Sibbach v. Wilson*, and *Schlagenhauf v. Holder*), there is a Federal Rule of Civil Procedure that covers the issue in dispute (*e.g.*, whether service of process was proper). In this second set of cases, *Hanna* stated that the Federal Rule should govern because of federal supremacy over control of its own judicial process so long as the Federal Rule regulated only procedure and was properly promulgated pursuant to the Enabling Act.

Hanna defined procedure as "the judicial process for enforcing rights and duties recognized by substantive law and for justly administering remedy and redress for disregard or infraction of them" (quoting *Sibbach* v. *Wilson & Co.*, 312 U.S. 1, 14 (1941)). But the *Hanna* opinion also noted that application of the Massachusetts service of process provisions would end the case—which was certainly outcome determinative. Responding to this argument, *Hanna* observed:

> The syllogism possesses an appealing simplicity, but is for several reasons invalid. . . . "Outcome-determination" analysis was never intended to serve as a talisman. Indeed, the message of York itself is that choices between state and federal law are to be made not by application of any automatic, "litmus paper" criterion, but rather by reference to the policies underlying the *Erie* rule. The *Erie* rule is rooted in part in a realization that it would be unfair for the character or result of a litigation materially to differ because the suit had been brought in a federal court.
>
> The decision was also in part a reaction to the practice of "forum-shopping" which had grown up in response to the rule of *Swift v. Tyson*. That the York test was an attempt to effectuate these policies is demonstrated by the fact that the opinion framed the inquiry in terms of "substantial" variations between state and federal litigation. Not only are nonsubstantial, or trivial, variations not likely to raise the sort of equal protection problems which troubled the Court in *Erie*; they are also unlikely to influence the choice of a forum. The "outcome-determination" test therefore cannot be read without reference to the twin aims of the *Erie* rule: discouragement of forum-shopping and avoidance of inequitable administration of the laws.

> [A service of process rule is] "outcome-determinative" in the sense
> that if we hold the state rule to apply, respondent prevails, whereas if
> we hold that Rule 4 (d)(1) governs, the litigation will continue. But
> in this sense *every* procedural variation is "outcome-determinative."
> . . . Petitioner, in choosing her forum, was not presented with a situ-
> ation where application of the state rule would wholly bar recovery.
> [By contrast,] a federal court's refusal to enforce the New Jersey rule
> involved in *Cohen* v. *Beneficial Loan Corp.*, requiring the posting of
> security by plaintiffs in stockholders' derivative actions, might well
> impel a stockholder to choose to bring suit in the federal, rather than
> the state, court.

The *Hanna* opinion then established the second category of *Erie* cases—
those involving Federal Rules—more clearly than had earlier cases like
Sibbach and *Murphree*.

> There is, however, a more fundamental flaw in respondent's syllo-
> gism: the incorrect assumption that the rule of *Erie R. Co. v. Tomp-*
> *kins* constitutes the appropriate test of the validity and therefore the
> applicability of a Federal Rule of Civil Procedure. The *Erie* rule has
> never been invoked to void a Federal Rule. . . . [I]n cases adjudicat-
> ing the validity of Federal Rules, we have not applied the York rule
> or other refinements of *Erie*, but have to this day continued to decide
> questions concerning the scope of the Enabling Act and the constitu-
> tionality of specific Federal Rules in light of the distinction [between
> cases involving a federal rule and cases in which there is no federal
> procedural rule on point].
>
>   * * *
>
> *Erie* and its offspring cast no doubt on the long-recognized power
> of Congress to prescribe housekeeping rules for federal courts even
> though some of those rules will inevitably differ from comparable
> state rules [because the systems are not identical]. Thus, though a
> court, in measuring a Federal Rule against the standards contained
> in the Enabling Act and the Constitution, need not wholly blind

> itself to the degree to which the Rule makes the character and result of the federal litigation stray from the course it would follow in state courts, it cannot be forgotten that the *Erie* rule, and the guidelines suggested in *York*, were created to serve another purpose altogether. To hold that a Federal Rule of Civil Procedure must cease to function whenever it alters the mode of enforcing state-created rights would be to disembowel either the Constitution's grant of power over federal procedure or Congress' attempt to exercise that power in the Enabling Act. Rule 4 (d)(1) is valid and controls the instant case.

380 U.S. at 468–72.

Although *Hanna* was unanimous, concurring Justice John Marshall Harlan took issue with the formalism and simplicity of the majority's test.

> I respect the Court's effort to clarify the situation in today's opinion. However, in doing so I think it has misconceived the constitutional remises of *Erie* and has failed to deal adequately with those past decisions upon which the courts below relied.
>
> *Erie* was something more than an opinion which worried about "forum-shopping and avoidance of inequitable administration of the laws," although to be sure these were important elements of the decision. I have always regarded that decision as one of the modern cornerstones of our federalism, expressing policies that profoundly touch the allocation of judicial power between the state and federal systems. . . .
>
> To my mind the proper line of approach in determining whether to apply a state or a federal rule, whether "substantive" or "procedural," is to stay close to basic principles by inquiring if the choice of rule would substantially affect those primary decisions respecting human conduct which our constitutional system leaves to state regulation. If so, *Erie* and the Constitution require that the state rule prevail, even in the face of a conflicting federal rule.

* * *

The Massachusetts rule provides that an executor need not answer suits unless in-hand service was made upon him or notice of the action was filed in the proper registry of probate within one year of his giving bond. The evident intent of this statute is to permit an executor to distribute the estate which he is administering without fear that further liabilities may be outstanding for which he could be held personally liable.

If the Federal District Court in Massachusetts applies Rule 4(d) (1) of the Federal Rules of Civil Procedure instead of the Massachusetts service rule, what effect would that have on the speed and assurance with which estates are distributed? As I see it, the effect would not be substantial. It would mean simply that an executor would have to check at his own house or the federal courthouse as well as the registry of probate before he could distribute the estate with impunity. As this does not seem enough to give rise to any real impingement on the vitality of the state policy which the Massachusetts rule is intended to serve, I concur in the judgment.

1. The Immediate Aftermath of *Hanna*

Hanna is seen by most observers as a reassertion of federal court power and federal authority generally that was largely welcome. Many shared Judge Clark's view that under *York* and its progeny, federal courts had been too constrained to follow any state law that would make a difference in case outcome, perhaps even something as silly as the difference between submitting a brief on green paper versus white paper. *Byrd v. Blue Ridge Electric Co.*, 356 U.S. 525 (1958) had cut back somewhat on the reach of *York* and the potential for excessively expansive application of the outcome determinative test but could be explained in large part by the influence of the Seventh Amendment and the strong federal policy in favor of jury trial (*see* Ch. 16). Because *Hanna* involved a Federal Rule rather than a statute or constitutional provision and because it seemed to say that federal rulemaking produced applicable federal procedure where the rules applied, it was viewed as a big victory for those favoring doing things the "federal way" in federal courts unless the matter was clearly one reserved for substantive state law.

2. The Limits of *Hanna*: *Walker v. Armco Steel*

But *Hanna* was eventually held not to be quite this strong a presumption in favor of following the federal method. In the immediate aftermath of *Hanna*, many wondered whether cases like *Ragan v. Merchant's Transfer & Warehouse Co.*, 337 U.S. 530 (1949) [p.203], were still good law. *Ragan* had rejected application of Fed. R. Civ. P. 3 governing filing in favor of a state practice measuring the commencement of litigation based on the date the defendants was served. *Hanna* had rejected a seemingly similar state law challenge to Fed. R. Civ. P. 4 governing service of process. A reasonable lawyer might be forgiven for seeing *Hanna* as a constructive overruling of *Ragan*.

But that reasonable lawyer would be proven wrong. In *Walker v. Armco Steel Corp.*, 446 U.S. 740 (1980), the Court reiterated the continued force of *Ragan* in holding that plaintiff had missed the applicable state (Oklahoma) statute of limitations in a suit alleging injury from use of defendant's allegedly defective nail. Plaintiff had filed his complaint in federal court prior to the expiration of the statute but had not served the defendant within 60 days of the expiration of the statute as required by state law.

As in *Ragan*, plaintiff Walker argued that he had "beaten" the running of the statute by filing prior to its expiration because Fed. R. Civ. P. 3 stated that an action in federal court is commenced by filing the complaint with the court. Although *Ragan* had rejected this argument, Walker contended that *Hanna* had changed the law and that Rule 3, like Rule 4, was a validly promulgated federal rule governing procedural matters and that it (and not state law regarding commencement of an action before expiration of the limitations period) should govern the case.

The Court rejected this argument and reaffirmed the authority of *Ragan*, holding that Rule 3 was merely a device for regulating deadlines under the federal rules and thus was not in conflict with Oklahoma law as Rule 4 had conflicted with Massachusetts service of process law in *Hanna*. Despite the reading many gave *Hanna*, *Ragan* was still good law, as it seems were other cases decided during the time between *York* and *Hanna*.

3. Applying *Erie* in Light of *Hanna*: The Two-Track Approach

After *Hanna*, it is important to first ask whether a Federal Rule of Civil Procedure applies to a dispute. If so, the Federal Rule presumptively governs unless (1) there was some defect in its promulgation; (2) it is not really a rule regulating "procedure" (loosely defined as the judicial process for enforcing rights and duties recognized by substantive law and for administering adjudication and remedies); or (3) it exceeds the authority of the Rules Enabling Act by acting to "abridge, enlarge or modify any substantive right." If there is no applicable Federal Rule, the judicial inquiry is restricted to determining whether the applicable state rule in question is one of substantive law (that which establishes the rights and duties of the litigants). If so, the state law applies.

EXAMPLES & ANALYSIS

EXAMPLE: Pete sues Daltry for unauthorized use of his rock songs in federal court in Florida—and loses. Pete appeals and loses again. Daltry seeks sanctions against Pete pursuant to a Florida statute stating that any unsuccessful appellant must pay a penalty of $5,000 or ten percent of the judgment at issue, whichever is greater. The Federal Rules of Appellate Procedure and federal statutes contain no such penalty. Pete protests, arguing that because the matter is in federal court, he is not responsible for any penalty payments merely because he lost his appeal. Will Pete prevail on this argument?

Analysis: Pete should prevail on this issue. Florida's appeal penalty, although it can create rights and impose duties, looks like a procedural statute. More important, there are federal rules governing appeals and they do not establish a penalty. Although one can argue that this leaves room for application of a state penalty, the better view is that the silence of the Federal Appellate Rules on this issue is in essence a rule implicitly stating that litigants cannot be penalized merely for losing an appeal. Federal Appellate Rule 38 provides for penalties where "an appeal is frivolous" but does not punish an appellant merely for losing, which suggests that the Federal Rules are inconsistent with the state's appeal penalty rule. This example is much like *Burlington Northern Railroad Co. v. Woods*, 480 U.S. 1 (1987), in which the Court declined to apply an Alabama statute imposing a ten percent penalty.

F. All Quiet on the *Erie* Front—Until *Gasperini*

After *Walker v. Armco Steel*, the Court went nearly 20 years without a major *Erie* decision. Then came *Gasperini v. Center for Humanities, Inc.*, 518 U.S. 415 (1996). Gasperini, a journalist, lent 300 photo transparency slides he made from covering unrest in Central America to the Center, which was to return the slides but lost them. Gasperini sued, contending that each slide was worth $1,500 (an industry standard testified to by his expert witness). The jury agreed, awarding $450,000 in damages, which the Center challenged as excessive.

The matter was in federal court in the Southern District of New York (Manhattan) and New York had a provision in its Civil Practice Laws and Rules (CPLR)—§ 5501(c)—that provided judges with power to reduce excessively high jury verdicts to a lower amount that does not "materially deviate" from an amount that would constitute reasonable compensation.

Invoking this statute/rule, the Center argued that $450,000 was too much for the lost transparencies, contending that most of the 300 were nothing special. The trial court agreed, reducing the award to $150,000, which was affirmed by the Second Circuit. Gasperini argued that instead of § 5501(c) the trial court should apply Fed. R. Civ. P. 59, which permits federal courts to order a new trial or grant a remittitur (*see* Ch. 18) if the verdict is excessive. Plaintiff Gasperini in essence argued that a federal court should use an on-point federal rule (Rule 59) which, pursuant to *Hanna*, should govern the matter notwithstanding *Walker v. Armco Steel*.

The Supreme Court disagreed and affirmed the Second Circuit and trial court holdings, ruling that although Rule 59 gave federal courts power to set aside or reduce jury awards, it did not set forth a specific standard or yardstick and was thus not a controlling federal rule. Thus, states were free to provide more specific standards for policing the size of jury verdicts without being in conflict with otherwise controlling federal procedure. New York's "materially deviates from reasonable compensation" standard in § 5501(c) was thus found applicable rather than the more amorphous Rule 59 criteria for reviewing verdict amounts.

However, the *Gasperini* majority also held that the manner in which § 5501 was applied to determine whether the verdict was excessive was a matter of federal procedural law, which vests with the trial judge the initial decision regarding whether to grant a new trial because the verdict is against the weight of the evidence. In the federal court, after the trial judge has ruled, the federal appellate court reviews the decision according to an "abuse of discretion" standard (*see* Ch. 19). This federal court approach was not supplanted by § 5501's requirement that New York state appeals courts make this determination de novo.

Thus, even though *Gasperini* was on the whole a victory for the state standard, an important part of the opinion followed the *Byrd v. Blue Ridge* tradition in finding a "countervailing federal interest" in federal court authority to apply federal procedural practice regarding the division of labor between trial and appellate courts. As in *Byrd*, the federal interest overcame the state law regarding the distribution of trial and appellate court authority. Consequently, the federal trial court was required to apply the state law materially-deviates-from-reasonable compensation standard in determining whether Gasperini's $450,000 award was excessive but the federal appellate court was required to use the deferential abuse-of-discretion standard of review in assessing the trial court decision and was not required to conduct a de novo review according to state court procedural practice.

G. *Shady Grove*—21st Century Approach to the *Erie* Doctrine?

Combined with *Walker v. Armco Steel*, *Gasperini* sent to many a message that the *York* approach was far from dead, even when there were Federal Rules (i.e, Rules 3 and 59, respectively) involved. Was it possible that, despite *Hanna*, state law seeming to govern litigation operations was likely to be held substantive under *Erie* after all in many cases?

> Although the opinion sets forth relevant text of Fed. R. Civ. P. 23 concerning class actions, it may be worth looking at Chapter 9's discussion of class actions prior to reading *Shady Grove*.

FROM THE COURT

Shady Grove Orthopedic Associates, P.A. v. Allstate Insurance Company

559 U.S. 393 (2010)

Supreme Court of the United States

Justice **Scalia** announced the judgment of the Court and delivered the opinion of the Court with respect to Parts I and II-A, an opinion with respect to Parts II-B and II-D, in which The **Chief Justice**, Justice **Thomas**, and Justice **Sotomayor** join, and an opinion with respect to Part II-C, in which The **Chief Justice** and Justice **Thomas** join.

SCALIA, J. New York law prohibits class actions in suits seeking penalties or statutory minimum damages. N. Y. Civ. Prac. Law Ann. § 901 provides:

> "(a) One or more members of a class may sue or be sued as representative parties on behalf of all if: "1. the class is so numerous that joinder of all members, whether otherwise required or permitted, is impracticable; "2. there are questions of law or fact common to the class which predominate over any questions affecting only individual members; "3. the claims or defenses of the representative parties are typical of the claims or defenses of the class; "4. the representative parties will fairly and adequately protect the interests of the class; and "5. a class action is superior to other available methods for the fair and efficient adjudication of the controversy.

> "(b) Unless a statute creating or imposing a penalty, or a minimum measure of recovery specifically authorizes the recovery thereof in a class action, an action to recover a penalty, or minimum measure of recovery created or imposed by statute may not be maintained as a class action."

We consider whether this precludes a federal district court sitting in diversity from entertaining a class action under Federal Rule of Civil Procedure 23. Rule 23(a) provides:

"(a) Prerequisites. One or more members of a class may sue or be sued as representative parties on behalf of all members only if: "(1) the class is so numerous that joinder of all members is impracticable; "(2) there are questions of law or fact common to the class; "(3) the claims or defenses of the representative parties are typical of the claims or defenses of the class; and "(4) the representative parties will fairly and adequately protect the interests of the class." Subsection (b) says that "[a] class action may be maintained if Rule 23 (a) is satisfied and if" the suit falls into one of three described categories (irrelevant for present purposes).

I

The petitioner's complaint alleged the following: Shady Grove Orthopedic Associates, P. A., provided medical care to Sonia E. Galvez for injuries she suffered in an automobile accident. As partial payment for that care, Galvez assigned to Shady Grove her rights to insurance benefits under a policy issued in New York by Allstate Insurance Co. Shady Grove tendered a claim for the assigned benefits to Allstate, which under New York law had 30 days to pay the claim or deny it. *See* N. Y. Ins. Law Ann. § 5106(a). Allstate apparently paid, but not on time, and it refused to pay the statutory interest that accrued on the overdue benefits (at two percent per month).

Shady Grove filed this diversity suit in the Eastern District of New York to recover the unpaid statutory interest. Alleging that Allstate routinely refuses to pay interest on overdue benefits, Shady Grove sought relief on behalf of itself and a class of all others to whom Allstate owes interest. The District Court dismissed the suit for lack of jurisdiction. It reasoned that N.Y. Civ. Prac. Law Ann. § 901(b), which precludes a suit to recover a "penalty" from proceeding as a class action, applies in diversity suits in federal court, despite Federal Rule of Civil Procedure 23. Concluding that statutory interest is a "penalty" under New York law, it held that § 901(b) prohibited the proposed class action. And, since Shady Grove conceded that its individual claim (worth roughly $500) fell far short of the amount-in-controversy requirement for individual suits under 28 U.S.C. § 1332(a), the suit did not belong in federal court. Shady Grove had asserted jurisdiction under 28 U.S.C. § 1332(d)(2), which relaxes, for class actions seeking at least $5 million, the rule against aggregating separate claims for calculation of the amount in controversy.

The Second Circuit affirmed. The court did not dispute that a federal rule adopted in compliance with the Rules Enabling Act, 28 U.S.C. § 2072, would control if it conflicted with § 901(b). But there was no conflict because (as we will describe in more detail below) the Second Circuit concluded that Rule 23 and § 901(b) address different issues. Finding no federal rule on point, the Court of Appeals held that § 901(b) is "substantive" within the meaning of *Erie R. Co.* v. *Tompkins* and thus must be applied by federal courts sitting in diversity. We granted certiorari [and reverse].

II

The framework for our decision is familiar. We must first determine whether Rule 23 answers the question in dispute. If it does, it governs—New York's law notwithstanding—unless it exceeds statutory authorization or Congress's rulemaking power. *Hanna* v. *Plumer.* We do not wade into *Erie*'s murky waters unless the federal rule is inapplicable or invalid.

A

The question in dispute is whether Shady Grove's suit may proceed as a class action. Rule 23 provides an answer. It states that "[a] class action may be maintained" if two conditions are met: The suit must satisfy the criteria set forth in subdivision (a) (*i.e.*, numerosity, commonality, typicality, and adequacy of representation), and it also must fit into one of the three categories described in subdivision (b). Fed. Rule Civ. Proc. 23(b). By its terms this creates a categorical rule entitling a plaintiff whose suit meets the specified criteria to pursue his claim as a class action. Thus, Rule 23 provides a one-size-fits-all formula for deciding the class-action question. Because § 901(b) attempts to answer the same question—*i.e.*, it states that Shady Grove's suit "may *not* be maintained as a class action" (emphasis added) because of the relief it seeks—it cannot apply in diversity suits unless Rule 23 is ultra vires.

The Second Circuit believed that § 901(b) and Rule 23 do not conflict because they address different issues. Rule 23, it said, concerns only the criteria for determining whether a given class can and should be certified; section 901(b), on the other hand, addresses an antecedent question: whether the particular type of claim is eligible for class treatment in the first place—a question on which Rule 23 is silent. Allstate embraces this analysis. We disagree. To begin with, the line between eligibility and certifiability is entirely artificial. Both are preconditions for maintaining a class action.

Allstate asserts that Rule 23 neither explicitly nor implicitly empowers a federal court "to certify a class in each and every case" where the Rule's criteria are met. But that is *exactly* what Rule 23 does: It says that if the prescribed preconditions are satisfied "[a] class action *may be maintained*" (emphasis added)—not "*a class action may be permitted*." Courts do not maintain actions; litigants do. The discretion suggested by Rule 23's "may" is discretion residing in the plaintiff: He may bring his claim in a class action if he wishes. And like the rest of the Federal Rules of Civil Procedure, Rule 23 *automatically* applies "in all civil actions and proceedings in the United States district courts," Fed. Rule Civ. Proc. 1.

Allstate points out that Congress has carved out some federal claims from Rule 23's reach, *see, e.g.,* 8 U.S.C. § 1252(e)(1)(B) [prohibiting use of class actions for judicial review of immigration removal]—which shows, Allstate contends, that Rule 23 does not authorize class actions for all claims, but rather leaves room for laws like § 901(b). But Congress, unlike New York, has ultimate authority over the Federal Rules of Civil Procedure; it can create exceptions to an individual rule as it sees fit—either by directly amending the rule or by enacting a separate statute overriding it in certain instances. The fact that Congress has created specific exceptions to Rule 23 hardly proves that the Rule does not apply generally. In fact, it proves the opposite. If Rule 23 did *not* authorize class actions across the board, the statutory exceptions would be unnecessary.

Rule 23 permits all class actions that meet its requirements, and a State cannot limit that permission by structuring one part of its statute to track Rule 23 and enacting another part that imposes additional requirements. Both of § 901's subsections undeniably answer the same question as Rule 23: whether a class action may proceed for a given suit.

    * * *

Unlike a law that sets a ceiling on damages (or puts other remedies out of reach) in properly filed class actions, § 901(b) says nothing about what remedies a court may award; it prevents the class actions it covers from coming into existence at all. . . .

[In a footnote, the plurality opinion observed that] The dissent all but admits that the literal terms of § 901(b) address the same subject as Rule 23—*i.e.*, whether a class action may be maintained—but insists the provision's *purpose* is to restrict only remedies. The dissent reaches this conclusion on the basis of (1) constituent concern recorded in the law's bill jacket [New York's official legislative history]; (2) a commentary suggesting that the Legislature "apparently fear[ed]" that combining class actions and statutory penalties "could result in annihilating punishment of the defendant," V. Alexander, *Practice Commentaries*, C901:11, reprinted in 7B *McKinney's Consolidated Laws of New York Ann.*, p. 104 (2006) (internal quotation marks omitted); (3) a remark by the Governor in his signing statement that § 901(b) 'provides a controlled remedy,' 176 L. Ed. 2d, at 346 (quoting *Memorandum on Approving* L. 1975, Ch. 207, reprinted in 1975 N. Y. Laws, at 1748; emphasis deleted), and (4) a state court's statement that the final text of § 901(b) 'was the result of a compromise among competing interests,' 176 L. Ed. 2d, at 346 (quoting *Sperry* v. *Crompton Corp.*, 8 N.Y.3d 204, 211, 863 N.E.2d 1012, 1015, 831 N.Y.S.2d 760 (2007)).]

This evidence of the New York Legislature's purpose is pretty sparse. But even accepting the dissent's account of the Legislature's objective at face value, it cannot override the statute's clear text. Even if its aim is to restrict the remedy a plaintiff can obtain, § 901(b) achieves that end by limiting a plaintiff's power to maintain a class action. The manner in which the law "could have been written," has no bearing; what matters is the law the Legislature *did* enact. We cannot rewrite that to reflect our perception of legislative purpose.

But while the dissent does indeed artificially narrow the scope of § 901(b) by finding that it pursues only substantive policies, that is not the central difficulty of the dissent's position. The central difficulty is that even artificial narrowing cannot render § 901(b) compatible with Rule 23. *Whatever* the policies they pursue, they flatly contradict each other. Allstate asserts (and the dissent implies) that we can (and must) *interpret* Rule 23 in a manner that avoids overstepping its authorizing statute.

If the Rule were susceptible of two meanings—one that would violate § 2072(b) and another that would not—we would agree. But it is not. Rule 23 unambiguously authorizes *any* plaintiff, in *any* federal civil proceeding, to maintain a class action if the Rule's prerequisites are met.

We cannot contort its text, even to avert a collision with state law that might render it invalid. What the dissent's approach achieves is not the avoiding of a "conflict between Rule 23 and § 901(b)," but rather the invalidation of Rule 23 (pursuant to § 2072(b) of the Rules Enabling Act) to the extent that it conflicts with the substantive policies of § 901.

B

Erie involved the constitutional power of federal courts to supplant state law with judge-made rules. In that context, it made no difference whether the rule was technically one of substance or procedure; the touchstone was whether it "significantly affect[s] the result of a litigation." *Guaranty Trust Co. v. York.* That is not the test for either the constitutionality or the statutory validity of a Federal Rule of Procedure. Congress has undoubted power to supplant state law, and undoubted power to prescribe rules for the courts it has created, so long as those rules regulate matters "rationally capable of classification" as procedure. *Hanna.* In the Rules Enabling Act, Congress authorized this Court to promulgate rules of procedure subject to its review, 28 U.S.C. § 2072(a), but with the limitation that those rules "shall not abridge, enlarge or modify any substantive right," § 2072(b).

We have long held that this limitation means that the Rule must "really regulat[e] procedure,—the judicial process for enforcing rights and duties recognized by substantive law and for justly administering remedy and redress for disregard or infraction of them," [citing cases]. The test is not whether the rule affects a litigant's substantive rights; most procedural rules do. What matters is what the rule itself *regulates:* If it governs only "the manner and the means" by which the litigants' rights are "enforced," it is valid; if it alters "the rules of decision by which [the] court will adjudicate [those] rights," it is not.

Applying that test, we have rejected every statutory challenge to a Federal Rule that has come before us. We have found to be in compliance with § 2072(b) rules prescribing methods for serving process, and requiring litigants whose mental or physical condition is in dispute to submit to examinations. Likewise, we have upheld rules authorizing imposition of sanctions upon those who file frivolous appeals (Fed. Rule App. Proc. 38), or who sign court papers without a reasonable inquiry into the facts asserted (Fed. Rule Civ. Proc. 11). Each of these rules had some practical effect on the parties' rights, but each undeniably regulated only the process for enforcing those rights; none altered the rights themselves, the available remedies, or the rules of decision by which the court adjudicated either.

Applying that criterion, we think it obvious that rules allowing multiple claims (and claims by or against multiple parties) to be litigated together are also valid. *See, e.g.*, Fed. Rules Civ. Proc. 18 (joinder of claims), 20 (joinder of parties), 42(a) (consolidation of actions). Such rules neither change plaintiffs' separate entitlements to relief nor abridge defendants' rights; they alter only how the claims are processed.

For the same reason, Rule 23—at least insofar as it allows willing plaintiffs to join their separate claims against the same defendants in a class action—falls within § 2072(b)'s authorization. A class action, no less than traditional joinder (of which it is a species), merely enables a federal court to adjudicate claims of multiple parties at once, instead of in separate suits. And like traditional joinder, it leaves the parties' legal rights and duties intact and the rules of decision unchanged.

Allstate contends that the authorization of class actions is not substantively neutral. . . . That has no bearing, however, on Allstate's or the plaintiffs' legal rights. The likelihood that some (even many) plaintiffs will be induced to sue by the availability of a class action is just the sort of "incidental effec[t]" we have long held does not violate § 2072(b).

As a fallback argument, Allstate argues that even if § 901(b) is a procedural provision, it was enacted "for *substantive reasons*," (emphasis added). Its end was not to improve "the conduct of the litigation process itself" but to alter "the outcome of that process." The fundamental difficulty with [this argument] is that the substantive nature of New York's law, or its substantive purpose, *makes no difference*. A Federal Rule of Procedure is not valid in some jurisdictions and invalid in others—or valid in some cases and invalid in others—depending upon whether its effect is to frustrate a state substantive law (or a state procedural law enacted for substantive purposes). . . . *Hanna* unmistakably expressed the . . . understanding that compliance of a Federal Rule with the Enabling Act is to be assessed by consulting the Rule itself, and not its effects in individual applications:

In sum, it is not the substantive or procedural nature or purpose of the affected state law that matters, but the substantive or procedural nature of the Federal Rule. [T]he validity of a Federal Rule depends entirely upon whether it regulates procedure. If it does, it is authorized by § 2072 and is valid in all jurisdictions, with respect to all claims, regardless of its incidental effect upon state-created rights.

C

A few words in response to the concurrence. [This portion of the Scalia plurality opinion engaged in extensive criticism of the methodology of the Stevens concurrence, which provided the crucial fifth vote in support of applying Fed. R. Civ. P. 23 to the dispute. Justice Stevens stopped short of the plurality's arguable view that "if a Federal Rule is procedural, it controls" as insufficiently appreciative of the limitation in the Enabling Act requiring that Federal Rules not abridge or modify substantive legal rights.]

[Unlike the dissenters, however, Justice Stevens did not see Federal Rule 23 as doing this to Allstate, even though in a state court action, Allstate would have been able to defeat class certification of the Shady Grove claim. Justice Scalia's plurality opinion faulted the concurrence's approach as inconsistent with precedents like *Hanna and Sibbach v. Wilson*, 312 U.S. 1 (1941) and unwise in that it made the *Erie/Hanna* inquiry too difficult, requiring judges to conduct an extensive analysis of state substantive goals.]

[This portion of the plurality opinion is harsher in attacking the concurrence than was the plurality's attack on the dissent, which may explain why Justice Sotomayor, although agreeing with the rest of Justice Scalia's analysis, did not join this portion of the plurality opinion.]

D

We must acknowledge the reality that keeping the federal-court door open to class actions that cannot proceed in state court will produce forum shopping. That is unacceptable when it comes as the consequence of judge-made rules created to fill supposed "gaps" in positive federal law. For where neither the Constitution, a treaty, nor a statute provides the rule of decision or authorizes a federal court to supply one, "state law must govern because there can be no other law." But divergence from state law, with the attendant consequence of forum shopping, is the inevitable (indeed, one might say the intended) result of a uniform system of federal procedure. Congress itself has created the possibility that the same case may follow a different course if filed in federal instead of state court.

The short of the matter is that a Federal Rule governing procedure is valid whether or not it alters the outcome of the case in a way that induces forum shopping. To hold otherwise would be to "disembowel either the Constitution's grant of power over federal procedure" or Congress's exercise of it.

JUSTICE STEVENS, concurring in part and concurring in the judgment.

The New York law at issue is a procedural rule that is not part of New York's substantive law. Accordingly, I agree with Justice Scalia that Federal Rule of Civil Procedure 23 must apply in this case and join Parts I and II-A of the Court's opinion. But I also agree with Justice Ginsburg that there are some state procedural rules that federal courts must apply in diversity cases because they function as a part of the State's definition of substantive rights and remedies.

I

[W]hile Congress may have the constitutional power to prescribe procedural rules that interfere with state substantive law in any number of respects, that is not what Congress has done. Instead, it has provided in the Enabling Act that although "[t]he Supreme Court" may "prescribe general rules of practice and procedure," § 2072(a), those rules "shall not abridge, enlarge or modify any substantive right," § 2072(b). Therefore, "[w]hen a situation is covered by one of the Federal Rules, . . . the court has been instructed to apply the Federal Rule" unless doing so would violate the Act or the Constitution.

Although the Enabling Act and the Rules of Decision Act "say, roughly, that federal courts are to apply state 'substantive' law and federal 'procedural' law," the inquiries are not the same. The Enabling Act does not invite federal courts to engage in the "relatively unguided Erie choice," but instead instructs only that federal rules cannot "abridge, enlarge or modify any substantive right," § 2072(b). The Enabling Act's limitation does not mean that federal rules cannot displace state policy judgments;

it means only that federal rules cannot displace a State's definition of its own rights or remedies.

Congress has thus struck a balance: "[H]ousekeeping rules for federal courts" will generally apply in diversity cases, notwithstanding that some federal rules "will inevitably differ" from state rules. But not every federal "rul[e] of practice or procedure," § 2072(a), will displace state law. To the contrary, federal rules must be interpreted with some degree of "sensitivity to important state interests and regulatory policies," *Gasperini*, and applied to diversity cases against the background of Congress' command that such rules not alter substantive rights and with consideration of "the degree to which the Rule makes the character and result of the federal litigation stray from the course it would follow in state courts . . . ."

II

I thus agree with Justice Ginsburg that a federal rule, like any federal law, must be interpreted in light of many different considerations, including "sensitivity to important state interests." . . . I disagree with Justice Ginsburg, however, about the degree to which the meaning of federal rules may be contorted, absent congressional authorization to do so, to accommodate state policy goals.

If the federal rule is "sufficiently broad to control the issue before the Court," such that there is a "direct collision," the court must decide whether application of the federal rule "represents a valid exercise" of the "rulemaking authority . . . bestowed on this Court by the Rules Enabling Act." That Act requires, *inter alia*, that federal rules "not abridge, enlarge or modify *any* substantive right." 28 U.S.C. § 2072(b) (emphasis added).

When a federal rule appears to abridge, enlarge, or modify a substantive right, federal courts must consider whether the rule can reasonably be interpreted to avoid that impermissible result. *See, e.g., Semtek Int'l Inc. v. Lockheed Martin Corp.*, 531 U.S. 497, 503 (2001) (avoiding an interpretation of Federal Rule of Civil Procedure 41(b) that "would arguably violate the jurisdictional limitation of the Rules Enabling Act" contained in § 2072(b)). And when such a "saving" construction is not possible and the rule would violate the Enabling Act, federal courts cannot apply the rule.

A federal rule, therefore, cannot govern a particular case in which the rule would displace a state law that is procedural in the ordinary use of the term but is so intertwined with a state right or remedy that it functions to define the scope of the state-created right. And absent a governing federal rule, a federal court must engage in the traditional Rules of Decision Act inquiry, under the *Erie* line of cases. This application of the Enabling Act shows "sensitivity to important state interests" and "regulatory policies," but it does so as Congress authorized.

Justice Scalia believes that the sole Enabling Act question is whether the federal rule "really regulates procedure." This understanding of the Enabling Act has been the subject of substantial academic criticism, and rightfully so. . . .[Justice Scalia's] interpretation of the Enabling Act is consonant with the Act's first limitation to "general rules of practice and procedure," § 2072(a). But it ignores the second limitation that such rules also "not abridge, enlarge or modify *any* substantive right," § 2072(b) (emphasis added), and in so doing ignores the balance that Congress struck between uniform rules of federal procedure and respect for a State's construction of its own rights and remedies. It also ignores the separation-of-powers presumption, and federalism presumption that counsel against judicially created rules displacing state substantive law.

Justice Scalia ['s approach misses a key point.] In some instances, a state rule that appears procedural really is not. A rule about how damages are reviewed on appeal may really be a damages cap. *See Gasperini*. A rule that a plaintiff can bring a claim for only three years may really be a limit on the existence of the right to seek redress. A rule that a claim must be proved beyond a reasonable doubt may really be a definition of the scope of the claim. These are the sorts of rules that one might describe as "procedural," but they nonetheless define substantive rights. Thus, if a federal rule displaced such a state rule, the federal rule would have altered the State's "substantive rights."

The plurality's interpretation of the Enabling Act appears to mean that no matter how bound up a state provision is with the State's own rights or remedies, any contrary federal rule that happens to regulate "the manner and the means by which the litigants' rights are enforced," must govern. . . .

I do not see why an Enabling Act inquiry that looks to state law neces-sarily is more taxing than Justice Scalia's. But in any event, that inquiry is what the Enabling Act requires. While it may not be easy to decide what is actually a "substantive right," "the designations substantive and procedural become important, for the Enabling Act has made them so."

The question, therefore, is not what rule *we* think would be easiest on federal courts. The question is what rule Congress established. Although, Justice Scalia may generally prefer easily administrable, bright-line rules, his preference does not give us license to adopt a second-best interpreta-tion of the Rules Enabling Act. Courts cannot ignore text and context in the service of simplicity.

It will be rare that a federal rule that is facially valid under 28 U.S.C. § 2072 will displace a State's definition of its own substantive rights. Justice Scalia's interpretation, moreover, is not much more determinative than mine. Although it avoids courts' having to evaluate state law, it tasks them with figuring out whether a federal rule is really "procedural." It is hard to know the answer to that question and especially hard to resolve it without considering the nature and functions of the state law that the federal rule will displace. The plurality's " 'test' is no test at all—in a sense, it is little more than the statement that a matter is procedural if, by revelation, it is procedural."

III

Justice Ginsburg views the basic issue in this case as whether and how to apply a federal rule that dictates an answer to a traditionally procedural question (whether to join plaintiffs together as a class), when a state law that "defines the dimensions" of a state-created claim dictates the opposite answer. I readily acknowledge that if a federal rule displaces a state rule that is "'procedural' in the ordinary sense of the term," but suf-ficiently interwoven with the scope of a substantive right or remedy, there would be an Enabling Act problem, and the federal rule would have to give way. In my view, however, this is not such a case.

* * *

The legislative history of § 901 thus reveals a classically procedural cali-bration of making it easier to litigate claims in New York courts (under any source of law) only when it is necessary to do so, and not making it *too* easy when the class tool is not required. This is the same sort of calculation that might go into setting filing fees or deadlines for briefs. There is of course a difference of degree between those examples and class certification, but not a difference of kind; the class vehicle may have a greater practical effect on who brings lawsuits than do low filing fees, but that does not transform it into a damages "proscription," or "limitation."

Justice Ginsburg asserts that class certification in this matter would "transform a $500 case into a $5,000,000 award." But in fact, class certification would transform 10,000 $500 cases into one $5,000,000 case. It may be that without class certification, not all of the potential plaintiffs would bring their cases. But that is true of any procedural vehicle; without a lower filing fee, a conveniently located courthouse, easy-to-use federal procedural rules, or many other features of the federal courts, many plaintiffs would not sue.

The difference of degree is relevant to the forum shopping considerations that are part of the Rules of Decision Act or *Erie* inquiry. If the applicable federal rule did not govern the particular question at issue (or could be fairly read not to do so), then those considerations would matter, for precisely the reasons given by the dissent. But that is not *this* case. . . .

JUSTICE GINSBURG, with whom JUSTICE KENNEDY, JUSTICE BREYER, and JUSTICE ALITO join, dissenting.

The Court today approves Shady Grove's attempt to transform a $500 case into a $5,000,000 award, although the State creating the right to recover has proscribed this alchemy. If Shady Grove had filed suit in New York state court, the 2% interest payment authorized by New York Ins. Law Ann. § 5106(a) (West 2009) as a penalty for overdue benefits would, by Shady Grove's own measure, amount to no more than $500. By instead filing in federal court based on the parties' diverse citizenship and requesting class certification, Shady Grove hopes to recover, for the class, statutory damages of more than $5,000,000.

The New York Legislature has barred this remedy, instructing that, unless specifically permitted, "an action to recover a penalty, or minimum measure of recovery created or imposed by statute may not be maintained as a class action." § 901(b). The Court nevertheless holds that Federal Rule of Civil Procedure 23, which prescribes procedures for the conduct of class actions in federal courts, preempts the application of § 901(b) in diversity suits.

The Court reads Rule 23 relentlessly to override New York's restriction on the availability of statutory damages. Our decisions, however, caution us to ask, before undermining state legislation: Is this conflict really necessary? Had the Court engaged in that inquiry, it would not have read Rule 23 to collide with New York's legitimate interest in keeping certain monetary awards reasonably bounded. I would continue to interpret Federal Rules with awareness of, and sensitivity to, important state regulatory policies. Because today's judgment radically departs from that course, I dissent.

I

[Section IA omitted]

B

In our prior decisions in point, many of them not mentioned in the Court's opinion, we have avoided immoderate interpretations of the Federal Rules that would trench on state prerogatives without serving any countervailing federal interest. "Application of the *Hanna* analysis," we have said, "is premised on a 'direct collision' between the Federal Rule and the state law." . . . In pre-*Hanna* decisions, the Court vigilantly read the Federal Rules to avoid conflict with state laws. In *Palmer* v. *Hoffman*, 318 U.S. 109, 117 (1943), for example, the Court read Federal Rule 8(c), which lists affirmative defenses, to control only the manner of pleading the listed defenses in diversity cases; as to the burden of proof in such cases, *Palmer* held, state law controls.

* * *

In *Hanna* itself, the Court found the clash "unavoidable," . . . Following *Hanna*, we continued to "interpre[t] the federal rules to avoid conflict with important state regulatory policies." In *Walker*, the Court took up the question whether *Ragan* should be overruled; we held, once again, that Federal Rule 3 does not directly conflict with state rules governing the time when an action commences for purposes of tolling a limitations period.

We were similarly attentive to a State's regulatory policy in *Gasperini*. That diversity case concerned the standard for determining when the large size of a jury verdict warrants a new trial. Federal and state courts alike had generally employed a "shock the conscience" test in reviewing jury awards for excessiveness. Federal courts did so pursuant to Federal Rule 59(a) which, as worded at the time of *Gasperini*, instructed that a trial court could grant a new trial "for any of the reasons for which new trials have heretofore been granted in actions at law in the courts of the United States." Fed. Rule Civ. Proc. 59(a).

In an effort to provide greater control, New York prescribed procedures under which jury verdicts would be examined to determine whether they "deviate[d] materially from what would be reasonable compensation." This Court held that Rule 59(a) did not inhibit federal-court accommodation of New York's invigorated test.

Most recently, in *Semtek*, [*Int'l, Inc. v. Lockheed Martin Corp.*, 531 U.S. 497 (2001)] we addressed the claim-preclusive effect of a federal-court judgment dismissing a diversity action on the basis of a California statute of limitations. The case came to us after the same plaintiff renewed the same fray against the same defendant in a Maryland state court. (Plaintiff chose Maryland because that State's limitations period had not yet run.) We held that Federal Rule 41(b), which provided that an involuntary dismissal "operate[d] as an adjudication on the merits," did not bar maintenance of the renewed action in Maryland. To hold that Rule 41(b) precluded the Maryland courts from entertaining the case, we said, "would arguably violate the jurisdictional limitation of the Rules Enabling Act," "would in many cases violate [*Erie*'s] federalism principle." * * *

Justice Stevens stakes out common ground on this point. Nevertheless, Justice Stevens sees no reason to read Rule 23 with restraint in this particular case; the Federal Rule preempts New York's damages limitation, in his view, because § 901(b) is "a procedural rule that is not part of New York's substantive law." This characterization of § 901(b) does not mirror reality. But a majority of this Court, it bears emphasis, agrees that Federal Rules should be read with moderation in diversity suits to accommodate important state concerns. The Court veers away from that approach—and conspicuously, its most recent reiteration in *Gasperini*, in favor of a mechanical reading of Federal Rules, insensitive to state interests and productive of discord.

C

Our decisions instruct over and over again that, in the adjudication of diversity cases, state interests—whether advanced in a statute, *e.g.*, *Cohen*, or a procedural rule, *e.g.*, *Gasperini*—warrant our respectful consideration. Yet today, the Court gives no quarter to New York's limitation on statutory damages and requires the lower courts to thwart the regulatory policy at stake: To prevent excessive damages, New York's law controls the penalty to which a defendant may be exposed in a single suit.

The story behind § 901(b)'s enactment deserves telling. [In this portion of the dissent, Justice Ginsburg reviews legislative history of § 901 reflecting concern by some that class treatment of statutory penalty cases might pose undue risks to business defendants, particularly small businesses. From this, she concluded that the New York law, in addition to regulating civil litigation procedure, also contained an important substantive element.]

D

* * *

The fair and efficient *conduct* of class litigation is the legitimate concern of Rule 23; the *remedy* for an infraction of state law, however, is the legitimate concern of the State's lawmakers and not of the federal rulemakers.

Suppose, for example, that a State, wishing to cap damages in class actions at $1,000,000, enacted a statute providing that "a suit to recover more than $1,000,000 may not be maintained as a class action." Under the Court's reasoning—which attributes dispositive significance to the words "may not be maintained"—Rule 23 would preempt this provision, nevermind that Congress, by authorizing the promulgation of rules of procedure for federal courts, surely did not intend to displace state-created ceilings on damages....

By finding a conflict without considering whether Rule 23 rationally should be read to avoid any collision, the Court unwisely and unnecessarily retreats from the federalism principles undergirding *Erie*.

II

Because I perceive no unavoidable conflict between Rule 23 and § 901(b), I would decide this case by inquiring "whether application of the [state] rule would have so important an effect upon the fortunes of one or both of the litigants that failure to [apply] it would be likely to cause a plaintiff to choose the federal court." . . . .

As this case starkly demonstrates, if federal courts exercising diversity jurisdiction are compelled by Rule 23 to award statutory penalties in class actions while New York courts are bound by § 901(b)'s proscription, "substantial variations between state and federal [money judgments] may be expected." *Gasperini.* The "variation" here is indeed "substantial." Shady Grove seeks class relief that is *ten thousand times* greater than the individual remedy available to it in state court.

As the plurality acknowledges, forum shopping will undoubtedly result if a plaintiff need only file in federal instead of state court to seek a massive monetary award explicitly barred by state law. In contrast, many "state rules ostensibly addressed to procedure,"—including pleading standards and rules governing summary judgment, pretrial discovery, and the admissibility of certain evidence—would not so hugely impact forum choices. It is difficult to imagine a scenario that would promote more forum shopping than one in which the difference between filing in state and federal court is the difference between a potential award of $500 and one of $5,000,000. The "accident of diversity of citizenship," should not subject a defendant to such augmented liability.

It is beyond debate that "a statutory cap on damages would supply substantive law for *Erie* purposes." In *Gasperini,* we determined that New York's standard for measuring the alleged excessiveness of a jury verdict was designed to provide a control analogous to a damages cap. The statute was framed as "a procedural instruction," we noted, "but the State's objective [wa]s manifestly substantive."

Gasperini's observations apply with full force in this case. By barring the recovery of statutory damages in a class action, § 901(b) controls a defendant's maximum liability in a suit seeking such a remedy. The remedial provision could have been written as an explicit cap: "In any class action seeking statutory damages, relief is limited to the amount the named plaintiff would have recovered in an individual suit." That New York's Legislature used other words to express the very same meaning should be inconsequential. . . .

III

The Court's erosion of *Erie*'s federalism grounding impels me to point out the large irony in today's judgment. Shady Grove is able to pursue its claim in federal court only by virtue of the recent enactment of the Class Action Fairness Act of 2005 (CAFA), 28 U.S.C. § 1332(d). In CAFA, Congress opened federal-court doors to state-law-based class actions so long as there is minimal diversity, at least 100 class members, and at least $5,000,000 in controversy.

By providing a federal forum, Congress sought to check what it considered to be the overreadiness of some state courts to certify class actions. . . . In other words, Congress envisioned fewer—not more—class actions overall. Congress surely never anticipated that CAFA would make federal courts a mecca for suits of the kind Shady Grove has launched: class actions seeking state-created penalties for claims arising under state law—claims that would be barred from class treatment in the State's own courts. It remains open to Congress, of course, to exclude from federal-court jurisdiction under the Class Action Fairness Act of 2005, 28 U.S.C. § 1332(d), claims that could not be maintained as a class action in state court.

Nearly 15 years after *Gasperini*, the Court answered in the negative. But, as in *Gasperini*, the Court was fractured, deciding the case on a 5-4 vote.

CASE ANALYSIS & QUESTIONS

1. One commentator has referred to Justice Scalia's opinion in *Shady Grove* as "*Hanna* on steroids"? Too strong? Why or why not?

2. Put another way: does the Scalia opinion in *Shady Grove* go farther than the Earl Warren majority opinion in *Hanna*?

3. Or does the Scalia position just seem a bit strident in light of post-*Hanna* developments like the reaffirmation of *Ragan* in *Walker v. Armco Steel* and *Gasperini*'s holding that a law embodied in procedural code was actually substantive law under *Erie* (and *York*)?

4. On that score, does *Gasperini* seem wrongly decided in light of *Shady Grove*? Or is the review of the size of jury verdicts in *Gasperini* really more substantive than the limits on class action treatment at issue in *Shady Grove*? Why or why not?

5. Which decision (*Gasperini* or *Shady Grove*) seems truer to the federalism, equal treatment, and restraint-on-forum-shopping rationale of *Erie*?

6. Note that Justice Scalia's opinion only commanded four votes. Justice Stevens provided the crucial fifth vote for the decision permitting use of Fed. R. Civ. P. 23 and according class action treatment that the New York statute denied. In light of this, one can reasonably ask whether the current doctrine is the strong form of *Hanna* espoused by Justice Scalia or the public policy-laden balancing of the Stevens concurrence and Ginsburg dissent. What do you think?

7. Which opinion in *Hanna* is most reminiscent of the Stevens concurrence in *Shady Grove*? Chief Justice Warren's majority opinion or the concurrence of Justice Harlan?

8. Justice Ginsburg's *Shady Grove* dissent is unsurprisingly consistent with her majority opinion in *Gasperini*. The roles of Justices Ginsburg and Scalia are reversed in the two cases, with Ginsburg prevailing in *Gasperini* and Scalia prevailing in *Shady Grove* a bit more than a decade later. Make the best factual distinction you can between the two cases and harmonize/reconcile the results as best you can. Are you convinced? Or is it more likely that changes in Court personnel or the change in thought of a Justice or two brought about the divergent results? Consult the changes in the Court between 1998 and 2010 to test this more legal realist hypothesis.

H. Applying *Erie* Today

Notwithstanding the many sociopolitical nuances occasionally presented in *Erie* cases, the basic *Erie* Doctrine principles are fairly straight forward and succinct:

- When cases are in federal court based on diversity jurisdiction, apply applicable state substantive law and federal procedure;

- To help make the substance/procedure determination, check to see if any Federal Rule of Civil Procedure is relevant;

- If there is a Federal Civil Rule on point, ask "Does the Rule really regulate procedure—or despite being in procedural garb does it actually embody a rule of federal substantive law?" If the answer is that the rule really regulates procedure and not substance, the Federal Rule controls;

- Unless, however, the rule, no matter how procedural it looks on the surface, operates to abridge, enlarge, or modify a state law substantive right that would otherwise belong to the litigants. This inquiry is essentially the same as the "does the Rule really regulate procedure" inquiry but asking the question in this second formulation can be helpful in clarifying your assessment of the Federal Rule in question and its operation;

- And, for those reading the various *Shady Grove* opinions closely, remember that one might argue that this follow-up question is not necessary under the approach outlined by Justice Scalia's plurality opinion. But Justice Ginsburg and the three dissenters as well as concurring Justice Stevens believe the follow-up question must be asked—and that's five votes to the plurality's four.

- If there is not a Federal Civil Rule on point, applicable state law will generally apply, particularly if it is determinative of the outcome of the case (*Hanna* and its progeny—unless, despite the absence of an on-point Federal Civil Rule, there is a strong and clearly discernable federal policy (a "countervailing federal interest") that overcomes the state law (such as the Seventh Amendment right to jury trial in *Byrd*).

EXAMPLES & ANALYSIS

EXAMPLE: Paloma Priceless, an investment banker domiciled in New York, is visiting her Vermont country home and finds Wood Rangers Troop 007 camping out in her back yard. Fortunately, for Paloma, her lawyer friend Lara Litigious, a member of the Vermont bar from her law clerking days, is one of the houseguests. She files a suit (in the federal courthouse) and seeks a preliminary injunction evicting the Troop pursuant to Fed. R. Civ. P. 65. Dick Daring, the troopmaster, is also a lawyer and responds by noting that mythical Vermont R. Civ. P. 65-x forbids entry of a preliminary injunction in any case involving trespass to land. He also notes that mythical Vermont Stat. Ann. § xxx provides that various scouting or camping groups may use anyone's private land for camping for a period of up to 72 hours once per year but shall be responsible for providing the owner compensation for any injury to land.

In adjudicating the injunction request, will the judge: Apply Fed. R. Civ. P. 65? Or Vermont R. Civ. P. 65-x? Or apply Vermont Stat. Ann. § xxx?

Analysis Unless there is a federal statute governing the camping rights of scout troops (and we know of none), Vermont Stat. Ann. xxx must apply. It is state substantive law (creating or limiting the rights and responsibilities of persons) just as the Pennsylvania rules on duties owed to persons on property were part of that state's substantive law in *Erie*. The Vermont statute is also "outcome determinative" under *York*. If the statute is not applied, the Troop is trespassing and has no right to use Paloma's land, even if fabulously wealthy Paloma is an unsympathetic character who may have helped cause the Recession of 2008. But if the statute is applied, the Troop may camp on Paloma's land with impunity for up to three days. And if the Wood Rangers are good stewards of the land, the Troop owes Paloma nothing (but must pay compensation if they do any permanent damage).

However, Vermont's mythical state rule governing injunctive relief would have to yield to Fed. R. Civ. P. 65, which is an on-point federal rule governing the procedural relief available in federal court. But even with the protections afforded to the Troop under state substantive law, another *Erie/Hanna* issue lurks: if the Troop has overstayed its statutory 3-day welcome, Paloma may have the right to immediately evict it. She certainly has the right to seek a preliminary injunction of eviction pursuant to Fed. R. Civ. P. 65. Federal Rule 65 governing the injunctions is clearly a rule regulating procedure—and we know by definition that it was promulgated pursuant to the Rules Enabling Act (28 U.S.C. § 2072) or it would not be in the rulebook. So it presumptively applies—but not if it abridges, enlarges, or modifies a substantive right.

> On appeal, a trial court's application of the *Erie* Doctrine is reviewed anew or "de novo." The application of *Erie* is a question of law for which review on appeal is plenary. The trial court is accorded no deference and the appeals court assesses the *Erie* question as though it was being heard in first instance.

The question then becomes whether the Troop's asserted right to camp without being subject to a preliminary injunction action (although it can concededly be ejected after a full trial and judgment under either Fed. R. Civ. P. 65 or Vt. R. Civ. P. 65-xxx), is one of state substantive law or is merely a procedural rule limiting the preliminary injunctive power of the state courts. If the former, Paloma will need to get a permanent injunction to get rid of the boys (which may take so much time that it becomes moot as the kids return to school). If the latter, the federal court retains power to issue the preliminary injunction on short notice so that Paloma can attempt to salvage what remains of her weekend.

Which of the two characterizations is more persuasive? Why?

I. "Horizontal" Choice of Law and *Erie*— Choosing Applicable State Law

Determining that a case is subject to state law is only part of the court's task. The court will then be required to determine which state law provides the rule of decision. In many cases, the applicable state law will be clear (*e.g.*, a California con artist visiting Nevada swindles a Nevada family out of their life savings, which were in a Nevada bank, in violation of Nevada criminal and civil law, with all operative aspects of the con job taking place in Nevada). In other cases (*e.g.*, a hypothetical four-car crash at the Four Corners area where Utah, Colorado, Arizona and New Mexico all meet at one spot), selecting applicable law will be more difficult.

A number of approaches exist for determining choice of law. However, by far the dominant approach is that of the American Law Institute's RE-STATEMENT (SECOND) OF CONFLICT OF LAWS (1971), which is not binding legislation but is followed by most courts, at least in large part. It and other choice of law methodologies are discussed later in this Chapter. There is no federal statute governing horizontal choice of law. Basic conflict of law methodology is reviewed in this Chapter.

In *Klaxon Co. v. Stentor Electric Mfg. Co.*, 313 U.S. 487 (1941), the Court sensibly clarified the relationship between the new *Erie* doctrine and the means by which federal courts presiding over diversity jurisdiction cases should determine the applicable state law when making a horizontal choice of law decision. The answer: follow the choice of law methodology of the state in which the federal court is located. Thus, a federal judge in the Southern District of New York utilizes New York's choice of law methodology—even if the underlying dispute has nothing to do with New York.

The rationale for this approach—a clearly correct one in the eyes of virtually all observers (even those who dislike the *Erie* doctrine itself) is that in this way the selection process for applicable state law will be the same in both federal and state courts within the same state—there will not be the problem of cases coming out one way in the federal court building and another way in the state court building across the street.

For example, if a case was filed in Clark County, Nevada, the state court deciding a choice of law question would utilize Nevada's choice of law methodology, which is essentially the ALI *Restatement* methodology. If the case were filed in federal court two blocks away, the federal court under *Klaxon* is required to use the same *Restatement* approach. Consequently, under *Klaxon*, there should be harmony of at least the applicable law of choice of law, even though Judge Jones in state court and Judge Smith in federal court might reach different results in applying the choice of law methodology.

Despite this potential for different outcomes based on different judges (a risk whenever there are two or more similar cases that can come out differently), the litigants have "equal protection of the laws" because the parties in state court and the parties in federal court are both subject to the very same choice of law methodology (the ALI *Second Restatement* approach, in the case of Nevada).

IN PRACTICE

Nevada at one time provided a good example of the occasional idiosyncrasy of state choice of law. In *Motenko v. MGM Dist., Inc.*, 921 P.2d 933 (Nev. 1996), the Nevada Supreme Court adopted a choice of law methodology particularly favorable to the adoption of Nevada law by holding the applicable law in a dispute was presumptively that of the forum state unless two or more of four factors pointed to the law of another state. The four factors were (1) the place of the conduct giving rise to the claim; (2) the place of the injury; (3) the domicile or residence of all parties, if in a state other than the forum state; and (4) the state where the relationship, if any, of the parties, is centered. In *GMC v. District Court*, 134 P.3d 111 (Nev. 2006), the Court overturned *Motenko* and adopted the "most significant relationship" test of the ALI *Restatement of Conflict of Laws*, discussed below. But during this 1997-2006 period, Nevada's peculiar choice of law rules provided an additional opportunity for lawyers seeking tactical advantage and (by virtue of *Klaxon v. Stentor Electric*) controlled in federal court as well.

1. The Mainstream Choice of Law Methodologies

Choice of law is often referred to as "conflict" of laws and the law school course governing this topic generally uses this latter title. But we prefer the former term. It is simply more accurate. Applicable law must always be selected for application even if it is not altogether clear whether the laws of the various jurisdictions under consideration really conflict. Indeed, a significant body of choice of law inquiry deals with the issue of whether there is a real difference between different state laws or whether there is only a "false conflict."

During the mid-20th Century, substantial harmonization of interstate law occurred as a result of the ALI *Restatements*, the promulgation of uniform laws by groups such as the National Conference on Uniform State Laws (*e.g.*, the Uniform Commercial Code and similar model statutes), and the National Association of Insurance Commissioners (*e.g.*, the model Unfair Claims Practices Act). Similarly, the ABA was promulgating Model Codes or Model Rules of lawyer professional conduct and judicial ethics during this time while the federal government was regulating extensively in ways that became models for most states.

However, for a variety of reasons, we still find occasionally pronounced differences in state law. Even if state law is technically "the same," precedents applicable to one's lawsuit in different states may produce dramatically different outcomes. Complicating matters is the degree to which choice of law technique may vary according to whether the case is one involving tort, contract, or property disputes.

The following categorization of choice of law approaches is necessarily oversimplified and context-specific. Interested readers will find the following materials useful when assessing choice of law issues in their own cases or exercises in other course: AMERICAN LAW INSTITUTE, RESTATEMENT (SECOND) OF CONFLICT OF LAWS (1971)(the FIRST RESTATEMENT (1923) has largely fallen out of favor relative to the *Second Restatement* but may still be relevant in a given dispute or jurisdiction); KERMIT ROOSEVELT, CONFLICT OF LAWS (2010); RUSSELL J. WEINTRAUB, COMMENTARY ON THE CONFLICT OF LAWS (6th ed. 2007). With these caveats, we review the following mainstream choice of law methods.

IN PRACTICE

The Practicalities of Choice of Law

 *Certeris parabis* (Latin for "all other things being equal"), courts sitting in a given state tend to apply the forum state's law if the question is reasonably close, for reasons that seem almost too obvious once considered. Judges in a given state, whether in federal court or state court, are almost always members of that state's bar. Consequently, they were trained in the forum state's law, are experienced in its application, tend to approve of it, and feel most comfortable applying it. Unless the case for using the law of another state is rather compelling, forum state judges will err on the side of applying forum state law. If nothing else, the source materials for assessing forum state law will be more accessible than those of other states, although this is less of a factor than was the case prior to the proliferation of electronic databases.

2. Choice of Law Methodology

- ***Lex Loci Delecti*** (Latin for "the place of the wrong"). This is the school of choice of law, most identified with Harvard Law Professor Joseph Henry Beale (1861-1943), that applies the law of the "place of the wrong" or "place of the injury" to decide cases. Its greatest use was primarily for tort actions. If an accident or battery or slander took place in State A, the applicable law was that of State A regardless of the citizenship of the parties or other factors. *Lex loci* was particularly popular during the early 20th Century and is largely the school of thought reflected in the ALI's First Restatement, issued in 1923. The Reporter for this Restatement was—you guessed it—Professor Beale. The strength of this approach is its simplicity and relative predictability. The weakness of this approach is its potential for arbitrary results. Because of the simple but rigid and sometimes odd application of *lex loci*, it fell out of favor, at least with legal scholars, due to the rise of Legal Realism during the 1930-1950 period. Notwithstanding this movement, states may continue to use *lex loci* in some form in many instances. *See* Patrick Borchers, *The Choice-of-Law Revolution: An Empirical Study*, 49 Wash. & Lee L. Rev. 357 (1992).

- ***The ALI Second Restatement.*** The ALI officially published its *Restatement (Second) of Conflict of Laws* in 1971. In varying forms or adaptations, the *Second Restatement* approach dominates American choice of law. Its oft-cited section on general principles sets forth the following objectives and values in determining applicable law:

  (1)   A court, subject to constitutional restrictions, will follow a statutory directive in its own state on choice of law.

  (2)   When there is no such directive, the factors relevant to the choice of the applicable law include:

  (a) The needs of the interstate and international systems,

  (b) The relevant policies of the forum,

    (c) The relevant policies of other interested states and the relative interest of those states in the determination of the particular issue,

    (d) The protection of justified expectations,

    (e) The basic policies underlying the particular field of law,

    (f) Certainty, predictability and uniformity of result, and

    (g) Ease in the determination and application of the law to be applied.

See RESTATEMENT (SECOND) OF CONFLICT OF LAWS § 6.

The "most significant relationship" test of the *Second Restatement* is also applied to most tort cases and to contract disputes, assuming there is no enforceable choice of law clause in the contract at issue. Regarding property disputes, the *Second Restatement* largely follows the traditional common law rule that such actions are governed by the law where the real property is located.

- **Center of Gravity.** Prior to and since the *Second Restatement*, courts have often focused on the total weight of state contacts with a dispute in determining applicable law, looking for the "center of gravity" of the controversy. For most lawyers (and in our view), the "most significant relationship" test is largely congruent with the center of gravity/weighing of contacts approach but for the *Second Restatement*'s somewhat greater willingness to examine public policy factors as well as the nature and quality of contacts rather than merely the amount or frequency of contact.[2]

- **Interest Analysis.** Similarly, although the degree of a state's interest in a matter can be thought of as a factor influencing the significance of a state's relationship to a dispute, government

---

2   Despite the similarities of the two methods, for reasons of history and nomenclature, "center of gravity" is usually regarded as its own school of choice of law despite its similarity to the *Second Restatement. See* Gregory E. Smith, *Choice of Law in the United States,* 38 HASTING L.J. 1041, 1043-49 (1987)(treating center of gravity analysis as its own system of choice of law along with other recognized schools as *lex loci, First Restatement, Second Restatement,* Interest Analysis, and the Leflar/choice-influencing factors approach).

interest analysis is usually treated as a separate method of choice of law. Under this approach, the court focuses on which of the states connected to a case is most interested in the outcome of the matter.

- *Choice-Influencing Factors.* In a series of articles and a prominent treatise, Professor Robert Leflar argued that proper choice of law should consider a number of factors: predictability of results; maintenance of interstate and international order; simplification of the judicial task; advancement of the forum's governmental interests; and application of the better rule law. *See* ROBERT A. LEFLAR, ET AL., AMERICAN CONFLICTS LAW (4th ed. 1986). Under this approach, courts were to be less concerned with physical connections and more focused on substantive policy concerns when weighing the associations of different states with the dispute before the court. Leflar's approach was very sympathetic to the government interest analysis approach but was distinguished by its advocacy that courts expressly consider whether one state espoused a "better rule of law" and apply that better rule unless other factors strongly pointed to another state.

- *Consequences-Based Choice of Law.* The late Russell Weintraub was the logical intellectual successor to Leflar in that Prof. Weintraub openly advocates that courts use a "consequences-based" approach when selecting controlling law. *See* RUSSELL J. WEINTRAUB, COMMENTARY ON THE CONFLICT OF LAWS § 6.2 (6th ed. 2010). He advocates that courts not only consider the better rule of law but expressly determine what outcomes will ensue in the case depending on the application of competing law—and that the choice of law decision be made with a healthy regard for the difference it will make in the case.

3. An Area of Pronounced Discretion

Whatever the merits or demerits of different approaches to choice of law, one thing is almost certain—trial court decisions in this area are rarely overturned. There are so many "moving parts" in choice of law analysis that any decision in a reasonably close or complex case can ordinarily be deemed reasonable or within the court's discretion. As a result, choice of law decisions are unlikely be overturned on appeal.

Parties on the losing end of a choice of law decision have tried to argue that such decisions are not only simple error but also are a failure to give "full faith and credit" (required by Article IV of the U.S. Constitution) when a state court refuses to follow another state's law in cases where that other state has a strong interest in the matter. (The Full Faith and Credit Clause by its terms applies only to the states but 28 U.S.C. § 1738 holds federal courts to the same standard). For the most part, these challenges have failed.

The U.S. Supreme Court in particular has been largely unreceptive to such arguments. *See, e.g., Allstate Insurance, Co. v. Hague*, 449 U.S. 302 (1981) (Minnesota courts did not act unconstitutionally in applying Minnesota law to Wisconsin auto accident involving Wisconsin citizens; basis for applying Minnesota law was constructive attachment of insurance policy by Minnesota courts); *Keeton v. Hustler Magazine, Inc.*, 465 U.S. 770 (1984)(no full faith and credit problem when New Hampshire courts apply state law with six-year statute of limitations for defamation claim when plaintiff sues in New Hampshire despite center of gravity of suit in Ohio or New York because much shorter statute of limitations in those states had already run).

IN PRACTICE

The Procedural and Substantive Nature of Statutes of Limitations. The treatment of statutes of limitations seems initially counter-intuitive or inconsistent to many law students and can present both conundrum and opportunity for lawyers. For example, we know from *Guaranty Trust v. York,* 326 U.S. 99 (1945) that in diversity cases, controlling state law on limitations periods is outcome determinative and must be applied in the absence of an on-point federal statute or rule of procedure (of which there is none). But this aspect of the *Erie* Doctrine does not prohibit state-to-state forum shopping seeking a longer limitations period.

EXAMPLES & ANALYSIS

EXAMPLE: Patty Parton filed a defamation suit against *Daxim* Magazine (over unflattering comments made about Parton on the pages of *Daxim*) in New Hampshire state court. *Daxim* was founded, incorporated, and published in Ohio, and Parton lived in New York. Yet, Parton filed in New Hampshire ostensibly to take advantage of the six-year long statute of limitations (which was much longer than provided in most states as defamation is a disfavored tort because it tends to chill free speech). Can she do so even when the dispute is more logically connected to Ohio or New York?

Analysis: Yes. The answer is that New Hampshire, like most states, treats its statutes of limitations as procedural in the sense that it applies them to its court cases even if other state substantive law will ultimately be applied to issues of liability, damages, immunity, defenses, and so on.

This hypothetical is based on *Keeton v. Hustler Magazine, Inc.*, 465 U.S. 770 (1984), which is most known as a personal jurisdiction case in which the Court upheld New Hampshire's exercise over the Ohio-based *Hustler* magazine on the basis of the company regularly shipping 10,000 to 15,000 magazines per issue (essentially each month) to New Hampshire. Lost in the usual discussion of the case is the concern that by so rigidly applying their own statutes of limitation to cases where they have personal jurisdiction over a defendant, states are arguably derogating the "laws" of other states more closely connected with the dispute even though there has been no other state court "judicial proceeding" being rejected by the forum state court. Whatever the merits of an argument against this extension of statutes of limitations, the train appears to have left the station. Absent a complete change in Supreme Court thinking on the topic, state courts may each apply their statute of limitations periods to state law disputes (and federal courts will be bound pursuant to *Klaxon v. Stentor Electric and York v. Guaranty Trust*). Lawyers should think of this not so much as an arguable constitutional problem or jurisprudential inconsistency but as a litigation opportunity. Because states offer a different statutes of limitations, forum shopping opportunities are dramatically expanded, limited only by the ability to obtain personal jurisdiction in a state court.

4. A Way Out of the Labyrinth? Choice of Law Agreements

After reading the summary of choice of law factors, students may rightly view choice of law as a relatively indeterminate, highly context specific area of law. True. But remember, in most cases, the context of the case will clearly point in the direction of a particular state's law.

When a contract contains a choice of law clause and neither the contract nor the clause was obtained through fraud, coercion, duress, or some other prohibited means, courts will generally enforce the agreement unless the jurisdiction chosen bears no relations to the parties or the transaction. In addition, the SECOND RESTATEMENT states that courts should disregard choice of law clauses when "application of the law of the chosen state would be contrary to a fundamental policy of a state which has a materially greater interest than the chosen state in the determination of the particular issue." *See* RESTATEMENT (SECOND) § 187(2)(b).

ADDITIONAL EXERCISES

1. In 1939, little Peter Peppy is playing in a local lot in New York, where a new home is under construction. Sure, enough, he steps on a nail, suffering significant injuries. His older brother Paul is attempting to remove some copper plumbing but slips, slicing his arm, which requires extensive surgery. Patriach Peppy, hearing the boys' screams, runs to their aid only to fall through a half-completed floor in the house, shattering his spine. The Peppys sue Diane's Construction Company, alleging negligent maintenance of the property.

   Under federal common law, there is no distinction in the duty of care owed third parties by a landowner. The standard is one of negligence. Under New York state law, owners are strictly liable to business and social invitees and good Samaritans but owe only a duty of reasonable care to informal licensees who use the property at the sufferance of the owner, which being liable to trespassers only for reckless conduct. No duty is owed at all to criminal trespassers. The owner may willfully injure a criminal trespasser without civil penalty. ***What law applies to the plaintiffs in this case?***

2. Perry Loose Cannon, a wild and crazy comedian, has just finished performing at the Desolation Casino in Laughlin, Nevada, which is adjacent to the Arizona border. Perry slides his overpowered vintage Chevy Impala into an AxHandle gas station in Arizona to top off the tank and take in some junk food snacks before heading back into Nevada and to Las Vegas, where he is booked to perform the next night at the Stir-Crazy.

Cruising up U.S. Highway 93 toward Searchlight, Nevada, Perry downs a few "Bad-N-Scanty" candies and immediately becomes violently ill. At the same time, his car engine alternately sputters and surges due to excess moisture in the AxHandle gas. Distracted and having difficulty controlling his car, Perry attempts to avoid an oncoming Blaze Transportation Truck but the Chevy brakes, which had recent maintenance at ClickClack's of Beverly Hills, fail. The Blaze Truck, which is going 20 m.p.h. over the posted 60 m.p.h. speed limit smashes head first into Perry's Chevy, effectively ending his performing career.

Perry, catastrophically injured, sues Blaze Transportation, a New Mexico company, Bad-N-Scanty, a Pennsylvania company, AxHandle, a Texas-based company and the state of Nevada (due to alleged poor road conditions and misleading signage that contributed to the collision). The action is filed in Southern California, Perry's home state as well as the location of his beach convalescence. **What law would be applied under the following choice of law methods:**

- *Lex loci delecti*?

- The *Second Restatement*'s most significant relationship approach?

- The center of gravity or weighing of contacts test?

- Interest analysis?

- Choice-influencing factors?

- Consequences-based assessment?

Can the consequences-based approach or the Leflar choice-influencing factors/better rule of law approach be applied based on the information available? What else would you need to know?

3. A former cabinet secretary, Don Dilly, who authored of a best-selling book, The Virtues of Discipline, after leaving office, talks a better game than he plays. Dilly, a Californian, enjoys coming to Las Vegas and gambling. But even the joys of Vegas can become too much of a good/bad thing. Turns out Dilly loves the high limit slot machines and has run up nearly $6 million in debt at The Place, a luxury casino. Owner Pat Place loves Dilly's political message and is loathe to put the hammer down on a high profile patron, but even Place's patience has its limits.

   The casino sues Dilly in Nevada state court. Dilly promptly removes to federal court and the case languishes for six years. Dilly moves for involuntary dismissal, invoking Nev. R. Civ. P. 41 (e), which provides for mandatory dismissal with prejudice of any action that has not been brought to trial within five years of the date the action was commenced. The Place Casino opposes the motion, arguing that Nevada Rule 41(e) has no application to federal litigation and that Fed. R. Civ. P. 41(b), which provides for involuntary dismissal in the court's discretion "[i]f the plaintiff fails to prosecute" the action in timely fashion, governs the matter. **Which Rule 41 applies?**

4. Reality television star Deena Dramaqueen marries pro basketball player Paul Pituitary in Texas. After 45 days of marriage, Deena filed for divorce.

   Paul's brother Peter had catered the wedding but was stiffed on the $500,000 bill by Deena's family, which is particularly annoying because the Dramaqueens also stiffed Peter on the more modest $150,000 bill for the rehearsal dinner, which was held in California the weekend before the wedding. Peter sues to collect on both debts, filing in federal court in Texas.

   In addition, Peter makes a claim under the Racketeer Influenced and Corrupt Organizations Act (RICO), alleging that Deena and her family have violated this federal statute by engaging in mail and wire fraud on two or more occasions in swindling Peter, which makes for a "pattern of racketeering activity" under the statute. In addition to stating a claim for compensatory damages under the statute, Peter also seeks trebling of the damages, which is permitted under the statute (reflect- ing congressional intent to deter criminal and fraudulent activity).

Assume, rightly or wrongly, that Peter's litigation proceeds to judgment in Texas and that he prevails on all claims. Peter obtains an award of $650,000 against Deena and her family for unpaid bills in connection with the wedding and the rehearsal dinner and for RICO fraud. Judge Reasonable trebles the damage award (to $1.95 million) and then adds two years of prejudgment interest at the rate provided by Texas state law.

Texas has a state rule of civil procedure stating that any party obtaining a judgment is entitled to pre-judgment interest at the rate of 10 percent per annum from the time of the infraction to the date of judgment-pursuant to Texas R. Civ. P. 54. Afterwards, a state statute provides for post-judgment interest at the rate of 8 percent per annum.

Deena objects, arguing that the trebling and the imposition of the Texas interest rate is inapt and that the court should award no prejudg- ment interest because there is no authorization for it under the Federal Rules of Civil Procedure or any federal statute. In the alternative, Deena argues that the California prejudgment interest rate of 4 percent (found in California Rev. Stat. Ann. § 0001), or the Arizona (which is Deena's state of domicile) prejudgment interest rate of 5 percent (found in Arizona R. Civ. P. 54) should apply. Peter opposes the motion. In addition, Deena argues that the federal post-judgment interest rate of 3 percent, established by mythical Fed. R. Civ. P. 100, should govern interest on the award from the date of judgment to the date of payment. *What laws of prejudgment and post-judgment interest should be applied by the court?*

Quick Summary

Determining Applicable Law: Choosing Between Federal and State Law and Choosing Among Competing State Laws.

- Courts must determine applicable law in order to decide disputes. Adjudication requires application of law to contested facts.

- The process may be one of "vertical" or "horizontal" selection.

- In federal litigation, issues of "vertical" choice of law can arise. This involves whether to apply otherwise controlling state law (as part of ordinary horizontal choice of law) or whether federal law must be applied. Where the case is in federal court because of federal question jurisdiction, federal substantive law generally applies except as to particular subquestions such evidentiary privilege. But where the case is in federal court because of diversity jurisdiction or supplemental jurisdiction, applicable state substantive law applies even though the case will be administered and processed according to federal procedural rules. Difficulty can arise in distinguishing the procedural from the substantive.

- The "*Erie* doctrine," so named because of its genesis in *Erie Railroad Co. v. Tompkins*, requires that state substantive law be used in diversity cases so that there is no difference in applicable law and case outcomes based on whether the dispute is litigated in state or federal court.

- Application of *Erie* (or vertical) choice of law generally requires determining whether potentially applicable state law is in fact substantive (in which case it applies) or procedural, in which case it does not and yields to an applicable Federal Rule of Civil Procedure or an important federal policy.

- "Horizontal" choice of law involves selection of which state law applies to a dispute and may be required in either state or federal court litigation.

- Horizontal choice of law, sometimes referred to as "conflict" of laws (often a separate course in law school), generally involves determining which state has the most contacts with, interest in, or closeness to the parties and issues of the case.

II

> ## Unit Overview:
> ## Commencement of a Case
>
>

Unit II comprises six chapters that deal generally with topics taken up either immediately before a case is filed or during its early stages. The topics are related and deal with what has to be done to start a case, how claims and defenses are asserted in a case, and what claims and parties may be brought into a particular case. These issues might be viewed as mechanical in nature, but they are important and have become only more important as courts move towards applying stricter scrutiny of the forum and detail with which the parties plead their cases.

Chapter 5 addresses investigation and Rule 11 of the Rules of Civil Procedure. The rules place an affirmative duty on a party signing a pleading to conduct an investigation to determine that there is an adequate basis to make the claims asserted in the complaint. This duty of investigation is important and failure to follow it leads to sanctions against parties and lawyers that may be significant or, in some cases, career-ending.

Chapters 6 and 7 address the rules of pleading for parties asserting claims and parties defending against them. Although the rules of pleading in the modern era are not highly formalistic, as they were in the days of common law pleading, there are several rules that must be followed and failure to do so potentially results in the loss of claims. Although the courts are generally reluctant to decide cases on pleading formalities rather than the merits, it is more important today than it was twenty years ago that parties set forth claims that are understandable and plausible. These chapters address those issues, as well as the more practical questions of how one actually prepares a complaint that will withstand judicial scrutiny or how one prepares any of the related pleadings, such as answers, third-party complaints, or other basic pleadings.

Chapters 8 and 9 both address joinder. Joinder is the process whereby two (or more) separate claims can be brought in the single lawsuit. In a simple joinder, questions include whether a party can assert additional claims that it may have against another party in the case. Those questions get more complex if the claims are sought to be brought against a different party, or if the claims are different, or if there are different subject-matter jurisdiction aspects governing the different claims. If one of several claims has an independent basis for federal jurisdiction, can the other claims be joined in the federal lawsuit? This is not always an easy question to answer, but Chapters 8 and 9 will attempt to explain this complex area of the law.

Chapter 10 addresses amendment of pleadings. It comes later, mainly because amendment issues generally arise later. Parties draft pleadings to be accurate and complete when they are filed, but the process of litigation results in learning additional information and as that information becomes available, parties may want to or need to amend their pleadings so that they are accurate or effective. Chapter 10 addresses the rules governing this step in the proceedings.

The Rulemaking Process and How to Read a Rule

Before examining Rule 11 and the other Civil Rules, it is imperative to understand how the rulemaking process works and how to best read procedural rules.

A. The Civil Rulemaking Process.

The Rules Enabling Act, 28 U.S.C. § 2072, was passed in 1934. According to that Act, courts of equity and law were merged into one court. In addition, Congress delegated authority to the Supreme Court to draft the procedural rules governing all of the federal courts. This gave the Supreme Court the opportunity to define the procedural rules for the entire federal system.

> The statute explicitly carves out substantive law— it is limited to procedural rules. As already discussed in Chapter 4 regarding *Erie* and choice of law, the dividing line between substance and procedure is a murky one.

In response to the Enabling Act, the Court created an Advisory Committee on the Federal Rules of Civil Procedure. That committee consisted of a number of practitioners and academics who drafted the Rules that are largely in place today. Since that time, the rulemaking process has changed quite a bit. Instead of having one advisory committee to draft the Rules of Civil Procedure, the Court (through a body called the Judicial Conference) created a Standing Committee on the Federal Rules of Practice and Procedure (the "Standing Committee").

The Judicial Conference is the national policy-making body for the federal courts. The Chief Justice of the United States Supreme Court presides over the Judicial Conference. The conference itself is made of the chief judge from each judicial circuit, the Chief Judge of the Court of International Trade, and a district judge from each regional judicial circuit. The Conference is responsible for overseeing the operation of the federal court, and this includes being a part of the federal rulemaking process.

That committee sits above five other advisory committees: Appellate Rules Committee, Bankruptcy Rules Committee, Civil Rules Committee, Criminal Rules Committee, Evidence Rules Committee. Each of these committees, like the Standing Committee, is led by a federal judge and made up of additional federal judges, practitioners, and academics.

The Civil Rules Committee meets at least twice a year. Its purpose is to review and revise the Federal Rules of Civil Procedure as appropriate. The rulemaking process is a multi-step, multi-year process. It starts with the idea for a new rule or an amendment to an existing rule. These ideas can originate from the committee itself or from a suggestion by a judge, practitioner, group, or member of the public.

A proposal to amend, delete, or add a rule is considered by the Civil Rules Committee, and if the Committee believes it is appropriate to propose a rule, it will draft and publish it for public comment. Once it receives public comments, the Civil Rules Committee will make further revisions to the rule, leave the rule as is, or table it. If it decides to proceed with a rule amendment, it forwards its proposal to the Standing Committee.

The Standing Committee considers the rule and votes on it. If approved, the rule is sent to the Judicial Conference. If the Judicial Conference approves the rule, it sends it to the Supreme Court for its approval. The Court then votes on the rule, and if a majority of the justices approve, the rule is sent on to Congress. The Court generally does this in May of any given year. Congress then has until December 1 of that year to vote to reject, modify, or defeat the rule. If Congress does not act, then the new rule becomes effective on December 1. All told, this process takes roughly three years from start to finish, but sometimes as much as four or five years.

B. How to Read a Federal Rule of Civil Procedure

Unlike other first year doctrinal classes where most of the content of the class revolves around common law cases, Civil Procedure requires students to understand how to read codified rules. The Rules of Civil Procedure are not contracts—they are not agreements among parties regarding how to conduct litigation. To the contrary, the rules are positive law, meaning these are man-made rules that have the force of law. However, it is important to note that the rules themselves are not statutes. They sit below Congressional statutory law in the hierarchy of authority, but unless there is a federal statute that conflicts with a rule, the Civil Rules are the law of the land when practicing in federal courts.

That said, being able to effectively read the rules is a critical skill for any law student. There are many ways to approach reading a rule, but there are some key approaches that should help any student better understand the rules during their studies. Here are some of those practical pointers:

- When reading a rule for the first time, read the entirety of the rule first from start to finish.

- Once you have read the rule through entirely, go back to the specific section that is being studied and read it again. Ask yourself what you think the rule requires.

- Outline the rule in your own words, setting forth what the rule requires and how and when it requires it. One test of your facility with the rule: can you describe it in plain English to another person, perhaps even one with no legal training, and be understood?

> A common error made by first-year law students (and sometimes second- and third-year students) is to focus almost exclusively on the black letter of a statute or rule and the major cases that are excerpted in the coursebook. Resist this tendency. Be sure to look at the Advisory Committee Notes to the Rules as well as the notes and commentary in your coursebooks. You will be missing a lot if you don't.

- Re-read the section of the rule and think about whether it makes sense policy-wise. Is this the best way to accomplish the rule's particular goal or might other requirements work better?

- Consult the advisory committee notes for clarification. The notes do not have the authority of legislative history, and they are not intended to be a binding part of the rule. But, the committee notes often give examples of how the rule is meant to work, as well as background on the rule's goal.

5

Pre-Filing Investigation and Sanction Rules

Key Concepts

- Signing requirement and what that signature means
- Criteria for "non-frivolous"
  · Evidentiary support
  · Legal support (existing law or a valid law reform argument)
- Safe-harbor waiting period before filing a Rule 11 motion
- Court's discretion to award or reject sanctions

Introduction

Rule 11 is a rule about sanctions. Its purpose is to discourage frivolous litigation that might result from the federal rules' grant of increased access and simplified procedures. But to cast the rule as being only about sanctions understates its import. Rule 11 serves as a reminder to lawyers about the essential steps they must take before filing a lawsuit. In that way, the rule is also one about professional responsibility. It requires lawyers to stop and think before they file a case.

> Model Rule 3.1 provides that a "lawyer shall not bring or defend a proceeding, or assert or controvert an issue therein, unless there is a basis in law and fact for doing so that is not frivolous...." This means that certain violations of Rule 11 may also violate the rules of professional conduct.

Rule 11 also has to contend with difficult policy questions. It attempts to strike a delicate balance between zealous advocacy on the one hand and the need for an efficient use of the courts' resources on the other. In other words, the rule has to efficiently monitor court filings for frivolousness, but it also has to allow parties and their lawyers to make innovative claims. The difference sounds straightforward, but many a heroic lawyer has been criticized for bringing a frivolous case. Where to strike the balance in Rule 11 has always been, and continues to be, a point of debate.

A. Rule 11 and The Rulemaking Process

Rule 11 was a part of the original set of federal rules adopted in 1938, but it has undergone two serious revisions since that initial adoption. Thus, the rule is often cited as an example of both the success and failure of the federal civil rulemaking process described in the overview.

Under the original Rule 11, an attorney who signed the pleadings certified that he believed there were "good grounds" for the allegations in the document. The signature also certified that the filing was not being made for delay. If it turned out that this was not the case, Rule 11 allowed the court to strike the paper. In practice, courts did not use this rule very often, largely because that version of the rule required subjective bad faith by a party or counsel to justify sanctions. Critics labeled this the "pure heart/empty head" standard. Even though courts occasionally found constructive bad faith based on circumstantial evidence (there were almost never any confessions by Rule 11 targets), the rule was considered a toothless tiger. It also did not contain much of an enforcement mechanism, and many viewed the rule's purpose as a way to remind attorneys of their duties, not as a way to punish them for bad behavior.

As a result, in the late 1970s, there was a push to amend Rule 11 to provide courts with more power to punish attorneys who ran afoul of the rule. Some practitioners, judges, and policymakers believed that a more robust Rule 11 would thwart some of the frivolous lawsuits that were being filed by reckless attorneys and their clients. Thus, in 1983, Rule 11 was amended to adopt an objective standard (*i.e.*, would a reasonable attorney or litigant submit the paper in question) and to require courts to decide whether an argument to change existing law was made in good faith. This meant that, in the latter case, judges determined the subjective intent of attorneys. Also, where a judge found that the attorney had violated the rule, she was required to sanction the attorney. Finally, the rule was silent as to procedures for utilizing the rule, and it did not provide any way for the filing party to escape sanctions once the offending paper was filed.

The 1983 version of Rule 11 became extremely controversial. Some hailed it as a success because they were concerned about a perceived increase in baseless litigation and believed sanctions would reduce those types of suits.

Others questioned the empirical assumption that there was such a problem and also worried that Rule 11 excessively empowered courts to not only reject a claim but to punish lawyers and clients in a way that chilled further advocacy. There was a particular concern that claims viewed as disfavored by some judges (*e.g.*, employment discrimination, police abuses, product liability, securities fraud) would be unduly targeted under the revised rule. There were a number of problems that arose after the rule's adoption—confusion over procedures for using the rule, additional litigation that arose in adjudicating the rule (called "satellite litigation"), and the impact the rule had on plaintiffs with fewer resources or with novel claims.

Because of these issues and sustained criticism, Rule 11 was amended in 1993. To address the concerns raised by the 1983 version of the rule, the attorney's subjective intent in arguments to change existing law was removed as an issue, and the sanctions became discretionary. In addition, the rule's purpose was clearly stated as deterrence, not punishment. Finally, the rule provided for procedures to implement the rule, including procedures intended to facilitate out-of-court resolution, resulting in less litigation. This version of Rule 11 is still in effect today and is the subject of this chapter.

The Rule 11 revisions from 1979—when serious work began on drafting the 1983 Amendment—to 1993 provide a good illustration of the workings of the federal rulemaking process discussed in the Overview. At first, critics who thought the original rule too soft prevailed on the Advisory Committee on the Civil Rules to adopt the 1983 version, which after drafting by the Advisory Committee was approved by the Standing Committee on Rules of Practice and Procedure and the Judicial Conference of the United States and then promulgated by the U.S. Supreme Court. Congress took no action to amend or reject the Court's action during the 180-day window provided by the Rules Enabling Act, 28 U.S.C. § 2072.

When the 1983 version of Rule 11 proved problematic and unpopular with many, the process was reversed, with critics this time convincing the Advisory Committee, the Standing Committee, and the Court that changes were warranted, producing the 1993 Amendment or current Rule 11 (to which Congress did not object). Along the way, there was plenty of the "politics" of law displayed as the profession argued the merits of different approaches to deterring baseless or inadequately vetted litigation. At the Supreme Court, Justices Scalia and Thomas dissented by questioning the efficacy of the 1993 Amendment in discouraging weak cases.

There will probably always be some professional division over Rule 11. Yet, this episode reflects well on the profession because it reveals lawyers and litigants showing concern about the litigation system and making good faith efforts to improve the system, with rulemakers gathering information and making a considered and responsive decision to complaints and problems. During the course of all this, certain individual lawyers, law professors (perhaps particularly Duke Law Professor Paul Carrington, who was the Reporter of the Civil Rules Advisory Committee at the time of the 1993 Amendment), and judges were influential in changing the law.

Those interested in additional background on the evolution of Rule 11 and its reflection on policymaking by bench and bar can find additional information in Gregory P. Joseph, *Sanctions: The Federal Law of Litigation Abuse* (6th ed. 2013); Carl Tobias, *Reconsidering Rule 11*, 46 U. Miami L. Rev. 855 (1992); and Stephen Burbank, *The Transformation of American Civil Procedure: The Example of Rule 11*, 137 U. Pa. L. Rev. 1929 (1989).

B. The Rule

Rule 11 has four main sections. The first section, 11(a), requires signatures on "every pleading, written motion, and other paper…."

Second, section 11(b) outlines the required steps when an attorney makes "representations to the court."

The third section, 11(c), explains the sanctions procedure a court will follow in the event of a Rule 11 violation. It is important to note that, although it was different in a past version of the rule, the court has discretion to impose sanctions should it find a violation. In other words, it may impose sanctions but it does not have to.

Finally, section 11(d) clarifies that Rule 11 does not apply to discovery.

1. Rule 11(a): Signature

This subsection is solely concerned with the requirement that counsel (or the party if he or she is unrepresented) sign any paper that is filed with the court.

THE RULE   Rule 11(a)

Signature

Every pleading, written motion, and other paper must be signed by at least one attorney of record in the attorney's name—**or by a party personally if the party is unrepresented . . .** Unless a rule or statute specifically states otherwise, a pleading need not be verified or accompanied by an affidavit. The court must strike an unsigned paper unless the omission is promptly corrected after being called to the attorney's or party's attention.

EXPLANATION

Historically, some courts required an attorney to verify a filing made with the court. The move to a signature requirement was deemed sufficient to put the attorney on notice that he was attesting to the contents of the filed papers without the additional formality of verification. If the paper is unsigned, the court will notify the party. If it is fixed quickly, the court will consider the paper. If it not fixed promptly, however, the court must strike it.

> **Verification** of a pleading is the swearing to its veracity under oath by either the attorney or party. Historically it was widely required; several states still require verification for certain types of cases. Typically, verification is accomplished by adding a provision for swearing to the accuracy of the factual statements before someone authorized to administer an oath, most often a Notary Public.

2. Rule 11(b): Representations to the Court

Rule 11(b) concerns four things that an attorney must certify "to the best of [their] knowledge, information, and belief" are true with respect to his or her representations to the court. The standard for judging whether this standard has been met is an objective one, meaning what a reasonable attorney would do.

EXPLANATION

 A representation includes a "pleading, written motion, or other paper." Statements made for the first time during oral presentations to the court are not covered by Rule 11 because oral advocacy often requires lawyers to address new matters without much opportunity for study and reflection. The rule

THE RULE   Rule 11(b)

Representations to the Court

By presenting to the court a pleading, written motion, or other paper—whether by signing, filing, submitting, or later advocating it—an attorney or unrepresented party **certifies that to the best of the person's knowledge, information, and belief,** formed after an inquiry reasonable under the circumstances:

  (i) it is not being presented for any **improper purpose**, such as to harass, cause unnecessary delay, or needlessly increase the cost of litigation;

  (ii) the claims, defenses, and other legal contentions are **warranted by existing law** or by a **nonfrivolous argument** for extending, modifying, or reversing existing law or for establishing new law;

  (iii) the **factual contentions have evidentiary support** or, if specifically so identified, will likely have evidentiary support **after a reasonable opportunity for further investigation or discovery**; and

  (iv) the **denials** of factual contentions are **warranted on the evidence** or, if specifically so identified, **are reasonably based on belief or a lack of information**.

is intended to ensure that claims brought in federal court have merit, not to discourage creative and zealous lawyering. There are some oral statements, however, that are subject to Rule 11. An attorney may make a written statement that was, after a reasonable inquiry, true at the time, and thus did not violate Rule 11. If the attorney later finds out that the statement was not true, then the attorney cannot affirm that original statement orally in court. If the attorney affirms that now-violative statement by "later advocating" it orally in court, she could be sanctioned under Rule 11.

EXAMPLES & ANALYSIS

EXAMPLE: Delia submitted an answer to Patricia's complaint. In Delia's answer, she alleged that Patricia failed to file the suit within the relevant statute of limitations. Between Delia filing her **answer** and a pre-trial hearing, Delia learned that a relevant event in Patricia's claim occurred more recently than she had previously thought. Therefore, the statute of limitations had not run. If Delia orally asserts the statute of limitations as a defense at the pre-trial hearing, has she violated Rule 11?

> An **answer** is the pleading that responds to a complaint. Pleadings are discussed in greater detail in Chapter 6.

Analysis: Yes, Delia has violated Rule 11 because she affirmed a now-violative statement by advocating it orally in court. It is a violation of Rule 11 to make an oral argument that affirms a writing she knows is no longer valid.

EXAMPLE: Assume that Patricia's case moves forward. Delia filed a motion to dismiss, arguing that Patricia failed to state a claim upon which relief could be granted. During oral argument for the motion, Delia told the judge that she believed a recent Supreme Court decision supported the arguments made in her motion. She was not able to include the case in her briefs because of the timing of the decision. The judge noted that she would take that argument under advisement. It turns out that Delia was wrong about the Supreme Court decision helping her argument. Has she violated Rule 11?

Analysis: No, she has not. She made an off-the-cuff argument orally, and Rule 11 does not reach such arguments. If she were to put that argument into a paper that she then filed with the court, and the court determined that it was frivolous, then she might be subject to Rule 11 sanctions. But, as long as the statement was only made orally and not filed with the court, she should not suffer a Rule 11 consequence for her mistake. Best practice would be to file a paper with the court noting that upon further research, the case is inapposite. Better to clarify this for the judge than leave her to figure it out on her own.

A "certification" is to be made "after an inquiry reasonable under the circumstances." This "reasonable inquiry" is a context-specific exercise. It does not have to be carried out to the point of absolute certainty, but the attorney must satisfy herself that she has made a sufficient investigation in order to make any particular factual or legal contention. The bounds of a "reasonable inquiry" will be explored in each of the subsections of Rule 11(b) described below.

> Federal courts have an inherent power to sanction for misconduct. *See Chambers v. NASCO, Inc.*, 501 U.S. 32 (1991). Additional statutes also provide courts with the power to sanction in particular substantive contexts. In other words, Rule 11 is not the only authority governing how and when attorneys are sanctioned. A filing may clear Rule 11, but may violate other sanction rules.

a. Improper Purpose

This section is intended to force the attorney (or party, if filing pro se) to "stop and think" before filing the paper. In other words, the requirement to certify that the paper is not being filed for an improper purpose forces the filer to carefully consider his or her motives for filing the documents. Improper purpose is a general term, but it can cover papers filed for the purpose of harassment, delay, or embarrassment. Papers filed solely to make one's adversary spend more money can also fall into the category of improper purpose.

IN PRACTICE

In most jurisdictions, the filing of a "mixed-purpose" case—a case that has a proper purpose either factually or legally, but may also cause embarrassment or is harassing—will not be sanctionable. However, some jurisdictions may impose sanctions for a case that has an improper purpose in part unless the party can show that it would have filed even in the absence of any improper purpose.

EXAMPLES & ANALYSIS

EXAMPLE: Patrova is suing Dustin, a contractor, for shoddy work on a house he was building for her. Dustin thought he had done a great job on the house and had given Patrova a discount because she referred him for more work. In addition to filing a motion to dismiss, Dustin also submitted documents showing that Patrova had filed bankruptcy nine years ago. Could Dustin be sanctioned under Rule 11 for filing a paper for an improper purpose?

Analysis: It is likely a court would find the bankruptcy documents had been filed for an improper purpose. This could easily fall under the category of embarrassment or harassment. However, if Dustin could show the bankruptcy documents served a proper purpose, such as establishing that Patrova was fiscally irresponsible and it was that fiscal irresponsibility that forced him to use lower quality materials, then his filing might not be sanctionable.

b. Warranted by Existing Law

Rule 11(b)(2) implicates the policy concerns outlined in the introduction to this chapter. That is, how to structure a rule that will discourage frivolous filings, but without chilling innovative legal argumentation.

The text of the rule requires that "after an inquiry reasonable under the circumstances," an attorney must be sure that her representations are warranted (i) "by existing law" or (ii) by "a nonfrivolous argument for extending, modifying, or reversing existing law or for establishing new law."

The first category—arguments that are "warranted by existing law"—does not require that the argument ultimately succeed. This standard requires that the attorney have credible authority for the arguments he is making. However, reasonable people can disagree about the particular outcomes under credible authority, and the rule allows for the disagreement to take place without making it sanctionable. Instead, the rule is meant to capture arguments that are simply not tenable under existing law. Yet, drawing the line between reasonable readings of binding authority and unreasonable readings of binding authority is necessarily difficult.

Similarly, the second category—arguments that are warranted by "a non-frivolous" argument for changing the law—is difficult to define. The policy behind this part of the rule is to encourage and allow for legal reform to take place. To achieve this policy goal, the rule has to allow for some flexibility in challenging existing precedent. The rule intends to capture arguments that are advocating for "frivolous" changes in the law, but defining when an argument is novel versus when it is frivolous is quite difficult. Both of these requirements are judged objectively, meaning that whether an argument is frivolous or not is judged from the perspective of a reasonable attorney. If a reasonable attorney in a particular circumstance, after reasonable investigation, would have known that his legal argument was making a frivolous argument for changing existing law, then he may be subject to sanctions for that argument.

EXAMPLES & ANALYSIS

EXAMPLE: Prim, Poe's attorney, filed a complaint on Poe's behalf against Dale Corporation, a private Delaware company. Prim alleged Poe worked for Dale Corporation, but he had recently provided adverse testimony in a civil action against Dale Corporation. Prim further alleged that Dale Corporation terminated Poe in retaliation for that testimony. Prim argued that this was a violation of 28 U.S.C. § 1983. Section 1983 claims require that the claim be made against a party that is acting under color of state law; yet, there is nothing in the complaint alleging that Dale Corporation was acting in such a way. Prim didn't know that § 1983 required the party to act under color of state law. She just learned a bit about it in law school and knew that when something was unfair, most cases were filed under § 1983. Should Prim be sanctioned under Rule 11(b)(2)?

Analysis: Yes. This is a classic example of an attorney who did not do her homework. No reasonable attorney, given these circumstances, would file a § 1983 claim. Moreover, Prim did not do any research that would indicate she was arguing for a valid extension of § 1983 to private corporations with no apparent ties to the state.

EXAMPLE: Pantheon School Teachers sued the District School Board for violating the state's Teacher Tenure Act. Pantheon alleged the District forced seven teachers to transfer to new schools. In its complaint, Pantheon stated that the teacher transfers were completely arbitrary and motivated by personal and political vendettas. The District's alleged violation is not explicitly carved out in the state's Teacher Tenure Act, nor is there any case law in the state to support Pantheon's claim. However, Pantheon has found a recently decided and nearly identical case in a neighboring state, *Principal v. Dean*. In *Principal,* the court found the teachers' transfers to be an unnecessary violation of that state's Teacher Tenure Act. Pantheon's claims are not warranted by existing law, but does the position in *Principal v. Dean* set forth a colorable argument for extension of the law sufficient to satisfy Rule 11?

Analysis: Yes, probably. Pantheon may not win its case on the merits, but Pantheon has done a reasonable investigation and has made a reasonable argument in favor of extending the law. In other words, it is making an argument with *some* legal basis. The policy behind Rule 11 is to thwart baseless claims (either factually or legally). Rule 11 is not supposed to chill creative or novel claims under the law. This scenario is likely more novel than it is frivolous. Thus, Pantheon probably did not violate Rule 11 by filing this claim.

EXAMPLE: Diamond Construction Company needed financial backing to build a new gated community in the very posh South Hills neighborhood of Littleput. Diamond went to Premium Capital, Inc. and borrowed $67,000,000. Premium acquired a lien on all of Diamond's real and personal property in exchange for the loan. Just as Diamond was finishing the new community, the housing market crashed, and Diamond was unable to sell any of its new properties. In an attempt to save itself as the economy worsened,

Diamond issued unsecured promissory notes to Premium. After recouping as much as it could on the lien, Premium sued Diamond under Section 12 of the Securities Act of 1933. In its complaint, Premium argued that the notes supplied by Diamond were securities for the remaining balance of the loan. Premium relied on *Pompous Securities v. Daily Commodities*, which was decided in its Circuit and concluded that the promissory notes provided by Daily were securities. However, in *Pompous*, the plaintiffs accepted the notes only as part of their investment *and* they retained the right to all of their options. In other words, the *Pompous* notes fit the already accepted definition of securities. Is Premium's complaint warranted by existing law?

Analysis: Maybe. It is a close call. Because Premium's claim is only supported by a case where the facts do not match the instant matter particularly well, Premium is pushing it a bit in this case. However, it is unlikely a court would find Premium's contentions *unreasonable* under existing law. The facts may be a bit different, but if Premium can construct a reasonable (even if not successful) argument that the policy underlying the decision in *Pompous* applies equally to its situation, it is probably making an argument for an extension of the law that would be acceptable under Rule 11(b)(2). While Diamond could file a motion for sanctions, a court probably would not grant the motion.

EXAMPLE: Poet believes he was discharged from his job because he complained about the presence of toxic materials. Poet's attorney, Lois, filed suit against Poet's employer pursuant to Title VII of the Civil Rights Act. This section of the Civil Rights Act protects employees who are retaliated against for claiming discrimination on the basis of race, color, national origin, religion, or sex. Poet did not allege a discrimination claim; however, she believed that a Title VII cause of action was appropriate because the action shielded an employee from retaliation, regardless of the discrimination claim's merit. The employer moved for Rule 11 sanctions because Poet invoked the retaliation provision of Title VII without even asserting a discrimination claim. Should the court impose sanctions under Rule 11?

Analysis: Yes. A court will likely impose Rule 11 sanctions because Poet's claim was not warranted under existing law. By invoking Title VII of the

Civil Rights Act, Lois should have known that the retaliation provision only covered retaliation resulting from discrimination claims. Even the most minimal inquiry into Title VII would have revealed that Poet had no cause of action because a discrimination claim was not even made.

EXAMPLE: Penelope, a pregnant woman, had worked for Deave City's Department of Education for ten years. When she was seven-months pregnant, she received a letter from the city informing her that she would have to cease working because of her condition, *i.e.*, her pregnancy. Penelope was outraged, but learned that other women in the office had been asked to do the same once they reached the seven-month mark in their pregnancies. Penelope went to an attorney to find out whether she could bring a claim of gender discrimination against the city. Her attorney explained that Penelope might be able to seek injunctive relief against the city—forcing them to end their pregnancy policy—but she was not likely to receive damages under existing precedent. Current law, Penelope's lawyer explained, did not allow individuals to seek monetary damages for Constitutional violations against municipalities. Penelope's lawyer went on to explain, however, that she believed there was a reasonable argument that the prohibition against monetary damages should change and that some judges and lawyers believed that existing cases had gotten it wrong. According to Penelope's lawyer's research, federal trial courts had started to split on this issue. No federal case had held that damages were allowed, but more and more dissents were being written to state that damages should be permitted. If Penelope's lawyer goes forward with the case and seeks monetary damages, should she be sanctioned?

Analysis: Not necessarily. This is a question that puts the issue of frivolity versus innovation to the test. While the precedent is against Penelope obtaining damages, if her lawyer has done the research to argue for a well-grounded change to existing law, then the claim might not be sanctionable. If, however, her lawyer has not done any research and does not have a well-founded argument for changing existing law, the lawyer might be sanctioned. In reality, this case was brought, and it completely changed the law regarding municipal liability. *See Monell v. Dep't. of Soc. Servs.*, 436 U.S. 658 (1978).

c. Factual Contentions Have Evidentiary Support

In addition to filing a case for a proper purpose and having a legal basis for the claim, an attorney must also certify that the factual contentions presented to the court have "evidentiary support." In other words, the attorney must do her homework before filing the case. She can do this in one of two ways. First, she can find actual evidentiary support through pre-filing investigation. Second, if she cannot get to the information because of the particular circumstances of the case, she can file the case and admit that she does not yet have the necessary evidentiary support, but hopes to find it through discovery in the case.

The first standard is easy enough to meet, assuming that the information necessary to make a valid claim is available. Even then, however, there are variations across cases. Some claims may only need a couple of pieces of information in order to have the necessary evidentiary support, while other cases may require more. The standard requires that the attorney have some support for the assertion when she made it, but it does not require that the factual support be right from start to finish. As long as the factual contention was reasonable at the time it was made, Rule 11 is satisfied.

As to the second standard—pleading the case based on information and belief—it does not absolve the attorney of any duty to investigate. To the contrary, the attorney must do enough research under the circumstances to assure herself that she is making a valid claim. If one or two pieces of key information are not readily available, she can admit as much. This does not give the attorney carte blanche to file a case without doing any factual investigation at all. In other words, the attorney is not allowed to file a case in the hopes of finding support for her allegations through discovery and simply engage in a "fishing expedition." Instead, she must have done the investigation necessary to find reasonable support for all of her allegations and use this provision only when she simply couldn't find particular facts without the benefit of discovery.

EXAMPLES & ANALYSIS

EXAMPLE: A client, Peeta, came to an attorney, Paul, and asked him to file a suit against Durum for breach of contract. Prior to filing his client's complaint, Paul got a copy of the contract between Peeta and Durum. The contract stated that Durum would bake a wedding cake for Peeta for his June wedding. Peeta paid for the cake in-full on May 15, and gave a copy of the receipt to Paul. After meeting with Peeta about the potential suit, Paul spoke with Durum's assistant at the bakery who verified that they never baked a wedding cake for Peeta and that there were no valid excuses for this failure to deliver the cake, such as a cancellation order or a failure of Peeta to make a required advance deposit. The next day Paul filed a complaint. Has Paul made a reasonable inquiry, such that his factual contentions have evidentiary support?

Analysis: Yes. Paul's inquiry is sufficient and his factual contentions have evidentiary support. Rule 11 does not require that Paul complete all his research or investigation prior to filing. It does, however, require that Paul have a factual basis for his representations beyond a mere opinion. Paul has met this standard based on Peeta's statement that Durum never fulfilled his obligation and the "evidentiary support" provided by the contract between Peeta and Durum and Peeta's receipt.

IN PRACTICE

The rules of professional conduct in each state are often adopted based on the ABA Model Rules of Professional Conduct. When deciding whether to interview an individual informally, an attorney must be aware of ABA Rule of Professional Conduct 4.2, which provides that "a lawyer shall not communicate . . . with a person the lawyer knows to be represented by another lawyer in the matter" absent the other lawyer's consent or a court order. With an entity, the question of who an attorney can informally interview can be difficult.

Some states use a "control group" test, meaning that an attorney is free to talk to everyone but top management. Other states place even rank-and-file workers off limits. The key is to know the rule that applies in your state and proceed accordingly and cautiously.

EXAMPLE: Assume the factual scenario is the same as above, except this time, Paul files the complaint without getting a copy of the contract or interviewing Durum's assistant. He still has the information provided by Peeta, including the receipt. Has Paul made a reasonable inquiry, such that his factual contentions have evidentiary support?

Analysis: This is a closer call. Paul still has a factual basis for his representations. He has a receipt showing that Peeta paid for a wedding cake and Peeta's statement that the cake was never made. This could be sufficient to meet the standards set out in Rule 11. However, if it turns out that a simple visit to the bakery would have revealed that Durum had a delivery invoice signed by Peeta, as well as photos of the finished cake, then Paul might be sanctioned under Rule 11 for failing to perform an "inquiry reasonable under the circumstances." The point is to do the amount of investigation required by the particular claim. An attorney has to believe his client, but he also has to do his own groundwork before filing a claim and signing his name to it.

EXAMPLE: Penelope is trying to get a very large security deposit back from her client's landlord, Dallas. Prior to filing a complaint, Penelope attempted to get a copy of the lease and any receipts for the security deposit and rent. Penelope could not get copies from her client, Pat, because they were destroyed by a fire in the storage unit where her client kept all her financial records. Dallas refused to provide copies of any documents or answer any of Penelope's questions. Unfortunately, Dallas is not part of any larger management company that might have copies of the documents. Penelope files the complaint. Has she performed a reasonable inquiry under the circumstances?

Analysis: Under these circumstances, yes, Penelope has done a reasonable inquiry. Penelope has exhausted all means possible to acquire verifying documentation, which meets the reasonable inquiry standard. When she files the complaint, she should state that she was not able to obtain the lease, but hopes to through discovery. The rest of her investigation should be sufficient to support the claims made. If other potential sources of evidence—such as Dallas—refuse to cooperate, this logically eases the attorney's duty of inquiry.

EXAMPLE: Bruce Pinkman worked for DialUs, a cellular telephone company. Pinkman is a man of Hispanic descent. He alleged that he was subject to racial hostility at DialUs and that the company's two top executives conspired to terminate him because of his race. Pinkman claims that he heard the executives discussing how to terminate him in a way that wouldn't get them into trouble, but that they didn't want a Hispanic person working for them. Pinkman hired an attorney, Sally, who investigated and discovered that the facility where Pinkman worked was "known to be racially hostile" against Hispanics. She filed a complaint, alleging the discrimination and conspiracy. Additionally, throughout the discovery process, Sally investigated and gathered evidence in support of Pinkman's claims through deposition testimony, and Pinkman even testified in a deposition to the conversation that he overheard. Unfortunately for Pinkman, the defendants filed a motion for summary judgment, which was granted. Additionally, after the safe-harbor period, the defendants filed a motion for Rule 11 sanctions, saying that Sally failed to conduct a proper investigation, and that Sally could not have held a reasonable belief that a conspiracy existed given the dearth of evidence to support a conspiracy theory. Will the court sanction Sally under Rule 11?

Analysis: Probably not. Just because the court did not find that there was a "genuine dispute of material fact" and granted summary judgment in the case does not mean that the claims were frivolous. The question is whether she conducted a reasonable investigation under the circumstances. In this case, she had her client's story and information regarding DialUs's reputation. It is difficult to say what else Sally could have done before filing the complaint. While some attorneys may have ultimately not chosen to file a suit with such little evidence, Sally arguably conducted a reasonable investigation under the circumstances, and did not violate Rule 11.

IN PRACTICE

Experienced lawyers frequently state that shrewd case selection is the key to avoiding legal ethics problems or civil litigation sanctions and to running a profitable law office. A lawyer need not accept every potential case that "walks in the door." While many prospective clients have been genuinely aggrieved by others, some potential clients have an unreasonable sense of entitlement or have only tenuous connections with empirical reality. Do not accept these clients—including prospective clients that sound credible but whose stories break down upon further Rule 11 investigation. And remember to send each of these rejected potential clients a letter summarizing the situation and your decision not to accept the retention, including a warning to the rejected prospective client that possible claims are subject to statutes of limitations and that they should consult another lawyer for a second opinion before the limitations period expires.

EXAMPLE: Paige sued Dalton, a caterer, for negligently serving spoiled potato salad. Paige claimed that everyone who ate the potato salad become violently ill within 30 minutes of eating it, and only people who ate the potato salad became ill. Paige has statements from every guest at her event detailing whether they ate the potato salad and whether they got sick. Are these statements enough to satisfy the requirement that Paige's factual contentions have evidentiary support?

Analysis: Yes, the statements are enough to satisfy the requirement that Paige's factual contentions have evidentiary support. The standard of "evidentiary support" is a relatively low hurdle. But remember, Paige must also have performed a reasonable inquiry given the circumstances of her case. Furthermore, Paige must keep in mind that her complaint must also meet the pleading requirements of Rule 8(a)(2). *See* Chapter 6. Rule 11(b)(3) does not relieve Paige from meeting other requirements under the rules.

EXAMPLE: Patrick's client, Panthea, wants to sue the Dolan Police Department for police brutality. According to Panthea, she was at a bar when a fight broke out between her friend and another regular at the bar. Panthea tried to break it up, and when the police arrived she was caught in the scuffle and her nose and eye socket were broken. What should Patrick do before filing a complaint to make sure he is compliant with Rule 11(b)?

Analysis: Patrick should perform a reasonable investigation under the circumstances. In this case, that would mean getting a copy of the police report, and maybe interviewing some of the witnesses. If this evidence supports Panthea's claims, Patrick would probably meet the requirements of Rule 11 by filing the complaint with just this information. However, if the new evidence raises doubts about Panthea's claims or contradicts her assertions, Patrick should conduct further inquiry. Remember, the standard in Rule 11 is an objective standard: a reasonable inquiry conducted by a reasonable attorney. If a reasonable attorney would be inclined to do further investigation, then Patrick should as well.

Remember also that Rule 11 requires that claims have legal support as well. Although most lawyers have a good general idea of what may be actionable at law, there should always be at least rudimentary research to confirm counsel's instincts—and more extensive research in difficult, troublesome, or complex matters. For example, police liability is often more limited than the liability that would befall persons outside of law enforcement for the same activity. Under federal civil rights law (42 U.S.C. § 1983), the government can only be liable for policy misconduct if it reflects a government policy (*e.g.*, a shoot-on-sight order for any curfew violators) or a systematic government failing (*e.g.*, inadequate training of officers in the proper use of force). There still may be an assault-and-battery or other state law tort liability claims against the individual officers or the police force, but this requires some legal research as well.

d. Denials of Factual Contentions

Rule 11(b)(4) is the section of Rule 11 that applies to a party's answer to the complaint. When answering allegations in the complaint, the party must admit, deny, or state that he lacks the necessary knowledge or information to respond to the specific allegation. These responses cannot be based on mere conjecture. The responding party, like a party filing a complaint, must make a reasonable inquiry before responding to the complaint. Further, the party cannot feign ignorance about or otherwise deny an allegation that he knows to be true.

EXAMPLES & ANALYSIS

EXAMPLE: Portia sued Drucilla for medical bills from a hit-and-run accident. Portia's evidence included photos from the traffic camera that showed Drucilla's car hitting Portia and driving away. However, Drucilla has evidence that she was in a different state when the accident occurred. Portia's complaint includes an allegation that Drucilla was driving the car that hit Portia. If Drucilla denies the factual contention that she was driving the car that hit Portia, will she have violated Rule 11?

Analysis: No, if Drucilla denies that allegation in her answer, she would not be violating Rule 11. Drucilla's denial is warranted because she has evidence that contradicts Portia's assertions. She was not in the state at the time of the accident, so she could not have been driving the car. However, if she knew the allegation was true, she would violate Rule 11(b)(4) by denying it.

EXAMPLE: Same situation as above, but what if Portia's complaint also contains an allegation that the car that hit Portia was owned by Drucilla. Drucilla does not know if anyone drove her car while she was out of town. She has not seen the traffic camera photos, so does not know anything about what happened that weekend. Her car was undamaged and in her garage when she returned from being out of town. Thus, she denies this allegation. Has she violated Rule 11?

Analysis: Maybe. It depends on whether Drucilla has done enough investigation under the circumstances. If she had ready access to the traffic camera photos so that she could identify whether it was her car or not, she probably needed to look at those before filing her answer. However, if she did not have access to the photos and did not otherwise have any indication that her car had been involved in an accident, her denial may be appropriate. The best course would probably be for her to answer by saying that she "lacks the knowledge and information sufficient to form a belief as to whether the allegation is true." By doing so, she effectively denies the allegation, but indicates that she simply does not know whether the allegation is true at this point.

3. Rule 11(c): Sanctions

Rule 11(c) addresses the details of Rule 11 sanctions. This section clarifies that sanctions are discretionary and requires the court to clearly explain its sanction decisions. Moreover, in an effort to encourage cooperation between attorneys, this part of the rule mandates that the parties take time to potentially resolve any issues under Rule 11 before a motion ever gets filed with the court.

THE RULE   Rule 11(c)

Sanctions

(1) **In General.** If, after notice and a reasonable opportunity to respond, the court determines that Rule 11(b) has been violated, the court may impose an **appropriate sanction** on any **attorney, law firm, or party** that violated the rule or is responsible for the violation. Absent exceptional circumstances, a law firm must be held jointly responsible for a violation committed by its partner, associate, or employee.

(2) **Motion for Sanctions.** A motion for sanctions must be made separately from any other motion and must describe the specific conduct that allegedly violates Rule 11(b). The motion must be served under Rule 5, but it must not be filed or be presented to the court if the challenged paper, claim, defense, contention, or denial is withdrawn or appropriately corrected within **21 days after service** or within another time the court sets. If warranted, the court may award the prevailing party **the reasonable expenses, including attorney's fees**, incurred for the motion.

(3) **On the Court's Initiative.** On its own, the **court may order** an attorney, law firm, or party to **show cause** why conduct specifically described in the order has not violated Rule 11(b).

(4) Nature of a Sanction. A sanction imposed under this rule **must be limited to what suffices to deter repetition of the conduct or comparable conduct by others similarly situated**. The sanction may include nonmonetary directives; an order to pay a penalty into court; or, if imposed on motion and warranted for effective deterrence, an order directing payment to the movant of part or all of the reasonable attorney's fees and other expenses directly resulting from the violation.

(5) Limitations on Monetary Sanctions. The court **must not** impose a monetary sanction:

    (A) against a represented party for violating **Rule 11(b)(2)**; or

    (B) on its own, unless it issued the **show-cause order** under Rule 11(c)(3) **before voluntary dismissal or settlement** of the claims made by or against the party that is, or whose attorneys are, to be sanctioned.

(6) Requirements for an Order. An order imposing a sanction **must describe the sanctioned conduct and explain the basis for the sanction**.

EXPLANATION

Rule 11(c) outlines the parameters for sanctioning attorneys and their clients. Recall that when the rule was amended in 1983, sanctions became mandatory. Where the filing was determined to be frivolous, the court had to impose sanctions. This changed with the 1993 amendments. Now, the court has discretion in deciding when and how to grant sanctions. Moreover, the sanctions cannot be punitive; they are supposed to be what is necessary to achieve deterrence.

There are six sections to this rule that are briefly outlined below:

- **Lawyers and Law Firms:** Courts can impose sanctions on parties, the attorneys, and the attorneys' law firm, provided that the parties have all had reasonable notice and chance to respond (11(c)(1)).

Individual versus law firm liability was one of the issues addressed in the 1993 amendments. In *Pavelic & LeFlore v. Marvel Entertainment Group*, 493 U.S. 120 (1989), the Supreme Court in applying the 1983 version of the rule refused to find a law firm subject to sanctions for a pleading found to violate Rule 11 even though the signing lawyer was a very junior associate who was simply signing the complaint at the behest of a senior partner. The Court's construction struck many as a reflection on the Court's lack of sense for the practice of law in the real world but is now moot because the current version of Rule 11 allows for law firm "vicarious" liability for pleadings signed by individual attorneys. But this aspect of the rule only applies to the firm that employed the signing attorney at the time of the Rule 11 violation. A lawyer who violates Rule 11 does infect all firms with which he is subsequently affiliated, although this aspect of his job experience may make him less employable or may even cost him his job with the firm he was with at the time of the offense.

- **21-day Safe Harbor:** A party may only make a motion for sanctions after she has given the opposing party a 21-day "safe harbor" in which to withdraw or modify the allegedly offending filing (11(c)(2)). This is the technical section of the rule because it outlines the requirements for a party who wants to file a Rule 11 motion against her opposition. The party making the motion cannot file the motion directly with the court. Instead, she must serve the motion on her opposition and wait 21 days before filing the motion. If during that 21-day period, her opposition withdraws the alleged offensive filing (or the suit altogether) or amends the alleged offensive filing, the party cannot file the motion and no sanctions can be granted. This 21-day "safe harbor" period can be extended by the court if appropriate.

- **Sua Sponte Sanctions:** The court may issue an order to show cause as to why

The safe harbor was added in the 1993 amendments to Rule 11. Under the 1983 version of Rule 11, litigation about whether a particular filing was frivolous increased immensely. The rulemakers wanted to change the rule to allow for necessary sanctions to be issued without chilling individuals from filing their claims and without creating so much additional litigation. With the safe harbor, a plaintiff can file her claim without the concern of immediate sanctions. If it turns out that her filing violates Rule 11, Rule 11(c)(2) allows her to pull back the filing before any negative impact. If she does not believe that her filing violates Rule 11, she can oppose the motion for sanctions. Note that the court has discretion to award expenses and attorney's fees to the party that ultimately prevails on the Rule 11 motion.

a party, her lawyers, or her lawyers' law firm should not be sanctioned (11(c)(3)). It does not have to wait for a party to make a motion seeking them. However, when a court wants to sanction a party, it must first issue an order to show cause, meaning that it must tell the alleged offending party why the court thinks it has violated Rule 11 and ask the party to explain why it should not be sanctioned under Rule 11.

- **Deterrence:** A court has ample discretion in deciding what kind of sanction to apply, however, that sanction cannot be solely punitive—it has to have a deterrent effect (11(c)(4)). It is easy to think of sanctions as monetary, but the rule is meant to give the court broad discretion in fashioning a sanction that fits the sanctionable activity. This means that some sanctions will be monetary in nature, but some will require some other action, such as referring an attorney to the local bar association or requiring further training for an attorney and his firm. In other words, the court is encouraged to be thoughtful about creating a sanction that will deter future offensive activities by that particular lawyer. Moreover, the court cannot order a party to pay monetary sanctions to the opposing party. Any monetary sanctions are payable only to the court. The only money that can be exchanged between the parties in a Rule 11 motion are the costs and attorney's fees associated with bringing the motion itself and/or the costs and attorney's fees associated with addressing the alleged overall Rule 11 violation.

> In addition, a goal of the 1993 amendments to Rule 11 was that courts impose only the "least severe" sanction necessary to vindicate the deterrent purpose of the rule in light of the conduct at issue.

- **Monetary Sanctions:** A court's ability to issue monetary sanctions is limited in two ways. First, it cannot issue monetary sanctions against a party for violations of Rule 11(b)(2). This makes sense. Where a party is represented, it is difficult to see how sanctioning a lawyer's client for a mistake of the law would have any deterrent effect. Instead, the court can only issue monetary sanctions against the attorney. Second, it cannot otherwise issue monetary sanctions on its own without first issuing a show-cause order (11(c)(5)).

- When it imposes sanctions, a court must explain its reasoning (11(c)(6)). An order of sanctions is reviewed on appeal under an **abuse of discretion** standard. The rule requires that any sanction order provide both the parties and any appellate court with the information necessary to assess the validity of the court's decision.

> **Abuse of discretion** is a standard of review that is quite deferential to the court that made the initial decision. Unless the appellate court believes that the trial court abused its power and imposed a sanction far beyond what was warranted under the circumstances, the appellate court will generally let the trial court's decision stand. This standard of review is in sharp contrast to other standards of review, such as de novo, which allows the appellate court to review the decision anew, without any necessary deference to the lower court's decision. Chapter 19 regarding Appeals provides a more extensive discussion of standards of review.

EXAMPLES & ANALYSIS

EXAMPLE: Judge Fisher issued a show cause order to Pewter after determining that the lawsuit Pewter had filed was only filed to harass his ex-employer after he had quit. Pewter's response to the show cause order did not sway Judge Fisher. Judge Fisher ordered that Pewter pay monetary sanctions to the court in order to deter Pewter from filing another claim for the purpose of harassment. Were these sanctions appropriate?

Analysis: Yes. Monetary sanctions are appropriate so long as they are used as a deterrent (Rule 11(c)(4)). The court ordered the sanctions *sua sponte*, but she issued an order to show cause before doing so (Rule 11(c)(5)), and she explained her reasoning in an order (Rule 11(c)(6)).

EXAMPLE: Piper filed a complaint against Duff. Duff believed the claim was baseless and frivolous. Duff filed a motion for Rule 11 sanctions. Will Duff's motion succeed?

Analysis: No, Duff's motion for sanctions will not be successful because he did not first serve Piper properly under Rule 5 and then give her 21 days to correct or withdraw her complaint prior to filing the motion. The safe harbor period allows counsel to withdraw or correct the paper at issue within 21 days. If a party fails to comply with the 21-day safe harbor requirement, a court must deny the motion for sanctions. Courts are vigilant about enforcing the safe harbor. They will refuse to grant sanctions, even if they think an act is sanctionable, if the 21-day safe harbor is not met. Failure to wait 21 days is not a basis in itself for sanctions against the movant. However, a party's failure to comply with the safe harbor requirement does not preclude the court from issuing sanctions *sua sponte* under Rule 11(c)(3).

IN PRACTICE

Attorneys should not take the decision to file a Rule 11 motion lightly. Like all procedural moves a party can make, the attorney has to make a strategic decision about how the court will view the motion before making it. The seeking of sanctions is likely to lessen the other side's willingness to "turn the other cheek" on litigation errors or slights. It is also not uncommon for cases to devolve into motions for sanctions, filed by all parties.

Remember, attorneys are agents of their clients. The general rule of agency is that the principal (*i.e.*, the client) is bound by actions of the agent (*i.e.*, the attorney) done within the scope of employment. Unless the attorney exceeded her authority, counsel's errors generally bind the party regarding litigation and negotiation. But this does not mean that clients should be sanctioned because of attorney errors. Losing a case is usually punishment enough. In extreme cases of attorney error regarding applicable law and litigation practice, clients may have a claim for malpractice and be able to avoid or recoup counsel fees even if they cannot show they would have prevailed in the absence of counsel's error.

4. Rule 11(d) Inapplicability to Discovery

Rule 11 *does not* apply to discovery. The discovery rules contain their own set of sanction rules as explained in Chapter 14 (discussing availability of sanctions pursuant to Rules 26 and 37).

ADDITIONAL EXERCISES

1. Pan was involved in a car accident with another vehicle driven by a man who identified himself as Robert Diron. Because Pan was injured in the accident, she decided to file suit against Robert for damages and medical expenses. Her attorney, Dave, was initially unable to serve Robert, because he had provided Pan with a false address. In order to serve him, Dave decided to look for "Robert Diron" in the telephone book, and, not finding anyone by that name, decided that "Roberto Diron" was close enough. Dave gave the address to Pan, who then went to Roberto Diron's house to observe him to make sure he was the one who had been in the accident with Pan. Pan told Dave that she "was uncertain," but Dave decided to file a complaint against "Robert Diron" and served "Roberto Diron" as the driver of the car. Following service of summons, Roberto Diron informed Dave that he was not involved in the accident, and also furnished a statement from his employer indicating that Roberto was at work on the date and at the time of the accident. Nevertheless, Dave moved forward with the litigation. ***Has Dave conducted sufficient investigation to avoid being sanctioned under Rule 11?***

2. Marion Pratt, an employee at Consulting Firm, was denied certain medical benefits as part of his benefit plan as an employee. He retained an attorney, Forest Green, to compel payment. Green filed a complaint, which named several defendants, including the consulting firm, the medical plan, and the medical plan's general attorneys, one of whom is named Violet Durge. Green alleged that Durge advised the plan to adopt certain provisions challenged in the suit and counseled the plan's administrators not to make certain payments to Pratt. Durge moved to dismiss the complaint and requested sanctions under Rule 11. She included several affidavits from her colleagues, which stated that Durge played no role in the adoption, implementation or administration of the medical plan, and in fact was unaware of the existence of the plan prior to the filing of the action. Green offered no evidence to rebut the affidavits. It is undisputed that Durge played no role in the actions of the plan that gave rise to the claims against the other defendants. Green amended the complaint and deleted the allegation that Durge had given advice to adopt the medical plan, but continued to name Durge as a defendant and to allege that Durge was involved in the conduct for which Pratt sought relief. ***Can Green be sanctioned under Rule 11?***

3. Bryan, a technician at Dericon, was terminated for getting into an accident with a company vehicle while under the influence of alcohol. Upset about being fired, Bryan hired Sara, an attorney that was well known for her work with workers' compensation claims. Sara filed a workers' compensation claim for Bryan's injuries sustained in the accident. The court denied the claim, concluding that Bryan could not prove that Dericon's conduct proximately resulted in his injuries. Sara filed a second workers' compensation claim based on the same facts, but that claim also failed. As a last resort, Sara filed a claim against Dericon for negligent infliction of emotional distress. In Dericon's answer, it stated that this claim was barred by the well-known exclusivity rule, which limits remedies for work related injuries to workers' compensation claims even if those workers' compensation claims ultimately fail. Sara argued that because Bryan's workers' compensation claim failed, he was entitled to sue again. Dericon then filed a motion for sanctions pursuant to Rule 11. **_Has Sara violated Rule 11?_**

4. Pete's lawyer, Plantre, sued Davea for breach of contract in June. The court granted Davea's motion for summary judgment because there was no consideration for the contract. During the litigation, Plantre joined the law firm Pearson Hardman. After Davea's motion for summary judgment was granted, the judge issued monetary Rule 11 sanctions against Plantre and Pearson Hardman. **_Assuming the judge issued a proper show-cause order, were these sanctions appropriate?_**

5. Pablo has sued Demarcus under Title VII of the Civil Rights Act of 1964 for discrimination. Pablo worked for Demarcus's construction company as a carpenter for the last three years. A position for a shift-manager opened up, and Pablo applied for the promotion; he was not given the job. In his complaint, Pablo asserted that the only reason he was not given the job was because he was too attractive. Pablo stated that he was the most qualified applicant, and he had been with the company the longest of all the applicants. Demarcus denied all of the allegations in the complaint and filed a motion to dismiss for failure to state a claim upon which relief could be granted. The judge granted the motion, and in his order, included an order to show cause as to why sanctions should not be imposed for a violation of Rule 11(b)(2). (There is no legal claim under Title VII for discrimination based on being too good-looking.)

Has the court followed the proper procedures for sanctions under Rule 11(c)(3)?

6. Same facts as the previous example, but assume that the court does not issue an order to show cause with the grant of the motion to dismiss. Following the grant of the motion to dismiss, Demarcus then files a motion seeking sanctions under Rule 11(b). **Can the court rule on that motion?**

7. Same facts as above, except assume that instead of Pablo alleging he was passed over for a promotion because of his good looks, he alleged that he was discriminated against on the basis of race. Following discovery, Demarcus moved for summary judgment and submitted multiple papers showing that Pablo was actually the least qualified of the applicants, and that Pablo had been written up on two occasions for violating company policy. The judge granted Demarcus's motion. **Should he also issue an order to show cause under Rule 11(c)(2)?**

8. Peggy's attorney Paulina sued Doris in federal court. Paulina's complaint stated that the final divorce decree her client agreed to in state court violated her First Amendment rights of free speech. The divorce decree contained no references to what Paulina's client could or could not say about the divorce or the other partner. The federal court issued an order to show cause as to why sanctions should not be made against Paulina. The court explained that Paulina was trying to collaterally attack a state's divorce decree, which the federal court did not have subject matter jurisdiction to hear. Moreover, the First Amendment claim was inextricably linked to that state claim, and a reasonable attorney would have done enough research to determine that the court could not assert jurisdiction over that claim. Finally, the court explained that it did not believe there was evidentiary support for the claim, nor would the parties be able to find any through discovery. Paulina was unable to respond to the order to show cause, so the court issued sanctions. The sanctions required Paulina to pay the court a monetary sanction for filing a frivolous claim. The court also ordered both Paulina and Peggy to pay a nominal monetary sanction for submitting a complaint that completely lacked any evidentiary support at the time of filing, and would not have gained any evidentiary support during discovery. **Were these sanctions proper?**

9. Pi has come to you for representation. Pi wants to sue Dom for stealing a song (copyright infringement). Pi has told you that he and Dom used to be in a band together, and Pi was the songwriter for the group. He shows you his notebooks from when the band was together and other songs that the band had copyrighted together. Pi says that the song in question is one he wrote after he left the band. Additionally, Pi confides in you that the reason he left the band was because Dom broke off their romantic relationship. You move forward and file a complaint against Dom.

>   *(a) Are you potentially in violation of Rule 11 by filing this complaint?*

>   *(b) Dom wants to file a 12(b)(6) motion to dismiss and a motion for Rule 11 sanctions. What steps, and in what order, does Dom need to take to successfully file these motions?*

Same facts as above, except you have now done more investigation prior to filing the complaint. You have found out that the song was actually written while Pi was still part of the band, and the song was included on an album that was copyrighted as a whole. (Relevant Law: A joint copyright owner cannot sue his co-owner for infringement.) *Are there any new Rule 11 issues?*

10. Palti wanted to sue his landlord, Dalila, for various damages caused when Palti was constructively evicted. Palti said that there was black mold growing throughout his unit, the heat had been broken for six weeks, the hot water heater would only produce about eight gallons of hot water a day, and the roof was leaking over the kitchen. Palti said he notified Dalila of each issue, in writing, and she refused to fix anything. Palti also said that when he brought the issues up verbally while he was delivering his rent, Dalila told him to "stop being so sensitive."

Two weeks after that incident Palti became so ill—he believes from his living conditions—that he left and is now staying in a motel. As his attorney, Pam asked Palti for copies of the notices he gave Dalila, but he said he didn't make copies and didn't take any pictures. Furthermore, he didn't have a "lease," only a verbal agreement that he can stay in this unit for $500 a month. He always paid his rent in cash, and he never asked for or received a receipt for his rent or deposit payments. *Under these circumstances, how much investigation should Pam do prior to filing a complaint on behalf of Palti? What would a court deem to be reasonable under the circumstances?*

IN PRACTICE

Although it may seem exciting on television when lawyers get out of the office and investigate cases, in real life attorneys need to be careful about this. If a lawyer is required to testify at trial about a finding, she could be disqualified from the case pursuant to ABA Model Rule of Professional Conduct 3.7. The rule has some escape hatches but even so, most lawyers will want to avoid these risks and have fact investigations conducted by non-lawyers working for the attorney such as legal assistants, private investigators, and expert witnesses.

Quick Summary

- Rule 11 is a lawyer's conscience. By signing papers filed with the court, a lawyer certifies that the filing was properly made.

- A filing is proper if it has evidentiary and legal support. Thus, Rule 11 requires that the lawyer and her client consider carefully the basis of the claims or defenses being made, both factually and legally.

- Rule 11 attempts to strike a balance between creating a disincentive to cheat and creating a disincentive to file a potentially meritorious case at all. The 21-day safe-harbor period allows the party to withdraw its filing before being sanctioned.

- The court has discretion to award or reject sanctions. When it grants sanctions, it has further discretion to fashion sanctions that appropriately meet the sanctionable offense.

6

Pleading

Key Concepts

- Pleading claims or defenses
- Admitting or denying allegations
- Pleading in the alternative, hypothetically, or inconsistently

Introduction

There are three basic types of pleadings. First, the complaint is the document that presents the allegations that a party is making. A federal civil action is commenced by filing a complaint with the court. Second, the answer responds to those allegations. The answer must precisely and fairly admit those allegations in the complaint that are true, deny those allegations that are not true, or state that the party does not have the requisite knowledge to respond to the claim, which is treated as a denial. The answer is also where the responding party will assert any affirmative defenses it may have. Third, the court may require or permit a party to respond to an answer by filing a document known as a reply. The reply may serve to clarify or supplement an allegation.

The primary goal of the pleadings is to put the parties on notice of each other's claims and defenses. Rule 8 itself explicitly requires the parties to say very little. This kind of pleading is called notice pleading, meaning that a party need only plead enough information to put the opposing party on notice of the claims against her and/or the defenses being raised. Notice pleading is designed to facilitate the resolution of civil disputes on their merits rather than based on a hyper-technical pleading defect. Plaintiffs often are unable to include detailed factual allegations in their complaint because such information may be under the control of the defendant who cannot be compelled to disclose it before the complaint is filed. As a result, any pleading regime that requires detailed factual allegations in a complaint may prevent meritorious civil cases from being filed or from being successfully litigated. Notice pleading was designed to ensure that such meritorious claims will not be blocked at the initial pleading stage of the lawsuit.

Over the years, however, courts and parties have challenged these bare-bones pleading requirements as they pertain to the complaint. Critics argued that plaintiffs were able to make frivolous claims in the hopes of extracting a coerced settlement from the defendant. Because the pleading requirements were so low, they argued, plaintiffs could count on defendants to settle instead of taking their chances with the overwhelming cost and risk of the litigation process. For many years, the Supreme Court rebuffed challenges to the pleading requirements. It argued that any changes to Rule 8 had to go through the rulemaking process, as required by the Rules Enabling Act, 28 U.S.C. § 2072. *See* Unit II Overview. Thus, the Court repeatedly held that until that process changed the rule, notice pleading was the law of the land. Recently, however, the Supreme Court's construction of this rule has led to more rigorous requirements than what one might think is required from the face of the rule itself. What is required under Rule 8 is still unsettled, but this chapter will explore the most recent Supreme Court decision in this area and will discuss what the effect of this decision might be on pleading requirements going forward.

A. Rule 8(a): The Claim for Relief

Rule 8(a) explains what a complaint must contain in order to move the case forward.

THE RULE	Rule 8(a)

Claim for Relief

A pleading that states a claim for relief must contain:
(1) **a short and plain statement** of the grounds for the court's jurisdiction, unless the court already has **jurisdiction** and the claim needs no new jurisdictional support;
(2) **a short and plain statement** of the claim showing that the pleader is **entitled to relief**; and
(3) a **demand for the relief** sought, which may include relief in the alternative or different types of relief.

EXPLANATION

 Rule 8(a)(1) requires the party to set forth the basis for the court's jurisdiction over the cause of action. This generally means that the pleader needs to state that jurisdiction is based on federal question, diversity, and/or supplemental jurisdiction. *See* Chapter 2. For example, in diversity cases, the party must allege the citizenship of each of the parties and that the amount in controversy exceeds $75,000. For federal question jurisdiction, the party must allege the provision of the Constitution, federal law, or treaty that serves as the basis of her claim. Finally, for supplemental jurisdiction, the party must allege that a particular claim is part of the same case or controversy as a claim for which there is a primary jurisdictional basis such that the court will have jurisdiction under 28 U.S.C. § 1367.

Rule 8(a)(2) requires the party to set forth a "short and plain statement" of the claim—one that will demonstrate that the party is entitled to relief. This concept will be explored in greater detail, but the basic requirement is that the pleader must set forth enough information for the defending party to know the basis of the claim against it.

Finally, Rule 8(a)(3) requires that the pleader set out the remedy it is seeking.

> The rule does not speak in terms of plaintiffs and defendants. Instead, it refers to each side as a party. While it is true that a plaintiff generally files a complaint and a defendant generally files an answer, it is not always the case. The pleading requirements of Rule 8 apply to parties who assert claims or defenses under a host of different joinder rules as third-parties, intervenors, indispensable parties, and class members. *See* Chapters 8 and 9. The rule provides the necessary flexibility to apply to all of these potential situations. For example, a defendant can file counterclaims or crossclaims, in which case it effectively becomes both a defendant and a counterclaim or crossclaim plaintiff. Similarly, a plaintiff may become a defendant in a counterclaim such that it will be both a plaintiff and a counterclaim defendant.

EXAMPLES & ANALYSIS

EXAMPLE: Purses, Inc., a fine purveyor of handbags, discovered that Discount Bags is selling allegedly counterfeit Purses, Inc. products. Purses, Inc. filed a complaint with the United States District Court for the District of Columbia. Its complaint included only the following: "Discount Bags has engaged in copyright infringement under the Copyright Act, 17 U.S.C. § 101 *et seq.*" Does this meet the requirements of Rule 8(a)?

Analysis: No. Although this section meets the requirement of Rule 8(a)(1), because the complaint sets forth the basis for jurisdiction—in this case the federal question presented by the Copyright Act—the complaint is silent as to the requirements of 8(a)(2) and 8(a)(3). Thus, it fails under Rule 8(a).

EXAMPLE: Assume the same factual situation, but now Purses, Inc.'s complaint reads as follows: "Discount Bags has engaged in copyright infringement under the Copyright Act, 17 U.S.C. § 101 *et seq.* Purses, Inc. has a valid copyright registered with the Copyright Office for several notable features of its handbags, including but not limited to, a valid copyright for its 'Regal Stripe' design (registration number Tau555202555). Discount Bags has available for purchase approximately ten counterfeit Purses, Inc. items, including handbags that bear multiple Purses, Inc. registered copyrights. Discount Bags is not an authorized retailer or manufacturer of Purses, Inc. handbags, and thus is violating Purses, Inc. copyright(s)." Does Purse's complaint meet the requirements of Rule 8(a)?

Analysis: No. Although it meets Rule 8(a)(1) and 8(a)(2), it does not meet Rule 8(a)(3). The requirement under Rule 8(a)(1) is met, as described above. The requirement under Rule 8(a)(2) is met because Discount Bags is on notice regarding the nature of the claims against it. (The sufficiency of this allegation is a complicated question, as discussed later in this chapter.) However, the complaint is silent as to the remedy that Purses, Inc. is seeking and thus does not satisfy Rule(a)(3).

EXAMPLE: Assume the same factual situation, but now in addition to the language in the previous example, the following is added: "Discount Bags is liable to Purses, Inc. and requests that the court order Discount Bags to account to and pay to Purses, Inc. all profits realized by their wrongful acts and also award Purses, Inc. its actual damages. Purses, Inc. also requests that the court enter an injunction requiring Discount Bags to immediately cease producing its infringing product." Does Purses complaint meet the requirements of Rule 8(a)?

Analysis: Yes. Purses has met all three requirements of Rule 8(a)—the jurisdictional statement, the statement of its claim, and the request for damages.

Further Explanation: The Evolution of Pleading Standards

As the examples above suggest, Rule 8(a) seems simple enough on its face. However, pleading requirements—specifically what Rule 8(a)(2) requires—have long been controversial and, to some degree, unsettled. When the rules were originally adopted in 1938, the drafters chose a "notice pleading" regime. The drafters made this choice in light of experience under two other pleading systems—common law and code.

Parties in the common law pleading system used various writs to make their cases. Writs are particular forms of action that English courts used to hear common law cases. When an individual had a grievance, he chose a writ that most closely matched what had happened to him. So, for example, if he had been in an accident and wanted to sue the person who injured him, he would file a writ in trespass (the precursor to the modern tort). The writ essentially provided all of the rules and requirements for making that particular claim. This made the process predictable, but it also meant that failure to choose the correct writ or any attempt to vary what was required under the writ was fatal. The writ system was also inefficient because the parties had to go back and forth over the facts until one single issue—either factual or legal—was ready to be resolved by the judge or jury. This back and forth could take an inordinate amount of time and could often leave other issues unresolved. Moreover, the system became so technical that many felt it was unfair.

American colonies adopted the writ system when they settled in the United States, but by the mid-1800s, some states began experimenting with other forms of pleading. Code pleading emerged as the major alternative to common law pleading. For instance, David Dudley Field, a New York City attorney, led the effort to adopt code pleading in New York, so the practice in that state was referred to as the Field Code. The purpose of code pleading was to get rid of the substantive divisions created by the writ system and to focus instead on the pertinent facts of the claim. Plaintiffs were not required to fit their case into a writ. Instead, they could file a case as one civil action and plead facts giving rise to potentially several causes of action. Some of the negative aspects of the writ system were thus avoided. The plaintiff was able to plead multiple causes of action, and the defendant was able to respond to all of them, eliminating the need for the back and forth created by the writ system. However, code pleading also had its shortcomings. It was not clear which facts needed to be pled, and even then, which facts were pure facts and which were simply legal conclusions. Code pleading did not favor the pleading of evidence, yet it also did not favor pleading legal conclusions. The line between these two concepts—the facts necessary to state a claim and evidentiary or conclusory facts—was fuzzy. This created great confusion among lawyers and courts alike.

> England also had a separate equity system that allowed for the resolution of claims that could not otherwise be resolved under law. The United States adopted the same system, providing separately for courts of law and courts of equity. When the Enabling Act was adopted in 1934 in the United States, it merged law and equity into one civil action. The Federal Rules of Civil Procedure thus reflect many procedures that had evolved under the equity system, including joinder and discovery, and other procedures that can be traced to common law.

Thus, when the rulemakers met to adopt a pleading regime, they rejected both the writ and code pleading systems. In their place, the rulemakers decided to adopt notice pleading. The point of notice pleading was not to require that every fact be pleaded or even that every potential legal theory be specifically stated. The goal was to put the opposing party on notice of the essential nature of the claims made against him. Whether the facts could be proven at trial was not decided at the pleading stage. Factual allegations were assumed to be true and the question of the sufficiency of the complaint was whether the party stated enough to entitle him to relief under applicable law.

The notice pleading regime worked quite well, but some lawyers and judges began to question whether such loose pleading requirements allowed frivolous and/or coercive lawsuits to be filed. Some courts began reading the pleading requirements more strictly, but the Supreme Court pushed back on such a narrow reading numerous times. The most notable case was decided in 1957, *Conley v. Gibson*, 355 U.S. 41. In that case, African American railroad employees were fired when their jobs were "abolished." In reality, those jobs remained, and they were refilled by white employees. The African American employees sued the railroad union, alleging that it did nothing to aid them and instead only protected the white union members. The case was dismissed at both the district and appellate court levels because the complaint failed to state a claim upon which relief could be granted.

> In order to challenge whether the case is properly pleaded under Rule 8, a defendant must bring a Rule 12(b)(6) motion. This motion is brought before the answer is filed, and in essence, it states that the complaint has failed to meet the requirements of Rule 8(a)(2)—it has failed to state a claim upon which relief can be granted. The cases discussed in this chapter and the case excerpted are all decisions regarding a defendant's Rule 12(b)(6) motion, or a motion to dismiss for failure to state a claim. In Chapter 7, the timing and other limitations of Rule 12(b)(6) will be discussed.

The Supreme Court reversed this decision, finding that the complaint should have survived. The Court disagreed with the lower courts' view that general allegations of discrimination were insufficient because the plaintiffs needed to set out specific facts. Instead, the Court reasoned that Rule 8 only required notice; after all, this was not a fact or code pleading regime. *Conley's* most important contribution to this area of the law was its use of talismanic language that since became the hallmark of all cases involving pleading. First, the Court wrote that "a complaint should not be dismissed for failure to state a claim unless it appears beyond doubt that the plaintiff can prove no set of facts in support of his claim which would entitle him to relief." *Conley*, 355 U.S. at 45-46. Second, the Court wrote that "[a]ll the Rules require is a 'short and plain statement of the claim' that will give the defendant fair notice of what the plaintiff's claim is and the grounds upon which it rests." *Id.* at 47. *Conley* and its key language set the bar quite low for pleading. As long as there were some set of facts that could entitle the plaintiff to relief, the complaint would survive.

Conley did not stop courts and parties from continuing to challenge the breadth of the notice pleading regime. At least two other cases challenged this regime, but once again the Supreme Court appeared to push back. The first was *Leatherman v. Tarrant County Narcotics Intelligence and Coordination Unit*, 507 U.S. 163 (1993). In that case, the plaintiffs alleged that their Fourth Amendment rights had been violated by a division of the local police department. Plaintiffs brought what is called a § 1983 claim, which allows private individuals to bring claims against particular government actors for constitutional violations. The thrust of their allegation was that Tarrant County should be held accountable because it had failed to properly train its officers. The district and appellate courts dismissed the complaint because they found that civil rights cases

> Liability against a municipality for its policies, customs, or laws is called *Monell* or municipal liability, arising from a case called *Monell v. Department of Soc. Servs.*, 436 U.S. 658 (1978). One way to prove municipal liability is to show that the municipality failed to properly train its employees.

like the one at issue in *Leatherman* required "heightened pleading requirements." The reasoning was that heightened pleading was necessary in this context in order to protect municipalities from frivolous lawsuits. The Court rejected this conclusion and held that Rule 8 required only a "short and plain statement." 507 U.S. at 168. It further held that the lower courts were requiring higher pleading standards, yet the only rule requiring such specificity was Rule 9, and Rule 9 was not implicated in this case.

> Rule 9, discussed later in this chapter, requires that when a plaintiff makes a claim of fraud or mistake, he must plead particularized facts. The rule does not require that the plaintiff specifically plead the defendant's state of mind, but he must plead the who, what, when, where, and why of the events giving rise to the claim of fraud or mistake.

The next Supreme Court case to challenge the pleading standards of Rule 8 was decided in 2002. *Swierkiewicz v. Sorema N.A.*, 534 U.S. 506 (2002), was an employment discrimination case. Once again, the lower courts dismissed the complaint because it failed to allege particularized facts that would prove a prima facie case of discrimination. Once again, the Court rejected the requirement of particularity. It held that the plaintiff had pleaded enough. The plaintiff had stated that he believed he was terminated because of his national origin and because of his age. He had also provided some dates and relevant information regarding the names and ages of the individuals involved in his termination. The Court determined that these "allegations [gave] respondent fair notice of what petitioner's claims are and the grounds upon which they rest." 534 U.S. at 514. The Court also observed that to hold otherwise would require a change to Rule 8, a change that would have to be obtained through the Rules Enabling Act rulemaking process. *See* Richard L. Marcus, *The Puzzling Persistence of Pleading Practice*, 76 Tex. L. Rev. 1749 (1998) (summarizing how pleading under Rule 8 was challenged by parties and courts alike).

The issue of pleading seemed well-settled following *Leatherman* and *Swierkiewicz*, but in 2007, the Court decided a case called *Bell Atlantic Corp. v. Twombly*, 550 U.S. 544 (2007). In *Twombly*, the plaintiffs, a group of local telecommunication companies, alleged that the Baby Bell telephone companies tacitly agreed not to compete in order to keep monopolies in their respective regions. (In 1984 after an action by the Department of Justice, AT&T divested itself of the Bell Operating Companies. This led to the creation of regional telephone companies, referred to as Baby Bells.) The effect of this conspiracy, the plaintiffs alleged, was to prevent them from effectively competing in those same markets. The Court determined that the complaint was rightly dismissed because the bare allegation of parallel conduct by the telephone companies was not enough to show that the companies conspired. The plaintiffs needed to state facts that would make the claim of conspiracy plausible. The Court expressed concern about meritless cases, and it rejected the argument that judges could effectively manage discovery to prevent defendants from needlessly settling a case—the fear being that the high costs of discovery often coerce innocent defendants into settling. Instead, the plaintiff must state a plausible claim at the outset; if she does not, then her complaint must be dismissed. Thus, in *Twombly*, the Court "retired" the talismanic *Conley* "no-set-of-facts" language, and instead required that in order to survive a motion to dismiss, a plaintiff's claim must be "plausible." 550 U.S. at 556, 563.

> Note that the word **plausible** does not appear in the text of Rule 8, but it is now a critical term when evaluating pleadings under the rule.

After *Twombly*, the question was whether it was a case that could be limited to its antitrust facts or whether it was a decision of greater impact. The answer came in *Ashcroft v. Iqbal*, 556 U.S. 662 (2009).

FROM THE COURT

Ashcroft v. Iqbal
556 U.S. 662 (2009)
Supreme Court of the United States

Justice KENNEDY delivered the opinion of the Court.

Respondent Javaid Iqbal is a citizen of Pakistan and a Muslim. In the wake of the September 11, 2001, terrorist attacks he was arrested in the United States on criminal charges and detained by federal officials. Respondent claims he was deprived of various constitutional protections while in federal custody. To redress the alleged deprivations, respondent filed a complaint against numerous federal officials, including John Ashcroft, the former Attorney General of the United States, and Robert Mueller, the Director of the Federal Bureau of Investigation (FBI). Ashcroft and Mueller are the petitioners in the case now before us. As to these two petitioners, the complaint alleges that they adopted an unconstitutional policy that subjected respondent to harsh conditions of confinement on account of his race, religion, or national origin.

In the District Court petitioners raised the defense of qualified immunity and moved to dismiss the suit, contending the complaint was not sufficient to state a claim against them. The District Court denied the motion to dismiss, concluding the complaint was sufficient to state a claim despite petitioners' official status at the times in question. . . . [T]he Second Circuit . . . affirmed the District Court's decision.

This case . . . turns on a narrow[] question: Did respondent, as the plaintiff in the District Court, plead factual matter that, if taken as true, states a claim that petitioners deprived him of his clearly established constitutional rights. We hold respondent's pleadings are insufficient.

I

Following the 2001 attacks, the FBI and other entities within the Department of Justice began an investigation of vast reach to identify the assailants and prevent them from attacking anew. The FBI dedicated more than 4,000 special agents and 3,000 support personnel to the endeavor. By September 18 "the FBI had received more than 96,000 tips or potential leads from the public...."

In the ensuing months the FBI questioned more than 1,000 people with suspected links to the attacks in particular or to terrorism in general. Of those individuals, some 762 were held on immigration charges; and a 184-member subset of that group was deemed to be "of 'high interest'" to the investigation. The high-interest detainees were held under restrictive conditions designed to prevent them from communicating with the general prison population or the outside world.

Respondent was one of the [high-interest] detainees. According to his complaint, in November 2001 agents of the FBI and Immigration and Naturalization Service arrested him on charges of fraud in relation to identification documents and conspiracy to defraud the United States. Pending trial for those crimes, respondent was housed at the Metropolitan Detention Center (MDC) in Brooklyn, New York. Respondent was designated a person "of high interest" to the September 11 investigation and in January 2002 was placed in a section of the MDC known as the Administrative Maximum Special Housing Unit (ADMAX SHU). As the facility's name indicates, the ADMAX SHU incorporates the maximum security conditions allowable under Federal Bureau of Prison regulations. ADMAX SHU detainees were kept in lockdown 23 hours a day, spending the remaining hour outside their cells in handcuffs and leg irons accompanied by a four-officer escort.

Respondent pleaded guilty to the criminal charges, served a term of imprisonment, and was removed to his native Pakistan. He then filed a *Bivens* action in the United States District Court for the Eastern District of New York against 34 current and former federal officials and 19 "John Doe" federal corrections officers. See *Bivens v. Six Unknown Fed. Narcotics Agents*, 403 U.S. 388 (1971). The defendants range from the correctional officers who had day-to-day contact with respondent during the term of his confinement, to the wardens of the MDC facility, all the way to petitioners-officials who were at the highest level of the federal law enforcement hierarchy.

* * *

The allegations against petitioners [Ashcroft and Mueller] are the only ones relevant here. The complaint contends that petitioners designated respondent a person of high interest on account of his race, religion, or national origin, in contravention of the First and Fifth Amendments to the Constitution. The complaint alleges that "the [FBI], under the direction of Defendant Mueller, arrested and detained thousands of Arab Muslim men ... as part of its investigation of the events of September 11." It further alleges that "[t]he policy of holding post-September-11th detainees in highly restrictive conditions of confinement until they were 'cleared' by the FBI was approved by Defendants Ashcroft and Mueller in discussions in the weeks after September 11, 2001." Lastly, the complaint posits that petitioners "each knew of, condoned, and willfully and maliciously agreed to subject" respondent to harsh conditions of confinement "as a matter of policy, solely on account of [his] religion, race, and/or national origin and for no legitimate penological interest." The pleading names Ashcroft as the "principal architect" of the policy, and identifies Mueller as "instrumental in [its] adoption, promulgation, and implementation."

Petitioners moved to dismiss the complaint for failure to state sufficient allegations to show their own involvement in clearly established unconstitutional conduct. The District Court denied their motion. Accepting all of the allegations in respondent's complaint as true, the court held that "it cannot be said that there [is] no set of facts on which [respondent] would be entitled to relief as against" petitioners. *Id.* (relying on *Conley v. Gibson*, 355 U.S. 41 (1957)). Invoking the collateral-order doctrine petitioners filed an interlocutory appeal in the United States Court of Appeals for the Second Circuit. While that appeal was pending, this Court decided *Bell Atlantic Corp. v. Twombly*, 550 U.S. 544 (2007), which discussed the standard for evaluating whether a complaint is sufficient to survive a motion to dismiss.

The Court of Appeals considered *Twombly*'s applicability to this case. Acknowledging that *Twombly* retired the Conley no-set-of-facts test relied upon by the District Court, the Court of Appeals' opinion discussed at length how to apply this Court's "standard for assessing the adequacy of pleadings." 490 F.3d, at 155. It concluded that *Twombly* called for a "flexible 'plausibility standard,' which obliges a pleader to amplify a claim with some factual allegations in those contexts where such amplification is needed to render the claim plausible." *Id.* at 157-158. The court found that petitioners' appeal did not present one of "those contexts" requiring amplification. As a consequence, it held respondent's pleading adequate to allege petitioners' personal involvement in discriminatory decisions which, if true, violated clearly established constitutional law. *Id.* at 174.

* * *

III

In *Twombly*, the Court found it necessary first to discuss the antitrust principles implicated by the complaint. Here too we begin by taking note of the elements a plaintiff must plead to state a claim of unconstitutional discrimination against officials entitled to assert the defense of qualified immunity.

* * *

In the limited settings where *Bivens* does apply, the implied cause of action is the "federal analog to suits brought against state officials under Rev. Stat. § 1979, 42 U.S.C. § 1983." *Hartman*, 547 U.S., at 254, n. 2. Based on the rules our precedents establish, respondent correctly concedes that Government officials may not be held liable for the unconstitutional conduct of their subordinates under a theory of respondeat superior.... Because vicarious liability is inapplicable to *Bivens* and § 1983 suits, a plaintiff must plead that each Government-official defendant, through the official's own individual actions, has violated the Constitution.

The factors necessary to establish a *Bivens* violation will vary with the constitutional provision at issue. Where the claim is invidious discrimination in contravention of the First and Fifth Amendments, our decisions make clear that the plaintiff must plead and prove that the defendant acted with discriminatory purpose.... It instead involves a decisionmaker's undertaking a course of action "'because of,' not merely 'in spite of,' [the action's] adverse effects upon an identifiable group." [*Church of Lukumi Babalu Aye, Inc. v. Hialeah*, 508 U.S. 520, 540-541 (1993)]. It follows that, to state a claim based on a violation of a clearly established right, respondent must plead sufficient factual matter to show that petitioners adopted and implemented the detention policies at issue not for a neutral, investigative reason but for the purpose of discriminating on account of race, religion, or national origin.

Respondent disagrees. He argues that, under a theory of "supervisory liability," petitioners can be liable for "knowledge and acquiescence in their subordinates' use of discriminatory criteria to make classification decisions among detainees." That is to say, respondent believes a supervisor's mere knowledge of his subordinate's discriminatory purpose amounts to the supervisor's violating the Constitution. We reject this argument. Respondent's conception of "supervisory liability" is inconsistent with his accurate stipulation that petitioners may not be held accountable for the misdeeds of their agents. In a § 1983 suit or a *Bivens* action-where masters do not answer for the torts of their servants-the term "supervisory liability" is a misnomer. Absent vicarious liability, each Government official, his or her title notwithstanding, is only liable for his or her own misconduct....

* * *

IV

A

. . . Under Federal Rule of Civil Procedure 8(a)(2), a pleading must contain a "short and plain statement of the claim showing that the pleader is entitled to relief." As the Court held in *Twombly*, the pleading standard Rule 8 announces does not require "detailed factual allegations," but it demands more than an unadorned, the-defendant-unlawfully-harmed-me accusation. *Id.* at 555. A pleading that offers "labels and conclusions" or "a formulaic recitation of the elements of a cause of action will not do." *Id.* Nor does a complaint suffice if it tenders "naked assertion[s]" devoid of "further factual enhancement." *Id.* at 557.

To survive a motion to dismiss, a complaint must contain sufficient factual matter, accepted as true, to "state a claim to relief that is plausible on its face." *Id.* at 570. A claim has facial plausibility when the plaintiff pleads factual content that allows the court to draw the reasonable inference that the defendant is liable for the misconduct alleged. The plausibility standard is not akin to a "probability requirement," but it asks for more than a sheer possibility that a defendant has acted unlaw-fully. Where a complaint pleads facts that are "merely consistent with" a defendant's liability, it "stops short of the line between possibility and plausibility of 'entitlement to relief.'" *Id.* at 557.

Two working principles underlie our decision in *Twombly*. First, the te-net that a court must accept as true all of the allegations contained in a complaint is inapplicable to legal conclusions. Threadbare recitals of the elements of a cause of action, supported by mere conclusory state-ments, do not suffice. *Id.* at 555 (Although for the purposes of a motion to dismiss we must take all of the factual allegations in the complaint as true, we "are not bound to accept as true a legal conclusion couched as a factual allegation."). Rule 8 marks a notable and generous departure from the hyper-technical, code-pleading regime of a prior era, but it does not unlock the doors of discovery for a plaintiff armed with nothing more than conclusions. Second, only a complaint that states a plausible claim for relief survives a motion to dismiss. Determining whether a complaint states a plausible claim for relief will, as the Court of Appeals observed, be a context-specific task that requires the reviewing court to draw on its judicial experience and common sense. But where the well-pleaded facts do not permit the court to infer more than the mere possibility of misconduct, the complaint has alleged—but it has not "show[n]"—"that the pleader is entitled to relief." Fed. Rule Civ. Proc. 8(a)(2).

In keeping with these principles a court considering a motion to dis-miss can choose to begin by identifying pleadings that, because they are no more than conclusions, are not entitled to the assumption of truth. While legal conclusions can provide the framework of a complaint, they must be supported by factual allegations. When there are well-pleaded factual allegations, a court should assume their veracity and then deter-mine whether they plausibly give rise to an entitlement to relief.

Our decision in *Twombly* illustrates the two-pronged approach. There, we considered the sufficiency of a complaint alleging that incumbent telecommunications providers had entered an agreement not to compete and to forestall competitive entry, in violation of the Sherman Act, 15 U.S.C. § 1. Recognizing that § 1 enjoins only anticompetitive conduct "effected by a contract, combination, or conspiracy," *Copperweld Corp. v. Independence Tube Corp.*, 467 U.S. 752, 775 (1984), the plaintiffs in *Twombly* flatly pleaded that the defendants "ha[d] entered into a contract, combination or conspiracy to prevent competitive entry ... and ha[d] agreed not to compete with one another." 550 U.S. at 551. The complaint also alleged that the defendants' "parallel course of conduct ... to prevent competition" and inflate prices was indicative of the unlawful agreement alleged. *Id.*

The Court held the plaintiffs' complaint deficient under Rule 8. In doing so it first noted that the plaintiffs' assertion of an unlawful agreement was a "'legal conclusion'" and, as such, was not entitled to the assumption of truth. *Id.* at 555. Had the Court simply credited the allegation of a conspiracy, the plaintiffs would have stated a claim for relief and been entitled to proceed perforce. The Court next addressed the "nub" of the plaintiffs' complaint-the well-pleaded, nonconclusory factual allegation of parallel behavior-to determine whether it gave rise to a "plausible suggestion of conspiracy." *Id.* at 565-66. Acknowledging that parallel conduct was consistent with an unlawful agreement, the Court nevertheless concluded that it did not plausibly suggest an illicit accord because it was not only compatible with, but indeed was more likely explained by, lawful, unchoreographed free-market behavior. *Id.* at 567. Because the well-pleaded fact of parallel conduct, accepted as true, did not plausibly suggest an unlawful agreement, the Court held the plaintiffs' complaint must be dismissed. *Id.* at 570.

B

Under *Twombly*'s construction of Rule 8, we conclude that respondent's complaint has not "nudged [his] claims" of invidious discrimination "across the line from conceivable to plausible." *Id.*

We begin our analysis by identifying the allegations in the complaint that are not entitled to the assumption of truth. Respondent pleads that petitioners "knew of, condoned, and willfully and maliciously agreed to subject [him]" to harsh conditions of confinement "as a matter of policy, solely on account of [his] religion, race, and/or national origin and for no legitimate penological interest." The complaint alleges that Ashcroft was the "principal architect" of this invidious policy, and that Mueller was "instrumental" in adopting and executing it. These bare assertions... amount to nothing more than a "formulaic recitation of the elements" of a constitutional discrimination claim, namely, that petitioners adopted a policy "'because of,' not merely 'in spite of,' its adverse effects upon an identifiable group." *Feeney*, 442 U.S. at 279. As such, the allegations are conclusory and not entitled to be assumed true. To be clear, we do not reject these bald allegations on the ground that they are unrealistic or nonsensical. We do not so characterize them any more than the Court in *Twombly* rejected the plaintiffs' express allegation of a "contract, combination or conspiracy to prevent competitive entry," *Id.* at 551, because it thought that claim too chimerical to be maintained. It is the conclusory nature of respondent's allegations, rather than their extravagantly fanciful nature, that disentitles them to the presumption of truth.

We next consider the factual allegations in respondent's complaint to determine if they plausibly suggest an entitlement to relief. The complaint alleges that "the [FBI], under the direction of Defendant Mueller, arrested and detained thousands of Arab Muslim men ... as part of its investigation of the events of September 11." It further claims that "[t]he policy of holding post-September-11th detainees in highly restrictive conditions of confinement until they were 'cleared' by the FBI was approved by Defendants Ashcroft and Mueller in discussions in the weeks after September 11, 2001." Taken as true, these allegations are consistent with petitioners' purposefully designating detainees "of high interest" because of their race, religion, or national origin. But given more likely explanations, they do not plausibly establish this purpose.

The September 11 attacks were perpetrated by 19 Arab Muslim hijackers who counted themselves members in good standing of al Qaeda, an Islamic fundamentalist group. Al Qaeda was headed by another Arab Muslim—Osama bin Laden—and composed in large part of his Arab Muslim disciples. It should come as no surprise that a legitimate policy directing law enforcement to arrest and detain individuals because of their suspected link to the attacks would produce a disparate, incidental impact on Arab Muslims, even though the purpose of the policy was to target neither Arabs nor Muslims. On the facts respondent alleges the arrests Mueller oversaw were likely lawful and justified by his nondiscriminatory intent to detain aliens who were illegally present in the United States and who had potential connections to those who committed terrorist acts. As between that "obvious alternative explanation" for the arrests, *Twombly*, 550 U.S. at 567, and the purposeful, invidious discrimination respondent asks us to infer, discrimination is not a plausible conclusion.

But even if the complaint's well-pleaded facts give rise to a plausible inference that respondent's arrest was the result of unconstitutional discrimination, that inference alone would not entitle respondent to relief. It is important to recall that respondent's complaint challenges neither the constitutionality of his arrest nor his initial detention in the MDC. Respondent's constitutional claims against petitioners rest solely on their ostensible "policy of holding post-September-11th detainees" in the ADMAX SHU once they were categorized as "of high interest." To prevail on that theory, the complaint must contain facts plausibly showing that petitioners purposefully adopted a policy of classifying post-September-11 detainees as "of high interest" because of their race, religion, or national origin.

This the complaint fails to do. Though respondent alleges that various other defendants, who are not before us, may have labeled him a person "of high interest" for impermissible reasons, his only factual allegation against petitioners accuses them of adopting a policy approving "restrictive conditions of confinement" for post-September-11 detainees until they were "'cleared' by the FBI." Accepting the truth of that allegation, the complaint does not show, or even intimate, that petitioners purposefully housed detainees in the ADMAX SHU due to their race, religion, or national origin. All it plausibly suggests is that the Nation's top law enforcement officers, in the aftermath of a devastating terrorist attack, sought to keep suspected terrorists in the most secure conditions available until the suspects could be cleared of terrorist activity. Respondent does not argue, nor can he, that such a motive would violate petitioners' constitutional obligations. He would need to allege more by way of factual content to "nudg[e]" his claim of purposeful discrimination "across the line from conceivable to plausible." *Twombly*, 550 U.S. at 570.

To be sure, respondent can attempt to draw certain contrasts between the pleadings the Court considered in *Twombly* and the pleadings at issue here. In *Twombly*, the complaint alleged general wrongdoing that extended over a period of years, *Id.* at 551, whereas here the complaint alleges discrete wrongs-for instance, beatings-by lower level Government actors. The allegations here, if true, and if condoned by petitioners, could be the basis for some inference of wrongful intent on petitioners' part. Despite these distinctions, respondent's pleadings do not suffice to state a claim. Unlike in *Twombly*, where the doctrine of respondeat superior could bind the corporate defendant, here, as we have noted, petitioners cannot be held liable unless they themselves acted on account of a constitutionally protected characteristic. Yet respondent's complaint does not contain any factual allegation sufficient to plausibly suggest petitioners' discriminatory state of mind. His pleadings thus do not meet the standard necessary to comply with Rule 8.

It is important to note, however, that we express no opinion concerning the sufficiency of respondent's complaint against the defendants who are not before us. Respondent's account of his prison ordeal alleges serious official misconduct that we need not address here. Our decision is limited to the determination that respondent's complaint does not entitle him to relief from petitioners [Ashcroft and Mueller].

* * *

V

We hold that respondent's complaint fails to plead sufficient facts to state a claim for purposeful and unlawful discrimination against petitioners. The Court of Appeals should decide in the first instance whether to remand to the District Court so that respondent can seek leave to amend his deficient complaint.

The judgment of the Court of Appeals is reversed, and the case is remanded for further proceedings consistent with this opinion.

It is so ordered.

Justice Souter, with whom Justice Stevens, Justice Ginsburg, and Justice Breyer join, dissenting:

* * *

I

A

Iqbal claims that on the day he was transferred to the special unit, prison guards, without provocation, "picked him up and threw him against the wall, kicked him in the stomach, punched him in the face, and dragged him across the room." He says that after being attacked a second time he sought medical attention but was denied care for two weeks. According to Iqbal's complaint, [for more than six months while he was held in the

Special Housing Unit] prison staff in the special unit subjected him to unjustified strip and body cavity searches, verbally berated him as a "'terrorist'" and "'Muslim killer,'" refused to give him adequate food, and intentionally turned on air conditioning during the winter and heating during the summer. He claims that prison staff interfered with his attempts to pray and engage in religious study and with his access to counsel.

* * *

II

Given petitioners' concession, the complaint satisfies Rule 8(a)(2). Ashcroft and Mueller admit they are liable for their subordinates' conduct if they "had actual knowledge of the assertedly discriminatory nature of the classification of suspects as being 'of high interest' and they were deliberately indifferent to that discrimination." Iqbal alleges that after the September 11 attacks the Federal Bureau of Investigation (FBI) "arrested and detained thousands of Arab Muslim men," that many of these men were designated by high-ranking FBI officials as being "'of high interest,'" and that in many cases, including Iqbal's, this designation was made "because of the race, religion, and national origin of the detainees, and not because of any evidence of the detainees' involvement in supporting terrorist activity." The complaint further alleges that Ashcroft was the "principal architect of the policies and practices challenged," and that Mueller "was instrumental in the adoption, promulgation, and implementation of the policies and practices challenged." According to the complaint, Ashcroft and Mueller "knew of, condoned, and willfully and maliciously agreed to subject [Iqbal] to these conditions of confinement as a matter of policy, solely on account of [his] religion, race, and/or national origin and for no legitimate penological interest." The complaint thus alleges, at a bare minimum, that Ashcroft and Mueller knew of and condoned the discriminatory policy their subordinates carried out. Actually, the complaint goes further in alleging that Ashcroft and Mueller affirmatively acted to create the discriminatory detention policy. If these factual allegations are true, Ashcroft and Mueller were, at the very least, aware of the discriminatory policy being implemented and deliberately indifferent to it.

Ashcroft and Mueller argue that these allegations fail to satisfy the "plausibility standard" of *Twombly*. They contend that Iqbal's claims are implausible because such high-ranking officials "tend not to be personally involved in the specific actions of lower-level officers down the bureaucratic chain of command." But this response bespeaks a fundamental misunderstanding of the enquiry that *Twombly* demands. *Twombly* does not require a court at the motion-to-dismiss stage to consider whether the factual allegations are probably true. We made it clear, on the contrary, that a court must take the allegations as true, no matter how skeptical the court may be.... The sole exception to this rule lies with allegations that are sufficiently fantastic to defy reality as we know it: claims about little green men, or the plaintiff's recent trip to Pluto, or experiences in time travel. That is not what we have here.

Under *Twombly*, the relevant question is whether, assuming the factual allegations are true, the plaintiff has stated a ground for relief that is plausible. That is, in *Twombly*'s words, a plaintiff must "allege facts" that, taken as true, are "suggestive of illegal conduct." 550 U.S. at 564, n.8. In *Twombly* we were faced with allegations of a conspiracy to violate § 1 of the Sherman Act through parallel conduct. The difficulty was that the conduct alleged was "consistent with conspiracy, but just as much in line with a wide swath of rational and competitive business strategy unilaterally prompted by common perceptions of the market." *Id.* at 554. We held that in that sort of circumstance, "[a]n allegation of parallel conduct is . . . much like a naked assertion of conspiracy in a § 1 complaint: it gets the complaint close to stating a claim, but without some further factual enhancement it stops short of the line between possibility and plausibility of 'entitlement to relief.'" *Id.* Here, by contrast, the allegations in the complaint are neither confined to naked legal conclusions nor consistent with legal conduct. The complaint alleges that FBI officials discriminated against Iqbal solely on account of his race, religion, and national origin, and it alleges the knowledge and deliberate indifference that, by Ashcroft and Mueller's own admission, are sufficient to make them liable for the illegal action. Iqbal's complaint therefore contains "enough facts to state a claim to relief that is plausible on its face." *Id.* at 570.

I do not understand the majority to disagree with this understanding of "plausibility" under *Twombly*. Rather, the majority discards the allegations discussed above with regard to Ashcroft and Mueller as conclusory, and is left considering only two statements in the complaint: that "the [FBI], under the direction of Defendant Mueller, arrested and detained thousands of Arab Muslim men ... as part of its investigation of the events of September 11," and that "[t]he policy of holding post-September-11th detainees in highly restrictive conditions of confinement until they were 'cleared' by the FBI was approved by Defendants Ashcroft and Mueller in discussions in the weeks after September 11, 2001." I think the majority is right in saying that these allegations suggest only that Ashcroft and Mueller "sought to keep suspected terrorists in the most secure conditions available until the suspects could be cleared of terrorist activity," ante, and that this produced "a disparate, incidental impact on Arab Muslims". . . . And I agree that the two allegations selected by the majority, standing alone, do not state a plausible entitlement to relief for unconstitutional discrimination.

But these allegations do not stand alone as the only significant, nonconclusory statements in the complaint, for the complaint contains many allegations linking Ashcroft and Mueller to the discriminatory practices of their subordinates. *See* Complaint ¶ 10 (Ashcroft was the "principal architect" of the discriminatory policy); *Id.* ¶ 11 (Mueller was "instrumental" in adopting and executing the discriminatory policy); *Id.* ¶ 96 (Ashcroft and Mueller "knew of, condoned, and willfully and maliciously agreed to subject" Iqbal to harsh conditions "as a matter of policy, solely on account of [his] religion, race, and/or national origin and for no legitimate penological interest").

The majority says that these are "bare assertions" that, "much like the pleading of conspiracy in *Twombly*, amount to nothing more than a 'formulaic recitation of the elements' of a constitutional discrimination claim" and therefore are "not entitled to be assumed true." The fallacy of the majority's position, however, lies in looking at the relevant assertions in isolation. The complaint contains specific allegations that, in the aftermath of the September 11 attacks, the Chief of the FBI's International Terrorism Operations Section and the Assistant Special Agent in Charge for the FBI's New York Field Office implemented a policy that discriminated against Arab Muslim men, including Iqbal, solely on account of their race, religion, or national origin. Viewed in light of these subsidiary allegations, the allegations singled out by the majority as "conclusory" are no such thing. Iqbal's claim is not that Ashcroft and Mueller "knew of, condoned, and willfully and maliciously agreed to subject" him to a discriminatory practice that is left undefined; his allegation is that "they knew of, condoned, and willfully and maliciously agreed to subject" him to a particular, discrete, discriminatory policy detailed in the complaint. Iqbal does not say merely that Ashcroft was the architect of some amorphous discrimination, or that Mueller was instrumental in an ill-defined constitutional violation; he alleges that they helped to create the discriminatory policy he has described. Taking the complaint as a whole, it gives Ashcroft and Mueller "'fair notice of what the ... claim is and the grounds upon which it rests.'" *Twombly*, 550 U.S. at 555 (quoting *Conley v. Gibson*, 355 U.S. 41, 47 (1957)).

* * *

I respectfully dissent.

CASE ANALYSIS & QUESTIONS

> Following *Iqbal*, many commentators and judges have since referred to the pleadings standards under Rule 8 as being governed by "Twiqbal."

Following *Twombly* and *Iqbal*, courts, practitioners, and academics have struggled to agree on what the two cases mean and how the requirements of Rule 8 have changed, if at all. It may be years before there are satisfactory answers to these questions, but in the meantime, courts and lawyers have done their best to adhere to the holding of *Twombly* and *Iqbal* on a case-by-case basis. They have done so based on *Iqbal*'s test for gauging the plausibility of a plaintiff's claim. That test is essentially the following:

1. Does the complaint include conclusory allegations unsupported by well-pleaded facts? If so, they are excluded from the analysis.

2. Considering all of the remaining well-pleaded facts, does the party state a plausible claim for relief?

This test, which can certainly be articulated in different ways, asks the essential questions posed in *Twombly* and *Iqbal*. First, are there conclusory allegations like the ones in *Iqbal* that are unsupported by well-pleaded facts? These are generally formulaic recitations of claims like *Iqbal*'s "knew of, condoned, and willfully and maliciously agreed" that do not have any factual content to support them. If there are, those allegations will not be accepted as true for the purpose of assessing the sufficiency of the complaint.

The second inquiry is whether the well-pleaded facts that remain (after ignoring any unsupported conclusory allegations) state a plausible claim for relief. Plausibility is a tricky term to pin down, and it is not stated in Rule 8, nor is it well-defined in the cases. What *Twombly* and *Iqbal* tell us, however, is that the facts do not have to state a probable claim, but they do have to state something more than the possibility of a claim. Moreover, under these cases, the plausibility of the complaint is to be determined by the judge's judicial experience and common sense.

Where there are well-pleaded facts that go to each element of a claim, this standard is not problematic. So, for example, suppose in a claim for breach of contract the plaintiff pleads that there was a valid contract. The contract was formed on the basis of valid consideration ($10 for the promise), the offer was made and accepted, and the whole agreement was memorialized in a document signed by both individuals. However, the promise was not fulfilled because the plaintiff did not receive the good for which she paid $10. Every element of the claim—valid contract (offer, acceptance, and consideration) and breach—has a fact that is well-pleaded. Moreover, there is no doubt about the plausibility of this breach of contract claim. Thus, there are no issues under *Twombly* and *Iqbal*.

> **Direct evidence** is evidence that tends to prove the issue without drawing any inference. For example, the credible eyewitness testimony of a person who states under oath that it is raining. **Circumstantial evidence** is evidence from which there are at least two reasonable inferences. For example, evidence that a person entered a house with an umbrella can be used to establish that it was raining outside. Or, it can mean that it was not raining, but that the person carries an umbrella all of the time because she lives in Seattle. For a more detailed discussion of the distinction between direct and circumstantial evidence, see Chapter 16.

The trouble arises under *Twombly* and *Iqbal* when the plaintiff does not have direct evidence going to each element of her claim. That is when she has to plead circumstantial evidence that might give rise to an inference that each element of the claim is met. It is where courts are asked to make such inferences that the rubber meets the road under

Twombly and *Iqbal.* To use an example from *Iqbal*, the plaintiff did not have a document from Ashcroft showing that he ordered his subordinates to

The effect of *Twombly* and *Iqbal* on pleading practice is being studied by academics and rulemakers alike. For example, in a recent study, Professor Patricia Hatamyar found that the number of motions to dismiss that are granted has increased from forty-six percent under *Conley* to forty-eight percent under *Twombly* and, ultimately, to sixty-one percent under *Iqbal*. Patricia Hatamyar, *An Updated Quantitative Study of Iqbal's Impact on 12(b)(6) Motions*, 46 U. Rich. L. Rev. 603, 613 tbl.1, 614 (2012). The Federal Judicial Center ("FJC") conducted a study as well, at the request of the Civil Rulemaking Committee. *See* Joe S. Cecil, et al., Fed. Judicial Ctr., Motions to Dismiss For Failure to State a Claim After Iqbal, Report to the Judicial Conference Advisory Committee on Civil Rules 2 (2011), *available at* http://www.fjc.gov/public/pdf.nsf/lookup/motioniqbal.pdf/$file/motioniqbal.pdf. The FJC Study found that, in its statistical sample, there was little or no increase in grants of motions to dismiss without leave to amend in civil rights and employment discrimination cases. Cecil et al. at 14. However, the granting of motions to dismiss with leave to amend in civil rights cases increased from 21.1 percent to 32.8 percent, and in employment discrimination cases increased from 17.9 percent to 23.5 percent. *See also* Lonny Hoffman, *Twombly and Iqbal's Measure: An Assessment of the Federal Judicial Center's Study of Motions to Dismiss*, 6 Fed. Cts. L. Rev. 1, 8–9 (2012) (challenging the findings of the FJC).

detain individuals on the basis of their religion, race, or national origin. Nor did he have an eye-witness account of Ashcroft ever having such a conversation. Thus, a key element of Iqbal's claim—Ashcroft's instruction to his subordinates that they discriminate—did not have direct evidence to support the allegation. Instead, Iqbal tried to rely on other facts—the race and religion of individuals detained following September 11, the treatment of those individuals, the use of immigration charges to detain only individuals of a certain race and religion, etc.—to create an inference that Ashcroft was complicit in the alleged discrimination. The Court rejected this inference and determined, in its judicial experience and common sense, that the more likely explanation for the actions taken after September 11 was law enforcement and not discrimination. The Court did not think it was plausible to infer discriminatory animus from the facts that Iqbal pleaded. The question that remains following *Iqbal* is how a claim like this can ever go forward if the plaintiff does not have the opportunity to potentially obtain a document or key eyewitness testimony through discovery because his pleading is dismissed before discovery can start.

Given all this uncertainty, the problems below attempt to cover the broad array of decisions that can be reached under *Twombly* and *Iqbal*. When working through them, try to apply the test described above to determine whether the pleadings are sufficient to meet the requirements of Rule 8.

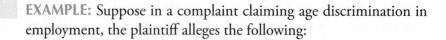

EXAMPLES & ANALYSIS

EXAMPLE: Suppose in a complaint claiming age discrimination in employment, the plaintiff alleges the following:

1. Plaintiff is an adult female citizen in the federally protected age group under the ADEA, 29 U.S.C. § 621 *et seq.* She is over the age of forty.

2. Defendant is an Oregon corporation that does business in Portland, Oregon.

3. Plaintiff worked for Defendant as an Executive Administrative Assistant from 11/28/05 to 2/2/09.

4. Plaintiff was involuntarily terminated from her position by Defendant.

5. At all material times her performance was satisfactory or better. She received consistently good performance reviews.

6. At the time of her termination there were five comparators employed by Defendant in Oregon of which Plaintiff was the oldest.

7. Plaintiff's younger comparators kept their jobs.

8. Age was a determining factor in the decision to terminate Plaintiff.

9. Prior to her termination, Plaintiff requested Family Medical Leave for a serious illness. She qualified for both Oregon Family Medical Leave and federal Family Medical Leave.

10. In so doing, Plaintiff was pursuing a right of public importance that belonged to her as an employee.

Does this complaint satisfy the pleading requirement in Rule 8(a)(2)?

Analysis: Probably yes. The courts have concluded that a claim for employment discrimination like this one is fairly straightforward. The plaintiff must allege the following factual ingredients of the claim: the plaintiff was a member of the class protected by the statute (above the age of 40); the plaintiff performed the duties of the job well; the plaintiff suffered an adverse employment action (was fired); and a person who is not a member of the protected class (a younger employee) maintained his employment. If those allegations are in the complaint, courts have found this kind of claim of employment discrimination to be sufficiently "plausible" to survive a motion to dismiss. *See, e.g., Sheppard v. David Evans and Assoc.*, 694 F. 3d 1045 (9th Cir. 2012).

EXAMPLE: Paul was a member of a prison review board, meaning that he sat on a board that reviewed whether parole should be granted to incarcerated individuals. When one prisoner, Henry Baleman, came before the board, Paul voted in support of the inmate's parole petition. The other board members, Dan, Dane, and David, all voted against granting Baleman parole. Following that vote, Paul was indicted for misconduct in the hearing because it was alleged that he received bribes on Baleman's behalf. Paul was eventually acquitted. Following his acquittal, he sued his fellow parole board members arguing that they had conspired to have him wrongfully prosecuted and that this conspiracy had denied him due process.

In his complaint, Paul alleged that the defendants assisted, encouraged and participated in the investigation. Dan participated in the investigation by providing investigative reports arising out of the hearing. Dane and David assisted in the investigation by giving interviews to the investigating authorities. Paul further alleged that "defendants actively assisted, encouraged, and participated in the investigation of Paul; positively contributing to the investigation and prosecution by advising, cooperating, and encouraging each and every phase of the prosecution." He also alleged the following:

> Plaintiff is informed, believes, and alleges that the defendants, while acting in concert with other state officials and employees, did knowingly, intentionally, and maliciously prosecute Plaintiff in retaliation for Plaintiff exercising his rights and privileges protected under the Constitution.

Has Paul pleaded enough in his complaint to survive a motion to dismiss?

Analysis: This is a close question, but a court is likely to grant the motion to dismiss. First, Paul's allegations regarding how the defendant participated in the investigation are problematic. In *Twombly*, the Court found that plaintiff's allegations of parallel conduct among the defendants "were consistent with conspiracy, but just as much in line with a wide swath of rational and competitive business strategy unilaterally prompted by common perceptions in the market." *Twombly*, 550 U.S. at 554. Similarly, Dan providing investigative reports and Dane and David granting interviews to investigators is just as consistent with purely lawful behavior as it is with wrongdoing. The other allegations regarding the defendants knowing and intentional behavior gets Paul a lot closer to alleging unlawful conduct. However, under *Iqbal*, it is just a formulaic recitation of the cause of action. They are just conclusory allegations without any facts to support them. Without more, under *Iqbal*, a court might find that Paul has not stated a plausible claim for relief.

EXAMPLE: Pamela sued her employer Drug Co. for racial discrimination. Pamela stated that she is an Asian-American female and was employed by Drug Co. Pamela alleged that throughout her employment she complained about mismanagement and discriminatory practices and that these complaints led to further discriminatory practices against her in retaliation. She also claimed that these practices kept her in a lower position than she would normally be in. Pamela alleged the discrimination included forcing her to work in a cold and drafty hallway, not reimbursing her for additional training, and denying her promotional opportunities. Has she sufficiently pleaded enough under Rule 8?

Analysis: Probably not. Her allegations of racial discrimination and retaliation are probably conclusory under *Iqbal* because they only state the elements of those claims. And, the factual allegations on their own are simply general grievances that are not specific enough to push her claim to be plausible. A judge, citing her judicial experience and common sense, could conclude that these events could occur in any workplace, not just one where there is discrimination. Pamela would need to provide more information to make her claim plausible. For example, Pamela could point to disciplinary actions that were done in retaliation, some promotional opportunities that she was denied, or she could specifically list the additional training for which she was not reimbursed. She needs some facts to help the court infer that these actions were motivated by racial animus and not just by lawful conduct.

EXAMPLE: Non-profit advocacy organization Polaris Plan, whose individual members opposed Governor Douglas's financial restructuring plan, decided to protest at a town hall meeting. At the meeting, the members of Polaris Plan had their signs and pamphlets taken away by security. It was the only group whose items were confiscated by security. Polaris Plan filed a complaint against Governor Douglas, claiming that its First Amendment rights were violated because the governor's security restricted its use of signs and distribution of leaflets at a state-sponsored town hall meeting held at a high school, while permitting another organization to give a similar speech approving the governor's plan. Is Polaris Plan's claim sufficient under Rule 8?

Analysis: Probably not. This is another close call. This claim is possible because it appears that only Polaris Plan was targeted by security. A judge, using her judicial experience and common sense, may infer that because other groups did not have their materials confiscated, Polaris Plan was discriminated against. However, the allegations against the governor could fail under *Iqbal*. There are no factual allegations connecting the confiscation of the materials by security to the governor. Moreover, like Attorney General Ashcroft's law enforcement purpose in *Iqbal*, the more plausible reason for taking the materials was that they represented a security threat. *Iqbal* required not just that the acts or omissions of the supervising official have a discriminatory effect, but that that the decisions be the consequence of purposeful discrimination. If Polaris Plan could point to specific facts where Governor Douglas permitted a policy to be executed that had discriminatory effects or some facts suggesting that he ordered such a discriminatory policy to be carried out, its complaint would likely survive. For example, if Governor Douglas had explicitly ordered security to enforce restrictions solely on Polaris Plan, that would likely be sufficient. Without something along these lines, however, there is a good chance that a court would dismiss the complaint.

EXAMPLE: Pedro was the ticket sales manager of the Dudleytown Dorights, a minor-league baseball team. He was very popular with the local fans and well respected throughout the league. The Dudleytown Dorights decided to cancel its season, causing all kinds of confusion and problems related to getting the fans refunds. The team also terminated Pedro. However, following his termination, the team sent an email informing the fans of this season's cancellation; that email appeared to have been sent by Pedro. Pedro brought a claim against the owner, Dante, and the general manager, Darren, for misappropriating his name. Pedro alleged that Dante and Darren sent the email to fans, but falsely designated Pedro as the sender of the email. He alleged that they did this in order to capitalize on Pedro's good reputation in the industry and with the fans. In other words, they used Pedro's identity to soften the blow of cancelling the season. Pedro alleged that he did not send the email. He further alleged that Dante and Darren's actions—falsely sending the email from Pedro's account—resulted in a loss of reputation for him among the public and his fans. He has a commercial interest in his name, which was harmed by Dante and Darren's falsely designated email. Has Pedro pleaded enough under Rule 8?

> Traditionally, plaintiffs who had a good faith basis for believing a particular fact alleged in the complaint, but did not have first-hand knowledge of that fact, could allege the fact based upon "information and belief." In the wake of *Twombly* and *Iqbal*, the courts have confronted the issue whether it is possible to allege facts only on "information and belief."
>
> The courts generally allow such pleadings, but only if the plaintiff can allege that the facts alleged are peculiarly in the control of the defendant or can allege a specific basis for the belief that demonstrates the plausibility of the fact alleged. *See, e.g., Arista Records, LLC v. Doe 3*, 604 F.3d 110, 120 (2d Cir. 2010).

Analysis: Probably. Pedro pleaded that as a direct and proximate result of Dante and Darren's falsely sending the email from Pedro, he suffered a loss of reputation and goodwill among the public and the team's fans. Pedro's complaint alleges Dante and Darren falsely designated the origin of the email either to soften the blow of an unfavorable message and/or to apportion some of the blame to someone else by trading upon Pedro's good name and reputation among the fan base and season ticket holders. He has provided more than the bare accusations of the elements of the claim. Further, a judge in her judicial experience and common sense could infer that the email was sent from Pedro's account in order to capitalize on his reputation. In other words, unlike the previous example, there are more facts connecting the people in charge—in this case, Dante and Darren—to the harmful acts. This is probably sufficient to show that Dante and Darren misappropriated Pedro's name.

B. Rule 9: Pleading Special Matters

Rule 9 governs how the substantive claims of fraud and mistake must be pleaded.

THE RULE   **Rule 9(b)**

Pleading Special Matters

(b) **Fraud or Mistake; Conditions of Mind.** In alleging **fraud or mistake**, a party must state **with particularity the circumstances** constituting fraud or mistake. Malice, intent, knowledge, and other **conditions of a person's mind may be alleged generally**.

EXPLANATION

Under Rule 9(b), a party pleading fraud or mistake must state the particularities of that claim. This has been described as providing the "who, what, when, where, why, and how" of the substantive claim. Why the original rulemakers chose to require this level of particularity for only fraud and mistake is not settled. Some argue that allegations of fraud can so harm one's reputation, the pleading requirements should be higher. As for mistake, it may be that the rulemakers wanted a higher threshold before potentially setting aside an otherwise valid contract. In any event, while scholars and jurists have suggested that additional categories be added to Rule 9, the rulemakers have not yet done so. There are, however, statutory regimes adopted by Congress that require this same level of particularity. One example is the Private Securities Litigation Reform Act. Private Securities Litigation Reform Act of 1955 (PSLRA), Pub. L. No. 104-67, 109 Stat. 737 (1995) (codified in scattered sections of 15 U.S.C.) (requiring, among other things, heightened pleading for securities violations, PSLRA § 101(a)). Finally, it is notable that Rule 9(b) allows a party to plead the defendant's state of mind generally. This seems to be in contrast to the Supreme Court's requirement in *Iqbal* that the defendant's intent be pleaded specifically. This has led many scholars to question the significance of Rule 9 in a post-*Twombly* and *Iqbal* pleading regime.

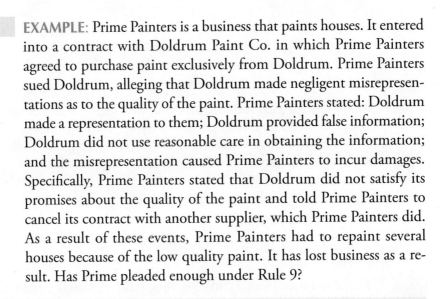

EXAMPLES & ANALYSIS

EXAMPLE: Prime Painters is a business that paints houses. It entered into a contract with Doldrum Paint Co. in which Prime Painters agreed to purchase paint exclusively from Doldrum. Prime Painters sued Doldrum, alleging that Doldrum made negligent misrepresentations as to the quality of the paint. Prime Painters stated: Doldrum made a representation to them; Doldrum provided false information; Doldrum did not use reasonable care in obtaining the information; and the misrepresentation caused Prime Painters to incur damages. Specifically, Prime Painters stated that Doldrum did not satisfy its promises about the quality of the paint and told Prime Painters to cancel its contract with another supplier, which Prime Painters did. As a result of these events, Prime Painters had to repaint several houses because of the low quality paint. It has lost business as a result. Has Prime pleaded enough under Rule 9?

Analysis: Probably. Because Prime Painters can point to specific instances of misrepresentations about the quality of the paint, the claim is likely sufficiently pleaded. Prime Painters stated the alleged false representations (the paint quality), showed that they relied on these representations (canceled their contract with another supplier), and demonstrated that they suffered harm (losing customers because of the low-quality paint). These facts should be enough to survive a motion to dismiss. Prime Painters has pleaded facts going to each element of its claim.

C. Rule 8(b): Defenses; Admissions and Denials

Once the complaint is done, Rule 8(b) tells the opposing party what it must do in response. In short, the party must file an answer, and Rule 8(b) governs what the party has to include in that document.

THE RULE   Rule 8(b)

Defenses: Admissions and Denials

(1) In General. In responding to a pleading, a party must:

  (A) state in short and plain terms its defenses to each claim asserted against it; and

  (B) admit or deny the allegations asserted against it by an opposing party.

(2) Denials—Responding to the Substance. A denial must **fairly respond** to the substance of the allegation.

(3) General and Specific Denials. A party that intends in good faith to deny all the allegations of a pleading—including the jurisdictional grounds—may do so by a general denial. A party that does not intend to deny all the allegations must either specifically deny designated allegations or generally deny all except those specifically admitted.

(4) Denying Part of an Allegation. A party that intends in good faith to deny only part of an allegation **must admit the part that is true and deny the rest.**

(5) Lacking Knowledge or Information. A party that **lacks knowledge or information sufficient to form a belief** about the truth of an allegation must so state, and the statement has the effect of a **denial**.

(6) Effect of Failing to Deny. An allegation—other than one relating to the amount of damages—is **admitted** if a responsive pleading is required and the **allegation is not denied**. If a responsive pleading is not required, an allegation is considered denied or avoided.

EXPLANATION

As Rule 8(b)(1) explains, when a party responds to a complaint in its answer, it must (i) assert any and all defenses that it has and (ii) admit or deny the allegations made against it. Rule 8(c) provides further information about how the party can assert its defenses. The balance of Rule 8(b) provides the responding party with three options in responding to the specific allegations in the complaint. First, it can admit the allegation. Second, it can deny the allegation. And, finally, it can state that it does not have enough information to respond to the allegation, a response that will be treated like a denial.

> Where applicable and advantageous, a defendant's first course of action is to file any relevant Rule 12 motions, discussed in Chapter 7, in response to a complaint. Rule 12 also governs the timing for filing the answer.

The most important element of an answer is its correlation with the complaint. A Rule 8(b) answer is written in direct response to a Rule 8(a) complaint. If a complaint alleges one cause of action, for example assault, but makes 20 allegations about that assault, the answer must respond to each of those 20 allegations. A party can do this by responding to each allegation individually or by doing what is called a **general denial**. *See* Rule 8(b)(3). Note that Rule 8(b) appears more comprehensive in content than 8(a), but it is important to remember that the two parallel one another in practice.

> A **general denial** means that the responding party chooses to just deny all of the allegations and not address each allegation individually. This is a very risky move because the responding party is less likely to address each allegation in accordance with the rule. Thus, general denials are unusual.

EXAMPLES & ANALYSIS

EXAMPLE: Peyton sued Dockworkers Inc., alleging Peyton was injured by a truck owned by Dockworkers Inc. and operated by Dockworkers Inc.'s employee, George. In one allegation, Peyton alleged that Dockworkers Inc. owned and operated the truck, knew of the negligent use by its employee, George, and that such negligent use resulted in Peyton's injuries. In its answer, Dockworkers Inc. generally denied this allegation, meaning that it did not deal with each allegation specifically (ownership, operation, injury), but just generally denied them all. After the statute of limitations had passed, discovery revealed that Dockworkers Inc. did not own the truck and that George was not its employee. Instead, Dockworkers Inc.'s partner Dunce Co. and Dunce Co.'s employee, George, operated the truck that injured Peyton. Both Dockworkers Inc. and Dunce Co. are represented by the same insurance company and lawyers. The insurance company learned of Peyton's injuries from a report that Dockworkers filed prior to litigation. In other words, Dockworkers knew that Peyton had been injured.

Peyton sought an order stating that Dockworkers Inc. admitted ownership of the truck and agency of the operator of the truck, on the grounds that Dockworkers Inc.'s general denial was ineffective in denying the allegation. Will the court grant this order?

Analysis: Yes. The court would find that Dockworkers' failure to address each allegation specifically was inadequate. Certainly, Dockworkers knew that Peyton had been injured by the truck, as it had made a report about the accident to its insurance company. Thus, because it did not effectively deny the allegations, the court would deem the whole allegation as admitted. In order to avoid this problem, Dockworkers Inc. should have specifically denied that it owned the truck. This case illustrates the potentially fatal consequences of generally denying allegations in a complaint. In most cases, best practice is to answer a complaint allegation by allegation. This hypothetical is based on *Zielinski v. Philadelphia Piers, Inc.*, 139 F. Supp. 408 (E.D. Pa. 1956). In that case, estoppel was an additional ground for deeming the facts to be admitted because the defendant knew who owned the truck, yet failed to apprise plaintiff of that fact until after the statute of limitations had run.

EXAMPLE: The Potters are suing Dore Contractors, seeking damages for claims arising out of a home improvement contract. The Potters alleged that Dore Contractors breached the contract by failing to perform and complete the work in a timely and workmanlike manner and by refusing to compensate the Potters for damages and costs.

The Potters also specifically alleged that Dore Contractors were unlicensed to perform the work. Dore Contractors denied this allegation on the grounds that it lacked information sufficient enough to form a belief as to whether the allegation was true or not. Is this denial on the grounds of a lack of information or knowledge proper?

Analysis: Generally, an assertion of lack of information or knowledge has the effect of a denial under Rule 8(b)(5). However, because a contractor or business should know whether it is licensed to perform the work, this denial would not be acceptable. Here, Dore Contractors has attempted to distance itself from the Potters' allegation that it is unlicensed; but because this is a matter it should obviously know, it would be deemed admitted. A party may not deny sufficient information or knowledge with impunity. It is subject to the requirements of honesty in pleading, and a denial will be deemed admitted when the matter is obviously one as to which a defendant has knowledge or information. *See* Chapter 5 regarding Rule 11 and its application to pleadings.

EXAMPLE: Danielle executed a promissory note to secure a loan in the amount of $100,000 from the United States Department of Education. Danielle defaulted on her obligation to repay her loan. After a period of several years of Danielle being in default, Postgraduate Loan Co. asked Danielle for the amount owed. She did not pay, so Postgraduate Loan Co. filed a complaint. The complaint made appropriate allegations regarding the loan, the fact that Danielle took out the loan, and the fact that Danielle has failed to repay it. Postgraduate Loan Co. requested that the court enter judgment against Danielle for the total amount of the loan. Danielle filed an answer, but did not deny any of the allegations in the complaint and only stated that she "always intended to pay back my student loans." Has Danielle admitted to the allegations in the complaint?

Analysis: Yes. Danielle failed to deny the allegations in the complaint. Thus, each allegation in the complaint is deemed admitted under Rule 8(b)(6). She might be able to amend her answer to change her response under Rule 15. *See* Chapter 10.

D. Rule 8(c): Affirmative Defenses

Rule 8(c) requires that a responding party state any affirmative defense it may have. It also allows for the court to reclassify an affirmative defense as a counterclaim (or vice versa) as appropriate.

THE RULE   Rule 8(c)

Affirmative Defenses

(1) In General. In responding to a pleading, a party **must affirmatively state any avoidance or affirmative defense**, including:

- accord and satisfaction; ...

- contributory negligence; ...

- fraud; ...

- statute of limitations; and

- waiver.

(2) Mistaken Designation. If a party mistakenly designates a defense as a counterclaim, or a counterclaim as a defense, the court must, if **justice requires**, treat the pleading as though it were correctly designated, and may impose terms for doing so.

EXPLANATION

An affirmative defense is different from a defense. A defense seeks to negate an element of the plaintiff's claim. An affirmative defense is a way to avoid liability even assuming the claim is valid. These are often called "yes, but" defenses because the party is saying that, "Even if I did what I am accused of in the complaint, I am not liable because of the defense." An affirmative defense is also different from a counterclaim. An affirmative defense directly relates to an opposing party's claim. For example, if a plaintiff sues a defendant for breach of contract, the defendant may assert the affirmative defense of failure of consideration, which essentially purports there is no valid contract and therefore the plaintiff's claim is illegitimate. A counterclaim does not have to be related to the original claim. For example, a plaintiff may sue a defendant for damages based on contract 1 and the defendant can subsequently counterclaim against the plaintiff for damages based on contract 2. However, some counterclaims must be made or they are waived. *See* Chapter 8 regarding Rule 13. Confusion among these three concepts, however, is not unusual so the rule is quite flexible in allowing any mislabeling of these concepts to be easily cured. Rule 8(c)(2) provides that when a party mistakenly designates an affirmative defense as a counterclaim, or vice versa, the court must consider the mistaken defense or counterclaim in its correct form, if justice so requires. Finally, Rule 8(c) provides a nonexhaustive list of affirmative defenses parties may raise in their answer. This means that there might be additional affirmative defenses that are not listed in the rule. The party seeking to take advantage of an affirmative defense must raise the defense in its answer, and then will bear the burden of proving the defense. Affirmative defenses are generally listed in the answer following the admission or denial of the allegations in the complaint.

> If a party fails to include an affirmative defense altogether, it can cure that omission by amending the pleading according to the requirements of Rule 15. *See* Chapter 10. As explained in this chapter, if this mistake is not fixed, however, the party risks waiving the defense. While the waiver may be cured in some instances in federal court, some state courts do not permit the waiver to be cured.

EXAMPLES & ANALYSIS

EXAMPLE: Perry is riding on a boat owned and operated by Deluge Boat Co. A storm comes in, and Perry falls out of the boat and is injured in the fall. Perry sues Deluge Boat Co. Deluge Boat Co. wishes to assert several arguments. They include the following:

    a. Deluge Boat Co. is not liable to Perry.

b. Deluge Boat Co. is not liable to Perry because Perry was not wearing a life jacket after Deluge Boat Co. told him to wear it.

c. Perry damaged the boat when he fell off and thus owes Deluge Boat Co. the cost of any repairs.

d. Deluge Boat Co. is not liable to Perry because Perry interfered with the ship's navigation system, causing damage to the boat, the navigation system, and himself.

For each argument, evaluate whether it is a denial, affirmative defense, or counterclaim.

Analysis: Argument (a) is a denial. Deluge Boat Co. is denying any liability. Argument (b) is an affirmative defense. Assuming the jurisdiction is a contributory negligence regime in which a plaintiff's negligence can be a defense, this is an assertion of contributory negligence. Argument (c) is a counterclaim. Deluge Boat Co. is making a separate claim for damages against Perry. Finally, argument (d) is arguably both an affirmative defense and a counterclaim. The assertion that Perry interfered with the navigation system could be another argument in the spirit of contributory negligence, but it is also a claim for damages for any harm done by Perry to the navigation system.

EXAMPLE: Preston was riding his bike on the side of the road. A truck driven by a Delmont Trucking employee was driving in the same direction on the same road. As the truck began passing Preston, he lost control of his bike, fell back into the roadway, and landed under the truck's tires. The truck hit Preston, and he died instantly. Preston's family sued Delmont Trucking. Delmont Trucking's answer did not contain the affirmative defense of comparative negligence, even though that defense was available in the jurisdiction. Delmont amended its answer, but it still did not assert the affirmative defense of comparative negligence. Shortly before trial, Delmont Trucking asked to amend its answer to include the affirmative defense of comparative negligence. Will the court allow Delmont Trucking to amend its answer to include the affirmative defense?

Analysis: Probably not. Failure to plead an affirmative defense generally results in the defense being waived. Delmont Trucking had ample time to plead the defense and it is likely Preston's family would suffer undue prejudice if Delmont were allowed to amend its answer at this late stage in the proceedings. It is so close to trial and Delmont is attempting to substantially change the theory on which the defense has been proceeding. However, it is not always the case that failure to plead an affirmative defense results in waiver. Most circuits do not enforce waiver relentlessly. It is common to allow a party to amend its answer to include an affirmative defense if the defendant seeks the amendment early in the proceeding. Moreover, if the defense would not have prejudiced the plaintiffs, the court would have likely allowed Delmont to raise the defense later. In other words, where the plaintiff would not suffer prejudice, most courts will allow the affirmative defense to be added. This response is closer to the spirit of allowing flexibility in the pleading regime. Note, however, that some state courts do not have rules allowing for this flexibility, so a waiver may not be curable in state court.

E. Rules 8(d) and 8(e): Pleading to Be Concise and Direct; Alternative Statements; Inconsistency; Construing Pleadings

These two rules govern when a party can offer alternative or inconsistent statements in its pleadings and how a court should generally construe pleadings.

THE RULE   **Rule 8(d) & 8(e)**

(d) Pleading to Be Concise and Direct; Alternative Statements; Inconsistency

(1) In General. Each allegation must be **simple, concise, and direct**. No technical form is required.

(2) Alternative Statements of a Claim or Defense. A party may set out 2 or more statements of a claim or defense **alternatively or hypothetically**, either in a single court or defense or in separate ones. If a party makes alternative statements, the pleading is sufficient if any one of them is sufficient.

(3) Inconsistent Claims or Defenses. A party may state as many **separate claims or defenses** as it has, **regardless of consistency**.

(e) Construing Pleadings

Construing Pleadings. Pleadings must be construed so as to do **justice**.

EXPLANATION

Rule 8(d)(2) states that the parties can advance numerous theories or claims and defenses. Further, Rule 8(d)(3) provides that the theories or claims do not have to be consistent. For example, a plaintiff can plead in the alternative or for different types of relief. The only restraint on pleading this way is that a party cannot plead in the alternative if it knows or has reason to know what actually happened. Moreover, a party cannot plead conflicting facts. It can plead that it does not know which set of facts are true, but it cannot plead one fact in one allegation and a completely opposite fact in the next allegation. There is a difference between not knowing which facts are accurate and trying to assert that two polar opposite facts can be true at the same time. Finally, Rule 8(e) requires that pleadings must be read to do justice. This part of the rule is largely unused, however, and tends to stand for the general proposition that the rules should be construed so as to achieve the "just, speedy, and inexpensive" determination of every action. *See* Fed. R. Civ. P. 1.

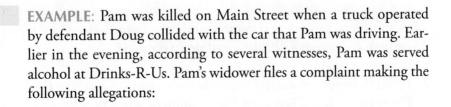

EXAMPLES & ANALYSIS

EXAMPLE: Pam was killed on Main Street when a truck operated by defendant Doug collided with the car that Pam was driving. Earlier in the evening, according to several witnesses, Pam was served alcohol at Drinks-R-Us. Pam's widower files a complaint making the following allegations:

Allegation 1: Defendant Doug negligently drove his truck across the median and collided with Pam's car, which was the proximate cause of Pam's death.

Allegation 2: Defendant Drinks-R-Us negligently continued to serve Pam before she drove, which was the proximate cause of her death.

Does this complaint comply with Rule 8(d)?

Analysis: Yes. Although the two counts are directly conflicting, Rule 8 allows alternative or even inconsistent pleading. In this case, Pam's widower was not at the accident or with her before the accident occurred. Thus, he cannot know whether the accident was a result of her being intoxicated (and thus the fault of Drinks-R-Us) or whether she was sober (and the accident was the fault of Doug). Rule 8(d) allows Pam's widower to plead both potential factual scenarios and lets the trial process work out which, if any, are accurate. For example, a jury might conclude that Pam's intoxication, and not Doug's negligent driving, contributed to the accident. If Pam's widower knew or had reason to know which factual scenario occurred, however, he would not be allowed to plead these conflicting facts.

ADDITIONAL EXERCISES

1. Penn is a small town farm owner living in rural Oklahoma. Penn sued the major television network, DBA, for slander, invasion of privacy, and defamation of character. In his complaint, Penn claimed that for the past two years DBA's primetime sports highlights program, Downtown Daily, "has been falsely stating at the beginning and ending of every program that Penn is a poor farmer and that his produce is the poorest in Oklahoma." Penn alleged that these are false statements that have ruined his reputation as a small town produce farmer. **Has Penn pleaded enough to survive a 12(b)(6) motion to dismiss?**

2. Plaintiff buyers of digital music brought suit against Da-Da Music, Dum Dum Beats, Doowop Entertainment and Digital Music Corp. ("DMC"), alleging the defendants had agreed to conspire to fix the prices of downloadable music. Plaintiffs allege several facts that allegedly

support their claim. First, defendants Da-Da and Dum Dum agreed to launch a website together to distribute their music. Doowop and DMC also agreed to create a website for the same purpose, and these two websites charged the same allegedly unreasonably high prices. Second, all defendants signed distribution agreements with the websites and sold music directly to consumers over the internet through these sites. Third, none of the defendants reduced its prices for download-able music (in comparison to CDs), despite the fact that all defendants experienced cost reductions in producing digital music. Fourth, when defendants began to sell downloadable music through entities they did not own or control, they maintained the same alleged unreasonably high prices. Fifth, all defendants refused to do business with the second larg-est downloadable music retailer. Sixth, all defendants raised wholesale prices from $0.65 per song to $1.00 per song at the same time. **Have the plaintiffs pleaded enough facts under Rule 8?**

3. Paul Perkins, as part of a routine physical examination for his military employer, had blood tests done. The lab reported back to Perkins that he had tested positive for HIV. Perkins had to disclose the information to his employer. It was not until after he had done so that the lab dis-covered it had confused Perkins's blood with another patient. Perkins did not, in fact, have the virus. Perkins filed suit for, among other things, intentional infliction of emotional distress, alleging in the com-plaint that the false reporting caused him "intentional distress so severe that no reasonable person could be expected to endure it." To establish a claim for the intentional infliction of emotional distress, the plaintiff must demonstrate: (1) that the defendant either intended to inflict emotional distress, or knew or should have known that emotional dis-tress was likely to result from its conduct; (2) that the defendant's con-duct was extreme and outrageous; and (3) that the defendant's conduct caused emotional distress so severe that no reasonable person could be expected to endure it. The laboratory has filed a motion to dismiss under 12(b)(6). **Will the lab prevail?**

4. Paul Pettigrew works in the maintenance department of the Lincoln County School District. He has submitted numerous complaints to the superintendent, claiming that the departments of the school district are operated in a racially discriminatory manner. He has filed suit against the district, claiming that the treatment of the maintenance depart-

ment is done in a racially discriminatory manner, as the maintenance department employs mostly black workers. He claims that the management office, which is comprised of mostly white employees, is well maintained and air-conditioned, while the maintenance department is not. He also claims that supervision is racially divided, with white foremen supervising the white employees and black foremen supervising the black employees. Additionally, Paul has evidence showing that the departments that employ mostly white workers were, on average, paid more, and not required to go through the same intensive training process as the departments that employed mostly black employees. In his complaint, Paul pleads all of these facts alleging discrimination. The district moves for dismissal under 12(b)(6), claiming that Paul has not stated a claim upon which relief can be granted. **What should the court decide?**

5. Pruitt filed a claim against the Watertown School District for employment discrimination. She claims that she also suffered retaliation. Under a retaliation claim, the plaintiff must prove that: (1) she engaged in protected participation or opposition; (2) that the employer was aware of the activity; (3) that the employer took adverse actions; and (4) that there was a causal connection between the protected activity and the adverse action. Pruitt is a forty-year-old woman who has a certificate in teaching for elementary school students. In 2007, she held a temporary teaching position in the Watertown School District. Pruitt claims she received outstanding reviews from both parents and faculty. In the years that followed, Pruitt worked in temporary positions, but repeatedly applied for and was denied tenure-track positions. In January 2008, Pruitt complained to the superintendent that the Watertown School District was only hiring younger and less-qualified applicants for its tenure-track positions. In September 2008, Pruitt was not hired for any position within the district. Pruitt has alleged that the district's failure to rehire her was retaliation for her age discrimination allegations. Watertown School District has moved to dismiss Pruitt's retaliation claim. **What should the court decide?**

6. Peter is a fifty-year-old employee at DFPG, a major accounting firm. In his complaint, he asserts a discrimination claim under Title VII of the Civil Rights Act. To state a claim for discrimination, a plaintiff must establish that: (1) he belongs to a protected class; (2) he was qualified for the position; (3) he was subject to adverse employment action; and

(4) similarly situated individuals outside his protected class were treated more favorably. Peter alleges that he always received positive performance evaluations. He also alleges that he was placed on a performance improvement plan (PIP) because he was late on one audit. All of the auditors in the office, save one, turned their audits in late, but only Peter and other older auditors were placed on a PIP. The younger auditors were not only given a pass for their late audits, DFPG also gave them extra support on their audits—support that was not provided to Peter and other older auditors. **If DFPG moves to dismiss Peter's claim, what will the court decide?**

7. **A Hypothetical—Exam-Like Question:** Pam and Pete Parza, members of the Alliance Against President Smith (AAPS), participated in a number of peaceful protests against President Smith and his policies during the 2012 presidential election. On October 14, 2012, just weeks before the election, President Smith paid a visit to Elko, Nevada for a campaign event. While there, he stayed at the Miners Inn in Elko.

The Miners Inn is located on, and faces, California Street, between Third and Fourth Streets. There is patio dining behind the hotel. The patio is quite large and can be seen clearly from both Third and Fourth Streets. There is an obstructed view of the patio from California Street. There is also a fence surrounding the patio, but it is only about three feet high. Although it can be chilly in Elko in mid-October, the weather is usually clear, and the Miners Inn patio is a very popular dining destination. To combat the cold, heat lamps are placed throughout the patio dining area.

On October 14, 2012, Pam and Pete and two hundred other concerned citizens gathered in Elko to protest against President Smith. Pam and Pete brought their young children to the protest—young Sally, nine months old, was safely affixed to her mother's back in a sling and little Aiden, 3 years old, was in a stroller bedecked with AAPS paraphernalia. The protestors congregated on the public sidewalks adjacent to and across the street from the Miners Inn (on California Street and around the corner onto Fourth Street). The protest started at 8:00 am that day.

One of the organizers of the AAPS protest, Shelley Vicker, spoke with Elko City Police Chief Joe Rin and Elko County Sheriff Cindi Greene before the protest and advised them of their plans. Ms. Vicker specifically informed the officials that the protest would be multi-generational, with many parents bringing small children. Police Chief Rin and Sheriff Greene told them the protestors would be okay if they remained on the designated sidewalks and did not obstruct traffic.

The AAPS protestors dutifully followed these instructions. They carried signs and chanted slogans for most of the day. The protest was peaceful, but it was quite loud. The police received a few complaints that day from neighboring businesses regarding the noise. A smaller group of individuals, supporters of President Smith (members of the Four More Years Alliance (FMYA)), were also gathered near the Miners Inn. However, the FMYA protestors congregated on Third Street, and they were not nearly as large a group, nor were they as loud, as the AAPS protestors.

The protest lasted the entire day without incident. However, around 5:00 pm, the atmosphere changed. News spread through the crowd that President Smith had changed his dinner plans and had decided to dine on the patio at the Miners Inn. President Smith entered the Miners Inn through the back kitchen door and was escorted to the patio by his two lead Secret Service Agents Daveen Duggins and Darrah Dell. Secret Service Agent Donny Driggs was waiting for the President and his fellow agents on the patio. There were already a number of individuals eating on the patio when the President arrived, but Agents Duggins, Dell, and Driggs did not sense a threat. Thus, they did not search or otherwise bother the diners upon the President's arrival.

Once the AAPS protestors learned that President Smith was at the Miners Inn, they escalated their protest. The protest remained peaceful, but the noise increased. About twenty minutes after the President's arrival, Chief Rin and a large number of police officers arrived at the protest site in full riot gear. An armored personnel carrier was located behind the police line. An announcement was made instructing the protestors to vacate California Street and Fourth Street. The following reason was given for moving the protestors: Secret Service Agents did not want anyone who might have a handgun or explosives within range of the President.

The police officers forced the AAPS protestors to move east along California Street, past Fourth Street and onto Fifth Street, in some cases shoving plaintiffs and striking them with clubs. According to Pam and Pete Parza, when the police officers arrived and attempted to move the demonstrators, plaintiffs and a number of other protestors employed "passive resistance" techniques to impede their arrest, including going limp, refusing to identify themselves, and refusing to unlock arms with one another. Accordingly, the officers had to employ some degree of physical coercion in order to move, and in some cases, arrest the protesters. Once the protestors were moved, the police split the group of protestors into two groups, and in some instances, separated family members from fellow family members, including parents from children. In fact, Pam and Sally were separated from Pete and Aiden. Finally, some of the protestors, including Pam and Pete, were arrested.

Following the protests and arrests, some of the AAPS protestors noted that the FMYA protestors were allowed to remain on Third Street and were not otherwise caught up in the attempts to relocate the protestors to Fifth Street.

On April 2, 2013, Pam and Pete Parza (plaintiffs) filed a complaint in the District Court for the District of Nevada against the Elko City Police Department, Elko City Police Chief Joe Rin, Elko City Police Officers "Don Doe I" and "Dana Doe I," and Secret Service Agents Duggins, Dell, and "Dave Doe I."

This exercise will only address the claim against the Secret Service Agents. The gravamen of the plaintiffs' complaint against the Secret Service Agents was that the agents violated plaintiffs' First Amendment rights by requiring them to be moved because of their anti-Smith views. The plaintiffs believe that the Secret Service either had an understood policy or de facto practice of keeping anti-Smith protestors away from the President. The statute of limitations for this claim is two years.

The key parts of the complaint alleged the following:

¶1 Plaintiffs are Pam and Pete Parza, members of the group Alliance Against President Smith (AAPS).

¶2 Secret Service Defendants Duggins, Dell, and "Dave Doe I" unconstitutionally excluded anti-government demonstrators from a traditional public forum. This exclusion was pursuant to an unconstitutional Secret Service policy.

¶3 On October 14, 2012, after the plaintiffs' anti-Smith chants and slogans could be heard within the patio where the President was dining, Secret Service Defendants Duggins, Dell, and "Dave Doe I" requested or directed Chief Rin and other police officers to clear California Street of all persons and to move them to the east side of Fourth Street and subsequently to the east side of Fifth Street.

¶4 The police officers forced the anti-Smith protestors to move east along California Street.

¶5 During the entire time these actions were being taken against the plaintiffs, the Secret Service Defendants did not take action to move the pro-Smith demonstrators on Third Street or the unscreened guests and diners in the Miners Inn.

"'[V]iewpoint discrimination' occurs when the government prohibits 'speech by particular speakers,' thereby suppressing a particular view about a subject." *Gieb v. Sylvester.* The Supreme Court has made clear that government suppression of speech based on the speaker's motivating ideology, opinion, or perspective is impermissible. *See Rosen v. Visitors of Univ. of Va.* ("It is axiomatic that the government may not regulate speech based on its substantive content or the message it conveys."); *Maney v. Babbitt* (holding that the First Amendment does not permit the federal government to bar ideological opponents from peacefully protesting on the sidewalks of Pennsylvania Avenue during President Wesson's second Inaugural Parade).

Thus, to prevail on this claim against the individual agents, the plaintiffs must establish that the Secret Service Defendants ordered the relocation of their demonstration because of, not merely in spite of, the demonstration's anti-Smith message. They can do this by (i) showing that the agents, on their own accord, impermissibly ordered the relocation of their demonstration; or (ii) showing that the agents, pursuant to an impermissible Secret Service policy, ordered the relocation of their demonstration.

Defendant Agents Duggins and Dell move to dismiss under Rule 12(b)(6), arguing that that the complaint failed to state a claim upon which relief can be granted because (i) plaintiffs did not show that the agents, *on their own accord*, impermissibly ordered the relocation of their demonstration; or (ii) plaintiffs did not show that the agents, *pursuant to an impermissible Secret Service policy*, ordered the relocation of their demonstration. Limiting your response to the complaint allegations provided, discuss whether the motion would be granted or denied and why. Assuming the motion would be granted, *briefly* discuss what additional facts might have been pleaded to save the complaint.

8. **An Exercise—Drafting a Complaint.** A friend from law school has recently called you and referred to you a new client. As she sits in your office, she describes what has recently happened to her:

> Two weeks ago I went to the Fifth Avenue and East 17th Department Store, Inc. and bought a new leather jacket. Last week I tried to return that jacket at the Department Store, Inc. in the bottom floor of my office building on Fifth Avenue and East 50th. After waiting in line at the customer service register, I gave the coat and my receipt to the man behind the register. He told me that they could only give me store credit instead of a full refund. Now, I knew he was wrong. I had returned things at that store before and I knew that they give a full refund within 14 days if you provide the clothing and receipt. So, in the politest way possible, I explained this to the guy behind the register. Pretty soon another guy, who turned out to be the manager of the store, jumped into the argument and told me that not only would I not receive the full refund, I was also trying to return merchandise that I hadn't even purchased. He told me this because the receipt said that the size of the jacket I was returning was 12, when in fact it was a size 6. He said I was trying to defraud the store. It was clear to me, and would have been to anyone else who was watching, that he said this because I was insisting on a full refund for the jacket.
>
> Then, store security arrived and grabbed me and prevented me from leaving the area in front of the register. Through all of this, I continued to reason with the manager, trying to get him to understand that the receipt I had presented was the one given to me from the other Department Store, Inc. store. During this time, someone from the

store must have called the police because, before I knew it, four officers arrived.

While the officers were arresting me, the manager told one of the police officers that I had created a fake receipt and was trying to return a coat that I had stolen. He also said that I had created the receipt from types of paper and ink that Department Store, Inc. does not use in making its receipts. I don't even know what kinds of paper and ink they use, let alone any other kinds someone could use to make a fake receipt. But, of course, the police believed the manager and arrested me.

Now, the back entrance of that Department Store, Inc. store leads to the lobby of my office building. I had to suffer the indignity of being falsely detained and arrested in a store I frequent and of being marched in handcuffs and placed in a police car in front of my coworkers and boss as they were returning from their lunch break. On top of being completely humiliated, I'm sure that it negatively impacted my chances of getting the promotion I'm up for later this month.

I was told that I have a case both for false imprisonment against the store and for intentional infliction of emotional distress against the manager of the store. I'd like you to pursue both of these suits.

To establish a cause of action to recover damages for false imprisonment, the plaintiff must show that:

(1) the defendant intended to confine him or her;

(2) the plaintiff was conscious of the confinement;

(3) the plaintiff did not consent to the confinement; and

(4) the confinement was not otherwise privileged.

To establish a cause of action to recover damages for intentional infliction of emotional distress, the plaintiff must show that:

(1) the defendant acted in an extreme and outrageous manner;

(2) the defendant intended to cause, or disregarded a substantial probability of causing, severe emotional distress;

(3) there is a causal connection between the defendant's extreme and outrageous conduct and the plaintiff's injury; and

(4) the plaintiff suffered severe emotional distress.

Draft a complaint for both causes of action requested by your client. A template complaint form will be made available to you.

9. **An Exercise—Drafting An Answer.** Assume that you now work for Department Store, Inc. Draft an answer to the complaint that you are given in class. A template answer form will be made available to you.

Quick Summary

- The pleadings initiate litigation.

- The drafters of Rule 8 envisioned a notice-pleading regime where these documents would provide the minimal amount of notice necessary to allow the parties to proceed with litigation. Recent Supreme Court cases have called the notice regime into question, but the extent to which the landscape has changed is still unclear. There is some certainty to some aspects of pleading, however. For a complaint to survive, it cannot rely on conclusory allegations unsupported by well-pleaded facts, and it must state a plausible claim for relief.

- Rule 9 requires a party alleging fraud or mistake to plead with particularity.

- The answer must admit, deny, or state a lack of knowledge for each allegation. It must address all of the allegations made in the complaint.

- Parties are allowed to plead alternative theories of recovery. They are also permitted to plead inconsistent facts when they are unable to know which facts actually occurred.

7

Responsive Pleadings &
Pre-Trial Motions

Key Concepts

- Timing for filing an answer to the complaint
- Requirement that certain motions be filed before the answer is filed
- Waiver of certain defenses and objections
- Default Judgment
- Voluntary & Involuntary Dismissal

Introduction

Rule 12 is central to pre-trial practice. The rule governs how defendants can respond to the complaint. They can file an answer within a specified time, or they can delay the filing of the answer by first bringing a pre-trial motion. In other words, when responding to a complaint, a defendant has a complex choice to make. It can answer the complaint, as discussed in Chapter 6, but it can also file a motion to dismiss under Rule 12, asking the court to adjudicate certain defenses before it answers the complaint. The goal of Rule 12 is to facilitate an efficient resolution of the claims. To the extent there are valid defenses that would resolve the case without the need for discovery and further litigation or that would eliminate some of the claims or issues in the case to allow the parties to litigate the remaining portions more efficiently, the rule allows, and sometimes requires, those defenses to be brought near the outset of the proceeding.

The first part of Rule 12 sets the deadline for responding to the complaint with an answer. Rule 12 also outlines the procedure for filing a pre-answer motion raising some of the most key procedural defenses in litigation. The content of those defenses—personal jurisdiction, for example—will be ex-

plored in other chapters specific to those
issues. This chapter will describe how
and when these defenses must be raised.
Some defenses, like subject matter jurisdiction, are never really waived, but other
defenses can be waived unwittingly under
Rule 12 if they are not properly asserted.
This chapter will discuss how the waiver
rules work and how the pre-trial motion
to dismiss interacts with the requirement
to file an answer. Finally, Rule 12 provides
other objections to the complaint, like a
request to strike an offensive statement in
the complaint (Rule 12(f)) or to require
a party to file a more clearly-stated complaint (Rule 12(e)).

The last part of this chapter will discuss
default judgments—the process by which
the court will enter judgment when a defendant is unresponsive. Relatedly, Rule
41, which governs how a case may be voluntarily and involuntarily dismissed, will
be discussed.

Rule 7 defines the difference
between a pleading and a
motion. Pleadings include
a complaint, an answer to a
complaint, an answer to a
counterclaim, an answer to a
crossclaim, a third-party complaint, an answer to a third-
party complaint, and a reply
(if the court orders one). This
list defines the limited universe
of "pleadings." Motions are
different because a motion, as
defined in Rule 7(b), is what a
party uses whenever it is making a request of the court for
a court order. In this chapter,
there will be a discussion
of a particular kind of motion—motions brought under
Rule 12. But, there are endless
variations of motions that can
be brought before the judge,
including motions to extend
time, amend a case management order, or even to allow
for a party to carry a dangerous
piece of evidence on a plane
for transport. In other words,
the types of pleadings are limited while the types of motions
are endless.

A. Rule 12

Rule 12 is the work horse of the federal
rules because it dictates how so many pertinent steps in the litigation process must be taken. The timing of filings, the content of those filings, and
how the filings must be presented to the court are all controlled by Rule 12.

1. Rule 12(a): Time to Serve a Responsive Pleading

As discussed in Chapter 6, following the filing of a complaint, the responding party must file a responsive pleading or an answer. While Rule 8 sets out
the requirements for what content must be included in that answer, Rule
12(a) provides the deadlines for filing a timely response.

THE RULE   Rule 12(a)

Time to Serve a Responsive Pleading

(1) In General. Unless another time is specified by this rule or a federal statute, the **time for serving a responsive pleading** is as follows:

(A) A defendant must serve an answer:

    (i) within **21 days** after being served with the summons and complaint; or

    (ii) if it has **timely waived service under Rule 4(d)**, within **60 days** after the request for a waiver was sent, or within **90 days** after it was sent to the defendant outside any judicial district of the United States.

(B) A party must serve **an answer to a counterclaim or crossclaim** within **21 days** after being served with the pleading that states the counterclaim or crossclaim.

(C) A party must serve a **reply to an answer** within **21 days** after being served with an order to reply, unless the order specifies a different time.

    * * *

(4) Effect of a Motion. Unless the court sets a different time, **serving the motion under this rule alters these periods as follows**:

(A) **if the court denies the motion or postpones its disposition until trial**, the responsive pleading must be served within **14 days** after notice of the court's action; or

(B) **if the court grants a motion for a more definite statement**, the responsive pleading must be served within **14 days** after the more definite statement is served.

EXPLANATION

Rule 12(a)(1) governs the temporal and procedural requirements for responding to a complaint. Upon service of the pleading, the defendant has 21 days to serve the plaintiff with an answer. If the defendant timely waived service, the time limit increases to 60 or 90 days depending on whether the defendant is outside the United States. The 21-day limit applies even if the pleading is a counterclaim or crossclaim (see Chapter 8). Rule 12(a)(4) states if the party makes a Rule 12 motion and the motion is denied or deferred, the party must serve a responsive pleading within 14 days of notice of the court's ruling. In other words, filing a pre-answer motion will delay the deadline for filing a responsive pleading until after the motion is re-solved. Additionally, if the court grants a motion for a more definite statement, under Rule 12(e)—a rule that will also be discussed later in this chapter—the responsive pleading must be served within 14 days after the more definite statement is served. For example, if the defendant makes a Rule 12(e) motion and it is granted, the defendant's response is due 14 days after the defendant receives the plaintiff's amended complaint.

> Rules 12(a)(2) and (3) provide for a longer period of time— 60 days—for the United States or any of its officers or employees to file a responsive pleading. This is because the United States is a large entity, so it may take extra time for it to determine who is being sued and under what theory.

IN PRACTICE

Rule 12 offers defendants a strategic choice in responding to the complaint. They may answer the complaint or file a motion. Numerous strategic concerns inform the decision as to whether to file a Rule 12 motion, including the likelihood of success, the cost in preparing and briefing the motion, and the benefits to be achieved if only a portion of the case is eliminated. If the responding party fails to file either a motion or a responsive pleading within the time limits set forth in Rule 12(a), the court may enter a default judgment against the party. This means that unless the party has a valid objection based on notice, the court's subject matter jurisdiction, or personal jurisdiction, the plaintiff will have a valid judgment to enforce against the party. Default judgments will be covered in greater detail later in this chapter.

EXAMPLES & ANALYSIS

EXAMPLE: Danny published an article in the local newspaper that was quite critical of Paul. Among other things, Danny called Paul a jerk. Paul, who believes he is not a jerk, decided to sue Danny for libel in federal district court. Paul filed a summons and complaint with the court on June 1. Danny was served with a copy of the summons and complaint on June 5. What is Danny's deadline to serve an answer on Paul? (Assume that the deadline you calculate is a weekday and does not fall on a holiday.)

Analysis: Rule 12(a)(1)(A)(i) requires that a defendant serve an answer within 21 days after being served with the summons and complaint. Danny was served on June 5. This means that Danny has until June 26 (21 days after the date Danny was served with the summons and complaint) to serve an answer on Paul.

> Rule 6 delineates how to count time under the rules. When the deadline is structured as days, the day of the event triggering the deadline is not counted. Counting begins on the following day and includes Saturdays, Sundays, and holidays. However, if the last day of the deadline is a Saturday, Sunday, or holiday, the deadline will effectively be the next business day. Rule 6 also sets the guidelines for extending deadlines under the rules.

EXAMPLE: Assume Danny was properly served with the summons and complaint on June 1. Danny did not believe that the federal district court had personal jurisdiction over him, so he filed a Rule 12(b)(2) motion to dismiss based on a lack of personal jurisdiction. Danny filed and served this motion on Paul on June 10. The court denied the motion to dismiss on September 14, and all parties received notice that same day. When does Danny have to file a responsive pleading? (Assume that the deadline you calculate is a weekday and does not fall on a holiday.)

Analysis: Under Rule 12(a)(4)(A), if the court denies the Rule 12 motion or postpones making a decision on the motion, the respondent (in this case, Danny) must serve an answer within 14 days after notice of the court's action. Because Danny found out that the court denied the motion on September 14, he must file a responsive pleading by September 28 (14 days later).

> Rule 4 governs the filing and service of a complaint. After the complaint, Rule 5 governs service and filing of papers. Rule 5 allows for more convenient forms of service like mail and email (if the parties consent).

EXAMPLE: Assume that Danny never filed a 12(b)(2) motion. Assume instead that Danny filed a Rule 12(e) motion for a more definite statement on June 12. On September 15, the court granted the motion, and all parties received notice of the decision the same day. When does Paul have to file an amended complaint that provides a more definite statement of his claim (assuming that the court order does not specify a time)? When does Danny have to file a responsive pleading to that amended complaint? (Assume that the deadline you calculate is a weekday and does not fall on a holiday.)

Analysis: As will be discussed in more detail later in the chapter, Rule 12(e) concerns when one party moves for a more definite statement. This can be done for any pleading that requires a responsive pleading. One example of this would be a complaint, which requires an answer. Since the court granted the motion and the parties got notice on September 15, Paul has until September 29 (14 days after getting notice of the order) to obey the order to serve a more definite statement on Danny. (Note that Rule 12(e) allows a court to set a different time limit on when the motion must be filed, if it chooses to.) Assuming that Paul filed and served his amended complaint on September 29, Danny has until October 13 (14 days after being served with the amended complaint) to serve his responsive pleading. Finally, if Paul does not serve the more definite statement, the court can strike the pleading, which in this case would end the litigation.

IN PRACTICE

All of these rule-based deadlines are generally superseded by a court's case management order, discussed in Chapter 11. So, in practice, these deadlines are often not as tightly timed.

2. Rule 12(b): How to Present Defenses

Rule 12(b) governs how to present defenses in a responsive pleading, including the Rule 8(c) affirmative defenses discussed in Chapter 6. It also delineates a sub-set of defenses that can be raised via motion before filing a responsive pleading.

THE RULE   Rule 12(b)

How to Present Defenses

Every defense to a claim for relief in any pleading **must be asserted in the responsive pleading** if one is required. But a party **may assert the following defenses by motion**:

(1) lack of subject matter jurisdiction;

(2) lack of personal jurisdiction;

(3) improper venue;

(4) insufficient process;

(5) insufficient service of process;

(6) failure to state a claim upon which relief can be granted; and

(7) failure to join a party under Rule 19.

A motion asserting any of these defenses **must be made before pleading if a responsive pleading is allowed**. If a pleading sets out a claim for relief that does not require a responsive pleading, an opposing party may assert at trial any defense to that claim. No defense or objection is waived by joining it with one or more other defenses or objections in a responsive pleading or in a motion.

EXPLANATION

As discussed in Chapter 6, the responding party must set forth his defenses (both affirmative and otherwise) in his responsive pleading under Rule 8. However, Rule 12(b) provides a narrow exception to this rule. Under Rule 12(b), a party may assert the listed sub-set of defenses in a pre-trial motion. This motion must be made before any responsive pleading is filed. Thus, a Rule 12 motion is the vehicle for asserting many of the defenses already discussed in this course book. These include personal jurisdiction in Chapter 1, subject matter jurisdiction in Chapter 2, and venue in Chapter 3. Most notably, the Rule 12(b)(6) motion is a critically important tool for defendants because it allows them to challenge the sufficiency of the pleadings under Rule 8 (and *Twombly* and *Iqbal*) before filing an answer or otherwise moving forward in the litigation process.

3. Rule 12(g): Joining Motions; Rule 12(h): Waiving and Preserving Certain Defenses

The titles of these rules may lull one into thinking that they are independent of one another, but they work together. Rules 12(g) and 12(h) control how particular Rule 12(b) defenses must be raised, and how they will be waived if they are not properly raised. These rules are difficult to decipher so time reading and re-reading these two sections of the rule is well spent.

> A court, when granting a motion to dismiss under Rule 12, will sometimes do so "without prejudice," meaning that if the plaintiff can amend the complaint to cure the alleged defect, it may do so. If the court grants the motion with prejudice, the party cannot amend and re-file in that court. However, if a case is dismissed for something curable like subject matter jurisdiction or venue, the party can re-file the case in an appropriate court and proceed on the merits.

THE RULE   Rule 12(g) & (h)

(g) Joining Motions

(1) Right to Join. A motion under this rule **may be joined** with any other motion allowed by this rule.

(2) Limitation on Further Motions. Except as provided in Rule 12(h)(2) or (3), a party that makes a motion under this rule **must not make another motion under this rule** raising a defense or objection that was available to the party but omitted from its earlier motion.

(3) Lack of Subject-Matter Jurisdiction. If the court determines **at any time** that it lacks subject-matter jurisdiction, the court must dismiss the action.

(h) Waiving and Preserving Certain Defenses

(1) When Some Are Waived. A party **waives any defense listed in Rule 12(b)(2)-(5)** by:

    (A) omitting it from a motion in the circumstances described in **Rule 12(g)(2)**; or

    (B) failing to either:

        (i) make it by motion under this rule; or

        (ii) include it in a responsive pleading or in an amendment allowed by Rule 15(a)(1) as a matter of course.

(2) When to Raise Others. Failure to **state a claim upon which relief can be granted, to join a person required by Rule 19(b), or to state a legal defense to a claim may** be raised:

    (A) in **any pleading** allowed or ordered under Rule 7(a);

    (B) by a motion under **Rule 12(c)**; or

    (C) at trial.

(3) Lack of Subject-Matter Jurisdiction. If the court determines **at any time** that it lacks subject-matter jurisdiction, the court must dismiss the action.

EXPLANATION

Before filing a responsive pleading, a party can raise any or all of the Rule 12(b) defenses through a motion under 12(g). However, once a party makes a motion under Rule 12(b), it must join any applicable defenses listed in Rule 12(b)(2)-(5).

If the party fails to raise those defenses in its Rule 12(b) motion, it will be prohibited from raising any of those defenses in the litigation under Rule 12(h)(1)(A). For example, if a party files a motion to dismiss for failure to state a claim under Rule 12(b)(6), but fails to make a motion for dismissal under 12(b)(2)—personal jurisdiction—that party cannot later raise a defense of personal jurisdiction. Rule 12(h)(1)(A) requires that once a Rule 12 motion is made, all of the defenses listed in Rule 12(b)(2)-(5) must also be raised. This rule furthers judicial economy by forcing parties to bring all the defenses that can be resolved early in the litigation at once.

If a party does not make a motion under Rule 12, it still risks waiving the defenses listed in Rule 12(b)(2)-(5) unless it includes them in the responsive pleading it files under Rule 12(a). *See* Rule 12(h)(1)(B)(ii). In other words, the defenses listed in Rule 12(b)(2)-(5)(the "waivable defenses") must be raised in either a Rule 12 motion or a responsive pleading. Notice though that once a party makes a Rule 12 motion, including any of the defenses listed in Rule 12(b)(2)-(5) in a responsive pleading will not save them. *See* Rule 12(h)(1)(A). Once the motion is made, any of the waivable defenses that are omitted are waived.

Rule 12(b)(1), (6), and (7) defenses are treated differently. These defenses can be raised at any time, including at trial, because of their procedural importance. As is discussed in greater detail in Chapter 2, a Rule 12(b)(1) defense—lack of subject matter jurisdiction—cannot be waived by the court or the parties. This is why under Rule 12(h)(3), the court can raise the issue of subject matter jurisdiction on its own at any time in the litigation. Rule 12(b)(6)—failure to state a claim upon which relief can be granted—allows a court to dismiss a claim before the parties proceed to trial, saving the parties and the court from wasting precious resources. Finally, a Rule 12(b)(7) defense—failure to join a party under Rule 19—ensures that all of the essential parties, as defined by that rule, are included in the litigation before it moves forward.

EXAMPLES & ANALYSIS

EXAMPLE: Peter sued Doug, and Doug was properly served with a summons and complaint. Doug did not think the court had subject matter jurisdiction over this type of case, so he brought a Rule 12(b)(1) motion to dismiss for lack of subject matter jurisdiction. The court considered this, but ultimately decided that it had subject matter jurisdiction over the case. Doug now believes that the court does not have personal jurisdiction over him, so he wants to file a motion to dismiss for lack of personal jurisdiction under Rule 12(b)(2). Can he do that?

Analysis: No. Doug cannot file a Rule 12(b)(2) motion after he has already brought a Rule 12(b)(1) motion. The defenses in Rules 12(b)(2) through 12(b)(5) are waived unless raised in the very first pleading or motion filed with the court. *See* Rule 12(h)(1)(A) and (B). In this case, since Doug already filed a motion to dismiss for lack of subject matter jurisdiction under Rule 12(b)(1), he waived his right to move to dismiss for lack of personal jurisdiction (Rule 12(b)(2)), improper venue (Rule 12(b)(3)), insufficient process (Rule 12(b)(4)), or insufficient service of process (Rule 12(b)(5)). Rule 12(g)(2) requires that he raise all of his Rule 12(b) defenses in one motion, unless there is an exception under Rules 12(h)(2) or (3). Those exceptions do not apply here, so he waived his personal jurisdiction defense.

EXAMPLE: Peter sued Doug for battery, and Doug was properly served with a summons and complaint. Doug filed a Rule 12(b)(2) motion to dismiss for lack of personal jurisdiction, which was denied. After the motion was denied, Doug realized that Peter was suing him in federal court on the basis of diversity jurisdiction, yet Peter and Doug are citizens of the same state. Doug now wants to raise a Rule 12(b)(1) defense, arguing that the court lacks subject matter jurisdiction. Can he do that?

Analysis: Yes. Doug can raise a Rule 12(b)(1) defense at any time, because if the court does not have subject matter jurisdiction over a case, it has no authority to adjudicate the proceedings at all. Rule 12(h)(3) provides that if a court determines that it lacks subject matter jurisdiction, the court must dismiss the action *sua sponte* even if neither party raised the issue. The implication of that rule is that the parties may also raise the issue of subject matter jurisdiction at any time.

EXAMPLE: Pablo sued Don. Don filed a motion to dismiss for lack of personal jurisdiction (Rule 12(b)(2)) and for improper venue (Rule 12(b)(3)). Don properly joined these motions under Rule 12(g)(1). However, the court denied the motions. Now Don wants to file motions to dismiss for insufficient process (Rule 12(b)(4)), insufficient service of process (Rule 12(b)(5)), and failure to join a required party under Rule 19 (Rule 12(b)(7)). Can he file any of those motions?

Analysis: No, but he can assert some of the defenses in his responsive pleading, by a Rule 12(c) motion, or at trial. *See* Rule 12(h)(2)(A), (B) and (C). Rule 12(b)(7) is a non-waivable defense, so even though he did not raise that defense in his original Rule 12(b) motion to dismiss, he can still raise the defense in his responsive pleading, by a motion under Rule 12(c), or at trial. In practice, were he to include the defense in his answer, he could then move to have the defense resolved before trial under Rule 12(i). The other defenses—Rule 12(b)(4)(motion to dismiss for insufficient service) and Rule 12(b)(5)(motion to dismiss for insufficient service of process)—are another story. Rule 12(h)(1) states that those defenses were waived when Don did not include them in his original motion to dismiss for lack of personal jurisdiction (12(b)(2)) and for improper venue (12(b)(3)). Unlike the non-waivable defenses, these defenses cannot be raised later in a pleading, via Rule 12(c), or at trial.

EXAMPLE: Paige sued Donna. In her answer, Donna raised several defenses, including insufficient process (Rule 12(b)(4)), insufficient service of process (Rule 12(b)(5)), and failure to join a required party under Rule 19 (Rule 12(b)(7)). Can Donna include these defenses in her answer and not file a motion?

Analysis: Yes. Rule 12(h)(1)(B)(ii) allows Rule 12(b) defenses to be included in a responsive pleading. An answer is a responsive pleading, so this is completely acceptable. However, note that she would not be able to raise any additional waivable defenses like personal jurisdiction or venue. Because she did not include those in her answer, she has waived them under Rules 12(h)(1)(b)(i) and (ii).

EXAMPLE: Payton sued Dominique. Dominique wants to file a motion to dismiss raising all seven 12(b) defenses at once. Can she do that?

Analysis: Yes, but only if she has a good faith basis to assert all seven defenses. Rule 12(g)(1) provides that when a party makes a motion under Rule 12, she can join any other motion allowed by Rule 12 with that motion. This means that Dominique (or any defendant) can bring all seven motions at once. The only limitation is Rule 11. *See* Chapter 5. The motion must meet the requirements of Rule 11, or Dominique might be subject to sanctions.

4. Rule 12(i): Hearing Before Trial

Under Rule 12(i), a party may require the court to make a decision regarding any Rule 12(b) defenses properly raised in a responsive pleading or Rule 12 motion.

THE RULE	Rule 12(i)

Hearing Before Trial

If a party so moves, any defense listed in Rule 12(b)(1)-(7)—whether made in a pleading or by motion—and a motion under Rule 12(c) must be heard and decided before trial unless the court orders a deferral until trial.

EXPLANATION

 When a defendant uses Rule 12(b)(1)-12(b)(7) motions, the court must "hear" the motions under Rule 12(i), unless the court orders a deferral, postponing a decision on the motion until trial. The purpose of this rule is to force the pre-trial resolution of any defenses that might make reaching the merits of the case unnecessary. Note that the court may satisfy this requirement for a hearing by reading the briefs, and courts frequently rule on Rule 12 motions without oral argument.

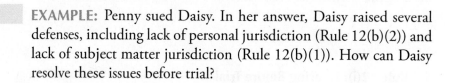

EXAMPLE: Penny sued Daisy. In her answer, Daisy raised several defenses, including lack of personal jurisdiction (Rule 12(b)(2)) and lack of subject matter jurisdiction (Rule 12(b)(1)). How can Daisy resolve these issues before trial?

Analysis: Daisy could move for a hearing on both of these issues before trial using Rule 12(i). However, the court can decide to defer the issue until trial if, for example, the defenses raise issues that need to be determined at trial anyway.

EXAMPLE: Using the same example as above, what if Daisy already raised a motion to dismiss for lack of personal jurisdiction under Rule 12(b)(2) that was denied, and now Daisy includes a defense of lack of subject matter jurisdiction (Rule 12(b)(1)) in her answer. How can this be resolved before trial?

Analysis: Rule 12(b)(1) is a non-waivable defense, and under 12(h)(3) a party may raise the issue of lack of subject matter jurisdiction at any time. Daisy can move for a hearing on the issue of subject matter jurisdiction using Rule 12(i) to get a hearing before trial.

IN PRACTICE

Depending on the judge, a party may have oral argument regarding a Rule 12 motion filed before the responsive pleading, even though the rule does not specifically provide for one. Practice varies from state to state and from court to court. Again, it is in the judge's discretion to hold an argument (or to allow a party requesting an argument to have one).

5. Rule 12(e): Motion for a More Definite Statement;
   Rule 12(f): Motion to Strike

A motion for a more definite statement and motion to strike are objections to the pleadings. They are subject to the same issues raised by the Rule 12(b) defenses and, therefore, can be waived if not properly raised.

THE RULE   Rule 12(e) & 12(f)

(e) Motion for a More Definite Statement

A party may move for a **more definite statement of a pleading** to which a responsive pleading is allowed but which is so **vague or ambiguous** that the party cannot reasonably prepare a response. The motion must be made **before filing a responsive pleading** and must point out **the defects complained of and the details desired**. If the court orders a more definite statement and the order is not obeyed within 14 days after notice of the order or within the time the court sets, the court may strike the pleading or issue any other appropriate order.

(f) Motion to Strike

The court may strike from a pleading an insufficient defense or any **redundant, immaterial, impertinent, or scandalous matter**. The court may act:

(1) on its own; or

(2) on motion made by a party either before responding to the pleading or, if a response is not allowed, within 21 days after being served with the pleading.

EXPLANATION

If a party receives a complaint that is so lacking in detail as to cause problems in proceeding, it can move for a more definite statement, meaning that it is asking the complaining party to clarify its claims. For example, the responding party may not know which of the claims are made against it as opposed to other defendants or it may not understand what the substantive claims are. More commonly, the responding party may feel that the complaint fails to include sufficient factual detail to place it on notice of the actual claims against it. Essentially the responding party is arguing that the complaint is written in a way that renders the party incapable of responding to the complaint. Rather than dismissing the complaint, the court may order a more definite statement. Under the rule, the responding party must point out what it needs to know that is not included in the complaint. A Rule 12(e) motion must be made before filing a responsive pleading. After all, if the party can respond to the complaint, then there is no need for a more definite statement. If the court orders a more definite statement and the order is not obeyed within the time the court sets, or within 14 days after notice of the order if the court does not set a time, the court may strike the pleading or issue any other appropriate order. If the court orders a more definite statement and the party files one, the responding party must respond to the amended pleading within 14 days of that amended pleading being served (Rule 12(a)(4)(B)).

A motion to strike is made when a part of the complaint does not comply with the rules or is intended to harass or embarrass. In that case, the court may strike out the offending language, defense, or allegation in the complaint. A court may do this *sua sponte* or by motion.

EXAMPLES & ANALYSIS

EXAMPLE: Prisoner Paul sued Damage Magazine for libel. Prisoner Paul is a *pro se* plaintiff, and wrote the complaint himself. The complaint stated only that Damage Magazine published an article that, when read as a whole, was libelous and that Prisoner Paul was damaged by the article. He claimed general damages of $1,000,000. Damage Magazine filed a Rule 12(e) motion. How should the court respond?

Analysis: The court should probably grant the Rule 12(e) motion and require that Prisoner Paul clarify his complaint. This complaint does not give Damage Magazine adequate notice of what it is being sued for. It does not specify what article was allegedly libelous; it does not explain what specific part of the article was libelous; it does not specify how Prisoner Paul was damaged; and it does not explain how the $1,000,000 in damages was calculated.

EXAMPLE: Pansy entered into a contract with Devious Industries in order to buy widgets. In the contract, Devious Industries promised to use its "best efforts" to ensure delivery of the widgets. Devious Industries did not deliver the widgets, and Pansy sued for breach of contract. In her complaint, Pansy cited a Security and Exchange Commission ("SEC") complaint that had been filed against Devious Industries for altering balance sheets it submitted to the SEC. Devious Industries filed a Rule 12(f) motion to strike the reference to the SEC complaint in Pansy's complaint. How should the court rule?

Analysis: Pansy sued Devious Industries for breach of contract. The elements of breach of contract do not involve whether or not the defendant has been sued by the SEC, so this part of the complaint is immaterial. Under Rule 12(f), upon a motion by a party (or *sua sponte),* the court may strike any redundant, immaterial, impertinent, or scandalous matter from the pleading. Here, the court would likely delete the parts of Pansy's complaint that referenced the SEC complaint. If the allegation is not pertinent or material to her breach of contract claim, it should be struck.

EXAMPLE: Pricilla sued Damon for assault. Damon received the summons and complaint and immediately filed an answer denying every allegation in Pricilla's complaint. After filing the answer, Damon looked more closely at Pricilla's complaint and realized that it was missing some key information, such as when the alleged assault occurred and how Pricilla was injured (if she was injured at all). Damon now wants to file a motion for a more definite statement under Rule 12(e). Can he do so?

Analysis: No. Damon has already filed his answer, so he cannot file a motion for a more definite statement. Rule 12(e) requires that motions for a more definite statement be made before a responsive pleading is filed. If Damon raised failure to state a claim as an affirmative defense in his answer, however, he may still be able to challenge the complaint based on the missing allegations.

EXAMPLE: Parker sued Donovan for trademark infringement. Before filing his answer, Donovan filed a motion for a more definite statement because he could not identify what trademark Parker alleged that he infringed. The motion was granted, and Parker filed an amended complaint. Now, Donovan wants to file a motion raising a Rule 12(b)(2) defense of lack of personal jurisdiction and a Rule 12(b)(4) defense of insufficient process. Can he do so?

Analysis: The answer depends on whether either of these defenses were "available to the party" at the time Donovan filed his Rule 12(e) motion. The Rule 12(e) motion is a motion under Rule 12, so it triggers the requirements of Rules 12(g) and (h). Donavan was probably aware of the service of process issues when he filed his Rule 12(e) motion, so he probably waived the service defense. However, the personal jurisdiction defense probably survives if the lack of information in the complaint regarding Parker's claim made it impossible for Donovan to decipher Parker's alleged basis for personal jurisdiction. If the basis for personal jurisdiction was apparent in the original complaint, however, Donovan may have waived that defense as well. This issue is a bit unsettled, but this is probably the best reading of the rule.

**6. Rule 12(c): Motion for Judgment on the Pleadings;
Rule 12(d): Result of Presenting Matters Outside
the Pleadings**

Under Rule 12(c), a court can decide a case based on the pleadings alone. Under Rule 12(d), the court can take a motion to dismiss and consider it as a motion for summary judgment.

THE RULE   **Rule 12(c) & 12(d)**

(c) Motion for Judgment on the Pleadings

After the pleadings are closed—but early enough not to delay trial— a party may move for **judgment on the pleadings**.

(d) Result of Presenting Matters Outside the Pleadings

If, on a motion under Rule 12(b)(6) or 12(c), **matters outside the pleadings are presented to and not excluded by the court**, the motion must be treated as one for summary judgment under Rule 56. All parties must be given a reasonable opportunity to present all the material that is pertinent to the motion.

EXPLANATION

After the pleadings are closed, a party may move for a judgment on the pleadings by using Rule 12(c). However, if evidence outside of the pleadings is presented with a Rule 12(b)(6) motion or a Rule 12(c) motion, and the court does not exclude that evidence, the court must treat the motion as one for summary judgment under Rule 56.

EXAMPLES & ANALYSIS

EXAMPLE: Pearl sued her employer, the Delicious Diner Inc., for age discrimination. In her complaint, Pearl said that when she was terminated her employer told her she was too old, and the diner only wanted young employees to serve their customers. Delicious Diner Inc. filed an answer, which raised an affirmative defense of statute of limitations. Assume the statute of limitations for an age discrimination suit is two years, and Pearl did not file her complaint until five years after her termination. Delicious Diner Inc. moves for judgment on the pleadings under 12(c). How should the court respond?

Analysis: Assuming that there were no facts that would require the statute of limitations to be tolled, the court has everything it needs to make a judgment based on the pleadings. More than two years passed between the time her cause of action accrued at her termination and the filing of her complaint. Therefore, the judge should rule on the pleadings under Rule 12(c) because she has all the information she needs to rule.

EXAMPLE: Poe sued Buses-R-Us for damages. In his complaint, Poe said that a bus rear-ended his car. Buses-R-Us responded with an answer denying any liability, and filed a Rule 12(c) motion for judgment on the pleadings. Attached to the answer was a picture of Poe's car shortly after the accident. The picture showed damage to the passenger side of Poe's car (and not the back, as one would expect when a car has been rear-ended). Buses-R-Us argued that the picture demonstrated that it had not rear-ended Poe, as alleged in the complaint. How should the court handle this motion?

Analysis: While Buses-R-Us may have made a Rule 12(c) motion, Rule 12(d) forces the court to treat a 12(c) motion like a summary judgment motion when matters outside the pleadings are presented to and not excluded by the court. Assuming the court does not exclude the picture of Poe's car, the court must treat the Buses-R-Us motion as one for summary judgment under Rule 56 and allow Poe to respond accordingly. *See* Chapter 15.

B. Rule 55: Default Judgment

If a party fails to appear in an action, a default will be ordered and a default judgment entered. Once the default or default judgment order is entered, the only recourse available to the defaulted party is a motion for relief pursuant to Rules 55(c) and 60(b). See Chapter 18 for a discussion of setting aside default judgments under Rule 60.

> Although appeal is another available way to attack a default judgment, assuming the party learns of the judgment while it is appealable, it is not entirely satisfactory. Since the defaulted party was not a part of the trial court proceedings, the record on appeal is unlikely to urge reversal. Appellate courts are generally not receptive to appeals raising issues that have not been presented to the trial court. Thus, relief from the default should usually be sought in the trial court. *See* Chapter 18.

THE RULE   Rule 55

Default; Default Judgment

(a) Entering a Default. When a party against whom a judgment for affirmative relief is sought **has failed to plead or otherwise defend**, and that **failure is shown by affidavit or otherwise**, the **clerk must** enter the party's default.

(b) Entering a Default Judgment.

(1) By the Clerk. If the plaintiff's claim is for **a sum certain or a sum that can be made certain by computation**, the clerk—on the plaintiff's request, with an affidavit showing the amount due—**must enter judgment for that amount and costs against a defendant** who has been defaulted for not appearing and who is neither a minor nor an incompetent person.

(2) By the Court. In all other cases, the party must apply to the court for a default judgment. A default judgment may be entered against a minor or incompetent person only if represented by a general guardian, conservator, or other like fiduciary who has appeared. If the party against whom a default judgment is sought has appeared personally or by a representative, that party or its representative must be served with written notice of the application at least 7 days before the hearing. The court may conduct hearings or make referrals—preserving any federal statutory right to a jury trial—when, to enter or effectuate judgment, it needs to:

(A) conduct an accounting;

(B) determine the amount of damages;

(C) establish the truth of any allegation by evidence; or

(D) investigate any other matter.

(c) Setting Aside a Default or a Default Judgment. The court may **set aside an entry of default for good cause**, and **it may set aside a default judgment under Rule 60(b).**

EXPLANATION

Obtaining a default judgment is generally a two-step process—obtaining a default and then obtaining a judgment based upon the default. The distinction between default and default judgment is this: default is a failure to respond that may be determinative of an issue (because the adversary system requires a response); default judgment is the entry of a judgment, which is a court order giving a party monetary or other relief. The mere failure of the opponent to respond is a default but does not itself result in default judgment. Before that happens, the party seeking the default judgment must make a motion and demonstrate that it is entitled to the relief requested.

1. Obtaining Default

Rule 55(a) contains the procedure for obtaining a default—essentially a determination that the defendant has not answered or responded to the complaint. Rule 55(a) requires the **clerk** to enter default when the plaintiff, by affidavit or other proof, demonstrates that the defendant has not answered or otherwise re-

> **"Clerk"** in this instance refers to the clerk of the court (or an assistant), the chief bureaucratic officer of the court. In other contexts, "clerk" may refer to the law clerks who work with individual judges or the court as a whole in performing legal research and related tasks.

sponded to the complaint (typically by a Rule 12 motion). The court can also enter default if it chooses to do so. However, obtaining a default does not entitle the plaintiff to recover money from the defendant. To recover damages, the plaintiff must move for default judgment under Rule 55(b).

2. Obtaining Default Judgment

If the complaint contains a demand for a sum certain or a sum that can be made certain by calculation and the plaintiff submits an affidavit showing the amount due, the clerk must enter a default judgment against a defendant who has been defaulted. The judgment will include that sum certain plus costs. If the complaint does not contain a demand for a sum certain (such as, for example, in a case involving pain and suffering), the plaintiff must move the court for a default judgment. Although "winning" a case and proving damages is usually easier when there is no opponent, even in the absence of opposition, the judge will require the movant to present sufficient evidence to convince the court that it is entitled to judgment. Where a plaintiff's claim is for a "sum certain" or a sum that can be "made certain by computation," the clerk "must" enter judgment when presented with a proper affidavit showing the sum to which the movant is entitled from a defaulting defendant. *See* Rule 55(b)(1).

3. Setting Aside a Default or Default Judgment

If the defendant wants to challenge a default or default judgment, the defendant may move to set aside the default or default judgment under Rule 55(c). The court will grant the motion if the defendant can show "good cause." In order to set aside default judgment, the party must use Rule 60. Rule 60 and setting aside judgments is discussed in Chapter 18.

IN PRACTICE

In general, courts prefer to have cases resolved on the merits, and if a defendant moves promptly to set aside the default or default judgment, most courts will grant the motion. That does not mean, however, that it is a good idea to miss the deadline for answering and hope that the court will set aside any default that is entered.

EXAMPLES & ANALYSIS

EXAMPLE: Parker sells his house to Dan for $100,000. Dan pays by check, and the check bounces. Parker sues Dan in federal court. Two months after Dan is properly served, he still has not answered the complaint or filed any papers. Can Parker take advantage of a Rule 55 default? If so, how?

Analysis: Parker may first seek a default under Rule 55(a). Parker must submit an affidavit or other evidence demonstrating that Dan failed to respond to the complaint. Because he is seeking a sum certain—$100,000—Parker may then seek a default judgment from the clerk for $100,000 plus his costs in the litigation, again supported by an affidavit.

EXAMPLE: In the above example, after the complaint is filed, Parker learns that Dan is planning to knock down the house in order to build a bigger house on the lot. Parker is concerned that the property will lose value if Dan does not complete a new house, and that Parker may not be able to use the property to satisfy his default judgment. Can Dan move the court for an injunction as part of the default judgment under Rule 55(b)?

Analysis: No. Defaults are limited to the relief requested in the complaint.

IN PRACTICE

Many courts have specific additional rules applicable to setting aside default. The party seeking to set aside defaults or default judgments often must submit an "affidavit of merit" stating that there is a meritorious defense to the claim. The court will not be inclined to set aside a default if the outcome of the claim is a foregone conclusion. In addition, by local rule or custom and practice, the court often requires a party to pay a modest fee (*e.g.*, $500) as a condition of setting aside default.

EXAMPLE: Pete sues Diane over a past due debt but Diane's side of the story is that the merchandise he sold her was substandard. Pete uses Paul as a process server. Assume that Paul timely gave the summons and complaint to Diane's husband, Don, who then left on a month-long business trip with the complaint in his briefcase and forgot about it until he returned home. Diane seeks to set aside the resulting default and asserts that Don's inadvertence is why she did not interpose a timely answer to the complaint. What would the court do in this case?

Analysis: Although Diane's plight is not entirely sympathetic, most courts would find this to be good cause. Diane should not lose her day in court because of the negligence of her husband. But in a case like this, the court might impose a significant fee (*e.g.*, $1,500) as a condition of setting aside default because of the inconvenience and weaker excuse for non-response.

C. Rule 41: Voluntary and Involuntary Dismissal

As already discussed, Rule 12 provides for dismissal near the beginning of the case for various reasons, such as for failure to state a claim in the complaint. Rule 41 contains provisions for dismissal in two other circumstances. First, Rule 41(a) allows for voluntary dismissal—when the plaintiff is seeking to dismiss its own complaint. Rule 41(b) allows for involuntary dismissal at the behest of the defendant or the court. The overall purpose and effect of Rule 41 is to permit claimants broad leeway in dropping claims, but to provide a means of compensating defendants who incurred expenses prior to claimants' termination of the matter.

THE RULE   Rule 41(a) & (b)

Dismissal of Actions

(a) Voluntary Dismissal.

    (1) *By the Plaintiff.*

        (A) *Without a Court Order.* Subject to Rules 23(e), 23.1(c), 23.2, and 66 and any applicable federal statute, the plaintiff may dismiss an action without a court order by filing:

        (i)   a notice of dismissal **before the opposing party serves either an answer or a motion for summary judgment**; or

        (ii) a **stipulation** of dismissal **signed by all parties who have appeared.**

   (B) *Effect*. **Unless the notice or stipulation states otherwise**, the dismissal is **without prejudice**. But if the plaintiff previously dismissed any federal- or state-court action based on or including the same claim, a notice of dismissal operates as an adjudication on the merits.

  (2) *By Court Order; Effect*. Except as provided in Rule 41(a)(1), an action may be dismissed at the plaintiff's request only by court order, on terms that the court considers proper. If a defendant has pleaded a counterclaim before being served with the plaintiff's motion to dismiss, the action may be dismissed over the defendant's objection only if the counterclaim can remain pending for independent adjudication. Unless the order states otherwise, a dismissal under this paragraph (2) is without prejudice.

(b) Involuntary Dismissal; Effect. If the plaintiff **fails to prosecute or to comply with these rules or a court order**, a defendant may move to dismiss the action or any claim against it. **Unless the dismissal order states otherwise**, a dismissal under this subdivision **(b)** and any dismissal not under this rule—except one for lack of jurisdiction, improper venue, or failure to join a party under Rule 19—**operates as an adjudication on the merits.**

EXPLANATION

1. Voluntary Dismissal

Voluntary dismissal typically occurs in two situations: when the plaintiff decides not to proceed with the case; and when the parties settle the case. If the voluntary dismissal occurs at the beginning of the case, when the defendant has not yet answered or filed a motion for summary judgment, the plaintiff can unilaterally dismiss the case by filing a notice of dismissal. This notice does not require consent by the defendant, and is automatically effective without action by the court. Note that a Rule 12 motion does not preclude a notice of dismissal. Thus, if the plaintiff is persuaded by a defendant's Rule 12 motion, the plaintiff can file a notice of dismissal under Rule 41(a)(1)(A)(i).

If the case has proceeded to the stage where the defendant has answered or filed a motion for summary judgment, then the plaintiff cannot dismiss the case unilaterally. In such circumstances, the plaintiff has two options. First, if the defendant agrees, the plaintiff can file a stipulation of dismissal signed by all parties. If the defendant will not agree, however, then the plaintiff must file a motion to dismiss. While it might seem odd for a defendant to refuse to consent to the dismissal, there are some strategic reasons to do so. Often, a plaintiff will want to dismiss a case without prejudice—meaning that he can refile at a later date or in a different court. In that case, a defendant may refuse the voluntary dismissal in order to resolve the case in the current litigation, rather than starting over in another forum. When the defendant opposes the voluntary dismissal, the court can grant the motion, deny the motion, or grant the motion with conditions—such as making the dismissal with prejudice or ordering the plaintiff to pay the defendant's fees and/or costs. The plaintiff can decline the dismissal if it is not willing to agree to the conditions.

As already noted, a case may be voluntarily dismissed through a signed stipulation by all parties. This is typical when a case is completely settled. Where settlement involves fewer than all defendants, the plaintiff and settling defendants can craft the agreement so that the settlement does not prejudice the plaintiff's remaining claims. Different jurisdictions have different names for the types of settlement agreements and releases that have been approved for such purposes. This area of litigation requires great care and local knowledge by counsel so that some claims are not inadvertently released or recoverable damages limited.

2. Involuntary Dismissal

A defendant who believes that the plaintiff has failed to comply with the rules or with a court order can seek involuntary dismissal under Rule 41(b). Typically, such orders are only granted when the defendant's conduct is repeated and egregious. The court may involuntarily dismiss a case under

Rule 41(b) for want of prosecution. It can do so at the request of the defendant or on its own.

3. Prejudice in Dismissals

Whether a dismissal is with or without prejudice becomes a critical issue in dismissals under Rule 41. As a general rule, when a plaintiff voluntarily dismisses a case, the dismissal will be presumed to be without prejudice unless otherwise specified. Conversely, an involuntary dismissal is presumed to be with prejudice.

> Although a plaintiff whose claim has been dismissed without prejudice can generally refile it, the "two dismissal rule" prevents repeated filings and dismissals. That rule provides that the second dismissal of the same action is with prejudice, regardless of whether it is voluntary or involuntary (and regardless of whether the first dismissal was in state or federal court).

EXAMPLES & ANALYSIS

EXAMPLE: Priscilla files a complaint against Danielle. Danielle responds with a motion to dismiss. Can Priscilla voluntarily dismiss her complaint, and if so how?

Analysis: Rule 41(a)(1) allows for dismissal by filing a notice of dismissal before an answer or motion for summary judgment is filed. Priscilla can voluntarily dismiss her complaint by filing a notice of dismissal. She does not need to seek consent from Danielle or the court.

EXAMPLE: Priscilla files a complaint against Danielle. Danielle responds with an answer. Can Priscilla voluntarily dismiss her complaint without court involvement, and if so how?

Analysis: Rule 41(a)(1) allows dismissal after an answer by stipulation, so if Danielle agrees, Priscilla can dismiss by filing a stipulation of dismissal.

EXAMPLE: Priscilla files a complaint against Danielle. Danielle responds with an answer. Priscilla asks Danielle to consent to dismissal without prejudice, but Danielle refuses. Can Priscilla voluntarily dismiss her complaint, and if so how?

Analysis: Because Danielle will not consent, Priscilla must file a motion to dismiss with the court under Rule 41(a)(2). The court can grant the motion, deny the motion, or grant the motion with conditions. If the court grants the motion with conditions, Priscilla will have the option of declining the dismissal.

IN PRACTICE

In addition to the grounds for involuntary dismissal set forth in Rule 41(b), particularly in state court practice, there may be additional grounds for involuntary dismissal such as failure to post necessary security required to go forward with the case or failure to follow a particular state requirement, local rule, or judge's standing order. Counsel must be alert to these somewhat "hidden" requirements that can pose a trap for the unwary.

ADDITIONAL EXERCISES

1. You are the general counsel for Department Store, Inc. and have just been informed about a lawsuit against your client. *See* Additional Exercise in Chapter 6. With the complaint in front of you, the manager of the store gives you a very different version of the story. The plaintiff has two potential claims against Department Store, Inc.: (1) false imprisonment, and (2) intentional infliction of emotional distress. Based on the following facts, how will you respond under Rule 12?

   As the general counsel, you are the properly designated agent to accept service of summons on behalf of Department Store, Inc. You return from lunch to find your administrative assistant a little nervous. When you ask him what is wrong, he tells you that while you were out, a teenager came into the office looking for you. When your assistant told the teen that you were out, the teen said "Well, they told me to find the general counsel, but I guess you'll do" and dropped a complaint on your assistant's desk, then left the office.

You look at the complaint itself, and are surprised to find it devoid of important details. The complaint lists a bankruptcy court as the court, but it does not list a date for a hearing. Additionally, you look at the date of when the alleged false imprisonment occurred and realize that it happened three years ago. After a quick search of the relevant law, you discover that the statute of limitations for a false imprisonment claim in your jurisdiction is one year. **How would you advise Department Store, Inc. to respond to this complaint?**

2. Pippy sues Damien and Dane for battery, claiming both Damien and Dane pushed Pippy into oncoming traffic. Damien and Dane are both served with the summons and complaint on March 1, 2008. Dane files a crossclaim against Damien, arguing that Damien punched Dane so hard that Dane flew into Pippy, causing Pippy to be pushed into oncoming traffic. Damien is served with the crossclaim on April 1, 2008. **How long does Damien have to respond to Pippy's complaint? How long does Damien have to respond to Dane's crossclaim?** (Assume that the deadline you calculate is a weekday and does not fall on a holiday.)

3. Paolo files suit against Dax for infringing on Paolo's intellectual property. Dax is served with a copy of the complaint on November 1. Dax timely raises a motion for a more definite statement under Rule 12(e), which is granted by the court, with leave to amend. Paolo fixes the complaint and serves Dax again, this time with a complaint that is more definite. Dax is served with Paolo's first amended complaint on December 1. **How long does Dax have to respond to the first amended complaint?** (Assume that the deadline you calculate is a weekday and does not fall on a holiday.)

4. The National Professional Bowlers Union, a union representing professional bowlers, sues the Division of Professional Bowling, the professional bowling league, for unfair labor practices. The Division of Professional Bowling immediately files a motion for improper venue under Rule 12(b)(3). The court denies the motion on August 3. The Division of Professional Bowling receives a copy of the order denying the motion on August 7. **When must the Division of Professional Bowling serve the responsive pleading on the National Professional Bowlers Union?** (Assume that the deadline you calculate is a weekday and does not fall on a holiday.)

5. Patricio sues Doughboy Restaurant in federal court after Patricio became very ill from eating at the restaurant. Doughboy Restaurant brings a motion to dismiss based on lack of personal jurisdiction under Rule 12(b)(2), which the court denies. Doughboy Restaurant then realizes that the complaint and summons do not comply with the requirements of Rule 4, and files a Rule 12(b)(4) motion asking the court to dismiss the claim based on insufficient process. ***How should the court respond?***

6. Pierre and his three siblings are left a substantial amount of money to be held in trust. Dean is named the trustee, the person who is in charge of looking after the money for the benefit of Pierre and his siblings. One day Pierre learns that Dean has been embezzling money from the trust. Pierre personally sues Dean for embezzlement and in his prayer for relief asks for monetary damages and to be named the new trustee. Dean first tries and fails to have the suit dismissed for insufficient service of process under Rule 12(b)(5). Dean then decides to file a motion under Rule 12(b)(7), asking the court to dismiss the case because Pierre failed to join his siblings, who are required parties under Rule 19. ***How should the court respond?***

7. Pierce sues Daria for breach of contract. Daria files several motions asking the court to dismiss the suit, including a 12(b)(2) motion for lack of personal jurisdiction, a 12(b)(3) motion for improper venue, and a 12(b)(5) motion for insufficient service of process. Pierce argues that there could not possibly have been insufficient service of process because Daria knew enough about the suit to challenge personal jurisdiction and venue, which meant that the service of process was good enough for her to receive actual notice of Pierce's allegations. ***How should the court respond?***

8. Victor was riding a motorcycle on the highway, and was involved in a collision. After the collision, Victor fell into a persistent vegetative state. Victor's wife, Pilar, investigated the collision and found out that Victor was wearing a defective helmet sold by Doffle Co. Pilar decided to sue Doffle Co. under a product liability theory in federal court. Doffle Co. initially raised several defenses under Rule 12, including failure to state a claim upon which relief could be granted and insufficient process, but the motions were denied and the case proceeded to trial. While the trial was underway, Congress passed the "Protect Our Manufacturers" bill, which prohibits federal courts from hearing any cases based on product liability. The "Protect Our Manufacturers"

bill was signed into law before a verdict was reached in Pilar's case. Immediately before the judge announced the verdict, Doffle Co. brought a 12(b)(1) motion to dismiss for lack of subject matter jurisdiction. **Assuming the "Protect Our Manufacturers" law is constitutional and applies to pending cases, how should the court respond to Doffle Co.'s 12(b)(1) motion?**

9. Princess sues Duchess for false imprisonment. In her responsive pleading, Duchess raises the affirmative defense of duress, claiming that she was being threatened by the mafia to keep Princess imprisoned. After submitting her responsive pleading, Duchess now wants to bring a motion to dismiss the claim under Rule 12(b)(3) for improper venue. **How should the court respond?**

10. On May 1, Pete's Quickie Loan lends Diane $1,000 at the rate of two percent per month with simple interest. The full payment is due in 60 days. July 2 arrives with no payment from Diane. Pete files a complaint on August 1. Diane does not reply. On October 1, Pete moves for entry of default and for default judgment, submitting an affidavit describing the transaction and Diane's failure to pay. It includes as exhibits the loan agreement, a copy of the $1,000 check tendered to Diane on May 1, and a worksheet showing that the simple interest on the loan for the May 1 to October 1 period is $100. **Can the Clerk of Court enter default judgment for Pete and against Diane? In what amount?**

11. Assume that instead of taking out a cash loan from Pete, Diane rents Pete's prize pickle-pepperer for six months at a stated rental price of $500. Six months later, Diane returns the pickle-pepperer and pays the rent, but the machine is completely unusable. Pete sues Diane, alleging improper use and maintenance of the equipment. Diane is served and sends Pete a nasty email stating that she should not be responsible for the poor durability of Pete's machine—but she does not answer the complaint or make a Rule 12 motion. **Is Diane in default? What are Pete's procedural and substantive remedies?**

12. Continuing the saga of Pete and Diane, assume that default has been entered against Diane but a hearing on the default judgment has not yet been held. Diane moves to set aside the default, contending that she never received service of the complaint. In response, Pete produces Paul

Process Server's certificate of service. Diane brings to the stand a police officer who testifies that Paul has been charged with fraud for taking service fees from lawyers and completing certificates of service without actually serving the complaints upon defendants as required by Rule 4. *Will the Court set aside the default?*

13. Pismo's lawyer filed a complaint against the city's Sewer and Water Authority. Pismo had 120 days to serve the Sewer and Water Authority. Before the time of service expired, Pismo's lawyer asked for an extension. The court granted Pismo an extra 45 days. After the 45 days expired, Pismo failed to serve the Sewer and Water Authority, and did not request a second extension. The court dismissed Pismo's claim for failure to provide service to the city's Sewer and Water Authority. *Did the court properly dismiss Pismo's claim?*

14. Bo Pule, a police officer, filed a complaint against the Dard County Sheriff's Department. Pule was fired after becoming a whistleblower and exposing corruption within Dard County Sherriff's Department. Pule is alleging that his First Amendment rights were violated. He also filed a claim under the state's whistleblower law, as well as a wrongful termination claim. Pule would like to withdraw his wrongful termination claim and dismiss the claim without prejudice. Dard County has yet to submit an answer or a motion for summary judgment in the case. *May Pule ask the court to withdraw his wrongful termination claim and dismiss that claim without prejudice?*

15. Pali filed a suit against Deadwood, a papermaking corporation. Before going to trial, Pali and Deadwood settled and would like to dismiss the case. *Can Pali and Deadwood have the claim dismissed? How?*

Quick Summary

- Responding parties have a strategic choice to make when determining whether to answer the complaint or file a motion under Rule 12.

- Rule 12 governs when particular defenses must be made. These defenses are ones that, as a matter of policy, should be resolved well before the case reaches disposition on the merits. In other words, in the interest of efficiency, issues such as personal jurisdiction, service of process, and venue should be resolved early in the process.

- Because of this interest in efficiency, parties are required to raise and resolve these defenses early or risk waiving them.

- Some defenses, like subject matter jurisdiction, can never be waived.

- Under Rule 12, the responding party can request a more definite statement of the claims being made against her and can also strike parts of the pleading that are embarrassing or immaterial.

- In addition to Rule 12 motions, there are other ways to dismiss or resolve a case before reaching the merits. These include default judgment under Rule 55 and dismissals under Rule 41.

8

Basic Joinder

Key Concepts

- The concept of "joinder," which refers to what types of claims and which parties may be added or "joined" in a single lawsuit
- The joinder of claims in a single lawsuit under Rule 18
- The joinder of parties in a single lawsuit under Rule 20
- The filing of counterclaims against the plaintiff and crossclaims against codefendants under Rule 13
- A party's ability to join or "implead" additional claims against additional parties under Rule 14

Introduction

In the simplest of lawsuits, one plaintiff sues one defendant for one cause of action. Paul buys a house from Diane, after Diane represents that the roof is relatively new and water tight. After the sale, Paul discovers that the roof had a pre-existing problem that will be very expensive to repair. In the most simple action, Paul sues Diane for breach of the representation. One plaintiff, one defendant, one claim.

Now suppose that the real estate broker, Bill, also made representations about the roof. Can Paul name Diane and Bill as defendants in a single action? Suppose Bill also sold Paul another property for a vacation home and there is a problem with that property too. Can Paul combine his claim against Diane and Bill related to the first property with his claim against Bill only for the second property? Suppose Paul did not make some of his scheduled payments on the second property. Can Bill assert a claim back against Paul? Answering these questions may entail an analysis of personal jurisdiction, subject matter jurisdiction, and the joinder rules. This chapter will examine these questions under the joinder rules.

A. The Rules

Rule 18 answers the basic question of which types of claims a party may join together in a single suit. Essentially, it provides that a plaintiff may join all the claims it has against another party in one action, without any requirement that the claims be related.

Rule 20 answers the other basic questions regarding who may join together as plaintiffs and whom the plaintiffs may name as defendants. In order for two parties to join as plaintiffs, they must have claims arising out of the same transaction or occurrence—or series of transactions or occurrences—and there must be a question of law or fact common to all plaintiffs. The rule governing multiple defendants is almost identical—in order for the plaintiffs to name two or more parties as defendants, there must be a claim against each defendant arising out of the same transaction or occurrence or series of transactions or occurrences and there must be a question of law or fact common to all defendants.

Rule 13 contains the provisions for counterclaims—claims that a defendant asserts back against the plaintiff. Some counterclaims are compulsory—generally those that arise out of the same transaction or occurrence as the plaintiff's claim. All others are permissive, and may or may not be brought at the defendant's discretion. Rule 13 also contains the provisions for crossclaims—claims by one defendant against a co-defendant. A crossclaim must arise out of the same transaction or occurrence as the original claim, and all crossclaims are permissive.

> Defendants who bring in third-party defendants are referred to as "**third-party plaintiffs**" in the context of the third-party claims. If a third-party defendant brings in another party, that party would be referred to as a "fourth-party defendant," and the third party defendant is referred to as the "fourth-party plaintiff." And so on.

Rule 14 provides parties with a right to join new parties as "third-party defendants." A "third-party defendant" is someone who may be liable for all or part of the liability asserted against the original defendant. Rule 14 also specifies which claims may be asserted between the plaintiff and a third-party defendant.

B. Joinder of Claims

THE RULE   Rule 18(a)

Joinder of Claims

In General. A party asserting a claim, counterclaim, crossclaim, or third-party claim may join, as independent or alternative claims, as many claims as it has against an opposing party.

EXPLANATION

Rule 18(a) is quite simple and straightforward. It provides that if a party is asserting one claim, counterclaim, crossclaim, or third-party claim, the party may join any other claims it has against the opposing party, without regard to whether the claims are related in any fashion.

EXAMPLE: Patrick brings an age discrimination claim against his employer, Donna's Accountants, under the federal civil rights statutes. Patrick also wants to assert a copyright claim against Donna's Accountants on the grounds that Donna's Accountants used a computer program that Patrick wrote without his permission and without compensating him. Can Patrick bring both claims in a single action in federal court?

Analysis: Patrick is authorized to bring both claims under Rule 18(a). Once Patrick is bringing one claim against Donna's Accountants, he can join any other claims he has against the company.

1. Subject Matter Jurisdiction

Remember that each claim must have an independent basis for federal court subject matter jurisdiction—generally federal question jurisdiction, diversity jurisdiction, or supplemental jurisdiction. So the fact that Rule 18(a) authorizes a plaintiff to join additional claims does not relieve the plaintiff from having to establish federal court subject matter jurisdiction over each claim that is joined in the case, as discussed in Chapter 1.

EXAMPLES & ANALYSIS

EXAMPLE: Patrick brings an age discrimination claim against his employer, Donna's Accountants, under the federal civil rights statutes. Patrick also wants to assert a breach of contract claim against Donna's on the grounds that Donna's failed to reimburse him for certain travel expenses, which he contends was in violation of his employment contract. Can Patrick bring both claims in a single action in federal court?

Analysis: Patrick is authorized to bring both claims under Rule 18(a), but must also establish federal court subject matter jurisdiction over each claim. The federal court will have federal question jurisdiction over the age discrimination claim because it is based on a federal statute. The breach of contract claim, however, would not be based on a federal statute, but rather would be based on state common law. Therefore, federal question jurisdiction will not support the claim. The example does not include enough facts to determine whether diversity jurisdiction exists, but Patrick and Donna are probably citizens of the same state and it is unlikely that the travel expenses exceed $75,000, so diversity jurisdiction is not likely. For the court to exercise supplemental jurisdiction over a claim, the claim must arise out of the same case or controversy as a claim over which the court has original jurisdiction. Therefore, for supplemental jurisdiction, the question would be whether the age discrimination claim and the travel expense reimbursement claim arise out of the same case or controversy. Although one could fashion an argument that they do, a court would probably conclude that these claims are not closely enough related to be deemed to arise out of the same case or controversy. Therefore, a federal court would likely conclude that there is no basis for subject matter jurisdiction over the breach of contract claim.

C. Joinder of Parties as Plaintiffs

THE RULE	Rule 20(a)(1)

Permissive Joinder of Parties

Plaintiffs. Persons may join in one action as plaintiffs if:

(A) they assert a right to relief jointly, severally, or in the alternative with respect to or **arising out of the same transaction, occurrence**, or series of transactions or occurrences; and

(B) any **question of law or fact common to all plaintiffs** will arise in the action.

EXPLANATION

 There are two requirements for parties to join together as plaintiffs in a single action. First, they must each assert a right to relief that arises out of the same transaction or occurrence, or series of transactions or occurrences. Second, their claims must implicate common issues of fact or law. The point of these requirements is to prevent two plaintiffs with entirely unrelated claims from joining together in one action, which could lead to significant inefficiencies.

1. Subject Matter Jurisdiction

As with joinder of claims, if two or more parties want to join together as plaintiffs, they must establish federal court subject matter jurisdiction over each of their claims.

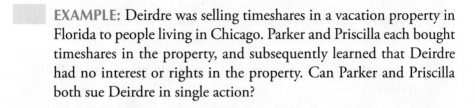

EXAMPLE: Deirdre was selling timeshares in a vacation property in Florida to people living in Chicago. Parker and Priscilla each bought timeshares in the property, and subsequently learned that Deirdre had no interest or rights in the property. Can Parker and Priscilla both sue Deirdre in single action?

Analysis: From a joinder perspective under Rule 20(A)(1), yes. Both of their claims arise out of the same series of transactions—ongoing sales of timeshares in the Florida property—and there are likely many common factual and legal issues that will arise in their claims. They will still each need to establish federal court subject matter jurisdiction over their claims. If Deirdre is a Florida citizen and Parker and Priscilla are Illinois citizens, and if they each paid more than $75,000 for the timeshares, then diversity jurisdiction will exist.

2. Separation of Claims

If the court determines that conducting a single trial of all of the claims may result in embarrassment, delay, expense, or other prejudice, the court can order separate trials under Rule 42.

3. Same Transaction or Occurrence

What does it mean for two claims to arise out of the same transaction or occurrence? There is no "bright line" test, but courts often look at:

- Whether the claims involve the same issues of fact and law;

- Whether substantially the same evidence will be required to support or refute the claims; and

- Whether there is a "logical relationship" between the claims.

D. Joinder of Parties as Defendants

THE RULE   Rule 20(a)(2)

Defendants. Persons . . . may be joined in one action as defendants if:

(C) any right to relief is asserted against them jointly, severally, or in the alternative with respect to or **arising out of the same transaction, occurrence**, or series of transactions or occurrences; and

(D) any **question of law or fact common to all defendants** will arise in the action.

EXPLANATION

 Plaintiffs may join parties as defendants subject to the same two requirements that pertain to joinder of parties as plaintiffs. First, the plaintiff or plaintiffs must assert a right to relief against each defendant that arises out of the same transaction or occurrence, or series of transactions or occurrences. Second, the claims must implicate common issues of law or fact.

1. Subject Matter Jurisdiction

Once again, if a plaintiff wants to join multiple defendants in a single law suit, the plaintiff must establish federal court subject matter jurisdiction over each claim.

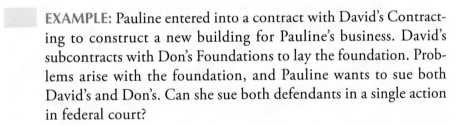
EXAMPLES & ANALYSIS

EXAMPLE: Pauline entered into a contract with David's Contracting to construct a new building for Pauline's business. David's subcontracts with Don's Foundations to lay the foundation. Problems arise with the foundation, and Pauline wants to sue both David's and Don's. Can she sue both defendants in a single action in federal court?

Analysis: From a joinder perspective, yes. Pauline's claims against both defendants arise out of the same transaction or occurrence—the construction of the foundation—and there are likely many common factual and legal issues that will arise in her claims against them. Pauline will still need to establish federal court subject matter jurisdiction over each of her claims though. Diversity jurisdiction seems most likely, but the example does not contain enough facts to determine whether diversity jurisdiction will exist.

2. Separation of Claims

Just like with multiple plaintiffs, if the court determines that conducting a single trial of the claims against all the defendants may result in embarrassment, delay, expense, or other prejudice, the court can order separate trials.

E. Counterclaims

1. The Rule

Rules 13(a) and (b) govern counterclaims, which are claims asserted back against the claiming party. There are two kinds of counterclaims—compulsory and permissive.

THE RULE   **Rule 13**

Counterclaim and Crossclaim

(a) Compulsory Counterclaim.

   (1) In General. A pleading **must** state as a counterclaim any claim that—at the time of its service—the pleader has against an opposing party if the claim:

      (A) arises out of the **transaction or occurrence** that is the subject matter of the opposing party's claim; and

      (B) does not require adding another party over whom the court cannot acquire jurisdiction.

   (2) Exceptions. The pleader need not state the claim if: (A) when the action was commenced, the claim was the subject of another pending action; or * * *

(b) Permissive Counterclaim. A pleading **may** state as a counterclaim against an opposing party any claim that is not compulsory.

(c) Relief Sought in a Counterclaim. A counterclaim need not diminish or defeat the recovery sought by the opposing party. It may request relief that exceeds in amount or differs in kind from the relief sought by the opposing party.

EXPLANATION

 "Counterclaims" are claims that a party asserts back against an opposing party. Typically, a defendant asserts counterclaims against a plaintiff, but any party against whom a claim is asserted can assert counterclaims against the claiming party.

1. Compulsory Counterclaims

Rule 13(a) governs compulsory counterclaims. As the name suggests, compulsory counterclaims are those claims that must be asserted. The rule defines compulsory counterclaims as those counterclaims that arise out of the same transaction or occurrence as the opposing party's claim. Rule 13(a) also creates an exception from the definition of compulsory counterclaims for claims that would require adding a party over whom the court does not have jurisdiction (for reasons of personal jurisdiction, subject matter jurisdiction, or notice).

EXAMPLES & ANALYSIS

EXAMPLE: Pam, a Florida citizen, and Derek, a Georgia citizen, have a car accident. Pam sues Derek, contending that he caused the accident, totaling her car and causing her to incur $100,000 in medical bills. Derek believes the accident was Pam's fault, and believes he has a claim against her for $25,000 in damage to his car (Derek was not injured in the accident). Can, and must, Derek assert his claim as a counterclaim in the action that Pam filed?

Analysis: Derek's claim arises out of the same car accident, and thus arises out of the same "transaction or occurrence," as Pam's claim against him. Therefore, Derek's claim is a compulsory counterclaim under Rule 13(a)(1), and must be asserted in Pam's action. Although Derek's claim is less than $75,000, and thus does not meet the amount in controversy requirement for diversity jurisdiction, the federal court would have supplemental jurisdiction over Derek's claim because it forms part of the same "case or controversy" under 28 U.S.C. § 1367. *See* Chapter 1.

a. Non-Parties Necessary for Counterclaim

As we will learn in the next chapter, sometimes the Rules require that additional parties be joined to the litigation if possible—generally parties whose interest will potentially be prejudiced if the lawsuit proceeds without them. Rule 13(a) provides that a counterclaim is not compulsory if the counterclaim would require the joinder of another party over whom the court does not have jurisdiction. This section of the rules refer to Rule 19, which is discussed in greater detail in Chapter 9.

2. Permissive Counterclaims

The second classification of counterclaim is the "permissive counterclaim," which is any counterclaim that is not a compulsory counterclaim. Rule 13(b) allows, but does not require, a party to assert its permissive counterclaims against an opposing party, regardless of whether the counterclaim has any relationship to the original claim, so long as the court has subject matter jurisdiction over the counterclaim and personal jurisdiction over any parties that need to be joined.

EXAMPLES & ANALYSIS

EXAMPLE: Petrochemical, Inc, a Texas corporation, and Drilling Corp, a Texas corporation, both use a new drilling technology. Petrochemical claims to have patented the technology, and asserts a patent infringement claim under federal law in a complaint filed in federal court. Drilling believes that Petrochemical is inducing property owners to breach their leases with Drilling and enter into new leases with Petrochemical, which creates a cause of action for tortious interference with contractual relations under Texas state law. Can, and must, Drilling assert its claim as a counterclaim in the action that Petrochemical filed?

Analysis: Drilling's claim for tortious interference does not appear to relate to the patent issue, and therefore probably does not arise out of the same transaction or occurrence as Petrochemical's patent infringement claim.

Accordingly, Drilling's claim is probably a permissive counterclaim, not a compulsory one. Under Rule 13(b), Drilling may assert its claim, but is not required to do so. However, in order to assert its claim in federal court, Drilling must also establish subject matter jurisdiction. Both parties are Texas corporations, so diversity jurisdiction will not exist. Drilling's claim is a state law claim, so federal question jurisdiction will not exist. Drilling's claim does not appear to be part of the same case or controversy as Petrochemical's claim, so supplemental jurisdiction probably will not exist. Therefore, although Rule 13(b) permits Drilling to file its counterclaim, it cannot do so because there does not appear to be subject matter jurisdiction over the counterclaim.

3. Relief Sought in a Counterclaim

Rule 13(c) clarifies that there does not need to be any relationship between the relief sought in the counterclaim and the relief sought by the opposing party. Thus, if the plaintiff is seeking money damages against the defendant, the defendant could counterclaim for an injunction. Likewise, if the plaintiff is seeking money damages in the amount of $100,000, the defendant could counterclaim for $200,000, or any other amount.

F. Crossclaims

THE RULE   **Rule 13(g)**

Crossclaim Against a Coparty

A pleading may state as a crossclaim any claim by one party against a coparty if the claim arises out of the **transaction or occurrence** that is the subject matter of the original action or of a counter-claim, or if the claim relates to any property that is the subject matter of the original action. The crossclaim may include a claim that the coparty is or may be liable to the crossclaimant for all or part of a claim asserted in the action against the cross-claimant.

EXPLANATION

Crossclaims are different from counterclaims in a couple of important aspects. While counterclaims are claims asserted back "across the v" against an opposing party who has already asserted a claim, a crossclaim is asserted against a coparty who is on the same side of the "v." The most common type of crossclaim occurs when a plaintiff has sued multiple defendants and the defendants choose to assert crossclaims against each other, contending essentially that if the defendant/crossclaim plaintiff is found liable to the original plaintiff, then the crossclaim defendant is liable to the crossclaim plaintiff for some or all of the crossclaim plaintiff's liability to the original plaintiff.

Crossclaims are also different from counterclaims because the Rules do not establish compulsory and permissive crossclaims. Rather, a party is only authorized to assert a crossclaim if the crossclaim arises out of the same "transaction or occurrence" as the original claim. Even then, crossclaims are always permissive—a party may choose to allow the original claims to proceed to their conclusion, and only bring its claims against coparties in a subsequent action if the primary claims resolve unfavorably.

IN PRACTICE

Codefendants often agree, formally or informally, to refrain from asserting crossclaims against each other, on the theory that they would be "doing the plaintiff's work" by trying to establish liability on each other's part.

EXAMPLES & ANALYSIS

EXAMPLE: Pete is a roofer who works as an independent contractor for Dario Construction. Dario Construction was hired by Design Architects to serve as general contractor on a new commercial office building. Pete is injured while working on the roof of the new building and sues Dario Construction and Design Architects in federal court (assume diversity jurisdiction exists). Dario also has a claim against Design for money due on three earlier construction projects. Can Dario Construction crossclaim against Design Architects?

Analysis: Dario Construction's claims against Design Architects do not arise out of the same transaction or occurrence—the construction of the office building and the injury on the roof—as Pete's claim. Therefore, Dario may not assert the crossclaim. Note that even if it did arise out of the same transaction or occurrence, Dario Construction would still need to establish subject matter jurisdiction over the crossclaim.

Crossclaims are not restricted to the original defendants. If two plaintiffs sue a defendant, and the defendant asserts a counterclaim, the plaintiffs may assert crossclaims against each other, so long as the crossclaims are related to the same transaction or occurrence as the counterclaim.

G. Third-Party Practice

THE RULE	Rule 14

Third-Party Practice

(a) When a Defending Party May Bring in a Third Party.

    (1) *Timing of the Summons and Complaint.* A defending party may, as third-party plaintiff, serve a summons and complaint on a nonparty who is or may be liable to it for all or part of the claim against it. But the third-party plaintiff must, by motion, obtain the court's leave if it files the third-party complaint more than 14 days after serving its original answer.

    (2) Third-Party Defendant's Claims and Defenses. The person served with the summons and third-party complaint—the "third-party defendant":

        (A) must assert any defense against the third-party plaintiff's claim under Rule 12;

        (B) must assert any counterclaim against the third-party plaintiff under Rule 13 (a), and **may assert** any counterclaim against the third-party plaintiff under Rule 13(b) or any crossclaim against another third-party defendant under Rule 13(g);

        (C) may assert against the plaintiff any defense that the third-party plaintiff has to the plaintiff's claim; and

       (D) may also assert against the plaintiff **any claim arising out of the transaction or occurrence** that is the subject matter of the plaintiff's claim against the third-party plaintiff.

(3) Plaintiff's Claims Against a Third-Party Defendant. The plaintiff **may assert** against the third-party defendant **any claim arising out of the transaction or occurrence** that is the subject matter of the plaintiff's claim against the third-party plaintiff.

      * * *

The third-party defendant **must then assert** any defense under Rule 12 and any counterclaim under Rule 13(a), and may assert any counterclaim under Rule 13(b) or any crossclaim under Rule 13(g).

       (D) may also assert against the plaintiff **any claim arising out of the transaction or occurrence** that is the subject matter of the plaintiff's claim against the third-party plaintiff.

(3) Plaintiff's Claims Against a Third-Party Defendant. The plaintiff **may assert** against the third-party defendant **any claim arising out of the transaction or occurrence** that is the subject matter of the plaintiff's claim against the third-party plaintiff. The third-party defendant **must then assert** any defense under Rule 12 and any counterclaim under Rule 13(a), and **may assert** any counterclaim under Rule 13(b) or any crossclaim under Rule 13(g).

      * * *

(5) Third-Party Defendant's Claim Against a Nonparty. A third-party defendant may proceed under this rule against a nonparty who is or may be liable to the third-party defendant for all or part of any claim against it.

      * * *

(b) When a Plaintiff May Bring in a Third Party. When a claim is asserted against a plaintiff, the plaintiff may bring in a third party if this rule would allow a defendant to do so.

      * * *

EXPLANATION

 Assume there is a hunting accident in which Hunter A is wounded, and Hunter A sues Hunter B for negligence. Hunter B believes that Hunter C also shot Hunter A. Hunter B has no direct claim against Hunter C—Hunter C has not injured Hunter B. However, Hunter B has what is sometimes referred to as a derivative claim against Hunter C—a claim that is derivative of Hunter A's claim against Hunter B, asking the court to find Hunter C liable to Hunter B for some of any amount for which Hunter B is found liable to Hunter A.

In such a situation, Rule 14 allows Hunter B to join, or "implead" Hunter C into the litigation. Hunter B files a "third-party complaint" against Hunter C, bringing Hunter C into the case. Once Hunter C is properly impleaded or joined into the case, Rule 14 controls the manner in which all of the parties may assert and defend claims against one another.

Third-party practice is used when the defending party has a claim that derives from the original claim between the plaintiff and defendant. The substantive basis for the third-party claim can vary, but third-party practice is generally used when the defendant has a claim for **contribution** or **indemnity** against a nonparty.

> "**Contribution**" refers to a claim that the contribution defendant is responsible for some portion of the contribution plaintiff's liability. Contribution claims are common in tort cases. "**Indemnity**" refers to a claim that the indemnity defendant is responsible for 100% of the indemnity plaintiff's liability. Contracts frequently create indemnity rights.

A defendant usually has a choice of bringing its third-party claims as part of the existing lawsuit or waiting until the original claim is adjudicated and then bringing its claims against the third parties in a separate action in the event that the defendant is found liable to the plaintiff. The decision is typically a strategic one, balancing the advantages of having more defendants contribute to settlement against the potential harm of having to develop evidence that benefits the plaintiff as much as the defendant.

IN PRACTICE

Third-party practice is most common in tort actions, where an injury is caused by a combination of actions, but the plaintiff does not sue all of the actors. Third-party practice is also common in environmental litigation, where the state or federal government sues the current owner or operator of contaminated property and forces that entity to seek contribution or indemnity from other responsible parties.

1. **Timing.** A defendant may bring a third-party complaint within 14 days of its original answer as of right, or after that time by leave of court.

IN PRACTICE

The court's scheduling order often sets a deadline for adding third parties, in which case a defendant does not need leave of court to file a third-party complaint before that deadline, even if more than 14 days after its original answer.

2. **Defenses by the Third-Party Defendant.** A third-party defendant files an answer to the third-party complaint just like an ordinary defendant, and must assert any defenses against the third-party plaintiff's claims under Rule 12.

3. **Counterclaims.** A third-party defendant must assert any compulsory counterclaims against the third-party plaintiff under Rule 13(a), and may assert any permissive counterclaims against the third-party plaintiff under Rule 13(b).

4. **Crossclaims.** A third-party defendant may assert any crossclaims against another third-party defendant under Rule 13(g).

5. Claims Against the Plaintiff. In order to assert a claim directly against the original plaintiff, a third-party defendant must have a claim against the plaintiff arising out of the transaction or occurrence that is the subject matter of the plaintiff's claim against the defendant/third-party plaintiff. If the third-party defendant has one such "transactionally related" claim, it may join any other claims it has under Rule 18(a), even if those other claims are unrelated.

6. Claims by the Plaintiff Against the Third-Party Defendant. In order to assert a claim directly against a third-party defendant, the plaintiff must have a claim against the third-party defendant arising out of the same transaction or occurrence that is the subject of the plaintiff's claim against the defendant/third-party plaintiff. Again, if the plaintiff has one such transactionally related claim, it may join any other claims it has under Rule 18(a).

7. Responding to Claims Between the Plaintiff and Third-Party Defendant. Following a claim between a plaintiff and a third-party defendant, the process proceeds in the same manner as a claim by a plaintiff against a defendant. The defendant to the claim asserts defenses by motion or answer under Rule 12, and asserts counterclaims as governed by Rule 13.

8. Third-Party Claims by the Plaintiff. If a defendant has asserted a counterclaim against the plaintiff or a third-party defendant has asserted a claim against the plaintiff, the plaintiff may implead a third-party defendant to that claim.

9. Fourth-Party Claims. If a third-party defendant believes a nonparty may be liable for some or all of the liability asserted against the third-party defendant, the third-party defendant may file a fourth-party complaint impleading the nonparty.

10. Subject Matter Jurisdiction. Each of these various claims must have an independent basis for federal court subject matter jurisdiction. Often, supplemental jurisdiction will exist over third-party claims, but remember the exception to supplemental jurisdiction that applies to diversity jurisdiction if a plaintiff tries to add a claim against a third-party defendant it could not have included in the original complaint. *See* Chapter 1.

EXAMPLES & ANALYSIS

EXAMPLE: Penny sues Dotty's Brick Oven Pizzeria under a federal statute that allows claims for damages caused by air emissions, asserting that soot from the Pizzeria is regularly deposited onto her car, drying laundry, and house. Dotty's believes that the soot is coming mostly or entirely from Tristate Power Plant and Trevor's Incinerator, which are both located nearby. Tristate has a claim against Penny because she attended a protest rally at Tristate and videotape shows her throwing a brick through a window at Tristate. Which claims might be asserted among these parties in the action that Penny commenced?

Analysis: Dotty's can bring a third-party complaint against Tristate and Trevor's under Rule 14(a), asserting that, to the extent Dotty's is found liable to Penny, Tristate and Trevor's are liable to Dotty's for some or all of that liability. Both federal question and supplemental jurisdiction would likely exist over the third-party claims. Tristate and Trevor's could each assert crossclaims against each other under Rule 13(g), and again federal question and supplemental jurisdiction would allow the claims. Because a third-party complaint only seeks contribution, there is no need for Tristate or Trevor's to assert a counterclaim against Dotty's. Penny could assert claims directly against Tristate or Trevor's for depositing soot on her property under Rule 14(a)(3) because such claims would arise out of the same transaction or occurrence as Penny's original claim against Dotty's. Again, federal question and supplemental jurisdiction would apply. Finally, Tristate could consider a claim against Penny relating to damage caused during the protest rally under Rule 14(a)(2)(D). However, Rule 14(a)(2)(D) only authorizes claims that arise out of the same transaction or occurrence as the plaintiff's claim against the defendant/third-party plaintiff, and here the brick throwing incident is unrelated to the deposit of soot on Penny's property. Furthermore, Tristate would need a basis for federal court jurisdiction. Under the facts in the example, federal court jurisdiction seems unlikely—the brick throwing does not likely create a cause of action under a federal statute, it is not likely to have caused $75,000 in damages to support diversity jurisdiction, and it does not likely arise out of the same case or controversy as the other claims in the case to support supplemental jurisdiction. Therefore, Tristate probably could not bring its claim against Penny.

IN PRACTICE

Joinder issues arise quite frequently in federal litigation, although they are typically not contested or controversial. Complaints routinely include multiple claims among multiple parties. In fact, a complaint where one plaintiff asserts one claim against one defendant is not common in federal court.

Most of the time, complaints contain multiple claims involving multiple parties without any controversy regarding the joinder rules. However, it is critical to keep the federal court's limited subject matter jurisdiction in mind and to evaluate subject matter jurisdiction for each claim. Thus, you must always go through a two-step evaluation under the joinder rules and the jurisdictional statutes.

Third-party practice is not quite as frequent, but is still relatively common. As with joinder of parties and claims, third-party joinder is typically not controversial. It can become more complex and challenging in the context of new claims asserted between the original plaintiff and the third-party defendant.

ADDITIONAL EXERCISES

Example: On a dark and stormy night, there is a five-car pileup on Route 1. Paul was rear-ended by Devin. Paul says he stopped because Tracy was wandering on the street in what appeared to be a drunken state. Devin says that Paul's rear lights were out, so Devin could not see Paul's car in the storm. The accident happened near a turn, and Tim came around the turn and ran into Devin's car. Tammy then ran into Tim's car, and Trevor ran into Tammy's car. Devin is a citizen of New York, and everyone else is a citizen of New Jersey. Paul knows Tim well, and had previously loaned him $40,000 to start up a business, which Tim was refusing to repay, claiming that the money was an investment in the business, not a loan. Tracy says that she was simply crossing the street, not wandering, and that Paul came around the corner at an excessive rate of speed, then slammed on his brakes and honked his horn repeatedly, causing her to have anxiety attacks since the time of the accident. Paul filed suit against Devin in federal court. **Be prepared to discuss the following:**

1. Devin wants to assert a claim against Tracy for causing the accident by wandering in the street, causing damage to his car. Can Devin join his claim against Tracy procedurally and what is the subject matter jurisdiction analysis? Assuming that Devin can successfully join Tracy, can Paul also bring a claim against Tracy for damaging his car?

2. If Devin also wants to seek the same damages from Tim, would Devin be able to assert his claims against Tracy and Tim in the same action?

3. If Devin has impleaded Tim, may Tim join Tammy and Trevor and assert claims for damage to his car? Assuming Tim successfully joins Tammy and Trevor, can Devin bring claims against Tammy and Trevor for damage to his car too?

4. Assume Tim properly impleaded Tammy and Trevor. If Tammy believes that she stopped in time, and then was propelled into Tim's car when Trevor's car hit the rear of her car, what type of procedural claim would Tammy assert against Trevor and what is the subject-matter jurisdiction analysis?

5. Assume Devin properly impleaded Tim. Now Paul wants to sue Tim for the money that Paul lent to Tim. Can Paul assert the claim as part of the original action, and if so, what type of procedural claim would Paul assert and what is the subject matter jurisdiction analysis?

6. If Paul is successful in asserting a claim against Tim for the $40,000, and Tim wants to assert that Paul's payment was an investment, and that as an owner of the business Paul has breached his obligation to help pay some outstanding debts, can Tim assert the claim in the original action, and if so, what type of procedural claim would Tim assert against Paul and what is the subject matter jurisdiction analysis?

7. If Devin has impleaded Tracy and Tracy wants to sue Paul for her anxiety attacks, can Tracy assert the claim in the original action, and if so what type of procedural claim would Tracy assert and what is the subject matter jurisdiction analysis?

Quick Summary

- The Rules provide almost no restriction on the joinder of additional claims to a claim properly in federal court.

- The Rules limit parties' ability to join together as plaintiffs and to join multiple parties as defendants to situations where the claims arise out of the same transaction or occurrence or series of transactions or occurrences and the claims raise common issues of fact or law.

- The Rules require a defendant to bring any counterclaims against the plaintiff that arise out of the same transaction or occurrence as the plaintiff's claim, unless the court cannot take jurisdiction over the claim or any necessary parties. The Rules permit, but do not require, a defendant to bring any other type of counterclaim.

- The Rules also authorize a crossclaim by one party against a co-party, if the crossclaim arises out of the same transaction or occurrence as the claim against the party asserting the crossclaim. All crossclaims are permissive.

- Third-party practice pertains to derivative claims—where a defendant to a claim is seeking contribution towards any liability imposed on that defendant. In such situations, the defendant can "implead" or join a nonparty as a third-party defendant by filing a third-party complaint.

- Once a third-party defendant is joined, it files an answer, Rule 12 motion, counterclaims, and crossclaims like any defendant.

- Claims between a third-party defendant and the original plaintiff are somewhat more limited, and must arise out of the same transaction or occurrence as the original claims.

- For each claim in any of these procedures, the federal court must have subject matter jurisdiction before the claim may proceed. Evaluation of subject matter jurisdiction is a critical stage of the analysis of any joinder situation.

9

Complex Joinder and Class Actions

Key Concepts

- Complex joinder rules that encourage, and sometimes require, the joinder of multiple parties in a single lawsuit to facilitate the full and fair adjudication of a civil action
- The intervention of nonparties into a lawsuit
- The court's power to compel the joinder of indispensable parties, and even to dismiss an action if those parties cannot be joined
- The complex joinder device termed "interpleader"
- Class actions

Introduction

In the previous chapter, we observed how the basic joinder rules generally allow plaintiffs and defendants to join claims and parties in a single lawsuit. In this chapter, we turn to a series of complex joinder devices that encourage, and sometimes require, the joinder of multiple parties in a single lawsuit in order to facilitate the fair and efficient adjudication of a civil action. These devices are designed to insure that all parties who may have an interest in the resolution of a case or controversy have an opportunity to become parties and to present their claims or defenses in a single action.

The Federal Rules of Civil Procedure generally allow parties who have not been joined to a lawsuit to "intervene" (to become parties) in that lawsuit if they have an interest that will be affected by the litigation. In addition, the court even has the power to enter an order forcing nonparties to be joined to a lawsuit, if their absence would make difficult the full and fair adjudication of the entire controversy. When the number of parties with a common interest in the resolution of a matter is so large that joinder of them all would be difficult, the complex joinder rules also allow the creation of a class action, whereby a named party represents a class of commonly situated absent parties. This chapter addresses the federal rules and the constitutional parameters for each of these complex joinder devices.

A. Intervention

Intervention is the act of a nonparty moving to participate as a party in an ongoing lawsuit. The nonparty will file a motion to intervene, asking the judge to allow it to become a party in the litigation.

Why would a nonparty want to become a party in an ongoing civil action? As a nonparty, the intervenor would not be legally bound by any judgment entered in that litigation. Nonetheless, the nonparty may have an interest in the ongoing lawsuit that—as a practical matter—would be harmed by that litigation. The nonparty might also recognize that none of the existing litigants can adequately protect that interest. The nonparty thus will move to intervene. For example, if a local environmental group sues to stop the renovation of an apartment building, a tenant in the building might want to intervene in the lawsuit to protect its interest in living in the renovated building.

> Intervention is different than appearing as an **amicus curiae.** A person who intervenes in a lawsuit becomes a party in the action, and therefore is bound by the judgment and has the right to appeal. An appearance as *amicus curiae,* by contrast, merely affords a "friend of the court" the opportunity to present arguments on behalf of a party already in the lawsuit.

Should the court allow the nonparty to intervene? Under the federal rules and those in virtually every state, there are two different types of intervention: (1) intervention as of right, by which the court must allow the intervenor to join the lawsuit; and (2) permissive intervention, by which the court may allow the intervenor to join the lawsuit.

THE RULE   Rule 24

Intervention

(a) Intervention of Right. On timely motion, the court must permit anyone to intervene who:

    (1) is given an unconditional right to intervene by a federal statute; or

    (2) claims an interest relating to the property or transaction that is the subject of the action, and is so situated that disposing of the action may as a practical matter impair or impede the movant's ability to protect its interest, unless existing parties adequately represent that interest.

(b) Permissive Intervention.

    (1) In General. On timely motion, the court may permit anyone to intervene who:

        (A) is given a conditional right to intervene by a federal statute; or

        (B) has a claim or defense that shares with the main action a common question of law or fact. . . .

(c) Notice and Pleading Required. A motion to intervene must be served on the parties as provided in Rule 5. The motion must state the grounds for intervention and be accompanied by a pleading that sets out the claim or defense for which intervention is sought.

EXPLANATION

1. Rule 24(a): Intervention of Right

Rule 24(a) requires the court to allow a nonparty to intervene in an ongoing action in two situations:

- if a federal statute grants the absolute right to intervene, or

- if the nonparty can show that it has an interest, that as a practical matter, will be adversely affected by the ongoing action and not adequately protected by the existing parties.

Where the intervenor demonstrates that a federal statute governing its claims explicitly grants it the absolute right to intervene, the court must allow the intervenor to join the lawsuit. For example, 2 U.S.C. § 288e(a), provides that the U.S. Senate's legal counsel "shall" intervene in an action when directed to do so by Senate resolution. Because this statutory language granting the right to intervene is unambiguous, the court must allow intervention.

The statutory right to intervene, however, must be "unconditional." As such, the courts have construed the right narrowly, and intervention as of right by statute applies only in exceptional circumstances.

More commonly, the intervenor will try to demonstrate that it should be granted the right to intervene. In making that demonstration, the intervenor must show that: (1) it has an **interest** in the subject matter of the litigation; (2) that interest may, as a practical matter, be **harmed** by the litigation, and (3) the interest will **not** be adequately **protected** by the existing parties.

a. Interest

The intervenor's interest in the litigation could be strong enough to give rise to a distinct case or controversy, or it could be strong enough that the judgment would legally preclude the intervenor from bringing a separate action to protect that interest. But it need not be that strong. Any significant financial or familial interest in the outcome of the adjudication typically is sufficient to satisfy this component of intervention as of right.

b. As a Practical Matter, Harmed by the Litigation

The intervenor can show that its interest will—as a practical matter— be harmed by the litigation by establishing that the impact of any court decision would affect its economic interests, injure its reputation, or deplete an existing litigant's resources that would otherwise be available to satisfy a subsequent judgment entered on the intervenor's behalf.

c. Not Protected by the Parties

The intervenor can readily establish that its interest will not be adequately protected by the existing parties by showing that its interests are distinct from, or in conflict with, those of the parties already in the litigation.

EXAMPLES & ANALYSIS

EXAMPLE: Petra brings a tort action against Danielle for negligently driving a vehicle that struck Petra. Danielle defends the action by alleging that the vehicle's brakes were defectively manufactured by Derekson Brakes, Inc. Does Derekson Brakes, Inc. have the right to intervene?

Analysis: Yes. Derekson Brakes, Inc. can show that it has an interest which as a practical matter will be adversely affected by the litigation and not protected by the existing parties. Here, although as a nonparty, Derekson Brakes, Inc. cannot be legally bound by any judgment, it nonetheless has an economic interest in its reputation for manufacturing safe brakes, which as a practical matter could be harmed by publicity about the litigation. Nor will any of the existing parties fully represent Derekson's interests. To the contrary, Danielle's defense involves allegations that Derekson was negligent.

EXAMPLE: Priscilla and Pablo were both injured when construction equipment designed by Dante Bros. Inc. malfunctioned. Priscilla sues Dante Bros Inc. for $10 million. Dante Bros Inc. has a $10 million cap on its liability insurance policy and no other assets. Pablo files a motion to intervene as of right in the lawsuit. Should the court grant the motion?

Analysis: Yes. Although Pablo will not be legally bound by the judgment, he has an economic interest in the lawsuit which as a practical matter will be impaired and not protected by the existing parties. Here, Dante Bros. Inc. has a limited fund of resources available to satisfy judgments against it, and that fund will likely be depleted before Pablo can assert his claims in a separate action.

In both of these examples, the nonparty has a tremendous incentive to intervene in an ongoing lawsuit. In the first example, the manufacturer of allegedly defective brakes is even willing to join the lawsuit as a defendant to protect its interests. In the second example, Pablo has an incentive to join the ongoing lawsuit to make sure that the limited funds available to satisfy his claim are not depleted. In both examples, there is a significant risk that these nonparties will lose something of value to them unless they are joined to the litigation.

> In the next section involving indispensable parties and compulsory joinder, we will see that the court in these situations has the power to force the joinder of such nonparties.

2. Rule 24(b): Permissive Intervention

Even if the nonparty cannot make the strong showing required for intervention as of right, that nonparty can seek permissive intervention. The court has broad discretion to allow a nonparty to intervene if:

(a) a federal statute supplies a **conditional** right to intervention; or

(b) there is a **commonality** of issues between those in the ongoing lawsuit and those affecting the intervenor.

Statutes that grant conditional intervention rights are relatively rare. Far more litigated are motions to intervene that invoke the court's discretion to permit intervention based on the existence of common questions of law or fact between those in the ongoing lawsuit and those affecting an intervenor's interests. The court's discretion is broad enough to allow permissive intervention even if the nonparty does not have a claim related to the ongoing lawsuit. That nonparty may intervene to assert an interest that will be implicated by the issues being litigated in the lawsuit, including, for example, an interest in the disclosure of material that the nonparty wants to protect.

The rule's grant of discretion to the judge carries with it an extremely deferential standard of review. Any order granting or denying permissive intervention will be affirmed by the appellate court unless the trial court has **abused its discretion**.

EXAMPLES & ANALYSIS

EXAMPLE: Pascal files a claim against Dennis in federal court, alleging that Dennis breached his contract to paint Pascal's house by taking a significant deposit and then skipping town. Pascal's neighbor, Juan, had the same experience with Dennis. Juan files a motion to intervene in the lawsuit. May the court grant intervention?

Analysis: Yes. Juan's claim may not satisfy the requirements for "intervention as of right" because there is no evidence that his interests will be adversely affected by the ongoing lawsuit. Nonetheless, the court has discretion to permit Juan to intervene in Pascal's lawsuit because there are common issues of fact or law between those in Pascal's lawsuit and those affecting Juan. The court's discretion would also allow it to deny the motion and require that Juan file his own lawsuit against Dennis.

3. Jurisdiction and Intervention

The federal rule governing intervention cannot expand the subject matter or personal jurisdiction of the federal court. A nonparty who voluntarily moves to intervene in an ongoing lawsuit as a defendant consents to personal jurisdiction.

Yet, what about the existence of subject matter jurisdiction over claims involving the intervenor? If those claims have an independent, primary jurisdictional basis such as "federal question" or "diversity" jurisdiction, there clearly will be subject matter jurisdiction. But, will "supplemental" jurisdiction supply a jurisdictional basis? Recall that 28 U.S.C. § 1367(b) provides a narrow exception to the use of supplemental jurisdiction. In cases where the only primary jurisdictional basis is diversity, there can be no supplemental jurisdiction over claims by plaintiffs against persons who intervene under Rule 24 or over claims by persons seeking to intervene as plaintiffs under Rule 24, where those claims would not otherwise meet the requirement of diversity jurisdiction. Accordingly, supplemental jurisdiction is generally not available for claims by or against intervenors.

IN PRACTICE

In order to make a motion to intervene, the intervenor must state the basis for the intervention and attach the intervenor's proposed pleading. The rule also requires that the motion be filed in a "timely" manner, which affords the court broad discretion to reject an intervenor's motion filed after the litigation has progressed through discovery.

B. Indispensable Parties

The joinder rules in federal and state court generally allow the joinder of claims and parties in a single lawsuit. The plaintiff may file as many claims as it has against a defendant and may generally join additional parties if the claims involving those parties derive from the same transaction or occurrence, or at least the same series of transactions or occurrences. The parties typically are given wide discretion to make the strategic decision of who to sue and who not to sue.

In some situations, however, the full and fair adjudication of a civil action will require the presence of parties who have not been joined in the lawsuit. In those situations, the joinder rules in federal and state court require the trial judge to compel the joinder of persons who are necessary for the full and fair adjudication of the action.

In order to facilitate the efficient resolution of an entire case or controversy in a single action, Federal Rule 19(a) requires a federal judge to compel the joinder of nonparties who are necessary for a full and fair adjudication. In some cases, however, that nonparty cannot be joined to an ongoing lawsuit because the court will lack personal jurisdiction over that nonparty or will lack subject matter jurisdiction over the claims involving that nonparty. These jurisdictional limits on joinder cannot be disregarded.

The court, therefore, faces a dilemma. On one hand, the nonparty must be joined for a full and fair adjudication. Yet, on the other hand, that nonparty cannot be joined because there is no jurisdiction. The court is left with two alternatives, neither of which is good. The court could proceed without the nonparty or the court could dismiss the entire action for failure to join that party. In selecting the lesser of these two evils, the court is instructed by Rule 19(b) to follow equity and its good conscience. As such, the court has virtually unbridled discretion to decide whether to dismiss an action for failure to join a party under Rule 19.

THE RULE   **Rule 19(a)-(c)**

Required Joinder of Parties

(a) Persons Required to Be Joined if Feasible.

    (1) Required Party. A person who is subject to service of process and whose joinder will not deprive the court of subject-matter jurisdiction **must be joined** as a party if:

        (A) in that person's absence, the court cannot accord complete relief among existing parties; or

        (B) that person claims an interest relating to the subject of the action and is so situated that disposing of the action in the person's absence may: **(i)** as a practical matter impair or impede the person's ability to protect the interest; or **(ii)** leave an existing party subject to a substantial risk of incurring double, multiple, or otherwise inconsistent obligations because of the interest.

    (2) Joinder by Court Order. If a person has not been joined as required, **the court must order** that the person be made a party. A person who refuses to join as a plaintiff may be made either a defendant or, in a proper case, an involuntary plaintiff.

    (3) Venue. If a joined party objects to venue and the joinder would make venue improper, the court must dismiss that party.

(b) When Joinder Is Not Feasible. If a **person** who is **required to be joined** if feasible **cannot be joined**, the court must determine whether, **in equity and good conscience**, the action should proceed among the existing parties or **should be dismissed**. The factors for the court to consider include:

(1) the extent to which a judgment rendered in the person's absence might prejudice that person or the existing parties;

(2) the extent to which any prejudice could be lessened or avoided by:

   (A) protective provisions in the judgment;

   (B) shaping the relief; or

   (C) other measures;

(3) whether a judgment rendered in the person's absence would be adequate; and

(4) whether the plaintiff would have an adequate remedy if the action were dismissed for nonjoinder.

(c) **Pleading the Reasons for Nonjoinder.** When asserting a claim for relief, a party must state:

(1) the name, if known, of any person who is required to be joined if feasible but is not joined; and

(2) the reasons for not joining that person.

* * *

EXPLANATION

Federal Rule 19 has two related, but distinct functions: (1) Rule 19(a) requires a federal judge to compel the joinder of persons who are necessary to a full and fair adjudication; and (2) Rule 19(b) guides the court's response to a situation in which such a person cannot be joined.

1. Parties Required to Be Joined If Feasible

Under Rule 19(a), a nonparty must be joined if its absence would be prejudicial to the plaintiff, the defendant or the nonparty itself.

First, Rule 19(a) directs the court to join a nonparty if the **plaintiff** cannot get "complete relief" in its absence. For instance, the party to be joined may have assets that are needed to satisfy any judgment obtained by the plaintiff, and its absence would leave the plaintiff without an adequate remedy against existing defendants with limited resources.

Second, the absence of the person might expose the **defendants** to multiple or inconsistent obligations. For example, the nonparty may have claims against the defendant's limited fund, and the defendant may be forced to litigate such claims in multiple forums, resulting in judgments in favor of multiple parties against the defendant for the same fund.

> These grounds for requiring the joinder of an additional party mirror the grounds for allowing such an additional party to intervene as of right.

Third, the **nonparty** itself may be prejudiced by its own absence because it may not be able—as a practical matter—to protect its interests. Here again, the nonparty may have a claim against the defendant, and the defendant may be left with insufficient assets to satisfy the nonparty's later-filed claims.

Accordingly, if the court finds that the absence of a person is prejudicial to the right of the plaintiff, the defendant or the nonparty to a full and fair adjudication, the court **must** order that the person be joined as a party.

The court typically will do so in response to a motion filed by an existing party to compel the joinder of the nonparty. Even if no such motion is made, however, the court must act on its own to order the joinder of the nonparty. The court also has the power to order that service of process be effectuated on the nonparty, and to **order the nonparty** to be joined to the action as a defendant, or even as an involuntary plaintiff.

Rule 19(a), however, makes clear that such a party must be joined as a plaintiff or a defendant **only if** its joinder would not deprive the court of subject matter jurisdiction or personal jurisdiction. Recall that if the only primary jurisdictional basis is diversity, 28 U.S.C. § 1367(b) precludes the use of supplemental jurisdiction over claims brought by parties joined, or proposed to be joined, under Rule 19, where those claims do not otherwise meet the requirements of diversity jurisdiction.

What happens if the joinder of a person required for full and fair adjudication would in fact deprive the court of jurisdiction? The federal court, of course, cannot alter the limits of jurisdiction to force the joinder of that person. The nonparty simply cannot be joined to the lawsuit if the court lacks personal jurisdiction over that nonparty or subject matter jurisdiction over its claims.

Accordingly, the court is left with only two options: (1) proceed without the absent party and risk the prejudice resulting from its absence; or (2) dismiss the entire action for failure to join an indispensable party.

2. Parties Who Are Required to Be Joined, but Who Cannot Be Joined

Rule 19(b) governs the unique situation in which a nonparty should be joined to a lawsuit, but cannot be joined because there is no personal jurisdiction over that nonparty or subject matter jurisdiction over its claims. The rule thus only applies if two predicates have been established:

(a) the court has decided that the nonparty's absence is so prejudicial that the nonparty must be joined; and

(b) the nonparty cannot be joined for the lack of jurisdiction.

In that circumstance, the court must decide whether to proceed without the nonparty, or to dismiss the litigation. Recognizing that neither result is desirable, the rulemakers have given federal judges discretion to use their "good conscience" in determining the least inequitable course of action. Rule 19(b) also provides a list of factors that the court should consider in deciding whether to proceed or dismiss.

The first factor simply asks the court to re-weigh the degree of prejudice caused by the nonparty's absence from the action.

The second factor directs the court to consider whether the prejudice might be mitigated by measures that tailor the litigation and the relief to protect the nonparty's interests.

The third factor leads the court to consider whether the judgment would be adequate without the nonparty.

The fourth factor, which is particularly important, directs the court to consider the practical consequence to the plaintiff if the action is dismissed. Will the plaintiff be able, for example, to re-file the action in a different forum where all of the parties can be joined? If there is no other forum available to the plaintiff, the court will most likely refuse to dismiss the action. See *Provident Tradesmens Bank & Trust Co. v. Patterson*, 390 U.S. 102 (1968) (emphasizing that the court must carefully consider these factors in the particular context of each case before deciding whether to dismiss the litigation).

EXAMPLES & ANALYSIS

EXAMPLE: Perry (a citizen of New York) and Penelope (a citizen of New York) each own 50% of the shares of Saturn Corporation (a Delaware corporation with its principal place of business in California). They each signed a contract with Jupiter Inc. in which they agreed to sell all of Saturn's assets to Jupiter. When Jupiter failed to pay for the assets, Perry filed an action for breach of contract against Jupiter in federal district court. Jupiter then moved the court to compel the joinder of Penelope under Rule 19(a). Should the court compel the joinder of Penelope?

Analysis: Yes. Jupiter would be prejudiced by the absence of Penelope. Penelope and Perry have identical breach of contract claims against Jupiter. The absence of Penelope from Perry's lawsuit could subject Jupiter to multiple or inconsistent obligations. Even if Perry loses his claim, Jupiter would be exposed to an identical claim brought by Penelope. Accordingly, the court should compel the joinder of Penelope.

EXAMPLE: Suppose, however, in that same prior example, Penelope was a citizen of Delaware. Jupiter moves to dismiss the action for failure to join Penelope under Rule 19(b). Should the court grant the motion?

Analysis: Probably yes. Because the absence of Penelope is prejudicial to Jupiter, the court must join Penelope if feasible. Yet, in this case, Penelope cannot be joined because she is a citizen of Delaware and there would be no diversity jurisdiction over her claim against Jupiter—a Delaware corporation. Nor could the court assert supplemental jurisdiction over Penelope's claim because 28 U.S.C. § 1367(b) bars the assertion of supplemental jurisdiction over claims brought by persons joined under Rule 19. The court therefore has discretion to decide in "equity and good conscience" to dismiss the entire litigation for failure to join Penelope. *See, e.g., Acton Co., Inc. v. Bachman Foods, Inc.,* 668 F.2d 76 (1st Cir. 1982).

IN PRACTICE

Federal Rule 19 is rarely employed by the court or the litigants. When coupled with Federal Rule 12(b)(7), however, this rule provides an under-utilized, potent tactic for defendants. Under Rule 12(b)(7), which is further discussed in Chapter 7, defendants may move to dismiss an action for failure to join a party required to be joined under Rule 19. That motion to dismiss proceeds along the following arguments:

(1) there is a nonparty whose absence is prejudicial to a full and fair adjudication;

(2) that nonparty cannot be joined because there is no personal or subject matter jurisdiction;

(3) the court—in equity and good conscience—must dismiss the entire action.

C. Interpleader

Interpleader is an extraordinary joinder device that allows the holder of a "common fund" to file an action as a plaintiff and to join ("interplead") as defendants all of the "rival claimants" to its common fund. The holder of a common fund typically is an insurance company that may be liable to certain beneficiaries for the payment of policy proceeds. The proceeds comprise the common fund. The beneficiaries are rival claimants to the policy proceeds fund.

The interpleader device is designed to protect the holders of a common fund, like insurance companies, from the risk that multiple claimants to that fund would expose it to multiple liability. In the absence of interpleader, one or more of the claimants might sue the fund holder to recover the fund in one court, while one or more other claimants may sue the holder for the same fund in another court. In that situation, the holder of the fund may be held liable to pay the full amount of its fund to multiple plaintiffs who have sued in multiple jurisdictions.

Interpleader avoids this problem of multiple exposure. The fund holder comes to court not as a defendant, but as a plaintiff. The holder need not wait to be sued in multiple jurisdictions by the claimants to its fund. Instead, the holder can initiate a lawsuit and file an interpleader action against all rival claimants to its common fund. If all of the rival claimants to the common fund are joined as defendants in one forum, the court can decide in one civil action (rather than multiple potentially inconsistent actions) which—if any—of the claimants should receive all or part of the fund.

In situations where the common fund is a limited pool of assets, interpleader also is beneficial to the rival claimants. If each of the claimants to a limited fund sues separately, it is possible that the first claimants to reach a judgment will recover the full amount of the fund, leaving nothing left for the later claimants. The rival claimants thus may have an interest in being joined as defendants to a single interpleader action along with all of the other rival claimants. In that single forum, all of the rival claimants will have the chance to present their claims in one action and to receive their proper share of the fund. Accordingly, interpleader protects fund holders from the risk of multiple liability, protects the judicial system from the risk of entering inconsistent judgments, and even protects the beneficiaries to a common fund from the risk that the fund will not be available to satisfy their claims.

The Federal Rules of Civil Procedure, and the rules in most states, authorize interpleader actions. Federal Rule 22 establishes interpleader by rule. In addition, Congress has encouraged the use of interpleader in federal court by enacting legislation establishing "statutory interpleader" and expanding the jurisdiction of the federal courts to adjudicate interpleader actions.

THE RULE   Rule 22

Interpleader

(a) Grounds.

   (1) By a Plaintiff. Persons with claims that may **expose** a plaintiff to double or **multiple liability** may be **joined as defendants** and required to **interplead**. Joinder for interpleader is proper even though:

      (A) the claims of the several claimants, or the titles on which their claims depend, lack a common origin or are adverse and independent rather than identical; or

      (B) the plaintiff denies liability in whole or in part to any or all of the claimants.

   (2) By a Defendant. A defendant exposed to similar liability may seek interpleader through a crossclaim or counterclaim.

(b) Relation to Other Rules and Statutes. This rule supplements—and does not limit—the joinder of parties allowed by Rule 20. The remedy this rule provides is in addition to—and does not supersede or limit—the remedy provided by 28 U.S.C. §§ 1335, 1397, and 2361. An action under those statutes must be conducted under these rules.

EXPLANATION

1. Rule Interpleader

Federal Rule 22 is a joinder rule that facilitates interpleader actions. In somewhat convoluted language, Rule 22(a)(1) allows "[p]ersons with claims" against the plaintiff to be joined as "defendants." The party exposed to the risk of multiple liability from those claims becomes a "plaintiff."

The rule also broadly allows interpleader any time there are claimants to that plaintiff's common fund, even if the claimants to the fund are "adverse" to each other. Thus, the rule allows the holder of a common fund to interplead all rival claimants to its common fund. If the holder of a common fund is sued by a particular claimant, the fund holder could also assert an interpleader action as a defendant in the lawsuit, by way of a counterclaim or a cross-claim.

Finally, Rule 22(a)(1)(b) makes clear that a plaintiff may initiate an interpleader action without admitting any liability to any one of the claimants. In some state courts, the fund holder who initiates an interpleader action must admit that it is liable to pay out the proceeds of its fund, and in some states the fund holder must relinquish control of its fund to the court. In those cases, the plaintiff fund holder acknowledges its liability to pay fund proceeds to one or more claimants, and effectively requests the court to allocate the fund proceeds properly among the rival claimants. In federal court, by contrast, the plaintiff fund holder can contest liability for the payment of all or part of the fund proceeds as part of the interpleader action.

As a rule of civil procedure, however, Rule 22 cannot expand the subject matter jurisdiction of the federal courts. The claims brought in the context of an interpleader do not typically "arise under" any federal law. Rather, they involve state law claims regarding insurance contracts or perhaps trust fund administration. Nor do these claims typically have diversity jurisdiction. The insurance companies who bring interpleader actions are commonly citizens of the same state as at least one of the rival claimants, making complete diversity unlikely. Accordingly, the application of the traditional rules governing diversity jurisdiction to interpleader actions would make it difficult to bring most such actions in federal court via Rule 22.

2. Statutory Interpleader and the Expansion of Federal Court Power

Congress has enacted a series of statutes that significantly expand the federal courts' subject matter jurisdiction over interpleader actions, and expand the federal courts' power to compel the joinder of all rival claimants in multiple jurisdictions into a single interpleader action.

a. Statutory Interpleader Diversity

THE STATUTE   **28 U.S.C. § 1335**

Interpleader

(a) The district courts shall have original **jurisdiction** of any civil action of **interpleader** or in the nature of interpleader filed by any person, firm, or corporation, association, or society having in his or its custody or possession money or property of the value of **$500 or more**, or having issued a note, bond, certificate, policy of insurance, or other instrument of value or amount of $500 or more, or providing for the delivery or payment or the loan of money or property of such amount or value, or being under any obligation written or unwritten to the amount of $500 or more, if

(1) **Two or more adverse claimants, of diverse citizenship as defined in subsection (a) or (d) of section 1332 of this title, are claiming or may claim to be entitled to such money or property**, or to any one or more of the benefits arising by virtue of any note, bond, certificate, policy or other instrument, or arising by virtue of any such obligation; **and** if

(2) **the plaintiff has deposited** such money or property or has paid the amount of or the loan or other value of such instrument or the amount due under such obligation into the registry of the court, there to abide the judgment of the court, or has given bond payable to the clerk of the court in such amount and with such surety as the court or judge may deem proper, conditioned upon the compliance by the plaintiff with the future order or judgment of the court with respect to the subject matter of the controversy. . . .

EXPLANATION

 This congressional statute is a special grant of original subject matter jurisdiction to the federal district courts for interpleader actions alone. That statute generally makes it easier to establish diversity jurisdiction for interpleader actions. Those actions do not have to satisfy the general 28 U.S.C. § 1332 statutory requirements of complete diversity and an amount in controversy in excess of $75,000. Rather, under 28 U.S.C. § 1335, the federal district courts have jurisdiction over an interpleader action if: (1) the amount in controversy is $500 or more, and (2) if any two of the rival claimants are citizens of different states. The requirement that any two of the adverse claimants be citizens of different states is termed "minimal diversity."

This grant of jurisdiction opens up the federal courts to many interpleader actions that would not otherwise acquire federal subject matter jurisdiction. They often involve an amount of $500 or more, and often involve at least two claimants who are from different states. In order to take advantage of statutory interpleader diversity, however, the plaintiff must deposit with the court the value of the fund at issue, although the plaintiff need not admit any liability.

1. Federal Power to Compel the Joinder of Claimants from Multiple Jurisdictions into One Interpleader Action

THE STATUTE   28 U.S.C. § 2361

Process and Procedure

In any civil action of **interpleader** or in the nature of interpleader under section 1335, * * * a district court may issue its process for all claimants and enter its order **restraining them from instituting or prosecuting any proceedings in any State or United States Court** affecting the property, instrument or obligation involved in the interpleader action until further order of the court * * * Such **district court** shall hear and **determine the case**, and may discharge the plaintiff from further liability, make the injunction permanent, and make all appropriate orders to enforce its judgment.

This congressional statute is an extraordinary grant of federal court power. In an interpleader action, a federal judge has the power to enjoin all pending and even future lawsuits in any federal or state court brought or to be brought by claimants to the fund being litigated in the federal court action. The district court then has the power to consolidate, and to adjudicate, all of the pending and prospective claims in one action.

Moreover, Congress provides that venue is proper for interpleader actions in any federal district where any one of the rival claimants resides. 28 U.S.C. § 1397. Equipped with this venue provision, with the jurisdictional power granted by 28 U.S.C. § 1335 and with the injunctive power granted by 28 U.S.C. § 2361, a federal court sitting in a district where any one claimant to a common fund resides may adjudicate virtually all claims to the common fund that have been or might be filed in any federal or state court throughout the country.

EXAMPLES & ANALYSIS

EXAMPLE: Prime Life Insurance Corporation issues a $10,000 life insurance policy on the life of Alice. When Alice dies, her sisters Clare and Claudia each claim to be the sole beneficiary of the $10,000 life insurance policy proceeds. May Prime Life Insurance Corporation file an interpleader action against Clare and Claudia?

Analysis: Yes. As the holder of a common fund, Prime Life Insurance Corporation may file an interpleader action against Clare and Claudia, who are rival claimants to its policy proceeds fund.

EXAMPLE: If Prime Life Insurance Corporation is a Delaware Corporation with its principal place of business in Wisconsin, Clare is domiciled in Wisconsin and Claudia is domiciled in Illinois, may Prime Life Insurance Corporation bring the action in federal district court?

Analysis: Yes. In this interpleader action, there are two alternative jurisdictional ways for the court to have diversity jurisdiction. Under traditional rule interpleader diversity, there must be complete diversity and the amount in controversy must exceed $75,000. Here, there is no complete diversity because the plaintiff insurance company is from Delaware and Wisconsin and one of the rival claimants (Clare) is domiciled in Wisconsin. Nor does the $10,000 policy amount exceed $75,000. Under statutory interpleader diversity, however, there is jurisdiction because $500 or more is at stake and there is "minimal diversity" because the rival claimants—Clare and Claudia—are citizens of different states.

D. Multiparty, Multiforum Jurisdiction Act

In its Multiparty, Multiforum Jurisdiction Act, Congress grants subject matter jurisdiction to federal district courts over civil actions that arise from a single accident at a discrete location in which at least 75 people have died. 28 U.S.C. § 1369. In such cases, the federal courts have subject matter jurisdiction if there is "minimal diversity" between any of the adverse parties, and if one of the following is also true: (1) the defendant resides in a state that is different from where a substantial part of the accident occurred; (2) any two defendants reside in different states; or (3) substantial parts of the accident took place in different states.

In the tragic circumstances envisioned by this statute, the federal courts are likely to acquire subject matter jurisdiction. 28 U.S.C. § 1369(a).

> This statute can work in tandem with the Judicial Panel on Multidistrict Litigation, which (as explored in Chapter 3) has the power to transfer multiple civil actions pending in multiple federal districts to a single federal district for consolidated pretrial proceedings.

Moreover, the statute gives additional persons with claims arising from the same accident the absolute right to intervene as plaintiffs, even if there is no other jurisdictional basis for their claims.

The statute, however, also prohibits the federal courts from accepting jurisdiction if a substantial majority of the plaintiffs are from the same state as the primary defendants and the plaintiffs' claims are governed primarily by the law of that state. 28 U.S.C. § 1369(b).

E. Class Actions

The rules of procedure in federal and state court generally encourage the joinder of multiple claims involving multiple parties in a single lawsuit. When those claims are joined in the same civil action, each one of them must be separately litigated on the merits. At some point, the number of parties and claims brought in a single lawsuit becomes so large as to make separate adjudication of each claim on the merits in the same action unmanageable.

In situations in which the number of parties in a lawsuit was so large as to make the joinder of them all impractical, the English Courts of Chancery developed a "bill of peace." The "bill of peace" allowed a named party to bring or defend an action on behalf of a group of commonly situated absent parties. This equitable device became the model for American "class actions," which were originally authorized by the Federal Equity Rules and the procedural rules of many state courts. In 1938, Federal Rule of Civil Procedure 23 was adopted, authorizing the use of class actions in both legal and equitable actions in federal court. That original rule recognized three different kinds of actions: a "true" class action in which the class asserted a "joint" or "common" interest; a "hybrid" class action in which the class asserted several rights to common property; and a "spurious" class action in which the class asserted claims involving common issues and common relief. These labels and distinctions, however, proved difficult to administer, and hindered the development of the class action device.

In 1966, Rule 23 was amended to clarify and expand the circumstances in which a class action could be maintained. The 1966 Amendment created a road map for federal judges to follow in determining whether to certify a class action and how to manage virtually all aspects of the litigation. The Amendment also made clear that a lawsuit seeking primarily monetary damages could be maintained as a class action where the common issues predominate over the individual issues. As a result, class action practice increased significantly in the federal courts and became a critical mechanism for prosecuting aggregate claims, particularly in civil rights cases, desegregation cases, mass tort cases and securities fraud cases.

In order for a class action to be effective, however, the result of the named party's adjudication must also govern the absent parties' claims. If the named party prevails, the absent parties must prevail as well. Conversely, if the named party loses its claims, the absent parties must lose their claims as well.

As we discovered in Chapter 2, however, the Due Process Clause of the Constitution prohibits state or federal courts from depriving persons of their property unless they have had an opportunity to be heard. In order to be bound by a judgment, therefore, a person must at least be a party to a lawsuit and have an opportunity to appear in court. Yet, for a class action to be effective, the result of the named party's action must be binding on all members of the class—even those class members who have not appeared in court. The maintenance of class actions therefore requires an exception to the usual requirements of due process. Should there be such an exception to the requirements of due process for class actions? What are the minimum constitutional requirements for a valid class action? How should the federal and state rules authorizing class actions incorporate those constitutional requirements?

As you grapple with these questions, consider also the myriad policy issues raised by class actions. In the absence of the class action device, many small claims challenging unlawful conduct would not be brought because the recovery would not justify the expense. By empowering individual claimants to aggregate their claims of misconduct, class actions are arguably vital to deterring wrongdoing. *See, e.g.,* Arthur Miller, *Of Frankenstein Monsters and Shining Knights: Myth, Reality, and the "Class Action Problem,"* 92 HARV. L. REV. 664, 665–66 (1979). On the other hand, critics of the class action process claim that it facilitates litigation that only benefits class action attorneys and results in "hydraulic" pressure on the defendant to settle the cases at amounts that are unrelated to the underlying merits of the suit. In fact, there is no empirical evidence to support the claim that class actions are abusive, or that certification creates inordinate settlement pressure. *See* Thomas E. Willging, et al., *Empirical Study of Class Actions in Four Federal District Courts: Final Report to the Advocacy Committee on Civil Rules* (1996); Allan Kanner & Tibor Nagy, *Exploding the Blackmail Myth: A New Perspective on Class Action Settlements,* 57 BAYLOR L. REV. 681, 697 (2005); Charles Silver, *"We're Scared to Death": Class Certification and Blackmail,* 78 N.Y.U. L. REV. 1357 (2003). Nonetheless, many courts and commentators remain skeptical of the class action device. The Supreme Court recently has rendered decisions that create barriers to the maintenance and efficacy of the class action device. In *AT&T Mobility LLC v. Concepcion,* 563 U.S. 321 (2011), for example, the Court held that the Federal Arbitration Act of 1925 preempts state laws that prohibit contracts containing provisions that waive the parties' right to seek class action relief. Moreover, in *American Express v. Italian Colors Restaurant,* 133 S. Ct. 2304 (2013), the Court concluded that the Federal Arbitration Act requires the courts to enforce strictly any provision in an arbitration agreement that waives the parties' right to seek class wide recovery for their damages. These decisions enable businesses to include in their consumer contracts provisions that require those consumers to forfeit their right to pursue their claims against the businesses through the cost-effective mechanism of a class action.

1. The Constitutional Requirements for Class Actions

a. Subject Matter Jurisdiction

i. Traditional Jurisdictional Bases for Class Actions

Because state courts are courts of general subject matter jurisdiction, class actions can virtually always be filed in state courts. The federal courts, by contrast, are courts of limited jurisdiction. Accordingly, there must be a constitutional and legislative jurisdictional basis for every class action filed in federal court. If the class action presents claims that "arise under" federal law, the action clearly may be filed in federal court based on "federal question" jurisdiction.

Class actions based on diversity jurisdiction, however, are more nuanced. First, the Supreme Court has consistently held that in determining whether there is diversity of citizenship in a class action, only the named parties must be diverse from the parties opposing the class.

EXAMPLES & ANALYSIS

EXAMPLE: Paula, a domicile of Nebraska, represents a class of commonly situated absent plaintiffs, most of whom are domiciled in Iowa. May Paula file a class action against Doll Corp., a Delaware corporation with its principal place of business in Iowa?

Analysis: Yes. Only the named party or parties must be diverse from the party or parties opposing the class. Paula is diverse from Doll Corp. It does not matter that some, or even most, of the absent plaintiffs may be domiciled in Iowa, where Doll Corp. has its principal place of business.

Second, the supplemental jurisdiction statute, 28 U.S.C. § 1367, also indicates that only the named party's claim must satisfy the requirements of diversity—even if the absent parties' claims do not separately satisfy those requirements. As we discussed in Chapter 1, that statute grants supplemental jurisdiction to the federal district court over nonfederal and nondiverse claims if they derive from a common nucleus of operative fact with a federal or a diverse claim. If the named plaintiff files a claim in which there is complete diversity and in which the amount in controversy exceeds $75,000, the federal court can generally assert supplemental jurisdiction over all of the other claims brought by the absent class members—even if those claims do not separately satisfy the requirements of diversity.

If the only primary jurisdictional basis in the action is diversity, however, 28 U.S.C. § 1367(b) precludes the use of supplemental jurisdiction over claims brought by plaintiffs against parties joined under explicitly enumerated joinder rules. But the statute's supplemental jurisdiction bar does not include class actions in those specifically delineated joinder devices. Accordingly, a federal court may assert supplemental jurisdiction over non-diverse class claims. In *Exxon Mobil Corp. v. Allapattah Services, Inc.*, 545 U.S. 546 (2005), the Supreme Court concluded that if the claims of one diverse plaintiff in a class action exceed $75,000, 28 U.S.C. § 1367(b) does not preclude a federal court from asserting supplemental jurisdiction over claims of additional class plaintiffs that do not themselves exceed $75,000.

ii. The Class Action Fairness Act

Many class actions will readily establish federal subject matter jurisdiction under the relaxed jurisdictional standards of the Class Action Fairness Act. That statute grants jurisdiction to the federal courts over most class actions in which: (1) there are one hundred or more class members; (2) the amount in controversy in the aggregate exceeds $5 million; and (3) any single member of the class is from a different state than any single party opposing the class. 28 U.S.C. § 1332(d).

The Class Action Fairness Act, however, specifically excludes class actions in which: (1) the primary defendants are states or governmental entities; or (2) the claims are based on the federal securities laws; or (3) the claims involve the internal affairs of a corporation which are governed by the law of the state of incorporation.

In addition, the statute bars the assertion of jurisdiction over class actions in which more than two-thirds of the class members are citizens of the forum state, at least one principal defendant is a citizen of the forum state, the principal injuries giving rise to the claims occurred in the forum state, and no similar class actions involving virtually the same parties have been filed in the prior three years. 28 U.S.C. § 1332(d)(4).

The district court also has **discretion** to decline jurisdiction over class actions in which: (1) more than one-third, but less than two-thirds, of the class members are citizens of the forum state, and (2) the primary defendants also are citizens of the forum state. 28 U.S.C. § 1332(d)(3).

Perhaps most significantly, the Class Action Fairness Act facilitates the **removal** of class actions from state to federal court. The expanded bases for federal jurisdiction allow defendants to remove many class actions to federal court. 28 U.S.C. § 1446. Moreover, the statute eliminates traditional impediments to the removal of diversity actions, including: (1) an action can be removed if **any** defendant (rather than **every defendant**) files a notice of removal; (2) removal is not precluded, even if a defendant is a citizen of the state where the action was filed; and (3) the one-year time limit that applies to removal of cases based on diversity jurisdiction does not apply to class actions. 28 U.S.C. § 1453(b).

IN PRACTICE

The primary import of the Class Action Fairness Act is in the context of removal. Congress perceived that class action plaintiffs through their attorneys were selecting beneficial state courts in which to file nationwide class actions. The removal provisions enable defendants easily to remove most such class actions to a proper federal court, where defendants believe they may have a more hospitable forum.

EXAMPLE: Portia, a domicile of Tennessee, files a class action in Tennessee state court on behalf of herself and thousands of other persons throughout the south who suffered more than $5 million in damages resulting from Delay Debt Loan Services, Inc.'s usurious lending practices in violation of Tennessee state law. Delay, which is a Delaware Corporation with its principal place of business in Tennessee, files a timely notice of removal to the federal court in the same location. Should the federal court remand the action back to state court?

Analysis: Probably Not. Under the Class Action Fairness Act, the federal courts have jurisdiction over this class action in which 100 or more plaintiffs together seek more than $5 million and the plaintiff Portia, from Tennessee, is from a different state than the defendant, Delay, which is a citizen of Delaware. Unless more than two-thirds of the plaintiffs are from Tennessee, the court will have federal jurisdiction and should not remand the action to state court.

b. Due Process Requirements for All Class Actions: Adequate Representation

A judgment in a class action is valid only if the parties receive due process. The Due Process Clause generally protects defendants by requiring that the court have personal jurisdiction over them, provide notice reasonably calculated to apprise them of litigation and afford them an opportunity to be heard. The same due process protections must be given to defendants in a class action.

Yet, what are the fundamental due process protections that must be given to plaintiffs in a class action? If the judgment in a class action governs all of the claims of the plaintiffs, the absent class members could each lose those claims in the action. A "claim" has value, and therefore constitutes a property interest. An adverse judgment in a class action deprives the plaintiffs of that property interest. The class plaintiffs thus are entitled to due process protections.

In *Hansberry v. Lee*, 311 U.S. 32 (1940), the Supreme Court addressed the issue of whether a class action could satisfy constitutional due process requirements even if it results in a binding judgment against parties who have had no opportunity to appear and be heard in the action. In that case, Lee sought to enjoin the sale of land governed by a racially restrictive covenant to Hansberry, a black man. Lee alleged that the binding effect of the covenant had been established in an earlier Illinois state court action finding that the covenant was valid. In response, Hansberry and his co-defendants argued that they were not bound by the earlier judgment because they were not parties to that suit or in privity with any of the parties to that action. They argued it would be a denial of due process to hold them to the first decree. The Supreme Court agreed, but in doing so declared that a person could be bound by a judgment entered in an action even if he were not a named party, if the action was a class action and if he received adequate representation.

FROM THE COURT

Hansberry v. Lee
311 U.S. 32 (1940)
Supreme Court of the United States

MR. JUSTICE STONE delivered the opinion of the Court:

The question is whether the Supreme Court of Illinois, by its adjudication that petitioners in this case are bound by a judgment rendered in an earlier litigation to which they were not parties, has deprived them of the due process of law guaranteed by the Fourteenth Amendment.

. . . [W]hen the judgment of a state court, ascribing to the judgment of another court the binding force and effect of *res judicata*, is challenged for want of due process it becomes the duty of this Court to examine the course of procedure in both litigations to ascertain whether the litigant whose rights have thus been adjudicated has been afforded such notice and opportunity to be heard as are requisite to the due process which the Constitution prescribes. . . .

> **Res judicata**, which will be discussed in Chapter 20, means that a claim which has been fully and fairly litigated to a final judgment on the merits cannot be re-litigated by the parties or those represented by the parties.

It is a principle of general application in Anglo-American jurisprudence that one is not bound by a judgment *in personam* in a litigation in which he is not designated as a party or to which he has not been made a party by service of process . . . A judgment rendered in such circumstances is not entitled to the full faith and credit which the Constitution and statute of the United States . . . prescribe, . . . and judicial action enforcing it against the person or property of the absent party is not that due process which the Fifth and Fourteenth Amendments require. . . .

To these general rules there is a recognized exception that, to an extent not precisely defined by judicial opinion, the judgment in a "class" or "representative" suit, to which some members of the class are parties, may bind members of the class or those represented who were not made parties to it . . . In such cases where the interests of those not joined are of the same class as the interests of those who are and where it is considered that the latter fairly represent the former in the prosecution of the litigation of the issues in which all have a common interest, the court will proceed to a decree. . . .

[T]here is scope within the framework of the Constitution for holding in appropriate cases that a judgment rendered in a class suit is *res judicata* as to members of the class who are not formal parties to the suit. . . . With a proper regard for divergent local institutions and interests . . ., this Court is justified in saying that there has been a failure of due process only in those cases where it cannot be said that the procedure adopted, fairly insures the protection of the interests of absent parties who are to be bound by it . . . .

It is familiar doctrine of the federal courts that members of a class not present as parties to the litigation may be bound by the judgment where they are in fact **adequately represented** by parties who are present, or where they actually participate in the conduct of the litigation in which members of the class are present as parties, . . . or where the interest of the members, some of whom are present as parties, is joint, or where for any other reason the relationship between the parties present and those who are absent is such as legally to entitle the former to stand in judgment for the latter. . . .

In all such cases, . . . we may assume for present purposes that such procedure affords a protection to the parties who are represented though absent, which would satisfy the requirements of due process and full faith and credit. . . .

We decide only that the procedure and the course of litigation sustained here by the plea of res judicata do not satisfy these requirements. . . .

CASE ANALYSIS & QUESTIONS

1. The *Hansberry* case actually involves two separate actions. The first action was a declaratory judgment action filed in Illinois state court by landowners seeking a declaration from the court that the racially restrictive covenant was valid. *Burke v. Kleiman*, 277 Ill. App. 519 (1934). That court entered a final judgment on the merits determining that the covenant was valid. The principle of *res judicata* would bar or preclude the parties and persons they represent in that first Illinois state court action from re-litigating any claim regarding the validity of the covenant.

The second lawsuit, from which the Supreme Court's opinion derives, sought to enjoin the sale of land to Hansberry. In seeking to enjoin that sale, the plaintiffs in the second lawsuit argued: (1) the sale to Hansberry violated the covenant; (2) the covenant already had been adjudged valid in the first Illinois action; and (3) the parties in the second Illinois action, including Hansberry, are precluded by *res judicata* from re-litigating the covenant's validity.

In response to these arguments, Hansberry and his seller argued that under the Constitution's Due Process Clause, they could not be bound or precluded by the *res judicata* effect of the judgment in the first lawsuit because they were not parties or represented by the parties in that first lawsuit. The Supreme Court agreed that they could not be bound in this case because they were not made parties and did not receive "adequate representation" in the first lawsuit. The parties who sought enforcement of the covenant in the first lawsuit were not of the same class and could not represent the parties in the second lawsuit who resisted its enforcement. In so holding, however, the Court declared that the Due Process Clause would permit persons to be bound by the *res judicata* effect of a prior judgment even if they were not made parties to the action, as long as they received "adequate representation" from those who were made parties.

How does this declaration of the scope of due process facilitate class actions? What would have happened to class actions if the Court had found that the Due Process Clause prohibits the entry of a judgment that is binding on persons who have not been made parties to an action?

2. What would have happened in the *Hansberry* case itself—and to the validity of similar racially restrictive covenants—if the Court had held that a judgment finding such a covenant valid is binding on persons like Hansberry who were not afforded adequate representation?

3. This case involves Carl Hansberry's attempt to live in a predominately white area of Chicago. His efforts are portrayed in his daughter Loraine Hansberry's play *A Raisin in the Sun*. The play chronicles the violence the Hansberrys encountered when they moved into the neighborhood. As Loraine Hansberry later wrote in her book *To be Young, Gifted and Black*, "I also remember my desperate and courageous mother, patrolling our household all night with a loaded German Luger, doggedly guarding her four children, while my father fought the respectable part of the battle in the Washington court."

c. Additional Due Process Requirements for Class Actions Seeking Primarily Monetary Damages

In *Hansberry,* the Supreme Court made clear that under the Due Process Clause a judgment entered in a class action could bind absent class members only if they received "adequate representation" from the parties in court.

In *Phillips Petroleum Co. v. Shutts*, 472 U.S. 797 (1985), the Court reaffirmed that **all** kinds of class actions must insure that absent parties receive "adequate representation." The Court in *Shutts*, however, also held that, although a court need not have proper personal jurisdiction over absent class plaintiffs, those plaintiffs must receive three additional due process protections in actions in which they seek primarily monetary damages: (1) notice reasonably calculated to apprise those class members of the litigation; (2) an opportunity to exclude themselves or to opt-out of the class action and pursue individual litigation by affirmatively submitting a request for exclusion; and (3) the opportunity to appear in the action and be heard in person or through counsel.

For all class actions, therefore, due process requires that the class members receive adequate representation. For class actions seeking primarily monetary damages, the class must receive not only adequate representation, but also notice, the right to opt-out and the right to appear and be heard.

2. Class Actions in Practice

Federal and state rules authorizing class actions incorporate the constitutional requirements for maintaining class actions, and also guide class action practice. Federal Rule 23 governs virtually all aspects of class action litigation in federal court. In particular, the rule establishes: (a) standards for determining whether a lawsuit should be "certified" as a class action; (b) guidelines for judicial discretion in managing a class action; and (c) parameters for resolving class actions through settlement.

a. Class Certification Requirements

THE RULE   Rule 23(a) & (b)

Class Actions

(a) **Prerequisites.** One or more members of a class may sue or be sued as representative parties on behalf of all members only if:

   (1) the class is so **numerous** that joinder of all members is impracticable;

   (2) there are questions of law or fact **common** to the class;

   (3) the claims or defenses of the representative parties are **typical** of the claims or defenses of the class; and

   (4) the representative parties will fairly and **adequately** protect the interests of the class.

(b) **Types of Class Actions.** A class action may be maintained if Rule 23**(a)** is satisfied and if:

   (1) prosecuting separate actions by or against individual class members would create a **risk** of:

      (A) inconsistent or varying adjudications with respect to individual class members that would establish incompatible standards of conduct for the party opposing the class; or

(B) adjudications with respect to individual class members that, as a practical matter, would be dispositive of the interests of the other members not parties to the individual adjudications or would substantially impair or impede their ability to protect their interests;

(2) the party opposing the class has acted or refused to act on grounds that apply generally to the class, so that final **injunctive** relief or corresponding declaratory relief is appropriate respecting the class as a whole; or

(3) the court finds that the questions of law or fact common to class members **predominate** over any questions affecting only individual members, and that a class action is **superior** to other available methods for fairly and efficiently adjudicating the controversy. The matters pertinent to these findings include:

(A) the class members' interests in individually controlling the prosecution or defense of separate actions;

(B) the extent and nature of any litigation concerning the controversy already begun by or against class members;

(C) the desirability or undesirability of concentrating the litigation of the claims in the particular forum; and

(D) the likely difficulties in managing a class action.

Rule 23(c) requires a federal district court to decide whether to certify a class action at "an early practical time." Before deciding to certify any kind of class action, the court must first determine that all four of the core requirements for class certification in **Rule 23(a)** are met. If so, the court must then determine whether the additional class certification requirements of **Rule 23(b)** are also met.

Rule 23(a) establishes four requirements for all kinds of class actions in federal court:

1. **Numerosity**—the class must be so numerous (usually at least forty) that joinder of them all as individual parties bringing their individual claims in one action would be difficult and inefficient;

2. **Commonality**—there must be questions of fact or law common to the class;

3. **Typicality**—the claims or defenses of the named party must be typical of those of the class, such that the named party does not have unique vulnerabilities; and

4. **Adequacy**—the named parties and their lawyers must, with fairness, competence, experience, perseverance, and without conflict protect the interests of the class.

EXPLANATION

In most class actions, the plaintiffs can establish these four core requirements. Class counsel does not typically bring a class action unless there are numerous plaintiffs who assert typical claims with common questions of fact or law. Although the court has an obligation to scrutinize class counsels' work in the case (including their knowledge, their experience and their resources), most courts find that attorneys bringing class actions will fairly and adequately protect the interests of the class. *See* Fed. R. Civ. P. 23(g).

In *Wal-Mart Stores, Inc. v. Dukes*, 131 S. Ct. 2541 (2011), however, the Supreme Court indicated that the "commonality" requirement of Rule 23(a) requires a heightened showing that the claims of the class members depend on a common contention which can be resolved on a class-wide basis. There, a class of about 1.5 million current and former female employees of Wal-Mart claimed that they were the victims of gender discrimination in violation of Title VII of the Civil Rights Act of 1964. They alleged that Wal-Mart gave to its local managers discretion over issues of pay and promotion, which they used in a way that disproportionately favored men over women.

Yet, the Supreme Court concluded that the class could not establish "commonality" because each of the class plaintiffs was victimized by a different employment decision and suffered a different injury. Nor could the plaintiffs establish that Wal-Mart operated under a general policy of discrimination that applied to all class members. In the wake of *Wal-Mart*, class members must be prepared to demonstrate that their claims involve common contentions, the resolution of which is central to the validity of all of their claims.

Even if the court finds that the four core requirements for all class actions under Rule 23(a) have been established, the court must then find that the action satisfies at least one of the additional requirements of Rule 23(b). That rule divides class actions into three categories.

First, the court may certify a class action under Rule 23(b)(1) if separate actions by individual class members would create a risk of prejudice either to members of the class or to parties opposing the class.

These so-called "prejudice" class actions have their roots in the joinder devices of interpleader and intervention. As with interpleader, the party opposing the class may be at risk of being exposed to multiple and inconsistent adjudications. For example, the defendant may have a limited fund that is being sought by multiple, rival claimants in multiple lawsuits. Those individual actions pose a risk of inconsistent results. When the rival claimants are so numerous that joinder of them all in one interpleader action is impracticable, the court may certify the action as a class action.

Alternatively, plaintiffs may, as a practical matter, lose their ability to recover damages for their losses if their individual lawsuits reach judgment only after the defendant's resources have been depleted. When those absent plaintiffs are too numerous to be joined as individual parties, the court may certify a class action.

Second, under Rule 23(b)(2), the court may certify a class action in which the plaintiffs seek primarily equitable relief in the form of an injunction or a declaratory judgment rather than monetary relief.

Third, under Rule 23(b)(3), the court may certify class actions seeking monetary damages. These class actions are by far the most common.

If the class seeks monetary damages, the court must make two additional findings before certifying the class: (1) the common issues of fact or law must **predominate** over the individual issues; and (2) the class action device must be a **superior** method of adjudicating multiple claims. In assessing predominance, the court must weigh the number and nature of the issues that are common to all class members against the number and nature of issues that are unique to each individual class member. For example, in *Comcast Corp. v. Behrend*, 133 S. Ct. 1426 (2013), the Supreme Court found the lack of predominance where the plaintiffs were unable to show that their damages could be measured on a common, class wide basis. In determining superiority, the court must consider whether the efficiencies of the class action method of adjudication outweigh any difficulties in managing the action.

EXAMPLES & ANALYSIS

EXAMPLE: Peter files a class action for monetary damages on behalf of himself and fifty other persons throughout the Midwest who were defrauded by Detour Travel, Inc. Peter alleges that Detour's travel agents fraudulently induced the class members, through various brochures, ads, and web contacts, into purchasing a two-week cruise package on a ship that was never sea-worthy. Should the federal court certify the class?

Analysis: Maybe. The class likely can establish the four core requirements of Rule 23(a): commonality, adequacy, numerosity, and typicality. In this action seeking monetary damages, however, the class must also satisfy the two additional requirements of Rule 23(b): predominance and superiority. In this case, the common issues may not "predominate" over the individual issues that inevitably arise in fraud actions. In addressing "superiority," the court must weigh the efficiency in resolving multiple claims in one forum against the potential difficulties in managing a complex class action.

b. Class Certification and Due Process

THE RULE   **Rule 23(c)**

Certification Order; Notice to Class Members; Judgment; Issue Classes; Subclasses

(1) Certification Order.

(A) Time to Issue. At an early practicable time after a person sues or is sued as a class representative, the court must determine by order whether to certify the action as a class action.

(B) **Defining the Class; Appointing Class Counsel.** An order that certifies a class action must define the class and the class claims, issues, or defenses, and must appoint class counsel under Rule 23(g).

(C) **Altering or Amending the Order.** An order that grants or denies class certification may be altered or amended before final judgment.

(2) Notice.

(A) **For (b)(1) or (b)(2) Classes.** For any class certified under Rule 23(b)(1) or (b)(2), the court may direct appropriate notice to the class.

(B) **For (b)(3) Classes.** For any class certified under Rule 23(b)(3), the court must direct to class members the best notice that is practicable under the circumstances, including individual notice to all members who can be identified through reasonable effort. The notice must clearly and concisely state in plain, easily understood language: (i) the nature of the action; (ii) the definition of the class certified; (iii) the class claims, issues, or defenses; (iv) that a class member may enter an appearance through an attorney if the member so desires; (v) that the court will exclude from the class any member who requests exclusion; (vi) the time and manner for requesting exclusion; and (vii) the binding effect of a class judgment on members under Rule 23(c)(3).

(3) Judgment. Whether or not favorable to the class, the judgment in a class action must:

(A) for any class certified under Rule 23(b)(1) or (b)(2), include and describe those whom the court finds to be class members; and

(B) for any class certified under Rule 23(b)(3), include and specify or describe those to whom the Rule 23(c)(2) notice was directed, who have not requested exclusion, and whom the court finds to be class members.

(4) Particular Issues. When appropriate, an action may be brought or maintained as a class action with respect to particular issues.

(5) Subclasses. When appropriate, a class may be divided into sub-classes that are each treated as a class under this rule.

Rule 23 incorporates the constitutional due process requirements for class actions in two ways. First, Rule 23(a) requires that in all kinds of class actions, the court must find that the named representative and class counsel will adequately represent the class. Second, Rule 23(c)(2) and Rule 23(c)(3) require that in actions seeking monetary damages which are certified under Rule 23(b)(3), the court must order "the best notice that is practicable under the circumstances" to the class, must offer the class members the opportunity to request exclusion from the class, and must afford them an opportunity to enter an appearance in the action. The federal rule thereby insures that class actions seeking monetary damages will meet the minimal requirements of due process.

Significantly, however, Rule 23(c)(2) and Rule 23(c)(3) do not require the court to provide these same due process protections for classes certified under Rule 23(b)(1) or 23(b)(2)—which do not seek monetary damages. In those non-monetary class actions, the court has **discretion** to provide notice, the opportunity to opt-out, and the opportunity to be heard; but the court is not required to do so. In fact, the class members pursuing Rule 23(b)(1) and Rule 23(b)(2) actions will be bound by the *res judicata* effect of the judgment, even if they received no notice. Why would the Due Process Clause not require the same protections in these class actions as those required in class actions seeking monetary damages?

IN PRACTICE

The decision by the court to certify a class is the most critical point in a class action. Defendants perceive that their exposure becomes so great when a class is certified that they often enter into serious settlement negotiations after the court makes that decision. Accordingly, the great bulk of class action litigation concentrates on the issue of whether the class should be certified. Although the district court has discretion in deciding whether to certify the class, the appellate court may permit an immediate appeal from that decision. *See* Fed. R. Civ. P. 23(f).

c. Judicial Discretion in Managing Class Actions

THE RULE   Rule 23(d)

Conducting the Action

(1) In General. In conducting an action under this rule, the court may issue orders that:

(A) determine the course of proceedings or prescribe measures to prevent undue repetition or complication in presenting evidence or argument;

(B) require—to protect class members and fairly conduct the action—giving appropriate notice to some or all class members of:

(i) any step in the action;

(ii) the proposed extent of the judgment; or

(iii) the members' opportunity to signify whether they consider the representation fair and adequate, to intervene and present claims or defenses, or to otherwise come into the action;

(C) impose conditions on the representative parties or on intervenors;

(D) require that the pleadings be amended to eliminate allegations about representation of absent persons and that the action proceed accordingly; or

(E) deal with similar procedural matters.

(2) Combining and Amending Orders. An order under Rule 23(d)(1) may be altered or amended from time to time and may be combined with an order under Rule 16.

Rule 23(d) grants broad discretion to federal judges to manage virtually all aspects of the class action. The court has the power to define the class, to appoint class counsel, to shape the content and timing of notice, to certify particular issues for class action treatment, to divide the action into sub-classes, to coordinate discovery, to streamline the presentation of evidence at trial, to monitor class counsel, to place conditions on the intervention of additional parties, to amend the pleadings, and to amend any of its prior orders to insure the just and efficient prosecution of the action.

d. Class Action Settlements

THE RULE   Rule 23(e)

Settlement, Voluntary Dismissal, or Compromise

The claims, issues, or defenses of a certified class may be settled, voluntarily dismissed, or compromised only with the court's approval. The following procedures apply to a proposed settlement, voluntary dismissal, or compromise:

(1) The court must direct notice in a reasonable manner to all class members who would be bound by the proposal.

(2) If the proposal would bind class members, the court may approve it only after a hearing and on finding that it is fair, reasonable, and adequate.

(3) The parties seeking approval must file a statement identifying any agreement made in connection with the proposal.

(4) If the class action was previously certified under Rule 23(b)(3), the court may refuse to approve a settlement unless it affords a new opportunity to request exclusion to individual class members who had an earlier opportunity to request exclusion but did not do so.

(5) Any class member may object to the proposal if it requires court approval under this subdivision (e); the objection may be withdrawn only with the court's approval.

In most civil litigation, the parties are free to enter into a settlement agreement disposing of the litigation without any judicial intervention. In a class action, by contrast, the court **must** approve of any settlement in order for it to become effective. Rule 23(e) prohibits the court from approving any settlement of the class action unless it: (1) orders reasonable notice to all class members bound by the settlement; and (2) conducts a hearing after which it determines that the settlement agreement is "fair, reasonable and adequate." In making its finding that the settlement is fair, reasonable, and adequate, the court typically will consider statements made in support of the agreement from the parties and their lawyers, as well as statements made by class members who object to the settlement as being inadequate.

As part of its resolution of the class action, the court also may award reasonable attorney's fees to class counsel after conducting a hearing to determine their propriety, at which objectors can be heard. *See* Fed. R. Civ. P. 23(h).

In some class actions, the parties reach a settlement agreement before the court has granted class certification. The court then may certify the class for settlement purposes, insuring that the resolution of the action is binding on all class members who do not properly request exclusion. These so-called "settlement classes" provide an efficient method of resolving multiple claims. The Supreme Court has made clear, however, that the federal courts may not certify a class for settlement purposes unless the class would otherwise satisfy the certification requirements of Rule 23. *See Ortiz v. Fibreboard Corp.,* 527 U.S. 815 (1999); *Amchem Products, Inc. v. Windsor,* 521 U.S. 591 (1997).

ADDITIONAL EXERCISES

1. Priscilla, a citizen of Wyoming, files a civil action for $100,000 in federal court in Michigan against Donald's Hair Salon, Inc., alleging the salon negligently caused her hair to become discolored. Donald's is a Delaware Corporation with its headquarters in Michigan. The defendant moves to dismiss the action for failure to join parties required to be joined by Rule 19. In particular, Donald's argues that Petra, a citizen of Michigan, must be joined because she has a similar claim against it for hair discoloration, and that Tonics Inc., a Hawaii Corporation with its headquarters and all of its activities in Hawaii, also must be joined because it created the hair lotion that may have contributed to the plaintiff's losses. ***How should the court rule?***

2. Perry, a citizen of New York, files a civil action for medical malpractice in the federal court in the District of Hawaii against his back surgeon, Dr. Ditmer (a citizen of Hawaii). Dr. Ditmer moves to dismiss the action for failure to join Dr. Thomas, who is Perry's chiropractor and who may be liable for all or part of Dr. Ditmer's liability to Perry. Dr. Thomas has never left his home state of New York. ***Should the court grant the motion to dismiss?***

3. Priscilla, a citizen of Wyoming, originally filed an action for $100,000 in federal court in Michigan against Donald's Hair Salon, Inc. alleging that the salon negligently caused the discoloration of her hair. Donald's Hair Salon, Inc. is a Delaware Corporation with its headquarters in Michigan. Priscilla's attorney discovers that at least 200 people have suffered various degrees of hair discoloration in the past two years at Donald's Hair Salon. Priscilla files a timely, amended complaint to assert a class action on behalf of herself and all other victims seeking damages from $50,000 to $4 million for their hair discolorations caused by Donald's Hair Salon, Inc. in the past two years.

   a. ***May the action be filed in federal court if several of the plaintiffs are domiciled in Michigan?***

   b. ***May the action be filed in federal court if some of the plaintiffs do not have claims exceeding $75,000?***

   c. ***Should the court certify the class?***

   d. ***To what extent should the court consider the underlying merits of the plaintiffs' claims in deciding whether to certify the class?***

   e. ***May the court certify the class without considering whether the plaintiff has introduced sufficient admissible evidence to show that damages can be awarded on a class-wide basis?***

   f. ***If the court certifies the class, must the court give the class notice, an opportunity to exclude themselves, and an opportunity to appear in the action?***

   g. ***Should the court create any sub-classes?***

   h. ***If the parties presented a settlement of this action that gives to the plaintiffs a total of $500,000 and awards attorneys' fees to the plain-***

tiffs' lawyers in the amount of $500,000, what factors should the court consider in determining whether to approve that settlement?

4. In its interpleader statute, its Multiparty, Multiforum Jurisdiction Act and its Class Action Fairness Act, Congress grants subject matter jurisdiction to its lower federal courts to adjudicate state law claims that do not have complete diversity. ***Does Congress have the constitutional power to do that?***

Quick Summary

- The rules of civil procedure in federal and state court encourage and sometimes require the joinder of parties needed for a full and fair adjudication.

- Nonparties have the right to intervene if they have an interest that, as a practical matter, will be adversely affected by a lawsuit and not protected by the existing parties. They may also seek permission from the court to allow them to intervene if there is a commonality of issues between those in the ongoing litigation and those affecting them.

- The court also has the power to compel the joinder of nonparties who are required for a full and fair adjudication. If a nonparty cannot be joined because there is no jurisdiction, the court may, in equity and good conscience, dismiss the entire litigation for failure to join an indispensable party.

- The holder of a common fund that is concerned about multiple claims to its fund may file an action as a plaintiff and interplead all rival claimants to its common fund. Congress has granted the federal courts broad jurisdiction over such interpleader actions.

- Congress has given expansive jurisdiction to its federal district courts to adjudicate claims on behalf of the victims of an accident in which at least 75 people have died.

- A named party may file an action on behalf of a class of commonly situated absent parties. The absent parties will be bound by the judgment if the court provides minimal due process protections, including that the named party will adequately represent the interests of the class.

10

Rule 15: Amended and
Supplemental Pleadings

Key Concepts

- Amending pleadings once as a matter of course and thereafter obtaining permission
- Amending pleadings after the statute of limitations has run
- Amending pleadings during or after the trial
- Supplementing pleadings

Introduction

Rule 15 allows a party to amend its pleading after it has been filed with the court. In keeping with the flexibility of the federal rules, Rule 15 is generous. The policy is that by allowing the parties to "fix" their pleadings as they go along, the merits of the case will more readily be resolved. The parties will not waste precious time and resources squabbling over the mechanics of amending their pleadings. However, Rule 15's flexibility must also be balanced with fairness concerns for the opposing party.

The need to amend generally arises when a party has made an inadvertent omission or mistake in its pleading. In that case, if the party realizes its mistake fairly quickly, the amendment will generally be allowed under the rule. But, a party may also learn of new information and want to amend its pleading to add a new party or claim accordingly. Whether an amendment is allowed in that situation often turns on whether the statute of limitations for the underlying action has run. If it has, the rule requires more complex analysis to determine whether the amendment will be allowed. If it does, the new pleading will "relate back" to the original date of filing.

A. The Rule

Rule 15 has four main sections:

- The first section (15(a)) sets out when and how a party can amend its pleading before trial;

- The second section (15(b)) allows the parties to amend the pleadings during and after trial;

- The third section (15(c)) prescribes when a party can amend to add a new claim or party even after the statute of limitations has run;

> The **statute of limitations** is the amount of time in which a particular cause of action can be brought. *See* Chapter 1 for a detailed description.

- Finally, the fourth section (15(d)) explains when a party can add claims that arise out of an event that occurred after the original pleading was filed.

B. Rule 15(a): Amendments Before Trial

Rule 15(a) addresses two issues:

- the one and only time a party can amend the complaint without the permission of either the court or the opposing party; and

- how a party can amend a pleading once it has already filed an amendment under Rule 15(a)(1) or if the time period for filing a Rule 15(a) amendment has passed.

THE RULE	Rule 15(a)

Amendments Before Trial

(1) *Amending as a Matter of Course.* A party may amend its pleading **once as a matter of course** within:

(A) 21 days after serving it; or

(B) if the pleading is one to which a responsive pleading is required, 21 days after service of a responsive pleading or 21 days after service of a motion under Rule 12(b), (e), or (f), whichever is earlier.

(2) *Other Amendments*. **In all other cases**, a party may amend its pleading only with the **opposing party's written consent** or the **court's leave**. The court should freely give leave **when justice so requires**.

EXPLANATION

1. Rule 15(a)(1): Amendments as a Matter of Course

 A party wishing to amend its pleading without permission of the court or the opposing party has a limited time in which to do so. This is called amending as a "matter of course" or an amendment "as of right." There are three specific moments listed in Rule 15(a)(1) in which a party can amend its pleading. They are:

> Remember Rule 7 (discussed in chapter 7). It tells us what counts as a "pleading" and what counts as a "motion." It is important to understand that while there are three distinct "amendment moments," a party has the right to amend without permission only once. For example, if a party amends its pleading within 21 days of serving that pleading, it cannot use Rule 15(a)(1) to amend again. Instead, it must seek permission of the court or the opposing party under Rule 15(a)(2).

(a) within 21 days of serving the pleading;

(b) 21 days after a responsive pleading is served; or

(c) 21 days after a Rule 12 motion is served.

EXAMPLES & ANALYSIS

EXAMPLE: Paula filed her complaint against Devon on October 1. She alleged that he negligently ran over her toe with his scooter. Devon did not file an answer, but instead filed and served a Rule 12(b)(6) motion to dismiss on October 11, arguing that Paula failed to state a claim upon which relief could be granted. In the meantime, Paula realized that she also wanted to state a claim against Devon's brother Dillon. She alleges that right after Devon ran over her right toe, Dillon ran over her left one. She would like to file an amended complaint to add Dillon. The statute of limitations does not run for two more years.

Analysis: Paula has 21 days from the date of filing of Devon's 12(b)(6) motion to file her amended complaint under 15(a)(1). This means that she has to file the complaint adding Dillon as a party by November 1. If she misses that deadline, she will not be able to file the amendment as a matter of course under Rule 15(a)(1).

IN PRACTICE

If a plaintiff files an amended complaint under Rule 15(a)(1) while a motion to dismiss is pending, the court has discretion to "transfer" the motion to the new complaint (assuming the motion is still responsive to the amended complaint) or it can require the defendant to file a new motion (if, for example, resolving the motion in light of the new complaint would cause confusion or delay).

EXAMPLE: Assume that Paula successfully amended her complaint before November 1 to add Dillon as party. Dillon filed his answer on November 15, but a few days later he realized that he mistakenly denied an allegation when he intended to admit it. He filed an amended answer on November 20. Is he allowed to do so without court permission or without Paula's consent?

Analysis: Yes. The answer is a pleading, so Rule 15(a)(1)(A) applies. Dillon has 21 days from serving his answer to amend. And, as a policy matter, this makes sense. His mistake is ministerial and the sooner it is fixed, the better it is for all parties involved.

EXAMPLE: Assume again that Paula successfully amended her complaint before November 1 to add Dillon as a party. After filing that amendment, Paula realized that she mistakenly listed the wrong street names when describing where the accident occurred. Can she amend her pleading without permission from the court or the opposing party in order to replace the wrong street names with the correct ones?

Analysis: No. Paula has already amended her complaint once as a matter of course under Rule 15(a)(1). Although her proposed amendment is fairly innocuous, she will have to seek permission to amend under Rule 15(a)(2).

2. Rule 15(a)(2): Amendments by Party Consent or Court Approval

Like Rule 15(a)(1), Rule 15(a)(2) is a generous rule. Even when the amending party has already amended once under Rule 15(a)(1) (or missed the window to amend under the same), that party can still amend its pleading as long as the opposing party consents in writing or the court grants the party leave to amend.

With respect to the first option—obtaining written consent from the opposing party—the calculus is fairly straightforward. The attorney for the opposing party should generally agree to the amendment unless doing so would violate the duties owed to her client. In other words, most reasonable requests for written consent for an amendment will be given. The attorney for the opposing party will in all likelihood want to avoid a protracted battle before the judge over a potential amendment and will often just allow the amendment out of professional courtesy.

> On appeal, the court's decision to deny the request for an amendment is reviewed for abuse of discretion. *See* Chapter 19 for a discussion of standards of review. If the court fails to explain why it denied the request, that omission alone could qualify as an abuse of discretion.

However, if the opposing party will not consent, the amending party must ask for the court's approval. Such a request should be made by motion, with the proposed amendment attached.

The language of Rule 15(a)(2) states that the amendment should be allowed "when justice so requires." Most courts have interpreted this language to require them to allow an amendment unless one of the following justifies denial:

(a) undue delay;

(b) bad faith or dilatory motive by the moving party;

(c) repeated failure to cure deficiencies by previous amendments;

(d) undue prejudice to the opposing party; or

(e) futility.

See *Foman v. Davis*, 371 U.S. 178, 192 (1962) (providing this basic set of factors for denying an amendment).

EXAMPLES & ANALYSIS

EXAMPLE: Parachute Corp. filed a complaint against Drexel Corp. in a breach of contract claim two years ago. In the past two years, the parties have completed a significant amount of discovery. The parties are set to go to trial in a month, but Parachute Corp. has asked to amend its complaint to add an additional claim of tortious interference. Drexel Corp. refused to consent to the amendment, so Parachute Corp. has sought permission from the court. Should the court allow the amendment?

Analysis: It depends, but probably not. The court will likely find that amending a month before trial to add this additional claim would result in prejudice to Drexel Corp. The court will have to determine whether Drexel Corp. would have done anything differently over the past two years. In other words, would it have conducted different discovery had it known of the tortious interference claim? If not, then the court may not find prejudice. But, if so, then the court will likely deny the amendment. The court will also have to consider whether the new claim added by the amendment would be futile. Or put a different way, the court will have to determine whether the tortious interference claim would survive a 12(b)(6) motion to dismiss. If it would not, then the court could deny the amendment on the basis of futility.

Rule 15(a)(2) does not prescribe a deadline for requesting permission from the court to amend the pleading. But, the factors to be considered certainly become more pronounced as time wears on. If a request to amend is made early in the litigation process, it is more difficult for a court to determine that the party was dilatory or that there was undue delay. However, if the request is made later in the process, the court may have a harder time avoiding that conclusion.

> While the denial of the request for amendment is reviewed for abuse of discretion on appeal, a finding that the amendment would have been futile is a legal conclusion that is subject to de novo review. *See* Chapter 19 for a discussion of standards of review.

It is worth pointing out, however, that just because an amendment will be bad for the opposing party on the merits— meaning, an amendment adding a meritorious claim might be harder for a defendant to disprove—it does not mean that the court should not grant leave to amend. Rule 15(a)(2)'s requirement of justice is just that. As long as the proposed amendment does not prejudice the opposing party's preparation, it should be allowed.

IN PRACTICE

While Rule 15(a)(2) does not contain a time limit on amendments to the pleading, the court's scheduling order under Rule 16(b) might. If a party attempts to amend its pleading after the deadline in a Rule 16(b) scheduling order has run, then the party must meet the requirements of both Rule 15(a)(2) and Rule 16(b)(4) (requiring good cause and the judge's consent to modify a Rule 16(b) scheduling order). *See* Chapter 11 for a discussion of scheduling orders.

C. Rule 15(b): Amendments During and After Trial

Rule 15(b) addresses amendments to the pleading during and after trial. Remember that up to now, we have only been looking at when and how pleadings might be amended before trial. With Rule 15(b), the rule addresses what to do when an issue that was not explicitly covered in the pleading is brought up at trial. This can happen in two situations. First, when the issue comes up in trial and the opposing party objects to allowing an amendment to the pleading. Second, when the issue is litigated in trial and neither party has objected to it. In the first situation, the court must determine whether the opposing party would suffer prejudice from adding the issue at that time. In the second, the parties and the court will treat the issue as if it had been properly pled from the beginning. However, a party may move to formally amend the pleading to "conform to the evidence."

THE RULE	Rule 15(b)

Amendments During and After Trial

(1) **Based on an Objection at Trial.** If, at trial, a party objects that evidence is not within the issues raised in the pleadings, the court may permit the pleadings to be amended. The court **should freely permit an amendment** when doing so will aid in presenting the merits and the objecting party fails to satisfy the court that **the evidence would prejudice that party's action or defense on the merits.** The court may grant a continuance to enable the objecting party to meet the evidence.

(2) **For Issues Tried by Consent.** When an issue not raised by the pleadings **is tried by the parties' express or implied consent,** it must be treated in all respects as if raised in the pleadings. A party may move—at any time, even after judgment—**to amend the pleadings to conform** them to the evidence and to raise an unpleaded issue. But failure to amend does not affect the result of the trial of that issue.

EXAMPLES & ANALYSIS

EXAMPLE: Pierre attended a baseball game at Danger Field, home of the Dangers. At the game, Pierre decided to check the scores of the other games being played that day on his phone. Unfortunately, while Pierre was looking at his phone, Sam Slugger (a star player for the Dangers) hit a foul ball that hit Pierre in the face. Pierre decided to sue Danger Field for negligently failing to have a net to stop foul balls from going into the stands. He did not include any other claims in his complaint.

At trial, Pierre tried to introduce evidence that a Danger Field security guard told Pierre that he was an idiot for checking his phone during an at-bat. Danger Field objected, arguing that the statement was not within the original claim and that introducing the statement into evidence would prejudice its defense. Pierre moved to amend his complaint to include a claim of intentional infliction of emotional distress. How should the judge rule?

Analysis: It is likely that a court would find that the security guard's statement will aid in Pierre's presentation of the merits of both claims. However, it is also likely that introducing this evidence would prejudice Danger Field's defense. The evidence was only introduced at trial, and Danger Field hasn't had an opportunity to investigate the alleged statement. It would also be difficult for Danger Field to adequately defend against the new claim of intentional infliction of emotional distress. If the court believes the claim should be added, however, it can lessen the prejudice that Danger Field might suffer by granting a continuance to give it more time to prepare.

EXAMPLE: Polly the Popstar wanted to film a music video for her new hit song, "I'm Rich." For the video, Polly rented very expensive jewelry from Dane the Jeweler. Unfortunately, while Polly was wearing the jewelry, she was robbed at gun point. Dane sued Polly alleging negligence in her complaint.

Before trial, Dane filed a brief with the court alleging that Polly also could be found liable for a breach of contract claim because Polly was contractually bound to return the jewelry. She did not amend the complaint at that time; it still only alleged negligence. Polly filed a response brief with the court, saying that she had no such duty to return the jewelry under the contract, and even if she did, she was excused from performance because of the extenuating circumstances. The trial ensued, and Polly was found liable for only the breach of contract claim. After the trial, Dane moved to amend her complaint to include the breach of contract claim. Should the court allow Dane to do so?

Analysis: Dane would be permitted to amend her complaint. By responding to Dane's brief with arguments disputing her breach of contract theory of liability, Polly impliedly consented to litigate that issue. Polly treated the breach of contract claim as if it was in the complaint. Assuming the court found that the issue was tried by implied consent, it must treat the issue as having been raised in the pleading under Rule 15(b)(2). Thus, Dane may amend her complaint to conform to the evidence that was presented in trial and raise the unpleaded breach of contract issue. Even if the court does not formally allow the amendment, however, Rule 15(b)(2) ensures that such failure to amend will not affect the results of the trial.

D. Rule 15(c): Relation Back of Amendments

This rule comes into play when a party wants to add either a new claim or a new party to a pleading, but the statute of limitations has run. It is key to remember that this rule only arises when the statute of limitations has expired. If a party is trying to amend a pleading and the statute of limitations on the action has not yet run, then the party should use only Rule 15(a) or (b) as discussed above.

Rule 15(c) often creates confusion for courts and students alike. But, it need not be that way. In short, Rule 15(c) creates a legal fiction. If a party satisfies the rule,

When a party seeks to amend his pleadings and wants the amendment to relate back, he technically makes the request under Rule 15(a)(2)—he seeks the consent of the court to amend the pleadings. He also uses Rule 15(c) to argue that the amendment is allowed because it relates back under that rule. In other words, the court will only consent to the amendment under Rule 15(a)(2) if it relates back under Rule 15(c). The same is true for amendments under Rule 15(a)(1), although that situation is less common.

then a new party or claim is added to the complaint. The court and the parties act as if the new party or claim has been there since the date the pleading was originally filed and thus before the statute of limitations ran. That is why the amendment is said to "relate back." Because such a legal fiction could potentially be unfair to either the existing parties (if a new claim is added) or to the new party (if she has just been added), the rule is drafted to have a fairly narrow application.

The rule itself consists of three main sections: (1) a section that defers to the relation back provisions of the substantive law being used if they are more generous than the federal rule; (2) a section that explains how a new claim can be added; and (3) a section that explains how a claim against a new party can be added.

THE RULE   Rule 15(c)(1)(A)

Relation Back of Amendments

(1) *When an Amendment Relates Back.* An amendment to a pleading relates back to the date of the original pleading when:

(A) the law that provides the applicable statute of limitations allows relation back; . . .

1. Relation Back Under the Applicable Law's Statute of Limitations

The first section is often overlooked by attorneys. It allows the party to use the relation-back provisions of the substantive law. This means, for example, that if the underlying limitations rule allows for relation back of an amendment that is more generous than Rules 15(c)(1)(B) or (C), then the party can use that state law to amend her pleading and relate her new claim back to the original date of filing. This, of course, only applies if the applicable law of the state includes a provision that governs relation back.

2. Relation Back When Adding a Claim

THE RULE   Rule 15(c)(1)(B)

Relation Back of Amendments

(1) *When an Amendment Relates Back.* An amendment to a pleading relates back to the date of the original pleading when: . . .

    (B) the amendment asserts a claim or defense that arose out of the **conduct, transaction, or occurrence** set out—or attempted to be set out—in the original pleading; or . . . .

Assuming that the applicable substantive law does not provide a more generous relation-back provision, the rule then provides for two different tests depending on whether the amending party is adding a new claim against an existing party or whether the amending party is adding a whole new party to the action. In the first instance—adding a new claim against an existing party—the rule requires that the new claim arise out of the same "conduct, transaction, or occurrence" that gave rise to the claims in the original pleading. The policy behind this language is that if the opposing party had notice of the facts that gave rise to a new claim, she would not suffer prejudice if that claim were added.

> The terminology "**transaction or occurrence**" might sound familiar. For instance, a version of this language appeared in Chapter 1 discussing supplemental jurisdiction. While the meaning is not exactly the same in all of these contexts, it is fairly similar. Where this language is found in a rule (or case law setting forth doctrine), courts will make similar inquiries such as whether the parties and evidence are the same.

EXAMPLES & ANALYSIS

EXAMPLE: Mr. Pond worked as an industrial engineer for Dooly Inc. for over thirty years. Pond was shocked last year when he was terminated by the company. The Dooly executive who terminated

Pond explained that due to some restructuring within the company, there were no longer any positions for which Pond was qualified. Pond was sorely disappointed and filed suit against Dooly in federal court. In his complaint, he alleged that he had been terminated in violation of the Age Discrimination in Employment Act. His factual allegations explained that he was terminated solely because he was over 50 years of age, not because he was unqualified for any positions in the company. Two years after filing his complaint, Pond sought leave to amend his complaint to add a tort claim. He alleged that in the ten years leading up to his termination, he had eaten lunch daily in the Dooly Inc. cafeteria. He alleged that he developed food allergies from the spoiled food he ate there. There is a two-year statute of limitations on a tort claim, and that time has passed. Can Pond amend his complaint to add this claim and will it relate back?

Analysis: Probably not. Rule 15(c)(1)(B) requires that the new claim arise out of the same conduct, transaction or occurrence set out in the original pleading. Here, Pond only originally alleged that he was terminated because of his age. In essence, that allegation covered only the day he was actually terminated. There were no allegations made about the time leading up to his termination when the allegedly defective food was served. From the perspective of Dooly, it would not have been on notice of this potential tort claim from the allegations supporting Pond's age discrimination claims. The alleged tort occurred at different times and involved different transactions and occurrences than the alleged act of age discrimination. So, it is unlikely that a court would find that the tort claim arose out of the same conduct, transaction, or occurrence as the age discrimination claim. This amendment would probably not relate back, so his request to amend would be denied.

3. Relation Back When Adding a Party

THE RULE   Rule 15(c)(1)(C)

Relation Back of Amendments

(1) **When an Amendment Relates Back.** An amendment to a pleading relates back to the date of the original pleading when: ...

> **(C)** the amendment **changes the party or the naming of the party** against whom a claim is asserted, if **Rule 15(c)(1)(B) is satisfied** and if, **within the period provided by Rule 4(m)** for serving the summons and complaint, the party to be brought in by amendment:
>
> **(i)** received such notice of the action that it will **not be prejudiced** in defending on the merits; and
>
> **(ii) knew or should have known** that the action would have been brought against it, **but for a mistake** concerning the proper party's identity.

Statutes of limitations exist to provide a potential defendant with "repose," meaning that after a certain amount a time that individual should be able to get on with her life and not worry about being sued. This policy clashes a bit with the liberality of amending pleadings under the federal rules. In the section governing how new parties are added, the rule attempts to strike a balance between these two policies. The new party can only be added when three distinct requirements are met.

> Under **Rule 4(m)**, the plaintiff generally has 120 days from the date of filing the complaint to serve the summons, although that time is subject to extension at the discretion of the court. Any extension granted in a particular case will apply to how Rule 15(c) is applied to a new defendant. In other words, if existing defendants in the action received notice within 150 days because the court granted an extension under Rule 4(m), then a new defendant's window of notice will similarly be 150 days under Rule 15(c).

- First, the new claim must arise out of the same conduct, transaction or occurrence as set out in the original pleading.

- Second, the new party must have received notice of the action such that it would not suffer prejudice in defending against that claim. This notice must have been received within the period provided under Rule 4(m) for serving the summons and complaint.

- Finally, the new party must have known (or should have known) that it would have been named as a defendant in the suit were it not for a mistake. All of these requirements combine to make it difficult to add a new party when doing so would be unfair.

EXAMPLES & ANALYSIS

EXAMPLE: Louise Shaffer was appointed to the position of Secretary of Labor by the President. She was a former executive at Pestin Construction, a large construction company in the state of New Jersey. While Shaffer awaited Senate confirmation of her appointment, Dollars Magazine ran a scathing article about her qualifications. In that same article, the author insinuated that both Shaffer and Pestin Construction had links to organized crime. Company president George Pestin was outraged at this article, but he did not act immediately to respond. He eventually decided that he wanted to take action, however, so ten days before the statute of limitations ran on his alleged libel claim, he filed a complaint against Dollars Magazine. The complaint listed Dollars Magazine as the defendant, with its principal place of business in the Dime and Nickel Building in New York. The summons and complaint were served on Dime, Inc.'s registered agent within 120 days of filing the complaint under Rule 4(m). Pestin quickly discovered, however, that he had sued the wrong entity. Dollars was only a trademark of Dime, Inc.—it was not a separate entity. In order for the suit to go forward, Pestin needed to sue Dime, Inc. However, the statute of limitations for the libel action had already run by the time he made this discovery.

Consider the requirements of Rule 15(c)(1)(C). Does the libel claim against Dime Inc. arise out of the same conduct, transaction, or occurrence that was set out in the original complaint?

Analysis: Yes. The libel action is the same. The only thing that is changing is that a new party is being added. Thus, the first requirement of relating back an amendment when adding a new party is met.

EXAMPLE: Did Dime, Inc. receive notice of the action within the 120-day period set out in Rule 4(m) such that it will not suffer prejudice in defending on the merits?

Analysis: Yes. Its registered agent received a copy of the complaint and summons within the 120-day period set out in Rule 4(m). Thus, it received notice and would not suffer prejudice in defending against the action. It is worth noting, however, that there are limited factual situations where a new party would have had the notice required under this part of the rule. The notice must be from the complaint itself. It cannot be met by general knowledge about a suit gleaned from a newspaper article or from a passing conversation. The complaint itself must have been actually seen or such knowledge must be imputed. What this means in practice is that there is a narrow category of situations where the notice requirement will be met. The first is where the party that was properly served with the complaint and the proposed new party share an "identity of interest," meaning generally that the parties are so related in their business interests that they are essentially one in the same. A parent and its wholly-owned subsidiary are often found to share an identity of interest. The second is when the parties share an attorney. In some situations, the knowledge of the complaint will be imputed to the new party if two parties share legal counsel.

EXAMPLE: Should Dime, Inc. have known that but for a mistake it would have been named as a defendant?

Analysis: Probably yes. It knew that Dollars was its trademark, and from the allegations in the complaint, it was clear that Pestin intended to sue Dime for libel. In other words, Dime knew or should have known that Pestin meant to sue it, especially since it knew that Dollars was not an entity against which one could file suit. It is not as if Pestin knew that both Dime, Inc. and Dollars were entities and chose strategically to sue one

> In the actual case upon which this illustration is modeled, relation back of amendment was not permitted. See *Schiavone v. Fortune*, 477 U.S. 21 (1986). This is because Rule 15(c) was differently worded at the time of *Schiavone*. Perception that the actual *Schiavone* result was unjust fueled reconsideration of the Rule, which was changed pursuant to the procedures set forth in the Rules Enabling Act—28 U.S.C. § 2072). (*See* Unit Overview, discussing the rulemaking process).

over the other. That would not be a mistake; it would be a strategic choice. This is certainly a fuzzy line and one that is sometimes difficult to determine. Courts do not always agree, but the general consensus is that when a party intended to sue another party, but failed to recognize a technical distinction between entities, that is a mistake. Where a party understood those technical distinctions, but chose to sue one party instead of the other, that is not a mistake. Finally, most courts have held that simple lack of knowledge is not a mistake. This means that when a party sues "John Doe" defendants, it will not be able to relate an amendment back to add the proper defendant after the statute of limitations has run. That is considered to be a lack of knowledge, not a mistake under the rule.

IN PRACTICE

As previously noted, state rules of civil procedure are often nearly the same as their federal counterparts. But not always. In general, it appears that the text, numbering, and organization of the civil rules in about half the states is almost completely identical to the Federal Rules. In most of the other states, the concepts and basic ground rules are very similar, but the nomenclature and numbering of the state rules differs from the federal model. In a small number of states, there can be significant divergence between state practice and its federal counterpart.

E. Rule 15(d): Supplemental Pleadings

Rule 15(d) allows parties to add claims to their original pleading for facts that have arisen after the date the original complaint was filed. This is the important distinction between amended and supplemental pleadings. Amended pleadings allow the party to add claims or parties based on facts that occurred before the original pleading was filed. Supplemental pleadings allow the party to add claims based on facts that occurred after the original complaint was filed. Courts have discretion to allow a party to supplement its pleading, and the inquiry is very similar to that in Rule 15(a)(2).

THE RULE   Rule 15(d)

Supplemental Pleadings

(d) Supplemental Pleadings. On motion and reasonable notice, **the court may, on just terms**, permit a party to serve a supplemental pleading setting out any transaction, occurrence, or event that happened after the date of the pleading to be supplemented . . . .

EXAMPLES & ANALYSIS

EXAMPLE: Ellen Piza has filed a suit alleging that she suffered gender discrimination while working for her employer, Dawn Co. Piza's complaint alleged that her supervisor berated her with sexist slurs, that the company knew about it, and that the company did not do anything to stop this behavior. She filed her complaint a year ago, but she has continued to work at Dawn Co. during the litigation. Since filing her complaint, however, she has been demoted from her position and has been transferred to a less-prestigious division of Dawn Co. She would like to add a claim of retaliation to her claims against Dawn Co. Can she do so?

Analysis: Yes, she probably can. As long as the court is assured that Dawn Co. will have an opportunity to prepare its defense to these new claims, it will allow the supplemental pleading to be filed. The new claims are absolutely related to the claims in the original pleading, and there is no evidence that Piza delayed bringing these additional claims. They simply arose after her original complaint was filed.

ADDITIONAL EXERCISES

1. Panera files a complaint against Dark Airways, a national airline, in a diversity action on December 13, 2010. He amends the complaint once under Rule 15(a)(1) to change the name. In the complaint, Panera alleges that he injured his ankle while returning to his seat during extreme turbulence on a flight from San Juan, Puerto Rico, to Philadelphia, Pennsylvania. Dark Airways operated the flight. Panera attributes his injury to Dark Airways' negligence in failing to warn passengers of the impending turbulence. Panera's claim against Dark Airways is based on a state theory of negligence. However, after his lawyer does further research, he realizes that Panera cannot bring a state negligence claim against a national airline because that claim is preempted by federal law. He must instead bring a claim under the Federal Aviation Administration's Air Traffic and General Operating Rules. ***Can Panera amend his complaint to make this change?***

2. Phillip Pry was convicted for failing to pay a parking ticket issued 5 years ago and was sent to Dew City State Prison to serve his time. Pry files a complaint alleging numerous violations of his constitutional rights by prison staff. Specifically, he alleges violations of his First Amendment right of access to the courts, freedom of speech and exercise of religion; the Eighth Amendment right to be free from cruel and unusual punishment; and the Fourteenth Amendment right to procedural due process. Pry seeks declaratory and injunctive relief as well as awards of compensatory and punitive damages against the Dew City State Prison System. The court has already granted Pry leave to amend his complaint twice in the face of motions to dismiss by Dew City. Pry would like to amend his complaint a third time with information that he believes will help his case survive. Dew City has filed a 12(b)(6) motion to dismiss the case stating that Pry's proposed amended complaint still fails to state a claim. ***Should the court allow Dry to file a third amended complaint?***

3. On April 9, 2013, Field Agent Ray Pillette filed a claim seeking to recover damages from his employer Dalton Industries. Pillette alleges Dalton discriminated against him under the Americans with Disabilities Act (ADA) after he was confined to a wheelchair from injuries stemming from a space shuttle crash. Pillette was fired from his job on May 3,

2011. Prior to being fired, his supervisor at Dalton removed him from fieldwork and did not give him a reason as to why. Pillette believes it is because of his disability. Dalton argues that Ray's claim under the ADA fails because he was not "qualified" under the ADA and additionally was not fired because of a disability. On May 23, 2013, Pillette learned he could have received accommodations under the Family and Medical Leave Act (FMLA). Dalton did not believe Pillette qualified for FMLA so it did not inform him of the accommodations. The statute of limitations for ADA and FMLA claims is two years. Pillette filed his ADA claim in time, but his FMLA claim is beyond the two-year statute of limitations. ***Can Pillette still amend his complaint to add the FMLA claim?***

4. Polly, a city transit employee who was a member of the Local 180 Transit Union believed the union discriminated against him in the last round of salary negotiations. On June 8, 2009, Polly filed an Equal Employment Opportunity Commission (EEOC) charge against his Local 180 Transit Union. Before Local 180 could retain counsel, the EEOC dismissed the charge and gave Jimmy the opportunity to re-file in 90 days. On September 18, 2009, Jimmy filed a suit and this time he named the Global Transit Union (GBU) as the defendant. GBU is the national organization for the Local 180 Transit Union. Polly served GBU at their headquarters in Washington D.C. A week later, Polly sent a letter to the Local 180 explaining that he was filing charges against Local 180 as well. Local 180 retained Mark Doffa to represent them. On November 29, 2009, GBU also retained Mark Doffa. Doffa, in answering the complaint, asserted that GBU and Local 180 were two distinct entities. On February 4, 2010, Polly sought to amend his complaint against GBU, by replacing GBU with Local 180 as the defendant. Polly stated he had named the wrong defendant and was seeking to name the correct defendant under rule 15(c). Doffa contends that Polly chose to sue GBU instead of the Local 180 and is seeking to have the complaint dismissed. Doffa asserts that under Rule 15(c), Jimmy's amendment does not relate back to his original claim. ***Can Jimmy amend his complaint to replace GBU with Local 180?***

5. Parker filed a tort claim for negligence and product liability against his employer, a package facility, International Delivery Packages (IDP), based in Kentucky. Parker's right arm was amputated after it became

caught between two rollers while he was trying to clear an obstruction off of a conveyor belt. Parker's complaint names IDP, D-Convey, the conveyor belt manufacturer, and Delta Co., the manufacturer of the rollers on the conveyor belt machinery as defendants. The statute of limitations for filing a negligence or product liability claim is two years. Parker filed his complaint right before the statute of limitations ran out. During discovery, Parker discovered another manufacturer of the rollers, Dodin. Even though the statute of limitations on the negligence and product liability claims against Dodin have run, Parker hopes to amend his complaint to add Dodin and ask that the claims relate back. **Will the court allow Parker to do this?**

6. Paloma, a protester, filed a claim against Agent Morgan, a Secret Service Officer and another Agent, who he could not identify ("Jane Doe"). The claim alleges a violation of Paloma's right to freedom of expression under the First Amendment. Paloma filed his claim right before the statute of limitations ran and served Agent Morgan with the complaint. He has requested that the Secret Service provide him with the name of Agent "Jane Doe" so that he can also serve her with the complaint. The Secret Service is moving to dismiss the claim against "Jane Doe" because the statute of limitations has run. **Can Paloma still request that the Secret Service provide him with the name for Agent Jane Doe?**

7. In July 1972, Jerry Peck attended his company's annual summer picnic at Lake Erie Water Village. He had a good time at the party: eating, drinking, and swimming a few laps in the main pool. He helped run the family relay races and the pie eating contest. Late in the afternoon, he went over to the water slide to help supervise the children there. Timmy, one of his coworker's children, was a little scared to go down the slide, so Peck offered to go down a few times to show him how fun it was. Unfortunately, he did not see the small sign beside the slide, partially obscured by a shrubbery, stating "Children only, please." He slid down a waterslide head first into four feet of water and was injured terribly. His injuries were so serious that they caused him to become a paraplegic.

Peck was no longer able to work. His entire home had to be redesigned to accommodate his disability. He lost complete movement in his legs and could only move his arms downwards, using the force of gravity. His wife had to be trained to care for him. She even had to quit her own job so that she could help Peck attend to his needs throughout the day.

Peck's prognosis is not good; it does not seem likely that he will ever regain full use of his limbs again.

Peck brought suit against Dippyslide, the company that allegedly designed and manufactured the slide. The manufacturer's label on the slide said "Dippyslide" in the typeface commonly used by the company at that time. However, Dippyslide has changed its label several times in the past few years after a series of consumer surveys. In addition, Thompson, the owner of Lake Erie Water Village, stated that he had had to re-attach the label when the slide was delivered and that the slide had been delivered in plain packaging. He suggested that Peck confirm who actually manufactured the slide.

In its answer, Dippyslide admitted that it had manufactured the slide. Three separate insurance companies determined that the slide had been produced by Dippyslide: Peck's employer's insurance company, Lake Erie Water Village's insurer, and Dippyslide's insurer. Without inspecting the slide himself, Meyer, the president and owner of Dippyslide, also admitted that the slide was manufactured by his company.

Dippyslide was a pioneer of the waterslide business; at the time of the accident, it made nearly ninety percent of all waterslides sold in the United States. However, it had been experiencing problems with competitors producing slides that were almost indistinguishable from its own and selling them under the Dippyslide name. It began to design slides that had a slightly unusual width, so that it could more readily identify which slides were genuine Dippyslide products. Not infrequently, a consumer would return a slide under warranty to Dippyslide that turned out to have been made by a competitor. Dippyslide would then have to track down the actual manufacturer and bill it for the repairs and the shipping. Meyer identified the slide in question without seeing it, despite the company's difficulty in ascertaining the true manufacturer of the slides in its daily business.

Two and a half years after originally filing suit, in January of 1975, Peck requested that Meyer look at the slide before Meyer gave his deposition in anticipation of trial. Meyer was asked to inspect the slide firsthand to see if it had been properly installed. Meyer agreed and drove over to Lake Erie Water Village from his Lake Erie home. After this inspection, he declared that the slide had not, if fact, been made by his company. He claimed that the slide had been made by Dorner Slides. Dorner

Slides had gotten into the slide-making business a few years after Dippyslide did. It hired a mold maker away from Dippyslide so as to better compete in the water slide business. Thus, its slide looked remarkably similar to the Dippyslide original.

After it realized that it had not manufactured the slide that injured Peck, Dippyslide moved for leave to amend its answer to deny manufacture of the slide. Assume that you are the judge presiding over this case. **Should the court allow Dippyslide to amend its answer?**

8. Panda bought a ticket to go on a cruise from Florida to Jamaica. Panda initially heard about the cruise line through a series of television advertisements, which boasted "Delago Cruises: Your Ticket to Paradise." When Panda received her travel documents, she noticed that they prominently identified Delago Cruises as the company responsible for the tickets and gave a Florida address for the company. Later, she would learn that the Florida Department of State listed Delago Cruises as the only "Delago" company registered to do business in Florida.

   Panda finally arrived in Florida on February 1, 2010, and picked up her ticket moments before she boarded the boat. The front of the ticket advertised that "Delago Cruises" was the first cruise company in the world to obtain a certification of quality. However, the back of the ticket explained that it was the sole contract between Panda and a "Carrier." The ticket identified the Carrier as "DelagoCrociereS.p.A." The ticket went on to explain that it was DelagoCrociere who owned, chartered, and operated the ship. Panda, having already made her first visit to the all-you-can-eat buffet upon boarding the boat, did not bother to read the back of the ticket. She instead set about to signing up for the all-ship shuffleboard tournament.

   On February 5, 2010, Panda won the shuffleboard tournament. She was so excited that she began skipping along the deck of the boat, boasting of her shuffleboard skills. However, due to her exuberance, she did not notice that there was a large cable on the deck. Unfortunately for Panda, her celebrations were stopped when she fell over the cable and fractured her femur. While the cruise doctor was treating her injuries, Panda tried to explain that she did not have money to pay for a doctor, nor did she have medical insurance. The doctor told her to contact the cruise claims administrator to get reimbursed for any medical expenses she would incur.

After arriving home from her eventful cruise, Panda hired a lawyer and decided to file suit for negligence against Delago Cruises. The lawyer started by contacting Delago Cruises to inquire whether it would settle before Panda filed suit. While negotiating a potential settlement with Delago Cruises, the Delago Cruises claims administrator clarified that Delago Cruises was a subsidiary of DelagoCrociere. The same claims administrator pointed out the back of Panda's ticket—the part that said that DelagoCrociere owned and operated Delago Cruises—and told Panda and her lawyer that she should contact DelagoCrociere (and not Delago Cruises). Settlement negotiations broke down, and the complaint was filed on February 1, 2011, just in time to meet the 1-year statute of limitations period for a negligence action in Florida.

On February 25, Delago Cruises filed an answer to Panda's complaint, asserting that it was not the proper defendant because it was just an agent for DelagoCrociere. Delago Cruises was represented by Rob Stone. Over the next few months, Panda and her attorney met with Mr. Stone several times. Each time Stone stressed that Delago Cruises was the wrong company to sue, and that DelagoCrociere was the parent company and proper defendant. After some investigation, Panda's lawyer determined that Stone was correct, and that Panda needed to amend her complaint to add DelagoCrociere as a defendant. In addition, her lawyer's investigation turned up a 2007 case in which a similarly situated plaintiff had tried unsuccessfully to sue Delago Cruises instead of DelagoCrociere.

On June 9, 2011, Panda's attorney moved to amend her complaint to add DelagoCrociere as a defendant. The trial court granted her motion to add DelagoCrociere as a defendant and dismissed Delago Cruises from the suit.

After being properly served, DelagoCrociere, represented by Rob Stone (the same attorney that represented Delago Cruises), moved to dismiss because the statute of limitations had run and therefore DelagoCrociere could not be properly joined. After firing the attorney who originally suggested she could sue Delago Cruises, Panda has now hired you as her lawyer. ***Can you defeat DelagoCrociere's motion to dismiss by arguing that DelagoCrociere can be added to her complaint under Rule 15?***

Quick Summary

- Rule 15 is an excellent example of how the federal rules provide parties with the necessary flexibility to pursue their claims.

- When a party acts within a specified time frame, it is free to amend its pleading once as a matter of course under Rule 15(a)(1).

- Even if it misses this deadline or even if it has already filed an amendment as a matter of course, it can still generally amend under Rule 15(a)(2). Either the opposing party or the court, in its discretion, can allow the amendment under this provision. Assuming the amendment is not futile, and assuming the party is not engaging in gamesmanship, the amendment will generally be allowed.

- Under Rule15(b), when an issue comes up in trial and the opposing party objects to allowing an amendment to the pleading, the court will allow the amendment if the opposing party would not suffer prejudice. Or, if the issue is litigated in trial and neither party has objected to it, the parties and the court will treat the issue as if it had been properly pled since the beginning.

- There is a narrowing of the right to amend, however, when the statute of limitations has run. In that case, the rule attempts to balance the need for flexibility under the federal rules with the policy of fairness and repose that underlies statutes of limitations.

- Finally, when facts arise after a complaint has been filed, a party may seek to supplement her pleading. The court has discretion as to whether that supplemental filing should be allowed.

III

Unit Overview:
Development of the Case

The four chapters in Unit III all address the steps that are taken between the commencement of the case and the actual trial of it. The most important part of this process may be the planning and management of the case, a topic addressed in Chapter 11. The most time-consuming part, however, at least for most cases, is discovery, and discovery is analyzed in Chapters 12, 13, and 14 dealing with the scope of discovery, the broad methods used to obtain information from the other side or from nonparties, and in Chapter 14, the process for enforcing discovery rights. The power to conduct discovery can be intrusive and very important to the success of the case. Discovery is not always willingly given up, despite the importance of it under the rules; and it is frequently necessary to bring a motion to compel a party, or nonparty, to comply with discovery requests.

Disclosure and discovery are important in most civil actions. They are important to all the parties and they consume a substantial part of the resources devoted to many cases. Disclosure—also called "automatic disclosure"—is the required disclosure of information without request. It has been a part of the federal rules for over a decade and is intended to make the exchange of information between the parties occur sooner and at lower cost.

Chapter 12 explores the scope of discovery—the definition of the limits on discovery and method for imposing those limits. These limits apply to all forms of discovery. Chapter 13 explores the specific tools for requesting information. These include interrogatories (written requests that must be signed under oath by the party to whom they are directed), requests for production of documents (including electronically stored information), tangible things, and for entry upon real property. The rules also provide for obtaining medical examination of a party, if that party has placed his or her medical condition at issue. Chapter 13 also covers the use of depositions—sworn testimony of a witness in traditional question-and-answer format.

11

Case Management

Key Concepts

- Courts manage cases, and don't just decide issues
- Different cases are managed in different ways
- Rule 16 pretrial conferences and pretrial orders are key parts of litigation process
- Pretrial orders set deadlines and limits on discovery, motion practice, and other pre-trial actions
- Pretrial orders may fully supplant pleadings
- The goal is often to reach a settlement

Introduction

Case management is an integral part of the litigation process. Clients manage their cases, lawyers manage their cases, and judges are likely to be managing them as well.

A. Background and Policy

It would be easy to view the litigation process as being governed by a group of rules that are routinely applied in assembly-line ways to process cases toward their conclusion, the court only responding to motions from the parties or requests for a trial. Very little "management" of cases would take place. This may fairly describe the "old days" of litigation, before the adoption of the rules of civil procedure in 1938. Since then, however, the role of the courts has changed and the changes have had a transformative impact on civil cases.

A seminal article describing, and not really applauding, the transformation of judges to case managers was Judith Resnik's, *Managerial Judges*, 96 HARV. L. REV. 374 (1982). Prof. Resnik really coined the term "managerial judge" and was critical of this development. Others had reacted more favorably to this change. *See, e.g.*, Hon. Robert F. Peckham, *The Federal Judge as a Case*

Manager: The New Role in Guiding a Case From Filing to Disposition, 69 Calif. L. Rev. 770 (1981); Hon. William W Schwarzer, *Managing Civil Litigation: The Trial Judge's Role*, 61 Judicature 400 (1978). What cannot be disputed at this point is that judges in many courts have embraced at least some aspects of the managerial role, and as a result spend a substantial portion of their time and energy managing cases. One goal of "case management" is encouraging the cases to settle rather than be tried.

Despite this trend of judges becoming "case managers," there remain many judicial approaches to litigation. The rules provide a common construct for handling all cases, but some judges are much more aggressive than others in setting deadlines, convening pretrial conferences, encouraging settlement, and otherwise managing their dockets. There are outstanding judges in virtually every camp on these questions. In addition, individual judges approach individual cases on their dockets differently—one case may strike the judge as simple and straightforward and not needing a lot of discovery or management; a different case may strike the same judge as complex and fact-intensive, and therefore warranting another approach.

One lingering problem with the managerial judge is the pressure that management actions may create on the lawyers representing parties in the cases. For example, insisting on a trial may require the lawyer to resist pressure from the judge, a tactic that risk because it may annoy the judge who will then hear the case. But the lawyer who succumbs too easily may give away what could have been obtained at trial. The key to making the right decision is a realistic appraisal of the case.

In many cases, particularly more complex cases, the court will enter a comprehensive case management order or "CMO." In most instances the court will ask the parties to meet and confer about what terms should be included in a CMO. Those conferences and the resulting order may be as important to the course of the litigation as any motions that would once have been used to accomplish the same constraints on the case.

A sample Case Management Order is set forth on this coursebook's website. In addition, David F. Herr, Annotated Manual for Complex Litigation Fourth (West 2015), collects numerous actual case management orders from a wide variety of types of complex cases in its Appendix A; these are orders entered in actual cases, and many of them are the result of agreement by the parties rather than imposition by the court.

B. Rule 16 and Pretrial Conferences and Orders

The most important rule change contributing to the case-management revolution was the adoption of Rule 16. This rule was innovative, with no real precursors in the earlier rules. Its impact was not immediately felt, and its drafters probably never contemplated the changes it would bring.

Rule 16(a) establishes the authority of the court to convene pretrial conferences and establishes goals for managing the litigation. This approach differs from sitting back and waiting for the parties to bring motions or ask for a trial. Under Rule 16, judges affirmatively expedite cases, establishing control over the proceedings, and facilitate settlement, among other things.

THE RULE   Rule 16(a)

Pretrial Conferences; Scheduling; Management

(a) **Purposes of a Pretrial Conference.** In any action, the court may order the attorneys and any unrepresented parties to appear for one or more pretrial conferences for such purposes as:

(1) expediting disposition of the action;

(2) establishing early and continuing control so that the case will not be protracted because of lack of management;

(3) discouraging wasteful pretrial activities;

(4) improving the quality of the trial through more thorough preparation; and

(5) facilitating settlement.

EXPLANATION

The rule does not require that the conference address each of the topics listed in the rule,, but it defines the types of issues that should be considered.

Courts hold pretrial conferences in various ways. Some prefer informal conferences in chambers, off the record—essentially engaging counsel in a discussion about the case and its needs with a fair amount of give-and-take. Other judges favor more formal proceedings, in the courtroom, and on the record, with lawyers speaking in turn. Most judges do not insist on either approach for all conferences, favoring an informal conference for some cases and more formal ones for others. Complex cases with multiple parties may require use of the courtroom, but may still be more or less formal in nature depending on the case.

The important corollary of the pretrial conference is the court's power to enter pretrial orders. This power is set forth in Rule 16(c), and is an important fount of judicial authority. Pretrial orders under this rule establish ground rules for the litigation that are fully as important—arguably more important—than any of the provisions of the rules of procedure. In practice, pretrial orders set case-specific deadlines and establish procedures. It is now well-established that the court has the authority to require particular lawyers —typically lead counsel—to attend, and also to require the parties (or designated representatives of corporate parties) to attend. Failure to heed such an order, in extreme situations, can result in dismissal of a case or a similarly serious sanction against a defendant. *See Link v. Wabash R.R. Co.*, 370 U.S. 626, 82 S. Ct. 1386, 8 L.Ed.2d 734 (1962).

THE RULE   Rule 16(c) & (d)

(c) Attendance and Matters for Consideration at a Pretrial Conference

    (1) Attendance. A represented party must authorize at least one of its attorneys to make stipulations and admissions about all matters that can reasonably be anticipated for discussion at a pretrial conference. If appropriate, the court may require that a party or its representative be present or reasonably available by other means to consider possible settlement.

    (2) Matters for Consideration. At any pretrial conference, the court may consider and take appropriate action on the following matters:

        (A) formulating and simplifying the issues, and eliminating frivolous claims or defenses;

(B) amending the pleadings if necessary or desirable;

(C) obtaining admissions and stipulations about facts and documents to avoid unnecessary proof, and ruling in advance on the admissibility of evidence;

(D) avoiding unnecessary proof and cumulative evidence, and limiting the use of testimony under Federal Rule of Evidence 702;

(E) determining the appropriateness and timing of summary adjudication under Rule 56;

(F) controlling and scheduling discovery, including orders affecting disclosures and discovery under Rule 26 and Rules 29 through 37;

(G) identifying witnesses and documents, scheduling the filing and exchange of any pretrial briefs, and setting dates for further conferences and for trial;

(H) referring matters to a magistrate judge or a master;

(I) settling the case and using special procedures to assist in resolving the dispute when authorized by statute or local rule;

(J) determining the form and content of the pretrial order;

(K) disposing of pending motions;

(L) adopting special procedures for managing potentially difficult or protracted actions that may involve complex issues, multiple parties, difficult legal questions, or unusual proof problems;

(M) ordering a separate trial under Rule 42(b) of a claim, counterclaim, crossclaim, third-party claim, or particular issue;

(N) ordering the presentation of evidence early in the trial on a manageable issue that might, on the evidence, be the basis for a judgment as a matter of law under Rule 50(a) or a judgment on partial findings under Rule 52(c);

(O) establishing a reasonable limit on the time allowed to present evidence; and

(P) facilitating in other ways the just, speedy, and inexpensive disposition of the action.

(d) Pretrial Orders

(6) After any conference under this rule, the court should issue an order reciting the action taken. This order controls the course of the action unless the court modifies it.

EXPLANATION

 Pretrial orders are important in one way that isn't obvious from the rule. Courts frequently define the issues to be litigated or tried—consistent with Rule 16(c)(2)(A)—in a way that the pretrial order ultimately replaces the pleadings as the definitive statement of the claims being tried. It is thus important that the parties ensure that any claims or defenses they are interested in asserting be included in such an order. A party must typically show "good cause" before a court will amend its pretrial order.

In addition to the topics enumerated in Rule 16(c), there are many more subjects that may be considered at pretrial conferences. Examples of these include:

- The necessity or desirability of a further conference of the parties prior to the final pretrial conference;

- The method of jury selection and number of peremptory challenges by individual parties in multi-party cases;

- Proposed voir dire questions or consideration of jury questionnaires or other means of collecting information on venire members;

> **Venire members** are prospective jurors summoned potentially to serve for a case. The term comes from the old venire writ or writ *venire facias,* which directed the Sheriff to summon prospective jurors. Jurors (jury members) are chosen from the venire or jury panel to sit on a case.

- Requested preliminary instructions to the jury;

- Specification of theories of claims or defenses;

- Specification of special damages;

- Identification of any statutes, regulations, or ordinances applicable to the claims or defenses relied upon;

- Specific acts of negligence claimed by any party;

- Identification of all expert witnesses and exchange of reports;

- Limitation on the number of expert witnesses;

- Disclosure of interested parties or insurers;

- Disclosure and review of any demonstrative evidence for the trial (*e.g.,* charts, models, video);

- Consideration of other evidentiary issues, such as use of summaries; and

- Requested jury instructions.

C. Settlement

The most dramatic change in the focus of civil litigation over time has been the focus on settlement as the ultimate goal. The goal was once adjudication of the issues and the entry of a judgment in the case. What was once an incidental result in some cases has become, at least for many judges, the main objective. Settlement has many attributes that make it a tantalizing goal. In particular, settlement may:

1. Empower the parties—allowing them to decide their own destiny, rather than abdicating that power to strangers;

2. Offer a wider range of remedies—in many cases, money damages gained or lost is the only adjudicative remedy realistically available. By settlement, the parties may be able to effect a mutually valuable remedy the court could never order;

> One particularly important opportunity that settlement presents relates to "business solutions" to disputes. These may reflect modification of existing contractual relations, agreements to buy or sell additional products or services on favorable terms, or otherwise compromise the dispute in a "win/win" manner. Sometimes the parties may be able to reach an agreed result that would provide preferential tax treatment of the settlement in a way no court order could provide.

3. Conserve judicial resources, as well as the resources of the parties; and

4. Render appellate review moot.

Not all commentators view this transformation of the process as welcome or helpful for the parties. One early and thoughtful article expressing this view is Owen Fiss, *Against Settlement*, 93 YALE L.J. 1073 (1984). Professor Fiss questions whether settlements are always in the parties' interest, and makes a number of arguments concerning the public interest in having disputes resolved within the litigation process, including the creation of precedent at the end of the case that is the foundation of the common law.

EXAMPLES & ANALYSIS

EXAMPLE: Pat Ponder is injured in a freak accident involving a nose-hair clipper manufactured and sold by Diversified Dental Supplies, Inc. In a suit brought in federal court for damages in excess of $100,000, the court orders a pretrial conference to discuss, among other things, settlement. At the time of the conference the judge has under advisement several motions of the parties—Ponder's motion to amend the complaint to add a count seeking punitive damages, and Diversified's motion for summary judgment based on Ponder's deposition testimony in which she admitted she didn't have any proof that the clippers she used, and subsequently lost, were manufactured by Diversified.

After discussing the issues with both sides, the judge inquires about the last settlement demand and offer of each party. Upon learning that Ponder had agreed to accept $15,000 in settlement of all claims, and that Diversified had offered to pay nothing, relying on a corporate policy not to pay anything to settle cases unless a liability had been established, the court ordered Diversified to make a meaningful compromise settlement offer.

Acting as counsel for Diversified, how do you address the judge's apparent intent to overrule your client's policy on settlement? What if the judge orders that the hearing be adjourned to the next day so Diversified's President can be in court to explain the company's "recalcitrance," as the judge puts it? How would you respond to the judge's statement that the court will rule on the pending motion to amend later in the day if the case has not settled?

Analysis: It certainly is unusual for a judge to require the President of a party to attend a settlement proceeding in a modest product liability case. It is also rare that a judge would overtly threaten to issue a ruling because of settlement conduct. (Is the judge threatening to deny the motion to amend, do you think?)

Ultimately this example presents difficult challenges to the litigant. As a general rule, judges are free to require parties and counsel to attend settlement conferences. They probably cannot properly order the parties to make an offer of settlement. At least some appellate courts would view that as crossing a line. Similarly, courts could probably require a party representative with full settlement authority to attend a settlement conference of a major case that unquestionably would be directly within the President's responsibility—say, a high-stakes antitrust or patent case that would fit in the "bet the company" category. But for a minor nose-hair case?

The probable course of action for orders requiring the party to do something is to comply with the order and to object to it. As to the judge's threat to decide the motion that day, there is much less to do—there is nothing wrong with the court deciding pending motions. Most likely, there is nothing really to put on the record, except that the court announced an intention to rule on the motion.

Note that Ponder is not immune to similar pressures. What if the judge announced an intention to rule on both motions, and it was prompted, or apparently prompted, by Ponder's refusal to accept anything less than the $100,000 sought in the complaint?

In reality, judges would likely be much less manipulative than this, but might still point out to both parties (or each party in a confidential settlement meeting without the other side present) that the other side's motion has apparent merit, and the court was thinking about granting it. Would this be an effective, and acceptable, means of helping the parties understand the risks inherent in the litigation?

Advocacy opportunities abound in the case management process. CMOs may be a very effective way to obtain relief that would be hard to obtain by motion, or at trial. CMOs are so important to the future progress and direction a case will take that it is imperative that the lawyers treat them as the important things they are. Only a foolish lawyer would delegate the preparation of the CMO to a lawyer unfamiliar with the case or the needs of the particular litigation. Once in place, a CMO can establish important deadlines and other requirements than can only be changed upon a showing of good cause. It may be difficult to obtain modification of the order; it is prudent to seek an order in the first instance with which the party can comply.

EXAMPLE: In Pat Ponder's action in the foregoing example, the judge's agenda for the pretrial conference was more limited. The court sought to define the issues in the dispute and establish a schedule for the case, including setting deadlines for completing fact discovery, disclosing final expert reports, and exchanging requested jury instructions, verdict forms, and trial briefs. The judge directed the parties to meet and confer before the conference to attempt reach agreement on these issues. The parties agreed to a joint statement of the claims and defenses in the case, and that they would all be tried to a jury. Each party identified the theories it would advance at trial and the witnesses and exhibits it would produce to advance the case. The parties did not agree on a discovery cut-off, with Pat Ponder requesting a trial in six months, with fact discovery to be completed in three months. Diversified insisted that it needed nine months to complete fact discovery and to complete expert depositions. Each side agreed to call a single expert on damages. The court accepted the parties' stiputlations as to the claims, defenses, and theories to be tried, ordered four months to complete discovery, and set a trial date seven months later. The order included language that the order would bind the parties unless modified for good cause shown.

Shortly after the conclusion of the discovery period, Diversified decided it needed to assert a defense of waiver it had identified in its Answer, but had thought would not apply at the time of the submission of stipulated issues and defenses. At the final pretrial conference Diversified advised the court of its intent to offer evidence on waiver at trial. At that conference, Ponder objected to consideration of the waiver defense and additionally sought to offer expert evidence from a different damages expert because the expert he had intitially designated was not going to be available for trial because she would be on leave from her consulting firm.

How does the court handle these requests from the parties?

Analysis: Courts would probably vary in their response to these requests. As to the waiver defense, that fact that it had originally been asserted in Diversified's Answer would probably have little impact on the analysis, because the pretrial order defining the issues, defenses, and theories would essentially supplant the pleadings. The court could allow the amendment of that order to include the waiver defense, but it is not clear that good cause is demonstrated for that amendment. Mere regret that it had been abandoned would not likely be viewed as good cause. Ponder's request to designate a new expert presents a different issue. Good cause would still be required, but there are two factors that militate toward a finding of good cause. The court would likely take a dim view of a request to add a second expert, to testify on additional issues. Here, however, the expert appears to be just a substitute for the expert originally designated. Diversified would be hard-pressed to argue that significant prejudice would occur to it if it had to face a new witness testifying to the same opinions as the originally designated expert. (If expert depositions had already occurred, then Diversified would be able to argue prejudice because it hadn't examined the witness it would face at trial. It would likely at least be allowed an opportunity to depose the new witness, probably at Ponder's cost.) Additionally, the first expert's unavailability does not appear to be caused by Ponder. The court might want to know the reason for the expert's leave of absence—certainly medical reasons would be likely to be viewed as good cause, and other reasons might as well.

Issues that may be addressed in pretrial orders and at pretrial conferences include the following:

- **Service issues.** The court can provide for service of the summons if that has not occurred, or can extend the 120-day limit for service contained in Rule 4(m) as to an unserved defendant, without requiring a formal motion.

- **Jurisdictional issues.** Courts generally desire to resolve any questions relating to jurisdiction promptly. These issues can be teed up for appropriate resolution in a CMO. For example, in a case where a plaintiff faces a claim of lack of personal jurisdiction and believes that discovery is necessary to frame that issue for decision, the court can order the appropriate discovery and establish a schedule for completing it and hearing the dismissal motion.

- **Timing.** Virtually every CMO will establish at least some of the deadlines the parties will face as the case progresses. These almost invariably include a discovery cutoff for the case, and may establish the process and deadlines for exchanging expert information. The lawyers should be prepared to argue for the deadlines they think the case warrants. This may be a very important, especially if a party believes that the case requires extra time or presents unusual urgency requiring short deadlines. Other deadlines include cutoffs for any amendment of the pleadings or the addition of new parties, bringing summary judgment motions; and submission of a trial brief and proposed jury instructions and verdict form if the case will be tried to a jury, and proposed findings if a court trial.

- **E-discovery.** E-discovery plays an important role in virtually every case these days. Both sides should be motivated to agree on appropriate e-discovery protocols and document retention requirements for the litigants, as agreement may save the parties massive amounts of money and may assure access to the information needed for the case. Additionally, many courts require the parties to discuss a variety of e-discovery topics prior to the first pretrial conference.

- **Discovery limits.** The court frequently discusses a variety of discovery topics at the initial pretrial conference. For example, discovery topics might include:

  — Whether five depositions per side would be more appropriate for this case than the ten allowed under Rule 30(a)(2);

  — Whether it would be helpful to have an order establishing where witnesses will be produced;

  — Whether the parties anticipate a dispute over who would be allowed to attend depositions?

Issues like these can easily be covered by a short discussion at a pretrial conference and provided for in the pretrial order. Virtually any anticipated discovery dispute might be preemptively addressed in this way at a pretrial conference. Most judges would be happy to address these topics in the more informal context of a pretrial conference and the parties are often well-served by this expedited and less-expensive process.

- **Dispositive motions.** It is often worthwhile to address the summary judgment motion schedule for the case. A party might obtain an order postponing the bringing of these motions until certain discovery is completed. Mapping this process out in a CMO is easy and much more efficient than filing a motion for summary judgment, responding with a request (supported by an affidavit) to postpone consideration until certain discovery is completed, arguing that request, awaiting a ruling, then briefing and arguing the summary judgment motion. Thoughtful consideration of timing in the CMO may avoid arguments that a motion is either premature or untimely.

The rules don't really catalog what can possibly be addressed at a pretrial conference. The point is that the pretrial conference can be treated as an obligation the court imposes on the parties, or as an opportunity for the advocate to help make the system work to advance the client's interests. Good lawyers choose the latter approach.

D. ADR and Its Role in Settlement

Settlement is a topic of many pretrial conferences and may be addressed in pretrial orders. If the case is not going to be settled by the parties immediately, the court or parties may want to explore alternative dispute resolution (ADR) methods. In addition to the discussion in this chapter, the Overview Chapter at the end of the book addresses dispute resolution generally. Even if ADR is not an immediate topic of discussion, the judge will at least want to establish a plan for when and how settlement or ADR will be considered. The judge's options for conducting the settlement process are many, but the following would be typical options:

- The judge would inquire whether the parties have attempted to settle their disputes; regardless of the answer to that question, the judge would likely encourage the parties to get together to see if they can settle;

- The judge can offer to assist in settlement by convening a settlement conference, with the judge presiding;

- In federal courts, the judge can offer the services of a magistrate judge or special master to assist in settlement. (Most state court judges do not have magistrates available to assist in this way, but they may be able to call on another judge for this task.) Special masters may be appointed by federal or state courts to serve this role, (and a wide variety of other roles);

- Some courts have standing ADR mechanisms that are conducted by court rule and are available in every case. For many of these court-annexed processes, the parties will be required to use the court's process before the case can proceed to trial;

- If the parties express the view that the case is not ready for serious settlement discussions, the judge can probe to determine whether the parties' view that settlement discussions would be premature is in fact a reasonable position;

- If settlement is not ripe for discussion, the judge may want to explore when the parties think settlement would be worth discussing. Judges recognize that some discovery may be required before settlement discussions are likely to be worthwhile. Even where the parties make this point, the judge may want to encourage that only the discovery needed for this purpose take place before settlement efforts are undertaken. In this situation, the court will want to ensure the parties have a plan in place when that point is reached:

a. How will settlement discussions be initiated?

b. What neutral will be used? (This could be a mediator, arbitrator, special master, or some other individual.)

c. Who will be in attendance? The judge may feel the need to exert the court's authority to require participation in the settlement process.

> There is pretty wide agreement that a judge can properly require the parties and attorneys to participate in reasonable settlement conferences. The court cannot, however, require the parties to settle the case or to make any particular settlement offers or demands.

There are myriad settlement mechanisms available. Parties often find that mediation using a mediator experienced in the particular type of case or with whom the parties have experience with is a more promising alternative to the court-annexed system.

Quick Summary

- The rules suggest that cases proceed in the same way and possibly on the same timetable. In reality the courts actively manage their caseloads and many cases proceed on completely different schedules.

- Available management tools are myriad, but nearly always involve setting deadlines and may include imposing limits on discovery, motion practice, and other pre-trial actions.

- Courts use Case Management Orders (CMOs) to establish guidelines that take precedence over the rules, and often define the issues being litigated in a way that takes precedence over the parties' pleadings.

- The overarching goal of this process is not necessarily a decision on the merits—it may be reaching a settlement that satisfies all parties.

- Courts resort to a wide variety of tools to encourage the parties to settle disputes that can reasonably be settled.

12

The Scope of Discovery

Key Concepts

- The discovery process, where a party learns about the other party's facts and evidence

- The 3 primary objectives of discovery:

  · To understand the other party's case;

  · To cabin the other party's evidence; and

  · To obtain concessions and admissions

- The general parameters for the discovery process

Introduction

"Discovery" refers to the stage of litigation where each party has the opportunity to obtain information and documents from other parties. Although discovery is a relatively modern process—historically, parties did not have the right to conduct discovery—it has become the most time-intensive and expensive stage of the litigation process.

Discovery includes a number of processes for this exchange of information. Rule 26 provides for some automatic disclosures of some of the basic categories of information—witness names, document categories, expert reports, etc.—without waiting for a request from another party. Rule 33 authorizes the use of interrogatories—written questions that another party must answer. Rule 34 authorizes requests to inspect (or copy) documents and other things. Rules 30 and 32 provide for depositions—oral interrogation of witnesses under oath. Rule 35 allows a party to request that a doctor conduct a mental or physical examination of another party. Rule 36 provides for requests for admissions. Finally, Rule 37 contains procedures for the court to police compliance with the discovery rules.

Chapter 13 will explore the individual discovery mechanisms. This chapter covers Rule 26, the omnibus discovery rule. In addition to the automatic disclosures mentioned above, Rule 26 defines the scope of discovery—what a party can and cannot obtain from other parties. It also contains limits on what must be produced, based on considerations like the attorney-client privilege. It contains some special provisions related to electronic discovery, and sets forth procedures for initial discovery planning.

A. The Rule

Rule 26 has seven sections:

- The first section, 26(a), requires parties to make specified disclosures at three junctures: at the outset of a case; at the expert phase of the case; and shortly before the trial—these are covered in the next chapter;

- The second section, 26(b), describes the scope of discovery and the limitations on what is discoverable;

- The third section, 26(c), allows a party to seek a protective order when the party believes the other party is being unreasonable;

- The fourth section, 26(d), addresses the timing and sequence of discovery;

- The fifth section, 26(e), requires parties to supplement discovery responses;

- The sixth section, 26(f), establishes procedures for a discovery planning conference among the parties; and

- The seventh section, 26(g), holds the signer of discovery requests, responses, and objections responsible for any abuse or misuse of the discovery process.

Rather than consider these sections in the order that they appear in the Rule, we will start with a discussion of what is and is not discoverable.

B. Discovery Scope

1. Rule 26(b): Discovery Scope and Limits

Rule 26(b) creates a broad definition of what is discoverable, then carves out some categories of information and documents that are not discoverable.

THE RULE   Rule 26(b)(1)

Scope in General

(1) Unless otherwise limited by court order, the scope of discovery is as follows: Parties may obtain discovery regarding any **non-privileged** matter that is **relevant to any party's claim or defense** and **proportional** to the needs of the case, considering the importance of the issues at stake in the action, the amount in controversy, the parties' relative access to relevant information, the parties' resources, the importance of the discovery in resolving the issues, and whether the burden or expense of the proposed discovery outweighs its likely benefit. **Information within this scope of discovery need not be admissible in evidence to be discoverable.**[1]

EXPLANATION

The scope of discovery is intended to be very broad or liberal, and the reporters are full of cases that expressly discuss how broad discovery is in federal court. Thus, Rule 26(b) allows discovery of any matter that is "**relevant** to any party's claims or defenses."

> The FRCP do not define **"relevant,"** but evidence is deemed relevant under the rules of evidence if it has **any tendency** to make a fact more or less probable.

---

1 Note: the language printed here is the language proposed in the amendments that were, at the time of this printing, scheduled to go into effect on December 1, 2015, unless vetoed or modified by Congress. One of the effects of these amendments is to move the concept of proportionality from a limitation on the frequency and extent of discovery in Rule 26(b)(2) to a part of the core definition of the scope of discovery in Rule 26(b)(1). The amendment also adds a list of factors the court may consider in making the proportionality analysis.

The definition was actually narrowed somewhat in 2000—it used to allow discovery of any matter that was relevant to "the subject matter" of the litigation. In response to criticism that discovery was too broad (and too expensive), Rule 26(b)(1) was amended to limit discovery to matters relevant to "claims or defenses" in the case. Thus, a party cannot file a complaint asserting one claim, then conduct discovery designed to support a related second claim. Many states continue to use the "relevant to the subject matter" standard for determining the scope of relevancy.

EXAMPLES & ANALYSIS

EXAMPLE: Pablo buys a car from Dan's Discount Cars based in part on Dan's warranty that the car would run properly for three months and in part on Dan's representation that the car had only been driven by a little old lady on Sundays. One month later the car dies, Dan refuses to fix it, and Pablo files a breach of warranty action in federal court. Pablo believes that the car was not driven only on Sundays by a little old lady, but has no evidence to support such an accusation yet. May Pablo serve discovery asking for Dan's proof that the car was only driven by a little old lady on Sundays?

Analysis: The issue is whether the discovery relates to a claim in the case. The case currently does not have a claim or defense related to the representation about the little old lady, so discovery about that representation is outside the scope of discovery—Pablo cannot conduct discovery to develop a new claim. Pablo might argue that the alleged representation is related to the warranty claim. This would ultimately be a matter of the court's discretion, but would probably be deemed outside the scope of discovery.

The last sentence of Rule 26(b)(1) is also important. It provides that the information sought in discovery does not need to be **admissible to be discoverable**.

EXAMPLE: In discovery in Pablo's suit against Dan's Discount Cars, Dan asks Pablo whether any mechanics have offered opinions as to the cause of the problems with Pablo's car. At trial, the rule against hearsay—essentially, out-of-court statements—might prevent Pablo from testifying about a mechanic's statements. Pablo objects to the request on the basis that it calls for hearsay. Is this a proper objection?

Analysis: Although the rule against hearsay might prevent Dan from asking Pablo to describe the mechanic's words at trial, Dan could call the mechanic to the stand to testify. This live first-hand testimony would not be hearsay, and would therefore be admissible. Accordingly, the discovery is proper because it is relevant to a claim or defense in the case, regardless of whether it would be admissible.

Note the use of the word "nonprivileged" in the standard for discoverable information. Rule 26(b)(1) excludes privileged matter from the scope of discoverable material, and Rule 26(b)(5) provides the procedures for handling privileged matters.

C. Limits on Discovery

After defining the scope of discovery, Rule 26(b) proceeds to impose a number of limits on discovery.

Rule 26(b)(2)(A) provides that the court may alter the limits that the subsequent rules set for the number of interrogatories and depositions or the length of depositions, and may limit the number of requests for admission, which are not limited by Rule 36 (the rule addressing requests for admission). Some courts have adjusted these limits by local rule.

Rule 26(b)(2)(B) allows a party not to produce "**electronically stored information**" if it would be unreasonably burdensome or expensive to produce it. It also establishes a process for asking the court to require the party to produce information withheld on this basis.

> **Electronically Stored Information**, or ESI, is the term of art for all electronic data under the Rules. All litigators should be familiar with this term.

It is now settled law that ESI is discoverable just like paper documents. The Rules are deliberately vague about what is included, in recognition that the forms of storing data will change more rapidly than the Supreme Court can amend the rules. So Twitter feeds are covered even though the Rules do not mention Twitter (in fact, Twitter was in its infancy when the ESI rules were written, so the concept is working). As are word processing documents, spreadsheets, databases, electronic calendar entries, etc. A party must produce such ESI found in the party's file and email servers and backup systems, on any shared or internet based storage systems (*e.g.*, the "cloud"), on employees' desktops, laptops, smart phones, and home computers, and anywhere else ESI is stored.

IN PRACTICE

Electronic discovery frequently dominates the discovery process, both in terms of time and cost. Most "smoking gun" documents are found in ESI these days—in part because most communications, internal and external, are now electronic and in part because people are less thoughtful about what they say in emails, text messages, and other forms of electronic communication. Many large firms have ESI specialists, and there is an industry of consultants who support litigators and companies in managing ESI.

Rule 26(b)(2)(C) provides that the court "must" limit discovery if the discovery is unreasonably cumulative or duplicative or is outside the scope of discovery permitted by Rule 26(b)(1).

1. Trial Preparation Materials

Rule 26(b)(3) protects "documents and tangible things that are prepared in anticipation of litigation or for trial" by a party or its representative (including its attorney).

> What the Rules call "**Trial Preparation Materials**" is the rough equivalent of what is often called "Attorney Work Product."

The protection for trial preparation materials has its origin in a 1947 decision from the United States Supreme Court, *Hickman v. Taylor*. Because this case created the work product doctrine, now embodied in Rule 26(b)(3), an excerpt is reprinted below.

FROM THE COURT

Hickman v. Taylor

329 U.S. 495 (1947)

Supreme Court of the United States

This case presents an important problem under the Federal Rules of Civil Procedure, 28 U.S.C.A. following section 723c, as to the extent to which a party may inquire into oral and written statements of witnesses, or other information, secured by an adverse party's counsel in the course of preparation for possible litigation after a claim has arisen.

Examination into a person's files and records, including those resulting from the professional activities of an attorney, must be judged with care. It is not without reason that various safeguards have been established to preclude unwarranted excursions into the privacy of a man's work. At the same time, public policy supports reasonable and necessary inquiries. Properly to balance these competing interests is a delicate and difficult task.

On February 7, 1943, the tug 'J. M. Taylor' sank while engaged in helping to tow a car float of the Baltimore & Ohio Railroad across the Delaware River at Philadelphia. The accident was apparently unusual in nature, the cause of it still being unknown. Five of the nine crew members were drowned. Three days later the tug owners and the underwriters employed a law firm, of which respondent Fortenbaugh is a member, to defend them against potential suits by representatives of the deceased crew members and to sue the railroad for damages to the tug.

A public hearing was held on March 4, 1943, before the United States Steamboat Inspectors, at which the four survivors were examined. This testimony was recorded and made available to all interested parties. Shortly thereafter, Fortenbaugh privately interviewed the survivors and took statements from them with an eye toward the anticipated litigation; the survivors signed these statements on March 29. Fortenbaugh also interviewed other persons believed to have some information relating to the accident and in some cases he made memoranda of what they told him. At the time when Fortenbaugh secured the statements of the survivors, representatives of two of the deceased crew members had been in communication with him. Ultimately claims were presented by representatives of all five of the deceased; four of the claims, however, were settled without litigation. The fifth claimant, petitioner herein, brought suit in a federal court under the Jones Act on November 26, 1943, naming as defendants the two tug owners, individually and as partners, and the railroad.

One year later, petitioner filed 39 interrogatories directed to the tug owners. The 38th interrogatory read:

> State whether any statements of the members of the crews of the Tugs 'J. M. Taylor' and 'Philadelphia' or of any other vessel were taken in connection with the towing of the car float and the sinking of the Tug 'John M. Taylor'. Attach hereto exact copies of all such statements if in writing, and if oral, set forth in detail the exact provisions of any such oral statements or reports.

Supplemental interrogatories asked whether any oral or written statements, records, reports or other memoranda had been made concerning any matter relative to the towing operation, the sinking of the tug, the salvaging and repair of the tug, and the death of the deceased. If the answer was in the affirmative, the tug owners were then requested to set forth the nature of all such records, reports, statements or other memoranda.

The tug owners, through Fortenbaugh, answered all of the interrogatories except No. 38 and the supplemental ones just described. While admitting that statements of the survivors had been taken, they declined to summarize or set forth the contents. They did so on the ground that such requests called 'for privileged matter obtained in preparation for litigation' and constituted 'an attempt to obtain indirectly counsel's private files.' It was claimed that answering these requests 'would involve practically turning over not only the complete files, but also the telephone records and, almost, the thoughts of counsel.'

In connection with the hearing on these objections, Fortenbaugh made a written statement and gave an informal oral deposition explaining the circumstances under which he had taken the statements. But he was not expressly asked in the deposition to produce the statements. The District Court for the Eastern District of Pennsylvania, sitting en banc, held that the requested matters were not privileged. 4 F.R.D. 479. The court then decreed that the tug owners and Fortenbaugh, as counsel and

agent for the tug owners forthwith 'Answer Plaintiff's 38th interrogatory and supplemental interrogatories; produce all written statements of
witnesses obtained by Mr. Fortenbaugh, as counsel and agent for Defendants; state in substance any fact concerning this case which Defendants
learned through oral statements made by witnesses to Mr. Fortenbaugh
whether or not included in his private memoranda and produce Mr.
Fortenbaugh's memoranda containing statements of fact by witnesses
or to submit these memoranda to the Court for determination of those
portions which should be revealed to Plaintiff.' Upon their refusal, the
court adjudged them in contempt and ordered them imprisoned until
they complied.

The Third Circuit Court of Appeals, also sitting en banc, reversed the
judgment of the District Court. 153 F.2d 212. It held that the information here sought was part of the 'work product of the lawyer' and hence
privileged from discovery under the Federal Rules of Civil Procedure.
The importance of the problem, which has engendered a great divergence of views among district courts, led us to grant certiorari.

The pre-trial deposition-discovery mechanism established by Rules 26
to 37 is one of the most significant innovations of the Federal Rules of
Civil Procedure. Under the prior federal practice, the pre-trial functions
of notice-giving issue-formulation and fact-revelation were performed
primarily and inadequately by the pleadings. Inquiry into the issues and
the facts before trial was narrowly confined and was often cumbersome
in method. The new rules, however, restrict the pleadings to the task of
general notice-giving and invest the deposition-discovery process with a
vital role in the preparation for trial. The various instruments of discovery now serve (1) as a device, along with the pre-trial hearing under Rule
16, to narrow and clarify the basic issues between the parties, and (2)
as a device for ascertaining the facts, or information as to the existence
or whereabouts of facts, relative to those issues. Thus civil trials in the
federal courts no longer need be carried on in the dark. The way is now
clear, consistent with recognized privileges, for the parties to obtain the
fullest possible knowledge of the issues and facts before trial.

In urging that he has a right to inquire into the materials secured and
prepared by Fortenbaugh, petitioner emphasizes that the deposition-
discovery portions of the Federal Rules of Civil Procedure are designed
to enable the parties to discover the true facts and to compel their disclosure wherever they may be found. It is said that inquiry may be made

under these rules, epitomized by Rule 26, as to any relevant matter which is not privileged; and since the discovery provisions are to be applied as broadly and liberally as possible, the privilege limitation must be restricted to its narrowest bounds. On the premise that the attorney-client privilege is the one involved in this case, petitioner argues that it must be strictly confined to confidential communications made by a client to his attorney. And since the materials here in issue were secured by Fortenbaugh from third persons rather than from his clients, the tug owners, the conclusion is reached that these materials are proper subjects for discovery under Rule 26.

As additional support for this result, petitioner claims that to prohibit discovery under these circumstances would give a corporate defendant a tremendous advantage in a suit by an individual plaintiff. Thus in a suit by an injured employee against a rail-road or in a suit by an insured person against an insurance company the corporate defendant could pull a dark veil of secrecy over all the pertinent facts it can collect after the claim arises merely on the assertion that such facts were gathered by its large staff of attorneys and claim agents. At the same time, the individual plaintiff, who often has direct knowledge of the matter in issue and has no counsel until some time after his claim arises could be compelled to disclose all the intimate details of his case. By endowing with immunity from disclosure all that a lawyer discovers in the course of his duties, it is said, the rights of individual litigants in such cases are drained of vitality and the lawsuit becomes more of a battle of deception than a search for truth.

But framing the problem in terms of assisting individual plaintiffs in their suits against corporate defendants is unsatisfactory. Discovery concededly may work to the disadvantage as well as to the advantage of individual plaintiffs. Discovery, in other words, is not a one-way proposition. It is available in all types of cases at the behest of any party, individual or corporate, plaintiff or defendant. The problem thus far transcends the situation confronting this petitioner. And we must view that problem in light of the limitless situations where the particular kind of discovery sought by petitioner might be used.

We agree, of course, that the deposition-discovery rules are to be accorded a broad and liberal treatment. No longer can the time-honored cry of 'fishing expedition' serve to preclude a party from inquiring into the facts underlying his opponent's case. Mutual knowledge of all the relevant facts gathered by both parties is essential to proper litigation. To that end, either party may compel the other to disgorge whatever facts he has in his possession. The deposition-discovery procedure simply advances the stage at which the disclosure can be compelled from the time of trial to the period preceding it, thus reducing the possibility of surprise. But discovery, like all matters of procedure, has ultimate and necessary boundaries. As indicated by Rules 30(b) and (d) and 31(d), limitations inevitably arise when it can be shown that the examination is being conducted in bad faith or in such a manner as to annoy, embarrass or oppress the person subject to the inquiry. And as Rule 26(b) provides, further limitations come into existence when the inquiry touches upon the irrelevant or encroaches upon the recognized domains of privilege.

We also agree that the memoranda, statements and mental impressions in issue in this case fall outside the scope of the attorney-client privilege and hence are not protected from discovery on that basis. It is unnecessary here to delineate the content and scope of that privilege as recognized in the federal courts. For present purposes, it suffices to note that the protective cloak of this privilege does not extend to information which an attorney secures from a witness while acting for his client in anticipation of litigation. Nor does this privilege concern the memoranda, briefs, communications and other writings prepared by counsel for his own use in prosecuting his client's case; and it is equally unrelated to writings which reflect an attorney's mental impressions, conclusions, opinions or legal theories.

But the impropriety of invoking that privilege does not provide an answer to the problem before us. Petitioner has made more than an ordinary request for relevant, non-privileged facts in the possession of his adversaries or their counsel. He has sought discovery as of right of oral and written statements of witnesses whose identity is well known and whose availability to petitioner appears unimpaired. He has sought production of these matters after making the most searching inquiries of his opponents as to the circumstances surrounding the fatal accident, which inquiries were sworn to have been answered to the best of their information and belief. Interrogatories were directed toward all the events prior to, during and subsequent to the sinking of the tug. Full and honest answers to such broad inquiries would necessarily have included all pertinent information gleaned by Fortenbaugh through his interviews with the witnesses. Petitioner makes no suggestion, and we cannot assume, that the tug owners or Fortenbaugh were incomplete or dishonest in the framing of their answers. In addition, petitioner was free to examine the public testimony of the witnesses taken before the United States Steamboat Inspectors. We are thus dealing with an attempt to secure the production of written statements and mental impressions contained in the files and the mind of the attorney Fortenbaugh without any showing of necessity or any indication or claim that denial of such production would unduly prejudice the preparation of petitioner's case or cause him any hardship or injustice. For aught that appears, the essence of what petitioner seeks either has been revealed to him already through the interrogatories or is readily available to him direct from the witnesses for the asking.

The District Court, after hearing objections to petitioner's request, commanded Fortenbaugh to produce all written statements of witnesses and to state in substance any facts learned through oral statements of witnesses to him. Fortenbaugh was to submit any memoranda he had made of the oral statements so that the court might determine what portions should be revealed to petitioner. All of this was ordered without any showing by petitioner, or any requirement that he make a proper showing, of the necessity for the production of any of this material or any demonstration that denial of production would cause hardship or injustice. The court simply ordered production on the theory that the facts sought were material and were not privileged as constituting attorney-client communications.

In our opinion, neither Rule 26 nor any other rule dealing with discovery contemplates production under such circumstances. That is not because the subject matter is privileged or irrelevant, as those concepts are used in these rules. Here is simply an attempt, without purported necessity or justification, to secure written statements, private memoranda and personal recollections prepared or formed by an adverse party's counsel in the course of his legal duties. As such, it falls outside the arena of discovery and contravenes the public policy underlying the orderly prosecution and defense of legal claims. Not even the most liberal of discovery theories can justify unwarranted inquiries into the files and the mental impressions of an attorney.

Historically, a lawyer is an officer of the court and is bound to work for the advancement of justice while faithfully protecting the rightful interests of his clients. In performing his various duties, however, it is essential that a lawyer work with a certain degree of privacy, free from unnecessary intrusion by opposing parties and their counsel. Proper preparation of a client's case demands that he assemble information, sift what he considers to be the relevant from the irrelevant facts, prepare his legal theories and plan his strategy without undue and needless interference. That is the historical and the necessary way in which lawyers act within the framework of our system of jurisprudence to promote justice and to protect their clients' interests. This work is reflected, of course, in interviews, statements, memoranda, correspondence, briefs, mental impressions, personal beliefs, and countless other tangible and intangible ways—aptly though roughly termed by the Circuit Court of Appeals in this case (153 F.2d 212, 223) as the 'Work product of the lawyer.' Were such materials open to opposing counsel on mere demand, much of what is now put down in writing would remain un-written. An attorney's thoughts, heretofore inviolate, would not be his own. Inefficiency, unfairness and sharp practices would inevitably develop in the giving of legal advice and in the preparation of cases for trial. The effect on the legal profession would be demoralizing. And the interests of the clients and the cause of justice would be poorly served.

We do not mean to say that all written materials obtained or prepared by an adversary's counsel with an eye toward litigation are necessarily free from discovery in all cases. Where relevant and non-privileged facts remain hidden in an attorney's file and where production of those facts is essential to the preparation of one's case, discovery may properly be had. Such written statements and documents might, under certain circumstances, be admissible in evidence or give clues as to the existence or location of relevant facts. Or they might be useful for purposes of impeachment or corroboration. And production might be justified where the witnesses are no longer available or can be reached only with difficulty. Were production of written statements and documents to be precluded under such circumstances, the liberal ideals of the deposition-discovery portions of the Federal Rules of Civil Procedure would be stripped of much of their meaning. But the general policy against invading the privacy of an attorney's course of preparation is so well recognized and so essential to an orderly working of our system of legal procedure that a burden rests on the one who would invade that privacy to establish adequate reasons to justify production through a subpoena or court order. That burden, we believe, is necessarily implicit in the rules as now constituted.

Rule 30(b), as presently written, gives the trial judge the requisite discretion to make a judgment as to whether discovery should be allowed as to written statements secured from witnesses. But in the instant case there was no room for that discretion to operate in favor of the petitioner. No attempt was made to establish any reason why Fortenbaugh should be forced to produce the written statements. There was only a naked, general demand for these materials as of right and a finding by the District Court that no recognizable privilege was involved. That was insufficient to justify discovery under these circumstances and the court should have sustained the refusal of the tug owners and Fortenbaugh to produce.

But as to oral statements made by witnesses to Fortenbaugh, whether presently in the form of his mental impressions or memoranda, we do not believe that any showing of necessity can be made under the circumstances of this case so as to justify production. Under ordinary conditions, forcing an attorney to repeat or write out all that witnesses have told him and to deliver the account to his adversary gives rise to grave dangers of inaccuracy and untrustworthiness. No legitimate purpose is served by such production. The practice forces the attorney to testify as to what he remembers or what he saw fit to write down regarding witnesses' remarks. Such testimony could not qualify as evidence; and to use it for impeachment or corroborative purposes would make the attorney much less an officer of the court and much more an ordinary witness. The standards of the profession would thereby suffer.

Denial of production of this nature does not mean that any material, non-privileged facts can be hidden from the petitioner in this case. He need not be unduly hindered in the preparation of his case, in the discovery of facts or in his anticipation of his opponents' position. Searching interrogatories directed to Fortenbaugh and the tug owners, production of written documents and statements upon a proper showing and direct interviews with the witnesses themselves all serve to reveal the facts in Fortenbaugh's possession to the fullest possible extent consistent with public policy. Petitioner's counsel frankly admits that he wants the oral statements only to help prepare himself to examine witnesses and to make sure that he has overlooked nothing. That is insufficient under the circumstances to permit him an exception to the policy underlying the privacy of Fortenbaugh's professional activities. If there should be a rare situation justifying production of these matters, petitioner's case is not of that type.

We fully appreciate the wide-spread controversy among the members of the legal profession over the problem raised by this case. It is a problem that rests on what has been one of the most hazy frontiers of the discovery process. But until some rule or statute definitely prescribes otherwise, we are not justified in permitting discovery in a situation of this nature as a matter of unqualified right. When Rule 26 and the other discovery rules were adopted, this Court and the members of the bar in general certainly did not believe or contemplate that all the files and mental processes of lawyers were thereby opened to the free scrutiny of their adversaries. And we refuse to interpret the rules at this time so as to reach so harsh and unwarranted a result.

We therefore affirm the judgment of the Circuit Court of Appeals.

Mr. Justice JACKSON, concurring.

* * *

The primary effect of the practice advocated here would be on the legal profession itself. But it too often is overlooked that the lawyer and the law office are indispensable parts of our administration of justice. Law-abiding people can go nowhere else to learn the ever changing and constantly multiplying rules by which they must behave and to obtain redress for their wrongs. The welfare and tone of the legal profession is therefore of prime consequence to society, which would feel the consequences of such a practice as petitioner urges secondarily but certainly.

* * *

It seems clear and long has been recognized that discovery should provide a party access to anything that is evidence in his case. It seems equally clear that discovery should not nullify the privilege of confidential communication between attorney and client. But those principles give us no real assistance here because what is being sought is neither evidence nor is it a privileged communication between attorney and client.

To consider first the most extreme aspect of the requirement in litigation here, we find it calls upon counsel, if he has had any conversations with any of the crews of the vessels in question or of any other, to 'set forth in detail the exact provision of any such oral statements or reports.' Thus the demand is not for the production of a transcript in existence but calls for the creation of a written statement not in being. But the statement by counsel of what a witness told him is not evidence when written plaintiff could not introduce it to prove his case. What, then, is the purpose sought to be served by demanding this of adverse counsel?

Counsel for the petitioner candidly said on argument that he wanted this information to help prepare himself to examine witnesses, to make sure he overlooked nothing. He bases his claim to it in his brief on the view that the Rules were to do away with the old situation where a law suit developed into 'a battle of wits between counsel.' But a common law trial is and always should be an adversary proceeding. Discovery was hardly intended to enable a learned profession to perform its functions either without wits or on wits borrowed from the adversary.

The real purpose and the probable effect of the practice ordered by the district court would be to put trials on a level even lower than a 'battle of wits.' I can conceive of no practice more demoralizing to the Bar than to require a lawyer to write out and deliver to his adversary an account of what witnesses have told him. Even if his recollection were perfect, the statement would be his language permeated with his inferences. Every one who has tried it knows that it is almost impossible so fairly to record the expressions and emphasis of a witness that when he testifies in the environment of the court and under the influence of the leading question there will not be departures in some respects. Whenever the testimony of the witness would differ from the 'exact' statement the lawyer had delivered, the lawyer's statement would be whipped out to impeach the witness. Counsel producing his adversary's 'inexact' statement could lose nothing by saying, 'Here is a contradiction, gentlemen of the jury. I do not know whether it is my adversary or his witness who is not telling the truth, but one is not.' Of course, if this practice were adopted, that scene would be repeated over and over again. The lawyer who delivers such statements often would find himself branded a deceiver afraid to take the stand to support his own version of the witness's conversation with him, or else he will have to go on the stand to defend his own credibility—perhaps against that of his chief witness, or possibly even his client.

Every lawyer dislikes to take the witness stand and will do so only for grave reasons. This is partly because it is not his role; he is almost invariably a poor witness. But he steps out of professional character to do it. He regrets it; the profession discourages it. But the practice advocated here is one which would force him to be a witness, not as to what he has seen or done but as to other witnesses' stories, and not because he wants to do so but in self-defense.

And what is the lawyer to do who has interviewed one whom he believes to be a biased, lying or hostile witness to get his unfavorable statements and know what to meet? He must record and deliver such statements even though he would not vouch for the credibility of the witness by calling him. Perhaps the other side would not want to call him either, but the attorney is open to the charge of suppressing evidence at the trial if he fails to call such a hostile witness even though he never regarded him as reliable or truthful.

* * *

I agree to the affirmance of the judgment of the Circuit Court of Appeals which reversed the district court.

CASE ANALYSIS & QUESTIONS

1. What was the plaintiff seeking in discovery?

2. Was it protected by the attorney-client privilege? Why or why not?

3. Was there any other way for the plaintiffs to get the information?

4. What did Fortenbaugh do at the trial court level to protect his documents?

5. Why did the Court feel that the plaintiffs were not entitled to the documents in question?

6. What was the legal source of authority for the protection that the Court announced?

7. Does the protection established in *Hickman* prevent the plaintiffs from learning the facts of the dispute?

8. What content was the Court protecting?

9. Did the Court create any exceptions?

10. Is the protection set forth in *Hickman* any different from the one codified in Rule 26(b)(3)?

After *Hickman* was decided, the federal Rules were modified in 1970 to add Rule 26(b)(3), which essentially codified the work product protection. Rule 26(b)(3) uses the term "trial preparation materials" and is similar, but not identical, to the protection established in *Hickman*.

THE RULE   Rule 26(b)(3)

Trial Preparation: Materials

(A) Documents and Tangible Things. Ordinarily, a party may not discover **documents and tangible things that are prepared in anticipation of litigation** or for trial by or for another **party or its representative** (including the other party's attorney, consultant, surety, indemnitor, insurer, or agent). But, subject to Rule 26(b)(4), those materials may be discovered if:

   (i) they are otherwise discoverable under Rule 26(b)(1); and

   (ii) the party shows that it has **substantial need** for the materials to prepare its case and cannot, without undue hardship, obtain their substantial equivalent by other means.

(B) Protection Against Disclosure. If the court orders discovery of those materials, it must protect against disclosure of mental impressions, conclusions, opinions, or legal theories of a party's attorney or other representative concerning the litigation.

a. Contours of the Rule 26(b)(3) Trial Preparation Materials Protection

As in *Hickman*, the concept behind the protection is that opposing parties are not entitled to the litigation strategy of the party or its attorneys. There are some important aspects of the trial preparation materials protection worth noting. First, the protection is limited to "documents and tangible things"—this doctrine does not apply to oral communications (but if oral communications involve an attorney, they may be protected under the attorney-client privilege). Also note that the protection applies only to the documents themselves, not to the underlying facts. So if the defendant saw that the light was red, the defendant cannot shield that fact from discovery by putting it in a document prepared in anticipation of litigation.

b. In Anticipation of Litigation

Another critical requirement is that the documents have been prepared "in anticipation of litigation." Courts generally require that the primary purpose of the preparation of the document was litigation, and that it was not prepared in the ordinary course of business. The litigation need not have been actually filed, so long as it was reasonably anticipated—so a threatening letter can support the protection. Documents that are prepared in the ordinary course of business or for some reason other than in anticipation of litigation are not protected, even if they are material to the litigation and are provided to the attorney—a party cannot shield a document from discovery by providing it to counsel.

c. Obtaining Trial Preparation Materials

The protection that Rule 26(b)(3) creates is not absolute. A party may obtain another party's trial preparation materials by showing that the materials are otherwise discoverable and that the party has "substantial need" for the materials, and cannot obtain their substantial equivalent without undue hardship. If a party is required to produce trial preparations materials, the party will be

> **"Redact"** means to remove, edit out, or excise, so that the balance of the document can be produced without revealing the protected or privileged matter.

permitted to **redact** the mental impressions, conclusions, opinions, or legal theories of the attorney or representative concerning the litigation.

d. Statements

There is an exception to the trial preparation material protection for statements made by a party. Any party or other person may obtain a copy of the person's own prior statement about the action or its subject matter. A statement is a signed or adopted written statement or any recording of the person's oral statement.

EXAMPLES & ANALYSIS

EXAMPLE: Prime Pinball Machines sues Delaney Distributor for losses caused by a fire at Delaney's warehouse. Prior to the filing of the lawsuit, Delaney had asked its attorney to investigate the cause of the fire and prepare a report, using consultants the attorney would hire. Prime seeks the report in discovery, and Delaney objects that it is trial preparation material. Is Delaney correct?

Analysis: The question is whether litigation was reasonably anticipated at the time of the investigation, since litigation was not yet filed. Given the hiring of an attorney, the answer is likely yes.

EXAMPLE: Suppose that the attorney gave an oral presentation to upper management at Delaney about the investigation and the potential outcome of any ensuing litigation. Is that presentation protected as trial preparation materials?

Analysis: No. Trial preparation materials must be documents or other tangible things, not oral statements. But, the presentation would likely be an attorney-client privileged communication.

EXAMPLE: The lawyer also interviewed two eyewitness employees of Delaney, and typed up statements which they signed. Can Prime obtain copies of the statements?

Analysis: The exception regarding statements only applies to a statement of the person seeking a copy of the statement. Therefore, this exception does not allow Prime to obtain a copy of the statements. If the witnesses are still available and still remember their observations, this information is available to Prime—Prime can interview the witnesses itself or depose them—and thus the statements are protected trial preparation materials. If the witnesses are no longer available and there are no additional witnesses with the same information, then Prime can likely obtain copies of the statements.

EXAMPLE: Suppose that the attorney took photographs of the warehouse during the investigation and incorporated them into the report. After the investigation Delaney hired a company to clean up and repair the warehouse so Delaney could resume operations. Are the photographs protected trial preparation materials or can Prime obtain them?

Analysis: Since they are "other tangible things" that were prepared in anticipation of litigation, they are trial preparation materials. However, because the condition of the warehouse after the fire is no longer observable or photographable because the warehouse was cleaned and restored, Prime has no other source of equivalent information, and can likely obtain copies of the photos. If so, any notes by the attorney could be redacted.

EXAMPLE: Now suppose in the above Example that the investigation was not conducted by an attorney, but rather by an engineer employed by Delaney. Is the report still trial preparation material?

Analysis: Yes. Trial preparation material is protected if created by any representative of a party, not just attorneys. Delaney would still need to demonstrate that it reasonably anticipated litigation at the time of the investigation, which might be more difficult since counsel was not involved. Remember, the attorney-client privilege and the trial preparation materials protection are not co-extensive; some trial preparation materials are not protected by the attorney-client privilege, and some privileged materials are not trial preparation material.

2. Trial Preparation: Experts

Most information regarding the party's testifying experts is exchanged pursuant to the automatic disclosures in Rule 26(a), as discussed in the next chapter. Rule 26(b)(4) imposes the following limitations regarding discovery of experts:

a. Depositions

A party may only depose an expert engaged by another party if the other party has identified the expert as someone who may testify at trial.

b. Drafts

Drafts of an expert's reports are not discoverable.

c. Communications Between a Party and its Experts

Such communications are protected from discovery unless they: relate to the expert's compensation; identify facts or data that the attorney provided to the expert and that the expert considered in forming the opinions; or identify assumptions that the attorney provided to the expert and that the expert relied on in forming the opinions.

d. Consulting Experts

Ordinarily, a party does not need to provide information in discovery regarding an expert who is retained or specially employed in anticipation of litigation if the expert is not expected to testify at trial. There is an exception to this limit for "exceptional circumstances." An example would be where the consulting expert was the only one to examine the scene of an incident and the scene was not adequately preserved, so that opposing counsel has no other source of the information observed at the scene.

IN PRACTICE

Trial attorneys often initially hire experts as consulting experts to shield them from discovery. Then, if the expert's opinions are helpful and circumstances otherwise so warrant, the attorney will convert the expert to a testifying expert, notifying opposing counsel and disclosing the required information at that time. This conversion typically occurs at the time when expert disclosures are due.

EXAMPLE: Attorney Albert is representing Toxic Chemicals R Us in a tort claim brought by a plaintiff claiming his illness was caused by exposure to the company's chemicals. Albert hires Edmund, a toxicologist, to review the scientific literature and give Albert his unbiased, non-advocacy opinions about whether the company's chemicals could have caused the illness. During the course of this relationship, Edmund sends Albert articles and they discuss the articles on telephone calls. Opposing counsel Amy serves interrogatories asking for the identity of all of Toxic Chemicals' experts, document requests seeking communications with such experts, and a request to schedule the depositions of such experts. Is Amy entitled to this discovery?

Analysis: No. Edmund is a consulting expert. Under Rule 26(b)(4)(D), no discovery is allowed for consulting experts unless it is impracticable to obtain that information from any other source. No such circumstances are present for Edmund.

EXAMPLE: In the above Example, Edmund concludes that the science does not support causation, and Albert decides to use Edmund as a testifying expert. What discovery is permitted regarding Edmund at that point?

Analysis: Once Edmund is converted to a testifying expert, Edmund will have to produce an expert report (discussed in the next chapter), Amy can take his deposition, and Amy can obtain any communications relating to Edmund's compensation, facts that Albert provided to Edmund and that he considered in forming his opinions, and assumptions that Albert provided to Edmund that Edmund relied upon. Albert does not need to produce any other types of communications or any drafts of Edmund's report.

EXAMPLE: Edna is a traffic accident reconstruction expert. She is hired as a consulting expert by the plaintiff's attorney shortly after an accident, and examines the scene. The plaintiffs file suit 11 months later. By the time the defense counsel hires an expert, the skid marks and broken glass are no longer present at the scene. The defendant now wants to depose Edna. Is this allowed?

Analysis: This is the type of situation where the exception for consulting experts applies. Edna has information about the scene that is not available from any other source. The plaintiff may have to make Edna available for deposition, although if Edna has photographs of the scene the court might deem those sufficient. If Edna is deposed, she will not be required to testify about the plaintiff's legal strategy.

3. Protecting Privileged or Trial Preparation Materials

Rule 26(b)(5) describes the procedure for withholding information based on a privilege or the trial preparation doctrine. It requires that the party expressly assert the privilege and describe the nature of the documents or information withheld on the basis of the privilege in sufficient detail that other parties can assess the assertion of the privilege. Privileged communications are typically listed in a "privilege log"—a chart that lists the document, the nature of the privilege asserted, all of the participants in the communication, and enough of a description of the document to support the privilege without actually disclosing the communication.

"Privileged communications" refers to communications subject to a formal evidentiary privilege, and ordinarily does not extend to confidential, embarrassing, or proprietary information like trade secrets. Some privileges are codified by federal or state law, and others are based on **common law**. Under Federal Rule of Evidence 501, privileges may be determined by state law even if a case as a whole is governed by federal law.

> **"Common law"** refers to legal principles that are developed by the courts through case law, in contrast to laws developed by the legislature in statutes.

a. The Attorney-Client Privilege

The attorney-client privilege is the most commonly asserted privilege. It protects communications but does not shield the facts underlying the communication from discovery. The following are the typical elements of the attorney-client privilege:

- A communication;

- Between an attorney and client;

- Designed to facilitate legal representation;

- Made in confidence; and

- Not waived.

The leading attorney-client privilege case in the federal courts is *Upjohn v. United States*, 449 U.S. 383 (1981), in which the Supreme Court deemed privileged a company's use of questionnaires and interviews conducted in response to a government inquiry.

b. Other Privileges

In addition to the attorney-client privilege, other commonly recognized privileges include the:

- Fifth Amendment Privilege against self-incrimination;

- National Security Privilege (which allows the government to resist disclosures that might endanger foreign policy objectives and especially citizens or soldiers);

- Priest-Penitent Privilege (which applies to confessions made to religious authority figures);

- Marital Testimonial Privilege (which prevents disclosure of communications between spouses);

- Critical Self-Examination Privilege (where entities are assessing what went wrong following an incident or conducting a critical examination of potential problems in their processes); and

- Deliberative Process Privilege (which protects the internal deliberative process of governments and governmental agencies).

c. Inadvertent Production

Although parties generally strive to identify and withhold privileged documents, sometimes they produce privileged documents despite these efforts. As a general rule, disclosure of a privileged communication to persons who do not have a legitimate need to be privy to the communication results in waiver of the privilege. Thus, disclosure to an adverse party would constitute waiver. However, if a privileged document is inadvertently produced in discovery despite good faith efforts to screen for privileged documents, the producing party may be able to recall or "claw back" the privileged document and preserve the privilege. See the discussion of document production under Rule 34 for a more detailed discussion of this process.

EXAMPLES & ANALYSIS

EXAMPLE: Carl hires Andrew as his attorney in connection with a lawsuit alleging that Carl shot his neighbor's dog, which barked all night. They meet and Carl describes the situation for Andrew and gives Andrew his gun. Carl asks Andrew to prepare a short memorandum summarizing the law. The opposing counsel serves discovery asking for the facts relating to the shooting, the discussion between Carl and Andrew, and the memo. Andrew objects that the facts were discussed between counsel and the facts and the discussion are privileged. Is Andrew correct?

Analysis: Andrew is two-thirds right. The discussion between Andrew and Carl is privileged, and Andrew's memorandum to Carl is also privileged. However, the facts themselves are not privileged, and describing the facts to counsel does not render the facts privileged. Thus, Andrew and Carl would have to respond to discovery inquiring about the facts.

EXAMPLE: In the above Example, opposing counsel requests an opportunity to examine the gun. Andrew objects on the grounds that Carl provided the gun to him during an attorney-client privileged meeting. Is Andrew correct?

Analysis: No. A party cannot shield relevant evidence by turning it over to the party's lawyer.

D. Protective Orders

Rule 26(c) authorizes a party from whom discovery is sought to obtain an order from the court preventing or limiting the discovery.

THE RULE   Rule 26(c)

Protective Orders

(1) In General. A party or any person from whom discovery is sought may move for a protective order in the court where the action is pending—or as an alternative on matters relating to a deposition, in the court for the district where the deposition will be taken. The motion must include a certification that the movant has in good faith conferred or attempted to confer with other affected parties in an effort to resolve the dispute without court action.

* * *

EXPLANATION

When a party feels that the discovery sought by an opposing party is unreasonable, overly burdensome, or inappropriate in some fashion, Rule 26(c) allows the party to seek a protective order from the court. The order can prohibit the discovery altogether or it can limit the scope or terms and conditions of the discovery.

Protective orders are not necessary for individual interrogatories or document requests that a party deems objectionable. Rather, a party only needs to state an objection to such requests, and the burden shifts to the seeking party to file a motion to compel a response. Instead, protective orders are more commonly aimed at conduct at depositions or when a party believes that entire topics of discovery should be limited or excluded.

IN PRACTICE

One of the most common types of protective order addresses confidential information, such as trade secrets or other intellectual property or sensitive information. While confidential information is discoverable, parties do not want confidential information used or distributed outside the litigation. Often, the parties will enter into a stipulated protective order specifying how confidential information is to be handled.

1. Meet and Confer. Rule 26(c) requires a party to "meet and confer" with opposing counsel to attempt to resolve its discovery dispute with the other party before seeking a protective order, and to certify to the court that it has done so. This is a common obligation throughout the discovery process, and **local rules** often add additional "meet and confer" obligations.

> In addition to the federal rules, each district has **local rules** which supplement (but cannot contradict) the federal rules. Practitioners must comply with both sets of rules.

2. Attorney's Fees. The prevailing party in a motion to compel is entitled to its attorney's fees under Rule 26(c) (3), which provides that the provisions of Rule 37 governing the award of attorney's fees apply to Rule 26(c) motions. Under these provisions, the court must award the prevailing party its attorney's fees in bringing or defending the motion unless the court finds the losing party's position was "substantially justified" or other circumstances make an award of fees unjust.

IN PRACTICE

Most courts do not like to award attorney's fees. Furthermore, most motions involve multiple issues and the court often rules in favor of each party on at least one issue. Accordingly, although the award of attorney's fees is technically mandatory under Rule 37, fee awards are the exception.

EXAMPLES & ANALYSIS

EXAMPLE: Percy has sued Del's Discount for unfair trade practices. Percy serves an interrogatory asking Del's for information regarding every transaction it has made since it started conducting business in 1924. Responding would be enormously expensive, and Del's believes that anything happening more than five years ago is irrelevant. Can, and should, Del's seek a protective order limiting its obligation to respond to the prior five years?

Analysis: Technically, Del's could seek a protective order, but typically Del's would just object to the interrogatory as unreasonably burdensome to the extent it seeks information more than five years old, and provide only information from the past five years. If Percy feels strongly, he can seek an order compelling Del's to produce earlier information under Rule 37 (as discussed in Chapter 14). If Del's thought the issue was likely to be an ongoing problem, that might cause Del's to seek a protective order generally limiting the scope of discovery to the past five years.

EXAMPLE: Now suppose Percy seeks to take the deposition of a series of customers of Del's from the 1980s? Can, and should, Del's seek a protective order prohibiting those depositions?

Analysis: Yes—assuming research supports the argument. Del's has no ability to instruct these customers not to answer questions at the depositions, so the only way to prevent them is to obtain a protective order.

E. Conference of the Parties

In most cases in federal court (and in some state court cases), the parties must meet near the beginning of the case and before discovery has started to conduct a conference to discuss a variety of discovery issues and develop a discovery plan to submit to the court.

EXPLANATION

1. Timing. The parties must conduct the discovery conference at least 21 days before the court conducts its initial Rule 16 status conference.

2. Topics. At the conference, the parties should discuss the following topics:

- The amount of time needed for discovery (and the resulting deadline for completing discovery);

- Preservation of evidence;

- Any changes to the timing, form, or requirement for the automatic disclosures under Rule 26(a);

- The subjects for discovery and whether discovery should be conducted in phases;

- The handling of electronically stored information;

- Issues related to privileged information, including any agreements for the handling of inadvertently produced privileged matter;

- Any changes to the limits on various forms of discovery;

- Any protective orders contemplated; and

- Settlement.

3. Discovery Plan. Following the conference, the parties must prepare a written discovery plan that memorializes their agreement on the issues upon which they have reached agreement, and states their different positions on issues where they cannot reach agreement. Most judges or districts have standard forms for the discovery plan, and require the parties to complete and submit that form as their discovery plan.

F. Timing and Sequence of Discovery

Discovery does not commence until the parties have conducted the initial discovery conference required by Rule 26(f). After that conference, Rule 26(d) provides that each party can conduct discovery in any sequence it chooses.

EXPLANATION

1. Motion to Set Sequence. If a party believes that a certain sequence is appropriate, or that certain discovery phases should not occur until others are completed, the party must file a motion for a protective order under Rule 26(c) setting the sequence or timing for discovery.

2. Each Discovery Event Is Independent. Discovery by one party does not require any other party to delay its discovery—each party's discovery is independent of other discovery. Even an overdue discovery response by party A does not excuse other parties from responding timely to party A's discovery.

EXAMPLES & ANALYSIS

EXAMPLE: Pippa serves document requests on Darlene. Darlene then issues a deposition notice to Pippa. Pippa does not believe it is fair to begin depositions until the documents have been produced, to avoid surprises. May Pippa refuse to participate in the deposition until the documents have been produced?

Analysis: No. If Darlene insists on beginning depositions before she has produced her documents, Pippa's recourse is to file a motion for a protective order under Rule 26(c), not to simply refuse to appear for the deposition.

EXAMPLE: Pippa serves interrogatories on Darlene. The date for Darlene's response passes and she does not serve responses. Darlene then serves interrogatories on Pippa. May Pippa refuse to respond to Darlene's interrogatories until she responds to hers?

Analysis: No. One party's failure to respond to discovery does not excuse opposing parties from responding to similar discovery. If Pippa believes she is prejudiced and Darlene is not willing to give Pippa an extension of time, Pippa's recourse is to file a motion for a protective order asking the court to allow her to defer responding until Darlene responds to her interrogatories.

IN PRACTICE

Typically, parties conduct basic written discovery first—interrogatories and document requests—followed by depositions. The idea is that you can typically only depose a witness one time, so you want to have the documents and certain information in hand before you start the depositions. However, in some cases, it makes sense to take certain depositions at the outset of the case to pin the witness's story down or to preserve recollections.

G. Stipulations Modifying Discovery Procedures

Rule 29 authorizes the parties to enter into stipulations modifying the time periods for taking or responding to discovery, the limits on discovery, the manner of taking depositions, and most other aspects of the discovery process. The primary limitation on such stipulations is that the parties may not, without court approval, make a stipulation that interferes with the time set by the court for the close of discovery, for a motion, or for trial.

H. Supplementing Discovery Responses

Parties have a duty under Rule 26(e) to supplement their disclosures and discovery responses if they learn that the disclosure or response was "incomplete or incorrect."

EXPLANATION

1. Timing. Rule 26(e) does not set a time for supplementing disclosures or responses. Rather, it vaguely requires that the supplements be served "in a timely manner." If there is a dispute, it would ultimately be up to the judge's discretion as to whether the supplement was served in a timely manner.

2. Information Already Disclosed. There is no requirement that a party formally supplement a prior response if the information rendering a disclosure or response incomplete or incorrect has already come out during the discovery process or in writing.

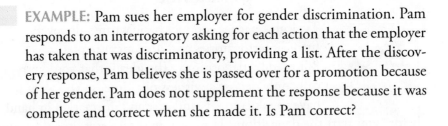

EXAMPLES & ANALYSIS

EXAMPLE: Pam sues her employer for gender discrimination. Pam responds to an interrogatory asking for each action that the employer has taken that was discriminatory, providing a list. After the discovery response, Pam believes she is passed over for a promotion because of her gender. Pam does not supplement the response because it was complete and correct when she made it. Is Pam correct?

Analysis: No. The duty to supplement applies to information obtained after the disclosure or response. Pam will not be allowed to offer evidence regarding the promotion at trial unless she supplements the disclosure in a timely manner.

> EXAMPLE: Pam responds to an interrogatory asking about her years of employment by stating that she worked at her prior job for seven years. During her deposition, she testifies that she worked at her prior job for five years, which was the accurate length of time. Must Pam supplement her incorrect interrogatory response?

Analysis: No. Because the information has already been brought out in the deposition, there is no need to supplement the response, even though incorrect.

I. Signing Disclosures and Discovery Requests, Responses and Objections

Every disclosure and every discovery request, response, and objection must be signed by an attorney of record under Rule 26(g). The signature certifies that the disclosure is complete and accurate, and that the discovery request, response, or objection is not unreasonably burdensome or expensive, is served for a proper purpose and not to harass or delay, and is based on existing law or a good faith basis for extending or modifying existing law.

EXPLANATION

1. Certification as to Disclosures. With respect to the disclosures required by Rule 26(a), the attorney's signature certifies that the disclosure is complete and correct as of the time it is made.

2. Certification as to Discovery Requests, Responses, and Objections. By signing a discovery request, response, or objection, the attorney is certifying that the document is:

- consistent with the rules and warranted by existing law or a non-frivolous argument for extending, modifying, or reversing existing law;

- not made for any improper purpose such as to harass, cause delay, or increase the cost of litigation; and

- neither unreasonable nor unduly burdensome or expensive.

3. Sanctions. If a certification violates this rule, the court must sanction the signer, the party, or both. The nature of the sanction is not specified, except to say that it should be an "appropriate sanction" and may include attorney's fees incurred as a result of the violation.

EXAMPLES & ANALYSIS

EXAMPLE: Pilar sues her employer, Data Management, alleging a pattern of discrimination against women over the past ten years of her employment. Pilar serves an interrogatory asking Data to list for each employee over the past ten years that employee's starting salary, starting position, and gender. Data Management has had 8,000 employees over that period of time, and Pilar's attorney, Amy, knows that gathering that information would be expensive and burdensome for Data. Has Amy violated Rule 26(g) by serving an interrogatory that is unduly burdensome and expensive?

Analysis: No. This information is clearly relevant to the litigation, and there is a proper purpose for it, so it would be quite unlikely to be deemed a violation of the certification. The issue would more likely play out by Data objecting to the interrogatory as being unreasonably burdensome and expensive, and then providing a more limited scope of information. Pilar could then file a motion to compel a more complete response, and the court might ultimately have to determine whether ten years of data about all employees was warranted under all the circumstances or whether a more limited scope was appropriate.

EXAMPLE: In the Example above, Amy serves interrogatories asking for the salaries of the top officers of Data. Amy believes she can justify this request by arguing that the information may enable her to prove that the gender discrimination extends all the way to the top. Amy does not really believe that this data is relevant to whether Pilar received discriminatory treatment, but believes that the officers will be reluctant to have that information become public knowledge, and hopes that they will make a settlement offer to avoid disclosing the information. Has Amy violated Rule 26(g)?

Analysis: Likely yes. Amy can recognize that a side effect of conducting legitimate discovery is to create settlement leverage, but if her sole or primary purpose is to harass or embarrass the officers, that is not a "proper purpose" of conducting discovery. Of course, proving her primary purpose may be difficult.

EXAMPLE: In the Example above, Data objects to the request for the salary information of the officers on the grounds of an "officer privilege." Data admits that there is no legal authority supporting an "officer privilege," but contends that there should be one to prevent this exact type of dirty litigation tactic. Has Data's attorney violated Rule 26(g) by interposing that objection?

Analysis: The issue is whether Data really has a good faith basis for contending that the law should be extended to create an "officer privilege." Given the reluctance in the law to establish new privileges, this might be difficult for Data to establish.

IN PRACTICE

Allegations of violations of Rule 26(g) are rare, and an award of sanctions is even rarer. Moreover, courts do not like sanctions motions. Therefore, attorneys should reserve sanctions motions for truly outrageous conduct.

IN PRACTICE

Although perhaps not as glamorous as trial, discovery is where the vast majority of cases are won or lost, and where most litigators spend the majority of their time. Only a small fraction of cases actually make it to trial—some estimates put the number below 2% of the cases filed. Therefore, an attorney's skill at obtaining and mastering the important documents, taking and defending the important depositions, and serving thoughtful interrogatories and requests for admission often makes the difference between a favorable outcome and a disappointed client.

In order to conduct discovery effectively, it is important to plan the discovery thoroughly at the outset of the case. In general, it is difficult to take effective depositions until you have all the documents, so attorneys typically conduct written discovery prior to conducting depositions. Parties have 30 days to respond to written discovery, and often ask for extensions of time. So if the court gives you 4 months to conduct fact discovery, you need to plan carefully in order to conduct written discovery, review and digest the responses and documents, and conduct depositions in that time frame.

A good discovery plan will analyze each of the elements of the claims and defenses, and identify the evidence that the party will need to establish its claims and defenses. It will specify where there are gaps in the evidence, and what discovery techniques the party will use to fill those gaps. In this fashion, discovery can be conducted with focus and purpose.

Flow Chart of Discovery Sequence

Judge Schedules the Rule 16 Conference
(Triggering event)

Rule 26(f) conference
(21 days before the Rule 16 Conference)

↓

The parties may conduct discovery
(starting immediately after the Rule 26(f) conference
and ending at the court established deadline)

↓

Rule 26(f) discovery plan and Rule 26(a) initial disclosures
(14 days after the 26(f) Conference)

↓

Rule 16 Conference

↓

Judge issues a pretrial order, which sets deadlines for discovery

Judge schedules trial to commence
(Triggering event)

↓

Rule 26(a)(2) expert disclosures
(90 days before trial, unless set by the court)

↓

Rule 26(a)(3) pretrial disclosures
(30 days before trial, unless set by the court)

↓

Trial Date

ADDITIONAL EXERCISES

Dennis sells Paula a baseball that, he said, Babe Ruth hit out of the park in Boston in 1916, before he was traded to the Yankees. Paula learns that the ball is not genuine and sues Dennis for fraud and breach of contract. Consider the following questions that arise during discovery in this action:

1. Dennis files a motion to dismiss for lack of personal jurisdiction. Paula sends interrogatories relating to Dennis's contacts with the forum state. **Must Dennis respond to these interrogatories?**

2. While the motion to dismiss is pending, Paula serves interrogatories and document requests. Dennis objects on the ground that it is improper and unduly burdensome to require him to respond to discovery until the court rules on the motion to dismiss. Paula moves to compel Dennis to respond. **How would a court likely rule?**

3. Paula asks Dennis to identify any sports memorabilia authenticators that he took the ball to prior to the sale. Dennis objects on the grounds that any statement by an authenticator would be inadmissible hearsay. Assume Dennis is correct about the hearsay issue—**is this a proper basis for Dennis to decline to respond to the discovery?**

4. Paula's attorney photographed the baseball and took it to a consulting expert who scanned it with an imaging device which revealed the nature of the core and windings (to see if they were consistent with baseballs in 1916). The baseball was subsequently lost. **Must Paula provide the photographs and images in discovery? Must she make the consulting expert available for deposition?**

5. Paula learned that the ball was not genuine when she took it to a sports memorabilia shop to try to sell it. She would like to call the store owner as a witness to testify as to the lack of provenance for the ball. **Must Paula disclose him as an expert and have him prepare an expert report?**

David sues Peggy, his boss and the owner of the bar where David worked as a bartender, claiming that Peggy fired him because he refused to engage in sexual conduct with her. Peggy answers the complaint, contending that David was sexually harassing the customers at the bar and stealing money from the cash register. Consider the following questions that arise during discovery in this action:

1. Peggy sends an interrogatory to David asking for the name of all of his sexual partners during the past five years while he worked at the bar. *Is this information discoverable? What measures can David take to avoid or limit disclosure of this information?*

2. David notices Peggy's deposition. Peggy sends a letter to David stating that she needs his documents and interrogatory answers in order to prepare for her deposition, and that she objects to a deposition prior to his discovery responses. David responds with a letter stating that he intends to go forward with the deposition, and expects her to appear as noticed. *Who is right, and what should each party do to protect his or her rights in this situation?*

3. Peggy sends an interrogatory to David asking for his income tax returns for the past five years while he worked at the bar. *Is this information discoverable? What measures can David take to avoid or limit disclosure of this information?*

4. Peggy hires an investigator to try to find customers who have been harassed by David. The investigator interviews ten customers and prepares notes of the interviews. David seeks the notes in discovery. *Is David entitled to them? Why or why not?*

5. Peggy's attorney asks her to prepare a memorandum summarizing the facts that support her claim against David. Peggy prepares the memorandum and sends it to her attorney. Attached to the memorandum is a video tape that Peggy believes shows David harassing a customer. David sends document requests that would cover both the memorandum and the tape, and Peggy lists them as attorney-client privileged on a privilege log. *Is David entitled to them? Why or why not?*

6. Peggy tells her attorney that she told David that "a relationship with his boss could be good for his career," but says that she was just joking. David sends an interrogatory asking whether Peggy ever made any remarks linking David's continued employment to a sexual relationship with Peggy. Peggy says to her attorney, "Our conversion was privileged, right? I don't want to disclose those facts." ***Can Peggy's attorney object on the grounds of attorney-client privilege and decline to respond?***

7. Peggy asks David for any records reflecting tips that he received while working at the bar. David used an app on his phone to track his tips, but never printed the data or transferred it to his computer. ***Must David produce the data from his phone?***

Quick Summary

- The scope of discovery is limited to information related to claims and defenses in the case, but is very broadly construed.

- Privileged documents and documents prepared in anticipation of litigation may be withheld, but should promptly be listed on a privilege log, and certain communications with experts are shielded from discovery.

- At the outset, the parties confer to make a discovery plan, which is submitted to the court and forms the basis of the court's Case Management Order, which governs the course of discovery.

- Discovery may proceed in any sequence.

- A party must supplement disclosures and discovery responses that it subsequently learns were or have become incomplete or incorrect.

> • Each discovery document must be signed, and the signature acts as a certification that the disclosures are accurate and that the discovery documents are consistent with the law and the Rules, not served for an improper purpose, and not unreasonably burdensome or expensive.

13

Discovery Techniques

Key Concepts

- The disclosures under Rule 26(a) that occur automatically without waiting for a discovery request from the opposing party

- The three primary mechanisms for conducting written discovery:

  · Interrogatories, which are written questions that other parties must answer under oath under Rule 33;

  · Document requests under Rule 34; and

  · Requests for admission under Rule 36, which are designed to narrow the issues for trial by requiring parties to either admit or deny specified facts, with sanctions for bad faith denials

- Depositions, or oral examinations, of parties and witnesses under Rules 30 and 32

- Physical and mental examinations of parties under Rule 35

Introduction

This chapter will cover the various discovery techniques that parties use to exchange information related to the litigation. The first step in the process is the initial disclosure of documents, witnesses, and other basic information under Rule 26(a).

After the initial disclosure, written discovery is usually the next phase. Written discovery is best suited for obtaining any relevant documents not already disclosed, identifying additional fact witnesses, and obtaining specific pieces of information or very specific admissions. The written discovery techniques are interrogatories (which are just written questions), document requests, and requests for admission.

Because of the volume of documents in many federal court cases, and in particular the volume of electronically stored documents and information, the process of requesting, gathering, and producing documents has become a time-intensive and expensive part of the litigation process. Additionally, young attorneys are often heavily involved in written discovery at the start of their careers. Accordingly, a sound understanding of the rules and practices in this area is important.

The next phase of discovery in a typical lawsuit is depositions. A deposition is a proceeding in which counsel for the parties can ask questions of other parties and non-party witnesses. The witness is placed under oath at the beginning of the proceeding, and every word spoken during the deposition is transcribed or recorded in some fashion. Typically, a stenographer is present, and the stenographer types the proceeding into a written transcript. Sometimes, a deposition is also videotaped or recorded in some other fashion.

Lawyers for all parties have the right to be present during a deposition, and questioning proceeds much like at trial, with one key difference. Most objections are stated on the record, but because no judge is present, the witness then answers the objected-to question. Later, if someone attempts to move the testimony into evidence, the objecting party can ask the court to rule on the objection. The primary exception to this rule is objections relating to privileged information, because disclosing the information would waive the privilege.

For example, suppose the question at a deposition is: "What did you tell your lawyer about the cause of the car accident?" If the witness must answer the question at the deposition, a subsequent court ruling that the information is privileged provides little comfort—the "cat is already out of the bag." Accordingly, witnesses may decline to answer questions calling for privileged information. In fact, this is one of the few circumstances where a lawyer may properly instruct a witness not to answer a question at a deposition.

Depositions are an extremely important discovery tool. The rules of ethics prevent an attorney from speaking directly to an opposing party who is represented by counsel in most circumstances, so depositions are one of the few opportunities to hear from the opposing party without the filter of opposing counsel. In addition, they are dynamic, so that if a particular question does not elicit the desired information, or if the answer suggests another line of inquiry, the attorney can immediately ask follow-up questions.

There are a number of objectives in taking a deposition. Learning the facts and avoiding being surprised at trial are, of course, important goals. In addition, an attorney will often try to pin down the witness's story, so that if the witness tries to change his or her testimony at trial, the deposition transcript can be used to impeach the witness's credibility. Furthermore, an attorney may try to obtain helpful admissions at a deposition, and may try to establish facts and documents for use in motion practice or at trial. Finally, a deposition is a good opportunity to assess how witnesses would present at trial—do they come across as honest and forthcoming, or do they appear evasive and deceptive?

At the same time, depositions can be expensive. The cost includes not only the time spent in the deposition and the costs for the court reporter, but also the cost to prepare for the deposition (which should involve a mastery of the relevant documents and careful planning of the objectives for the deposition). Therefore, some balancing of the cost and benefit is important.

Subpoenas are the tool for obtaining documents or testimony from nonparties, who are not required to respond to document requests or deposition notices. Attorneys have the extraordinary power of issuing subpoenas which require nonparties to appear and give testimony or produce documents.

Depositions occur in most federal court cases that proceed through discovery. Mental or physical examinations of a party by a medical professional under Rule 35 are less common, but can also be an important tool. Such examinations are only available by motion for "good cause," which generally exists whenever the party's mental or physical condition is at issue in the litigation.

A. Initial Disclosures

Rule 26(a) requires each party to make three sets of disclosures automatically, without waiting for a request from another party. The first of these three disclosures is the initial disclosure of certain basic information at the beginning of the case. The other two disclosures, relating to expert testimony and trial witnesses and exhibits, occur near the end of the case and are discussed at the end of this chapter.

EXPLANATION

Rule 26(a)(1) requires all parties—plaintiffs and defendants—to disclose four categories of information at the outset of the litigation. Those categories are:

- The names and addresses of witnesses that the disclosing party may use to support its claims or defenses;

- A copy, or a description by category and location, of all documents, electronically stored information, and tangible things that the disclosing party may use to support its claims or defenses;

- A computation of each category of damages that the disclosing party claims, together with the documents supporting the damages; and

- Any insurance policies that may cover all or part of a judgment in the case.

1. Timing. The deadline for the initial disclosures is triggered by the mandatory discovery meeting that parties must conduct under Rule 26(f). The parties must make the initial disclosures within 14 days of that discovery conference.

2. Scope of Initial Disclosures. In contrast to the other affirmative discovery techniques, the scope of the disclosure obligations is somewhat limited. A party is only required to disclose the witnesses and documents that it may use to support its claims and defenses—the initial disclosure requirements do not apply to witnesses and documents that might support an opponent's case. Documents and the identity of witness that might support an opponent's case may be obtained through the affirmative discovery techniques discussed later in this chapter.

3. Impeachment Evidence. The disclosure obligation is further limited to exclude witnesses or documents that the disclosing party may use solely for **impeachment** purposes.

> **"Impeachment"** refers to evidence that will be used to discredit the witnesses offered by the opposing party.

IN PRACTICE

Rule 26(a)(1) allows a party to describe categories of documents instead of producing them. Because it can be challenging to have the client gather all of the documents, review them, and produce them at the outset of the case, parties often take advantage of this option.

EXAMPLES & ANALYSIS

EXAMPLE: Paisley sues Danielle for breach of a contract to sell Danielle's house, claiming that Danielle told her that the basement never leaked. Danielle has in her possession a bill from a cleaning company that removed mold from the basement carpet while Danielle owned the house. Danielle is planning to call her sister, Wanda, as a witness to testify that Paisley knew about the prior water damage before she purchased the house. Must Danielle disclose the cleaning bill and Wanda's identity?

Analysis: The cleaning bill is not something that Danielle would ever use to support her defenses in the case—if anything, the bill supports Paisley's case. Therefore, Danielle does not have to disclose it as part of the initial disclosure (although it will likely come out in discovery). One could argue that Wanda's testimony would be used to impeach Paisley if she claims not to have known about the water damage, but Wanda's testimony would likely be part of Danielle's defense, so the better approach would be to disclose her identity.

B. Interrogatories

Rule 33 governs the use of interrogatories.

THE RULE   Rule 33

Interrogatories to Parties

(a) **In General.**

(1) **Number.** Unless otherwise stipulated or ordered by the court, a party may **serve on any other party** no more than 25 written interrogatories, **including all discrete subparts**.

* * *

(2) **Scope.** An interrogatory may relate to any matter that may be inquired into under Rule 26(b). An interrogatory is not objectionable merely because it asks for an **opinion or contention** that relates to fact or the application of law to fact, but the court may order that the interrogatory need not be answered until designated discovery is complete, or until a pretrial conference or some other time.

* * *

(d) **Option to Produce Business Records.** If the answer to an interrogatory may be determined by examining, auditing, compiling, abstracting, or summarizing a party's business records (including electronically stored information), and **if the burden of deriving or ascertaining the answer will be substantially the same for either party**, the responding party may answer by:

(1) specifying the records that must be reviewed, **in sufficient detail to enable the interrogating party to locate and identify them as readily as the responding party could**; and

(2) giving the interrogating party a reasonable opportunity to examine and audit the records and to make copies, compilations, abstracts, or summaries.

EXPLANATION

1. Interrogatories

a.   Number of Interrogatories. Rule 33 limits each party to 25 interrogatories on another party. Note that the restriction is on the number of interrogatories served on each other party—thus, if there are 4 defendants, a plaintiff may serve up to 25 interrogatories on each defendant.

Rule 33 further specifies that discrete subparts count as separate interrogatories. Thus, a party cannot expand the number of allowable interrogatories by including an interrogatory that reads, "Please state the following:" followed by a series of separate questions formatted as subparts. However, if the subparts are closely related to one topic, they may not be counted as separate interrogatories. Thus, for example, an interrogatory that reads, "For each witness you may call at trial, please list: the witness's name; the witness's address; and a general description of the witness's testimony" would likely be counted as one interrogatory.

IN PRACTICE

When there are multiple plaintiffs or defendants, they will often coordinate to make good use of their 25 interrogatories, making sure they do not duplicate each other's topics.

b.   Scope of Interrogatories. The scope of interrogatories is tied to the scope of discovery generally permitted under Rule 26(b) (which is discussed in detail in Chapter 12). Rule 33 specifically provides that "contention interrogatories"—asking for a party's position on an issue of fact or the application of the facts to the law—are expressly authorized. Contention interrogatories asking for a pure conclusion of law, totally divorced from the facts of the case, are not permitted.

c. Format for Interrogatories. A set of interrogatories typically has the following parts:

- The caption;

- An introductory paragraph, typically identifying the parties, referring to Rule 33, and requesting responses within 30 days;

- A set of general instructions and definitions. The instructions typically address issues like the information that should be included when witness or documents are identified and the rules for construing the language in the interrogatories. The definitions should define terms that are used frequently throughout the interrogatories;

- The interrogatories, with the word "Response" or "Answer," followed by a space for the response;

- The signature of the attorney representing the party propounding the interrogatories; and

- A certificate of service.

IN PRACTICE

When drafting interrogatories, attorneys typically start with a preexisting set of discovery, to avoid having to draft the instructions and definitions from whole cloth. In addition, there are resources available that have typical sets of interrogatories for various types of cases. At the same time, it is important not to use form interrogatories mindlessly—it looks unprofessional to include stock interrogatories that have no bearing on the case.

To facilitate the process, parties will often agree to exchange interrogatories in a word processing format, so that the responding party can add the responses directly into the document, which then shows each interrogatory followed by the response.

d. Time for Service. Interrogatories may not be served before the parties have conducted their discovery conference under Rule 26(f). The court sets the deadline for the end of discovery, and all interrogatories must be served in sufficient time for the response to be due before the end of discovery. Typically, this means that all interrogatories must be served 30 days before the discovery cutoff.

e. No Filing. Unless otherwise ordered by the court, interrogatories are not **filed** with the court, they are just **served** on all other parties. If a dispute arises, the disputed interrogatories and responses are attached to the motion filed with the court.

> **"Filing"** refers to submitting a document to the clerk's office, where it is entered into the official docket, and then is provided to the judge. **"Serving"** refers to providing a copy to other counsel.

2. Responses to Interrogatories

a. Time for Response. Responses to interrogatories and any objections must be served (not filed) within 30 days (unless extended by agreement of counsel or order of court). If discovery is not complete, a party can request leave to defer responding to contention interrogatories until a later point in time.

IN PRACTICE

Requests for extension are quite common for interrogatories, and the professional courtesy of granting these requests is quite common unless there is genuine prejudice as a result of the extension.

b. Format for Responses. The response to a set of interrogatories typically has the following parts:

- The caption;

- An introductory paragraph, typically identifying the parties and stating that the document is a response to the interrogatories;

- Any objections to the general instructions and definitions;

- Responses to the individual interrogatories as discussed below, including any objections;

- A verification or some other method of satisfying the requirement that the answers be "under oath," plus the signature of the attorney representing the responding party if there are any objections; and

- A certificate of service.

Each interrogatory must be answered separately and fully under oath. To the extent that an interrogatory is objectionable in part, the responding party must respond to the extent it is not objectionable.

The "under oath" requirement is unique in federal written discovery to interrogatories—the other responses do not need to be verified by the party. Typically, a verification signed by the party is attached to the answers, which satisfies both the "under oath" and the signature requirements. The attorney also signs the response if there are any objections.

c. **Objections.** If the responding party wants to object to the interrogatories, the objection must be stated with specificity. Any objections that are not asserted timely with such specificity are deemed waived. Typical grounds for objections include an assertion that the interrogatory:

- is overly broad;

- is unreasonably burdensome;

- is vague and ambiguous;

- is not related to a claim or defense in the case;

- calls for a pure legal conclusion; and/or

- seeks privileged information.

Conversely, the following are some common improper objections:

- the information requested is already known by the requesting party (a party is required to provide all responsive information within its possession, custody, or control, regardless of whether another party also may have the same information);

- the information is available from a public source (again, a party must produce all responsive information in its possession, custody, or control); and

- the request seeks information that may be primarily in another party's possession, custody, or control (a party is generally not required to produce information in another party's possession, custody, or control, but that is not a basis for objection to a request for any such information in the responding party's possession, custody, or control).

If an interrogatory is objectionable in part, the responding party must respond to the non-objectionable parts. If the party sending the interrogatories believes the objections are improper, the party can file a motion to compel an answer to the objected portion.

IN PRACTICE

The last thing a practicing attorney wants to do is to waive anything unintentionally. Therefore, it is critical within the 30-day time period to either serve an answer to the interrogatories asserting any objections or obtain an extension from opposing counsel. If the 30-day period passes without either of those occurring, there is a substantial risk that objections have been waived.

d. Duty to Gather Information. A party's duty in responding to interrogatories extends beyond simply providing the readily available information. Rather, a party has an affirmative obligation to diligently gather the responsive information in the party's possession, custody, or control.

3. Use of Interrogatory Answers. Rule 33 states that the answers can be used to the extent authorized by the Federal Rules of Evidence. In practice, this means that the answers are like any other written statement by the party—they are generally admissible as party admissions, but can be contradicted or explained at trial (see the discussion of Rule 36 below for the evidentiary distinction between this type of admission and an admission in response to a request for admission).

4.   Option to Produce Documents. Rule 33(d) allows a party to refer to documents containing the requested information in lieu of compiling it in an interrogatory response, so long as the burden of finding the answer is "substantially" equal for either party. The responding party must describe the documents containing the information with sufficient detail that the propounding party can find the information as easily as the responding party could. Thus, a party cannot point to a warehouse of documents containing the answer.

IN PRACTICE

The option to produce documents in lieu of answering under Rule 33(d) is a very powerful and appealing option when another party is seeking to require the responding party to compile detailed information located in documents. The battleground on this process is typically whether the burden of ascertaining the information is "substantially equal."

EXAMPLES & ANALYSIS

EXAMPLE: Darcy forms a company named "Goggle, Inc." which hosts a search engine called Goggle. Darcy and Goggle are sued under a variety of intellectual property claims including trademark infringement for the name and patent infringement for the search algorithms. Darcy and Goggle answer the complaint, contending that Goggle is an English word that cannot be trademarked, and is descriptive of the process of looking for websites containing the searched-for terms. During discovery, Goggle receives an interrogatory that reads: "With respect to the Goggle search engine, please identify the primary developer of the Code (Code is a defined term) and all other programmers who worked on the Code. Is this interrogatory objectionable? If so on what grounds?

Analysis: Depending on Goggle's employee classifications, some of the terms may be ambiguous. For example, the identity of the "primary developer" may or may not be clear, and it is not a defined term. Additionally, depending on the length of time and the number of people working on the development of the Goggle search engine, it may or may not be unduly burdensome to identify everyone who worked on the project.

EXAMPLE: Goggle asserts an objection based on the vagueness of the term "primary developer." Having objected to the interrogatory, must Goggle also respond substantively?

Analysis: Yes. An objection only excuses a response to the extent of the objection. At a minimum, Goggle must respond to the other parts that do not use the objectionable term.

EXAMPLE: Goggle sends an interrogatory to the plaintiff asking whether the plaintiff contends that Goggle's home-page design violates any of the plaintiff's intellectual property rights. Can the plaintiff object to this as seeking a pure legal conclusion?

Analysis: This is a contention interrogatory. While contention interrogatories seeking pure legal conclusions are prohibited, this interrogatory seems to entail the application of law to fact (intellectual property law applied to the facts of Goggle's home page), which is explicitly authorized.

EXAMPLE: Goggle sends the plaintiff an interrogatory asking the plaintiff to identify any third parties who were misled by the name "Goggle." The plaintiff objects on the ground that the interrogatory calls for information outside Goggle's possession, custody, or control, in the form of information held by these third parties. Is this a proper objection, and must the plaintiff respond?

Analysis: The interrogatory does not, on its face, call for the production of information held by others. While there is no harm if the plaintiff asserts the objection, there is no need to do so. Regardless of whether the plaintiff asserts the objection, however, it must provide the responsive information in its possession, custody, or control.

C. Requests to Inspect Documents and Things

Rule 34 contains the provisions for requests to inspect documents and other things.

THE RULE   **Rule 34**

Producing Documents, Electronically Stored Information, and Tangible Things, or Entering Onto Land, for Inspection and Other Purposes

(a) In General.

    (1) A party may **serve** on any other party a request within the scope of Rule 26(b): to produce and permit the requesting party or its representative to inspect, copy, test, or sample the following items in the responding party's **possession, custody, or control**:

        (A) any designated documents or **electronically stored information**—including writings, drawings, graphs, charts, photographs, sound recordings, images, and other data or data compilations * * * or

        (B) any designated **tangible things**; or

    (2) to permit entry onto designated land or other property possessed or controlled by the responding party, so that the requesting party may inspect, survey, photograph, test, or sample the property or any designated object or operation on it.

    * * *

EXPLANATION

1. Document Requests

a. Scope of Requests.

As with interrogatories, the scope of **document requests** is tied to the scope of discovery generally in Rule 26(b). A party may request inspection of tangible things (the allegedly dangerous product, for example) or property, as well as documents.

> Although the technical scope of Rule 34 extends to inspection of things and property, documents (and their electronic counterparts) are by far the most commonly requested, and Rule 34 requests are commonly referred to as "**document requests**." That shorthand term will sometimes be used in this text.

The terms "document" and "electronically stored information" are deliberately broad and vague so as to encompass the variety of information that is potentially relevant to the litigation.

b. Time for Service.

At the front end, document requests may be served 21 days after the complaint and summons are served, but will be considered served at the parties' discovery conference under Rule 26(f). This gives the parties an opportunity to discuss document issues at the conference. At the back end, document requests must be served in sufficient time for the response to be due before the end of discovery.

c. Form for Requests.

A set of document requests typically has the same parts as a set of interrogatories. However, in contrast to interrogatories, the document requests are not set out as questions, but rather as descriptions of the documents or things sought to be inspected.

IN PRACTICE

As with interrogatories, when drafting requests for documents, it is best to start with a preexisting set of requests or a form and modify it to fit the particular facts of the new case. Think of the forms as an efficient way to draft and as a checklist to help counsel get started and minimize the risk of forgetting important topics.

d. Service. Like interrogatories, document requests and responses are generally served on all parties but not filed with the court.

e. Number of Requests. There is no limit on the number of requests for inspection. If a party believes that an opponent has served an excessive number of requests for inspection, the party must file a motion for a protective order, and the court will exercise its discretion to determine whether the requests are appropriate or abusive.

f. Format for Electronically Stored Information (ESI). When ESI is sought, the requests may, but are not required to, specify the form for production (*i.e.*, paper or electronic, and if electronic, native format, searchable pdf, etc.). If the requests do not specify the form, then the responding party can pick the form, so long as the form is either the form the ESI is ordinarily stored in or in a reasonably accessible form. In other words, the responding party cannot convert the data into an obsolete or obscure format to make things more difficult for the requesting party. The choice about the form of the ESI also implicates the issue of whether metadata is to be preserved and produced. Typically, parties will discuss this issue during the Rule 26(f) conference.

> "**Metadata**" means, roughly, data about the data. It refers to the data that computers store about the author of a file, the dates that the file was created or edited, etc., and can be very important.

IN PRACTICE

The form for production of ESI is an important issue. This issue is often addressed in the discovery conference under Rule 26(f), and is often the subject of an informal agreement. In any event, an attorney requesting ESI will want to select the format in which it is produced. Typically, this will be an electronic format that is searchable and compatible with any litigation software that the attorney uses. If the requesting party fails to specify a form, then the producing party can produce the ESI in paper form (which is generally disadvantageous to the requesting party).

Metadata can also be an important issue when the timing, legitimacy, or accessing of documents is at issue. At the same time, preserving and producing metadata can be cumbersome and expensive, and thoughtful litigators often agree to forgo discovery of metadata.

2. Responses to Document Requests

a. Time for Response. The written response must be served within 30 days from service of the requests, in the absence of an extension of time. However, the inspection of the documents does not necessarily occur at the time of the service of the written response, and responses frequently state that responsive documents will be made available at a mutually convenient time and location. The parties then coordinate regarding the actual inspection.

IN PRACTICE

Requests for extension are quite common for document requests, and the professional courtesy of granting these requests is quite common unless there is genuine prejudice as a result of the extension. This issue has two different aspects—the time for the service of the written response and the time for making the documents available for inspection. The latter process can take considerable time, depending on the volume of ESI, the number of custodians, the way that ESI is stored, and the need to search laptops, PDAs, and web-based storage, etc.

For documents that are going to be produced or made available for inspection, the preferred response states, "Subject to [or without waiving] these objections, all non-privileged responsive documents in [the responding party's] possession, custody, or control will be made available for inspection at a mutually convenient time and location." The important concepts in this phrasing are that privileged documents will be withheld, that the response is limited by the objections, that the responding party is only purporting to produce documents within its possession, custody, or control. The parties then typically work out the logistics of the production.

b. Form for Requests. The response to a set of document requests typically has the same parts as the response to a set of interrogatories, except that the responses to individual requests include an indication of whether responsive documents will be produced or are being made available for inspection.

c. Objections. Objections to the requests should be included as part of the response. If there is an objection to part of a request, the responding party should produce those documents requested by the non-objectionable part of the request. A responding party risks waiver by not serving objections within 30 days or within the time established in an extension granted within the initial 30 days.

A party interposing an objection must state whether any responsive documents are being withheld on the basis of the objection. This serves to help the opposing party evaluate whether it is worth challenging the objection.

Grounds for typical objections to document requests are similar to those for interrogatories. The following are some common improper objections to document requests:

- The documents requested are already in the possession of the requesting party (a party is required to provide all responsive documents within its possession, custody, or control, regardless of whether another party also may have the same documents).

- The documents are available from a public source (again, a party must produce all responsive documents in its possession, custody, or control).

- The request seeks documents in another party's possession, custody, or control (a party is generally not required to produce documents in another party's possession, custody, or control, but that is not a basis for objection to producing those documents in the responding party's possession, custody, or control).

3. Making Documents Available for Inspection

a. Scope of Documents Produced. The obligation to gather and make documents available for inspection only extends to documents in a party's **possession**, **custody**, or **control**. Thus, there is generally no obligation to create documents or to obtain documents from third parties in response to a document request.

b. No Obligation to Make Copies. The Rules do not require a responding party to produce a copy of the documents to the requesting party.

Rather, the responding party may make them available for inspection. The requesting party can then inspect them and copy any documents it chooses at its expense. However, the rules allow the responding party to produce a copy rather than make the documents available for inspection, and that is the common practice.

> The term **"possession, custody, or control"** is frequently used in discovery documents, and one that every litigator should know.

c. Organization of Documents. Documents or ESI may be produced "as they are kept in the ordinary course of business" or they may be organized and labeled to correspond to the categories in the request. Thus the options are essentially to say, "there is the section of our file room where we keep the responsive documents, you may inspect them," or to group and label them according to which request they are responsive to. It is not permissible to produce documents that are not organized in one of these two fashions. Although the rules do not require it, most parties **Bates label** documents they are producing or making available for inspection so that they have a record of what they have produced.

> **"Bates label"** is the term commonly used for an identifying set of letters and numbers that is added to each page of documents (and often ESI) that is produced. There is often an alpha prefix identifying the producing party and a sequential number—such as PL0001.

IN PRACTICE

 If the parties are going to have roughly equivalent numbers of documents to produce, they will often agree that the producing party will simply copy and produce the documents that would otherwise be made available for inspection. If the production volumes are disparate, but not too large, then parties often forgo the process of inspection and the requesting party simply agrees to reimburse the producing party for the costs of making a copy or arranges for a vendor to make a copy.

d. Privileged Documents. If the producing party withholds any documents on the basis of privilege, the producing party should promptly list those documents on a privilege log. A privilege log is a chart that lists each privileged document, the nature of the privilege asserted, and all of the participants in the communication. It must contain enough information that the requesting party (and the court) can evaluate the merits of the privilege without actually disclosing the privileged information.

If a party inadvertently produces privileged documents, Rule 26(b)(5) establishes a process for "clawing back" the privileged documents. Under that process, the producing party notifies the requesting party of the contention that the producing party inadvertently produced privileged material and the nature of the privilege assertion. The requesting party must then return, sequester, or destroy all copies of the privileged documents, and may not use the privileged information until the privilege claim is resolved. The producing party must preserve the privileged information until the status of the privilege is resolved. If the requesting party does not agree with the privilege assertion, the requesting party may present the matter to the court for a determination of the validity of the assertion.

Substantive law on privileges and the particular facts and documents at issue will determine both whether the documents were originally privileged and whether the privilege was waived by the production. If the producing party did not exercise sufficient diligence in conducting a privilege review, the "inadvertent" production may result in a waiver, even though the producing party properly followed the "claw back" provisions of Rule 26(b)(5).

IN PRACTICE

Prior to producing documents, the responding party must review them for privileged content and must withhold or redact the privileged documents. Even with proper review, however, inadvertent production of privileged documents is becoming more common with the exploding volume of ESI. Gathering and reviewing gigabytes of ESI is very time consuming, and it is difficult not to miss any privileged documents. Many requesting attorneys will affirmatively bring to the attention of the producing attorney any plainly privileged documents they encounter in their review of the produced documents, and many will agree to return inadvertently produced privileged documents without contest.

e. **Inspection of Property or Things.** Although requests for inspection typically pertain to documents, they can be used to gain access to things or property too. So, for example, in a products liability case, the party or its representative (such as its expert) can examine the product in question. Likewise, in a property boundary dispute, a party's surveyor can come onto the property to conduct a survey.

The inspection can include measuring, testing, sampling, and photographing. The request for inspection should describe the "manner" of inspection, including whether any testing, sampling, or photographing is anticipated.

IN PRACTICE

It is not uncommon for logistical issues to arise regarding the scope or manner of the inspection, such as when a party seeks to conduct destructive testing or to take pictures of proprietary processes or equipment. Typically, these issues can be resolved through cooperation by both sides in a way that does not interfere with the necessary gathering of evidence but also protects the concerns of the responding party. If not, the court can resolve the dispute through a motion for protective order or a motion to compel.

f. Duty to Preserve. Another important concept in document discovery is the duty to preserve evidence. A party is required to preserve documents that are potentially relevant to litigation starting at the time the litigation has been filed **or is reasonably anticipated**. Lawyers and clients should work together to send out "litigation hold letters" advising all employees likely to have relevant documents that they must preserve the documents. Parties should also suspend any automatic destruction of paper documents or ESI (so that documents that are scheduled to be destroyed pursuant to a document retention policy are not destroyed, and documents that are automatically deleted by the party's computer systems are preserved). A party who fails to preserve evidence in this manner may be subject to sanctions for **"spoliation,"** as described in Chapter 14.

> **"Spoliation"** is the term that refers to the destruction of evidence.

IN PRACTICE

Spoliation can result in substantial sanctions, including an instruction to the jury that they may assume that the evidence that was not preserved was adverse or harmful to the party not preserving it.

It is therefore extremely important that attorneys advise their clients to send litigation hold letters at the outset of a dispute, and take steps to ensure compliance with the instruction to preserve evidence.

EXAMPLES & ANALYSIS

EXAMPLE: In the Goggle intellectual property lawsuit described above, the plaintiff serves a request to inspect the Code that Goggle uses in its search algorithm. Goggle serves a timely response that objects to the request on the basis that the request improperly seeks protected information because Goggle has a patent application pending for its algorithm and because it would give the plaintiff a competitive advantage to examine Goggle's Code. Is this a proper objection, and may Goggle decline to produce the Code?

Analysis: This is not a proper basis for an objection. The Code is both within the scope of discovery—relevant to a claim in the litigation—and is not covered by any evidentiary privilege (confidentiality issues are legitimate concerns, but are not evidentiary privileges). Goggle may not withhold the Code based on this objection. If Goggle does not want to produce the Code or wants to produce it under restricted conditions, it must either reach an agreement with the plaintiff or move for a protective order under Rule 26(c). That request might ask that the plaintiff be limited in how the information could be used and distributed, or might ask that only the attorney and the expert witness be permitted to examine the Code.

EXAMPLE: When requesting a copy of the Code, the plaintiff does not specify the form in which the Code should be produced. What are Goggle's options for making the code available?

Analysis: Because the request did not specify the form, Goggle may choose either the form in which the Code is normally maintained or a form that is reasonably usable. Presumably, the code is normally maintained in an electronic format, but it may also be maintained in a paper format. If the Code is not normally maintained in paper format, then Goggle may produce it in paper format only if paper format would be reasonably usable to the plaintiff.

EXAMPLE: Goggle receives a request for inspection that asks for "all correspondence with actual or potential employees or independent contractors regarding the development of the Algorithm." The "Algorithm" is a term defined in the definitions. Goggle has letters in paper form, copies of drafts of the same letters on its computer system, emails with independent contractors, and records of communications with potential independent contractors from postings on an electronic bulletin board for computer contractors. Which, if any, of these documents must Goggle make available for inspection?

Analysis: Assuming that there are no instructions or definitions that bear on this request (other than the meaning of "Algorithm"), the issue turns on the interpretation of the term "correspondence." Although there is room for debate, a court would likely conclude that the paper letters and emails were correspondence, and might reasonably conclude that the bulletin board postings were too. They are certainly communications, and could be considered correspondence. Absent a request for drafts, the drafts of the letters are not likely correspondence, as they were not sent to anyone.

EXAMPLE: Goggle receives a request for all documents discussing, referring, or relating in any way to the issue of whether its Algorithm copies or infringes on the plaintiff's algorithm. Goggle has some memoranda and correspondence with an attorney who is a Goggle employee in the company's legal department. What should Goggle do in response to this request?

Analysis: The memoranda and correspondence with the in-house attorney are likely attorney-client privileged communications—the privilege extends to in-house counsel in the same manner as to outside counsel, assuming the in-house counsel are acting in a legal capacity. Goggle should serve a timely response to the request objecting to the request to the extent that it seeks documents protected by the attorney-client privilege. Goggle should produce any non-privileged responsive documents in its possession, custody, or control, and should list the privileged documents on a privilege log that it provides to the plaintiff.

EXAMPLE: Goggle receives a request to inspect any documents that Goggle gathered from the patent office before applying for a patent for its search Algorithm. Goggle objects that the request is unreasonably burdensome because the documents are equally available to the plaintiff and describes how Goggle did its search so that the plaintiff can check for itself. Is this a proper response?

Analysis: No. The plaintiff is entitled to know what documents Goggle reviewed, and Goggle is not relieved of its obligations to comply with a legitimate discovery request simply because the documents are available from another source.

EXAMPLE: Goggle receives a request to inspect documents relating to its patent application. Goggle provided a file to its patent attorney, who prepared and filed the application. Goggle did not maintain copies of the file it sent to its counsel, and did not receive a copy of the application. Can Goggle take the position that it does not have any responsive documents in its possession, custody, or control?

Analysis: Probably not. It is likely that any documents held by Goggle's counsel would be deemed in its control. The application and any documents that the attorney provided to the patent office would not be privileged or trial preparation material. Any internal memoranda or correspondence between Goggle and the attorney would likely be privileged, and could be withheld and listed on a privilege log.

D. Requests for Admission

Rule 36 establishes procedures for requests for admission.

THE RULE   Rule 36

Requests for Admission

(a) In General.

 (1) **Scope.** A party may **serve** on any other party a written request to admit, for purposes of the pending action only, the truth of any matters within the scope of Rule 26(b)(1) relating to:

   (A) facts, the application of law to fact, or opinions about either; and

   (B) the genuineness of any described documents. * * *

* * *

 (3) **Time to Respond; Effect of Not Responding. A matter is admitted unless**, within 30 days after being served, the party to whom the request is directed serves on the requesting party a written answer or objection addressed to the matter and signed by the party or its attorney.

* * *

(4) Answer. If a matter is not admitted, the answer must **specifically deny it** or **state in detail why the answering party cannot truthfully admit or deny it. A denial must fairly respond to the substance of the matter**; and when good faith requires that a party qualify an answer or deny only a part of a matter, the answer must specify the part admitted and qualify or deny the rest. The answering party may assert lack of knowledge or information as a reason for failing to admit or deny only if the party states that it has made reasonable inquiry and that the information it knows or can readily obtain is insufficient to enable it to admit or deny.

(b) Effect of an Admission; Withdrawing or Amending It. A matter admitted under this rule is **conclusively established** unless the court, on motion, permits the admission to be withdrawn or amended. * * * [T]he court may permit withdrawal or amendment if it would promote the presentation of the merits of the action and if the court is not persuaded that it would prejudice the requesting party in maintaining or defending the action on the merits. An admission under this rule is not an admission for any other purpose and cannot be used against the party in any other proceeding.

EXPLANATION

Requests for admission are statements that one party makes, and that the other party is obligated to admit or deny (or explain why the party cannot admit or deny). They can be an important tool in narrowing the disputed issues that need to be resolved at trial.

1. Requests to Admit

a. Scope of Request. As with interrogatories and document requests, the scope of requests for admission is tied to the scope of discovery generally in Rule 26(b). However, requests for admission are further limited to two areas:

- facts, the application of law to fact, or opinions about either; and

- the genuineness of any described documents.

i. Admissions as to Facts and Application of Law to Facts. The limitation to facts, the application of law to facts, or opinions about either parallels the similar provision about contention interrogatories. Thus, it is not proper to serve a request for admission relating to a pure legal conclusion (*e.g.*, admit that negligence has the following elements ...), but a mixture of law and fact is permissible (*e.g.*, admit that you were negligent when you failed to stop at the stop sign). Requests for admission typically are formatted like, and contain the same parts as, interrogatories, except that requests for admission include a place for the responding party to check whether it admits or denies the request.

ii. Admissions as to Document Authenticity. The purpose of seeking an admission of the genuineness of a document is to avoid having to lay an evidentiary foundation for the document at trial. In the absence of such an admission, it might be necessary to call a record custodian simply to authenticate the document.

> Under the evidence rules, "**authenticity**" and "**admissibility**" are two separate concepts, both of which must be satisfied before a document can be moved into evidence. Rule 36 requests typically go to authenticity, because admissibility often depends on the context in which a document is offered into evidence, and thus parties are generally reluctant to stipulate to admissibility in the abstract. In contrast, authenticity can typically be established by calling a record custodian to testify. When there is no genuine issue as to the authenticity of a document, it is a waste of everyone's time to call a record custodian, so parties often stipulate as to authenticity.

b. Service. Like most other discovery forms, requests for admission and responses are served on all other parties, but not filed with the court.

c. Time for Service . Like other written discovery, requests for admission may not be served before the parties have conducted their discovery conference under Rule 26(f) and must be served in sufficient time that the response is due before the discovery deadline.

d. Number of Requests. There is no limit on the number of requests for admission. If a party believes that an opponent has served an excessive number of requests for admission, the party must file a motion for a protective order, and the court will exercise its discretion to determine whether the requests are appropriate or abusive.

2. Responses to Requests

a. Time to Respond. Responses to requests for admission are due 30 days after service, unless the time period is changed by order of court or agreement of the parties. Failure to serve a timely, signed response results in an admission. Therefore, it is critical to file a timely response or obtain a timely extension—failure to do so can result in damaging admissions.

IN PRACTICE

The consequences of failing to respond timely to requests for admission are **extremely severe**. Having statements unintentionally deemed admitted can be harmful to a party's case and an attorney's career. Therefore, it is critical that attorneys promptly calendar the date for responding to requests for admission, and either serve the response or obtain an extension of time prior to the due date.

b. Response Options. A responding party has four choices in responding to a request for admission, which may be used individually or in combination:

i. **Admit the request;**

ii. **Deny the request**—a denial must respond to the substance of the matter, and may not sidestep the request or be evasive;

iii. **Object to the request**; or

iv. **Neither admit nor deny the request,** stating "in detail" the reason that the responding party can neither admit nor deny the request. If the reason for the lack of an admission or denial is lack of sufficient information, the responding party must state that after reasonable inquiry, the information the party knows or can readily obtain is insufficient to admit or deny.

c. Objections. Typical grounds for objections to requests for admission include an assertion that the request for admission: is vague and ambiguous; is not related to a claim or defense in the case; or calls for a pure legal conclusion. Rule 36(a)(5) specifically provides that it is not proper to object on the ground that the request presents a genuine issue for trial (outlawing an historic practice of making that objection). If there is an objection to part of a request, the responding party must specify the objectionable part and must respond to the remaining parts.

3. Effects of Admissions. A fact that is admitted under Rule 36 is "conclusively established." This means that a party cannot attempt to prove at trial that the fact is not correct. A Rule 36 admission is different from an **evidentiary admission**, which a party is free to attempt to disavow or explain away at trial (the admission comes into evidence and may be considered by the fact finder, but the admitting party is not precluded from attempting to prove a contrary fact).

> An **evidentiary admission** is typically an oral or written statement by the party. Such statements are excluded from the definition of hearsay, and typically are admitted into evidence.

EXAMPLES & ANALYSIS

EXAMPLE: In the Goggle example described above, Goggle receives this request for admission: "Admit that the Goggle search engine infringes on patent No. 9,999,999." Goggle objects on the grounds that the request goes to the ultimate issue to be resolved at trial, and is therefore inappropriate. Is this a proper objection?

Analysis: No. It is not grounds for objection that a request for admission addresses the ultimate issue to be resolved at trial. Rule 36 does prohibit requests that seek pure legal conclusions, but this request involves the application of fact to law.

> **EXAMPLE:** Goggle serves requests for admission, and does not receive a response. Should Goggle file a motion to compel a response or a motion for sanctions?

Analysis: Neither. Requests for admission are essentially self-policing—there is an automatic sanction for failing to respond: deemed admission. Goggle does not need to do anything.

> **EXAMPLE:** During discovery, Goggle's opponent admitted a request for admission that Goggle's search engine contains a fuzzy logic algorithm that is much more sophisticated than its competitor's. At trial, a witness for the opponent testifies that Goggle's fuzzy logic algorithm was similar to that of its competitor and did not contain any significant improvements or differences. What should Goggle do?

Analysis: Goggle should object to the testimony, and move to strike it. Admissions under Rule 36 are "conclusively established," and therefore cannot be contradicted by testimony at trial. If the opponent seeks to withdraw the admission, Goggle should oppose the motion on the grounds that it would be prejudiced by the late withdrawal, as it has planned its trial strategy assuming it could rely on the admission.

E. Depositions

Depositions implicate a number of the rules. Rule 30 contains the general provisions regarding the mechanics of the deposition proceeding. Rule 32 contains the provisions governing use of the deposition transcript at trial or in other proceedings. Rule 28, which we will not cover, addresses who may serve as the stenographer or otherwise administer the oath and record the deposition. Rule 27, which we will not cover, allows the taking of depositions when a case has not yet been commenced to perpetuate a witness's testimony. And Rule 31, which is rarely used and which we also will not cover, allows a party to conduct a deposition by written questions. Rule 45 governs subpoenas, which compel nonparties to attend depositions. We will start with Rule 30.

1. Procedures for Depositions: Rule 30

THE RULE   Rule 30

Depositions by Oral Examination

(a) When a Deposition May Be Taken.

(1) Without Leave. A party may, by oral questions, depose any person, including a party, without leave of court except as provided in Rule 30(a)**(2)**. The deponent's attendance may be compelled by subpoena under Rule 45.

(2) With Leave. A party must obtain leave of court, and the court must grant leave to the extent consistent with Rule 26(b)(2):

(A) if the parties have not stipulated to the deposition and:

   (i) the deposition would result in more than 10 depositions being taken under this rule or Rule 31 by the plaintiffs, or by the defendants, or by the third-party defendants;

   (ii) the deponent has already been deposed in the case; or

   (iii) the party seeks to take the deposition before the time specified in Rule 26(d), unless the party certifies in the notice, with supporting facts, that the deponent is expected to leave the United States and be unavailable for examination in this country after that time; or

(B) if the deponent is confined in prison.

* * *

(b)(6)Notice or Subpoena Directed to an Organization. In its notice or subpoena, a party may name as the deponent a public or private corporation, a partnership, an association, a governmental agency, or other entity and must describe with reasonable particularity the matters for examination. The named organization must then designate one or more officers, directors, or managing agents, or designate other persons who consent to testify on its behalf; and it may set out the matters on which each person designated will testify. A subpoena must advise a nonparty organization of its duty to make this designation. **The persons designated must testify about information known or reasonably available to the organization**. This paragraph **(6)** does not preclude a deposition by any other procedure allowed by these rules.

(c) Examination and Cross-Examination; Record of the Examination; Objections; Written Questions.

(1) *Examination and Cross-Examination.* The examination and cross-examination of a deponent proceed as they would at trial under the Federal Rules of Evidence, except Rules 103 and 615. After putting the deponent under oath or affirmation, the officer must record the testimony by the method designated under Rule 30(b)(3)(A). The testimony must be recorded by the officer personally or by a person acting in the presence and under the direction of the officer.

(2) Objections. An objection at the time of the examination—whether to evidence, to a party's conduct, to the officer's qualifications, to the manner of taking the deposition, or to any other aspect of the deposition—must be noted on the record, but the examination still proceeds; the testimony is taken subject to any objection. **An objection must be stated concisely in a nonargumentative and nonsuggestive manner**. A person may instruct a deponent not to answer only when necessary to preserve a privilege, to enforce a limitation ordered by the court, or to present a motion under Rule 30(d)(3).

* * *

EXPLANATION

1. Timing for Deposition. Like most discovery, depositions may be taken after the parties have conducted the discovery conference under Rule 26(f) and before the discovery deadline. These limits may be extended by motion or stipulation.

2. Limits on Depositions. Rule 30(a) establishes three limits on depositions. Leave of court or a stipulation by the parties is required to take:

a. More than ten depositions by each *side*. Note that this limitation is cumulative for each category of party, so that leave of court is required if the plaintiffs, defendants, third-party defendants, etc., want to take more than ten depositions;

b. A second deposition of the same person; or

c. The deposition of a person in prison (this requires a court order, even if the parties stipulate).

3. Deposition Notices. To initiate the deposition process, the party seeking to take the deposition serves a notice on all parties. The notice must specify the time and location of the deposition, the name and address (if known) of the witness, and the manner of recording.

IN PRACTICE

Typically, before noticing a deposition, a party will call or email opposing counsel and try to find a mutually convenient date. Alternatively, attorneys sometimes notice the deposition for a date that fits their schedule, but then adjust the date and send an amended notice if the selected date turns out to be inconvenient for another party. If the parties cannot agree, the party taking the deposition can notice it, and the opposing party's only recourse is a motion for a protective order under Rule 26(c).

4. Compelling Attendance. A deposition notice is sufficient to compel the attendance of a party. For a nonparty, a **subpoena** is necessary to compel attendance, and the deposition notice serves to put other parties on notice of the details of the deposition.

> A **subpoena** is a form of process that compels nonparties to appear to testify or to produce documents. Subpoenas are discussed in detail below.

5. Manner of Recording. The testimony at depositions is recorded in some fashion for future use. The party noticing the deposition can choose audio, audiovisual, or stenographic means of recording the deposition. Other parties may arrange for additional methods of recordation, but must give prior notice to the witness and all other parties.

IN PRACTICE

A stenographer is present at the vast majority of depositions. Videography is becoming more common, particularly when there is some question as to whether the witness will be available to testify at trial. In a video deposition, the camera focuses only on the witness, and the attorneys ask their questions and make objections off camera.

6. Cost of Recording. The party noticing the deposition must pay the costs of recording by the methods specified in the notice. Any party arranging for an additional method must pay the costs of that additional recording. The recording costs are separate from the costs of obtaining a copy of the recording. Thus, if the plaintiff notices a deposition and arranges for a stenographer to transcribe the deposition, the plaintiff pays the stenographer's fees. If the defendant wants a copy of the transcript, the defendant must pay for the copy.

7. Deposition Location. The rules do not specify where a deposition may occur. Generally, the party noticing the deposition picks the location and specifies it in the notice. If the opposing party disagrees with the location, it can (after trying to reach agreement) file a motion for a protective order, in which case the court has broad discretion to choose the location. Although there are no hard and fast rules, courts generally require plaintiffs to travel to the location of the jurisdiction (since they picked it) and allow defendants to be deposed at their place of business or residence. However, some courts are less sympathetic to complaints about travel from large corporations.

8. Who May Be Present. As a general rule, each party is entitled to have its attorney or attorneys present, and one party representative. Experts or others aiding counsel may also be present. Witnesses who have not yet been deposed can be "sequestered" or excluded.

9. Length of Depositions. A deposition is limited to one 7-hour day. This time limitation can be extended by agreement of counsel or upon motion to the court.

10. Telephone Depositions. Rule 30 authorizes depositions by "remote means," including by telephone. The court reporter or other officer administering the deposition will be present where the witness is located, and the deposition will be deemed to occur where the witness is located for purposes of enforcement and sanctions.

11. Depositions of Corporations. Rule 30(b)(6) contains procedures for taking the deposition of the designated representative of an organization like a corporation. This procedure was added to cure the inefficiencies and expense caused when a party notices the deposition of witness A, who defers the answer to certain questions to witness B, who then defers to witness C, and so on. Under the Rule 30(b)(6) procedure, a party can avoid having to serially depose one witness after another to find the right person, and can instead require the opposing party to designate a witness to present the collective information of the party on the designated topics.

> Attorneys commonly refer to the deposition of a representative of a corporation or other entity as a "**30(b)(6)**" deposition, and practitioners should be familiar with this term. Some state courts use the imprecise term "PMK" or "Person Most Knowledgeable" instead (but note that Rule 30(b)(6) requires a witness who is properly prepared, but need not be the most "knowledgeable").

The topics of the Rule 30(b)(6) deposition are typically attached as an exhibit to the deposition notice. The designated representative has an obligation to prepare for the deposition by gathering the corporation's information. This preparation often entails interviewing other witnesses and reviewing documents. There are consequences for presenting a representative who is not properly prepared, including having to present the witness a second time and paying for the noticing party's expenses for the second deposition.

The corporation can select the representative—thus, if the noticing party wants to depose a specific person, the party should notice the witness individually, not under Rule 30(b)(6). The representative need not be an officer, or even an employee, of the corporation, and need not be the most knowledgeable person. Rather, it must simply be a representative capable of presenting the corporation's collective knowledge. A party may designate more than one representative if it chooses.

The testimony of the designated representative is deemed the testimony of the corporation (and is thereby admissible as an admission of the party).

IN PRACTICE

The selection of the corporate representative is a very strategic decision, with the ability of the representative to present the testimony well and hold up under cross-examination being as important as the representative's personal involvement in the underlying events.

12. Manner of Examination. During the deposition, examination of the witness proceeds much like testimony at trial, with the party noticing the deposition asking questions first, and other parties having an opportunity to ask questions after the noticing party. Like at trial, parties adverse to the witness may ask **leading questions** and parties aligned with the witness are limited to non-leading questions.

> **"Leading questions"** are those that suggest the answer, often "yes" or "no" questions. At trial, leading questions are normally permitted only during cross-examination, but a party calling the witness may ask the court to declare the witness "hostile" and permit leading questions on direct examination.

IN PRACTICE

Although the attorney representing the witness or the witness's employer—the attorney "defending the deposition"—has the right to ask questions of the witness during the deposition, attorneys will rarely do so. The rationale is that if the witness is friendly and cooperative, the attorney can get testimony from the witness through an affidavit or at trial, and can learn information from the witness through an off-the-record conversation outside the hearing of opposing counsel. Exceptions to this rule of thumb are questions designed to correct inaccuracies in the witness's testimony or questioning when there is uncertainty as to whether the witness will be available at the time of trial.

13. Objections. Objections that can be cured by rephrasing the question must be stated at the deposition or they are waived. Objections that go to the substance or admissibility of the testimony need not be asserted, and are preserved until the time that a party seeks to introduce the testimony into the record.

Objections that must be asserted during the deposition are generally objections to the form of the question. This includes objections on the grounds that the question is leading (or suggests the answer), that the question is compound (includes two questions), that the question calls for speculation, that the question lacks foundation (assumes facts not in evidence), that the question is ambiguous or misleading, that the question mischaracterizes prior testimony, that the question is argumentative, and that the question calls for a legal conclusion.

Objections that are preserved and need not be asserted are those that cannot be cured by rephrasing the question, including objections on the grounds that the question calls for hearsay and that the question seeks irrelevant or inadmissible information.

Any attorney may make an objection to a question, even if the attorney does not represent the witness.

    a. Phrasing of Objections. Rule 30(c)(2) requires that objections be stated "concisely in a nonargumentataive and nonsuggestive manner." This means that the objection should articulate the grounds of the objection without suggesting the answer to the witness or disrupting the examination.

IN PRACTICE

Objections that violate this rule are often referred to as "speaking objections." For example, if the question to Walt is, "Why did Mark burn his house down," a properly phrased objection is "Objection, calls for speculation." A speaking objection might be, "Objection, calls for speculation. How is this witness supposed to know what was in Mark's head? Walt, you can respond if you know what Mark was thinking that night." This latter objection improperly coaches the witness as to the desired response—a dutiful, "I don't know what Mark was thinking."

564 • Learning Civil Procedure •

14. Testimony Following Objections. As a general rule, the witness will respond to the question after the objection is placed on the record. Then, at the time that a party seeks to use or introduce the testimony, the objecting party can ask the court to rule on the objection.

15. Instructions Not to Answer a Question. The circumstances in which an attorney may instruct a witness not to answer a question are EXTREME-LY LIMITED. An attorney is only allowed to instruct a witness not to answer a question in three circumstances:

   a. To preserve a privilege (because to answer would disclose the privileged information);

   b. To enforce a limitation on the scope of the deposition ordered by the court pursuant to a protective order under Rule 26(c); or

   c. To suspend the deposition to seek a court order terminating or limiting the deposition.

An instruction to a witness not to answer a question in any other circumstance is improper and subjects the attorney to potential sanctions. Thus, for example, it is improper to instruct a witness not to answer a question because the question has been asked and answered, because the question is harassing, because the information sought is irrelevant, or because the question seeks a legal opinion or an expert opinion. Furthermore, an attorney who does not represent the witness may not instruct the witness not to answer a question.

A motion to terminate a deposition may be based on the ground that it is being conducted in bad faith or in a manner that *unreasonably* annoys, embarrasses, or oppresses the deponent or party. Rule 30(d) authorizes the court to impose sanctions against any party who "impedes, delays, or frustrates the fair examination of the deponent."

IN PRACTICE

Instructions not to answer deposition questions on grounds other than privilege should be extremely rare. However, this is a rule that is often abused in practice, as attorneys often instruct witnesses not to answer questions in contravention of this rule. Many judges are willing to get on the phone to answer important questions that arise during a deposition. Thus, if the party defending the deposition believes that a line of questioning crosses the line, the parties can suspend the deposition and place a call to the court. Sometimes, the threat of such action will persuade the questioning attorney to move on.

Motions to terminate a deposition are also extremely rare. Such a motion should be brought only when the questioning is truly abusive or improper.

16. Review by the Witness. After a deposition, the witness has 30 days to review the transcript and make any necessary changes. These changes are denoted on an "errata sheet," which is signed by the witness.

The most common, and least controversial, changes, are corrections of typos or mistranscriptions, where the witness is asserting that the stenographer did not accurately capture the witness's testimony. However, substantive changes are also authorized—"I said the light was green in the deposition, but really it was red." When a witness makes substantive changes, the parties can generally recall the witness to take further deposition testimony regarding the reason for the change. At trial or any subsequent hearing, the witness can be impeached with the original testimony.

EXAMPLES & ANALYSIS

EXAMPLE: Pat sues Doug (a reporter) and the Daily News for defamation, because Doug wrote an op-ed column in the Daily News saying that Pat was abusive toward her children. Pat claims that she was fired as a result of the article. Doug wants to take the deposition of Pat's boss, Betty, and sends a deposition notice. Pat objects because Betty is not a party to the litigation. Does Pat's objection prevent the deposition from going forward?

Analysis: No. An objection by the party does not prevent the deposition from going forward. Rather, a motion for protective order is in the proper mechanism for preventing a deposition. Furthermore, the objection is not well-founded—Rule 30 authorizes depositions of "any person, including a party." However, because Betty is not a party, Doug will have to subpoena her in order to compel her attendance.

EXAMPLE: Doug also wants to take the deposition of Pat's co-worker, Carl. Doug learns that Carl is about to transfer to the company's London office, and will be very difficult to depose, so Doug sends a deposition notice scheduling the deposition for two days later. Pat does not believe that this is fair or reasonable. What can Pat do?

Analysis: Assuming Pat cannot work anything out informally with Doug, Pat's only recourse is to file a motion for a protective order. Rule 30 does not specify the amount of notice required, instead stating that notice must be "reasonable." The reasonableness of the notice depends on the circumstances. If Carl will be unavailable in the near future, then a much shorter notice period would likely be deemed reasonable.

EXAMPLE: When Pat deposes Carl, Carl's testimony is inconsistent with Betty's. Doug wants to depose Betty again to hear her explanation of the inconsistency. May Doug depose Betty again on the limited topic of this new evidence?

Analysis: Rule 30 only allows a person to be deposed one time without leave of court. If Doug believes a second deposition of Betty is important, then unless Pat consents, his only recourse is to file a motion for leave to take Betty's deposition a second time. The court would have discretion to allow or deny this request, balancing Doug's need and the burden on Pat and Betty.

EXAMPLE: Pat serves a deposition notice on the Daily News, asking it to designate a representative to testify regarding Doug's fact-checking, the basis for the allegations in Doug's column, past incidents where allegations were raised regarding the accuracy of Doug's columns, the paper's policies regarding sources and fact-checking, and review of the article by the paper's editorial staff. The Daily News does not have any single representative who can testify to all of these topics. What should the Daily News do?

Analysis: The Daily News can either designate more than one representative or it can pick one representative and have that individual gather and present the newspaper's collective information on all the topics. The information presented by the company representative does not need to be based on first-hand knowledge.

EXAMPLE: During Pat's deposition, Doug's attorney asks her a question. She gives an answer that Doug's attorney considers evasive, so he asks the question again, with slight rephrasing. Pat's attorney objects on the grounds that the question has been "asked and answered," but allows Pat to respond. Doug's attorney still considers the answer evasive, so he asks the question a third time. Pat's attorney objects again that the question has been asked and answered, and this time instructs Pat not to answer and Doug's attorney to "move on." Evaluate Pat's attorney's conduct.

Analysis: Pat's attorney is wrong across the board. "Asked and answered" is not a proper objection at a deposition (although it might succeed at trial)—an attorney can ask a question multiple times. And the instruction not to answer is also improper—Rule 30(d) limits the circumstances where an attorney can instruct a witness not to answer a question to three limited circumstances, none of which is present in this example. If Pat's attorney believes that the questioning has become abusive, her recourse is to suspend the deposition to seek a protective order, not to instruct Pat not to answer the questions.

EXAMPLE: During Pat's deposition, Doug's attorney asks Pat what explanation her boss, Betty, gave her regarding the reason she was fired. Assume that this testimony is hearsay. Should Pat's attorney object and/or instruct Pat not to respond?

Analysis: Pat's attorney does not need to object, and may not instruct her not to answer. The only objections that must be stated during a deposition are those that go to the form of the question—objections like relevance or hearsay may be made at the time the evidence is presented to the court. The attorney may not instruct Pat not to answer because this situation does not meet the limited criteria under Rule 30(d).

2. Use of Depositions: Rule 32

Once a deposition has been conducted and the testimony transcribed or recorded, the next question is how may the parties use the transcript or recording. Rule 32 answers that question. Deposition testimony may be used if it meets all three of the following criteria:

- **Representation at the Deposition**—A deposition transcript may only be used against a party who was either represented at the deposition or had an opportunity to be represented (in other words, if a party receives a deposition notice, the party cannot prevent use of the deposition by failing to appear);

- **Rules of Evidence**—to be admitted into evidence, deposition testimony must also be relevant and otherwise admissible under the Federal Rules of Evidence. Essentially, the effect of Rule 32 is to make it as if the witness were present in court and testifying, eliminating certain hearsay objections;

- **Rule 32 Criteria**—the deposition testimony must qualify under Rules 32(a)(2) through (8), which list conditions for admission that vary depending on whether the testimony is to be used for impeachment purposes (*i.e.*, to contradict the witness's testimony at trial) or as substantive evidence (*i.e.*, to prove a fact relevant to a claim or defense), as discussed below.

a. Use for Impeachment

A party may always use a deposition transcript for impeachment purposes.

b. Use for Substantive Evidence

A party may use a deposition transcript as substantive evidence (to help prove a fact at trial) in the following circumstances:

- **Party witness**—the deposition of a party is admissible against that party as substantive evidence.

- **Unavailable witness**—a party may use the deposition of a witness as substantive evidence if the witness is not available to testify live. Circumstances that render a witness unavailable are:

  1. The witness is dead;

  2. The witness is more than 100 miles from the place of hearing or trial or is outside the United States, unless the party offering the testimony caused the witness to be absent;

  3. The witness is unable to appear because of age, illness, infirmity, or imprisonment;

  4. The party offering the testimony could not obtain the witness's attendance by subpoena; or

  5. On motion, if the court finds that exceptional circumstances exist warranting admission of the testimony, taking into account the preference for live testimony.

c. Use of Part of a Deposition

A party may offer a portion of the deposition transcript. In that case, an adverse party can require the offering party to introduce other parts that, in fairness, should be considered with the part introduced. Additionally any other parties may introduce any other parts during their case.

Note the timing distinction. If a party attempts to introduce a portion of a transcript that is taken out of context, adverse parties can require that the portions necessary to supply the context are introduced right then, without waiting for their turn to introduce evidence, **an exception to the general rule**. If the additional testimony in question is not supplying context, then other parties may still introduce it, but must wait until their turn to examine the witness.

> Normally, while one party is examining a witness, other parties can object to questions, answers, and exhibits, but must wait until their turn to cross-examine the witness (after the first attorney finishes questioning the witness) to ask their own questions or introduce exhibits. This provision is an **exception to that general rule**.

d. Rulings on Objections

At the time that deposition testimony is offered, a party may ask the judge to rule on any objection that has not been waived. In general, the court will use the standard it would apply if the witness were present and testifying live.

IN PRACTICE

Often, the court will set a deadline shortly before trial for the designation of deposition testimony that the parties intend to offer at trial for other than impeachment purposes. Other parties can then counter-designate additional portions and identify objections to the offered testimony.

Depositions are typically transcribed on pages with numbered lines, so the designations typically list both the page and line numbers (*e.g.*, Smith Deposition, 12:5-13:2).

EXAMPLES & ANALYSIS

EXAMPLE: Pascal commissions Deter to prepare a website for his landscaping business. After the website goes live, Pascal encounters a number of problems with the site, including slow-loading of pages, non-working links, and crashes. Pascal sues Deter for breach of contract. During discovery, Pascal deposes a potential customer, Wendy, who was considering hiring Pascal and visited his website as part of her diligence. At trial, Wendy testifies that the website did not affect her decision to hire a different landscaper, which is different from her deposition testimony. Pascal seeks to introduce the deposition testimony, and Deter objects that the rules favor live testimony for a witness who is not "unavailable." Who is correct?

Analysis: Pascal is correct. This would be classic impeachment testimony, which is admissible even if the witness is present.

EXAMPLE: Pascal also seeks to introduce Wendy's testimony that when she clicked on various links, some did not work and others directed her to the wrong content. Deter again objects. Who is correct?

Analysis: Deter is correct this time. Pascal is seeking to introduce Wendy's testimony as part of his proof that the links did not work. Use of deposition testimony for substantive purposes is only allowed if the witness is a party or is unavailable. Wendy is not a party and is present at the trial, so her deposition testimony may not be used except for impeachment.

EXAMPLE: Deter seeks to introduce the testimony of another customer, Wanda, who hired Pascal after reviewing his website. She testified at her deposition that the website worked properly when she visited it, and that it had some influence on her decision to hire Pascal. Wanda lived nearby when she was deposed, but moved across the country before trial. May Deter introduce Wanda's testimony as substantive evidence?

Analysis: Yes. Wanda's availability is measured at the time of trial, not at the time of the deposition. Because she lived more than 100 miles from the courthouse at the time of trial, Deter may use her deposition for any purpose.

3. Depositions to Perpetuate Testimony: Rule 27

Occasionally, there is a need to preserve the testimony of a witness, but an action has not been, and cannot be, commenced so that the deposition can be conducted as part of normal discovery. In such circumstances, Rule 27 allows a party to preserve the testimony by deposition. Rule 27 requires a verified petition setting forth the circumstances that satisfy the Rule's criteria. Depositions under Rule 27 are relatively infrequent.

4. Subpoenas: Rule 45

The discovery rules discussed so far pertain to discovery from parties. A nonparty is not required to answer interrogatories or document requests or to appear in response to a deposition notice. Instead, a subpoena provides the means for obtaining discovery or testimony from a nonparty.

Subpoenas may only compel two types of activity—testimony (at a deposition or at trial) and **inspection of documents** or things (analogous in scope to a request to inspect under Rule 34). These two activities can be combined—a subpoena can compel a witness to appear for a deposition and bring the documents specified in the attached listing.

> A subpoena compelling the **inspection of documents** is sometimes referred to as a "subpoena duces tecum."

EXAMPLES & ANALYSIS

EXAMPLE: Perry has sued Dilys for negligence in connection with a car accident. Perry believes that Wanda witnessed the accident. Perry serves a subpoena on Wanda to attend a deposition and to answer the attached requests for admission. Is Perry's subpoena proper?

Analysis: No. The part requiring attendance at the deposition is fine, but subpoenas cannot be used to compel a witness to respond to requests for admission or interrogatories.

a. Procedures. Attorneys issue subpoenas simply by preparing and signing the form—no motion or involvement of the court is necessary. The subpoena must issue from the court where the case is pending. Generally, there are printed subpoena forms available that have all the required content and language.

IN PRACTICE

Because the attorney issues the subpoena without court involvement, the choice of court issue simply means that the attorney must use the subpoena form from the correct court.

b. Geographic Limitations. A subpoena for attendance at a deposition or production of documents may not require a witness to travel more than 100 miles from the place where the witness resides, is employed, or regularly transacts business in person. A subpoena for testimony at trial may also require a witness to travel from anywhere within the state where the trial will occur.

c. Notice. Rule 45 does not set a specific amount of notice that the party serving the subpoena must provide to the recipient, but rather requires "reasonable" time to comply. The amount of time that is reasonable depends on the circumstances, and is ultimately up to the discretion of the judge.

Rule 45 does require that a party issuing a subpoena for the inspection of documents serve the subpoena on other parties before serving it on the recipient, to allow opposing parties an opportunity to object to or move to quash the subpoena (when, for example, the subpoena seeks privileged or confidential information).

d. Witness Fees. The party serving a subpoena must also tender along with the subpoena the statutory fees for one day's attendance and the mileage allowed by law. Note that the attendance fee is quite small, and does not begin to compensate a witness for his or her time.

e. Duty to Avoid Undue Burden or Expense . Rule 45(d) imposes a duty on the party or attorney issuing a subpoena to take reasonable steps to avoid undue burden or expense to the party receiving the subpoena.

f. Electronically Stored Information. The provisions in Rule 45 governing inspection of ESI are similar to those in Rule 34, but Rule 45(e)(1)(D) contains an extra protection. It provides that the person responding to a subpoena does not need to provide ESI from sources that are not reasonably accessible because of undue burden or cost. An example might be

ESI that is only located on backup tapes from a legacy system that would be time-consuming and expensive to restore and search. If the responding party asserts this provision, the party issuing the subpoena can move for an order compelling production, in which case the court can order production, but also can order the party issuing the subpoena to pay the costs of producing the ESI.

g. Objections. Rule 45(d) provides the recipient with the right to object to the subpoena. This objection can be in the form of a simple letter stating that the witness objects. The objection relieves the recipient of the obligation to comply, and shifts the burden to the party issuing the subpoena to seek an order compelling the witness to comply.

h. Contempt. A subpoena is the equivalent of a court order, and the court may hold a person in contempt who fails to obey a subpoena without adequate cause.

EXAMPLES & ANALYSIS

EXAMPLE: Penelope sues her former employer, Diamond Software Development Corp., for gender discrimination. She wants to take the deposition of her former boss, Will, who is a mid-level manager. Should she send a deposition notice to Diamond, a subpoena to Will, both, or neither?

Analysis: Both. Because Will is not an officer, director, or control person at Diamond, Penelope must subpoena him to compel his attendance—a deposition notice would not be sufficient. But Penelope must also serve a deposition notice on all parties in advance of taking a deposition.

EXAMPLE: Penelope believes that Diamond is also interfering with her efforts to obtain a new position, and believes that Diamond sent harmful emails to Trident Software Development, where Penelope applied for a job. Penelope sends a subpoena to Trident asking for all emails to and from Diamond mentioning her. Trident has deleted all such emails from its server. It could likely locate copies on backup tapes, but it would be very time-consuming to try to find the relevant emails. What are Trident and Penelope's rights and options, and how would a court likely rule?

Analysis: Trident should send a letter objection, citing the provision in Rule 45 that protects a subpoena recipient from producing ESI that is not reasonably accessible because of undue burden and cost. Penelope will then have the option of filing a motion to compel compliance with the subpoena. If the court is persuaded that the emails are important, it would likely order Trident to gather them, and Penelope to pay Trident's reasonable costs in doing so.

F. Physical and Mental Examinations: Rule 35

Rule 35 authorizes a party to obtain an examination of an individual whose mental or physical condition is at issue. Unless the parties agree, a motion and court order is necessary to obtain the examination, unlike most discovery which is available without court involvement. Note that this rule only pertains to the examination of people—recall that examination of property, equipment, and other tangible things occurs under Rule 34.

1. Condition in Controversy. In order to obtain an examination, the condition of the witness must be "in controversy." If the plaintiff is claiming a back injury, the application of this requirement is straightforward. It becomes somewhat trickier when a party seeks a mental examination of the opposing party. If the plaintiff includes a routine emotional distress claim as part of a tort claim, the courts are divided as to whether an examination is available.

2. Who Conducts the Examination. The party moving for the examination gets to pick the examiner, as long as the examiner is licensed or certified. The responding party may challenge the examiner, in which case the court will evaluate the appropriateness of the examiner.

3. The Report. The examiner must prepare a written report. Upon request by opposing parties or the person examined, the party requesting the report must provide a copy of the report, and all other reports pertaining to the same condition. After delivering these reports, the party who had obtained the examination may then request all copies of reports pertaining to the same condition from the party who was ordered to submit to the examination.

EXAMPLE: Paris claims that she suffers from severe anxiety attacks since taking medication manufactured by Drugs R Us. Drugs seeks to have a psychologist examine Paris to determine if her condition was pre-existing or had a different etiology. Will a judge allow this examination even though it is designed to establish a defense, not a claim?

Analysis: Yes, a judge would likely allow this examination. Paris's mental condition is at issue, and it does not matter whether the examination is designed to establish a claim or defense, as long as the condition is at issue in the case.

G. Expert Disclosures: Rule 26(a)(2)

Rule 26(a)(2) requires each party to disclose the identity of any witness it may use at trial to present expert testimony. In addition, it requires most experts to produce a written expert report.

1. Timing. Unless the court sets a different deadline, the parties must make expert disclosures at least 90 days prior to the trial. Rebuttal experts may be disclosed within 30 days of the other party's disclosure. Typically, however, the court sets the dates for expert disclosures.

2. Expert Reports. Any witness who is either retained to testify or who is specially employed to testify must produce a written, signed expert report containing the following information:

- A complete statement of all opinions the expert will express and the basis and reasons for the opinions;

- The facts or data that the expert considered in forming the opinions;

- Any exhibits the expert will use;

- The expert's qualifications, including a list of all publications from the prior ten years;

- A list of all cases in which the expert testified at trial or in deposition during the previous four years; and

- A statement of the compensation that the expert will receive for the testimony.

3. Witnesses Not Required to Produce Reports. If an expert witness is not retained or specially employed to testify, then the party intending to call the witness does not need to disclose an expert report, and instead must disclose:

- The subject matter on which the witness is expected to testify; and

- A summary of the facts and opinions to which the witness is expected to testify.

EXAMPLES & ANALYSIS

EXAMPLE: Patil sues Douglas for negligence in connection with a car accident. Patil plans to call Dr. Wilson, his treating physician, to testify as to the permanent nature of his injuries and his painful procedures. What are Patil's disclosure obligations?

Analysis: Dr. Wilson is an expert, but not someone who Patil retained or specially employed. Therefore, Patil must disclose his identity and the subject matter, facts, and opinions of Dr. Wilson's expected testimony, but does not need to disclose a written report for Dr. Wilson.

EXAMPLE: Patil also intends to call Ward, a NASCAR driver who happened to be on the corner and saw the accident. Patil wants Ward to testify as to his observations of the accident. What are Patil's disclosure obligations?

Analysis: Although Ward has sufficient expertise that he would likely be qualified as an expert, he is really being called as a fact or "percipient" witness. Therefore, Patil likely does not have any expert witness disclosure obligation with respect to Ward.

EXAMPLE: Patil also sues Dynamo, which manufactured a metal part that failed during the accident, claiming that the metal was faulty. Dynamo employs Wanda, a metallurgist, who regularly testifies when Dynamo is sued. What are Dynamo's disclosure obligations?

Analysis: Wanda is a classic example of a witness who is specially employed to testify—testifying is a regular part of her duties. Therefore, Dynamo must disclose her identity and a written expert report.

H. Pretrial Disclosures: Rule 26(a)(3)

Rule 26(a)(3) requires the parties to disclose the identity of any witness, deposition testimony, and documents or exhibits it may use at trial.

1. Timing. Unless the court sets a different deadline, the parties must make the pretrial disclosures at least 30 days prior to the trial. Other parties then have 14 days after receiving the pretrial disclosures to serve and file objections to the testimony or evidence in the disclosing party's disclosure. Typically, however, the court sets the dates for pretrial disclosures.

2. Evidence a Party "May" Use. Rule 26(a)(3) requires the disclosing party to specify which witnesses or documents it "expects" to offer and which it "may" offer "if the need arises." This is an attempt to ameliorate the effects of the practice of listing every witness and document in order to avoid the risk of later being denied leave to use a witness or document not listed.

3. Failure to Disclose. As with the other automatic disclosures under Rule 26(a), the consequence of failing to disclose a witness, document, or deposition testimony is that the party will not normally be able to use that evidence at trial except for impeachment purposes.

IN PRACTICE

Written discovery, and in particular the document production process, can be enormously time-consuming and expensive. Therefore, it is important to be thoughtful and to plan carefully before you embark on written discovery, rather than making it up as you go along. Interrogatories, for example, are an effective tool for identifying witnesses and very specific pieces of information. Because the answers are drafted by opposing counsel, however, they are often carefully worded to convey only a small amount of generic information. Therefore, depositions are a better tool for obtaining helpful concessions and pinning down the other side's story.

The explosion of electronically generated and stored information has focused much of the discovery process on ESI. When the party is a large corporation, gathering and producing ESI is even more difficult, as the individuals likely to have discoverable information may be spread among different offices, using different servers, each with their own laptops, PDAs, portable storage devices, and other potential repositories for ESI. Once these record custodians have been identified, parties typically use search terms to identify potentially relevant documents from their files—the quantity of data is often simply too great to review each document individually. Parties sometimes agree on search terms in advance, in order to avoid disputes down the road and to avoid the risk of having to repeat the process if the court deems the original search inadequate.

Once the ESI has been collected, it must be reviewed for privilege and responsiveness. For privilege review, parties often conduct electronic searches using the names of in-house and outside attorneys and words like "privileged," "attorney," and "legal." Documents identified by the searches then need to be individually reviewed, and the privileged ones need to be logged on a privilege log.

The drafting process is important in discovery. When drafting discovery requests, you should be very precise in the wording, so that your opponent cannot avoid answering by objecting to ambiguities or loose language, and so that you ensure to the extent possible that you receive the information you are seeking. When drafting responses, you should be clear in what you are or are not providing in response. Thus, if you object to a discovery request as overly broad in time and you intend to produce information for a more limited period of time, make sure the response clearly states what information is being produced. That way, a court might order you to produce a greater scope of information, but will not sanction you for misleading your opponent or the court.

Similarly, when responding to discovery requests, there is a great temptation to read the requests very carefully to see if there is a construction of the words that allows you to deem damaging documents to be not responsive to the requests. While you have an obligation to represent your clients zealously, at the same time you cannot represent your clients effectively if you lose your credibility with the court. Therefore, before concluding that you can withhold a damaging document as non-responsive based on a tortured reading of the request, you should consider how your conduct will be perceived if you are in court one day explaining to the judge why you deemed it appropriate to withhold the document. If that prospect makes you cringe, you should probably produce the document.

While interrogatories and document requests are used in almost every case that proceeds past Rule 12 motions, requests for admission are not nearly as common, and are likely underutilized. Requests for admission can be powerful tools, either leading to helpful concessions and/or streamlining the case for trial.

Because depositions allow an attorney to ask questions directly to the opposing party and its witnesses, without advanced notice of the specific questions and time to prepare the answers and without the opposing counsel filtering or writing the responses, depositions can be an extremely important discovery tool. Before taking depositions, therefore, you will want to carefully plan what you hope to achieve in each deposition.

The obvious objective is to obtain all of the information held by the witness, so you can use the helpful information, strategize as to how to deal with the unfavorable information, and avoid surprises at trial. But your preparation should go beyond merely trying to obtain all of the witness's information.

Before you conduct depositions, you should have completed your discovery plan, and should have thought through where you will get the evidence you will need to establish each element of your claims or defenses. One of your objectives in a deposition may be to develop certain evidence to support one of your claims or defenses. You may also want to set up grounds for a motion for summary judgment or other planned motion.

Defending depositions is also challenging. It can take great concentration to participate in a deposition that lasts for seven hours, where the defending attorney's primary role is to listen to each question and object appropriately. Some discretion is also required. For example, "Where did you go to high school and college?" may technically be a compound question, but you don't look very good making that objection. It is better to save your objections for questions that matter, as you lose some credibility if you object too often. It is also important to learn how to make your objections in a non-suggestive or coaching manner. While it is tempting to guide your witness to the proper response, it can also get you in trouble with the court.

Subpoenas are also powerful tools in the discovery process, and are necessary whenever you need a nonparty's documents or testimony. Even when a nonparty is cooperative, and states that he or she will appear for a deposition, it is preferable to send a subpoena anyway. If the nonparty fails to appear and you have not issued a subpoena then you are potentially at some risk, whereas if you served a subpoena, then you are protected and the nonparty is at risk for contempt sanctions.

Although Rule 35 requires a motion to conduct an examination, most often, it is obvious when a Rule 35 examination is appropriate and the parties can work out the details cooperatively. The most common dispute concerns who may be present during the examination.

ADDITIONAL EXERCISES

A. Drafting Exercise—Drafting Discovery

1. Using the fact pattern from the complaint-drafting exercise involving Department Store and the sample complaint provided by your professor, draft three interrogatories, three document requests, and three requests for admission. These should be substantive discovery requests related to the specific facts of the case, not generic requests like "identify the witnesses you plan to call at trial" or "identify the documents you plan to use at trial." Think carefully about language, and try to draft requests that will not draw objections. You do not need to draft an instruction or definition section, but be sure to include a definition for any terms in your requests that require a definition.

2. Exchange electronic copies of your requests with another student in the class, as instructed by your professor. Draft responses to the document requests, interposing objections as appropriate and making substantive responses where appropriate (making up the facts necessary to respond where they are not specified in the book). Serve your responses on both the drafter of the discovery and your professor.

B. Evaluate Sample Discovery

Your professor may make available for you a sample set of discovery requests and responses to illustrate the typical format and the process. These discovery documents pertain to the fact pattern from the complaint-drafting exercise involving Department Store and the sample complaint provided by your professor. *Be prepared to discuss the following questions that relate to the sample discovery:*

1. What is the purpose of the instructions and definitions? What is the purpose of the general objections?

2. What would happen if the instructions required responses within 20 days? Is there a better mechanism to get quick responses?

3. Why did Department Store add the language to its response to Interrogatory No. 2 that states, "By way of further response, Department Store does not have a complete list of all employees, contractors, and representatives who were present at the 17th Street Store between 4:30 p.m. and 6:00 p.m. on the date referred to in paragraph 6 of the Complaint."?

4. Look at the response to Interrogatory No. 3. Do you agree with Department Store's objection? Is the objection necessary? Does Department Store answer the question as phrased? Is Department Store's answer fair?

5. Look at the response to Interrogatory No. 4. Do you agree with Department Store's objections? Why does Department Store include the language, "Without waiving its objections"? Does Department Store answer the question fully? Is Department Store's response proper under Rule 33? Is it fair?

6. Look at the response to Interrogatory No. 5. Is Department Store's response proper under Rule 33? Why did Department Store answer in that fashion?

7. Look at the response to Interrogatory No. 6. Does Department Store answer the question as phrased? What should Doe do if dissatisfied with the response?

8. Look at the response to Interrogatory No. 7. Why did Department Store answer in that fashion?

9. Look at the responses to Interrogatory No. 8. What kind of interrogatory is this? Do you agree with Department Store's objection?

10. In response to Interrogatory No. 9, Department Store admitted that its employees detained Doe. In response to Request for Admission No. 3, Department Store also admitted that its employees had detained Doe. Is there a difference in the effectiveness or permanence of these two admissions?

11. Look at Request to Inspect No. 1. Would you object to this request? Why or why not?

12. Look at Request to Inspect No. 2. Is this all Department Store needs to do to withhold its privileged documents?

13. Look at Request to Inspect No. 3. Is it proper to request a sample of the receipt paper and ink?

14. Look at the response to Request to Inspect No. 8. Is that a proper objection/response?

15. Look at the responses to Requests for Admission Nos. 1 and 2. Would you admit or deny these? What are the consequences of each option?

16. Department Store did not admit or deny Requests for Admission Nos. 4 or 5. Is this okay? Why or why not?

Example: Petroleum Exploration Network, Inc. (PEN) enters into a joint venture agreement (JVA) with Development of Resources, Inc. (DOR), pursuant to which PEN will drill exploratory and producing natural gas wells on acreage where DOR holds the lease rights. In the course of performance of this contract, issues arise regarding DOR's title to certain of the acreage covered by the JVA and the effect of these issues on PEN's drilling obligations. The following issues arise during discovery:

1. PEN wants to take the deposition of the president of DOR. *Should PEN use Rule 30(b)(6), which allows the deposition of a corporate representative?*

2. DOR wants to video-record the deposition of its president, but PEN states in the notice that it will be recorded by stenographer. *May DOR arrange for a videographer, and if so, how?*

3. During the deposition of DOR's president, PEN's attorney asks her what her religion is. Assume this has absolutely no bearing on the claims in the case. *What are the options for DOR's attorney, and may DOR's attorney instruct the president not to answer the question?*

4. DOR wants to take the deposition of PEN's president, and serves a deposition notice for a date ten days later. *What are PEN's options if the date is not convenient for its president?*

5. During the deposition of PEN's president, DOR's attorney asks PEN's president about conversations with PEN's in-house attorney. *What are the options for PEN's attorney, and may PEN's attorney instruct the president not to answer the question?*

6. DOR sends PEN a deposition notice under Rule 30(b)(6) asking PEN to designate a representative to testify about seven topics. Four of the topics relate to activities performed by PEN's land department in investigating the title issues related to the acreage at issue, and three of the topics relate to operational issues concerning the drilling of the acreage. PEN does not have any individual who can testify about all of the topics. **What are PEN's choices? What should PEN do if it believes that a former employee is the best person to testify regarding the title issues?**

7. At trial, DOR offers testimony from a deposition of PEN's president. PEN's attorney argues that the testimony cannot be admitted for substantive purposes because PEN's president is not "unavailable." **Will the court admit the testimony?**

8. PEN's attorney feels that DOR's attorney offered a misleading excerpt of a deposition. **What are his options?**

9. PEN's attorney wants to take the deposition of a low level employee of DOR, William. **What documents must PEN issue and serve in order to take William's deposition?**

10. DOR's attorney was very nervous about how William would testify, but to DOR's attorney's gratification, William does very well and DOR wants to use his testimony at trial. Concerned that William will not do as well the second time, DOR sends him to a job site in another state. DOR then offers William's testimony as substantive evidence, contending that he is unavailable because he is more than 100 miles from the place of trial. PEN's attorney wants to object. **Does she have a good objection, and how would a court likely rule?**

11. DOR's attorney wants to take the deposition of another employee, Erica. Erica works at PEN's office that is located in another state (California) hundreds of miles away. **Can DOR compel Erica's attendance at the deposition by subpoena, and if so, how? Can DOR compel Erica's testimony at the trial?**

12. DOR's attorney takes the deposition of another PEN employee, Wendy. At trial, Wendy gives testimony that is different from her testimony at the deposition. DOR's attorney wants to use the deposition transcript, but PEN's attorney objects that Wendy is not a

party and is available to testify (in fact, she is on the witness stand). *Will the court allow DOR's attorney to use the transcript at trial?*

13. PEN's attorney wants to take the deposition of a nonparty witness, Walter. Walter lives in New Mexico and the case is proceeding in Colorado. PEN's subpoena commands Walter to appear for a deposition in Colorado. *What should Walter do if he does not want to travel to Colorado? What are PEN's options?*

14. PEN wants its surveyor to come onto the land in question to conduct a survey. *Can PEN use Rule 35 to obtain the right to have this examination occur?*

Quick Summary

- **Interrogatories are governed by Rule 33.**

    · A party is limited to 25 interrogatories to any other party.

    · Interrogatories may seek facts or the application of law to fact (often referred to as "contention interrogatories"), but may not seek pure conclusions of law.

    · Otherwise, the scope is governed by Rule 26(b).

    · Answers are due within 30 days. Extensions are common, but should be documented before the 30 days expires, because failure to respond timely results in waiver of objections.

    · Answers must be verified.

- **Requests to inspect (or document requests) are governed by Rule 34.**

    · A party may serve an unlimited number of document requests. The scope is governed by Rule 26(b).

    · Like interrogatories, answers are due within 30 days, and extensions are common, but should be documented before the 30 days expire.

    · The responding party should provide a privilege log for any documents withheld on the basis of privilege.

    · The responding party may provide copies of responsive documents or may make them available for inspection by the requesting party, who may arrange for copies.

· If part of a document request is objectionable, the responding party must answer the non-objectionable parts.

• **Requests for admission are governed by Rule 36.**

· A party may serve an unlimited number of requests for admission.

· Responses are due in 30 days, and unanswered requests are deemed admitted.

· An admission may only be withdrawn or modified by motion.

· Admissions are considered evidentiary admissions, and may not be controverted at trial (except by motion to withdraw or amend).

· In order to decline to admit or deny based on lack of knowledge, a party must state that it has first conducted a reasonable investigation.

• **The procedures for depositions are set forth in Rule 30.**

· Each side is limited to 10 depositions.

· Each deposition is limited to one day of 7 hours.

· Rule 30(b)(6) allows a party to notice the deposition of a corporation on designated topics, and the corporation must then designate a representative and prepare the representative to testify to the party's collective information.

· The party noticing the deposition picks the manner of recording, and then other parties may select additional methods.

- Mental and Physical examinations are conducted under Rule 35.

  · Unlike most other discovery, a party may not obtain a mental or physical examination simply by serving a request, but instead must seek a court order.

  · The primary requirement for an examination is that the condition to be examined be in controversy in the litigation.

  · The examiner will prepare a report. The person examined or other parties can demand a copy of the report, and generally all other reports for the same condition will then be exchanged.

14

Enforcing Discovery Rights

Key Concepts

- The sanctions for violations of the discovery rules
- The general two-step process for enforcement and sanctions—from motion to compel to motion for sanctions
- Violations that allow for immediate sanctions, without going through the step of obtaining an order compelling compliance
- The recovery of attorney's fees incurred as a result of the violation
- The court's broad discretion in deciding whether sanctions are appropriate, and if so what sanctions to impose

Introduction

In order to work properly, discovery is dependent on good faith participation by the parties. Rule 37 provides the enforcement tools so that parties are motivated to participate in the proper spirit and so that the parties and the court can compel compliance when it is lacking.

For many situations, Rule 37 establishes a two-step process. First, a party must seek an order under Rule 37(a) compelling compliance with the discovery rules. Thus, if an opposing party provides insufficient responses to interrogatories, the first step for the party seeking the more complete responses is to file a motion to compel under Rule 37(a). If the recalcitrant party still fails to respond properly, then step two is to seek sanctions under Rule 37(b).

For other situations where a motion to compel is impractical, Rule 37 allows for immediate sanctions. Thus, for example, if an opposing party fails to appear for a properly noticed deposition, a motion to compel is an inadequate remedy—the attorney and court reporter have already shown up for the deposition and been harmed, so immediate sanctions are appropriate.

Courts do not like discovery sanctions motions, and particularly do not like lawyers who rush into court to complain about opposing counsel. Accordingly, attorneys should work together to resolve as many disputes as possible without court intervention. In many circumstances, the federal rules or local rules require parties to "meet and confer" before filing discovery motions. And even in the situations when the rules do not strictly require the parties to meet and confer before filing a discovery motion, courts will typically look more favorably on a motion where it is clear that the moving party has first tried to resolve the dispute informally.

The court has great discretion in ruling on a discovery motion, and the appellate courts typically give great deference to the trial court's discovery rulings. Within that framework, however, there has been a trend towards awarding sanctions that has coincided with the explosion in the generation and discovery of electronically stored information.

A. The Rules

Rule 37 contains all of the discovery sanctions provisions (other than Rule 26(g), which provides sanctions for violating the certification that is attendant to signing a discovery document).

- Rule 37(a) contains the procedures for motions to compel compliance with the discovery rules.

- Rule 37(b) establishes the sanctions for failure to comply with a Rule 37(a) order.

- Rule 37(c) contains the sanctions for failing to disclose information, failing to supplement an earlier response, or failing to admit something that turns out to be true.

- Rule 37(d) establishes automatic sanctions for a party's failure to attend its own deposition or failure to serve responses to interrogatories or requests for inspection.

- Finally, Rule 37(e) sets the rules for sanctioning the failure to preserve electronically stored information.

B. Motion to Compel

THE RULE   **Rule 37(a)**

Failure to Make Disclosures or to Cooperate in Discovery; Sanctions

(a) Motion for an Order Compelling Disclosure or Discovery.

(1) In General. On notice to other parties and all affected persons, a party may move for an order compelling disclosure or discovery. The motion must include a **certification** that the movant has in **good faith conferred** or attempted to confer with the person or party failing to make disclosure or discovery in an effort to obtain it without court action.

* * *

(4) Evasive or Incomplete Disclosure, Answer, or Response. For purposes of this subdivision (a), an evasive or incomplete disclosure, answer, or response must be treated as a failure to disclose, answer, or respond.

(5) Payment of Expenses; Protective Orders.

(A) **If the Motion Is Granted (or Disclosure or Discovery Is Provided After Filing).** If the motion is granted—**or if the disclosure or requested discovery is provided after the motion was filed**—the court **must**, after giving an opportunity to be heard, require the **party** or deponent whose conduct necessitated the motion, the party or **attorney** advising that conduct, **or both** to pay the movant's reasonable expenses incurred in making the motion, including **attorney's fees**. But the court **must not order this payment if**:

(i) the movant filed the motion before attempting in good faith to obtain the disclosure or discovery without court action;

> **(ii)** the opposing party's nondisclosure, response, or objection was substantially justified; or
>
> **(iii)** other circumstances make an award of expenses unjust.
>
> (B) **If the Motion Is Denied.** If the motion is denied, the court may issue any protective order authorized under Rule 26(c) and must, after giving an opportunity to be heard, require the movant, the attorney filing the motion, or both to pay the party or deponent who opposed the motion its reasonable expenses incurred in opposing the motion, including attorney's fees. But the court must not order this payment if the motion was substantially justified or other circumstances make an award of expenses unjust.

EXPLANATION

 Rule 37(a) authorizes a party to file a motion seeking to compel another party to perform its discovery obligations. Rule 37(a)(3) lists five specific situations where a motion to compel is appropriate. These are:

- To compel one of the disclosures under Rule 26(a);

- To compel a party to answer a deposition question;

- To compel a party to designate a representative under Rule 30(b)(6);

- To compel a party to answer an interrogatory; or

- To compel a party to permit an inspection of documents or things.

1. Procedures. A motion to compel should be filed with the court and served on all other parties.

2. Evasive or Incomplete Disclosure or Answer. Rule 37(a)(4) specifies that an evasive or incomplete disclosure or answer will be treated as a failure to disclose or answer.

3. Performance After the Motion is Filed. A party may not avoid the sanctions under Rule 37(a) by complying with the discovery request after the motion is filed—the rationale being that the moving party has already had to incur the expense of preparing the motion and is therefore entitled to its fees.

4. Expenses. The court must award the expenses incurred in connection with the motion, including attorney's fees, in favor of the prevailing party and against the losing party, the losing party's attorney, or both, unless the losing party was substantially justified in its position (such as having case law that arguably supported its position), or other circumstances render an award of sanctions unjust. However, the court must not award sanctions if the moving party failed to meet and confer.

5. Protective Order. If the motion to compel is denied, the court may enter a protective order under Rule 26(c) (protecting the non-moving party from the type of discovery that was the subject of the unsuccessful motion).

6. Motion Granted in Part and Denied in Part. If the court grants and denies parts of the motion, then it may apportion fees as it deems appropriate, and may also enter a protective order as it deems appropriate.

7. Meet and Confer. Prior to filing a motion to compel, a party must meet and confer, or at least make a strong effort to meet and confer, with the opposing party to try to resolve the dispute without court intervention. The motion must then contain a certification that the moving party complied with this obligation, and failure to include the certification will typically result in denial of the motion.

EXAMPLES & ANALYSIS

EXAMPLE: Priscilla sues Dana's Lawnmowers, asserting product liability/failure-to-warn claims based on an injury she sustained using a lawnmower she purchased at Dana's. Priscilla serves a set of interrogatories, and Dana's serves a timely response that consists primarily of a laundry list of objections to many of the interrogatories, with very little substantive information. If Priscilla believes that the objections are improper and the responses are inadequate, what should she do and what will the court do in response?

Analysis: Priscilla must first meet and confer with Dana's. If that is unsuccessful, Priscilla may file a motion to compel more complete responses—she may not yet file a motion for sanctions. The court will evaluate the merits of the parties' positions and make a ruling, and will award the successful party its attorney's fees unless the losing party's position was substantially justified or other circumstances make an award of fees unjust. If the court found that Priscilla's interrogatories were improper, it could also enter a protective order in favor of Dana's.

EXAMPLE: Page has sued Dylan in connection with a car accident. Page serves interrogatories on Dylan asking for the amount of alcohol consumed prior to the accident. Dylan objects on the basis of attorney–client privilege, which Page believes to be improper. Page calls Dylan to ask him to reconsider the objection, but Dylan does not answer and Page leaves a message. Page waits three days, and when Dylan has not returned the call, Page files her motion, certifying that she attempted to confer with Dylan. Is Page on solid ground?

Analysis: Probably not. Although there is no clear definition of the degree of effort required to attempt to confer, case law suggests that one attempted phone call is not sufficient. Rather, it should be clear from the record that the opponent is refusing to cooperate.

C. Failure to Comply with Court Order

THE RULE   **Rule 37(b)**

Failure to Comply with a Court Order

* * *

(2)(A) For Not Obeying a Discovery Order. If a party or a party's officer, director, or managing agent—or a witness designated under Rule 30(b)(6) or 31(a)(4)—fails to obey an order to provide or permit discovery, including an order under Rule 26(f), 35, or 37(a), the court where the action is pending may issue further just orders. They may include the following:

  (i) directing that the matters embraced in the order or other designated facts be taken as established for purposes of the action, as the prevailing party claims;

  (ii) prohibiting the disobedient party from supporting or opposing designated claims or defenses, or from introducing designated matters in evidence;

  (iii) striking pleadings in whole or in part;

  (iv) staying further proceedings until the order is obeyed;

  (v) dismissing the action or proceeding in whole or in part;

  (vi) rendering a default judgment against the disobedient party; or

  (vii) treating as contempt of court the failure to obey any order except an order to submit to a physical or mental examination [for which any of the above sanctions apply except contempt].

* * *

(A) Payment of Expenses. Instead of or in addition to the orders above, the court must order the disobedient party, the attorney advising that party, or both to pay the reasonable expenses, including **attorney's fees**, caused by the failure, unless the failure was substantially justified or other circumstances make an award of expenses unjust.

EXPLANATION

Once a party has obtained a motion to compel under Rule 37(a), Rule 37(b) establishes the sanctions for failing to comply with the order. The sanctions can be quite harsh, including dismissal of the action.

1. Sanctions for Disobeying an Order. Rule 37(b) states that, if a party fails to comply with a discovery order under Rule 37(a), 26(f), or 35, the court may impose any sanction it deems just. Rule 37(b) contains a non-exclusive list of sanctions that the court may consider:

- deeming certain facts as established;

- striking pleadings in whole or in part;

- staying the case until the order is obeyed;

- dismissing the action in whole or in part;

- rendering a default judgment; or

- treating the failure as a contempt of court (except in the case of an order for a Rule 35 examination, violation of which cannot be contempt).

IN PRACTICE

Courts have broad discretion as to what sanctions, if any, to impose. Sanctions that are case dispositive, like dismissal or default judgment, are rare, and case law suggests that courts must try lesser sanctions first, and only resort to dispositive sanctions when lesser sanctions prove insufficient.

2. Meet and Confer. Rule 37(b) does not contain a meet and confer requirement like that found in Rule 37(a), the rationale being that if a party has already gone through the process of obtaining an order and the opposing party does not comply, it is not necessary or reasonable to ask the party to try to cajole the opposing party into complying with the court order.

EXAMPLES & ANALYSIS

EXAMPLE: Prince's Plumbing Palace sues Dara's Drain Depot for breach of a supply contract. In its answer, Dara's asserts breach of conditions precedent as one of its affirmative defenses. Prince's serves discovery seeking the basis for the defense, and Dara's asserts an objection that the discovery seeks a conclusion of law. Prince's files a motion to compel a substantive response, and the court grants Prince's motion. On the date set for compliance, Dara's counsel sends a letter saying that he has been on vacation and is now very busy, but will respond as soon as his schedule allows. Counsel for Prince's sends a response demanding the discovery answers by the end of that week. Dara's does not respond by the end of that week, and Prince's files a motion for sanctions under Rule 37(b). Has Prince's satisfied its obligation to meet and confer? What sanctions might the court consider?

Analysis: There is no obligation to meet and confer under Rule 37(b). However, Prince's wisely went beyond its technical obligation and gave Dara's an extra opportunity to comply. Many of the sanctions listed in Rule 37(b) could come into play. The court could deem it established that Prince's complied with all conditions precedent (negating the affirmative defense that Dara's failed to support). The court could strike the affirmative defense from the answer. The court would be unlikely to stay the case until Dara's complied because Dara's is the defendant and would benefit from a stay. The court could enter judgment against Dara's (but would be unlikely to do so unless this event was the last in a series of violations by Dara's). Finally, the court could treat Dara's as being in contempt (which could entail fining Dara's or its counsel). If this is the first violation by Dara's, the most likely result would be striking the affirmative defense or deeming the conditions precedent established.

3. Attorney's Fees. Rule 37(b) provides that the court must require the disobedient party, its attorney, or both, to pay the attorney's fees of the moving party, either in addition to or in lieu of other sanctions, unless the court finds that the disobedient party's failure was substantially justified or other circumstances make an award of expenses unjust.

4. Preservation Orders. Parties wanting to increase the likelihood of sanctions in the event of **spoliation** will sometimes seek a court order requiring the parties to preserve evidence. Then, if a party fails to preserve evidence, other parties can seek Rule 37(b) sanctions. Such sanctions will often include an instruction to the jury to presume that the evidence would have been unfavorable to the party who failed to preserve it (called an "adverse inference"), and can also include monetary fines and case dispositive sanctions like dismissal or default judgment. Alternatively, some parties use simple notice letters, which do not require court involvement and do not implicate Rule 37(b) sanctions, but may cause the opposing party to collect and preserve relevant evidence.

> **"Spoliation"**
> (spō-lē-ʹā-shun) refers to the destruction of, or failure to preserve, evidence.

D. Immediate Sanctions for Failure to Disclose, Supplement, or Admit

---

THE RULE   **Rule 37(c)**

Failure to Disclose, to Supplement an Earlier Response, or to Admit

(1) Failure to Disclose or Supplement. If a party fails to provide information or identify a witness as required by Rule 26(a) or (e), the party is **not allowed to use that information or witness to supply evidence on a motion, at a hearing, or at a trial**, unless the failure was substantially justified or is harmless. In addition to or instead of this sanction, the court, on motion and after giving an opportunity to be heard:

(A) may order payment of the reasonable expenses, including attorney's fees, caused by the failure;

(B) may inform the jury of the party's failure; and

(C) may impose other appropriate sanctions, including any of the orders listed in Rule 37(b)(2)(A)(i)–(vi).

(2) Failure to Admit. If a party fails to admit what is requested under Rule 36 and if the requesting party later proves a document to be genuine or the matter true, the requesting party may move that the party who failed to admit pay the reasonable expenses, including **attorney's fees, incurred in making that proof**. The court must so order unless:

(A) the request was held objectionable under Rule 36(a);

(B) the admission sought was of no substantial importance;

(C) the party failing to admit had a reasonable ground to believe that it might prevail on the matter; or

(D) there was other good reason for the failure to admit.

EXPLANATION

Rule 37(c) establishes immediate sanctions, without the need for a motion to compel, in three circumstances: failure to disclose information that should have been disclosed; failure to provide information in a supplemental response as required by Rule 26(e); and failure to admit something that is later proven true at trial.

1. Sanctions for Failure to Disclose or Supplement. Rule 37(c) states that, if a party fails to provide information or the identity of witnesses by disclosure or supplement, the party is not permitted to use such information or witnesses in a motion, at a hearing, or at trial, unless the court finds the failure was substantially justified or harmless. In addition to this primary sanction precluding the evidence, the court may order the party to pay another party's expenses, including attorney's fees, caused as a result of the failure, may inform the jury that the party failed to provide the information, and may impose any other appropriate sanction, including those listed in

Rule 37(b) (except contempt, because the party being sanctioned has not violated a court order).

2. Sanctions for Failure to Admit. Rule 37(c) states that, if a party fails to admit something that is later proven, the party requesting the admission may move that the party who failed to admit pay the reasonable expenses, including attorney's fees, incurred in making that proof. The court must award such expenses unless: the request was held objectionable under Rule 36(a); the admission sought was of no substantial importance; the party failing to admit had a reasonable ground to believe that it might prevail on the matter; or there was other good reason for the failure to admit.

EXAMPLES & ANALYSIS

EXAMPLE: Pao brings a suit against Darren for defamation regarding a statement that Darren made to a reporter that Pao had stolen money from the state. In his Rule 26 disclosures, Pao did not list Walter as a witness. During his deposition, Pao was asked about who had knowledge regarding whether he stole the money, and Pao identified Walter as someone who would support his version of the relevant events. Pao did not supplement his disclosures or discovery responses to identify Walter. At trial, Pao calls Walter as a witness and Darren objects. Will the court allow Walter to testify?

Analysis: Pao had a duty to identify Walter, either through the original Rule 26 disclosures or by supplementation. However, if Pao identified Walter sufficiently during the deposition as someone he might call as a witness, a court might find that the failure to disclose his identity formally was "harmless" and might choose not to preclude Walter from testifying or award any other sanctions.

EXAMPLE: In the above Example, Darren asks Pao to admit the authenticity of certain documents, and Pao denies the request. At trial, Darren calls a record custodian to the witness stand, who authenticates the documents, and they are admitted into evidence. Darren then moves for his expenses in preparing the record custodian to testify and in subpoenaing him to testify. Will the court grant Darren's motion?

Analysis: Unless Pao can qualify for one of the four exceptions, the court would likely award Darren his expenses. Based on the facts provided, there is no indication that the request was held objectionable, that the admission was of no substantial importance, that Pao had a reasonable ground to believe that he might prove the documents to be fraudulent or improper, or there was other good reason for Pao's failure to admit. Therefore, the court would likely award Darren his expenses.

E. Immediate Sanctions for Failure to Attend Deposition or Answer Discovery

Rule 37(d) provides for immediate sanctions when a party fails entirely to respond to a discovery request. It applies when a party fails to appear for a deposition or altogether fails to respond to interrogatories or document requests.

1. Failure to Appear for a Deposition. Upon motion, the court may impose sanctions when a party, a party's officer, director, or managing agent, or a party's designated representative under Rule 30(b)(6) fails to appear for a deposition that has been properly noticed.

2. Failure to Respond to Interrogatories or Document Requests. Upon motion, the court may impose sanctions when a party fails to serve answers, objections, or a written response to properly served interrogatories or requests for inspection.

3. Failure to Respond to Requests to Admit. Rule 37(d) does not provide for immediate sanctions for failure to respond to requests for admission. Why not? Because Rule 37(c) provides the sanction—the requests are deemed admitted.

4. Meet and Confer. Before filing a motion for sanctions for failure to respond to interrogatories or document requests, a party must meet and confer, or at least make a strong effort to meet and confer, with the opposing party to try to resolve the dispute without court intervention. A motion under Rule 37(d) pertaining to interrogatories or document requests must include a certification that the moving party complied with its meet and confer requirements. The certification is not required when the opposing party fails to attend its deposition, with the rationale being that the party noticing the deposition has already been harmed by appearing for a deposition that did not occur, and that harm is not redressed by the party agreeing in a meet and confer conference to appear the next time.

5. Sanctions Available. The court may impose any of the sanctions listed in Rule 37(b)—such as deeming facts established, striking pleadings, dismissing claims, or entering default judgments—except contempt (because the disobedient party has not violated a court order). As with Rule 37(b), case dispositive sanctions like dismissal or default judgment are reserved for ongoing or egregious violations.

6. Attorney's Fees. Rule 37(d) provides that the court must require the disobedient party, its attorney, or both, to pay the attorney's fees of the moving party, either in addition to or in lieu of other sanctions, unless the court finds that the disobedient party's failure was substantially justified or other circumstances make an award of expenses unjust.

7. Improper Excuses. A party may not justify its failure to appear for a deposition or respond to interrogatories or document requests by contending that the discovery sought was objectionable, unless the party had a motion for a protective order pending. In other words, if a party believes discovery is objectionable, it may serve written objections or file a motion for a protective order, but simply declining to respond is not an acceptable option.

EXAMPLES & ANALYSIS

EXAMPLE: Pembroke Restaurant, Inc. sues Daniels Dishwashers, Inc. for breach of contract, asserting that Daniels' representation that its new model dishwasher used 40% less water was inaccurate. Daniels serves document requests on Pembroke, and Pembroke fails to respond in 30 days. Daniels then files a motion for sanctions. How would the court likely rule?

Analysis: The facts do not suggest that Daniels met and conferred with Pembroke before filing the motion. If that is true then the court would likely deny the motion. If they did meet and confer, then Pembroke would be subject to sanctions under Rule 37(d).

IN PRACTICE

Remember, the meet and confer process is critical in discovery disputes. Failure to conduct that process in good faith is the quickest way to doom your discovery motion—courts do not like discovery disputes, and lack of a meet and confer certification gives the court an easy out.

EXAMPLE: In the above Example, Daniels also served a deposition notice on Pembroke's president. He was on a truffle-gathering trip in France, so counsel for Pembroke sent a letter to counsel for Daniels stating that the president would not be able to appear for his deposition. Counsel for Daniels wrote back stating that the close of discovery was one week away, so he could not agree to postpone the deposition. Counsel for Pembroke wrote back stating that the president was already in France, and was physically unable to attend. The date of the deposition came, and counsel for Daniels appeared but no one appeared for Pembroke. Counsel for Daniels then filed a motion for sanctions. How would a court likely rule?

Analysis: Because this motion addresses failure to attend a deposition, Daniels was not required to meet and confer, and the court would address the motion on its merits. As a technical matter, a letter to opposing counsel providing notice that the witness is not available is not sufficient to avoid the obligation to appear. Rather, Pembroke should have filed a motion for a protective order if Daniels would not agree to reschedule the deposition. Therefore, Pembroke is subject to sanctions under Rule 37(d). At the same time, counsel for Daniels was arguably unreasonable in refusing to reschedule (unless there was some history of failure to cooperate). Accordingly, the court would be unlikely to impose any extreme sanctions on Pembroke, and might just award a modest amount of attorney's fees to Daniels for the time incurred to attend the deposition, or might simply issue an order controlling the rescheduling of the deposition.

IN PRACTICE

 Scheduling of depositions is often genuinely difficult, because it involves the schedule of the witness and counsel for each party. If there is a single plaintiff and four defendants, then each deposition involves finding an open date on at least six calendars (the witness plus five attorneys). To work smoothly, this process requires genuine cooperation among counsel, which is encouraged.

If it proves difficult to get open dates or cooperation from opposing counsel, a party can notice a deposition for a specific date, while at the same time advising counsel in a cover letter that the noticing party will agree to reschedule the deposition if all parties can agree on another date when the witness is available. That puts the onus on other parties to either cooperate or file a motion for a protective order.

F. Failure to Preserve ESI

THE RULE   Rule 37(e)

Failure to Provide Electronically Stored Information

If electronically stored information that should have been preserved in the anticipation or conduct of litigation is lost because a party failed to take reasonable steps to preserve the information, and the information cannot be restored or replaced through additional discovery, the court may:

(1) Upon a finding of prejudice to another party from loss of the information, order measures no greater than necessary to cure the prejudice;

(2) Only upon a finding that the party acted with the intent to deprive another party of the information's use in the litigation,

(a) presume that the lost information was unfavorable to the party;

(b) instruct the jury that it may or must presume the information was unfavorable to the party; or

(c) dismiss the action or enter a default judgment[1].

With the vast majority of all communications and documents originating on computers and being stored on electronic media, ESI is understandably the focus of most discovery. The ease with which ESI can be deleted has resulted in the loss of evidence—inadvertently or deliberately—and a concomitant increase in motions for spoliation sanctions.

The duty to preserve evidence is based in common law, and typically arises as soon as litigation is known or "reasonably anticipated." This duty certainly arises when the complaint is served, but can also arise if there is correspondence that threatens litigation or other signs that litigation is coming.

Once the duty to preserve has arisen, each party should send a "litigation hold" letter to all of the likely record custodians, including the party's technology department if applicable, instructing them to retain all documents and ESI that might be relevant to the litigation, and to suspend any automatic deletion policies or procedures. Both the party and the attorney have an obligation to send the litigation hold letter, and both are potentially subject to sanctions if the letter is not sent.

When a party does not follow this process or its employees fail to comply, the party is potentially subject to substantial sanctions. Phillip Morris was fined $2.75 million in a case for failing to preserve emails, and was not allowed to present testimony from any employee who failed to preserve emails. Prudential Insurance Company was fined $1 million plus attorney's fees for failing to preserve evidence.

Perhaps the most widely known and cited opinions involving the spoliation of ESI are from *Zubalake v. UBS Warburg*. In a series of opinions, Judge Scheindlin from the United States District Court for the Southern District of New York addressed allegations that the defendant, UBS, failed to pre-

---

1 Note that this language reflects the December 1, 2015 Amendments

serve emails and other ESI. The court held that both the party **and its attorneys** have a duty to take measures to ensure that relevant ESI is preserved, such as issuing a litigation hold letter **and then monitoring compliance.** Eventually, the court both awarded monetary sanctions and ruled that she would instruct the jury that it was permitted, but not required, to presume that destroyed documents would have been adverse to UBS (an "adverse inference"). Other courts, however, have taken less extreme approaches.

Rule 37(e) was amended to provide a uniform standard for adjudicating motions for spoliation of ESI. It provides that a court may only impose sanctions if another party was prejudiced by the loss of evidence. Furthermore, those sanctions must be no greater than necessary to cure the prejudice. Only if the court finds that a party acted with the intent to deprive another party of the information's use in the litigation may the court impose the following more severe sanctions on that party: presume that the lost information was unfavorable to the party; instruct the jury that it may or must presume the information was unfavorable to the party; or dismiss the action or enter a default judgment.

IN PRACTICE

Discovery is a process that largely relies on ethical behavior by parties and attorneys. In general, if an attorney deems a document not relevant or responsive to document requests, neither the opposing party nor the court ever see that document to double check the attorney's judgment. Therefore, if attorneys do not participate in the process in good faith, the process will not work.

In addition, if attorneys do not act professionally, cooperatively, and ethically, the cost of the discovery process—expensive even in the best-case scenario—can increase dramatically. Motion practice is expensive, and often results in an outcome that the parties could have and should have reached amicably.

Moreover, courts really do not like discovery disputes, which are often the legal system equivalent of adolescent squabbling. Thus, while adjudicating discovery motions is part of a judge's job, the judge will not look favorably on an attorney who is too quick to resort to sanctions motions. For all of these reasons, discovery motions are much more the exception than the rule.

Sometimes, however, either the parties have a good faith disagreement about the rules and applicable law or one side does not act in good faith. In such instances, Rule 37 can provide a powerful tool for the parties and the court to ensure that the relevant information is exchanged and that recalcitrant parties and attorneys are not rewarded for their transgressions.

While Rule 37 contains a wide range of sanctions, and suggests that attorney's fees should be a component of almost every sanction

award, in practice many judges are reluctant to award fees, and move cautiously with sanctions. Most of the more extreme sanctions arise from situations where a party persists in a pattern of disregard for the rules. Although these sanctions are not common, they can also be ruinous to an attorney's career, so attorneys should not take the discovery process or their obligations cavalierly.

The proliferation of ESI and the many issues associated with preserving, gathering, reviewing, and producing it has created a minefield for unwary or unprepared attorneys and parties. Even in this area, however, the risk of sanctions can be greatly mitigated by coordination, communication, and cooperation with opposing counsel.

ADDITIONAL EXERCISES

Example: Mr. Patterson lives near a plant that Defense Contract Corp. operated during the 1940s manufacturing munitions. Mr. Patterson has developed leukemia, and contends that his leukemia was caused by his exposure to chemicals released by Defense, and files a complaint asserting various tort claims. Analyze how the parties and/or the court should act in the following scenarios:

1. Mr. Patterson sends interrogatories to Defense. Defense sends a timely response that consists of a litany of objections to each interrogatory, and no substantive information. **What is the proper course for Mr. Patterson if he believes that Defense's objections are not proper?**

2. Defense serves amended responses to Mr. Patterson's interrogatories. Mr. Patterson still believes that the responses are inadequate and evasive. ***Does Mr. Patterson need to meet and confer? What should Mr. Patterson do, and what are the court's options if it agrees with Mr. Patterson? What will the court do if it agrees with Defense?***

3. Defense serves interrogatories on Mr. Patterson. After 30 days, when Mr. Patterson has not responded, counsel for Defense contacts counsel for Mr. Patterson and requests responses. Mr. Patterson still fails to respond. ***What should Defense do, and what will the court do if it agrees with Defense?***

4. Defense serves requests to admit on Mr. Patterson. 30 days pass, and Mr. Patterson has not responded. ***What should Defense do?***

5. Mr. Patterson notices the deposition of Defense's president. On the day of the deposition, Mr. Patterson's attorney appears for the deposition. While sitting waiting for Defense to appear, Mr. Patterson's attorney receives an email stating that the president had an emergency business matter arise, and would not be able to attend. ***What should Mr. Patterson do, and what would a court be likely to do? Can the court hold Defense in contempt?***

6. When Defense's president is eventually deposed, Defense's counsel makes speaking objections and improperly instructs the president not to respond to certain questions. ***What should Mr. Patterson do?***

7. Mr. Patterson also notices the deposition of a lab technician employed by Defense. The technician fails to appear for his deposition. ***What should Mr. Patterson do, and what would a court be likely to do?***

8. Mr. Patterson serves document requests on Defense. Counsel for Mr. Patterson believes that Defense has improperly objected to one of the document requests. Counsel for Mr. Patterson calls counsel for Defense, and gets voicemail. Counsel for Mr. Patterson leaves a message, and a week passes with no response. ***Can Mr. Patterson properly file a motion to compel a more complete response to the document request?***

9. Mr. Patterson files a motion to compel more complete responses to his document requests. Before its response is due, Defense provides a second response that does not contain some of the objections and contains additional substantive responses. ***What effect does the second response have on Mr. Patterson's motion?***

10. At trial, Defense offers a document into evidence that it did not disclose or produce during discovery. ***What are Mr. Patterson's options with respect to this surprise document?***

11. At trial, Defense calls a witness whose name was not disclosed under Rule 26(a)(1). Mr. Patterson objects. Defense argues that the witness's identity was disclosed during a deposition, when Mr. Patterson asked the company's Rule 30(b)(6) representative to identify the individuals with information supporting Defense's defenses. ***How would a court likely rule?***

Quick Summary

• Rule 37(a) is the first step in the typical discovery dispute, and allows a party to move for an order compelling another party to perform its discovery obligations. Rule 37(a) is generally for situations where the opposing party has made some sort of performance, but the moving party does not believe the performance was adequate—abject failure to perform is covered by other subsections of Rule 37.

• The movant must meet and confer with opposing counsel before filing the motion. The court must award attorney's fees to the prevailing party unless the court determines that the other party's position was substantially justified or circumstances make an award of fees unjust. Performance after the motion is filed does not avoid the award of attorney's fees.

- Rule 37(b) imposes sanctions for failure to comply with a discovery order—typically an order compelling performance un-der Rule 37(a). Rule 37(b) lists sanctions, although the court can fashion any sanction it deems appropriate. The listed sanctions are an order: directing that specified facts be taken as established; prohibiting the disobedient party from supporting or opposing specified claims or defenses or from introducing specified evidence; striking pleadings; staying the case until the order is obeyed; dismissing the action; entering default judgment; or treating the disobedience as contempt. Courts generally treat case-dispositive sanctions as matters of last resort. The court must also award attorney's fees against the disobedient party unless the court determines that the disobedient party's position was substantially justified or circumstances make an award of fees unjust.

- If a party fails to disclose information, fails to supplement an earlier response, or fails to admit something that is later proven true at trial, Rule 37(c) provides the sanctions. If a party fails to provide information by disclosure or supplement, the primary sanction is that the party will not be permitted to use that information at trial. The court may also order payment of the movant's attorney's fees, inform the jury of the party's failure, and impose any of the sanctions in Rule 37(b) except contempt.

- If a party fails to admit something that is later proven at trial, the party will be liable for the opponent's costs and fees in proving the matter, unless the request was objectionable, the admission was of no substantial importance, or the party had reasonable grounds to believe it would prevail on the issue at trial.

- If a party fails to appear for a deposition or fails altogether to respond to discovery requests, Rule 37(d) provides the sanctions. The movant must meet and confer with opposing counsel before filing the motion, except when the party has failed to appear for its deposition. Rule 37(d) does not apply to deficient answers to discovery requests, except when the responses are so inadequate as to be tantamount to no response at all.

- The sanctions may include any of the Rule 37(b) sanctions except contempt. The court will also award the movant its attorney's fees unless the court determines that the failure was substantially justified or circumstances make an award of fees unjust.

- Rule 37(e) governs sanctions for the destruction of ESI. It authorizes sanctions only when another party is prejudiced, and limits the sanctions to those necessary to cure the prejudice. If the court finds that a party acted with the intent to deprive another party of information contained in the destroyed ESI, the court may presume certain facts to be true, give an adverse inference instruction to the jury, or enter a ruling disposing of some or all of the case.

- Under all of the discovery sanction provisions, the court has considerable discretion, and an appellate court will be extremely reluctant to reverse a discovery sanction.

IV

Unit Overview:
The Adjudication Process

The six chapters in Unit IV address the parts of the process involving the court's actual decision in a case. Chapter 15 is devoted to a single, but very important, motion—the motion for summary judgment. This tool allows the court to decide a case without holding a trial at all and is a powerful tool to resolve cases. In some types of litigation, the bulk of the dispute is probably decided on summary judgment, at least in part. There are certainly cases where both sides want to have the case decided on a motion as neither side wants to try fact issues. This motion has the result, if successful, of deciding a case on the merits but without trial. It is thus terminally important for many cases. It is crucially important for litigants to understand the motion, both to obtain it when it is properly available and to avoid it lest they lose their case and their right to a trial as well.

Chapter 16 deals with the question of when a party has a right to a jury trial. Not all cases are tried to juries, and in many instances one party has a strong preference that the jury decide the case, its opponent will have an equally strong desire that the jury not hear the case. Chapter 15 addresses how that narrow dispute between the parties might get resolved.

Chapter 17 addresses trial itself and how a typical trial progresses to a decision. Despite the thought that this would be a step that the majority of cases would reach, the reality is that only a very small percentage of cases are tried. For those that do, however, the process of trial is important and it explains why many of the other procedures studied in this book are established and then undertaken.

Following trial, both sides may bring post-trial motions, and it may be necessary to do so to obtain the broadest appellate review possible. These motions are discussed in Chapter 18. These motions include motions typically brought by the defeated party—the motion for a new trial, for judgment as a matter of law, or for relief from an order or judgment. Post-trial motions also include motions the prevailing party may bring, motions to amend findings or modify the trial result, or, in some cases, for additional relief not ordered at trial, such as attorneys' fees.

Chapter 19 addresses the appellate process. It is an important part of the civil procedure world, although even fewer appeals are held than there are trials. The rules governing appeals are complex and different from the trial court rules, and it is important that anyone heading off to trial understands at least the broad outlines of how appeals work and how a party needs to take certain steps in the trial court to prepare for an eventual appeal.

Chapter 20 addresses judgments and preclusion. In some ways the judgment is the Holy Grail of the litigation process. A judgment is the ultimate end to all the procedures discussed in this book. Every party seeks to obtain the adjudication of claims and defenses in a valid judgment that can be enforced with legal process and will be given preclusive effect in any further efforts to litigate the same issues. In some ways, this chapter could be the first chapter studied in civil procedure—it is that important and that fundamental. But it probably makes more sense as a capstone rather than introduction.

15

Summary Judgment and Other Dispositive Motions

Key Concepts

- The role of dispositive motions, particularly summary judgment
- The ground rules governing summary judgment, including determining whether there is a genuine dispute of material fact and whether the moving party is entitled to judgment as a matter of law
- Summary judgment procedure and protocols, including use and assessment of supporting papers, consideration of the burden of proof in the underlying action, and appealability
- The availability and use of partial summary judgment
- Public policy concerns implicated by summary judgment practice

Introduction

A substantial number of cases are resolved via the granting of a dispositive motion such as the Rule 12(b)(6) motion to dismiss for failure to state a claim, which we examined in Chapter 7.

Grants of dispositive motions are final, appealable orders unless the grant extends only to some but not all claims in the case. Along with Rule 12(b)(6), summary judgment is a key dispositive motion. Other dispositive motions, such as motions for involuntary dismissal pursuant to Fed. R. Civ. P. 41 and motions for default judgment pursuant to Fed. R. Civ. P. 55, are discussed in Chapter 7 regarding responses to the complaint. This Chapter focuses on motions for summary judgment pursuant to Fed. R. Civ. P. 56.

Summary judgment originated in Nineteenth Century England as a procedural device to make it easier to collect essentially uncontested debts without requiring the time and inconvenience of trial.

A. The Summary Judgment Standard

THE RULE	Rule 56(a)

Motion for Summary Judgment or Partial Summary Judgment

A party may move for summary judgment, identifying each claim or defense—or the part of each claim or defense—on which summary judgment is sought. The court shall grant summary judgment if the movant shows that there is **no genuine dispute as to any material fact and the movant is entitled to judgment as a matter of law.** The court should state on the record the reasons for granting or denying the motion.

EXPLANATION

Simply put, summary judgment requires that there be no "genuine" (a/k/a legitimate, realistic) dispute regarding any "material" fact (a fact that must be established in order to decide the matter). As discussed below, a fact does not become disputed simply because of allegations but requires evidentiary support. Disputes over unimportant (*i.e.*, non-material) facts do not prevent summary judgment. If the material facts are not genuinely disputed, the second step of summary judgment analysis requires that—given the undisputed facts—the law clearly gives the movant the right to judgment in its favor. In reading older cases, students should be aware that significant amendments to Rule 56 became effective on December 1, 2010. Although these amendments did not change the substantive standard of the Rule, it was extensively rewritten and renumbered. Consequently, any summary judgment decision prior to late 2010 will be referring to the language and organization of the old rule. Because the substantive standards were not altered by the 2010 changes, the case law is still authoritative.

EXAMPLES & ANALYSIS

EXAMPLE: Vendor sells widget for $100. Buyer pays with a check that bounces, uses the widget and has no complaint. Vendor commences a lawsuit and moves for summary judgment, introducing via affidavit of the owner the evidence of the sale and nonpayment. Buyer does not contest these facts but simply states his checking account is overdrawn. Will summary judgment be granted?

Analysis: Yes. Whether the transaction occurred, whether the buyer paid, and whether the buyer has any legally cognizable excuse to avoid payment are all "material" facts—but the buyer has not contested any of these material facts. The buyer has an excuse of sorts (the check bounced) but the law considers this an inadequate defense just as laypersons would deem this an inadequate excuse. There are no "material" facts in dispute. Buyer admits he bought the widgets and has not paid. There is no "genuine" dispute about the sale of the widget, its performance, or the nonpayment. Under these facts, Vendor is entitled to judgment as a matter of law. Because there are no contested material facts, there is no need to conduct a trial (the purpose of which is to determine disputed facts).

A material fact is one made salient under the substantive law, if its existence might affect the outcome of the suit according to the governing law. *See Anderson v. Liberty Lobby, Inc.*, 477 U.S. 242, 248 (1986) ("Only disputes over facts that might affect the outcome of the suit under the governing law will properly preclude the entry of summary judgment. Factual disputes that are irrelevant or unnecessary will not be counted."). Irrelevant or unnecessary facts are not material.

Facts essential to establishing the elements of a claim for relief are common illustrations of material facts. For example, in a car accident case, the plaintiff must demonstrate: (1) existence of a duty; (2) breach of the duty; (3) that causes; (4) injury. Facts related to whether the driver was bound to stop at a red light, failed to stop, hit and injured the plaintiff are thus material facts. Thus, "the outcome of a car accident case might depend on whether the light was red or green, but it is unlikely to depend on whether the car itself was blue or black. That is to say, a dispute over the color of the car is unlikely to preclude summary judgment because the applicable substantive law is unlikely to prescribe one result if the car was blue but a different result if the car was black—the color of the car might be disputed, but it is not material." *See* STEVEN S. GENSLER, FEDERAL RULES OF CIVIL PROCEDURE: RULES AND COMMENTARY 955 (2011).

B. Partial Summary Judgment

In addition to granting summary judgment on the entire case, a court may also grant partial summary judgment as to specific claims or issues in the case.

> **EXAMPLE:** Let's develop the auto accident hypo some more. Assume Plaintiff Pilates's car is struck by Defendant Dragon's car after Dragon runs a red light. Pilates, who complains of a sore back, was returning home from a visit to an orthopedic surgeon. The medical records indicate that Pilates came to see the doctor because of—you guessed it—a sore back. Both Pilates and Dragon move for summary judgment, with Pilates submitting his medical bills incurred after the accident (including surgery and extensive physical therapy). Assuming these facts are not disputed, can Pilates obtain summary judgment?

Analysis: The court might grant partial summary judgment to Pilates re-garding the liability of Dragon, since it is undisputed that Dragon ran the red light. Dragon was negligent as a matter of law. If other facts do not create some genuine dispute about the respective negligence of the parties, a court could rule that Dragon was liable as a matter of law. The amount of Pilates' damages, and the effect of his pre-existing condition, is likely to be disputed, however, so Pilates could not obtain summary judgment as to damages.

Rather than entering an order establishing Dragon's negligence, the court might deny summary judgment altogether. Notwithstanding the literal language of Rule 56, Courts have discretion to deny summary judgment even when the motion seems meritorious if further litigation activity will enhance the court's legal analysis or better illuminate the facts and law at issue, increasing the odds of a more accurate outcome. *See Kennedy v. Silas Mason Co.* 334 U.S. 249 (1948); Steven S. Gensler, *Must, Should, Shall*, 43 AKRON L. REV. 1139, 1160 (2010) (concluding that despite use of "shall" in Rule 56(a), judges retain discretion regarding summary judgment).

Despite the Dragon's conceded negligence, the court cannot grant summary judgment in full to Pilates because of the questions surrounding the cause and extent of Pilates' back pain. Neither can the court grant summary judgment to Dragon based on the fact that Pilates had back problems before the incident. If the accident made Pilates' already bad back worse, Pilates may recover for this item of injury from Dragon—that's the "thin skull" or "you take the plaintiff as you find him" concept from tort law. There appears to be a genuine dispute of material fact regarding the amount of injury, if any, related to the car collision.

C. Historical Division over Application of the Standard

Summary judgment was made a part of the newly minted Federal Rules in 1938. Committee Reporter Charles Clark argued that the nonmovant must do more than make mere arguments, and must also submit sufficiently weighty, believable, or important facts precluding entry of judgment in favor of the movant. Because of the influence of the Federal Rules, all states provide for some form of summary judgment in their rules of procedure.

During the first two decades after adoption of the Federal Rules, there was some disagreement about the conditions under which summary judgment could be granted. Judge Jerome Frank resisted summary judgment and took the position that it should not be granted if there was any question as to the facts, including questions regarding the veracity of a single witness to an event. Clark opposed Frank, taking the view that it was too low a threshold for keeping a claim alive and that (assuming the movant had made out a prima facie case for summary judgment) the respondent needed to show that there was realistically enough evidence on its side to make a favorable jury verdict possible.

Despite Clark's stature as primary drafter of the Federal Rules, Frank (who was also a major figure in American law), won several battles on this point in actual cases, most famously in *Arnstein v. Porter*, 154 F.2d 464, 468 (2d Cir. 1946), where summary judgment was denied in a copyright infringement case alleging that famous composer Cole Porter had plagiarized material from the far less known Ira Arnstein. Despite Clark's stature, other judges often sided with Frank on this issue.

Judge Frank's approach became known as the "slightest doubt" test for assessing summary judgment motions—and it was widely criticized by not only the defense bar (which you would expect; consider why defendants tend to like summary judgment more than plaintiffs and why defendants are more likely to get summary judgment) but also by scholars. In particular, major academic authorities referred to the slightest doubt test as "**gloss**" on Rule 56 that was not only absent from the text but contradicted by the text.

> The term "gloss" originated in the middle ages when religious scholars delved into construction of often complex texts. Leading scholars developed a gloss to aid in interpretation. The ancient gloss was literally a physical template placedupon the text that contained interpretative notes on the text to aid the reader. Think of it as a precursor to *Cliff Notes* or interlinear editions of the classics. The gloss was developed by experts to aid the less expert readers.

In 1963, the Rules Committee responded in part to criticisms of the slightest doubt test to require that a party opposing summary judgment do more than merely cite to its pleadings to establish a sufficient factual dispute. The goal of this Rule change was to require something more than mere assertion to defeat a summary judgment motion.

Notwithstanding the change and scholarly criticism, it became the conventional wisdom that summary judgment was difficult to obtain and that even a well-made and supported summary judgment motion could be defeated by very weak evidence bordering on mere assertion. Perhaps the poster child for a case viewed as too resistant to summary judgment was *Poller v. Columbia Broadcasting System*, 368 U.S. 464 (1962), in which the Court supported denial of summary judgment in an antitrust case based almost solely on the view that the jury would be entitled to refuse to believe the defense witnesses because of their economic interest in avoiding liability for their company—even though the plaintiff appeared not to have put forth any information that contradicted the assertions of the defense witnesses.

The perceived reluctance of courts to grant summary judgment came under increasing criticism due to a perceived litigation "crisis," or "explosion" that allegedly counseled for greater use of pretrial dismissal devices in order to gain presumed savings of cost and time in avoiding trial. There were also criticisms made about perceived judicial reluctance to grant Rule 56 motions and concerns that Rule 12(b)(6) dismissal motions were underutilized—although this latter view tended not to enjoy scholarly support.

D. 1986: A Pivotal Year in Summary Judgment Practice

Consider this sociopolitical context as you consider the U.S. Supreme Court's 1986 trilogy of summary judgment cases discussed below. Most of the cases using slightest doubt language were decided in the 1950s and 1960s, with only a few during the 1970s. By then, the slightest doubt

> **The "Trilogy."** When lawyers talk about the summary judgment trilogy they are speaking about these three cases decided during 1986.

standard was losing ground. But the 1986 trilogy buried it completely.

1. *Matsushita*

Matsushita Elec. Indus. Co. Ltd. v. Zenith Radio Corp., 475 U.S. 574 (1986), decided in March, reinstated a trial court grant of summary judgment for defendants in a complex antitrust case reversed by the Third Circuit. The case involved allegations by U.S. electronic goods manufacturers contending that Japanese companies had illegally conspired to take over the field and drive the U.S. companies out of business through "predatory pricing"— the sale of goods below their actual cost of manufacture in order to deny sales to others, gain customers, and eventually starve the competitors into submission. The profit in predatory pricing is supposed to come after the competitors are driven out of business, at which time the surviving predators have the field to themselves and can raise prices at will. The defendants denied the allegations and contended that they were merely competing better in the consumer marketplace, making better products that sold for less. Essentially, the Japanese companies said it wasn't their fault if Americans preferred their products over clunkier, more expensive U.S. counterparts.

This argument was persuasive to the trial court and the Supreme Court (but not the Third Circuit), so much so that the Supreme Court approved summary judgment in favor of the Japanese companies, ending the case. The Court accepted the defendants' proffered economic theory positing that predatory pricing was highly unlikely because of the difficulties of maintaining discipline among the conspirators and because a would-be predator would have to have very deep pockets to keep selling goods below cost long enough to break the competition without itself going broke. Because of the posited unlikelihood of predatory pricing, the *Matsushita* majority insisted that the plaintiff would need to provide "direct" evidence of predatory pricing in order to survive the defendants' motion for summary judgment.

Matsushita was a controversial 5-4 decision that included a vigorous dissent expressing dismay that the majority was so willing to find as a matter of law that predatory pricing was too unlikely to be taken seriously in the absence of direct evidence. In addition, critics of the decision noted that insisting on direct evidence is at odds with normal American adjudication, in which circumstantial evidence alone can carry the burden of persuasion to demonstrate a violation of law.

As discussed in Chapter 6, "direct" evidence is evidence that definitively shows something without any need for the fact finder to make an inference from the evidence. For example, if a defendant admits murder or theft, nothing is left to the imagination of the fact finder. Similarly, if an eyewitness testifies that defendant struck plaintiff, this is conclusive. Only disbelief of the witness (*e.g.*, the witness is lying or there is a case of mistaken identity) could justify a refusal to find battery.

By contrast, "circumstantial" evidence is evidence from which there are at least two reasonable inferences that could be drawn by the fact finder. A fact finder could make inferences but is not required. Depending on the facts, even pretty powerful circumstantial evidence can be refuted while direct evidence can be refuted only if the source is disbelieved. Conversely, some circumstantial evidence can be just as powerful as direct evidence.

Requiring a plaintiff to have direct evidence of a price-fixing conspiracy raises some immediately apparent problems. What would constitute direct evidence of a price-fixing conspiracy? One possibility is a video or audio of a price-fixing meeting. But that's unlikely and was even less likely in an earlier era of less sophisticated electronics. Another possibility is that one of the conspirators decides to confess. But this is also unlikely (though not impossible). Can you think of anything else? Was the *Matsushita* majority serious when it insisted on direct evidence as a prerequisite to having a trial on a price-fixing claim?

EXAMPLES & ANALYSIS

EXAMPLE NO. 1: Certain "rare earths" used in making electronic components are found only in China and the Western United States. There are three miners/manufacturers in China and three in the U.S. In May 2010, the three Chinese companies all cut their prices in half. Electronics manufactures, who had previously purchased from both U.S. and Chinese manufacturers, begin buying almost all their rare earths from the Chinese companies because of the vast difference in price. The American companies, who cannot match the Chinese prices without operating at a loss, sue, alleging price-fixing. The Chinese companies move for summary judgment, citing *Matsushita*. What result?

Analysis: Under *Matsushita*, the defendants would win. The American rare earth companies, like the U.S. electronics manufacturers of 30 years ago in *Matsushita*, have the burden of proof. They have proffered some pretty strong looking evidence of illegal concerted activity by the defendants, but the evidence, however persuasive, is only circumstantial and not direct. Now you know why some scholars aren't very impressed by the *Matsushita* decision. *See, e.g.,* Michael J. Kaufman, *Summary Pre-Judgment: The Supreme Court's Profound, Pervasive, and Problematic Presumption About Human Behavior*, 43 LOYOLA L.J. 593, 595-602 (2012) (criticizing the decision and noting that its incorrect approach has had negative ripple effects on other areas of civil procedure).

EXAMPLE NO. 2: In 2012, the three Chinese companies are taken over by the government and begin operating as a state-owned monopoly—Rareco. In 2013, RareCo cuts the price of its products in half again and begins taking away the remaining customers from the only three U.S. companies selling these rare earths. The American manufacturers sue. RareCo moves for summary judgment, citing *Matsushita*. What result?

Analysis: The plaintiffs may be able to defeat summary judgment in spite of *Matsushita*. Recall that in *Matsushita*, the Court placed substantial weight on the economic theory positing that it is very hard to hold together a predatory pricing conspiracy not only because of the difficulties of coordination but also because it will be hard to keep selling products at a loss and remain in business. In turn, this may prompt one or more members of the conspiracy to exit the conspiracy or even blow the whistle. But while Example No. 1 is a lot like the alleged Japanese Electronics conspiracy in *Matsushita*, Example No. 2 involves a state-owned monopoly (RareCo), which removes the problem of coordination as well as extending the potential for the predatory pricer to sell at a loss for a long time in order to drive competitors out of business and then recoup the earlier losses with monopoly profits after the competitors are gone. Further, the facts of Example No. 2 state that RareCo now essentially has captured all of the rare earth sales in the world because of its ultra-low, allegedly below cost, prices. Another part of economic theory influential to the Supreme Court is that predatory pricing is unlikely to succeed because even if the predatory pricers drive out the competition, new competitors will enter the market as soon as the prices go back up, making predatory pricing a losing game. But in addition to being a state-owned monopoly, RareCo is dealing in a product that is very scarce, making it more difficult for competitors to emerge if RareCo drives the existing U.S. companies out of business. In light of the differences between Example No. 2 and the actual *Matsushita* case, the U.S. rare earth companies might defeat summary judgment with such powerful circumstantial evidence because under the facts of Example No. 2 there is no issue of parallel conduct due to the state-owned monopoly. But the question would be close, because it can be argued that despite the differences in the cases, *Matsushita* requires direct evidence—period.

EXAMPLE NO. 3: Assume that in 2014, Congress bans RareCo from selling its products in the U.S. The chief executives of the three American producers of rare earths meet at the Furnace Creek Inn in Death Valley, California on May 1, 2015. On May 4, all three manufacturers double the prices of their products. Purchasers repeatedly attempt to negotiate a lower price in return for long-term purchasing commitments but each of the producers refuses to negotiate and none lowers its prices to take business away from the others. Pro-Chip, a manufacturer of integrated circuits, sues the three Defendants alleging price fixing. The Defendants move for summary judgment. On this record, what result? Does *Matsushita* control?

Analysis: This example has moved from predatory pricing (the subject of *Matsushita*) to price fixing, which is a different type of anticompetitive activity. Unlike predatory pricing, which depends on driving others out of business to make money, price-fixing makes money right away for the conspirators. Consequently, different economic theory is at work and the "must have direct evidence" requirement of *Matsushita* should not apply to a price fixing case. In light of the strong circumstantial evidence in Example No. 3, Pro-Chip should be able to defeat summary judgment.

2. *Liberty Lobby*

Anderson v. Liberty Lobby, Inc., 477 U.S. 242 (1986), granted summary judgment in favor of newspaper defendants sued for libel by a right-wing organization and its founder who took umbrage when compared to Nazis in magazine articles.. *Liberty Lobby* illustrates the interplay between summary judgment procedure and the applicable substantive law of the case—although, like *Matsushita*, it is a controversial decision.

The substantive law was that of defamation. Because of the First Amendment and a strong socio-legal policy in favor of free expression, defamation claims are generally disfavored and subjected to more barriers than many types of cases. In *Liberty Lobby*, the defendants moved for summary judgment, supporting the motion with an affidavit of the primary author of the offending piece in which he detailed the research he had undertaken and the care with which he wrote the article. Under the substantive law of defamation, a plaintiff who is a public official or public figure must show that the defendant acted with "malice," which the Court has defined as publishing an article knowing it was false or with "reckless disregard" for its truth or falsity. *See New York Times Co. v. Sullivan*, 376 U.S. 254, 279–80 (1964). *Liberty Lobby* presented the question of whether, in the face of the reporter's denial of any malice, there was enough evidence of malice to create a genuine dispute of material fact—and whether in making this determination, the court should consider that the plaintiff at trial would need to demonstrate malice by clear and convincing evidence in order to win.

The *Liberty Lobby* majority concluded that a court deciding a summary judgment motion should consider the plaintiff's burden of proof at trial. Reviewing the summary judgment record, it concluded that the plaintiffs had not presented enough evidence of malice to satisfy (to the satisfaction of a reasonable jury) the clear and convincing evidence standard. Consequently, judgment was entered in favor of the media defendants.

Some saw *Liberty Lobby* as a great victory for freedom of the press and many had little sympathy for the plaintiffs, who exhibited extremist views, including racism. Others were concerned that by considering the burden of proof at trial, the Court majority was implicitly involving trial judges in the weighing of evidence, which was not supposed to happen at the summary judgment stage of trial. *Liberty Lobby* was a 6-3 decision in which the dissenters also noted that the majority was also unduly embracing the credibility of the newspaper affiants, who were of course something less than impartial observers. At least constructively, *Poller v. CBS*, 368 U.S. 464 (1962), was overruled, as were other "slightest doubt" style summary judgment decisions prior to the trilogy.

> In addition, per the discussion in the Overview Chapter, recall that there are three major **standards of proof** operating in U.S. law: **preponderance of the evidence, clear-and-convincing evidence,** and **beyond a reasonable doubt**. Ordinary tort and contract claims are subject to the preponderance standard. But defamation claims must be proven by clear and convincing evidence in order to provide greater protection for free expression.

Matsushita and *Liberty Lobby* arguably put the Court in the fact-finding business when assessing summary judgment motions and certainly made it necessary for nonmovants to show that there was more than merely a slight doubt. If the nonmovant wanted to survive a motion for summary judgment that included competent affidavits denying liability and supporting documents, the nonmovant would need to produce sufficient evidence to support the verdict of a reasonable jury. Because plaintiffs have the burden of persuasion at trial, this also as a practical matter requires them to show not only that there is some pretty good evidence in their favor but also that the evidence is good enough to satisfy their burdens of persuasion, which in some cases will be the higher clear and convincing standard.

EXAMPLES & ANALYSIS

EXAMPLE: Pam sues Doug when the golf club he sold her snaps in two on her first use of it at the driving range. The complaint alleges breach of contract and fraud. Doug moves for partial summary judgment, contending that Pam has no evidence to suggest any knowledge on his part that there was anything defective about the club. What result? Does *Liberty Lobby* impact the assessment?

Analysis: Like defamation, fraud is a disfavored claim of sorts in that one must prove wrongdoing by clear and convincing evidence rather than merely a preponderance of the evidence. Even under the preponderance standard, it appears Pam has no evidence that Doug made any knowingly false material representations about the golf club. Her fraud claim thus lacks any evidence on a crucial element (or elements, depending on how one lists the elements of a fraud claim). Assuming Pam has had an adequate opportunity for discovery, Doug's partial summary judgment motion should be granted, particularly when one considers the higher standard of proof Pam must shoulder to prevail in a fraud claim. Her breach of contract claim, however, can go forward. She might even be entitled to partial summary judgment on contract breach if it is undisputed that the golf club broke upon mere normal use and that Doug after discovery has no evidence that she misused or abused the club in any way.

3. *Celotex*

Celotex Corp. v. Catrett, 477 U.S. 317 (1986) was the least controversial of the trilogy decisions and was focused on the procedural protocols of summary judgment practice. It is one of the most cited cases in American law because it has become a fixture of most summary judgment motions and did not involve an "exotic" or highly specialized case like antitrust or defamation.

However, although *Celotex* was in some ways a straightforward tort/product liability case, it was something more than a Brand X tort case because the dangerous product involved was asbestos, a chemical that produced the largest mass tort in history. Asbestos was widely used as an insulating material during much of the 20th Century until it became known that under certain common conditions asbestos gave off microscopic airborne fibers that when ingested often caused serious damage to the lungs. By the 1970s, plaintiffs' lawyers had obtained incriminating documents establishing these dangers and were winning asbestos cases against both manufacturers and those using asbestos product such as insulation installation companies. Much of this was just beginning to become apparent during the mid-1980s when the *Celotex* case hit the Supreme Court.

When suing a product manufacturer, the plaintiff must be able to show that the plaintiff was in contact with the defendant's product and that this contact caused injury. A plaintiff who was exposed to asbestos while working at a factory, naval yard, or power plant still generally had to show that he was injured by a particular manufacturer's asbestos. As a result, a major battle in the tort cases became whether the plaintiff had sufficiently established the identity of the injurious asbestos at issue. Celotex did not argue that its asbestos was safe, but rather that the plaintiff had not shown that he was hurt by Celotex asbestos rather than that of Johns-Manville or some other manufacturer.

In response, Nell Catrett, the wife of the decedent Louis, produced three documents: a transcript of a deposition of Louis while he was still alive, a letter from an official of one of Louis's former employers whom Celotex planned to call as a trial witness, and a letter from an insurance company to Nell's attorney, all tending to establish that Louis had been exposed to Celotex's asbestos products in Chicago during 1970-1971. Celotex argued that the three documents were inadmissible hearsay and thus could not be considered in opposition to the summary judgment motion.

Hearsay is a statement made out of the courtroom that is offered to establish the truth of the statement. Statements in documents such as letters and ledgers are often hearsay. Hearsay is generally inadmissible at trial but statements of a party are not hearsay. For example, if it was a letter from Celotex reflecting use of its product at Louis Catrett's workplace, this would be admissible. In addition, Federal Rules of Evidence 803 and 804 establish roughly 30 exceptions to the hearsay rule, such as the business records exception.

The trial court granted Celotex's summary judgment motion because Nell was unable to produce evidence in support of her allegation that Louis had been exposed to Celotex asbestos. The D.C. Circuit reversed, holding that Celotex's failure to support its motion with evidence tending to negate such exposure precluded the entry of summary judgment in its favor. The Supreme Court reversed and remanded, holding that a summary judgment movant could succeed without submitting affidavits or other motion papers in cases where the non-movant lacked supporting evidence on an essential element of its claim.

In denying Celotex's motion, the D.C. Circuit stated that "the party opposing the motion for summary judgment bears the burden of responding only after the moving party has met its burden of coming forward with proof of the absence of any genuine issues of material fact" and declined to consider Celotex's hearsay argument. The Supreme Court disagreed, ruling that "the plain language of Rule 56 mandates the entry of summary judgment, after adequate time for discovery and upon motion, against a party who fails to make a showing sufficient to establish the existence of an element essential to that party's case, and on which that party will bear the burden of proof at trial." Continued the Court:

In such a situation, there can be "no genuine issue as to any material fact," since a complete failure of proof concerning an essential element of the nonmoving party's case necessarily renders all other facts immaterial. The moving party is "entitled to a judgment as a matter of law" because the nonmoving party has failed to make a sufficient showing on an essential element of her case with respect to which she has the burden of proof. . . .

Of course, a party seeking summary judgment always bears the initial responsibility of informing the district court of the basis for its motion, and identifying those portions of "the pleadings, depositions, answers to interrogatories, and admissions on file, together with the affidavits, if any," which it believes demonstrate the absence of a genuine issue of material fact. But unlike the Court of Appeals, we find no express or implied requirement in Rule 56 that the moving party support its motion with affidavits or other similar materials *negating* the opponent's claim. On the contrary, Rule 56 refers to "the affidavits, *if any*" (emphasis added), [which the Court read as suggesting that affidavits were unnecessary.] And if there were any doubt about the meaning of Rule 56 in this regard, such doubt is clearly removed by [other language in Rule 56 which provides] that claimants and defendants, respectively, may move for summary judgment *"with or without supporting affidavits."* (emphasis added).

The import of these subsections is that, regardless of whether the moving party accompanies its summary judgment motion with affidavits, the motion may, and should, be granted so long as whatever is before the district court demonstrates that the standard for the entry of summary judgment, as set forth in Rule 56(c), is satisfied. One of the principal purposes of the summary judgment rule is to isolate and dispose of factually unsupported claims or defenses, and we think it should be interpreted in a way that allows it to accomplish this purpose.

In cases like the instant one, where the nonmoving party will bear the burden of proof at trial on a dispositive issue, a summary judgment motion may properly be made in reliance solely on the "pleadings, depositions, answers to interrogatories, and admissions on file." Such a motion, whether or not accompanied by affidavits, will be "made and supported as provided in this rule," and Rule 56 therefore requires the nonmoving party to go beyond the pleadings and by her own affidavits, or by the "depositions, answers to interrogatories, and admissions on file," designate "specific facts showing that there is a genuine issue for trial."

We do not mean that the nonmoving party must produce evidence in a form that would be admissible at trial in order to avoid summary judgment. Obviously, Rule 56 does not require the nonmoving party to depose her own witnesses. Rule 56 permits a proper summary judgment motion to be opposed by any of the kinds of evidentiary materials listed in Rule 56(c), except the mere pleadings themselves, and it is from this list that one would normally expect the nonmoving party to make the showing to which we have referred.

* * *

> **Sua sponte** roughly translates to (and means) "on the court's initiative."

Our conclusion is bolstered by the fact that district courts are widely acknowledged to possess the power to enter summary judgments *sua sponte*, so long as the losing party was on notice that she had to come forward with all of her evidence. It would surely defy common sense to hold that the District Court could have entered summary judgment *sua sponte* in favor of petitioner in the instant case, but that petitioner's filing of a motion requesting such a disposition precluded the District Court from ordering it.

477 U.S. at 332–26. After this holding, Chief Justice Rehnquist's majority opinion continued with dicta that has become known as the Court's "Ode to Summary Judgment":

Summary judgment procedure is properly regarded not as a disfavored procedural shortcut, but rather as an integral part of the Federal Rules as a whole, which are designed "to secure the just, speedy and inexpensive determination of every action." Fed. Rule Civ. Proc. 1.

Before the shift to "notice pleading" accomplished by the Federal Rules, motions to dismiss a complaint or to strike a defense were the principal tools by which factually insufficient claims or defenses could be isolated and prevented from going to trial with the attendant unwarranted consumption of public and private resources. But with the advent of "notice pleading," the motion to dismiss seldom fulfills this function any more, and its place has been taken by the motion for summary judgment. Rule 56 must be construed with due regard not only for the rights of persons asserting claims and defenses that are adequately based in fact to have those claims and defenses tried to a jury, but also for the rights of persons opposing such claims and defenses to demonstrate in the manner provided by the Rule, prior to trial, that the claims and defenses have no factual basis.

477 U.S. at 327.

Justice Byron White, concurred, noting that the summary judgment "movant must discharge the burden the Rules place upon him" and that it "is not enough to move for summary judgment without supporting the motion in any way or with a conclusory assertion that the plaintiff has no evidence to prove his case." Further, the non-movant "need not also depose his witnesses or obtain their affidavits to defeat a summary judgment motion asserting only that he has failed to produce any support for his case. It is the defendant's task to negate, if he can, the claimed basis for the suit." 477 U.S. at 328. This concurrence also set up an interesting inquiry for the D.C. Circuit on remand. "[Catrett] does not contend that she was not obligated to reveal her witnesses and evidence but insists that she has revealed enough to defeat the motion for summary judgment. Because the Court of Appeals found it unnecessary to address this aspect of the case, I agree that the case should be remanded for further proceedings." 477 U.S. at 328–29.

Justice William Brennan and two others dissented, contending that Celotex did

Justice John Paul Stevens dissented on the basis of a flaw in the trial court decision in that it appeared the trial judge believed it was necessary for the plaintiff to show Louis's exposure to Celotex asbestos happened in the District of Columbia in order to win the case. Justice Stevens was correct in pointing out this flaw in the trial court's analysis. Because of the error, Justice Stevens favored a remand to determine if this error in thinking was crucial to the decision to grant summary judgment.

not meet its burden of production sufficiently to merit summary judgment. The dissent also went into some detail describing the choreography of summary judgment. Although this part of the opinion has become a staple of many law school classes, recent empirical scholarship suggests that the type of burden shifting outlined in the Brennan dissent seldom is relevant to summary judgment practice at the trial court level. *See* Linda S. Mullenix, *The 25th Anniversary of the Summary Judgment Trilogy: Much Ado About Very Little*, 43 Loyola L.J. 561 (2012). The Brennan dissent set forth the following template for making and responding to summary judgment motions.

The burden of production imposed by Rule 56 requires the moving party to make a prima facie showing that it is entitled to summary judgment. The manner in which this showing can be made depends upon which party will bear the burden of persuasion on the challenged claim at trial. If the *moving* party will bear the burden of persuasion at trial, that party must support its motion with credible evidence—using any of the materials specified in Rule 56—that would entitle it to a directed verdict if not controverted at trial. . . .

If the burden of persuasion at trial would be on the *nonmoving* party, the party moving for summary judgment may satisfy Rule 56's burden of production in either of two ways. First, the moving party may submit affirmative evidence that negates an essential element of the nonmoving party's claim. Second, the moving party may demonstrate to the court that the nonmoving party's evidence is insufficient to establish an essential element of the nonmoving party's claim. If the nonmoving party cannot muster sufficient evidence to make out its claim, a trial would be useless and the moving party is entitled to summary judgment as a matter of law.

Where the moving party adopts this second option and seeks summary judgment on the ground that the nonmoving party—who will bear the burden of persuasion at trial—has no evidence, the mechanics of dis- charging Rule 56's burden of production are somewhat trickier. Plainly, a conclusory assertion that the nonmoving party has no evidence is insufficient. Such a "burden" of production is no burden at all and would simply permit summary judgment procedure to be converted into a tool for harassment.

* * *

[A] party who moves for summary judgment on the ground that the nonmoving party has no evidence must affirmatively show the absence of evidence in the record. This may require the moving party to depose the nonmoving party's witnesses or to establish the inadequacy of documentary evidence. If there is literally no evidence in the record, the moving party may demonstrate this by reviewing for the court the admissions, interrogatories, and other exchanges between the parties that are in the record. Either way, however, the moving party must affirmatively demonstrate that there is no evidence in the record to support a judgment for the nonmoving party.

If the moving party has not fully discharged this initial burden of pro- duction, its motion for summary judgment must be denied, and the court need not consider whether the moving party has met its ultimate burden of persuasion. Accordingly, the nonmoving party may defeat a motion for summary judgment that asserts that the nonmoving party has no evidence by calling the court's attention to supporting evidence already in the re- cord that was overlooked or ignored by the moving party. In that event, the moving party must respond by making an attempt to demonstrate the inadequacy of this evidence. . . . Absent such a demonstration, summary judgment would have to be denied on the ground that the moving party had failed to meet its burden of production under Rule 56. . . . .

477 U.S. at 331-32.

4. An Example of the Intersection of Product Liability Claims and Procedure

As noted above, plaintiffs have to identify the offending product's origin and prove a causal link between product use or exposure and injury. This can make product description and identification a crucial stage of litigation. Another mass tort of the 1980s involved DES, a drug that when ingested by pregnant women sometimes led to birth defects. Plaintiffs were often the children born with the defects, which might not manifest themselves until adolescence (the statute of limitations on such claims does not begin to run until the child turns 18). This meant that by the time many DES actions were being tried, the taking of the drug was a relatively distant memory for the mother and the identity of the manufacturer might no longer be reflected in medical or pharmaceutical records. But different manufacturers of DES tended to color the pills differently. At the depositions of the plaintiffs' mothers, the on-the-edge-of-your-seat moment was when the mother was asked about the color of the pills she took during plaintiff's pregnancy. Her answer would inculpate some defendants and exculpate others.

EXAMPLES & ANALYSIS

EXAMPLE: You've just taken the deposition of one of these mothers. She testifies that she is positive that she took only blue DES pills during pregnancy and denies ever taking red, green, or yellow DES pills. You represent the Yellow DES Company and move for summary judgment. Will the court be likely to grant the motion? What else, if anything, do you need to know to answer the question?

Analysis: You need to know whether there is any other information tending to suggest use of Yellow pills by the plaintiff's mother, such as medical or pharmaceutical records. If there is not and she testifies firmly and consistently that she took only blue pills, you can make a summary judgment motion that should be granted. Point to any aspects of the record where there is an absence of anything suggesting use of Yellow pills by the mother. If the record shows no possibility of use of Yellow pills, your client should get summary judgment—unless the plaintiff establishes some issue for trial. For example, the plaintiff might introduce another affidavit from the pharmacist that filled the mother's prescriptions saying that during the time period in question, her pharmacy sold only Yellow pills. Or plaintiff might introduce evidence of the mother's faulty memory generally (*e.g.*, an Alzheimer's diagnosis) or contradictory testimony (in statements other than the deposition, she mentioned Yellow and Green pills). At the mother's deposition, other manufacturers or plaintiff probably challenged her recollection of taking only Blue pills. If she wavered or contradicted her earlier testimony, some courts would see this as a genuine dispute of material fact precluding summary judgment. And there's another wrinkle. Even if her testimony is unwavering, a court still has discretion to deny the motion if the judge is reluctant to think that people can be this accurate about the pills they took 15 or 20 years earlier (although this is unlikely).

EXAMPLE: What if Celotex was supporting its summary judgment motion with letters from all former plant managers at the places Mr. Cattrett had worked and all letters clearly stated, without contradiction or refutation, that Celotex product was never used at the plants. Would this be enough to support summary judgment for Celotex? Should the court insist that these statements by the plant managers be in affidavit form? Must the court permit Catrett to depose the letter authors? Or is it enough if Celotex states that it intends to call all the letter authors as witnesses at trial?

Analysis: In this variant of the actual case, what is "sauce for the goose" (*i.e.*, a plaintiff seeking to establish a genuine dispute of material fact) should be "sauce for the gander" (*i.e.*, a defendant seeking to establish undisputed facts that foreclose as a matter of law the possibility that the plaintiff was exposed to the defendant's asbestos). In both cases, a court should be permitted to accept assertions not contained in an affidavit or sworn declaration if the court is satisfied that the statements have sufficient credibility and the party proffering the statement can produce the information in admissible form at trial.

The trial court has great discretion to insist on an affidavit or **declaration** unless there are compelling reasons why the statement could not be put into this form. For example, the letter-writing witness may currently be traveling abroad or undergoing surgery. Usually, however, courts will want to see more than an unverified letter.

> A **declaration** is a statement signed under penalty of perjury that many states allow to be used in place of the traditional affidavit, which must be notarized. Use of a declaration allows the witness to avoid the burden of searching out a notary and perhaps paying a fee for the notarization.

Under almost all circumstances, the non-moving party will be permitted an opportunity to depose the letter writers to test their recollection and learn more about the bases for their opinions in order to assess their accuracy. For example, the letter writers may have been unaware that a particular brand name of asbestos they recall being used was a Celotex product.

If the court is willing to receive into the case record the statements of the former workers claiming a complete absence of Celotex product at their workplaces, the plaintiff fails to impeach their testimony at deposition, and the plaintiff offers no conflicting evidence, summary judgment should probably be granted.

EXAMPLE: What if Catrett had moved for summary judgment using letters stating that Celotex product was in widespread use at the places he had worked and that Nell Catrett intended to call all the letter authors as witnesses at trial? Assume that Celotex's only defense is lack of exposure to its product. Can Catrett, despite having the burden of persuasion, get partial summary judgment? Why is complete summary judgment for the plaintiff realistically impossible in this situation?

Analysis: Although Rule 56 applies to both plaintiffs and defendants, courts as a practical matter will be less inclined to end a case based on inadmissible submissions than to allow a case to continue if there is adequate promise that the submissions will be made admissible by the time of trial. In such cases, the argument that the factfinder might disbelieve the witness has more traction because the summary judgment movant must show that trial is unnecessary while the nonmovant merely must show that there are fact disputes requiring trial. A promise to produce a letter writer on the witness stand satisfies the latter burden fairly easily but does not necessarily satisfy the former burden. In the actual case, Catrett could not realistically obtain full summary judgment because it would remain open to the jury to conclude that Louis was either injured by asbestos made by a manufacturer other than Celotex or that his injuries resulted from a something other than asbestos.

E. The Wake of the Trilogy and Continuing Debate over Summary Judgment Practice

Most observers view the Trilogy as effecting a major revision of summary judgment practice and judicial attitudes toward summary judgment. *See, e.g.,* Steven Alan Childress, *A New Era for Summary Judgments: Recent Shifts at the Supreme Court,* 116 F.R.D. 183 (1987). It met mixed responses from the legal profession. Many hailed the cases for encouraging greater use of summary judgment, which they saw as not only more consistent with the Rule but also more efficient (avoiding trials where one side was seemingly sure to lose) and fairer to defendants, who might win at trial but were likely to settle rather than go to trial and likely to pay more in settlement because the claim had survived summary judgment.

Conversely, many others, particularly in the academy, argued that not only were the decisions flawed on their own terms but also that they established a regime in which plaintiffs would routinely need to invest more resources in order to do as well as they did prior to the Trilogy and in which judges intruded too much on the traditional jury prerogative of fact finding. These criticisms continued for the next two decades as the Court refused to back away from the Trilogy and it became firmly ensconced as controlling law. *See, e.g.,* Arthur R. Miller, *The Pretrial Rush to Judgment: Are the "Litigation Explosion," "Liability Crisis," and Efficiency Cliches Eroding Our Day in Court and Jury Trial Commitments?,* 78 N.Y.U. L. Rev. 982 (2003).

There is also substantial debate regarding whether aggressive pretrial disposition motion practice really saves any time at all compared to simply setting a case for trial. In more than 95 percent of cases, settlement results and the time expended to try the remaining one percent of cases may well be far less than the cumulative resources expended on summary judgment practice. *See* Jeffrey W. Stempel, *Taking Cognitive Illiberalism Seriously: Judicial Humility; Aggregate Efficiency; and Acceptable Justice,* 43 Loyola L.J. 627 (2012); John Bronsteen, *Against Summary Judgment,* 75 Geo. Wash. L. Rev. 522 (2007).

In particular, more aggressive summary judgment practice raised substantial concern that judges influenced by their own perception of facts may be inappropriately substituting their assessments for those of a jury by improperly reaching factual determinations influenced by the judges' own biases instead of merely looking for genuine disputes of material fact and submitting such disputes to jury trial.

Perhaps proving the ineffectiveness of academic criticism, the Supreme Court ushered in the third decade of post-Trilogy summary judgment with a decision that proved even more controversial and criticism-attracting than the Trilogy.

FROM THE COURT

Scott v. Harris
550 U.S. 372 (2007)
Supreme Court of the United States

Justice SCALIA delivered the opinion of the Court.

We consider whether a law enforcement official can, consistent with the Fourth Amendment, attempt to stop a fleeing motorist from continuing his public-endangering flight by ramming the motorist's car from behind. Put another way: Can an officer take actions that place a fleeing motorist at risk of serious injury or death in order to stop the motorist's flight from endangering the lives of innocent bystanders?

I

In March 2001, a Georgia county deputy clocked respondent's vehicle traveling at 73 miles per hour on a road with a 55-mile-per-hour speed limit. [R]espondent sped away, initiating a chase down what is in most portions a two-lane road, at speeds exceeding 85 miles per hour. The deputy radioed his dispatcher. . . . Petitioner, Deputy Timothy Scott, heard the radio communication and joined the pursuit along with other officers. In the midst of the chase, respondent pulled into the parking lot of a shopping center and was nearly boxed in by the various police vehicles. Respondent [Victor Harris, a college student returning home after work] evaded the trap by making a sharp turn, colliding with Scott's police car, exiting the parking lot, and speeding off once again down a two-lane highway.

Following respondent's shopping center maneuvering, which resulted in slight damage to Scott's police car, Scott took over as the lead pursuit vehicle. Six minutes and nearly 10 miles after the chase had begun, Scott decided to attempt to terminate the episode by employing a "Precision Intervention Technique ('PIT') maneuver, which causes the fleeing vehicle to spin to a stop." Having radioed his supervisor for permission, Scott was told to "'[g]o ahead and take him out.'" Instead, Scott applied his push bumper to the rear of respondent's vehicle. As a result, respondent lost control of his vehicle, which left the roadway, ran down an embankment, overturned, and crashed. Respondent [Harris] was badly injured and was rendered a quadriplegic.

Respondent filed suit against Deputy Scott and others under 42 U.S.C. § 1983, alleging, *inter alia*, a violation of his federal constitutional rights, viz. use of excessive force resulting in an unreasonable seizure under the Fourth Amendment. In response, Scott filed a motion for summary judgment based on an assertion of qualified immunity.

> *Inter alia* roughly translates as "among other things.

The District Court denied the motion, finding that "there are material issues of fact on which the issue of qualified immunity turns which present sufficient disagreement to require submission to a jury." On interlocutory appeal, the United States Court of Appeals for the Eleventh Circuit affirmed the District Court's decision to allow respondent's Fourth Amendment claim against Scott to proceed to trial.

[T]he Court of Appeals concluded that Scott's actions could constitute "deadly force" under *Tennessee* v. *Garner*, 471 U.S. 1 (1985), and that the use of such force in this context "would violate [respondent's] constitutional right to be free from excessive force during a seizure. Accordingly, a reasonable jury could find that Scott violated [respondent's] Fourth Amendment rights." The Court of Appeals further concluded that "the law as it existed [at the time of the incident], was sufficiently clear to give reasonable law enforcement officers 'fair notice' that ramming a vehicle under these circumstances was unlawful." The Court of Appeals thus concluded that Scott was not entitled to qualified immunity.

> In a footnote, the Court noted that:
>
> Qualified immunity is "an *immunity from suit* rather than a mere defense to liability; and like an absolute immunity, it is effectively lost if a case is erroneously permitted to go to trial." *Mitchell* v. *Forsyth*, 472 U.S. 511, 526 (1985). Thus, we have held that an order denying qualified immunity is immediately appealable even though it is interlocutory; otherwise, it would be "effectively unreviewable." Further, "we repeatedly have stressed the importance of resolving immunity questions at the earliest possible stage in litigation."
>
> Why did the Court find it necessary to include this in the opinion? Absent this substantive law of qualified immunity, what would have happened to the case after the Eleventh Circuit decision?

II

In resolving questions of qualified immunity, courts are required to resolve a "threshold question: Taken in the light most favorable to the party asserting the injury, do the facts alleged show the officer's conduct violated a constitutional right? This must be the initial inquiry." If, and only if, the court finds a violation of a constitutional right, "the next, sequential step is to ask whether the right was clearly established . . . in light of the specific context of the case." Although this ordering contradicts "[o]ur policy of avoiding unnecessary adjudication of constitutional issues," we have said that such a departure from practice is "necessary to set forth principles which will become the basis for a [future] holding that a right is clearly established." We therefore turn to the threshold inquiry: whether Deputy Scott's actions violated the Fourth Amendment.

III

A

The first step in assessing the constitutionality of Scott's actions is to determine the relevant facts. As this case was decided on summary judgment, there have not yet been factual findings by a judge or jury, and respondent's version of events (unsurprisingly) differs substantially from Scott's version. When things are in such a posture, courts are required to view the facts and draw reasonable inferences "in the light most favorable to the party opposing the [summary judgment] motion." In qualified immunity cases, this usually means adopting (as the Court of Appeals did here) the plaintiff's version of the facts.

There is, however, an added wrinkle in this case: existence in the record of a videotape capturing the events in question. There are no allegations or indications that this videotape was doctored or altered in any way, nor any contention that what it depicts differs from what actually happened. The videotape quite clearly contradicts the version of the story told by respondent and adopted by the Court of Appeals. For example, the Court of Appeals adopted respondent's assertions that, during the chase, "there was little, if any, actual threat to pedestrians or other motorists, as the roads were mostly empty and [respondent] remained in control of his vehicle." Indeed, reading the lower court's opinion, one gets the impression that respondent, rather than fleeing from police, was attempting to pass his driving test:

"[T]aking the facts from the non-movant's viewpoint, [respondent] remained in control of his vehicle, slowed for turns and intersections, and typically used his indicators for turns. He did not run any motorists off the road. Nor was he a threat to pedestrians in the shopping center parking lot, which was free from pedestrian and vehicular traffic as the center was closed. Significantly, by the time the parties were back on the highway and Scott rammed [Harris], the motorway had been cleared of motorists and pedestrians allegedly because of police blockades of the nearby intersections."

We are happy to allow the videotape to speak for itself. *See* Record 36, Exh. A, available at http://www.supremecourtus.gov/opinions/video/scott_v_harris.html and in Clerk of Court's case file.

The videotape tells quite a different story. There we see respondent's vehicle racing down narrow, two-lane roads in the dead of night at speeds that are shockingly fast. We see it swerve around more than a dozen other cars, cross the double-yellow line, and force cars traveling in both directions to their respective shoulders to avoid being hit. We see it run multiple red lights and travel for considerable periods of time in the occasional center left-turn-only lane, chased by numerous police cars forced to engage in the same hazardous maneuvers just to keep up. Far from being the cautious and controlled driver the lower court depicts, what we see on the video more closely resembles a Hollywood-style car chase of the most frightening sort, placing police officers and innocent bystanders alike at great risk of serious injury. . . .

When opposing parties tell two different stories, one of which is blatantly contradicted by the record, so that no reasonable jury could believe it, a court should not adopt that version of the facts for purposes of ruling on a motion for summary judgment.

That was the case here with regard to the factual issue whether respondent was driving in such fashion as to endanger human life. Respondent's version of events is so utterly discredited by the record that no reasonable jury could have believed him. The Court of Appeals should not have relied on such visible fiction; it should have viewed the facts in the light depicted by the videotape.

B

The question we need to answer is whether Scott's actions were objectively reasonable. Justice Stevens incorrectly declares this to be "a question of fact best reserved for a jury," and complains we are "usurp[ing] the jury's factfinding function." At the summary judgment stage, however, once we have determined the relevant set of facts and drawn all inferences in favor of the nonmoving party *to the extent supportable by the record*, the reasonableness of Scott's actions—or, in Justice Stevens' parlance, "[w]hether [respondent's] actions have risen to a level warranting deadly force," is a pure question of law.

1

Respondent urges us to analyze this case as we analyzed *Garner*. We must first decide, he says, whether the actions Scott took constituted "deadly force." (He defines "deadly force" as "any use of force which creates a substantial likelihood of causing death or serious bodily injury"). If so, respondent claims that *Garner* prescribes certain preconditions that must be met before Scott's actions can survive Fourth Amendment scrutiny: (1) The suspect must have posed an immediate threat of serious physical harm to the officer or others; (2) deadly force must have been necessary to prevent escape; and (3) where feasible, the officer must have given the suspect some warning. Since these *Garner* preconditions for using deadly force were not met in this case, [Harris argues that] Scott's actions were *per se* unreasonable.

Respondent's argument falters at its first step; *Garner* did not establish a magical on/off switch that triggers rigid preconditions whenever an officer's actions constitute "deadly force." *Garner* was simply an application of the Fourth Amendment's "reasonableness" test, to the use of a particular type of force in a particular situation. *Garner* held that it was unreasonable to kill a "young, slight, and unarmed" burglary suspect by shooting him "in the back of the head" while he was running away on foot and when the officer "could not reasonably have believed that [the suspect] . . . posed any threat," and "never attempted to justify his actions on any basis other than the need to prevent an escape."

Whatever *Garner* said about the factors that *might have* justified shooting the suspect in that case, such "preconditions" have scant applicability to this case, which has vastly different facts. "*Garner* had nothing to do with one car striking another or even with car chases in general. . . . A police car's bumping a fleeing car is, in fact, not much like a policeman's shooting a gun so as to hit a person." Nor is the threat posed by the flight on foot of an unarmed suspect even remotely comparable to the extreme danger to human life posed by respondent in this case. Although respondent's attempt to craft an easy-to-apply legal test in the Fourth Amendment context is admirable, in the end we must still slosh our way through the factbound morass of "reasonableness." Whether or not Scott's actions constituted application of "deadly force," all that matters is whether Scott's actions were reasonable.

2

In determining the reasonableness of the manner in which a seizure is effected, "[w]e must balance the nature and quality of the intrusion on the individual's Fourth Amendment interests against the importance of the governmental interests alleged to justify the intrusion." . . . Thus, in judging whether Scott's actions were reasonable, we must consider the risk of bodily harm that Scott's actions posed to respondent in light of the threat to the public that Scott was trying to eliminate. Although there is no obvious way to quantify the risks on either side, it is clear from the videotape that respondent posed an actual and imminent threat to the lives of any pedestrians who might have been present, to other civilian motorists, and to the officers involved in the chase.

It is equally clear that Scott's actions posed a high likelihood of serious injury or death to respondent—though not the near *certainty* of death posed by, say, shooting a fleeing felon in the back of the head or pulling alongside a fleeing motorist's car and shooting the motorist. So how does a court go about weighing the perhaps lesser probability of injuring or killing numerous bystanders against the perhaps larger probability of injuring or killing a single person? We think it appropriate in this process to take into account not only the number of lives at risk, but also their relative culpability. It was respondent, after all, who intentionally placed himself and the public in danger by unlawfully engaging in the reckless, high-speed flight that ultimately produced the choice between two evils that Scott confronted. Multiple police cars, with blue lights flashing and sirens blaring, had been chasing respondent for nearly 10 miles, but he ignored their warning to stop. By contrast, those who might have been harmed had Scott not taken the action he did were entirely innocent. We have little difficulty in concluding it was reasonable for Scott to take the action that he did.

But wait, says respondent: Couldn't the innocent public equally have been protected, and the tragic accident entirely avoided, if the police had simply ceased their pursuit? We think the police need not have taken that chance and hoped for the best. Whereas Scott's action—ramming respondent off the road—was *certain* to eliminate the risk that respondent posed to the public, ceasing pursuit was not. . . .

[W]e are loath to lay down a rule requiring the police to allow fleeing suspects to get away whenever they drive *so recklessly* that they put other people's lives in danger. It is obvious the perverse incentives such a rule would create: Every fleeing motorist would know that escape is within his grasp, if only he accelerates to 90 miles per hour, crosses the double-yellow line a few times, and runs a few red lights. The Constitution assuredly does not impose this invitation to impunity-earned-by-recklessness. Instead, we lay down a more sensible rule: A police officer's attempt to terminate a dangerous high-speed car chase that threatens the lives of innocent bystanders does not violate the Fourth Amendment, even when it places the fleeing motorist at risk of serious injury or death.

* * *

The car chase that respondent initiated in this case posed a substantial and immediate risk of serious physical injury to others; no reasonable jury could conclude otherwise. Scott's attempt to terminate the chase by forcing respondent off the road was reasonable, and Scott is entitled to summary judgment. The Court of Appeals' judgment to the contrary is reversed.

Justice GINSBURG, concurring.

I join the Court's opinion and would underscore two points. First, I do not read today's decision as articulating a mechanical, *per se* rule. The inquiry described by the Court is situation specific. Among relevant considerations: Were the lives and well-being of others (motorists, pedestrians, police officers) at risk? Was there a safer way, given the time, place, and circumstances, to stop the fleeing vehicle? "[A]dmirable" as "[an] attempt to craft an easy-to-apply legal test in the Fourth Amendment context [may be]," the Court explains, "in the end we must still slosh our way through the factbound morass of 'reasonableness.'"

Justice BREYER, concurring.

I join the Court's opinion with one suggestion and two qualifications. Because watching the video footage of the car chase made a difference to my own view of the case, I suggest that the interested reader take advantage of the link in the Court's opinion and watch it. Having done so, I do not believe a reasonable jury could, in this instance, find that Officer Timothy Scott (who joined the chase late in the day and did not know the specific reason why the respondent was being pursued) acted in violation of the Constitution. . . .

I disagree with the Court insofar as it articulates a *per se* rule. The majority states: "A police officer's attempt to terminate a dangerous high-speed car chase that threatens the lives of innocent bystanders does not violate the Fourth Amendment, even when it places the fleeing motorist at risk of serious injury or death." This statement is too absolute. As Justice Ginsburg points out, whether a high-speed chase violates the Fourth Amendment may well depend upon more circumstances than the majority's rule reflects. With these qualifications, I join the Court's opinion.

Justice STEVENS, dissenting.

Today, the Court asks whether an officer may "take actions that place a fleeing motorist at risk of serious injury or death in order to stop the motorist's flight from endangering the lives of innocent bystanders." Depending on the circumstances, the answer may be an obvious "yes," an obvious "no," or sufficiently doubtful that the question of the reasonableness of the officer's actions should be decided by a jury, after a review of the degree of danger and the alternatives available to the officer. A high-speed chase in a desert in Nevada is, after all, quite different from one that travels through the heart of Las Vegas.

Relying on a *de novo* review of a videotape of a portion of a nighttime chase on a lightly traveled road in Georgia where no pedestrians or other "bystanders" were present, buttressed by uninformed speculation about the possible consequences of discontinuing the chase, eight of the jurors on this Court reach a verdict that differs from the views of the judges on both the District Court and the Court of Appeals who are surely more familiar with the hazards of driving on Georgia roads than we are. The Court's justification for this unprecedented departure from our well-settled standard of review of factual determinations made by a district court and affirmed by a court of appeals is based on its mistaken view that the Court of Appeals' description of the facts was "blatantly contradicted by the record" and that respondent's version of the events was "so utterly discredited by the record that no reasonable jury could have believed him."

> A **de novo review** is one according no deference to the lower court's assessment. This contrasts with "clearly erroneous" review that disturbs a lower court determination only if the reviewing court is left with the definite and firm impression that a mistake was made. Where the lower court has discretion, review of its exercise may proceed according to an "abuse of discretion" standard.

Rather than supporting the conclusion that what we see on the video "resembles a Hollywood-style car chase of the most frightening sort," the tape actually confirms, rather than contradicts, the lower courts' appraisal of the factual questions at issue. More importantly, it surely does not provide a principled basis for depriving the respondent of his right to have a jury evaluate the question whether the police officers' decision to use deadly force to bring the chase to an end was reasonable.

> In a footnote, Justice Stevens stated:
>
> I can only conclude that my colleagues were unduly frightened by two or three images on the tape that looked like bursts of lightning or explosions, but were in fact merely the headlights of vehicles zooming by in the opposite lane. Had they learned to drive when most high-speed driving took place on two-lane roads rather than on superhighways—when split-second judgments about the risk of passing a slow poke in the face of oncoming traffic were routine—they might well have reacted to the videotape more dispassionately.

Was Justice Stevens being an old fogie of the "when I was your age, I used to walk five miles to school through snow drifts ten feet high" genre? (All of us except Coleman are old enough that we are allowed to use politically incorrect terms like old fogie.) Or is he on to something about differing perceptions of traffic danger? Do his observations suggest anything regarding the degree to which judges should exercise their power in determining the range of reasonable jury responses?

Omitted from the Court's description of the initial speeding violation is the fact that respondent was on a four-lane portion of Highway 34 when the officer clocked his speed at 73 miles per hour and initiated the chase. More significantly—and contrary to the Court's assumption that respondent's vehicle "forced cars traveling in both directions to their respective shoulders to avoid being hit"—a fact unmentioned in the text of the opinion explains why those cars pulled over prior to being passed by respondent. The sirens and flashing lights on the police cars following respondent gave the same warning that a speeding ambulance or fire engine would have provided. The 13 cars that respondent passed on his side of the road before entering the shopping center, and both of the cars that he passed on the right after leaving the center, no doubt had already pulled to the side of the road or were driving along the shoulder because they heard the police sirens or saw the flashing lights before respondent or the police cruisers approached. A jury could certainly conclude that those motorists were exposed to no greater risk than persons who take the same action in response to a speeding ambulance, and that their reactions were fully consistent with the evidence that respondent, though speeding, retained full control of his vehicle.

The police sirens also minimized any risk that may have arisen from running "multiple red lights." In fact, respondent and his pursuers went through only two intersections with stop lights and in both cases all other vehicles in sight were stationary, presumably because they had been warned of the approaching speeders. Incidentally, the videos do show that the lights were red when the police cars passed through them but, because the cameras were farther away when respondent did so and it is difficult to discern the color of the signal at that point, it is not entirely clear that he ran either or both of the red lights. In any event, the risk of harm to the stationary vehicles was minimized by the sirens, and there is no reason to believe that respondent would have disobeyed the signals if he were not being pursued.

My colleagues on the jury saw respondent "swerve around more than a dozen other cars," and "force cars traveling in both directions to their respective shoulders," but they apparently discounted the possibility that those cars were already out of the pursuit's path as a result of hearing the sirens. Even if that were not so, passing a slower vehicle on a two-lane road always involves some degree of swerving and is not especially dangerous if there are no cars coming from the opposite direction. At no point during the chase did respondent pull into the opposite lane other than to pass a car in front of him; he did the latter no more than five times and, on most of those occasions, used his turn signal. On none of these occasions was there a car traveling in the opposite direction. In fact, at one point, when respondent found himself behind a car in his own lane and there were cars traveling in the other direction, he slowed and waited for the cars traveling in the other direction to pass before overtaking the car in front of him while using his turn signal to do so. This is hardly the stuff of Hollywood. To the contrary, the video does not reveal any incidents that could even be remotely characterized as "close calls."

In sum, the factual statements by the Court of Appeals quoted by the Court were entirely accurate. That court did not describe respondent as a "cautious" driver as my colleagues imply but it did correctly conclude that there is no evidence that he ever lost control of his vehicle. That court also correctly pointed out that the incident in the shopping center parking lot did not create any risk to pedestrians or other vehicles because the chase occurred just before 11 p.m. on a weekday night and the center was closed. It is apparent from the record (including the videotape) that local police had blocked off intersections to keep respondent from entering residential neighborhoods and possibly endangering other motorists. I would add that the videos also show that no pedestrians, parked cars, sidewalks, or residences were visible at any time during the chase. The only "innocent bystanders" who were placed "at great risk of serious injury," were the drivers who either pulled off the road in response to the sirens or passed respondent in the opposite direction when he was driving on his side of the road.

I recognize, of course, that even though respondent's original speeding violation on a four-lane highway was rather ordinary, his refusal to stop and subsequent flight was a serious offense that merited severe punishment. It was not, however, a capital offense, or even an offense that justified the use of deadly force rather than an abandonment of the chase. The Court's concern about the "imminent threat to the lives of any pedestrians who might have been present," while surely valid in an appropriate case, should be discounted in a case involving a nighttime chase in an area where no pedestrians were present.

What would have happened if the police had decided to abandon the chase? We now know that they could have apprehended respondent later because they had his license plate number. Even if that were not true, and even if he would have escaped any punishment at all, the use of deadly force in this case was no more appropriate than the use of a deadly weapon against a fleeing felon in *Tennessee* v. *Garner*, 471 U.S. 1 (1985).

In any event, any uncertainty about the result of abandoning the pursuit has not prevented the Court from basing its conclusions on its own factual assumptions. The Court attempts to avoid the conclusion that deadly force was unnecessary by speculating that if the officers had let him go, respondent might have been "just as likely" to continue to drive recklessly as to slow down and wipe his brow. That speculation is unconvincing as a matter of common sense and improper as a matter of law. Our duty to view the evidence in the light most favorable to the nonmoving party would foreclose such speculation if the Court had not used its observation of the video as an excuse for replacing the rule of law with its ad hoc judgment.

Whether a person's actions have risen to a level warranting deadly force is a question of fact best reserved for a jury. Here, the Court has usurped the jury's factfinding function and, in doing so, implicitly labeled the four other judges to review the case unreasonable. It chastises the Court of Appeals for failing to "vie[w] the facts in the light depicted by the videotape" and implies that no reasonable person could view the videotape and come to the conclusion that deadly force was unjustified. However, the three judges on the Court of Appeals panel apparently did view the videotapes entered into evidence and described a very different version of events.

If two groups of judges can disagree so vehemently about the nature of the pursuit and the circumstances surrounding that pursuit, it seems eminently likely that a reasonable juror could disagree with this Court's characterization of events. Moreover, under the standard set forth in *Garner*, it is certainly possible that "a jury could conclude that Scott unreasonably used deadly force to seize Harris by ramming him off the road under the instant circumstances."

The Court today sets forth a *per se* rule that presumes its own version of the facts: "A police officer's attempt to terminate a dangerous high-speed car chase *that threatens the lives of innocent bystanders* does not violate the Fourth Amendment, even when it places the fleeing motorist at risk of serious injury or death." (emphasis added). Not only does that rule fly in the face of the flexible and case-by-case "reasonableness" approach applied in [prior Court decisions] but it is also arguably inapplicable to the case at hand, given that it is not clear that this chase threatened the life of any "innocent bystande[r]." In my view, the risks inherent in justifying unwarranted police conduct on the basis of unfounded assumptions are unacceptable, particularly when less drastic measures—in this case, the use of stop sticks [a device which can be placed across the roadway and used to flatten a vehicle's tires slowly to safely terminate a pursuit] or a simple warning issued from a loudspeaker—could have avoided such a tragic result. In my judgment, jurors in Georgia should be allowed to evaluate the reasonableness of the decision to ram respondent's speeding vehicle in a manner that created an obvious risk of death and has in fact made him a quadriplegic at the age of 19.

1. The Aftermath of *Scott v. Harris*

Justice Stevens made some wonderful points in his dissenting opinion but was unable to convince anyone else to join him. But as his dissent pointed out, the trial court judge and three Eleventh Circuit judges all saw it his way and thought the question of reasonable force was one for the jury. The Justice Stevens dissent had immediate support in the scholarly community as well.

The Court majority was sufficiently self confident in its view that the Court posted the chase video on its website and invited readers of the opinion to see for themselves. Three enterprising scholars took the Court up on the offer and arranged for viewing of the chase video by a random sample of potential jurors. The results added new fuel to the fire regarding the wisdom of summary judgment and the reliability of judicial determinations of the range of "reasonable" jury behavior. *See* Dan M. Kahan, David A. Hoffman & Donald Braman, *Whose Eyes Are You Going to Believe?,* Scott v. Harris *and the Perils of Cognitive Illiberalism,* 122 Harv. L. Rev. 837 (2009).

The authors found that although most viewers agreed with the majority's assessment there was wide variation according to the demographic traits of the respondents. For example, older persons, Caucasians, and men were more likely to see the video as did Justice Scalia, while younger persons, racial minorities, and women were more likely to see it as did Justice Stevens. This article made a huge splash when published and was something of an embarrassment to the Court majority. The chase video is no longer on the Court's website but remains widely available on the internet.

In addition, there is a fascinating short video titled "Why I Ran" in which Mr. Harris and Officer Scott give their respective sides of the story. The video shows that Mr. Harris is African-American and Officer Harris is white, facts completely ignored by the Court. Does that surprise you? Should it have been considered by the Court? Or do you think it not pertinent to the excessive use of force question arising out of law enforcement in a Deep South state that was part of the Confederacy?

An interesting and arguably overlooked aspect of the Kahan et al. study is that even within demographic groups generally supportive of the Court's view, there were significant subgroups who did not see the Harris flight as presenting a danger to the public that required police to ram his car. For example, 20 percent of older, white male conservative viewers agreed with Justice Stevens rather than Justice Scalia. Although this would still be a landslide victory in an election, remember that jury decisions usually must be unanimous or by a super-majority. Although this might not be much help to Mr. Harris (who bore the burden of proof to show unreasonable use of force), it certainly should make one less confident about the ability of judges to represent the views of jurors.

2. The Supreme Court's Recent Mixed Signals on Summary Judgment

Notwithstanding these cognitive pitfalls and criticism of its decision in *Scott v. Harris*, the Court in 2014 figuratively doubled-down on its view that judges could, at least in some instances, resolve disputed facts by watching a videotape (more precisely, a composite formed by multiple police car camera recordings) to determine with certainty whether police had gone beyond constitutional limits in using deadly force to stop a fleeing car. *See Plumhoff v. Rickard*, 134 S. Ct. 2012 (2014).

In *Plumhoff*, the driver sped away after a police stop in West Memphis, Arkansas prompted by a broken headlight, apparently because there were small amounts of illegal drugs in the car. The chase went into Memphis, Tennessee, where the car was nearly cornered in a shopping center parking lot. As the driver was pulling away from the police after a near stop, officers fired roughly 15 shots, killing the passenger and the driver, but not before he continued to drive, losing control of the car and crashing into a nearby home.

Despite what viewers of the video might describe as gratuitous violence (three or more of the shots were point blank through the passenger side window), the Court—without dissent—(Justice Stevens having retired) overruled a trial court and unanimous Sixth Circuit decision rejecting the police defendants' claims of qualified immunity. We urge students to take a look at the *Plumhoff* video and ask: could a reasonable jury, after having been instructed as to the applicable law, have viewed the shooting as excessive force? *See, e.g.,* www.cnn.com/2014/03/04/us/court-police-chase (news account of oral argument in case including composite video showing chase, parking lot, and close range shooting by police).

Interestingly, in another civil rights/excessive use of force case decided three weeks prior to *Plumhoff*, the Court in a per curiam opinion reversed a grant of qualified immunity to a police officer who shot a teenager when investigating a suspected car theft (the car was not stolen but appeared so because the investigating officer made a typographical error in searching police records). *See Tolan v. Cotton*, 134 S.Ct. 1861 (2014). In *Tolan*, the Court emphasized that even in a qualified immunity case, a court addressing a summary judgment motion must construe disputed facts in the light most favorable to the nonmovant. Perhaps police shootings in car chases have become their own subset of summary judgment cases, what one critic has deemed the "videotape exception" to the Seventh Amendment.

One takeaway for law students and lawyers: effective summary judgment practice requires knowledge of the applicable substantive law and sensitivity to the context of the case; procedural knowledge of Rule 56 is a necessary but not sufficient condition to litigating summary judgment questions effectively.

F. The "Mechanics" and Technique of Summary Judgment

1. Timing and Motion Papers

THE RULE	Rule 56(b)

Time to File a Motion

Unless a different time is set by local rule or the court orders otherwise, a party may file a motion for summary judgment at any time until 30 days after the close of all discovery.

EXPLANATION

Until the 2010 Amendment, summary judgment motions generally could not be made until 20 days after the action was commenced. Now, the motion may be made at the outset of the case. Although most cases require some opportunity for discovery before summary judgment is apt, consider how an immediate motion might be apt in the type of debt collection case that spawned the motion and was used for the initial illustration in this Chapter—or in other cases where the defendant has no legitimate defense to the claim.

At the other end of the process, the motion cannot be made more than 30 days after the close of discovery—unless permitted by the court. Some timing deadlines in the Rules are absolute and may not be altered but this deadline, like most, can be extended by court order. In most cases, however, the court overrides the default deadline in the Rules and sets the deadline for summary judgment motions in a case management order.

THE RULE   Rule 56(c)

Procedures

(1) *Supporting Factual Positions.* A party asserting that a fact cannot be or is genuinely disputed must support the assertion by:

  (A) citing to particular parts of materials **in the record**, including depositions, documents, electronically stored information, affidavits or declarations, stipulations (including those made for purposes of the motion only), admissions, interrogatory answers, or other materials; or

  (B) showing that the materials cited do not establish the absence or presence of a genuine dispute, or that an adverse party cannot produce admissible evidence to support the fact.

EXPLANATION

There are two ways to support a party's position in a motion for summary judgment. First, the party can submit record evidence—depositions, documents, electronically stored information, or affidavits—supporting the party's contentions. Second, if the opposing party would have the burden of proof on the issue at trial, the moving party can argue that the opposing party does not have sufficient evidence to meet that party's burden of proof. In *Celotex*, the defendant used the latter approach. It took the position that the record was devoid of any facts indicating the plaintiff's husband's exposure to the defendant's asbestos.

THE RULE   Rule 56(c)(2)

Objection That a Fact is Not Supported by Admissible Evidence

A party may object that the material cited to support or dispute a fact cannot be presented in a form that would be admissible in evidence.

EXPLANATION

Evidence does not need to be admissible in order for the court to consider it as part of its summary judgment analysis. Rather, the evidence must only be capable of being placed in an admissible form. For example, affidavits are typically not admissible at trial, they are hearsay. However, if the affiant comes into the courtroom and offers the statements in the affidavit as live testimony, the statements would no longer be hearsay and would be admissible (unless otherwise objectionable). Thus, statements in an affidavit are properly part of the summary judgment record because they are capable of being presented in an admissible form.

This provision was implicated in *Celotex* when the defendant challenged a letter regarding the plaintiff's husband's exposure to its product as inadmissible hearsay. The attempt ultimately failed on remand when the D.C. Circuit ruled that there was a sufficient indication that plaintiff could put the information in admissible form by calling to the witness stand the author of the letter. If the witness had been unavailable, what could the plaintiff have done? Consult Fed. R. Civ. P. 32 and Chapters 12 and 17.

2. Special Circumstances

THE RULE   Rule 56(d)

When Facts Are Unavailable to the Nonmovant

If a nonmovant shows by affidavit or declaration that, for specified reasons, it cannot present facts essential to justify its opposition, the court may:

(1) defer considering the motion or deny it;

(2) allow time to obtain affidavits or declarations or to take discovery; or

(3) issue any other appropriate order.

EXPLANATION

When a party moves for summary judgment, it generally does so because it believes it has the record it needs to prevail. By contrast, the respondent is forced to "play defense" and may be caught without the material it would like to use to demonstrate the need for trial. In such cases, the nonmovant can seek the court's permission for a delay in the proceedings for further investigation and discovery, or perhaps have the motion tabled until later in the case. Whether the nonmovant will be successful depends on the facts and circumstances of the case.

EXAMPLES & ANALYSIS

EXAMPLE: Pamela sues Dog Day Industries for gender discrimination after she was passed over for promotion in favor of Doogie, who she claims is a less skilled worker but a sycophant who spends his days talking sports and going to striptease clubs with the boss. Dog Day immediately moves for summary judgment submitting the Boss's affidavit in which he states that Doogie is a more productive worker and better liked by the customers. Will this be sufficient to obtain summary judgment for Dog Day? If Pamela seeks more time for discovery, will the Court grant her request?

Analysis: Although Pamela may have enough information from her pretrial Rule 11 investigation to effectively respond, plaintiffs in this position will often want an opportunity to conduct at least basic discovery. She will want to look at Doogie's annual evaluations, his sales record, his complaint log, etc. If Pamela has not had an opportunity to conduct that discovery yet, the court will likely give her that opportunity before ruling on the motion. Conversely, if discovery has been ongoing and Pamela has not exercised diligence in conducting her discovery, the court will likely be less sympathetic.

G. Some Potential Trouble Spots in Summary Judgment Practice

1. Local Rules and Standing Orders

Federal Rule 83 permits each district court (there are 94 in the federal system) to have its own local rules of procedure so long as they are "consistent with—but not duplicat[ive of]—federal statutes" and the Federal Rules and so long as they conform to the numbering system of the Federal Rules. In addition, individual judges usually have standing orders governing their customized adaptation of the Civil Rules. Although consistency is mandated, some standing orders and local rules take considerable liberty with the national rules.

Motion practice has been a significant area of local rulemaking and standing order emphasis. A particular "package" of motion papers may be required in specific form or certain items may be barred. A case in point is the use of a proposed order by the movant. Traditionally, the standard set of motion papers (*e.g.*, motion, memorandum of law, and any supporting affidavits, discovery materials, and other documents) also included a proposed order setting forth the relief requested by the movant with the hope that the court upon granting the motion would simply sign the proposed order. Some courts require such a proposed order while others ban such submissions, presumably out of a view that this is demeaning or opens the door to error in suggesting that the court merely rubber stamps the winning litigant's proposed order.

To be effective, counsel must follow applicable local rules and the standing order of the judge before whom a summary judgment motion (any motion for that matter) is made.

2. Statement of Uncontested Facts

A common standing order preference or local rule requires a summary judgment movant to accompany the motion with a numbered list of facts that it alleges are not genuinely disputed, including citations to the record to support each fact listed. The nonmovant must then respond using a corresponding numbering scheme, admitting or denying each fact and citing specific evidence showing that there is a genuine dispute as to each fact that is not admitted. The nonmovant may also raise additional facts with specific citations to the record if the nonmovant claims these additional facts are germane to the resolution of the motion. The movant then may reply to the additional facts, also in correspondingly numbered form.

In crafting the 2010 Amendment to Rule 56, the Rules Committee considered making statements of uncontested facts part of the national general Rule but was persuaded that such stylized practice might well unnecessarily increase legal costs or have an anti-claimant impact. Can you see why? Do you agree? Although rejected as a national rule, statements of uncontested facts are common and are viewed as an acceptable local or individual variant. A party's failure to comply can result in facts being deemed established or undisputed for purposes of the motion or can even constitute grounds for denial or dismissal of the motion. A court may not grant summary judgment merely because of failure to comply, but must assess the motion under the standard of Rule 56(a). A court may deny the motion, however, merely because of noncompliance.

3. Motions to Strike

Historically, lawyers often made motions to strike defective or objectionable materials in a summary judgment motion or response. Under the 2010 Amendment to Rule 56, motions to strike are not a proper procedure for attacking the opposition's motion papers. Instead, counsel should make a simple objection that the material in question cannot be presented in a form that would be admissible in evidence at trial. The Civil Rules Advisory Committee Notes specifically state that there is "no need to make a separate motion to strike."

4. Sham Affidavits

A longstanding tactic used by some counsel facing a summary judgment motion supported by deposition testimony was to respond to the motion with an affidavit of the deponent refuting or revising the testimony. Beginning in the 1980s, courts became increasingly hostile to such efforts and there is now a well-established "sham affidavit" doctrine stating that affidavits attempting to contradict sworn deposition testimony will be disregarded. If the deposition was properly conducted, there is no ambiguity in the testimony, and the deponent had fair opportunity to review and correct the transcript, testimony cannot be altered by affidavit. However, affidavits may be received to explain testimony and perhaps even to correct a misstatement if the affiant can show legitimate grounds as to why the mistake was not caught when reviewing the deposition transcript.

5. Changes to the Deposition Transcript

A related issue is the degree to which a deponent can, after review of the transcript, change her testimony pursuant to Rule 30(e). Traditionally, the rule was that the deponent could make any change desired for any reason, even to the point of saying the color of the traffic light was green rather than red as originally testified. The adequate remedy for such drastic deponent revisions was thought to be cross-examination at trial. More recently, however, many courts have stated that a deponent cannot engage in wholesale rewriting of her testimony in the face of a summary judgment motion but must instead make changes only on the basis of transcription error or misunderstanding regarding the question. These courts disregard "rewriting" types of changes to the transcript for purposes of avoiding summary judgment. Courts are not uniform in this area, however.

6. Judicial Notice

Federal Rule of Evidence 201 states that courts may, if properly informed on motion by a party, take judicial notice of a fact if it is "not subject to reasonable dispute" and either "[g]enerally known within the territorial jurisdiction of the trial court" or "[c]apable of accurate and ready determination by resort to sources whose accuracy cannot reasonably be questioned." Consequently, a party may support or oppose a summary judgment motion on the basis of facts subject to judicial notice rather than attempting to prove such facts by submitting record evidence.

For example, if defendant states that he should be excused from running into a school bus because he was blinded by the evening sun while driving home eastward from Santa Monica to Claremont, the Court could find this attempted excuse precluded because the sun would be in the west at this time and could not have blinded him at that time of day while traveling east.

A court may take judicial notice on its own but is not required to. Consequently, counsel normally request recognition or rejection of a fact via judicial notice and to provide the court with apt supporting material such as an official chart showing sunrise and sunset times or a physics or astronomy textbook (but remember to consider the hearsay rule of Fed. R. Evid. 803

662 • Learning Civil Procedure •

and whether the textbook is subject to the "learned treatise" exception to the hearsay rule or must be discussed by a live witness such as a science teacher).

ADDITIONAL EXERCISES

1. Paige teaches at a school for special needs children in Dawson, Oklahoma. For a treat, she takes her students to lunch at the Darryl's Sweet Shop. Darryl, afraid that the presence of so many special needs kids in the restaurant at once will be off-putting to his regular customers, refuses service to the group. As Paige and the children exit the Shop, Cam Constable of the Dawson Police Department, who has been in the shop the whole time, then arrests Paige for violating a local ordinance prohibiting more than a ten unrelated persons from dining out at once. The law was passed in order to make it possible to more easily shut down unruly fraternity outings from students at Dawson State College. The frats at Dawson State have been sedate for some time and the ordinance has not been enforced during the past five years.

    Paige sues, alleging a conspiracy in violation of her civil rights and those of the children. Her theory of the case is that Darryl and Dawson's Constable either discussed "teaching her a lesson" or had an implicit understanding that she and the kids would be arrested in order to keep them away in the future. Darryl (sole proprietor of the Sweet Shop) and the Dawson Police Department move for summary judgment on the ground that Paige has failed to prove any agreement at all, much less an agreement to deprive her of civil rights due to selective enforcement of the local ordinance. In addition, Darryl and Constable each submit affidavits denying any agreement between them or anyone associated with either of them. *How should the Court rule on the summary judgment motion?*

2. Pat sues Don, contending that Don defamed her by regaling Colleen with stories about Pat's days as a con artist selling counterfeit Gucci handbags in Venice after college. Pat concedes that she sold handbags to make ends meet after college but contends that they were real Gucci, although factory seconds. Pat alleges this happened when the three of them were driving from New York to Washington for a political rally. Don denies ever telling any such story and submits his affidavit and one

from Colleen, who swears that Don never told her such an anecdote. Pat deposes both Don and Colleen and they continue to deny making or hearing the statements. Neither has any obvious impeaching evidence such as a felony or perjury conviction or a medical condition affecting perception or memory. Don files a motion for summary judgment, and submits his and Colleen's affidavits stating that Don never told the story alleged in the complaint. Pat opposes the motion, submitting her affidavit that Don did tell the story **On this record, how should the court rule?**

A Further Wrinkle on Additional Exercise No. 2.

Assume that rather than attempting to win completely on the defamation claim, Don moves for partial summary judgment on the punitive damages issue, reiterating in an affidavit that he never told any such story about Pat and that he had no ill will toward Pat (at least not before the lawsuit). Colleen submits an affidavit reiterating that the story was unknown to her until the lawsuit, that she bears no ill will toward Pat, and that she does not think anything less of Pat because of the story. In response, Pat submits an affidavit stating that she did indeed hear Don tell Colleen the story she views as unflattering, that the story is false, and that Don had no information on which to assess the truth or falsity of the story. Pat also avers that she has suffered emotional distress but does not claim any tangible economic injury such as loss of a job or any concrete instances of public ridicule. **Under these circumstances, can Don get partial summary judgment on the punitive damages claim (which requires a showing, by clear-and-convincing evidence, that Don engaged in wilful disregard for Pat's rights)?**

3. Paula sues Dan, alleging that Dan groped her during 2014 when picking her up from the ground after she had tripped on a grate attempting to enter the subway through Grand Central Station. A security camera has captured Paula falling and Dan picking her up, with a moment of inaudible verbal exchange before Paula heads to the subway and Dan for his Metro North train.

Dan readily concedes picking Paula up but denies groping. The angle of the videotape is from the back of Dan and Paula but does show Dan's arms in front of Paula as part of the process of pulling her up (rather than by the shoulders, clothing, etc.). Paula called the police after arriving home and swore out a criminal complaint, upon which the local prosecutor chose not to take any action. The day after the incident, Paula scheduled an emergency session with her psychiatrist and related the story. She made an unscheduled visit to her primary care physician but he found no physical evidence of unwanted touching. Dan was twice convicted of lewd behavior in 2007 but has had no incidents since.

Paula and Dan each move for summary judgment, with both submitting detailed affidavits presenting their respective versions of events (including from Paula's doctors). In the alternative, Dan has also moved for partial summary judgment dismissing Paula's punitive damages claim, arguing that as a matter of law, the facts as shown on the videotape, even drawing all reasonable inferences in Paula's favor, could not as a matter of law constitute "willful or wanton indifference to the rights" of Paula, the jurisdiction's legal standard for assessing punitive damages. **What ruling on the motions and why?**

4. Don responds to a 911 call about someone acting strangely at the 42nd Street subway station. Upon arrival, Don observes Phien shouting at others on the platform. Don asks Phien to calm down but Phien appears not to understand English. Phien runs to his backpack and pulls out a knife. Standing 15 feet from Don, Phien holds the knife aloft and begins reciting what appears to be some sort of ritual incantation. The subway patrons have scattered, leaving Don and Phien alone on the platform.

According to the testimony of roughly 20 eyewitnesses who watched from approximately 40 feet away, Phien finishes reciting, lowers the knife, and takes two slow and deliberate steps toward Don. Don whips out his sidearm and shoots Phien dead with two bullets to the torso. Phien's widow sues Don and the Police Department, alleging unnecessary use of deadly force.

Under the prevailing law (modified for this Exercise), an officer acting in the line of duty can be held liable for "unnecessary use of force grossly disproportionate to what is necessary to subdue someone posing a threat of serious injury to an officer or a member of the public." The Department can be liable if it is found to have policies that do not adequately train officers in the applicable standard and proper protocols for dealing with such situations.

Notwithstanding this standard for liability, an individual police officer will be immune from suit unless the behavior at issue violated "clearly established law." The case reports are full of cases stating that it violates the constitutional rights of a person if an officer uses deadly force upon someone who is unarmed or fleeing on foot (unless it is clear the person in flight is about to hurt someone as part of the flight). The case reports also have many cases in which it is held not to be unconstitutional to use deadly force against someone who has a gun and is displaying it in a manner that indicates possible imminent use. There are no cases precisely involving a person holding a knife, much less any holding a knife on a subway platform, reciting incantations, etc. ***After discovery is complete, Don moves for summary judgment. The Phien Estate opposes. What result? Why? If this had all been captured on a security camera, would the result be different? Prior to the motion, what information would Don and Phien have sought to develop/confirm during discovery?***

Quick Summary

- Summary judgment is available where there is no genuine dispute of material fact between the parties and one of the parties is entitled to judgment as a matter of law.

- Courts may grant partial summary judgment or deem a fact established and also have discretion to deny summary judgment in appropriate cases even where the standard appears to be met.

- A denial of summary judgment is not a final, appealable order. Neither are partial grants or determinations of established fact.

- In determining whether there is a genuinely disputed material fact, the court is not to assess the credibility of witnesses.

- In deciding a summary judgment motion, the court may consider the parties' respective burdens of proof at trial, which may vary according to the type of case. Where the party with the burden of proof makes a claim viewed as implausible by the court, it may in some circumstances require a higher evidentiary showing by that party to preclude summary judgment such as some direct evidence supporting the claim rather than only circumstantial evidence.

- A party moving for summary judgment must properly make and support the motion as a prerequisite to requiring a response by the nonmovant. Where the motion is properly made and supported, the nonmovant must respond by submitting sufficient material to demonstrate that there exists a genuine dispute requiring trial

- Summary judgment practice was significantly changed by a trio of 1986 U.S. Supreme Court cases that generally made summary judgment more available. These decisions and their approach to summary judgment remain controversial.

- Defendants can shoulder their summary judgment burden by illustrating the lack of support for a necessary fact required to sustain the claim.

- A party can object to the inadmissibility of an opponent's materials submitted by the opponent if it does not appear that the materials can be put into admissible form at trial.

- The court need not consider anything outside the supporting materials submitted by the parties but is permitted to consider other materials in the record.

- Affidavits must be based on the affiant's personal knowledge and demonstrate that the facts presented can be put in admissible form at trial.

- Parties may move for additional time to respond to a summary judgment motion if they can show a need for the additional time.

- Courts can grant summary judgment on their own motion, but only if the Rule 56(a) standard is met and the parties are given notice of the court motion and adequate time to respond.

- If a party submits an affidavit in bad faith, the court may order an apt remedy, including fee shifting, and may even hold the offending party in contempt.

16

Jury Trial Right: The Seventh Amendment

Key Concepts

- The Seventh Amendment right to jury trial
- The distinction between "legal" and "equitable" matters
- The historical and remedial tests for applying the Seventh Amendment
- Functional and public policy factors affecting the right to jury trial
- Procedure for protecting the jury trial in Fed. R. Civ. P. 38
- The availability of jury trial and litigation strategy

Introduction

The national commitment to jury trial and passage of the Seventh Amendment stems from a variety of factors. The United States inherited the jury trial from its English colonizers—but in breaking away from the Crown, Americans exhibited a strong populist and anti-central government sentiment that persists today. Institutionalizing a layperson finder of fact (the jury) as part of the legal system was viewed as a protection against government oppression. Although the dispute resolution context has changed, the U.S. commitment to the jury remains strong, both because of the constitutional provision and prevailing attitudes. In similar fashion, criminal defendants enjoy a right to jury trial pursuant to the Sixth Amendment that is even more sacrosanct than the Seventh Amendment right to jury trial in civil litigation.

Because a high percentage of civil actions settle and because of the growth of arbitration and alternative dispute resolution generally, jury trials appear to be in decline in historical terms. However, there is still a robust collection of caselaw addressing the jury trial right.

A. The Historical Background of the American Jury

The history of the jury trial right is well-chronicled in many treatises and casebooks as well as in stand-alone historical studies of the genesis and development of the jury in Anglo-American law. The short version of the history is that the Anglo-Saxon tribes of what eventually became England often used a group of local laypersons to make factual determinations in disputes that arose. The early juries were persons familiar with the parties and the community and perhaps even the specific controversy. Over time, the jury evolved to the present system in which jurors are expected to have no connection to or pre-trial knowledge of the litigants or the controversy.

England developed the common law method of adjudication in which law develops primarily through case precedent rather than the more heavily codified European systems. To reduce the risk of local courts and juries resisting or subverting the Crown, England also developed a separate Court of Chancery that had jurisdiction over legal matters most important to maintaining the Crown's control—and vested decisionmaking power in the Chancellor (essentially a judge) without the involvement of a jury.

Consequently, England developed two separate judicial tracks: Equity (which was administered by the Court of Chancery) and Law (which was administered by the other courts). Depending on the type of action, it would be heard either by the court of equity or a court of law. If the former, the procedure was essentially what we now call a bench trial with decision by the judge. If the latter, the action was administered by a judge but factual determinations and ultimate decisions were made by a jury. This two-track system was what existed in England at the time of the American Revolution, when the United States set about drafting a Constitution.

The Bill of Rights was ratified in 1791 and Seventh Amendment right to jury trial has been constitutionally protected ever since. It has also been commonly used for more than 200 years. As we will see in Chapter 18 regarding post-verdict motions, judges continued to have significant control over trials and adjudication notwithstanding the role of the jury. Over time, judicial power increased relative to that of juries. But this is a different issue than whether a litigant has a constitutional right to demand a jury, the topic on which this Chapter focuses. The litigant may be clearly entitled to a jury. But as reflected in Chapters 7 (regarding responses to the complaint), 16 (regarding summary judgment), 17 (regarding trial), and 18 (regarding post-trial motions), the judge affects and may even limit the role of the jury through evidentiary rulings and decisions on motions (*e.g.,* Rule 12, Rule 50, Rule 56, Rule 59, Rule 60).

Despite whatever dilution may have occurred regarding jury power in the U.S., it remains the country with the greatest doctrinal and practical commitment to juries. England, despite its role as the jury's country of origin, has largely eliminated its use in civil cases (save for defamation claims), with former British colonies such as Australia and New Zealand exhibiting a similar if less extreme pattern. Ironically, however, a number of developing countries as well as Russia and former Soviet Union countries appear to be borrowing the jury concept from the U.S., at least for certain types of cases.

An important historical development in the U.S. was the 1938 merger of law and equity in the federal courts. Despite the merger of these systems, as discussed below, the right to a jury still hinges on this historical distinction. Although the Seventh Amendment applies only to federal court proceedings, most states have similar provisions in their constitutions or civil rules, making much federal jury trial caselaw relevant to determining the contours of the jury trial right in state courts.

B. The Division of Labor Between Judge and Jury: The Fact/Law Distinction

The right to a jury trial does not mean that the jury completely supplants the judge. Of necessity, the case is still administered by its presiding judge, most obviously in the pretrial phases of the matter that include motion practice, selection of applicable law, and decisions regarding the complaint and other pleadings and motions as well as amendments to pleadings, discovery, and case management orders. In addition, as reflected in this Chapter, even the decision as to whether juries will be involved is one made by judges.

The involvement of jurors thus has an important but confined impact; juries make findings of fact while judges make legal rulings as well as attending to the administration and processing of the case.

EXAMPLE: Pia Perturbed's car is T-boned at an intersection by Damian Daredevil's vehicle. Pia sues, seeking compensation for her physical injuries, damage to her vehicle, and mental anguish, including her post-collision fear of driving, which she claims has required her to hire a chauffeur for commuting to work in her small town that lacks mass transit (and where her workplace is far beyond walking distance from home). Of the core issues in this case, which are for the judge and which are for the jury?

Analysis: The question of whether Damian was negligent (*e.g.*, did he run a red light in striking Pia's vehicle) is one of fact for the jury. So are any questions as to Damian's speed, care, and attentiveness as well as whether Pia was comparatively negligent (perhaps she was the one who ran a red light). Similarly, the question of what harms Pia suffered, the extent of her injuries, and the cost of medical care, rehabilitation, and adjustment are questions of fact for the jury.

While these jury questions are important to determining the outcome of the case, the judge continues to play a crucial role in the case. For example, there is the question of whether under the prevailing law, Pia's alleged phobia about driving (even if completely true) is compensable. This is a legal question the judge must decide. Similarly, the judge must decide the degree of relief permitted under the law. A chauffer for commuting may be considered too expensive as a matter of law. Instead, the law may require Pia to mitigate damages by changing jobs (to one within walking distance) or moving closer to work.

Once the judge determines the legal parameters of permissible relief, the jury then decides whether Pia is so impaired that she cannot drive, whether the impairment is permanent or temporary, and whether the claimed costs are reasonable. For example, the jury may award only the cost of cab fare rather than that of a car service or personal chauffer. Or the judge may rule that under the law, only the least expensive mode of transit is compensable regardless of Pia's convenience or fears.

EXAMPLE: Proud Homeowner's house is struck by lightning, resulting in fire that consumes the house. When he makes a claim pursuant to his homeowner's insurance company, Denial Mutual, the insurer contends that the claim is not covered because the damage resulted from "electrical mishaps" which are excluded under the policy because lightning is static electricity. Denial also contends that the house was not a total loss and can be repaired for $75,000, and that even if there is coverage there is no need to pay the $200,000 required to build a new structure from the foundation up. Proud contends that the electrical mishap exclusion was meant to apply only to commercial alternating current electricity and that the actual cause of most of the destruction was fire. Which of these issues is for the judge and which are for the jury?

Analysis: The questions of the extent of the home's destruction and the cost of repair or replacement are fact questions for the jury. Similarly, the causes of the destruction (impact of lightning versus fire) are fact questions for the jury. The question of what is meant by the policy's exclusion for "electrical mishaps" is one of law for the judge. This flows from the general principle that contract construction is a question of law for the court (judge) but that questions of fact relevant to contract construction are questions of fact for the jury.

Similarly, if Proud asserted that Denial's agent had stated that lightning strikes were not what the company meant by "electrical mishaps," issues of what the agent said and whether Proud reasonably relied on the statement to his detriment (which would create a right of recovery under the law of promissory estoppel even if the court determined that the legally correct construction of the term electrical mishap included lightning), resolution of this dispute would involve determination of a question of fact by the jury. However, the judge would rule on any issues of agency law regarding the agent's authority.

C. Judges v. Juries: Conventional Wisdoms and Considerations

One widely held conventional wisdom is that juries tend to favor underdogs and individuals over corporations and governments. But a contradictory conventional wisdom posits that juries are also a little starstruck by the rich and famous, which may make them deferential to authority figures and their organizations. This area is still remarkably long on folklore and short on hard evidence. The choice of judge-vs.-jury is highly context specific and varies dramatically according to the type of case, the identity of the litigants, witnesses, and counsel, and the likely composition of the pool from which the jury will be selected. Each case needs to be assessed in its own context rather than according to traditional nostrums. Overall, however, it appears that in most cases juries and judges do not differ all that much in their perception of the evidence. *See* HARRY KALVEN & HANS ZEISEL, THE AMERICAN JURY (1966).

At a minimum, the presence or absence of a jury impacts the manner in which the case is tried (*e.g.,* the presence or absence of jury instructions, motions for pretrial evidence rulings, the use of visual aids, the presentation of witnesses and documents, etc.). Where a trial will be lengthy, a litigant may prefer a judge on the theory that jurors ripped away from their daily lives for weeks or months of trial will resent the imposition and punish the party perceived as having caused the imposition—or may render a slap-dash verdict merely to be done a bit sooner at the end of an exhausting process.

Note as you read the text of the Amendment below that its language is not clear on this point. Why, since the jury trial provision is part of the U.S. Constitution, does it not apply in all courts?

In assessing juries and strategizing about whether or not to insist on a jury trial, counsel must also recognize an additional limit. The Seventh Amendment is a two-way street. Unilateral waiver of a jury by itself accomplishes nothing. Your opponent can still insist on its constitutional right to jury trial.

D. The Seventh Amendment

The Seventh Amendment is pretty straight-forward. Textually, it simply says that the right to jury trial in "suits at common law" shall be "preserved," leaving courts to flesh out what constitutes a suit at common law and what suffices as preservation. The Amendment also provides for limitations on court re-examination of facts tried to a jury so that judges may not blithely set aside jury findings. But as we will see in Chapter 18, the law does provide for reversing jury trial outcomes or ordering new trials under certain circumstances.

THE CONSTITUTION: Amendment VII

In Suits at common law, where the value in controversy shall exceed twenty dollars, the right of trial by jury shall be preserved, and no fact tried by a jury, shall be otherwise reexamined in any Court of the United States, than according to the rules of the common law.

E. Testing the Basic Law vs. Equity Concept

The basic concept is that the Seventh Amendment guarantees a right to jury trial in matters "at law." For the moment, equate "at law" or "legal" with a claim for monetary relief and equate an action "in equity" as one seeking nonmonetary relief such as an injunction.

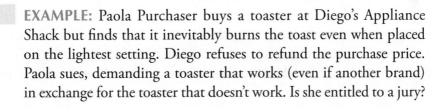

EXAMPLES & ANALYSIS

EXAMPLE: Paola Purchaser buys a toaster at Diego's Appliance Shack but finds that it inevitably burns the toast even when placed on the lightest setting. Diego refuses to refund the purchase price. Paola sues, demanding a toaster that works (even if another brand) in exchange for the toaster that doesn't work. Is she entitled to a jury?

Analysis: No. Paola is seeking the equitable relief of toaster replacement rather than the legal relief of monetary damages. Her claim is one for breach of contract, which has historically been a claim sounding in law rather than equity—but the relief she seeks is equitable. She wants the defendant to do something rather than pay something.

EXAMPLE: Assume that Paola does not seek a new toaster but instead seeks damages in the form of compensation for wasted time using the defective toaster, shopping for a functioning toaster, and the purchase price of the new, better toaster she buys to replace Diego's defective toaster.

Analysis: Now Paola is seeking legal relief in the form of monetary damages and makes no remedial request for return or repair of Diego's product—nor does she demand that any activity be conducted by Diego. Paola may obtain a jury trial.

> **EXAMPLE:** Assume instead that Paola sues Diego seeking return of the purchase price. Is she entitled to jury trial as a matter of right?

Analysis: This is a closer case. On one hand, Paola is seeking to obtain money, which makes the case look like an action at law. On the other hand, she simply wants money she already paid returned to her, which looks like equitable action for rescission rather than damages calculated based on injury from the toaster. Most courts would probably find the Seventh Amendment inapplicable, but this can vary depending on the court and the manner in which the complaint describes the claim and the relief requested.

> **EXAMPLE:** Assume instead that the toaster not only burned the toast but also burned Paola's house. She sues Diego for damages that include the cost of repairing the damage, lost income because of work she missed, mental anguish, and the value of her collection of exotic fish that perished in the blaze. Does the Seventh Amendment right to jury trial apply?

Analysis: Yes. Paola is making a product liability, tort negligence, breach of contract, or breach of warranty claim alleging injury from the product and seeking monetary compensation. She is seeking money damages, a classic form of "legal" relief, and may demand a jury trial pursuant to the Seventh Amendment.

> **EXAMPLE:** Assume instead that after the fire, Paola sues Diego seeking a court order that Diego, an accomplished carpenter, personally rebuild her home. May she obtain a jury trial?

Analysis: By requesting the specific relief of rebuilding and no additional damages, Paola is pursuing injunctive or equitable relief that falls outside the jury trial guarantee of the Seventh Amendment.

EXAMPLE: In Contracts class, you will read cases in which the victim of a breach by an entertainer was not permitted to force the entertainer to appear but could prevent performances at the same time on behalf of others—and could obtain dollar damages or a refund of previously paid fees. Consider this intersection between Contracts and Civil Procedure. Singer Perry Crooner was scheduled to perform on New Year's Eve 1999/2000 at the Divas Casino in Las Vegas but was unable due to illness. The Divas sought a refund of its advance on the fee and damages it incurred from refunding tickets, losing concession sales in the absence of the concert, etc. Perry took the position that he could keep the deal and his fee by rescheduling and performing at another time after he recovered. The Divas refused, arguing that the large fee was linked to the crowd draw presented by the "end of the millennium" and related festivities, which made Vegas ground zero for Year 2000 partying. Could either Perry or the Divas insist on a jury trial?

Analysis: Unless the Divas gives up its claim for damages allegedly flowing from the breach both the Divas and Perry may demand jury trial.

EXAMPLE: Assume instead that Perry signs on to perform at the Divas on New Year's Eve but then is offered more money by the Desert Air Casino. Perry advises the Divas that he intends to back out. The Divas sues, seeking to prevent Perry from performing at the Desert Air. If this is the only remedy it seeks, does either side have a right to jury trial?

Analysis: No. In this case, the Divas is seeking solely injunctive relief. It is not seeking any legal relief in the form of money damages and thus the Seventh Amendment is not triggered.

Federal Rule 38

THE RULE   Fed. R. Civ. P. 38

Right to Jury Trial; Demand

(a) **Right Preserved.** The right of trial by jury as declared by the Seventh Amendment to the Constitution—or as provided by a federal statute—is preserved to the parties inviolate.

(b) **Demand.** On any issue triable of right by a jury, a party may demand a jury trial by:

 (1) serving the other parties with a written demand—which may be included in a pleading—no later than 14 days after the last pleading directed to the issue is served; and

 (2) filing the demand in accordance with Rule 5(d).

(c) **Specifying Issues.** In its demand, a party may specify the issues that it wishes to have tried by a jury; otherwise, it is considered to have demanded a jury trial on all the issues so triable. If the party has demanded a jury trial on only some issues, any other party may—within 14 days after being served with the demand or within a shorter time ordered by the court—serve a demand for a jury trial on any other or all factual issues triable by jury.

(d) **Waiver; Withdrawal.** A party waives a jury trial unless its demand is properly served and filed. A proper demand may be withdrawn only if the parties consent.

(e) **Admirality and Maritime Claims.** These rules do not create a right to a jury trial on issues in a claim that is an admirality or maritime claim under Rule 9(h)

EXPLANATION

Rule 38 has several significant components:

- Rule 38(a) restates the Seventh Amendment and also provides for the enforcement of jury trial rights provided by federal statute.

- Rule 38(b) states that a party seeking jury trial must make a timely and specific demand for a jury trial.

- Rule 38(c) allows a party to demand jury consideration of only particular issues in the case.

- Rule 38(d) allows withdrawal of a prior demand for jury trial but notes that such a withdrawal will be effective only with the consent of the other parties to the case.

- Rule 38(e) exempts admiralty and maritime claims from the scope of Rule 38 and the rule-based right to jury trial. This is because admiralty actions have long been considered equitable and tried by judges rather than juries.

Assuming a litigant wants a jury trial, the Seventh Amendment establishes the criteria for demanding jury trial as a matter of right. Rule 38 then provides the means by which to preserve that constitutional right through a proper demand. Whether to seek a jury trial needs to be addressed at the outset of the case, or the right will be lost. There are also traps for the unwary regarding assertion of the right to jury trial.

Although a litigant may have a right to jury trial, that right is lost if jury trial is not demanded in timely fashion. Rule 38(b) states that a party "may" make such a demand by "serving the other parties with a written demand . . . no later than 14 days after the last pleading directed to the issue" of fact on which jury consideration is sought and "filing the demand in accordance with Rule 5(d)." The "may" language can be misleading if viewed in isolation. Rule 38(d) provides that a party "waives a jury trial unless its demand is properly served and filed."

Fortunately, Rule 38(b) also provides that the demand "may be included in a pleading" that is served on the opponent, which is the simplest and surest way for counsel not to waive the client's right to jury trial. Plaintiffs normally make a determination of whether they prefer a jury or bench trial and if a jury is sought, it is demanded in the complaint (usually in the caption or at the end of the complaint or in the prayer for relief).

Courts have occasionally been very liberal and permitted an indication of jury demand on the civil docket sheet or in a pretrial order to satisfy the demand requirement—even though these are not pleadings under the Rules— so long as the opponent was served in timely fashion. But the demand must be in some form of writing. An oral demand is ineffective.

Defendants usually assess their preference for jury trial and make a demand as part of the answer. They are also bound by the 14-day deadline after the close of the pleadings on an issue subject to jury trial. Counterclaims, cross-claims, and amended pleadings that raise new fact issues usually provide a new window of opportunity for demanding jury trial. But these sorts of changes do not eliminate a previously properly made jury trial demand. For example, plaintiff need not re-demand a jury when a third-party defendant is impleaded.

As provided by Rule 38, the demand can specify that jury trial is sought only on certain issues. The opponent can then demand jury trial of the issues on which the original demanding party sought to avoid a jury. Seeking jury trial is a two-way street. For example, if plaintiff demands a jury trial and then changes its mind, the demand can only be withdrawn with the consent of all parties. However, if the original demand sought a jury trial under circumstances where it was not available under the Seventh Amendment, there is no bar to dropping the demand. However, if a jury trial is demanded in an apt case, the demand cannot be withdrawn without consent of the other litigants.

1. Jury Trial Right and the Merger of Law & Equity: The *Beacon Theatres* Case

The 1938 Rules which merged law and equity included Rule 38 in substantially its current form. The 1993 Amendment clarified that one could demand a jury trial by noting this in the caption of a complaint or elsewhere in a pleading, constructively overruling a line of cases that held jury demands ineffective unless presented in a separate document. The 2009

Amendment expanded the time for making a demand after the close of the pleadings from 10 days to 14 days. But otherwise, Rule 38 has been largely the same nearly since its inception 75 years ago.

The 1938 adoption of one set of rules for both legal and equitable matters at least raised the question of whether there would be an attendant change in jury trial doctrine. Prior to the merger, the jury trial right depended largely on whether the action was classified as one at law or in equity. If the former, the Seventh Amendment conveyed a right to jury trial. If the latter, it did not. *See American Life Insurance Co. v. Stewart*, 300 U.S. 203 (1937). But now both legal and equitable claims could be tried together. The great procedural (and torts) scholar Fleming James (in *Trial by Jury and the New Federal Rules of Procedure*, 45 Yale L. J. 1022 (1936)) recognized the issue but it was otherwise largely ignored for the next 20 years. *But see* Note, *The Right to Jury Trial Under Merged Procedures*, 65 Harv. L. Rev. 453 (1952).

Beacon Theatres v. Westover, 359 U.S. 500 (1959) changed the legal landscape and effectively expanded the scope of the Seventh Amendment by holding that the merger had effectively enlarged the jurisdictional parameters of actions at law under the federal system and thereby enlarged the number of circumstances in which jury trial was required if properly demanded. In particular, if an action presented common questions of fact relevant to both legal and equitable claims, the fact question must be tried to a jury first so that a judge's determination of the fact did not deprive a litigant of the opportunity for juror assessment of the fact question.

In *Beacon Theatres*, the operator of a movie theater in San Bernardino, California (Fox) sued Beacon, which ran a drive-in theater eleven miles away. Fox was firing off a preemptive volley. It sought a declaratory judgment that Fox was not liable under the antitrust laws even though it was operating its theater at a closer distance to Beacon's than permitted by the theaters' agreements with the motion picture studios. Fox also sought an injunction to prohibit Beacon from suing it on antitrust grounds. Prior to Fox's suit, Beacon had threatened legal action.

The trial court ruled that because Fox's action was primarily an equity action seeking injunctive relief and that it could hear and decided Fox's request, making necessary fact findings as part of the process, even if this raised a real possibility that the judge's determinations would create a conclusive factual determination that would be binding on any jury trial of the antitrust damages action. Beacon sought immediate review of the trial judge's determination by the Ninth Circuit via a writ of mandamus, which was granted. But after review, a Circuit panel affirmed the trial court decision. *See* 252 F.2d 864, 874 (9th Cir. 1985). Beacon then sought certiorari, which was granted.

IN PRACTICE

Litigation as Ambush. By threatening Fox, Beacon "telegraphed its punch." Rather than waiting to be hit, Fox hit first by commencing its declaratory judgment action, which it framed as one seeking injunctive relief in an effort to gain a judge's determination of important factual issues and avoid a jury. Beacon could, of course, have simply sued Fox first in an available forum of its choice, framing the action as one solely for damages in order to obtain a jury trial. Lawyers in these situations often must make tough judgment calls about how extensively to announce positions, make communications, and negotiate because this raises the risk that a potential adversary, having been alerted to a dispute, will win the race to the courthouse and obtain a more favorable forum or framing of the issues.

The Supreme Court held that where there is a common question of fact pertinent to both equitable and legal actions, the fact must be heard and decided by a jury before the matter may be considered by a court of law. In other words, the trial court in *Beacon* could not hear the injunction first because it would necessarily decide jury questions before the jury had a chance to. The better course was to sequence the case to first allow a jury trial on the antitrust allegations and then to allow the judge to decide the injunction.

Most state constitutions have a jury trial guarantee similar to that of the U.S. Constitution, and most states take an approach similar to that of *Beacon Theatres* in requiring that judges structure fact finding in a mixed case so that jury determination not be foreclosed by earlier determinations by the bench. *See, e.g., Onvoy, Inc. v. ALLETE, Inc.*, 736 N.W.2d 611 (Minn. 2007). Further, "factual findings that are common to both claims at law and claims for equitable relief are binding" upon the court. *Id.* at 616. *Accord, Lee v. Aiu*, 936 P.2d 655 (Haw. 1997); *Wood v. Wood*, 693 A.2d 673 (Vt. 1997).

EXAMPLES & ANALYSIS

EXAMPLE: After a broken hose in the family washing machine leaves Pia's house soaked, she calls DrainPro, a clean-up company, which leads to further disaster. According to Pia's complaint, DrainPro placed innumerable gashes in the home, used toxic chemicals that injured her son and daughter, and failed to adequately dry out the home, leading to toxic mold problems, all of which forced Pia and her family to pay to stay in a motel and incur substantial medical bills. Pia's suit against DrainCo seeks an injunction requiring remedial work on the home as well as damages for medical and lodging expenses and for the family's pain and suffering. Despite Pia's demand for a jury trial on issues of DrainPro's alleged negligence and damages, the judge wants to preside over the injunction hearing without a jury. Does *Beacon Theatres* permit this?

Analysis: In order to determine whether to grant an injunction (*see* Ch. 20), the judge will need to engage in fact finding about DrainCo's alleged negligence and the injury asserted by Pia, facts that are in common with her damages action. *Beacon Theatres* thus requires that these common issues of fact be first presented to a jury so that a judge's decision on them does not become binding and preclude jury consideration (*see* Ch. 20).

EXAMPLE: What if Pia is seeking a preliminary injunction requiring DrainPro to immediately repair her home, at least enough to make it habitable? Can the judge decided the preliminary injunction motion without violating *Beacon Theatres*?

Analysis: Because this injunction is "preliminary" and does not constitute a final judgment on the merits, the fact finding necessary to sustain a preliminary injunction does not have preclusive effect (*see* Ch. 20) as would a permanent injunction. Consequently, the judge's decision on the preliminary injunction motion does not thwart the jury trial right in a merged system or run afoul of the *Beacon Theatres* holding. It also comports with the common sense of litigation that judges have power to rule on motions while the role of the jury is to determine facts at trial.

> **EXAMPLE:** Pat Promoter sues Donna Developer for beginning to build part of Donna's most recent office building on Pat's land. The suit also accuses Donna of erecting another building that blocked public access to Pat's restaurant. Pat is also suing Donna for failing to pay Pat for some 10,000 of Pat's famous cheesesteaks (at $8 per sandwich) provided to Donna's office holiday party. Can Judge Neutral preside without a jury over Pat's (1) request for for an injunction to halt construction of the encroaching building? (2) request for an injunction to provide access for Pat's customers? (3) claim for $80,000 in damages plus prejudgment interest?

Analysis: Pat's first claim can be decided by the judge sitting without a jury. It appears not to seek any "legal" relief because the aim of the injunction request is to halt construction without pursuing compensation. Pat's second claim is likewise one that seeks only equitable relief (the affirmative injunction) rather than legal relief such as money damages. Pat's third claim, however, is a straight-forward, failure-to-pay damages claim that constitutes legal relief in an action at law, entitling Pat to a jury trial (assuming one has been properly demanded). These three claims all involve different facts, so a judge's resolution of the first and second claims will not raise a *Beacon Theatres* problem regarding the third claim.

2. Jury Trial Rights and the Statutory and Administrative State

When the Seventh Amendment was ratified, common law case precedent was almost all the "law" there was. Actions were classed as equitable or legal based on the judiciary's characterization of such matters over time. Increasingly, the United States has become a nation of statutes and administrative regulation as well as common law.

There was considerable statute-making in the mid-late 19th Century, with a comparative explosion of legislation in the 20th Century. The enactment and amendment of statutes remains common—at both the federal and state levels. State legislative activity also increased markedly during the 20th Century. Administrative and regulatory agencies came somewhat later, and have continued to be created, reformed, and supported. We now live in a world where most of the law we encounter is administrative law. Examples include regulations of roads, driving, purchase of retail products, maintenance of the home and office, banking, etc.

Because today's web of statutes and regulatory agencies did not exist in 1791, courts have needed to adopt jury trial right jurisprudence. Regarding statutes, the general rule is that when a statute authorizes a **private right of civil action**, the right to jury trial is determined by analogy to analogous common law causes of action. *See Curtis v. Loether*, 415 U.S. 189 (1974)(jury trial available in action brought by plaintiff alleging race discrimination in housing).

> Not every statute gives individuals a **private right to sue** for damages for themselves. Some laws can only be enforced by an authorized government actor even if they are not criminal laws. If the law expressly provides such a right, there is no issue. But many laws are silent on the point. In such cases, courts decide whether to permit a **private right of action** by examining the legislative history and overall purpose of the statute along with whether traditional practice or public policy counsels for or against permitting individuals to sue in their own right for violations of the law.

One might think the same approach would apply to demands for jury trial in administrative enforcement actions. And for the most part this is correct. For example, in *Tull v. United States*, 481 U.S. 412 (1987), the Court required jury trial of a landowners' defense to an Environmental Protection Agency enforcement claim. But in *Atlas Roofing Co. v. Occupational Safety and Health Review Commn.*, 430 U.S. 442 (1977), the Court refused to require a jury trial when a business was fighting an OSHA enforcement action alleging an unsafe workplace. The *Atlas Roofing* Court found that where the government was enforcing "**public rights**," and that in this type of enforcement action, which post-dated enactment of the Seventh Amendment, there was no constitutional right to jury trial (although Congress or OSHA could certainly provide for one). Although a public rights exception of this type could potentially be a broad one, subsequent cases have seldom invoked it to deny jury trial, with courts preferring instead to look for historical analogy and at the remedy sought by the claimant.

In *Katchen v. Landy*, 382 U.S. 323 (1966), the Court ruled that jury trial was not available in certain bankruptcy administration proceedings because of the essentially equitable nature of a bankruptcy reorganization or the liquidation of an insolvent debtor. *But see Granfinanciera, S.A. v. Nordberg*, 492 U.S. 33 (1989), in which the Court found that a litigant disputing whether a transfer was an improper preference in bankruptcy was entitled to a jury trial because actions to recover a fraudulent conveyance had historically been available in the law courts of England, at least to an extent.

3. The *Ross v. Bernhard* Footnote—Are Juries Capable?

In *Ross v. Bernhard*, 396 U.S. 531 (1970), the Court ruled that a plaintiff making a "shareholder's derivative" claim (in which the shareholder argues that the directors and officers of the corporation have violated duties to the company and its shareholders) seeking monetary damages was entitled to a jury trial even though the derivative suit device (in which the shareholder "steps into the shoes" of the corporation) was much like equitable proceedings such as receivership, bankruptcy, or an accounting.

Ross v. Bernhard contained a famous footnote (*see* 396 U.S. at 538 n. 10) stating that in addition to considering history and remedy, courts also determine the right to jury trial by reference to the "practical abilities and limitations of juries." This footnote was read by some as supporting a "complexity" exception to the right to jury trial or at least making it permissible for courts to consider whether mandating a jury trial was prudent in light of the nature of the claim and the need for efficient processing of disputes.

Despite the *Ross* footnote, efforts to impose a complexity exception to the jury trial right (premised on the notion that a litigant was denied due process if lay jurors could not understand the case) was subsequently rejected by most lower courts, although the Supreme Court has never spoken definitively on the issue. *See Developments in the Law: The Civil Jury*, 110 HARV. L. REV. 1408, 1497 (1997). *See, e.g., In re U.S. Financial Securities Litigation*, 609 F.2d 411 (9th Cir. 1979)(rejecting complexity exception). *But see In re Japanese Electronic Products Antitrust Litigation*, 631 F.2d 1069 (3d Cir. 1980)(finding use of jury in lengthy, complex case would violate due process rights of defendants)(but premising decision as much on prospect of likely multi-month or even multi-

> **Juries in Discrimination Cases:**
> Prior to passage of the Civil Rights Act of 1991, it was generally thought that jury trials were not available in Title VII employment discrimination actions. Although the Supreme Court never expressed a definitive position on the issue, it suggested in dicta that the remedies of "back pay" or reinstatement were more equitable than legal. The 1991 Act, which was part of a congressional overruling of a series of Supreme Court cases decided in the 1989 term, also expressly provided for jury trial of job discrimination claims. *See* Pub. L. 102-166, codified in various sections of Title 42, U.S. Code; *Wooddell v. International Bd. of Elec. Workers*, 502 U.S. 93 (1991)(jury trial available for claim based on alleged discrimination in failure to hire plaintiff).

year trial that would fatigue and annoy jurors as much on technical complexity of the case); Graham C. Lilly, *The Decline of the American Jury*, 72 U. COLO. L. REV. 53 (2001)(suggesting that jurors do often misunderstand the law and complex factual disputes and that use of blue ribbon juries of higher education or court-appointed experts to assist the jury may be apt).

F. An Illustrative Case:
Teamsters v. Terry

Compared to other topics in Civil Procedure, the right to jury trial has an advantage in that there is one particularly good, relatively recent U.S. Supreme Court case that recaps the history of jury trial doctrine, cites leading precedent, explains the doctrine, and reveals the differing jurisprudential approaches of the Justices (and hence many judges) in the context of a brain-teasing hypothetical. For that reason, we excerpt *Teamsters v. Terry* at considerable length, including many of its citations to earlier cases and to leading scholarly articles regarding the jury trial right.

Despite some evolution of the Court away from its pro-jury views of the 1950-1990 period, *Teamsters v. Terry* remains good law and presents a methodology that is still used today in applying the Seventh Amendment. Some of the cases cited in *Teamsters v. Terry* have already been mentioned above and the decision can also be a helpful source for reviewing the modern development of the jury trial right. In reading *Terry*, consider it a bit of a review as well as a more detailed examination of the nature of "legal" versus "equitable"

> **Caveat:** *Teamsters v. Terry* was decided before passage of the 1991 Act and its change in the availability of the jury in Title VII claims. Keep this in mind when reading the Court's discussion of discrimination back pay as an equitable remedy even though it essentially involves the payment of monetary damages to a prevailing employee.

relief and this chapter's first (and only) extensive examination of the "historical" and "remedial" tests in applying the Seventh Amendment as well as a window on the judiciary's public policy preference in favor of jury trial rights in close cases.

FROM THE COURT

Chauffeurs, Teamsters and
Helpers Local No. 391 v. Terry
494 U.S. 558 (1990)
Supreme Court of the United States

JUSTICE MARSHALL delivered the opinion of the Court, except as to Part III-A.

This case presents the question whether an employee who seeks relief in the form of backpay for a union's alleged breach of its duty of fair representation has a right to trial by jury. We hold that the Seventh Amendment entitles such a plaintiff to a jury trial.

[R]espondents (truck drivers for McLean) filed an action in District Court, alleging that McLean had breached the collective-bargaining agreement in violation of § 301 of the Labor Management Relations Act, 1947, 29 U.S.C. § 185, and that the Union had violated its duty of fair representation. [§ 301(a) provides for suits by and against labor unions and that such suits "may be brought in any district court of the United States having jurisdiction of the parties, without respect to the amount in controversy or without regard to the citizenship of the parties."] Respondents requested a permanent injunction requiring the defendants to cease their illegal acts and to reinstate them to their proper seniority status; in addition, they sought, *inter alia*, compensatory damages for lost wages and health benefits. In 1986 McLean filed for bankruptcy; subsequently, the action against it was voluntarily dismissed, along with all claims for injunctive relief.

Inter alia is Latin for "among other things."

Respondents had requested a jury trial in their pleadings. The Union moved to strike the jury demand on the ground that no right to a jury trial exists in a duty of fair representation suit. The District Court denied the motion to strike. After an interlocutory appeal, the Fourth Circuit affirmed the trial court, holding that the Seventh Amendment entitled respondents to a jury trial of their claim for monetary relief. We granted the petition for certiorari to resolve a Circuit conflict on this issue, and now affirm the judgment of the Fourth Circuit.

II

The duty of fair representation is inferred from unions' exclusive authority under the National Labor Relations Act (NLRA), 29 U.S.C. § 159(a) to represent all employees in a bargaining unit. *Vaca v. Sipes*, 386 U.S. 171, 177 (1967). The duty requires a union "to serve the interests of all members without hostility or discrimination toward any, to exercise its discretion with complete good faith and honesty, and to avoid arbitrary conduct." A union must discharge its duty both in bargaining with the employer and in its enforcement of the resulting collective-bargaining agreement. Thus, the Union here was required to pursue respondents' grievances in a manner consistent with the principles of fair representation.

[A]n employee normally cannot bring a § 301 action against an employer unless he can show that the union breached its duty of fair representation in its handling of his grievance. Whether the employee sues both the labor union and the employer or only one of those entities, he must prove the same two facts to recover money damages: that the employer's action violated the terms of the collective-bargaining agreement and that the union breached its duty of fair representation.

III

We turn now to the constitutional issue presented in this case—whether respondents are entitled to a jury trial. The Seventh Amendment provides that "[i]n Suits at common law, where the value in controversy shall exceed twenty dollars, the right of trial by jury shall be preserved." The right to a jury trial includes more than the common-law forms of action recognized in 1791; the phrase "Suits at common law" refers to "suits in which *legal* rights [are] to be ascertained and determined, in contradistinction to those where equitable rights alone [are] recognized, and equitable remedies [are] administered." *Parsons v. Bedford*, 3 Pet. 433, 447 (1830). The right extends to causes of action created by Congress. *Tull v. United States*, 481 U.S. 412, 417 (1987). Since the merger of the systems of law and equity, this Court has carefully preserved the right to trial by jury where legal rights are at stake. . .

To determine whether a particular action will resolve legal rights, we examine both the nature of the issues involved and the remedy sought. "First, we compare the statutory action to 18th-century actions brought in the courts of England prior to the merger of the courts of law and equity. Second, we examine the remedy sought and determine whether it is legal or equitable in nature." The second inquiry is the more important in our analysis. *Granfinanciera, S. A. v. Nordberg*, 492 U.S. 33, 42 (1989). Justice Stevens' analysis [in his concurring opinion below] emphasizes a third consideration, namely whether "the issues [presented by the claim] are typical grist for the jury's judgment." This Court, however, has never relied on this consideration "as an independent basis for extending the right to a jury trial under the Seventh Amendment." *Tull v. United States*, 481 U.S. 412, 418, n. 4 (1987). We recently noted that this consideration is relevant only to the determination "whether Congress has permissibly entrusted the resolution of certain disputes to an administrative agency or specialized court of equity, and whether jury trials would impair the functioning of the legislative scheme." *Granfinanciera, S. A. v. Nordberg*, 492 U.S., at 42, n. 4. No one disputes that an action for breach of the duty of fair representation may properly be brought in an Article III court; thus, the factor does not affect our analysis.

A

An action for breach of a union's duty of fair representation was unknown in 18th-century England; in fact, collective bargaining was unlawful. We must therefore look for an analogous cause of action that existed in the 18th century to determine whether the nature of this duty of fair representation suit is legal or equitable.

The Union contends that this duty of fair representation action resembles a suit brought to vacate an arbitration award because respondents seek to set aside the result of the grievance process. In the 18th century, an action to set aside an arbitration award was considered equitable.

The arbitration analogy is inapposite, however, to the Seventh Amendment question posed in this case. No grievance committee has considered respondents' claim that the Union violated its duty of fair representation; the grievance process was concerned only with the employer's alleged breach of the collective-bargaining agreement. Thus, respondents' claim against the Union cannot be characterized as an action to vacate an arbitration award because "'[t]he arbitration proceeding did not, and indeed, could not, resolve the employee's claim against the union . . . . Because no arbitrator has decided the primary issue presented by this claim, no arbitration award need be undone, even if the employee ultimately prevails.'" *DelCostello*, 462 U.S., at 167 (quoting *Mitchell, supra*, at 73 (Stevens, J., concurring in part and dissenting in part) (footnotes omitted)).

The Union next argues that respondents' duty of fair representation action is comparable to an action by a trust beneficiary against a trustee for breach of fiduciary duty. Such actions were within the exclusive jurisdiction of courts of equity. This analogy is far more persuasive than the arbitration analogy. Just as a trustee must act in the best interests of the beneficiaries, a union, as the exclusive representative of the workers, must exercise its power to act on behalf of the employees in good faith. Moreover, just as a beneficiary does not directly control the actions of a trustee, an individual employee lacks direct control over a union's actions taken on his behalf, *see* [Archibald] Cox, *The Legal Nature of Collective Bargaining Agreements*, 57 Mich. L. Rev. 1, 21 (1958).

The trust analogy extends to a union's handling of grievances. In most cases, a trustee has the exclusive authority to sue third parties who injure the beneficiaries' interest in the trust, including any legal claim the trustee holds in trust for the beneficiaries, RESTATEMENT (SECOND) OF TRUSTS, *supra*, § 82, comment *a*. The trustee then has the sole responsibility for determining whether to settle, arbitrate, or otherwise dispose of the claim. RESTATEMENT (SECOND) OF TRUSTS, *supra*, § 192. Similarly, the union typically has broad discretion in its decision whether and how to pursue an employee's grievance against an employer. Just as a trust beneficiary can sue to enforce a contract entered into on his behalf by the trustee only if the trustee "improperly refuses or neglects to bring an action against the third person," so an employee can sue his employer for a breach of the collective-bargaining agreement only if he shows that the union breached its duty of fair representation in its handling of the grievance.

Respondents contend that their duty of fair representation suit is less like a trust action than an attorney malpractice action, which was historically an action at law, *see, e.g., Russell v. Palmer*, 2 Wils. K. B. 325, 95 Eng. Rep. 837 (1767). In determining the appropriate statute of limitations for a hybrid § 301/duty of fair representation action, this

Court [has] noted in dictum that an attorney malpractice action is "the closest state-law analogy for the claim against the union." Th[at] Court did not consider the trust analogy, however. Presented with a more complete range of alternatives, we find that, in the context of the Seventh Amendment inquiry, the attorney malpractice analogy does not capture the relationship between the union and the represented employees as fully as the trust analogy does.

The attorney malpractice analogy is inadequate in several respects. Although an attorney malpractice suit is in some ways similar to a suit alleging a union's breach of its fiduciary duty, the two actions are fundamentally different. The nature of an action is in large part controlled by the nature of the underlying relationship between the parties. Unlike employees represented by a union, a client controls the significant decisions concerning his representation. Moreover, a client can fire his attorney if he is dissatisfied with his attorney's performance. This option is not available to an individual employee who is unhappy with a union's representation, unless a majority of the members of the bargaining unit share his dissatisfaction. Thus, we find the malpractice analogy less convincing than the trust analogy.

Nevertheless, the trust analogy does not persuade us to characterize respondents' claim as wholly equitable. The Union's argument mischaracterizes the nature of our comparison of the action before us to 18th-century forms of action. As we observed in *Ross v. Bernhard*, 396 U.S. 531 (1970), "The Seventh Amendment question depends on the nature of the *issue* to be tried rather than the character of the overall action." *Id.*, at 538 (emphasis added) (finding a right to jury trial in a shareholder's derivative suit, a type of suit traditionally brought in courts of equity, because plaintiffs' case presented legal issues of breach of contract and negligence). As discussed above, *see supra*, at 564, to recover from the Union here, respondents must prove both that McLean violated § 301 by breaching the collective-bargaining agreement and that the Union breached its duty of fair representation. When viewed in isolation, the duty of fair representation issue is analogous to a claim against a trustee for breach of fiduciary duty. The § 301 issue, however, is comparable to a breach of contract claim—a legal issue.

Respondents' action against the Union thus encompasses both equitable and legal issues. The first part of our Seventh Amendment inquiry, then, leaves us in equipoise as to whether respondents are entitled to a jury trial.

B

Our determination under the first part of the Seventh Amendment analysis is only preliminary. In this case, the only remedy sought is a request for compensatory damages representing backpay and benefits. Generally, an action for money damages was "the traditional form of relief offered in the courts of law." *Curtis v. Loether*, 415 U.S. 189, 196 (1974). This Court has not, however, held that "any award of monetary relief must *necessarily* be 'legal' relief." *Ibid.* (emphasis added). Nonetheless, because we conclude that the remedy respondents seek has none of the attributes that must be present before we will find an exception to the general rule and characterize damages as equitable, we find that the remedy sought by respondents is legal.

First, we have characterized damages as equitable where they are restitutionary, such as in "action[s] for disgorgement of improper profits," The backpay sought by respondents is not money wrongfully held by the Union, but wages and benefits they would have received from McLean had the Union processed the employees' grievances properly. Such relief is not restitutionary.

Second, a monetary award "incidental to or intertwined with injunctive relief" may be equitable. Because respondents seek only money damages, this characteristic is clearly absent from the case . . . . Thus, the remedy sought in this duty of fair representation case is clearly different from backpay sought for violations of Title VII . . . .

Unlike the unfair labor practice provisions of the NLRA, which are concerned primarily with the public interest in effecting federal labor policy, the duty of fair representation targets "'the wrong done the individual employee.'" *Electrical Workers v. Foust*, 442 U.S. 42, 49, n. 12 (1979) (quoting *Vaca v. Sipes*, 386 U.S., at 182, n. 8) (emphasis deleted). Thus, the remedies appropriate for unfair labor practices may differ from the remedies for a breach of the duty of fair representation, given the need to vindicate different goals.

We hold, then, that the remedy of backpay sought in this duty of fair representation action is legal in nature. Considering both parts of the

Seventh Amendment inquiry, we find that respondents are entitled to a jury trial on all issues presented in their suit.

IV

On balance, our analysis of the nature of respondents' duty of fair representation action and the remedy they seek convinces us that this action is a legal one. Although the search for an adequate 18th-century analog revealed that the claim includes both legal and equitable issues, the money damages respondents seek are the type of relief traditionally awarded by courts of law. Thus, the Seventh Amendment entitles respondents to a jury trial, and we therefore affirm the judgment of the Court of Appeals.

JUSTICE BRENNAN, concurring in part and concurring in the judgment.

I agree with the Court that respondents seek a remedy that is legal in nature and that the Seventh Amendment entitles respondents to a jury trial on their duty of fair representation claims. I therefore join Parts I, II, III-B, and IV of the Court's opinion. I do not join that part of the opinion which reprises the particular historical analysis this Court has employed to determine whether a claim is a "Sui[t] at common law" under the Seventh Amendment, *ante*, at 564, because I believe the historical test can and should be simplified . . . .

I believe that our insistence that the jury trial right hinges in part on a comparison of the substantive right at issue to forms of action used in English courts 200 years ago needlessly convolutes our Seventh Amendment jurisprudence. For the past decade and a half, this Court has explained that the two parts of the historical test are not equal in weight, that the nature of the remedy is more important than the nature of the right. *Granfinanciera, S. A. v. Nordberg*, 492 U.S. 33, 42 (1989); *Tull v. United States*, 481 U.S. 412, 421 (1987); *Curtis v. Loether, supra*, at 196. Since the existence of a right to jury trial therefore turns on the nature of the remedy, absent congressional delegation to a specialized decisionmaker, there remains little purpose to our rattling through dusty attics of ancient writs. The time has come to borrow William of Occam's razor and sever this portion of our analysis.

We have long acknowledged that, of the factors relevant to the jury trial right, comparison of the claim to ancient forms of action, "requiring extensive and possibly abstruse historical inquiry, is obviously the most difficult to apply." *Ross v. Bernhard*, 396 U.S. 531, 538, n. 10 (1970). Requiring judges, with neither the training nor time necessary for reputable historical scholarship, to root through the tangle of primary and secondary sources to determine which of a hundred or so writs is analogous to the right at issue has embroiled courts in recondite controversies better left to legal historians . . . .

What Blackstone described as "the glory of the English law" and "the most transcendent privilege which any subject can enjoy," 3 W[illiam] Blackstone, *Commentaries* 379, was crucial in the eyes of those who founded this country. The encroachment on civil jury trial by colonial administrators was a "deeply divisive issue in the years just preceding the outbreak of hostilities between the colonies and England," and all 13 States reinstituted the right after hostilities ensued. [Charles] Wolfram, *The Constitutional History of the Seventh Amendment*, 57 Minn. L. Rev. 639, 654-655 (1973). "In fact, '[t]he right to trial by jury was probably the only one universally secured by the first American constitutions.'" *Id.*, at 655 (quoting L. Levy, *Freedom of Speech and Press in Early American History—Legacy of Suppression* 281 (1963 reprint)). Fear of a Federal Government that had not guaranteed jury trial in civil cases, voiced first at the Philadelphia Convention in 1787 and regularly during the ratification debates, was the concern that precipitated the maelstrom over the need for a bill of rights in the United States Constitution. Wolfram, *supra*, at 657-660.

This Court has long recognized the caliber of this right. In *Parsons v. Bedford*, 3 Pet. 433, 446 (1830), Justice Story stressed: "The trial by jury is justly dear to the American people. It has always been an object of deep interest and solicitude, and every encroachment upon it has been watched with great jealousy." Similarly, in *Jacob v. New York City*, 315 U.S. 752, 752-753 (1942), we said that "[t]he right of jury trial in civil cases at common law is a basic and fundamental feature of our system of federal jurisprudence . . . [a] right so fundamental and sacred to the citizen [that it] should be jealously guarded by the courts."

We can guard this right and save our courts from needless and intractable excursions into increasingly unfamiliar territory simply by retiring that prong of our Seventh Amendment test which we have already cast into a certain doubt. If we are not prepared to accord the nature of the historical analog sufficient weight for this factor to affect the outcome of our inquiry, except in the rarest of hypothetical cases, what reason do we have for insisting that federal judges proceed with this arduous inquiry? It is time we read the writing on the wall, especially as we ourselves put it there.

JUSTICE STEVENS, concurring in part and concurring in the judgment.

Because I believe the Court has made this case unnecessarily difficult by exaggerating the importance of finding a precise common-law analogue to the duty of fair representation, I do not join Part III-A of its opinion. Ironically, by stressing the importance of identifying an exact analogue, the Court has diminished the utility of looking for any analogue.

As I have suggested in the past, I believe the duty of fair representation action resembles a common-law action against an attorney for malpractice more closely than it does any other form of action. *See United Parcel Service, Inc. v. Mitchell*, 451 U.S. 56, 74 (1981) (opinion concurring in part and dissenting in part). Of course, this action is not an exact counterpart to a malpractice suit. Indeed, by definition, no recently recognized form of action—whether the product of express congressional enactment or of judicial interpretation—can have a precise analog in 17th- or 18th-century English law. Were it otherwise the form of action would not in fact be "recently recognized."

But the Court surely overstates this action's similarity to an action against a trustee. Collective bargaining involves no settlor, no trust corpus, and no trust instrument executed to convey property to beneficiaries chosen at the settlor's pleasure. Nor are these distinctions reified matters of pure form. The law of trusts originated to expand the varieties of land ownership in feudal England, and evolved to protect the paternalistic beneficence of the wealthy, often between generations and always over time. *See Scott on Trusts* § 1 (4th ed. 1987); L[awrence] Friedman, *A History of American Law* 212, 222-223 (1973). Beneficiaries are protected from their own judgment. The attorney-client relationship, by contrast, advances the client's interests in dealings with adverse parties. Clients are saved from their lack of skill, but their judgment is honored. Union members, as a group, accordingly have the power to hire, fire, and direct the actions of their representatives—prerogatives anathema to the paternalistic forms of the equitable trust.

Equitable reasoning calibrated by the sophisticated judgment of the jurist, the accountant, and the chancellor is thus appropriately invoked when the impact of a trustee's conduct on the future interests of contingent remaindermen must be reviewed. However, the commonsense understanding of the jury, selected to represent the community, is appropriately invoked when disputes in the factory, the warehouse, and the garage must be resolved. In most duty of fair representation cases, the issues, which require an understanding of the realities of employment relationships, are typical grist for the jury's judgment. Indeed, the law defining the union's duty of fair representation has developed in cases tried to juries. Thus, *Vaca v. Sipes*, 386 U.S. 171 (1967), was itself a jury trial as were, for example, *Electrical Workers v. Foust*, 442 U.S. 42 (1979), and *Bowen v. United States Postal Service*, 459 U.S. 212 (1983).

As the Court correctly observed in *Curtis v. Loether*, 415 U.S. 189, 195 (1974), "in an ordinary civil action in the district courts, where there is obviously no functional justification for denying the jury trial right, a jury trial must be available if the action involves rights and remedies of the sort typically enforced in an action at law." As I had occasion to remark at an earlier proceeding in the same case, the relevant historical question is not whether a suit was "specifically recognized at common law," but whether "the nature of the substantive right asserted . . . is analogous to common law rights" and whether the relief sought is "typical of an action at law." *Rogers v. Loether*, 467 F. 2d 1110, 1116-1117 (CA7 1972). Duty of fair representation suits are for the most part ordinary civil actions involving the stuff of contract and malpractice disputes. There is accordingly no ground for excluding these actions from the jury right . . . .

JUSTICE KENNEDY, with whom JUSTICE O'CONNOR and JUSTICE SCALIA join, dissenting.

This case asks whether the Seventh Amendment guarantees the respondent union members a jury trial in a duty of fair representation action against their labor union. The Court is quite correct, in my view, in its formulation of the initial premises that must govern the case. Under *Curtis v. Loether*, 415 U.S. 189, 194 (1974), the right to a jury trial in a statutory action depends on the presence of "legal rights and remedies." To determine whether rights and remedies in a duty of fair representation action are legal in character, we must compare the action to the 18th-century cases permitted in the law courts of England, and we must examine the nature of the relief sought. *See Granfinanciera, S. A. v. Nordberg*, 492 U.S. 33, 42 (1989). I agree also with those Members of the Court who find that the duty of fair representation action resembles an equitable trust action more than a suit for malpractice.

I disagree with the analytic innovation of the Court that identification of the trust action as a model for modern duty of fair representation actions is insufficient to decide the case. The Seventh Amendment requires us to determine whether the duty of fair representation action "is more similar to cases that were tried in courts of law than to suits tried in courts of equity." *Tull v. United States*, 481 U.S. 412, 417 (1987). Having made this decision in favor of an equitable action, our inquiry should end. Because the Court disagrees with this proposition, I dissent.

I

. . .[T]he trust analogy [should be] the controlling one here. A union's duty of fair representation accords with a trustee's duty of impartiality. The duty of fair representation requires a union "to make an honest effort to serve the interests of all of [its] members, without hostility to any." *Ford Motor Co. v. Huffman*, 345 U.S. 330, 337 (1953). This standard may require a union to act for the benefit of employees who, as in this case, have antithetical interests. *See* Cox, *The Legal Nature of Collective Bargaining Agreements*, 57 Mich. L. Rev. 1, 21 (1958). Trust law, in a similar manner, long has required trustees to serve the interests of all beneficiaries with impartiality. *See* RESTATEMENT, *supra*, § 183 ("When there are two or more beneficiaries of a trust, the trustee is under a duty to deal impartially with them).

A lawyer's duty of loyalty is cast in different terms. Although the union is charged with the responsibility of reconciling the positions of its members, the lawyer's duty of loyalty long has precluded the representation of conflicting interests. A lawyer, at least absent knowing waiver by the parties, could not represent both the respondents and the senior laidoff workers as the Union has done in this case.

The relief available in a duty of fair representation action also makes the trust action the better model. To remedy a breach of the duty of fair representation, a court must issue an award "fashioned to make the injured employee whole." The court may order an injunction compelling the union, if it is still able, to pursue the employee's claim, and may require monetary compensation, but it cannot award exemplary or punitive damages. This relief parallels the remedies prevailing in the courts of equity in actions against trustees for failing to pursue claims.

These remedies differ somewhat from those available in attorney malpractice actions. Because legal malpractice was a common-law claim, clients sued their attorneys for breach of professional obligations in the law courts. *See* R[onald] Mallen & V[ictor] Levit, *Legal Malpractice* §§ 4 and 5, pp. 14–18 (2d ed. 1981). No one maintains that clients could obtain from these courts the injunctive relief offered in duty of fair representation actions. The evidence suggests that compensatory damages in malpractice cases resembled the monetary relief now awarded in duty of fair representation actions. Yet, as a historical matter, juries did have the authority to award exemplary damages in at least some tort actions. Although the parties have not cited any punitive damages award in an attorney malpractice action prior to 1791, courts have awarded such damages since the 19th century.

II

The Court relies on two lines of precedents to overcome the conclusion that the trust action should serve as the controlling model. The first consists of cases in which the Court has considered simplifications in litigation resulting from modern procedural reforms in the federal courts. Justice Marshall asserts that these cases show that the Court must look at the character of individual issues rather than claims as a whole. The second line addresses the significance of the remedy in determining the equitable or legal nature of an action for the purpose of choosing the most appropriate analogy. Under these cases, the Court decides that the respondents have a right to a jury because they seek money damages. *See ante*, at 570-573. These authorities do not support the Court's holding.

A

In three cases we have found a right to trial by jury where there are legal claims that, for procedural reasons, a plaintiff could have or must have raised in the courts of equity before the systems merged. In *Beacon Theatres, Inc. v. Westover*, 359 U.S. 500 (1959), Fox, a potential defendant threatened with legal antitrust claims, brought an action for declaratory and injunctive relief against Beacon, the likely plaintiff. Because only the courts of equity had offered such relief prior to the merger of the two court systems, Fox had thought that it could deprive Beacon of a jury trial. Beacon, however, raised the antitrust issues as counterclaims and sought a jury. We ruled that, because Beacon would have had a right to a jury trial on its antitrust claims, Fox could not deprive it of a jury merely by taking advantage of modern declaratory procedures to sue first. The result was consistent with the spirit of the Federal Rules of Civil Procedure, which allow liberal joinder of legal and equitable actions, and the Declaratory Judgment Act, 28 U.S.C. §§ 2201, 2202, which preserves the right to jury trial to both parties. *See* 359 U.S., at 509–510.

In *Dairy Queen, Inc. v. Wood*, 369 U.S. 469 (1962), we held, in a similar manner, that a plaintiff, by asking in his complaint for an equitable accounting for trademark infringement, could not deprive the defendant of a jury trial on contract claims subsumed within the accounting. Although a court of equity would have heard the contract claims as part of the accounting suit, we found them severable under modern procedure.

In *Ross v. Bernhard*, 396 U.S. 531 (1970), a shareholder-plaintiff demanded a jury trial in a derivative action asserting a legal claim on behalf of his corporation. The defendant opposed a jury trial. In deciding the case, we recognized that only the courts of equity had procedural devices allowing shareholders to raise a corporation's claims. We nonetheless again ruled that modern procedure allowed trial of the legal claim to a jury.

These three cases responded to the difficulties created by a merged court system. *See* [John] McCoid, *Procedural Reform and the Right to Jury Trial: A Study of Beacon Theatres, Inc. v. Westover*, 116 U. Pa. L. Rev. 1 (1967). They stand for the proposition that, because distinct courts of equity no longer exist, the possibility or necessity of using former equitable procedures to press a legal claim no longer will determine the right to a jury. Justice Marshall reads these cases to require a jury trial whenever a cause of action contains legal issues and would require a jury trial in this case because the respondents must prove a breach of the collective-bargaining agreement as one element of their claim.

I disagree. The respondents, as shown above, are asserting an equitable claim. Having reached this conclusion, the *Beacon*, *Dairy Queen*, and *Ross* cases are inapplicable. Although we have divided self-standing legal claims from equitable declaratory, accounting, and derivative procedures, we have never parsed legal elements out of equitable claims absent specific procedural justifications. Actions which, beyond all question, are equitable in nature may involve some predicate inquiry that would be submitted to a jury in other contexts. For example, just as the plaintiff in a duty of fair representation action against his union must show breach of the collective-bargaining agreement as an initial matter, in an action against a trustee for failing to pursue a claim the beneficiary must show that the claim had some merit. But the question of the claim's validity, even if the claim raises contract issues, would not bring the jury right into play in a suit against a trustee.

B

The Court also rules that, despite the appropriateness of the trust analogy as a whole, the respondents have a right to a jury trial because they seek money damages. The nature of the remedy remains a factor of considerable importance in determining whether a statutory action had a legal or equitable analog in 1791, but we have not adopted a rule that a statutory action permitting damages is by definition more analogous to a legal action than to any equitable suit. In each case, we look to the remedy to determine whether, taken with other factors, it places an action within the definition of "Suits at common law."

In *Curtis v. Loether*, 415 U.S., at 195–196, for example, we ruled that the availability of actual and punitive damages made a statutory antidiscrimination action resemble a legal tort action more than any equitable action. We made explicit that we did not "go so far as to say that any award of monetary relief must necessarily be 'legal' relief." *Id.*, at 196. Although monetary damages might cause some statutory actions to resemble tort suits, the presence of monetary damages in this duty of fair representation action does not make it more analogous to a legal action than to an equitable action. Indeed, as shown above, the injunctive and monetary remedies available make the duty of fair representation suit less analogous to a malpractice action than to a suit against a trustee.

In *Tull v. United States*, 481 U.S., at 422, the availability of damages again played a critical role in determining the right to a jury trial. In an environmental suit by the Government for injunctive relief and a civil penalty, both an equitable public nuisance action and a legal action in debt seemed appropriate historical models. We decided between them by noting that only the courts of law could award civil penalties. In the present case, however, one cannot characterize both the trust analogy and the legal malpractice comparisons as appropriate; the considerations discussed above, including the remedy available, all make the trust model superior. As we stated in *Tull*, "[o]ur search is for a single historical analog, taking into consideration the nature of the cause of action and the remedy as two important factors." The trust action alone satisfies this standard.

In *Granfinanciera, S. A. v. Nordberg*, 492 U.S. 33 (1989), we again found the presence of monetary relief critical in determining the nature of a statutory action as a whole. We held that, despite some evidence that both the courts of law and equity had jurisdiction over fraudulent conveyances, only a court of law could entertain an action to recover an alleged fraudulent transfer of a determinate sum of money. As in *Curtis* and *Tull*, however, the particular importance of monetary damages in *Granfinanciera* does not carry forward into this case. The courts of equity could and did award the kind of damages sought by the respondents here. The respondents' mere request for backpay in no way entitles them to a jury under the Seventh Amendment.

III

The Court must adhere to the historical test in determining the right to a jury because the language of the Constitution requires it. The Seventh Amendment "preserves" the right to jury trial in civil cases. We cannot preserve a right existing in 1791 unless we look to history to identify it. Our precedents are in full agreement with this reasoning and insist on adherence to the historical test. No alternatives short of rewriting the Constitution exist . . . If we abandon the plain language of the Constitution to expand the jury right, we may expect Courts with opposing views to curtail it in the future.

I would hesitate to abandon or curtail the historical test out of concern for the competence of the Court to understand legal history. We do look to history for the answers to constitutional questions. Although opinions will differ on what this history shows, the approach has no less validity in the Seventh Amendment context than elsewhere.

If Congress has not provided for a jury trial, we are confined to the Seventh Amendment to determine whether one is required. Our own views respecting the wisdom of using a jury should be put aside. Like Justice Brennan, I admire the jury process. Other judges have taken the opposite view. *See, e.g.,* J[erome]. Frank, *Law and the Modern Mind* 170–185 (1931). But the judgment of our own times is not always preferable to the lessons of history. Our whole constitutional experience teaches that history must inform the judicial inquiry. Our obligation to the Constitution and its Bill of Rights, no less than the compact we have with the generation that wrote them for us, do not permit us to disregard provisions that some may think to be mere matters of historical form.

CASE ANALYSIS & QUESTIONS

1. After reading the Justices' debate about the utility of the historical prong of the Seventh Amendment test, are you persuaded by either position? Should the historical test continue to be used? Why?

2. Was the *Terry* majority wrong to look at issues presented rather than the entire case? By doing this, Justice Marshall's majority opinion made it easier to avoid the consequence of the majority's own conclusion that a union's breach of fair representation resembled the equitable action of enforcing a trust more than the legal action of legal malpractice or breach of contract.

3. Justice Stevens concurred alone—but is his point not well taken? Given the plasticity of the two-pronged historical and remedial tests, shouldn't courts also consider whether the issues at hand are of the type that have traditionally been decided by jurors?

4. Why did the plaintiff want a jury trial and the union oppose it?

G. Other Matters Related to the Jury Trial

1. Jury Composition

As discussed above regarding jury selection, a pool of citizens must be assembled before jurors can be drawn from the pool and impaneled for jury service in a particular case. For too many years in the nation's history there were express prohibitions against jury service by blacks and women. Even after these express barriers were lifted, the sources for drawing potential juror names were often slanted toward those with more resources or longer residence in the community, which tended to reduce racial and ethnic representation, if not also gender representation. *See, e.g., Rose v. Mitchell*, 443 U.S. 545 (1979)(addressing allegations of bias in selection of grand jurors in one Texas county that appears to have resulted in under-representation of Hispanics)(remember that the grand jury is a criminal law device and not part of civil procedure). Modern jury selection practice uses a variety of sources designed to enhance the prospects of obtaining a more complete cross-section of the community in jury representation.

2. Jury Size

Traditionally, a jury meant a twelve-person jury. The Supreme Court has ruled that jurors of fewer than twelve can be used in criminal matters (*Williams v. Florida*, 399 U.S. 78 (1970)) and civil matters (*Colgrove v. Battin*, 413 U.S. 149 (1973)). A jury smaller than six, however, violates the Constitution. *See Ballew v. Georgia*, 435 U.S. 223 (1978). As scholars have observed, however, the same arguments used to prohibit five-person juries also apply to juries of between six and twelve persons in size. *See* Hans Zeisel, *And Then There Were None: The Diminution of the Civil Jury*, 38 U. Chi. L. Rev. 710 (1971); Michael Saks, *Ignorance of Science is No Excuse*, 10 Trial 11 (1974). They observe that in juries of less than twelve, the odds of obtaining a cross-section of the community are greatly reduced and a greater likelihood exists that certain perspectives and demographic groups will be absent altogether. In addition, there is less likelihood that a dissenting juror will have an ally—and psychological research suggests that dissenters are much more willing to insist on being heard if faced with group opposition so long as they have at least one ally. Professor Zeisel's concern was that the minority position was less likely present and fully aired on smaller juries. In spite of this, most courts in civil cases use six and eight person juries, although judges have discretion to use a full complement of twelve jurors.

For decades, it was common practice to select alternates jurors but this practice was effectively abolished in the 1991 Amendments to the Civil Rules.

Pursuant to Rule 48, the trial judge impanels a jury of between six and twelve persons and if one or more jurors becomes unable to participate, the remaining jurors continue to conclusion. So long as there are six jurors left sitting, the jury is of sufficient size to satisfy constitutional concerns. Obviously, impaneling only six jurors can pose a risk as jurors may become ill during trial or have inappropriate contact with counsel such as overhearing a conversation or discussing the merits of the case. If the jury falls below six persons, the trial proceedings up to that time are for naught. Some states still use the alternate juror device and ordinarily forbid alternates from participating in the deliberations. But where this occurs with consent of the parties, many courts find the error to be harmless or the matter waived as a ground for challenging the verdict on appeal.

3. Unanimity

Traditionally, jury verdicts had to be unanimous. But this is not constitutionally required. *See Apodaca v. Oregon*, 406 U.S. 404 (1972) (unanimity not constitutionally required for state criminal verdicts) (reversing *American Publ. Co. v. Fisher*, 166 U.S. 464 (1897)). Rule 48(b) requires federal civil verdicts to be unanimous unless otherwise stipulated by the parties. As with juries of less than twelve, the majority vote jury (the majority required varies with the size of the jury and is always a super-majority such as ten of twelve jurors or six of eight jurors rather than a bare majority) has been criticized by scholars as discouraging the type of vigorous debate needed to achieve unanimity. *See, e.g.,* Valerie P. Hans & Neil Vidmar, *Judging The Jury* 175 (1986). Rule 48(c) permits the court to "poll" or question the jurors individually to confirm agreement with the announced verdict.

4. Jury Instructions and Deliberation

After presentation of the evidence and closing argument by counsel, jurors are instructed by the judge both as to the law and regarding their task. Then the jury retires to deliberate. Historically, jurors were not permitted to take notes or ask questions during the trial, although individual judges have authority over this and often permit note-taking and submission of written questions. During deliberations, jurors are shielded from contact with outsiders and are instructed not to discuss the case with others or read about the case during the time they are deliberating. In an extreme case, the court may even sequester the jurors in a hotel to insulate them from outside influences, lobbying, or intimidation efforts.

Jury instructions are an important part of the trial process. Prior to instructing the jury, the judge typically receives requested instructions from the parties and may modify or supplement the court's standard jury instructions in response to the parties' suggestions. If the jury instructions are in error, this may result in reversal and remand by an appellate court or grant of a new trial by the trial court. However, if an error in jury instruction is harmless (*see* Fed. R. Civ. P. 61), the verdict may stand despite the error. Chapter 17 provides further discussion of the role of the jury in the trial process.

ADDITIONAL EXERCISES

1. Deena Dramaqueen wed Paul Pituitary, a pro basketball player. But after only a month of actual marriage, the couple discovered that they were not all that compatible and filed for divorce.

   In addition to the divorce action, Paul sued the entire Dramaqueen family seeking return of a substantial amount of Pro League merchandise loaned by Paul to the family for use in their reality television show. The complaint alleges that the family has wrongfully continued to hold on to the "valuable" memorabilia or perhaps has already sold all or part of the merchandise at flea markets throughout the Sunbelt. Paul seeks return of the merchandise and compensatory damages. He really prefers return because most of it was not his and he wants to be able to give it back rather than try to prove particular market values for everything.

   Paul also seeks statutory penalties under the state's recently enacted "Memorabilia Respect Act," which provides a cause of action for punitive damages for owners of sports merchandise whose material is intentionally wrongfully detained by any borrower and also provides that the owner of record of sports memorabilia may obtain ex parte seizure of the memorabilia from those wrongfully detaining it. Paul elected not to seek an ex parte TRO (temporary restraining order) or try the surprise attack of a preliminary injunction (which does require notice but is something of an ambush) and to instead give notice and time to respond for Deena because he's still a lovesick sap mooning over her.

Assuming the case gets to trial without dispositive motion practice or settlement, can either Paul or Deena demand a jury trial?

2. The Penny Ante Casino in Las Vegas sues international gambler and tabloid magazine playboy heartthrob Devin Drama for allegedly ripping off millions during a complicated scam involving Drama and ten of his fellow rogues. It seems that whenever Drama was playing there was always some sort of distraction staged, which enabled Drama to evade casino security systems. He placed his winnings in the safe deposit box he maintains at ImmunityBank of Switzerland's Lugano branch office. Drama has been at this long enough that the safe deposit box now holds nearly 100 million Euros.

    The Penny Ante action seeks an injunction requiring Drama to turn over the safe deposit box and place it in the hands of a court-appointed receiver to sort out the contents, which Penny Ante suspects includes jewelry and documents as well as money that may have come from Drama's legitimate acting career. All Penny Ante wants is the money Drama allegedly swindled. Penny Ante intentionally is forbearing from a punitive damages claim or any express claim for damages because it does not want to appear to be hounding Drama, who is immensely popular. ***Drama, knowing that he is immensely popular, demands a jury trial. Penny Ante wants a bench trial. Who wins on that point?***

3. Perma Frost Refrigerators sues Darrell's Dealhouse, alleging that Darrell is dealing in counterfeit Perma Frost products, diluting the value of the Perma Frost trademark and damaging its reputation when the counterfeit fridges fail at high rates. Perma's counsel files a complaint seeking a permanent injunction against Darrell's practices and money damages for injury to Perma's reputation due to the failure of Darrell's counterfeit fridges, which buyers wrongly think are Perma products. The complaint says nothing about jury trial.

    Perma obtains a temporary restraining order, which is a form of injunctive relief granted by the judge. Rather than proceeding immediately to a preliminary injunction hearing after the TRO is granted, Darrell agrees to abide by the TRO and puts the allegedly offending goods in a locked warehouse (*see* Fed. R. Civ. P. 65(b)(2)). A month later, Perma's in-house counsel notes that she is eager for trial, expecting that a jury composed of consumers familiar with the high-quality Perma products will be supportive of the company's request to shut down distribution of fake goods of lower quality. ***Does Perma's outside counsel have a problem?***

4. Pat Client retains Daring Attorney to purchase land for use in Pat's planned construction of a shopping center, depositing $10 million in Daring's client funds account for use in purchasing the land. Pat then decides it will be cheaper to use a realtor for this work, fires Daring and demands return of the funds and the file papers in the matter. Daring refuses, citing an outstanding bill, and places an attorney's lien on the file (which is permissible in this particular state as a means of gaining leverage on a client who is in arrears on payment). Pat sues. Is Pat entitled to a jury trial? ***If Pat does not demand a jury trial, may Daring insist on a jury trial? How, if at all, does Teamsters v. Terry answer the question?***

5. Pam Pipefitter works on a job she obtains through Dan's Temporary Solutions, working on a building owned by Diane Developer and Doug Contractor. After a four days of work, she returns on Friday only to find herself barred by security guards while a crew from Dino's Pipefitting Solutions is finishing the job. Unable to obtain informal resolution, Pam sues Dan, Diane, Doug and Dino. She sues on theories of tort and contract, as well as the state's "Fair Pay for a Fair Day" statute providing that any worker "shall be adequately compensated for work done and contribution to a building project on which the worker has performed services." In addition, Pam makes a claim under the federal Fair Labor Standards Act. As relief, she seeks return of her tools (left on the job site Thursday night), payment for work done pursuant to both statutes and common law, and punitive damages. Her complaint includes a claim for relief sounding in fraud against Dan, Diane, and Doug and a tortious interference claim against Dino. ***Outline the claims and remedies sought and determine to what extent Pam is entitled to a jury trial. How, if at all, does Teamsters v. Terry answer the question?***

6. Paloma Participant is a member of the Dirt Demons Garden Society, the group in her neighborhood responsible for maintaining the common areas of the development such as parks, trails, median strips, benches—

and of course—gardens. Paloma is upset that the small flower garden and park next to her home has become overgrown, weedy, and ill-kept. Informal negotiation proves unavailing and Paloma sues, seeking clean-up of the park or alternatively payment of funds that she can use to hire a professional lawn service and aborist to whip the park into shape. She does not demand a jury trial but the Dirt Demons do, anticipating that a lay jury drawn from folks who live in more modest neighborhoods will be unsympathetic to Paloma's lament that the garden/park right by her house is somehow not good enough. ***To what extent, if any, is a jury required? How, if at all, does Teamsters v. Terry answer the question?***

Quick Summary

- Although studies show that judges and juries usually see the facts of cases in the same way, there are believed to be case-specific differences that make the issue of jury trial an important strategic consideration for litigants.

- In federal courts, the Seventh Amendment governs and it requires a jury trial in actions "at law" but not in equity actions. States often have a similar jury trial guaranty.

- Jury trial must be timely and appropriately demanded pursuant to Rule 38 in order to be preserved. If this is not done, the right is waived, although a court can impanel an actual or advisory jury if it chooses.

- In determining whether jury trial is warranted, courts look at whether the claim at issue has historically been deemed one at law or in equity. Where the claim is statutory or otherwise did not exist in 1791, courts analogize the instant action to historical actions.

- Courts also look at the remedy sought, generally viewing demands for monetary relief as legal and demands for injunctive relief as equitable.

- Courts also consider the federal policy favoring juries and may consider issues of practicality and feasibility if the case is conducted as a jury trial.

- Where a case presents both equitable and legal claims for relief, common facts are first tried to a jury so that judicial determinations do not preclude jury determination.

17
Trial

Key Concepts

- Preparing for trial—including negotiation and possible settlement
- Beginning at the end—working backward from the desired result to facilitate trial planning (as you did for pretrial planning)

- The phases of trial
- The adversarial but civilized nature of trial
- The "American Rule" on attorney's fees—and its exceptions
- Selecting a jury
- The role of the Rules of Evidence and objections
- Pretrial "*in limine*" evidence rulings
- The law and use of motions for judgment as a matter of law
- Issues related to the verdict form, jury instructions, juror misconduct, and lawyer misconduct

Introduction

Although most cases eventually settle, many settle on the very eve of trial, during trial, after trial, while appeal is pending or after an appellate decision. Although perhaps "vanishing" in relation to their frequency of a century ago, trials still happen, at least in part and with enough frequency that "litigators" still need to be adequately versed in the trial process. Even a lawyer who will never conduct a trial (some lawyers routinely hand off claims to associated counsel if the matter gets to trial) need to know enough to inform the litigator's strategy and tactics for the claim.

IN PRACTICE

Many in the legal profession distinguish between "litigators" who deal with the pretrial phase of a matter and "trial lawyers" who conduct the actual trials. Too much can be made of this apparent distinction. Most effective trial lawyers are also very good at pleading, discovery, and motion practice—things you need to do well to set the stage for a successful result at trial. But there is a trend toward specialization. Some very skilled lawyers are better used preparing cases rather than actually trying them just as others may excel at trial but be less proficient in preparation.

Within the litigation genre, there may be further specialization. For example, some lawyers may concentrate primarily on legal research and drafting while others focus on conducting depositions and arguing motions. To a large extent this is a good development for clients if the lawyers know their strengths and weaknesses. A personable lawyer quick on her feet may be wonderful examining witnesses or giving a closing argument before a jury but be a mediocre researcher and writer—or vice versa. Deploying personnel effectively is part of delivering effective legal services. A sole practitioner (and there are still tens of thousands in spite of a general trend toward consolidation) thus faces that problem of needing to be good (or at least adequate) at everything a lawyer does—unless he is willing to affiliate with other counsel. Wise solos do this when necessary.

We define the trial process as beginning in part with settlement efforts. Effective negotiation requires appreciation of the range of likely results at trial. In addition, the final stages of pretrial litigation—such as the final pretrial conference before the court—realistically are more a part of the trial process than true pretrial activity such as discovery. With that in mind, consider the following precursors to trial and phases of trial and its aftermath.

IN PRACTICE

Don't focus so hard on settlement or trial preparation that you forget legal ethics. Rules of professional conduct may preclude certain settlement arrangements. For example, one state bar has advised that a settlement offer cannot be conditioned on receiving an "acceptable" affidavit from opposing counsel for use in another matter. *See* Texas State Bar Prof. Ethics Comm. Op. 614 (2012). In one notorious case, a lawyer was disciplined for agreeing not to report opposing counsel to the bar as a condition of settlement. *See In re Himmel*, 533 N.E.2d 790 (Ill. 1988). Another too-common pitfall is an attorney agreeing to refrain from bringing future such cases in return for a settlement payment. The ethics rules forbid agreements limiting an attorney's right to practice law in the future.

A. The Path of Trial

Trial proceedings (as we broadly define them) generally come in the following order:

- The (Possible) Making of an Offer of Judgment (which, along with other settlement and ADR devices, was discussed in the Introduction/Orientation chapter)

- Settlement Efforts after the conclusion of discovery and decisions on dispositive motions

- Planning for trial and preparation of a final pretrial order

- Motions "*in limine*" (at the threshold of trial) regarding evidentiary matters and trial conduct

- The Final Pretrial Conference before the judge

- Jury Selection (unless it is a bench trial)

- Opening Statements

- Plaintiff's Case-in-Chief, which ordinarily includes direct and cross-examination of witnesses proffered by plaintiff along with any documents, "real" evidence or demonstrative evidence used as well as the testimonial evidence of witnesses

- Mid-trial motions for Judgment as a Matter of Law pursuant to Rule 50

- Defendant's Case-in-Chief (assuming defendant's Rule 50 motion is denied)

- Requests for Jury Instructions and determination of the Verdict Form

- Closing Arguments

- Administration of Jury Instructions

- Jury Deliberation (with possible questions to the court)

- The Verdict

- Post-Trial Motions (the topic of Chapter 18)

- Appeal (the topic of Chapter 19)

- Efforts to Satisfy the Judgment through collection or enforcement of the Court's order (which can also occur prior to conclusion of the appellate process). *See* Chapter 20.

B. Rule 68 and Counsel Fees Recovery

In approaching trial and considering any settlement offers or offers of judgment pursuant to Rule 68, counsel should remember that the "American Rule" regarding counsel fees is that each party is responsible for paying its lawyers. This is contrasted to the "English Rule" in which the losing party must reimburse the winner's reasonable legal fees. The English approach is not a blank check. The winner must submit an application for fees to a "taxing master" who determines the amount of recoverable fees and who frequently awards considerably less than the amount requested. But the British approach is still nonetheless a powerful incentive for settlement. It's bad enough to lose a case. Worse yet to lose and end up owing money to the adversary you claim harmed you in violation of the law. Under these circumstances, many lawyers and litigants reason that it makes sense to settle not only to diminish the risk of an unacceptably bad result but also to eliminate the risk of fee-shifting.

Because of the American Rule and because Rule 68 costs ordinarily do not encompass counsel fees, the conventional wisdom is that claimants in the U.S. can afford to be bolder than in England because there is less to lose if the case goes badly. (In addition, the U.S. is viewed as more claimant-friendly generally because of the jury system, the availability of extensive discovery, and generally broad liability rules recall that Rule 12 and Rule 56 have real teeth and are useful tools for defendants).

Counsel must also be aware that many state versions of Rule 68 (which may be in a state statute rather than the state's civil rules) do provide for fee shifting against the party that does worse at trial than a defendant's offer. In these states, counsel must think very seriously before rejecting any offer of judgment or its equivalent. Counsel must also be careful of such state law even when litigating in federal court. Pursuant to the Rules of Decision Act (28 U.S.C. § 2072) and *Erie* Doctrine, Fed. R. Civ. P. 68 governs in federal court actions and trumps state offer of judgment law that clashes directly with Rule 68. But in the absence of such direct collision, state law may apply. *See, e.g., MRO Communications, Inc. v. American Tel. & Tel. Co.*, 197 F.3d 1276, 1280 (9th Cir. 1999)(state law shifting fees to prevailing defendants even when plaintiff claim not frivolous a substantive state law applicable pursuant to *Erie*); *S.A. Healy Co. v. Milwaukee Metropolitan Sewerage Dist.*, 60 F.3d 305, 310 (7th Cir. 1995)(state law permitting plaintiffs to make offer of judgment, although different than Federal Rule allowing only defendants to use the device, was not in sufficient conflict with Federal Rule to preclude application of state law pursuant to *Erie*). *See also* Ch. 4.

Further complicating factors are exceptions to the American Rule, which are recognized under a few common law doctrines or established by some statutes. Where such exceptions are provided and the case is governed by a requirement that the losing party pay counsel fees, the fees may be counted as Rule 68 costs at least to the extent that a plaintiff rejecting an offer and then doing worse at trial may be denied the counsel fees to which it otherwise would be entitled under an exception to the American Rule. *See Marek v. Chesny*, 473 U.S. 1 (1985). But the treatment of counsel fees as costs under some statutes, such as employment discrimination and civil rights cases discussed below has generally not be used by courts to justify requiring this type of plaintiff to pay defendant's post-offer legal fees merely because plaintiff does less well at trial than the offer, provided that plaintiff at least prevails to some extent. "[S]hifting fees would impermissibly require a plaintiff who brought non-frivolous claims—and won—to pay defense fees." *See* Steven S. Gensler, *Federal Rules of Civil Procedure: Rules and Commentary* 1116-17 (2011)(footnote citing case omitted). But the Eleventh Circuit has authority permitting Rule 68 to be used to force the prevailing plaintiff to pay defendant's post-offer legal fees. *See Jordan v. Time, Inc.*, 111 F.3d 102, 105 (11th Cir. 1997).

Examples of exceptions to the American Rule of each side paying its own counsel fees (which must be considered when making settlement decisions regardless of the application of Rule 68) are:

- The Civil Rights Attorney's Fees Act, 42 U.S.C. § 1988, which provides that plaintiffs prevailing in certain actions alleging violations of federal civil rights (*e.g.*, 42 U.S.C. § 1983, for a government's deprivation of due process or lack of equal protection or 42 U.S.C. § 1981 for racial discrimination in contracting) are entitled to payment of their reasonable counsel fees by the losing defendant. The statute was passed in 1976 as a response to *Alyeska Service Pipeline Co. v. Wilderness Society*, 421 U.S. 240 (1975), which rejected the concept of a common law "private attorney general" exception to the American Rule for public interest lawsuits brought by private parties. Prevailing defendants can also recover § 1988 fees—but only if the plaintiff's position was baseless, an approach that largely replicates the Rule 11 standard (*see* Ch. 5) to which counsel and parties are subject in any event.

- The Equal Access to Justice Act, 28 U.S.C. § 2412(d)(1)(A), which permits targets of failed government regulatory actions to recover their counsel fees—but only if the government's position was not "substantially justified." In practice, this means fee shifting is unlikely unless the government enforcement action was over-the-top. So long as reasonable, even if unsuccessful, fee shifting is unlikely under this statute.

- Title VII of the Civil Rights Act of 1964, 42 U.S.C. §§ 2000e, *et. seq.*, which bars race, gender, religion, and national origin discrimination in employment. Prevailing job discrimination plaintiffs can obtain an award of counsel fees from the defendants. Prevailing defendants may recover fees if the plaintiff's claim is found to be frivolous. *See Christiansburg Garment Co. v. EEOC*, 434 U.S. 412 (1978). Other portions of the Civil Rights Act such as Title IX regarding gender equality also permit recovery of counsel fees for successful plaintiffs as does the Age Discrimination in Employment Act (ADEA).

- Various consumer/commercial laws such as securities statutes and antitrust statutes also may provide for fee-shifting to the prevailing party.

- Bad faith conduct by losing counsel or parties may prompt the court to order reimbursement of some or all of the prevailing party's counsel fees even if such fee-shifting is not otherwise authorized pursuant to Fed. R. Civ. P. 11 or 28 U.S.C. § 1927 (*see* Ch. 5).

- Class actions pursuant to Fed. R. Civ. P. 23 and state analogs (*see* Ch. 9) permit an award of fees.

- The Common Fund/Common Benefit Doctrine allows a court to require a losing defendant to pay a victorious plaintiff's counsel fees where the action has not only benefitted the individual plaintiffs but also tangibly benefitted others who are identifiable as well, particularly if a common fund is created that can be used to compensate others injured by the defendant's wrongful conduct. Simply making the world a better place is not enough. To get counsel fees, the plaintiff must make a concrete showing that there is tangibly traceable benefit to a particular group because of the plaintiff's actions (and payment of counsel fees to his or her lawyer).

EXAMPLES & ANALYSIS

EXAMPLE: Peter Pastoral successfully sues to prevent the construction of a high-rise building that would have left People's Park in constant shade. The Park has long been used by those living in Tree-Hugging Township as well as being the site for local Little League games and has no artificial lighting because this would create light pollution for those living near the Park. Peter petitions for counsel fees. Will he get them?

Analysis: Probably. Although Peter's action does not create a common fund that can be drawn upon by the area residents, it does preserve sunshine in the Park, which is a pretty tangible benefit to a fairly discreet, identifiable group. But in cases like this (and in fee shifting generally), the judge has considerable discretion. Many of us might think the discretion abused if the judge denies fees and forces Peter to shoulder the entire legal expense of an action that so clearly benefitted the neighborhood, but a significant number of appellate court panels would probably uphold a denial of fees on the ground that this benefit is a bit diffuse.

EXAMPLE: Peter Pastoral also wins a lawsuit requiring that all new construction in Tree-Hugger Township be subject to an environmental impact review before a permit can be granted. He petitions for fees. What result?

Analysis: This is the type of case that, prior to *Alyeska Pipeline v. Wilderness Society* might well have qualified for fee-shifting under the private attorney general rationale. Peter has accomplished something that should make future construction less detrimental to the environment and has acted in the public interest. It seems only fair that he not pay all the legal fees that helped achieve this result that help many others who did not pay these fees. But the benefit is diffuse. We don't know exactly what will happen with future projects and which residents will be affected. Although 42 U.S.C. § 1988 overruled *Alyeska Pipeline* in part, it did not address this type of case.

C. Bifurcation as Trial Tactic

Bifurcation is the process of first trying issues of liability prior to receiving any evidence of damages. If the jury renders a verdict of no liability, the trial is over. If the jury finds liability, the jury (usually the same jury) then hears evidence regarding damages. Courts also sometimes "trifurcate" a case by having separate consideration of liability, compensatory damages, and then any claim for punitive damages, including first considering whether plaintiff has shown the required willful indifference of the defendant to the rights of plaintiff by clear and convincing evidence.

The theory behind such choreography is that the jury should not be exposed to evidence related to the punitive damages claims (*e.g.*, similar past bad conduct by the defendant or the defendant's wealth) unless the jury has first found that punitive damages are in order. Evidence that is clearly relevant to the punitive damages questions may be arguably too prejudicial for the liability and compensatory damage stages of the case. As you might expect, plaintiffs tend to hate bifurcation/trifurcation while defendants like or even love it because it tends to present plaintiff's narratives in dribs and drabs that most think give the case less emotional impact and narrative force. Conversely, courts may be attracted to this approach precisely because they do not want the jury to be unduly influenced by emotion or narrative. *See generally* Steven S. Gensler, *Bifurcation Unbound*, 75 WASH. L. REV. 705 (2000) (reviewing history, development, rationale, and debate over bifurcation).

EXAMPLES & ANALYSIS

EXAMPLE: Petra sues Dave, alleging that he negligently rear-ended her vehicle at a stop sign, causing her neck and back injuries. The rear-ending part is true (Dave would violate Rule 11 to deny it) but the collision was at low speed and Dave's expert doctor thinks Petra's injuries, which involve no broken bones or permanent nerve damage, will heal well and that she will be fine after a couple months of healing and physical therapy. After reading this doctor's report, Dave makes an offer of judgment in the amount of $25,000. Petra rejects the offer and makes a $100,000 settlement demand. Her doctor believes the injury is permanent and, although not debilitating, will bother her for years. What happens if the jury's verdict is $15,000? Or $50,000? Or $150,000? More?

Analysis: If the verdict is for only $15,000, Petra may not recover the costs that normally go to the winner and will be responsible for paying Dave's costs as provided pursuant to Rule 54(d) and 19 U.S.C. § 1920, which basically means witness fees and the cost of preparing documents for use in the case. Because counsel fees are not included as "costs," this amount will not be large but may be significant enough to make Petra's counsel more cautious in the future about rejecting such offers. (Under the rules of legal ethics, the client has the final decision about accepting or rejecting a settlement but the lawyer's advice normally has a strong influence upon the client. Chapter 18 provides further discussion of recoverable costs.

If the verdict is for $50,000, Petra will be able to recover costs as provided by rule or statute because she is the prevailing party and did not reject an offer of judgment larger than what she achieved at trial. The same of course is true if the verdict is for $150,000 or any larger amount.

Depending on how much automobile liability insurance is possessed by Dave (some states require only as little as $15,000 per person or $30,000 per accident in coverage as a condition of licensing a vehicle), the verdict may be in "excess" of the policy limits, which could expose Dave's insurer to liability for bad faith failure to settle within the policy limits. Dave may then have a claim against his insurer, which defendants in this position often assign to a victorious plaintiff in order to avoid personal liability. *See* JEFFREY W. STEMPEL, PETER NASH SWISHER & ERIK KNUTSEN, PRINCIPLES OF INSURANCE LAW CH. 15 (4th ed. 2011).

Other Aspects of Settlement on the Verge of Trial. One famous dispute resolution article used the memorable phrase "bargaining in the shadow of the law" to describe settlement. For lawyers advising clients, the likely range of outcomes at trial is the "shadow" under which most negotiation takes place. Settlement offers or demands outside this range are unlikely to be effective, although a plaintiff with limited resources might settle too cheaply or a defendant may pay more than the highest realistic range of an adverse trial outcome because it wishes to avoid adverse publicity or because the consequences of a very high adverse judgment, no matter how unlikely, are too unpalatable (*e.g.*, it would bankrupt the company or make it uninsurable in the future).

D. The Final Pretrial Conference and Final Pretrial Order

After completion of discovery, counsel makes preparations for trial and attends a final pretrial conference during which the court seeks to get organized for the trial. As part of this process, the court requires the parties to collaborate in assembling a final pretrial order which will govern the administration of the case, supplanting any prior inconsistent rulings or proceedings. Typically, a final pretrial order includes a listing of each side's trial witnesses and exhibits as well as a summary of the case, indicating the matters on which the parties agree and diverge. The parties may also be required to submit requested jury instructions at the time of the final pretrial order but this is often done later in the trial just prior to closing arguments and submission of the case to the jury.

E. Jury Selection (Unless It Is a Bench Trial)

One phase of trial is **jury selection.** Court protocols for assembling a pool of prospective jurors may differ but in general the process involves randomly selecting names of jurisdiction residents and summoning them to come to the courthouse on a certain day. The assembled prospective jurors (the "venire" in legal parlance) then often complete a questionnaire regarding their backgrounds and attitudes and then are dispatched to the courtroom where a case is awaiting trial. This information may be used by counsel in determining whether to challenge a juror. In many jurisdictions, however, questionnaires are viewed as burdensome and used only in larger cases that are more likely to present jury selection difficulty. Each side is allowed a certain number of **peremptory** challenges that it can use to exclude a prospective juror for any reason. Counsel also may challenge a prospective juror **for cause** if counsel has grounds from which an objective observer would have reason to doubt the prospective juror's neutrality. Each side of a dispute is allotted a set number of "peremptory" challenges to prospective jurors. The peremptory challenge device gives counsel the right to eject a prospective juror for any reason at all, including the proverbial "hunch" that the juror would not be supportive of counsel's client. In federal court, each side is normally permitted three peremptory challenges. State court rules vary but 3-5 peremptory challenges per side is a common arrangement.

Counsel may potentially make an unlimited number of challenges "for cause" alleging that a prospective juror is biased, prejudiced, or otherwise unfit to serve as juror. However, unlike peremptory challenges, which are as the name implies granted without question, a juror can be excluded for cause only if the trial judge is persuaded that the juror is unable to be impartial. Potential grounds for a challenge for cause will vary with the case and litigants. Support for a challenge may be based on the contents of the questionnaire as well as statements made in court by prospective jurors.

Lawyers often complain that judges take too narrow a view of challenge for cause. For example, a prospective juror might say something pretty damning like "I think there's too much litigation and it's raising the cost of everything," a comment sure to strike terror into the heart of a plaintiff's attorney. Commonly, the judge deciding on a challenge for cause will respond by asking the juror if he nonetheless would be willing to follow the law as instructed and decide the instant case fairly without regard to whether other suits are meritorious. The juror almost always answers in the affirmative and is seated on the jury. Few would admit to disregarding the evidence in court or refusing to follow the law. But if you were the plaintiff in this situation, would you be very excited about having this juror in your case? The same thing is likely to happen if the juror states that "all drug manufacturers are vultures profiting off the misery of others through their overpriced, dangerous products," even if the juror answers "yes" to a "can you still be fair and follow the law?" question.

Now you know why peremptory challenges—counsel's ability to have jurors excused on motion with no questions asked—are so important. Lawyers use them not because they disapprove of the jurors' taste in clothing or hairstyle but because they are concerned the juror has a predisposition favoring the opponent but that there is not enough information to sustain a challenge for cause. But with only a few peremptory challenges, counsel's ability to truly shape a jury is limited, just as counsel's ability to really assess a prospective juror is limited.

The methodology of jury selection can vary by court. Many courts in the Western U.S. use the "Arizona method" in which a large group of prospective jurors (e.g., 50) is brought to the courtroom. The judge then asks about possible conflicts such as work or family commitments that remove the possible juror from the state at the time of trial and about obviously disqualifying matter such as a business or personal connection to a litigant or counsel. After jurors with compelling conflicts are excused, twice the number of necessary jurors and alternates are seated in the jury box (e.g., 20 prospective jurors in a jurisdiction that uses a system of eight jurors and two alternates).

The judge or counsel then asks questions designed to give counsel an idea as to the possible juror's inclinations. Some are straightforward (e.g., "Has anyone here ever been an insurance claims adjustor?")(although some judges may limit such questioning on the ground that it improperly suggests the presence of insurance coverage for any resulting judgment). Others are more ethereal but potentially revealing (e.g., "Who is your favorite President?" "What is your favorite book?"). Judges have wide discretion as to whether to permit such questions. After questioning, counsel makes any challenges for cause it wishes, which in turn may require the court to further question the challenged juror prior to ruling on the challenge. If prospective jurors are eliminated, another juror from the larger pool takes the seat. After challenges for cause, each side is permitted to exercise its peremptory challenges. After this is done, the first remaining jurors and alternates (e.g., those sitting in seats 1, 4, 5, 7, 9, 10, 11, 13, 14, and 15) are impaneled)(this example assumes three peremptory challenges per side).

Counsel's substantial discretion over the use of peremptory challenges is limited by the non-discrimination provisions of the U.S. Constitution. Counsel may not use peremptory challenges as a means of excluding prospective women jurors or prospective jurors from a particular racial group. *See Edmonson v. Leesville Concrete Co.*, 500 U.S. 614 (1991)(race); *J.E.B. v. Alabama*, 511 U.S. 127 (1993)(gender). As a practical matter, however, it may often be difficult to "prove" that a lawyer is using peremptory challenges in a biased manner. The landmark case *Batson v. Kentucky*, 476 U.S. 79 (1986) established this principle for criminal trials and it was extended to civil litigation in *Edmonson*.

EXAMPLES & ANALYSIS

EXAMPLE: The case involves a bad faith claim against an insurance company. Plaintiff seeks to exclude from the jury two members of the venire who work for insurance companies and another who works for the insurance company that is the defendant in the case.

Analysis: All courts would exclude the juror who works for the defendant company. Many courts would exclude the two that work for other insurers as well, finding it too improbable that an insurance company employees would not tend to favor all insurers to some degree. But other courts would first examine the prospective jurors and ask them what they thought about bad faith lawsuits, whether all insurers always behaved properly, whether the juror could be fair and listen to the evidence before making a decision, and so on. Depending on the answers, the judge might reject a challenge for cause directed at these two insurers. Some courts would not permit inquiry about work for insurers generally but only about specific companies that might be named parties. However, the modern emerging view seems to be to allow inquiry about insurance, including whether prospective jurors have seen insurer or business-sponsored advertisements advocating tort reform or stating that high jury verdicts lead to higher premiums or higher costs for consumer goods.

In federal court, it is almost always the judge that examines prospective jurors—but attorneys have input into the process and may seek the judge's permission to question prospective jurors directly even if that is not the court's normal practice. Even prior to any opportunity for a challenge for cause, the judge typically welcomes the jurors to the courtroom and asks general questions designed to see if any members of the venire may be inappropriate as jurors. For example, the judge may find that some persons in the pool cannot sit in court all day without undue discomfort. Others may have already made travel commitments and the court may excuse them out of concern that they will be annoyed if the trial displaces their travel plans and take it out on one or both parties. The attorneys can submit questions for the judge to ask the pool but the judge is not obliged to ask all the proposed questions or to ask them in the same form as submitted by counsel. When challenges are raised, normally the court does any questioning that might be required to rule on the challenge. In state court, lawyers do most of the questioning of the panel and are permitted more leeway than is usually the case in federal court.

IN PRACTICE

Judges have a natural resistance to granting juror challenges out of a desire to impanel a jury and move the case along as briskly as possible. When faced with a challenge for cause, judges will often engage in extensive questioning that seems designed to rehabilitate the challenged juror or minimize the seriousness of the challenge. Judges also are sympathetic to removing prejudiced jurors but less concerned about permitting the parties to stack the jury with jurors biased in favor of a given party's position.

This can be frustrating to counsel, particularly when there remains a room full of prospective jurors who do not have any colorable problems. One might reasonably ask why judges are so often so resistant to challenges for cause. Rather than complain in the abstract, counsel with a cause challenge must focus on particular problems with the prospective juror and her answers to the court's question, asking the court to follow up with additional questions from counsel that may be effective to highlight the alleged lack of impartiality. This may re-orient the judge in favor of removing the juror and can at least make a record for possible appeal.

Jury challenge rulings are not final, appealable orders. Trial judges have a fair amount of latitude in handling jury selection. Exceptions to the final order rule discussed in Chapter 20 are unlikely to apply. For the most part, counsel must simply take her best shot at juror exclusion and live with the result. Remember not to cross the line from vigorous advocacy to annoying the judge. A judge's procedural and evidentiary rulings may have a much greater impact on the matter than the presence of a single sub-optimal juror and judges, despite their honest efforts to be fair to counsel, may be less inclined to decide close issues in favor of counsel that the judge comes to see as pesky, annoying, or unreasonable. Similarly, a juror unsuccessfully challenged for cause may resent the lawyer that made the challenge. Counsel might therefore refrain from bringing any challenges for cause that are not certain to be successful.

F. Professional Responsibility Concerns Surrounding Jury Empanelment

Once a jury has been selected, counsel must be careful not to engage in behavior that might be deemed an improper influence upon the jury. For example, in recent cases, mistrials have been declared or verdicts set aside when jurors have felt intimidated ("creeped out" in the words of one juror) by monitoring efforts of a party or counsel. In one case where the result was later set aside, a lawyer monitoring the case for an insurer not only attended court each day (generally permissible absent some other misconduct of the observer; for example, wearing a "defense verdict or you all die" T-shirt would not be a good idea) but also followed the jurors on breaks, to lunch, etc. as if tailing a criminal suspect.

This admonition applies to jury selection as well. In another recent case, an entire jury panel was dismissed (requiring the court to start over on jury selection) when the lead lawyer representing the defendant dispatched an associate to sit in the jury assembly room (where prospective jurors gather to receive instruction in their duties, fill out paperwork, grab a cup of coffee, and wait to be called to the courtroom for jury selection) and observe (a/k/a spy on) the jury pool in this informal setting and report to the partner prior to the start of formal jury selection. Court personnel recognized the associate as someone who did not belong in the jury assembly room and ejected the lawyer. Plaintiff's counsel sought the notes that had been taken prior to the ejection but defense counsel refused, prompting the court's decision to bring in an entirely new pool of possible jurors.

The court would have been within its authority to sanction the offending lawyers but was lenient. Less experienced lawyers subject to partner supervision should be wary of such situations and be willing to refuse, informing the partner of the problems with this tactic. Better to earn partner wrath and even job loss than bar discipline. Also, a good supervising partner will thank you later for saving him or her from error and embarrassment. In the heat of battle, even decent lawyers can do stupid things – and this can really boomerang if it is perceived as jury tampering or unfair misconduct toward the opponent (who doesn't have access to the ill-gotten information) or the court (that wants an untainted, fairly selected jury).

A good rule of thumb is to avoid any conduct around juries or litigation that seems too cloak-and-dagger. It's a lawsuit, not an episode of "24" or a John Le Carre novel. That said, reasonable investigation of prospective and even actual jurors is permissible. For example, a recent ethics opinion states that it is permissible to research social media to find out about jurors (*e.g.*, a Facebook page; if it states "all plaintiffs are greedy losers" plaintiff's counsel might want to know) but it is not permissible to engage in deceptive conduct (*e.g.*, friending the juror to gain additional information, having ex parte contact with the juror).

A related danger during the trial itself is that counsel may be so heated in prosecuting and defending the case as to taint the jury with prejudicial material, resulting in a mistrial.

G. Opening Statements

Many trial lawyers consider the opening statement to be the most important part of the trial. Counsel cannot argue during the opening statement, characterize evidence, or criticize witnesses or the opposing party—at least not openly. For plaintiffs in particular, a standard but effective form of opening statement is to describe the events leading up to plaintiff's injury, including without editorial comment the poor conduct of defendant and its agents and the adverse impact suffered by plaintiff. If the story is well-presented, jurors will draw the conclusions sought by counsel—at least until defense counsel gives its opening or refutes this version of events with other evidence.

Because the trial is just starting, there is not yet any evidence of record. As a result, lawyers during the opening statement typically use terms such as "the evidence will show" and so on. In response, defense counsel's narrative will highlight planned presentation of facts tending to negate liability. It's an adversary system and the lawyers are allowed to spin on behalf of their clients. They are not however permitted to violate the "etiquette" of trial practice (*e.g.*, no overt argument during the opening, no misrepresentation of what witnesses will say or what documents will state, no direct attacks on opposing counsel or party testimony).

H. Presenting the Case-in-Chief: Use of Witnesses and Introduction of Evidence

After completion of the opening, plaintiff as the party with the burden of proof gets to present its side of the story first. A party's effort to present its case in full is referred to as the party's "case-in-chief." Litigants normally prove their cases with a mixture of live testimony and supporting documents, and may also introduce expert testimony, videotaped testimony, deposition testimony, demonstrative evidence (*e.g.*, a laboratory experiment that illustrates how something occurred), or real evidence (authenticated tangible objects relevant to the case such as a murder weapon or the allegedly defective medical device). Documents are ordinarily introduced through a witness who can establish their authenticity and explain them, although documents may also be admitted via stipulation of the parties.

Direct examination of the witness cannot involve leading questions except to speed things along regarding uncontested matters or to help a witness remember and compose her thoughts. Courts vary in the degree to which they will accept highly open ended questions (*e.g.*, "tell us how you came to be injured") or narrative answers. Many courts find that witnesses are entitled to describe what they saw or know in narrative fashion while other courts are concerned that this holds too much potential for the introduction of irrelevant or prejudicial information that can be limited if the witness is required to respond to a series of more cabined questions.

After plaintiff examines a witness, the defense is entitled to cross-examine. Here, leading questions are not only permitted but dominant because the witness is adverse. Counsel is entitled to probe the witness and attempt to impeach the testimony and control the witness's responses so that the witness does not ramble or evade the question. A party may also use leading questions on direct examination if the witness is hostile. During cross-examination, counsel may confront the witness with documents or prior testimony that may contradict the account given during direct examination. The scope of the cross-examination cannot go beyond the scope of the direct examination.

After cross-examination, the party originally calling the witness is permitted re-direct examination of the witness. The re-direct may not exceed the scope of the cross. Like direct examination, re-direct generally proceeds without leading questions but it is less likely than direct to involve broad, open-ended questions or narrative answers.

After plaintiff completes its case-in-chief, there may be a defendant's motion for judgment as a matter of law pursuant to Fed. R. Civ. P. 50 (more on that below). But assuming that the case is not ended on a mid-trial Rule 50 motion, defendant then presents its case-in-chief. Now it is defendant's turn to present witnesses for direct examination, cross-examination, and re-direct, including the introduction of documents and other types of evidence as appropriate.

During both cases-in-chief and all witness examination, there may be objections and rulings on the objections as well "curative" instructions to the jury if problematic testimony occurs. For example, the witness may blurt out something irrelevant or prejudicial, prompting the court to instruct the jury to disregard the testimony.

I. The Rules of Evidence and Battles over Objections and Admissibility

In federal court, evidentiary matters are governed by the Federal Rules of Evidence, which were promulgated in 1975. Before that, evidence law was largely based on common law precedent except for a few statutes governing particular evidentiary matter. Prior to the codification, treatises by notable scholars such as Wigmore and McCormick were particularly important in that era and continue to be influential secondary authority regarding evidence in updated versions of their treatises kept current by successor authors. *See, e.g.,* JOHN HENRY WIGMORE, WIGMORE'S EVIDENCE (first published in 1904, current through 2013); CHARLES T. MCCORMICK, MCCORMICK ON EVIDENCE (7th ed. 2013). With the codification, which stemmed from the work of a blue-ribbon committee of lawyers, judges, and scholars, focus shifted to the language of the Rules, the Advisory Committee Notes, and the legislative history of congressional consideration of the Rules (more on that in a minute). An influential treatise following the organization of the Rules emerged as well. *See* Jack B. Weinstein & Margaret Berger, *Weinstein's Evidence* (1975)(updated subsequently).

For the most part, state evidence law is similar to federal evidence law. But although much state evidence law is contained in sets of rules similar to the federal model, there are often many state statutes bearing on evidentiary questions, particularly regarding privilege or the use of certain documents such as police reports or other government investigations. Counsel trying cases in state court must become conversant in the similarities and differences from the Federal Rules.

In federal court, the evidence rules frame the acceptably boundaries for presentation of the case. Witness examination and the introduction of documents depends not only on customary practice, attorney style, and judicial tolerance but of course also depends on what is permitted by the Federal Rules. The Rules of Evidence are organized into several Articles. Article I deals with overall principles and protocol. Rule 103 is important because it sets groundrules for trial. Errors in evidence rulings do not support overturning the trial result "unless a substantial right of the party is affected" and there must be timely objection that either states the ground for the objection or makes the ground apparent. But if there is "plain error," a party may succeed in undoing an adverse result even absent timely objection. Rule 103 also empowers and counsels judges to conduct argument about evidentiary questions outside the hearing of the jury to avoid tainting the jury. The court also has power to admit evidence for one purpose but instruct the jury that it may not be considered for other purposes.

Article II (Rule 201) permits courts to take "judicial notice" and establish as facts of record facts that are not subject to reasonable dispute because they are generally known (*e.g.*, the sun rises in the East) or capable of accurate and ready determination from an authoritative source (*e.g.*, the melting point of pewter, which can be looked up in a textbook on metallurgy).

Article III (Rules 301 and 302) governs presumptions, extensive discussion of which we will leave to your evidence class (which we insist you take if you think you ever want to become a civil litigator). For now, appreciate that law often establishes rebuttable presumptions that govern unless refuted by the party against whom the presumption operates. Occasionally, law imposes irrebuttable or conclusive presumptions that a judge or jury must accept even if personally in disagreement.

Article IV (Rules 401-415) regarding relevancy and its limits is particularly important and governs much of the trial process. Rule 401 defines relevant evidence while 402 makes relevant evidence generally admissible and irrelevant evidence inadmissible. Rule 403 is an important one that you've probably seen invoked on TV. It provides that even relevant evidence can be excluded if the judge deems it more prejudicial than probative or if its admission will cause "undue delay, waste of time, or needless presentation of cumulative evidence."

EXAMPLES & ANALYSIS

EXAMPLE: Plaintiff stops by his favorite watering hole, The Crazy Bar, after work and quaffs a single 12-ounce beer, then heads home but is T-boned by Defendant at a nearby intersection that lacked any stop signs or stoplights. On the eve of trial, Plaintiff moves to forbid any mention of the name of the drinking establishment on the ground that "Crazy Bar" inevitably conjures up prejudicial visions of a raucous tavern and makes it unfairly less likely that a jury will believe Plaintiff (a 200-pound man) had only one beer and was not intoxicated or even impaired at the time of the collision.

Analysis: Most courts would probably grant the motion and restrict Defendant to simply establishing that Plaintiff stopped at a bar and had a drink shortly before the intersection collision. One court did so on very similar facts, and the decision has been cited approvingly through the years. Once the words "Crazy Bar" have been presented to the jury in association with the plaintiff, it is a bit hard to unring the metaphorical bell. Hence the ruling to prevent defense counsel from even mentioning it and forcing plaintiff to object and draw further attention to the establishment's unfortunate name. Defendant can offer evidence that it was more than one drink if Defendant has such evidence; a ban on mentioning the name of the bar does not preclude attacking Plaintiff's veracity. If the motion is granted, Defense counsel must be careful not to unwittingly violate it. This includes adequate preparation of witnesses in which each witness is properly informed of the order restricting testimony. For example, if Defendant is going to call another patron to testify that he saw Plaintiff down four beers and four shots of whiskey on the night in question, the witness must be told that he should not identify the bar by its potentially prejudicial name.

IN PRACTICE

The Potential Availability of "*In Limine*" Motions for Evidence Rulings Prior to Trial

A motion "*in limine*" (from the Latin) is one made "at the threshold" of the trial when dealing with evidentiary concerns such as the one described in the Example and Analysis. Technically, any motion made at the beginning of trial could be characterized as one made in limine but for the most part these are motions for pretrial evidence rulings. In addition, the motion can be made prior to the examination or cross-examination of the witness but the best lawyers tend to anticipate evidentiary trouble spots, particularly the risk of prejudicing the jurors, and make the motion well before the examination begins.

Most evidence rulings occur at the time evidence is being presented—and most judges want it that way most of the time so that they can make rulings sustaining or overruling objections in the context of the live courtroom proceedings. However, it may be wise to pursue pretrial evidence rulings not only where prejudice is a risk but also where an anticipated evidentiary issue is complex so that counsel can brief and argue the issue at length so that the judge may have more time to reflect on the issue. It may also be more efficient to determine certain evidence matters prior to trial in order to streamline the trial, particularly if an objection relates to an entire category of evidence.

Unlike an oral objection in the midst of trial, an in limine motion is normally in writing and supported by a memorandum of law. Depending on local rules and standing orders, it may also be accompanied by a proposed order and affidavits, discovery materials, or other supporting documents.

Particularly important in civil litigation are several rules that seek to avoid biasing the jury. For example, Rule 407 forbids evidence of subsequent remedial measures when used to prove negligence on the theory that this will discourage safety improvements after an accident because an owner is worried that repair will make liability more likely.

EXAMPLE: Paul rents a room in Damian's house that is reachable only through an outdoor stairway that has no handrail. After Paul slips and falls, sustaining injury, he sues Damian for negligent maintenance of the premises. While trial is pending, Damian has a handrail installed. Paul seeks to cross-examine Damian on this point. Damian objects. What ruling by the Judge?

Analysis: Plaintiff may not introduce evidence of defendant installing a handrail on a stairway to prove the stairway was defective without the handrail. Damian has engaged in a subsequent remedial measure protected by Rule 407. But a plaintiff may introduce this evidence to show that a defendant who denied control over the stairway does in fact manage the stairway. So if Damian had contended that stairway maintenance was Paul's responsibility, Paul would be able to use the installation of the handrail to demonstare Damian's dominion over the stairway.

Regarding Article V of the Rules of Evidence, Rule 501 deals with privilege, essentially punting the question to federal common law and applicable state law unless there is an on-point federal statute. Rule 502 deals with protection of work product (addressed at length in Ch. 13), primarily concerning experts.

Article VI is another important section of the Rules of Evidence, governing witness competency (Rule 601), the requirement of personal knowledge (Rule 602), administration of an oath or affirmation of truthfulness to the witness (Rule 603), use of interpreters (Rule 604), restrictions on the judge or jurors being a witness (Rule 605 and 606), and reference to the religious beliefs of a witness (there should ordinarily be none)(Rule 610). Rule 615 provides that witnesses can be excluded from the courtroom prior to their testimony to prevent them from shaping it to fit legal argument or the testimony of other witnesses.

Particularly important to the conduct of trials is Rule 611, which governs the method of witness examination and is the source of rules about direct and cross-examination. Also important is Rule 612, which addresses the use of documents to refresh a witness's recollection. Rule 613 governs the use of prior statements of a witness while Rule 614 permits the judge to call and examine witnesses, although in the American adversary system, the judge is usually quite content to leave this to the parties. Rule 608 deals with the bolstering or impeachment of witnesses based on character or conduct while Rule 609 deals with the use of prior criminal convictions for impeachment.

Article VII (Rules 701-705) governs the use of expert witnesses at trial while Article VIII (Rules 801-806) is the infamous hearsay rule which will receive a good deal of attention in Evidence class. The evidentiary rules generally prohibit the receipt into evidence of a statement to assert the truth of a matter unless an exception applies. The rationale of the Hearsay Rule is that such out-of-court statements by persons who are not under oath and subject to cross-examination about the statement are not sufficiently trustworthy. The rationale of exceptions to the Hearsay Rule (and there are many) is that certain types of hearsay (*e.g.*, an "excited utterance" or a "dying declaration") are sufficiently trustworthy to admit because the witness has neither the time, motivation, nor ability to fabricate. Importantly, the out-of-court statement of an adverse party or its agent is expressly defined as not being hearsay (Rule 801(d) (2)) while Rule 803 lists 23 exceptions that may apply regardless of whether the "declarant" (the person making the statement outside the court) is available and Rule 804 list five exceptions that may apply if the declarant is not available to testify on the witness stand. In addition, Rule 807 contains a "residual" or catch-all exception that although rarely applied may be available.

Article IX (Rules 901-903) governs authentication of documents while Article X (Rules 1001-1008) governs use of originals and duplicates and encompasses the real world version of the so-called "best evidence rule" (which is really an "original document rule" that is not much like what you often see on television). Article XI (Rules 1101-1103) contains miscellaneous rules about the rules and their applicability, including that the Federal Rules of Evidence apply in federal court (which you already knew). Remember, pursuant to *Erie v. Tomkins* and its progeny (*see* Ch. 4), evidentiary rules are largely procedural rather than substantive—but be careful about state law regarding privilege, which is expressly given precedence under Rule 501.

J. Use of Technology at Trial

Witness testimony can be presented by videotape, close-circuit television, Skype, or perhaps even phone or other voice transmission. In general, however, courts vastly prefer live testimony and testimony that includes jury opportunity to view the witness. The rationale is that the jury can better evaluate witness testimony when seeking the witness's demeanor. A large amount of psychological research suggests that demeanor evidence is highly over-rated. Most people simply are not that good at discerning a speaker who is lying from one telling the truth. Sometimes a truthful person is so nervous when testifying that they are wrongly thought to be evasive or untrustworthy. Sometimes pathological liars make convincing witnesses because they are so practiced at lying. Nonetheless, the preference in law for visual testimony, preferably live, in-person testimony, persists.

IN PRACTICE

"You win with your witnesses and their documents" was the saying of an accomplished trial lawyer. He meant that the opponent's documents would be crucial in undermining the self-serving testimony frequently delivered by litigants but that it was also important that counsel's own witnesses present well to the jury. If your honest witness is so nervous as to appear dishonest, part of your job as counsel is to make the witness comfortable and to structure the testimony to present the witness in the best light. Consider bolstering the testimony—even more than might ordinarily be the case—through use of documents consistent with the testimony and exhibits that emphasize the testimony in a calmer, more authoritative manner than does your nervous witness's answers to questions.

Fed. R. Civ. P. 43(a) specifically permits testimony from a remote location "by contemporaneous transmission" provided there has been a "showing of good cause" and there are "compelling circumstances" as well as "appropriate safeguards." Where bringing the witness to court would be expensive, the testimony is not crucial, or both, this may be a sound means of reducing the cost of litigation.

Notwithstanding the preference for live testimony, testimony may in some cases be submitted by deposition. In addition, depositions can be used for impeachment of witnesses even when they cannot be used as substantive evidence. Chapter 13 discusses in detail use of a deposition at trial.

K. Motions for Judgment as a Matter of Law (Rule 50)

Federal Civil Rule 50 provides that a court may grant judgment as a matter of law to a party and thereby remove a matter from further jury consideration or even reverse a jury outcome. Because most of the "action" in Rule 50 practice comes in the post-trial context, most of our discussion of Rule 50, particularly its substantive standards, is in Chapter 18. But Rule 50 practice is an important part of trial as well.

THE RULE   Fed. R. Civ. P. 50(a)

(a) Judgment As A Matter of Law

(1) In General. If a party has been fully heard on an issue during the jury trial and the court finds that a reasonable jury would not have a legally sufficient evidentiary basis to find for the party on that issue, the court may:

(A) resolve the issue against the party; and

(B) grant a motion for judgment as a matter of law against the party on a claim or defense that, under the controlling law, can be maintained or defeated only with a favorable finding on that issue.

(2) Motion. A motion for judgment as a matter of law may be made at any time before the case is submitted to the jury. The motion must specify the judgment sought and the law and facts that entitle the movant to the judgment.

Here's how Rule 50 practice typically works: after the close of plaintiff's case, defendant moves for judgment as a matter of law in its favor, contending that even though plaintiff has now been able to present its entire case-in-chief plaintiff has failed to present substantial evidence in support of its claim or on an essential element of the claim. Just as typically, this mid-trial Rule 50 motion is denied.

Query: Can you see why a judge would be reluctant to grant the motion unless it is very compelling and plaintiff's case very weak? Remember as well that plaintiff has by this time normally survived a summary judgment motion as well.

Assuming denial of the Rule 50 motion after plaintiff's case-in-chief, we then have defendant's case-in-chief. After that, both plaintiff and defendant are likely to make Rule 50 motions for judgment as a matter of law, with plaintiff alleging that it has presented adequate unrefuted evidence supporting each element of its claim for relief. Conversely, defendant will argue that plaintiff has failed to present sufficiently substantial evidence on at least one necessary element of the claim for relief. As with the earlier Rule 50 motion, the court is likely to deny both these motions made at the close of the evidence—and for largely the same reasons that the first Rule 50 motion usually is denied.

Prior to the 1988 Amendments to the Federal Rules of Civil Procedure, Rule 50 motions made during trial were called motions of "directed verdict" and this nomenclature still prevails in some jurisdictions. Even in states where the state procedural rule uses the language of the Federal Rule, older lawyers may continue to use this term. But "directed verdict" was always a misnomer. Judges very rarely actually instructed the jury to find in favor of the party that won a Rule 50 motion, even in cases where directed verdict was granted as to some claims but not the entire case. Instead, the judge simply entered an order dismissing a plaintiff's claim or entering judgment in favor of plaintiff on a claim.

By "as a matter of law," the legal system generally means that the result is commanded by the applicable law and is not subject to fact-based alteration. When a court finds something is the case "as a matter of law" it usually means that the matter can be decided only one way under the prevailing legal construct.

Example and Analysis: For example, a plaintiff may argue that he suffered emotional distress when a co-worker refused to greet him at work and instead scowled upon his arrival. This is not a winning claim because the court will rule as a matter of law that unfriendliness or even rudeness toward a co-worker is not actionable. Even if plaintiff was genuinely upset, there was no duty of cordiality and the law will not recognize liability when a defendant's mere unfriendliness causes upset. On the other hand, if the coworker played a humiliating practical joke on plaintiff in front of the entire office, plaintiff's emotional distress might be actionable under the applicable law because most jurisdictions would find a duty not to subject co-workers to this type of conduct. Different facts may create difficult line-drawing issues as to the existence of a duty. However, for mere rudeness or unfriendliness, this "as a matter of law" bar to such a claim would also apply in the context of a Rule 12(b)(6) motion (Ch. 7) or a Rule 56 summary judgment motion (Ch. 15). Consequently, if the system is functioning well, claims of this type that are totally foreclosed by the applicable law should not even make it to trial. But if they do, a Rule 50 motion should eliminate them prior to jury deliberation. And if that opportunity has been missed as well, a post-trial Rule 50 motion (Ch. 18) remains available.

After the evidence closes, final argument takes place and the jury renders its verdict, there can still be—and usually is—a Rule 50 motion for judgment as a matter of law made by the losing party. Often (as discussed in Ch. 18), it is coupled with a Rule 59 motion for a new trial. The post-trial Rule 50 motion seeks to turn defeat into victory while the Rule 59 motion simply seeks another chance.

The substantive standard (discussed at greater length in Chapter 18) is the same for both post-trial and in-trial Rule 50 motions: the movant must show a lack of substantial evidence supporting the opponent's claim and that on the basis of the record in court the movant is entitled to judgment in its favor. Since the Supreme Court's 1986 Trilogy on summary judgment (discussed in Chapter 15), Rule 50 by implication has effectively provided that the party with the burden of persuasion is less likely to prevail on a Rule 50 motion than the defending party. The party with the burden of proof must convince the court that no reasonable jury could fail to find its evidence sufficient to satisfy the burden of persuasion. By contrast, the party without the burden of proof merely needs to "play defense" and show a fatal gap in the evidence presented by the party saddled with the burden of persuasion.

Despite the congruence of substantive standards, the post-trial Rule 50 motion is more likely to be granted than the in-trial Rule 50 motion. Why?

By "more likely" we do not mean all that likely. Most post-trial Rule 50 motions are denied because courts defer to the jury process once it is under way. To completely reverse a jury verdict and turn loser into winner, the court must be convinced that the case for the movant was so strong as to preclude a reasonable jury from doing what an apparently reasonable jury just did. If the judge was that convinced, one would have expected a grant of summary judgment or an in-trial Rule 50 motion. But there are nonetheless cases where the court completely rejects a jury's findings and grants Rule 50 relief. Why?

By contrast, a Rule 59 new trial may be granted without any need to conclude that the jury was completely off base. For example, the court may become convinced that it gave a misleading jury instruction (although cognitive bias research makes this unlikely; the judge will be disinclined to admit a mistake—but the appellate court will not have this same bias, although it will have a custom of deference toward trial judge decisions) and that this tainted the result and requires a new trial. Or one of the lawyers may have made inflammatory and prejudicial statements during closing argument that the court is now convinced tainted the jury outcome, requiring retrial before an untainted jury. In addition, as discussed in Ch. 18, a new trial can be ordered if the judge deems a verdict "excessive," which is essentially a ruling that the jury's liability finding was reasonable but its award too high. In some states, verdicts that are so small as to be "inadequate" can be grounds for a new trial. A Rule 59 motion may also be granted where the verdict is against the weight of the evidence, a ruling that reflects that the court is skeptical about the result but not so offended as to completely reverse the jury's decision.

L. Requests for Jury Instructions and the Verdict Form

After presentations of the cases-in-chief and in-trial Rule 50 motions (assuming they are not granted), the case proceeds to jury consideration. The parties submit proposed jury instructions and the court determines what instructions it will in fact give to the jury. Many judges require this submission to take place prior to trial to give the court more time to review the requests (but counsel is not prohibited from supplementing requests prior to jury instruction based on additional issues that arise during trial). Although there can be occasional difficult areas of disagreement, jury instructions are for the most part standardized by either official jury charge books (in many states) or well-established by case law and judicial custom and practice. In addition, each judge has his or own particular preferred version of jury instructions used for the standard issues that come up in each case. Jury instructions regarding negligence, breach of contract, fraud, punitive damages, defamation, or issues particular to the case are adapted as necessary. For example, the judge will probably talk about "Mr. Smith" rather than "plaintiff" so that the jury has a clearer understanding.

But to the extent there are disagreements, counsel get to argue their positions before the judge and attempt to persuade the judge that one instruction is a better or clearer reflection of the law than that proposed by the other side. The judge does not have to show the parties its precise script for instructing the jury but will let counsel know whose instructions it is accepting on controversial points. In this way, the lawyers during closing argument will be able to anticipate the jury instructions and tailor the closing to the explanation of the law the judge will give to the jury. The parties also can propose a particular verdict form, although the court is likely to use the form it finds best based on past experience.

M. Special Verdicts, General Verdicts, and Questions

The verdict in a civil action can run the continuum from the judge's simple request for a conclusion (*e.g.*, "we find defendant liable to plaintiff in the amount of $200,000") to a very involved series of specific questions designed to force the jury to consider and make findings at multiple steps in their analysis of the case. Rule 49 governs verdict form and sets for the alternative methods of obtaining the jury's verdict.

Federal Rule 49 specifically recognizes two types of verdict forms: a general verdict based on written questions, and a special verdict. But there also exists the possibility of a general verdict, although these are becoming increasingly rare in both federal and state courts.

A **general verdict** simply asks the jury "who wins?" and if so, "how much?" *See Johnson v. Ablt Trucking Co.,* 412 F.3d 1138, 1142-43 (10th Cir. 2005). The general verdict in its pure form does not even require submitting a written form to the jury. The judge can simply ask the jury to find for plaintiff or defendant and to report its finding orally in open court (where the rendering of the verdict is transcribed by the court reporter). Commonly, however, the judge submits a short verdict form asking for a finding in favor of one party or another, particularly in cases with multiple parties.

A **general verdict based on written questions** seeks to bring more focus and precision to the inquiry by having the jurors answer particular fact-based questions that in turn lead to the rendering of a general verdict. The questions need not address all factual issues.

A **special verdict** propounds specific questions to the jury. Based on the answers to these questions, the judge determines the legal consequences and enters an appropriate judgment. *See Mason v. Ford Motor Co.*, 307 F.3d 1271, 1274 (11th Cir. 2002). Although Rule 49(a)(1) speaks only of questions addressing "each issue of fact," the special verdict form may include mixed questions of law and fact so long as the jury is adequately instructed on the legal aspects of the question.

As discussed in Chapter 15, there may be questions of "fact existence" (*e.g.*, whether car tires were slashed) or "fact inference" (*e.g.*, the tires were fine when the owner went into the convenience store; when he

> **Questions of Law, Questions of Fact & Mixed Questions of Law and Fact.** A question of law, as the name implies, is a question about the prevailing law, legal standards, and what the law requires. It is an assessment of the rights and obligations of the litigants. A question of fact is a question regarding what happened in a particular case. A "mixed" question is one in which the court's determination is ultimately one of law but may vary based on the fact findings of the proceeding.

emerged two minutes later he observed defendant walking away from his car and noticed the slashed tires). A mixed question of fact and law is one in which the factfinder is asked both to determine a fact and to assess its legal import. For example, a jury might be asked to determine whether a police officer used unreasonable force, which requires the jury to determine what happened (was force applied at all and in what context) and whether the amount of force was legally reasonable). As also discussed in Chapter 15 regarding summary judgment, when a court determines something "as a matter of law," it is in effect declaring that under the law it will not permit a jury to reach a contrary result.

If counsel does not make timely objection to a verdict form, the right to challenge the form is usually considered waived. In egregious cases, an appellate court may order a new trial but such circumstances are rare.

There can be confusion as to whether a verdict form is one for a general verdict with questions or is instead a special verdict. The test is whether the jury declares the final legal result of a claim or whether instead the jury is simply making findings of fact upon which the judge declares the legal result. *See Zhang v. American Gem Seafoods, Inc.*, 339 F.3d 1020, 1031 (9th Cir. 2003).

The trial court has substantial discretion as to which approach to use. Under the *Erie* doctrine (*see* Chapter 4), choice of verdict form is a matter of federal procedure rather than state substantive law. *See Evoy v. CRST Van Expedited, Inc.*, 430 F. Supp. 2d 775, 784 (N.D. Ill. 2006). Where cases are more complex, the verdict form is liable to have more questions regardless of whether it is propounded pursuant to Rule 49(a) or Rule 49(b) simply because there are more issues in the case.

One school of thought is that special verdicts reduce the risk that a new trial may be necessary because the jury's fact-finding (however bizarre) is largely sacrosanct and the judge's application of the law to the facts, even if incorrect, can be corrected on appeal without the need for a new trial. By contrast, jurors rendering a general verdict with questions may have made a mistake of law as to an aspect of the decision but because it is part of an indivisible whole, a new trial may be necessary.

Although this is a concern, it is probably overstated. Weighed against the risk of jury error is the argument that use of a special verdict deprives the jury of its traditional power to make a definitive declaration of the case outcome and raises Seventh Amendment concerns (although few would argue that Rule 49(a) is unconstitutional). Conversely, it can be argued that use of a special verdict is particularly apt where the case has emotional appeal (*e.g.*, a tragically injured child, a hugely popular or unpopular defendant) that may overwhelm the jury's rationality. In such cases, confining the jury's task to fact finding and limiting the jury's power to declare a winner outright may produce more dispassionate, reflective justice.

Regardless of whether proceeding pursuant to Rule 49(a) or Rule 49(b), the questions on the verdict form must be sufficiently accurate and clear. One trap for the unwary: If a party fails to request that an essential element of a claim be submitted to the jury, this may constitute a waiver of the Seventh Amendment right to jury trial and permit the judge to resolve fact issues not presented to the jury. *See* Rule 49(a)(3); *Givens v. O'Quinn*, 447 F. Supp. 2d 593, 601 (W.D. Va. 2006).

Where jury answers to Rule 49(a) questions are inconsistent with one another, the jury should be required to continue deliberating to resolve the inconsistency. This requires counsel to be vigilant when the special verdict answers are being read in court and to immediately bring any internal inconsistency to the court's attention. It is not a valid objection to argue that the answers are erroneous in light of the evidence—that's an argument for a post-trial Rule 50 motion or a Rule 59 motion.

Where jury answers to the fact questions in a Rule 49(b) verdict form are inconsistent with the general verdict on the same form, the court has three options: it may apply the fact findings in spite of the inconsistent general verdict; It may resubmit the issue to the jury for further consideration; Or it may order a new trial. The judge's decision in choosing among these options is reviewed under an "abuse of discretion" standard (*see* Ch. 19 regarding standards of review). This means that the trial court's resolution of the inconsistency will be affirmed so long as reasonable even if the appellate court thinks a different remedy was preferable. *See Wilbur v. Correctional Services Corp.*, 393 F.3d 1192, 1199 (11th Cir. 2004).

The court may not, however, enter judgment on the inconsistent general verdict and disregard the inconsistent fact findings. Why is this the case? What values does this approach serve?

N. Closing Arguments

After determination of the verdict form and jury instructions, the case proceeds to the closing statements by counsel. Unlike the opening statement, where argument is prohibited, the closing is all about argument. But the most effective closings are not exercises in name calling or accusation but instead review the evidence and argue that on the basis of the evidence presented and the applicable law upon which the judge will instruct, the verdict should be in favor of counsel's client. During closing argument, one sees some of the theatrics and storytelling that laypersons often think of as part of trial lawyering. But even argument in an adversary system has its limits. Counsel in closing argument may not misstate the evidence, suggest improper bases for decision, or use prejudicial rhetoric. Nonetheless, it is normally the responsibility of opposing counsel to object to improper material or conduct during the closing. If there is no objection, opposing counsel's rights (*i.e.*, the client's rights) are often considered waived and the verdict will stand even if there has been improper closing argument. An exception to this adversarial norm is that certain egregious misconduct during closing argument may be deemed "plain error" and be the basis for a new trial even if there was not a timely objection. See *Lioce v. Cohen*, 149 P.3d 916 (Nev. 2006) (court finds defense counsel's closing argument sufficiently prejudicial to require new trials even in the absence of objection.

O. Jury Instructions and Jury Deliberation

After the closing, the judge instructs the jurors in the law. The charge is read to the jury, which traditionally is not permitted to take notes (and could not take notes during the trial) or a copy of the instructions into the jury room. After instructions, the jury retires to deliberate. Until a verdict is reached, they cannot discuss the case with others or consider media accounts of the case. Jurors are "sequestered" (formally isolated from family and society) only in very high profile cases where the integrity of the process might be threatened by massive publicity or efforts to influence the jury (or in extreme cases where there is concern for the safety of the jurors).

Even without sequestering, jurors are isolated during the times they deliberate, confined to the jury room supervised by court personnel (which may be either a "civilian" administrator or a law enforcement officer). When out of the jury room, jurors are on their honor to follow the rules.

Prior to deliberation, jurors have had some practice with the ground rules. During trial, they are prohibited from talking with the parties, counsel, or witnesses and typically wear a small lapel pin reflecting their juror status so that passers-by do not unwittingly violate the rules by engaging them in conversation.

During deliberations—and during the trial presentation—jurors are to focus on the evidence and refrain from doing their own investigation of the matter. In one recent case, a trial judge's failure to follow-up on complaints that a jury was engaging in internet research resulted in a new trial. The rationale for such a strong reaction is not only concerns about an individual juror's research abilities or potentially erroneous spinning of the findings but the view that for the jury system to work as intended, the jury should be receiving information at one time as a unit rather than engaging in informational side trips that are not subject to scrutiny by the entire jury, counsel, and the court.

Procedures inside the jury room can vary. Historically, the jury was to elect a foreperson (once known as a "foreman") to preside over deliberations. Increasingly, judges simply pick the juror in the first chair to serve as foreperson.

As discussed in Chapter 16, jury size varies. U.S. Supreme Court decisions interpreting the Seventh Amendment require a jury of at least six, but judges are permitted to have larger juries. Most courts appear to opt for eight-person juries but some require a jury of twelve. In federal court, jury verdicts must be unanimous, as is the case in many state courts as well. In other states, a super-majority (*e.g.*, six of eight, nine or more of twelve) is permitted. When the jury has reached a verdict supported by the requisite minimum number of jurors, the foreperson notifies the judge, who then has the verdict read in open court.

P. The Verdict and Possible Challenges

When the jury returns a verdict and has it read in open court, any of the parties may request that the jury be "polled"—a process in which each juror is individually asked aloud if he or she supports the verdict given to the judge by the foreperson. This option probably arose out of historical fears that some jurors would be coerced into a verdict and then stand mute when the foreperson transmitted the verdict. Today, it seems a real relic. Collectively, the authors have seen a lot of polled juries. Never once has an individual juror disavowed the verdict. If it every happens, it will make good theatre à la Perry Mason. But we're not holding our collective breath. Jury verdicts may be subject to challenge, however, if there is something that suggests jury tampering or that the jury was subjected to improper influences or engaged in improper behavior. In addition, recall that there may be issues of inconsistency in a jury's answers to questions on the verdict form.

Q. From Verdict to Judgment and Beyond

As we have stressed, litigation is not final until the court enters a judgment that is binding on the parties and that permits a prevailing litigant to obtain monetary or other relief. After a favorable verdict, the claimant is almost home but, as shown in Chapter 18, there may still be vigorous post-trial motion practice, particularly by the verdict loser, who will seek a post-trial Rule 50 judgment as a matter of law or a Rule 59 new trial. If this is unsuccessful, judgment is entered for the verdict winner but an appeal (Ch. 19) likely follows. If the judgment is affirmed, the case moves to judgment enforcement. And at any step of the process, settlement remains a distinct possibility.

Although the jury is accorded wide latitude in determining facts, assessing behavior, and calculating damages, the law imposes constraints that may result in reversing or setting aside a jury verdict in violation of the law or in tension with legal norms. In addition, a jury verdict may be modified if required by law. For example, prevailing state law may put a cap on damages for a particular type of claim (*e.g.*, non-economic damages in a medical malpractice case)(although such limitations have been held to violate state constitutions in Alabama, Florida, Georgia, Illinois, Missouri, New Hampshire, Oregon, and Washington). If the jury award exceeds the legal cap, a court may reduce the amount of the award rather than ordering a full new trial.

ADDITIONAL EXERCISES

1. Percy Plaintiff is walking on a path alongside the railroad track and waives to his friend Wally Witness who is whiling away the time eating fried green tomatoes at the local Whistle Stop Cafe. While Wally looks down to read the paper, a train goes by. When Wally looks up, he sees Percy lying flat on the ground near the train tracks. Further inspection reveals Percy to be dead from a blow to the head. Percy's estate and spouse sue the railroad, contending that a mail hook or other protrusion from the side of a passing train car is what hit Percy. The Darn Railroad contends that the evidence is just as consistent with Percy negligently wandering too close to the passing train or having been hit on the head by a hobo trying to rob Percy. Defendant Darn fails to move for summary judgment but instead seeks Rule 50 judgment as a matter of law after the close of Plaintiff Percy's case-in-chief, which consists only of Wally's testimony. **What Result?**

2. Same situation. But assume instead that the incident occurs at 9 p.m. in October and Percy's body is discovered by Wally while Wally is walking his dog. **What ruling in response to the Darn Railroad's Rule 50 motion at the close of the evidence?**

3. Go back to the Problem No. 1 version of the facts and assume that in addition to Wally's testimony, Percy's counsel also presents his widow, the local police chief, and Percy's employer, all of whom testify Percy was by habit a very cautious person who had used the railroad path without incident for years. (In real life, there may be some evidence is-

sues with this testimony, but assume it all comes in.) The Darn Railroad again moves for Rule 50 JAML. ***What result?***

4. Assume (rightly or wrongly) that the Court denies the Railroad's Rule 50 motion. In its case-in-chief, the Railroad introduces evidence that Percy was an alcoholic who had talked of suicide. There is Percy's Doctor, an Industrial Psychologist who tested Percy and other workers at Percy's place of employment, and the local Bartender. The Railroad makes a Rule 50 motion at the close of the evidence. ***What result?***

5. Assume the same facts as in Practice Problem No. 4 but that on cross-examination, the Doctor admits to being convicted of Medicare fraud 15 years earlier, the Industrial Psychologist concedes that 50 percent of his income comes from work for the Railroad, and the Bartender has been convicted of manslaughter for beating an unruly patron to death some five years ago, for which the Bartender served a year in prison (nobody else in town much liked the decedent, either). The Railroad makes a Rule 50 motion. ***What result?***

6. Assume (rightly or wrongly) that the case is submitted to the jury, which renders a verdict in favor of Percy's estate in the amount of $22 million. Percy was 45-year-old father of two who worked on an assembly line. The Darn Railroad makes a Rule 50 motion for a defense judgment and in the alternative makes a Rule 59 motion on the ground that the verdict is excessive in amount. ***What result?***

   You cannot fully assess this Problem until after studying Chapter 18—but you should have an inkle, at least as to the Rule 50 decision because the legal standard is the same both during and after trial, even if as a practical matter, a court may hesitate to grant judgment as a matter of law until all the evidence has been received. ***As to the Rule 59 excessive verdict contention, what does you common sense tell you?***

7. Same as facts as in Problem No. 1 except that after the close of the evidence, defendant makes a Rule 50 motion after discovery through legal research the previous evening that the Darn Railroad is immune from any liability claims involving pedestrians within 50 yards of the track at time of alleged impact. The state abandoned the trespasser rule with which you are familiar from *Erie v. Tompkins* but the legislature later

restored much of the Railroad's immunity. The lawyers simply failed to notice this statute until late in the trial. **What result?**

8. Consider each of the following and whether the circumstances warrant setting aside the verdict or some other form of relief such as requiring the jury to continue deliberating.

   a. Donna Defendant, during a break, notices Juror No. 6 sneaking into the stairwell for a cigarette. Donna joins Juror No. 6. They have a smoke and talk about two recent movies they've seen.

   b. One of plaintiff's paralegals sees Juror No. 5 confronted at the drinking fountain by Harry Machete, one of the town's prominent hard-driving business leaders. Plaintiff is claiming injury from chemical runoff from a local manufacturing plant and worries that Machete, a former head of the local Chamber of Commerce, may have lobbied the juror to vote against the claim because it might make the town look "anti-business."

   c. Juror No. 4 slips a note to the judge stating "I'm frightened. A hulking man in a Lincoln Continental has been following my son home after school since the trial began."

   d. While eating at the Courtside Café, defense counsel strikes up a conversation with the waiter, who reveals that Jurors Nos. 1, 2, and 3 have been eating lunch there each day during trial, typically with three martinis apiece. Up until then, counsel thought he was just boring when he saw these three jurors staring blankly into space or nodding off during the afternoons at trial.

   e. Defense counsel is picking up a case of Bourbon to send out as Christmas gifts to court reporters when the clerk at Larry's Liquor recognizes him as the lawyer in the Smith case for which a jury is currently deliberating. "Man, can those jurors put it away. I've been delivering two bottles of this stuff and a case of beer to them each day of the trial." Until now, counsel thought they were nodding off because of overeating at lunch.

   f. The verdict of $50,000 for the plaintiff leaves both plaintiff and defendant scratching their heads. It was a breach of contract claim and they both agreed that either defendant owed $100,000 or nothing because widgets had indisputably been delivered, had never been paid for, but there was a disagreement over whether the widgets worked properly. "Great trial, both of you guys," pipes up Juror No. 7 as counsel are leaving the courtroom. "It's nice that we could just split the difference so that neither of you had to lose."

g. The verdict form asks whether defendant was negligent, whether plaintiff was negligent, and for a percentage of the negligence of each. The form then asks the jury, if it finds any negligence of defendant, to submit a calculation of damages. The jury answers "no" and "no" to both negligence questions, leaves the percentage question blank, and then writes the figure $100,000 in response to the damages question.

h. After three days of deliberation, the jury informs the court that it is hopelessly deadlocked and asks that it be discharged, hopefully before Thursday Night Football.

Quick Summary

- Final preparation for trial provides a last opportunity to evaluate the strengths and weaknesses of the case and to consider further efforts at negotiated settlement or ADR.

- Motions for pretrial evidence rulings can be used to prevent references to prejudicial material in the midst of trial and to resolve difficult evidentiary issues outside the spur-of-the-moment atmosphere of trial.

- Trial proceeds through a number of phases: jury selection; opening statements; plaintiff's case-in-chief (with direct examination, cross-examination, and attendant document introduction and use); Rule 50 motions at the end of plaintiff's case; defendant's case-in-chief; more Rule 50 practice; requested jury instructions and verdict forms; closing arguments; the actual instructions and submission of the case to the jury; verdict and (absent successful post-trial motions (*see* Ch. 18); and judgment.

- During trial, the Rules of Evidence, enforced through objections, argument, and rulings by the judge, play an important role.

- Rule 50—Judgment as a Matter of Law—can play an important role. A Rule 50 motion seeks a determination that on the basis of the trial record, the non-movant is legally precluded from prevailing.

- Excessive rhetorical liberties by counsel, particularly during closing argument, can result in a new trial—but normally this will require a timely objection by opposing counsel.

- Jury misconduct during deliberations can, in extreme cases, require a new trial.

- Inconsistent jury responses to verdict form questions can also result in a new trial—but courts are reluctant to set aside the prior work of trial unless the error is substantial and appears to have affected the result.

18

Post-Trial Motions

Key Concepts

- Reasons for post-decision motions
- Role of post-trial motions in obtaining appellate review
- Some cases are finally decided on post-trial motions, obviating the expense and delay that an appeal would entail
- Key post-trial motions: for judgment as a matter of law; for amended findings; for a new trial; or for relief from an order or judgment

Introduction

The rules permit parties to bring several important motions even after trial—indeed, both sides in a case may want or need to bring one or more of these motions. It is a rare case that is tried with neither side seeking some post-trial relief.

A. Background and Policy

The underlying policy reason for permitting—or even requiring—a party to bring post-trial motions is to give the court an opportunity to correct error. Appellate courts see an efficiency advantage in allowing the trial court to have a chance to take actions that may obviate an otherwise certain—or at least likely—appeal. This also recognizes that the trial judge may be in the best place to correct mistakes based on first-hand experience with the proceedings. This also comes partly out of a sense of fairness to the trial court—appellate courts recognize that many trial decisions must be made while the trial is underway and that neither the court nor the parties may have time to research fully and carefully all the issues presented. Examining these issues after trial and in the more relaxed schedule after trial allows the trial judge to give the question full consideration and the judge's best judgment as to the correct answers.

Post-trial motions are never literally necessary, but the consequences of not bringing them may be significant. Obviously, if a party does not ask for relief it is not likely to be granted. The federal rules allow much narrower review of issues by appellate courts if a motion for judgment as a matter of law is not brought (or doesn't raise the issues sought to be argued on appeal). Specifically, failure to bring the motion will prevent the consideration of the sufficiency of the evidence on appeal. Some state courts are less concerned about a motion for judgment as a matter of law, but may require a motion for a new trial in order to obtain broad appellate review of the multiple discretionary decisions made at trial. Even if there is no specific consequence to forgoing a post-trial motion, it may be a good idea to bring one or more.

Perhaps the best reason to bring a motion after trial probably is not with an eye toward the appeal, but to obtain the relief the rules allow. Some motions after trial are actually granted!

The great thing about post-trial motions is that the judge by this juncture knows the issues thoroughly. The challenge may be, however, that post-trial motions challenge the trial judge's earlier rulings but must be made to the same trial judge. Not all judges eagerly seek to correct their own errors—they may not even want to acknowledge that there could be errors.

B. Available Post-Trial Motions

A party who "loses" at trial has several available motions. The most important, at least in federal court, is the motion for judgment as a matter of law ("JAML" or, sometimes, "JMOL"). This motion, formerly a "motion for j.n.o.v.," allows the trial court to revisit the *legal* decisions made throughout the case. The procedure calls for renewing the motion after trial. (JAML motions made during trial are discussed in Chapter 17). This process requires that a JAML motion be brought at any time before the case is submitted to the jury; the post-trial JAML motion is considered the "renewal" of that earlier motion. This form of the motion replaces the former motion j.n.o.v.

> **J.N.O.V.** is shorthand for "judgment notwithstanding the verdict." Actually, it is the carryover of the abbreviation for that phrase in its Latin formulation, judgment *"non obstante veredicto."* JAML or JMOL carries forward the four-letter label.

> The rule refers to "renewing" the motion because it requires an earlier motion for JAML at the close of the evidence. This motion's precursor was called a "motion for directed verdict." The post-trial motion essentially raises the same issues in the context of the entire record.

A losing party (or possibly a prevailing party who did get the result sought), may bring a motion for new trial under Rule 59. The parties may also want to consider two mirror-image motions, motions for additur or remittitur (to increase or cut down the verdict result). These motions are discussed briefly, but given their rarity, are probably not worth more than passing familiarity.

A party who has won at trial—with no complaints about how the trial was conducted or the result—may bring a motion for the award of pre-judgment interest, costs, attorneys' fees, or other additional relief not submitted to the jury.

It is common to bring motions in the alternative. Following a jury trial the disappointed litigant may want to bring a motion for judgment as a matter of law or, in the alternative, for a new trial. There is no reason to elect between these motions unless the party really doesn't want a new trial even if the court would order one.

C. Renewed Motions for Judgment as a Matter of Law

THE RULE	Rule 50

(b) Renewing the Motion after Trial; Alternative Motion for a New Trial. If the court does not grant a motion for judgment as a matter of law made under **Rule 50(a)**, the court is considered to have submitted the action to the jury subject to the court's later deciding the legal questions raised by the motion. No later than 28 days after the entry of judgment—or if the motion addresses a jury issue not decided by a verdict, no later than 28 days after the jury was discharged—the movant may file a renewed motion for judgment as a matter of law and may include an alternative or joint request for a new trial under **Rule 59**. In ruling on the renewed motion, the court may:

(1) allow judgment on the verdict, if the jury returned a verdict;

(2) order a new trial; or

(c) Granting the Renewed Motion; Conditional Ruling on a Motion for a New Trial.

(1) In General. If the court grants a renewed motion for judgment as a matter of law, it must also conditionally rule on any motion for a new trial by determining whether a new trial should be granted if the judgment is later vacated or reversed. The court must state the grounds for conditionally granting or denying the motion for a new trial.

(2) Effect of a Conditional Ruling. Conditionally granting the motion for a new trial does not affect the judgment's finality; if the judgment is reversed, the new trial must proceed unless the appellate court orders otherwise. If the motion for a new trial is conditionally denied, the appellee may assert error in that denial; if the judgment is reversed, the case must proceed as the appellate court orders.

(d) Time for a Losing Party's New-Trial Motion. Any motion for a new trial under **Rule 59** by a party against whom judgment as a matter of law is rendered must be filed no later than 28 days after the entry of the judgment.

(e) Denying the Motion for Judgment as a Matter of Law; Reversal on Appeal. If the court denies the motion for judgment as a matter of law, the prevailing party may, as appellee, assert grounds entitling it to a new trial should the appellate court conclude that the trial court erred in denying the motion. If the appellate court reverses the judgment, it may order a new trial, direct the trial court to determine whether a new trial should be granted, or direct the entry of judgment.

The post-trial JAML motion attacks an adverse decision, in effect charging the factfinder of finding liability where none can exist as a matter of law. The Seventh Amendment requires jury trials in matters at law when so demanded by one of the parties.

It is not uncommon for a judge with strong inclination to grant a motion to dismiss at the close of the evidence nonetheless to allow the case to proceed to verdict. This allows the jury, possibly, to vindicate the judge's skepticism by returning a defense verdict. It also reduces the risk of reversal on appeal.

IN PRACTICE

What reason is there for the court "waiting to see" what the jury does? There are two good justifications. First, there is the chance a jury would vindicate the view that there is not enough evidence to support a verdict. On a very practical level, appellate review of the jury's decision is extremely limited, so the verdict is likely to end the litigation of the issue; an order taking the case away from the jury, however, is likely to be the focus of later appellate review. Second, by allowing the case to go to verdict, the trial court's later decision to grant judgment as a matter of law can be fully reviewed by the appellate court without requiring a new trial—if the appellate court disagrees with the trial court ruling, it can just reinstate the jury verdict, potentially saving days or weeks of trial time.

The question presented by a JAML motion is whether the evidence presented is sufficient to create an issue of fact for the jury to decide. The JAML motion should be granted when there exists no evidence or too little evidence upon which a jury could render a verdict for the nonmovant. The verdict winner may have a scintilla (or even a few shreds) of evidence in its favor, but the court may still grant JAML when this evidence is clearly insufficient to warrant jury determination of the case. Thus, the court will reverse a denial of a JAML motion "only when there is such a complete absence of evidence supporting the verdict that the jury's findings could only have been the result of sheer surmise and conjecture or where there is such an overwhelming amount of evidence in favor of the moving party that fair minded jurors could not have arrived at a verdict against the movant." *See, e.g., Song v. Ives Laboratories, Inc.*, 957 F.2d 1041, 1046 (2d Cir. 1992).

In assessing the evidence, the court must view it in the light most favorable to the verdict winner and nonmovant, who is entitled to all reasonable inferences from the evidence. Frequently, the standard is stated as whether the evidence is such that, without weighing the credibility of the witnesses or otherwise considering the weight of the evidence, there can be but one reasonable conclusion as to the verdict. Put another way, JAML should be granted only when the jury verdict is one that no reasonable jury could have reached on the evidence before it. *See, e.g., Anderson v. Liberty Lobby, Inc.,* 477 U.S. 242 (1986).

The motion for judgment as a matter of law has a special role in federal litigation—failure to bring the motion will result in narrower appellate review of the trial court decision. If the motion is not brought, the disappointed litigant will not be able to raise the issue of sufficiency of evidence on appeal. Fed. R. Civ. P. 50(b). The court will not test the sufficiency of the evidence to support a jury's verdict beyond application of the "plain error" doctrine in order to prevent a manifest miscarriage of justice. Questions of law are still preserved, however.

EXAMPLES & ANALYSIS

EXAMPLE: Pen sues Deller in federal court for breach of contract, contending that Deller's silence was acceptance of Pen's offer to sell his magician's equipment for $200,000. Pen testifies that he made the offer to Deller and that Deller nodded in agreement and they shook hands. During cross-examination, Pen admits to being convicted of felony trespass when arrested for sitting in at the South African Embassy 40 years ago as a protest against the then white supremacist apartheid regime. Pen also concedes that he bounced a check when making a contribution to the ACLU the previous year, a failing he attributes to oversight by his former business manager. At the close of Pen's case-in-chief (the time at which Pen has "been fully heard" within the meaning of Rule 50(a)), Deller moves for JAML, contending that Pen's testimony is unworthy of belief based on these blots on his record.

Analysis: Both these grounds for JAML are losers. Evidence of Pen's arrest 40 years ago (including cross-examination on the topic), even if a felony, would probably be excluded by most courts pursuant to Fed. R. Evid. 612. Of course, the judge in this case allowed the questioning. But it is an old arrest that can be characterized as justified civil disobedience rather than real crime, and it casts no doubt on Pen's credibility regarding business agreements.

The bounced check arguably has some connection to Pen's business veracity in that presenting a check is a representation that it is good and backed by funds in an account—which apparently was not the case. But even if Pen admitted to check fraud in another situation, this does not mean his claim of an agreed sale to Deller was part of a fraud. The issue of Pen's credibility is for the jury and cannot be decided by the judge "as a matter of law."

> **EXAMPLE:** Assume Deller's motion is denied. Deller takes the stand but does not deny nodding in agreement when Pen proposed the sale. Indeed, Deller, as is his wont, says almost nothing on the stand. He does, however, proffer Dr. Verne Value, the world's greatest appraiser of magician's equipment, who testifies that Pen's gear is worth at most $25,000. Dr. Value emerges unscathed from cross-examination. Deller again moves for JAML. Pen also moves for JAML in the amount of his claimed $200,000.

Analysis: Even if Dr. Value is unassailable regarding the value of the equipment, Deller has effectively conceded to an agreement to pay $200,000 for the gear. Unless Deller can invoke state law regarding unconscionable contracts, $200,000 will be the amount owed. For that reason, Pen's motion has a real chance of being granted. But Pen has the burden of persuasion, which will make most courts reluctant to enter a judgment in his favor with the jury waiting in the wings to consider the case, notwithstanding that Deller has all but conceded to the agreement. And if Deller had raised an unconscionability defense (*e.g.*, that $200,000 was an obscenely high amount for old magician's equipment), most state law would probably consider this a factor the jury could use to award less than the claimed amount, making a JAML grant for the plaintiff inappropriate. Certainly, the practicalities of the situation would prompt most judges to submit the case to the jury so that the jury could enter a verdict resulting in a judgment that would be nearly immune to attack on appeal.

> **EXAMPLE:** Despite Dr. Value's testimony, the jury (perhaps overwhelmed by Pen's charisma as well as the apparent absence of an unconscionability defense) renders a verdict for Pen in the amount of $200,000. Deller moves yet again for JAML, this time invoking the forum state's Super-Strong Statute of Frauds, which provides that "[t]here shall be no recovery upon any claimed contract in the absence of a signed writing if the amount at issue exceeds $500."

A **statute of frauds** requires that certain types of contracts be evidenced by a writing in order to minimize the chance that the claimant is simply making up an agreement. Modern state versions of these statutes are descended from a 1677 English law enacted out of concern that silver-tongued claimants were prevailing simply by lying about what had been promised by a defendant. The statute of frauds concept can be summarized as the notion that "big deals should be in writing" and the statute normally covers only contracts involving real estate sales, suretyship (the promise to guarantee the debt of another), marriage contracts, sales of goods in an amount more than $500, and contracts that are not to be performed within a year of the agreement.

Analysis: Here, the third time could likely the charm for Deller unless there is some precedent softening the clear and strong language of the statute—which appears to say that claims of this magnitude cannot prevail in court unless the contract is in writing and signed at least by Deller, the party against whom the agreement is to be enforced. Regardless of the parties' intent, the equities of the situation, or the relative believability of Pen and Deller, "the law" appears to clearly require a defense verdict based on the undisputed fact that this alleged contract has no signed writing to support its existence.

Pen's best hope of beating this seemingly ironclad defense is to argue that Deller has waived it by bringing it up so late. But the Super Strong Statute of Frauds defense is not one sounding in personal jurisdiction, venue, form of process, or service of process (see Rule 12 and ch. 7), so waiver would appear not to apply.

Alternatively, under the right set of facts, Pen might be able to argue that even absent a writing, he can enforce the agreement as one supported by promissory estoppel. As you will learn in Contracts class (or may have learned already), contracts can be formed by promissory estoppel and enforced as necessary to prevent injustice (pursuant to ALI RESTATEMENT OF CONTRACTS (SECOND) § 90, which is the law in most every state) provided that there has been a representation (Deller's nodding assent probably counts but an oral statement would be better) upon which Pen can show reasonable reliance. For example, if Pen bought new magician's equipment based on having thought he'd sold the old stuff to Deller, this would suffice.

But wait! There's another wrinkle. Pen can also argue that Deller in essence admitted the contract on the witness stand. In most states, an admission of the contract makes the statute of frauds irrelevant because the rationale for the statute is to prevent fraudulent assertion of an oral contract. If the forum state follows this rule (and if the forum state's substantive contract law is applicable to the dispute; (*see* Ch. 4 regarding choice of law)), Pen can perhaps prevail.

And here's the ultimate wrinkle, one that effectively prevents Deller from winning his JAML motion based on the statute of frauds—Deller failed to raise this ground in his earlier motions for JAML at the end of Pen's case and at the close of the evidence. Rule 50(b) allows the movant to "renew" after trial a previously made motion for JAML pursuant to Rule 50(a). But if Deller's previous Rule 50(a) JAML motion made no mention of the statute of frauds defense, there is nothing for Deller to renew. Having failed to raise this legal argument prior to the verdict, Deller is precluded from raising it after the verdict. What could have been a winning JAML motion based on the statute of frauds defense is now denied to Deller because he waited too long to articulate this legal ground in his favor. Post-verdict Rule 50(b) motions are limited to the grounds previously raised in an earlier 50(a) motion.

EXAMPLE: Assume that after Pen's case in chief, Deller in his JAML motion directed the court's attention to the forum state's "Almost Instant Statute of Repose," which provides that no contract for the sale of goods can be enforced by the courts more than eight weeks after the making of the contract. Although Pen did not wait long before bringing his breach of contract claim, we can safely assume that the deal was made more than eight weeks ago.

Analysis: Despite its seeming unfairness, the Statute of Repose would appear to guarantee Deller a Rule 50 JAML victory. Unless Pen can persuasively argue that such a short time for obtaining relief violates due process (*see* Ch. 2), the motion should be granted. In real life, most courts would probably find such a short statute of repose unduly unfair because it would effectively strip citizens of the ordinary contract rights many have come to expect. In addition, if this statute of repose was noticeably shorter than those provided for other types of legal claims, there could be equal protection problems—but in general, courts have not found it unconstitutional for legislatures to have differential limitations periods so long as there is some rational basis for the short statute.

As you know, a **statute of limitations** requires that claims be commenced before a certain amount of time has passed since the right of action accrued or became discovered by the plaintiff. A statute of repose is even stronger in that it provides that a claim cannot be effectively made after a certain number of years have passed since a particular event. The most common statute of repose is one barring lawsuits regarding building design more than a certain number of years (*e.g.*, 15) after the building's substantial completion. *Can you guess the rationale for such a statute? And who probably lobbied for such statutes in the state legislature?*

D. Motions for a New Trial

A party disappointed by decisions made during a trial that prevented a fair trial has versatile motion for relief available: the motion for a new trial. It is a motion available when a trial has been held, and may permit review of pretrial rulings that may have prevented a fair trial. While a JAML motion (if successful) will result in judgment in favor of the movant, a new trial motion will yield a do-over—a new trial.

THE RULE   Rule 59

New Trial; Altering or Amending a Judgment

(a) In General.

(1) Grounds for New Trial. The court may, on motion, grant a new trial on all or some of the issues—and to any party—as follows:

(A) after a jury trial, for any reason for which a new trial has heretofore been granted in an action at law in federal court; or

(B) after a nonjury trial, for any reason for which a rehearing has heretofore been granted in a suit in equity in federal court.

(2) Further Action After a Nonjury Trial. After a nonjury trial, the court may, on motion for a new trial, open the judgment if one has been entered, take additional testimony, amend findings of fact and conclusions of law or make new ones, and direct the entry of a new judgment.

(b) Time to File a Motion for a New Trial. A motion for a new trial must be filed no later than 28 days after the entry of judgment.

(c) Time to Serve Affidavits. When a motion for a new trial is based on affidavits, they must be filed with the motion. The opposing party has 14 days after being served to file opposing affidavits. The court may permit reply affidavits.

(d) New Trial on the Court's Initiative or for Reasons Not in the Motion. No later than 28 days after the entry of judgment, the court, on its own, may order a new trial for any reason that would justify granting one on a party's motion. After giving the parties notice and an opportunity to be heard, the court may grant a timely motion for a new trial for a reason not stated in the motion. In either event, the court must specify the reasons in its order.

(e) Motion to Alter or Amend a Judgment. A motion to alter or amend a judgment must be filed no later than 28 days after the entry of the judgment.

One very important limitation on this motion is the relief it offers—it only allows a new trial. If the party doesn't want a new trial, and that is often the case, the motion doesn't provide much benefit. But the motion is broad in possible scope, and can be based on any of these grounds:

- procedural error;

- evidentiary error;

- improper jury instructions that require setting aside verdict and repeating trial;

- verdict against the clear weight of the evidence;

- verdict resulting from passion or prejudice;

- inadequate damages award;

- excessive damages award;

- newly discovered evidence that justifies new trial; or

- available state law grounds for obtaining a new trial in cases where state law controls.

While JAML after trial is rarely granted, new trials sometimes are.

EXAMPLES & ANALYSIS

EXAMPLE: Return again to our contract squabble between Pen and Deller. Assume that Pen obtains a verdict in the amount of $2,000 and moves for a new trial. Assume as well that during closing argument, Deller's lawyer referred to Pen as "the magician's version of Hitler" who "bounced checks like he was Bernie Madoff [an infamous swindler]. Assume as well that the judge instructed the jury to "award an amount you think is commensurate with the character of the parties to the lawsuit" and also observed that "he has known and admired" Deller "since we were in Little League together," and Deller "saved my infant son from drowning." Pen moves for a new trial. What result?

Analysis: Pen will almost certainly get a new trial, particularly if the errors are viewed in totality rather than in isolation. First, the judge should probably have disqualified himself from the case. *See* 28 U.S.C. § 455(a) and ABA Model Rule of Judicial Conduct 2.11(a).

Unless the judge disclosed his partiality toward Deller and Pen's counsel waived further argument on the point, this would appear to require re-doing the trial in front of an impartial judge.

In addition, the closing argument of Deller's counsel was not only improper but so vividly prejudicial as to prompt most judges to grant a new trial. However, if Pen's counsel failed to make a timely objection (which would have allowed the judge to admonish Deller's counsel

> Section 455(a) and Rule 2.11(a) provide that a judge should recuse (a synonym for disqualify) himself where the judge's ability to be impartial is subject to reasonable question. In addition, these rules require disqualification if the judge or a family member has financial ties to a party or investments that could be impacted by the outcome of a case.

and issue a curative instruction; *see* Ch. 17), many courts would find this ground for new trial waived, although many others would regard improper closing argument of this type as such "plain error" that it requires a new trial even in the absence of a timely objection.

The award of $2,000 is so low as to suggest an inadequate award that makes the verdict against the clear weight of the evidence. Even Deller's expert witness (Dr. Value) thought that $25,000 was the ballpark value of Pen's magician's equipment. Where the jury awards less than 10 percent of the defense estimation of value, this would appear to support a new trial—although one perhaps limited only to the fair, non-unconscionable value of the gear that was "sold." But, as you learn in Contracts class, generally contracts are enforceable as agreed even if one of the parties made a bad deal, so long as it was not an unconscionable deal. Thus, if there was ironclad evidence of a $200,000 sales agreement, anything less than this could be viewed by the court as an inadequate award or a ground for JAML, depending on the clarity of the record. Similarly, a $2 million award in Pen's favor would almost certainly not withstand either a Rule 59 new trial attack or a Rule 50 JAML attack.

E. Motions to Amend Findings

Rule 52(b) permits a party to move the court to amend findings of fact and conclusions of law made in a bench trial. The rule specifically provides that the motion may be coupled with a Rule 59 new trial motion. At the outset, one should differentiate between these various motions. As previously discussed, a Rule 59 new trial motion may be made after either a jury or a bench trial. A Rule 59(e) motion to alter or amend a judgment can also be made after either a jury or a bench trial. A Rule 52(b) motion to alter or amend findings of fact can be made only after a bench trial or where the trial court is entering factual findings and is similar to a Rule 59(e) motion.

> ## THE RULE   Rule 52(b)
>
> ### Findings and Conclusions by the Court;
> ### Judgment on Partial Findings
>
> * * *
>
> **(b) Amended or Additional Findings**. On a party's motion filed no later than 28 days after the entry of judgment, the court may amend its findings—or make additional findings—and may amend the judgment accordingly. The motion may accompany a motion for a new trial under Rule 59.

Motions for amended findings are important for correcting certain types of error: findings of the trial court that contain factual errors that prejudice the party on appeal or in subsequent litigation. A Rule 52(b) motion may also be useful where the court's findings of fact include gratuitous conclusions adverse to a party but not material to the adjudication of the dispute. A timely motion to delete or amend the objectionable material should be made even in cases where no motion for a new trial is made. In these circumstances, the Rule 52(b) motion can be very helpful and should be promptly.

EXAMPLES & ANALYSIS

EXAMPLE: Past Prime Fruit Co. supplied grapes to Dead Head Wineries for making their bulk wine. Past Prime and Dead Head had a written contract they had made at the outset of their relationship. After three years of satisfactory business transactions, Dead Head started to complain about the grapes supplied by Past Prime, about the timeliness of deliveries, and the failure of Past Prime to certify that the grapes were grown in pesticide-free plantings. (The parties' contract did not specify pesticide-free grapes, but Past Prime had occasionally supplied grapes with that certification.) The parties' relationship deteriorated as Dead Head ceased payments to Past Prime and increased its complaints about the product delivered. Past Prime ultimately sued under the UCC and for breach of contract. Dead Head counterclaimed for damages for lost sales and complaints about its wine's trace contamination with a banned pesticide. The parties agreed to a trial to the court, and following a five-day trial, the court entered findings of fact and ordered judgment for Past Prime on its claim and the counterclaim. Dead Head believes the trial was unfair because of several evidence rulings, including the exclusion of its experts on the importance of pesticide-free certification and on its counterclaim damages. Additionally, Dead Head believes that there was no evidence to support the judge's findings that it had accepted the deliveries, and that the grapes were of sufficient quality to comply with the parties' contract. What motions might it want to bring?

Analysis: Dead Head's complaints about the evidence rulings could require a new trial, as they cannot be remedied by modification or reversal of the judgment. Its objections to the court's findings could be made by a motion for amended findings. To the extent it has an argument that there is no evidence to support the court's findings, it should also (if it has preserved it by an earlier motion), renew its JAML motion. In practice, it would want to bring a single "Motion for Judgment as a Matter of Law, or in the Alternative, for Amended Findings or for a New Trial." It covers all its grounds and seeks all the relief it might expect to receive.

F. Motions by the Victor

A party who prevails in the trial may want to seek additional relief. These motions are not required for appellate review, but if the relief is sought, the motion must be filed or the relief will not be available. These motions can broadly be viewed in three categories:

1. Motions seeking additional relief, such as motions seeking to tax costs and disbursements, or to award attorneys' fees or prejudgment interest.

2. Motions seeking to correct rulings that the moving party may be planning to appeal.

3. Motions seeking correction of rulings that are *too favorable*. These motions do not arise often, but there are occasions where the court may have awarded a remedy the party does not want to have to justify on appeal.

The rules apply to prevailing parties as well as the vanquished—if a party seeks to raise some issues on appeal, even as a cross-appeal, a post-trial motion may be necessary in order to have the best chance of prevailing on it.

This relief might include the "taxation" of costs, the award of attorneys' fees, and for the award of pre-judgment interest.

1. Taxation of Costs

A prevailing party is normally permitted to recover its costs and disbursements. Rule 54(d) of the Federal Rules of Civil Procedure permits the prevailing litigant to tax certain costs and disbursements against the defeated party unless the court directs otherwise or unless a statute or rule expressly prohibits the taxation of costs. Because of sovereign immunity, costs may be taxed against the United States only when expressly permitted by statute.

Taxation of costs is frequently not a matter of major concern to the parties because of the small amounts involved in "taxable" costs. Unless there is a special statute, counsel fees and other substantial items of litigation expense are not recoverable as taxable costs. The reality of taxation of costs, because of the limits on what may be recovered, is that taxation often does not justify the cost incurred in contesting taxation issues. In many cases, the winner may seek costs only to waive them in exchange for the defeated party's agreement not to appeal. Even without such agreements, there frequently is no opposition from the defeated party when costs are taxed.

The statute governing costs in federal court creates several limited categories of expense that may be recovered by a prevailing party. These categories invariably include only a fraction of the total costs incurred and most often do not include attorneys' fees.

THE STATUTE   28 U.S.C. § 1920

Taxation of Costs

A judge or clerk of any court of the United States may tax as costs the following:

(1) Fees of the clerk and marshal;

(2) Fees for printed or electronically recorded transcripts necessarily obtained for use in the case;

(3) Fees and disbursements for printing and witnesses;

(4) Fees for exemplification and the costs of making copies of any materials where the copies are necessarily obtained for use in the case;

(5) Docket fees under section 1923 of this title;

(6) Compensation of court appointed experts, compensation of interpreters, and salaries, fees, expenses, and costs of special interpretation services under section 1828 of this title.

    A bill of costs shall be filed in the case and, upon allowance, included in the judgment or decree.

To avoid confusion, one must distinguish between the various terms used to describe financial outlays related to litigation. "Expenses" include all funds expended by the litigant in connection with the case. "Fees" are funds paid to the court for particular charges, such as filing fees. These fees are usually defined by statute. "Costs" are the funds spent by the prevailing party that may be recovered from the opponent. Fees are almost always recoverable as costs, while many expenses are not recoverable. Taxation of fees and other items of expense are governed by general litigation costs statutes, specific statutes, common law rules, the facts of the case, the ability of the parties to pay, and the court's discretion. In *Marx v. General Revenue Corp.,*133 S. Ct. 1166, (2013), the Court held that a statute that allows the award of costs and fees for bad faith litigation does not limit the court's discretion to award costs without regard to bad faith.

If a statute provides for recovery of attorney's fees explicitly as costs, offers of judgment under Fed. R. Civ. P. 68 may affect recovery of fees as well. *See Marek v. Chesny*, 473 U.S. 1 (1985).

Costs involving interpreters and the costs of electronic scanning and imaging may be recoverable as "copies of papers" permitted by 29 U.S.C. § 1920. The cost of a litigation database and electronic evidence presentation at trial may also be taxable, although there is hardly a consensus on these extensions of the statutory language.

All of these categories are subject to the court's discretion to allow or deny costs, and each has been the subject of many decisions determining what is included within its ambit. A few decisions deal with numerous categories in a single case, and they may be particularly helpful in understanding the views of judges on various categories of costs.

Absent from the list of recoverable costs is any mention of attorney's fees. The exclusion is not an oversight but rather reflects the embodiment of the American rule, whereby each party normally bears its own attorney's fees regardless of the outcome of the case. Many states allow recovery of similar categories of costs. The amount of recoverable witness fees is limited currently by 28 U.S.C. § 1821(b) to $40 per day per witness, and this figure applies to taxation of expert witness fees as well.

EXAMPLES & ANALYSIS

EXAMPLE: In the earlier example, Past Prime seeks to recover as costs the following expenses it incurred:

- Costs of eight depositions taken in the case; one of which was read at trial in lieu of live testimony, two of which were used in the cross-examination of Dead Head's witnesses.

- Costs of bringing witnesses to the trial, including two employees and one former employee.

- Cost of daily transcript used by the lawyers, but not read in court nor provided to the judge.

- Subpoena and witness fees for 31 witnesses, 4 of whom were actually called to testify at trial.

- Charges for copying 11,240 pages of exhibits, including copies for the court, Past Prime, and opposing counsel.

- The cost of 140 graphic poster boards illustrating the wine-making process, the unpaid invoices at issue, and Past Prime's demands for payment.

- The costs of five expert witnesses, two of which did not testify because of the court's rulings excluding Dead Head's witnesses.

Which of these costs will it recover?

Analysis: None of these items will necessarily be recovered in the amount sought or the amount incurred. Past Prime can only recover the *reasonable amount* of its expenses, and then only if they were *reasonably incurred*. The likely rulings on the specific items will be discretionary with the court, and may well depend on the court's assessment of the need for them.

• Certainly the cost of the four depositions used at trial should be recovered. But the test does not require use at trial, only that they be necessarily incurred for use in the case. The judge might conclude that all the depositions fit that test, so they might be recoverable.

• The travel costs of witnesses at trial may be recoverable, and courts would be particularly inclined to award these costs of the non-party witness (the former employee).

• The daily transcript cost would be recovered if the judge thought it necessary for the case; in many cases the daily transcript would be view as a "luxury," and would not be taxed.

• Subpoena and witness fees for 4 of the 31 witnesses would nearly automatically be recovered—they were actual witnesses at trial. The remaining 27 would be more doubtful, but the court would again assess the reasonableness of arranging for them to appear if needed.

• Copying charges for exhibits are recoverable. Unless the court found the exhibits clearly irrelevant, duplicative, or similarly frivolous, the reasonable cost would be recoverable. The answer for the "blow-ups" would be essentially the same.

• Expert witness fees are regularly recovered as "fees for witnesses." These fees may be substantial, but if experts are reasonably needed to prove or rebut the claims in the case, the prevailing party will recover them. If reasonably incurred, the fact that they were made unnecessary by a ruling to exclude the other side's expert does not make them not reasonably incurred.

2. Recovery of Attorneys' Fees

In many cases, the most important post-trial motion is a request for an award of attorneys' fees. In a majority of these cases, attorneys' fees are not recoverable because there is no statutory, contractual, or common law basis for recovery. As a general rule in the United States, counsel fees are not recoverable in the absence of such a specific basis. *See Alyeska Pipeline Serv. Co. v. Wilderness Soc'y*, 421 U.S. 240 (1975). This rule is known as the "American Rule." An exception to this statement is contained in the federal bad-faith litigation statute, 28 U.S.C. § 1927, and in similar state statutes.

Rule 54(d)(2) requires that where attorneys' fees are sought, the requesting party must file a motion. If the basis for attorneys's fees is a substantive part of the claim, the request for fees may have to be made as part of the proof at trial. An example of this would be a claim for fees in a breach-of-contract case involving a contract that provides for recovery of attorney's fees against a party breaching the contract.

EXAMPLES & ANALYSIS

EXAMPLE: Prime Properties leases commercial space to Deluxe Development. The lease includes a provision for Prime to recover reasonable attorneys' in the event Deluxe fails to pay any monthly rent payment by the fifth of the month in which it is due. Deluxe falls months behind in paying its rent, resulting in a suit by Prime. Prime claims its four months' overdue rent, and seeks to terminate the lease as is provided as a remedy in the event of default. After the court grants Prime a default judgment following Deluxe's failure to appear in the case, it enters judgment for the total of four months' rent. Eight days later Prime files a motion to tax its costs, and for its attorneys' fees. Can it recover its fees pursuant to contract?

Analysis: The motion to tax costs is timely, but the request for fees probably is not. Contractual fees typically have to be proven as part of the damages proof. Failure to submit them to the court as part of the default judgment proof may be fatal to the recovery of fees.

Attorney fees may also be recovered under certain well-defined and long-standing judicial doctrines. Some of these exceptions are quite narrow in scope, while others have broader application.

Four important common law exceptions of general application are:

1. *The common-fund exception.* This exception applies when a plaintiff succeeds in obtaining through litigation a common fund in which others who did not actively prosecute the case may share, the litigant has established a "common fund" and may receive an award for fees. This exception is intended to prevent the entire group from "free-riding" on the actions of one member at that one member's expense. Each party is required to share the expenses of creating the fund on a basis proportionate to its share of the fund.

2. *The common-benefit exception.* This exception is similar to the common-fund exception, but it does not require the creation of a fund. It is enough that the plaintiff achieves a litigation result that brings common benefit to an identifiable group. Both the common-fund and the common-benefit exceptions are relied on in class actions to permit class counsel to recover fees.

3. *The contempt exception.* Courts have historically permitted the award of fees to a litigant who obtains a contempt order against an opposing party. The theoretical basis for this exception is that the party has vindicated the court's authority by directing its attention to the contemptuous conduct. Fees awarded under this exception may be awarded at the time the contempt order is entered and need not await the conclusion of the litigation. Similarly, the party obtaining the contempt order is permitted to recover fees even if it is not ultimately the prevailing party.

4. *The bad-faith exception.* The bad-faith exception to the American rule permits the court to award the expenses of litigation to a party who has endured litigation brought or defended in bad faith by an adversary.

This exception may be invoked on an interlocutory basis, although it is more frequently relied on at the conclusion of litigation. This exception has been in part codified by 28 U.S.C. § 1927, although that statute permits the award of fees against an attorney who "multiplies" the proceedings in a lawsuit, while the common law exception applies to the parties to the suit.

Courts may find constructive bad faith when an action is "frivolous" (usually defined as being devoid of arguable rationale) and award counsel fees as a sanction. This can occur for either the entire case or only a portion of it. Increasingly, courts have been willing to apply this basis to pro se litigants, who in the past were considered nearly exempt from procedural punishment.

The statutory and common law exceptions to the American rule are available only to a "prevailing party" in the litigation. Although the "winner" may be easily identified in some cases and situations, in others more than one party may claim that status. In class actions, in cases seeking fees on the common-benefit exception, and in cases that settled subject to the parties seeking a fee award, determining the "prevailing party" may be difficult.

EXAMPLES & ANALYSIS

EXAMPLE: If the litigation results in changes beneficial to the plaintiffs but not sought directly in the action, have the plaintiffs prevailed? If the plaintiffs achieve success in small part on one of many claims, have they prevailed?

Analysis: If the plaintiffs achieve success in small part on one of many claims, have they prevailed? Most courts have applied a liberal definition of victory in order to give full effect to the public policy underlying the attorney's fees exceptions, particularly in civil rights cases and class actions. Certainly obtaining meaningful relief caused by the litigation should be treated as a "success," even if economic relief was not accomplished.

G. Motions to Reduce Award or Increase Award

In some cases, a party will have a fundamental disagreement with the amount of damages awarded by the jury. The losing party may insist that the award is excessive, or the prevailing party may assert that the jury (or the judge in a bench trial) did not make a sufficient award of damages. "There's a motion for that," to paraphrase the electronics ad, though it is neither a straightforward nor simple matter.

The procedure for seeking a reduction in a jury award is simple, just not straight forward. The aggrieved litigant cannot merely move for reduction; instead, it must move for a new trial motion (within the strict 28—day limits of Rule 59) and move that the grant of a new trial be accompanied by remittitur, whereby the court gives the prevailing party the option of accepting a reduced judgment or having the motion for new trial granted. The relief may be imposed on the court's own initiative, though it rarely is.

> **Remittitur** is the name given for reduction of a verdict if the amount awarded is grossly excessive as a matter of law.

Remittitur is not specifically provided for in the federal rules or statutes, although some states specifically provide for it. The relief has common law roots approved by the Supreme Court as early as the 1800s. *See Northern Pac. R.R. v. Herbert*, 116 U.S. 642 (1886). When last extensively discussed by the Court more than seventy-five years ago, the Court concluded that remittitur was constitutional, since it gave the verdict winner the option of accepting reduced damages or proceeding with a second trial, thus preserving the litigant's jury trial options under the Seventh Amendment. *See Dimick v. Schiedt*, 293 U.S. 474 (1935).

> **Additur** is the process for directing that, as a matter of law, the amount recovered be increased from the amount awarded by a jury.

Additur, relief giving the verdict loser the option of either accepting an increase in the damage award or proceeding with a new trial, has a somewhat different status.

Additur was held to violate the Seventh Amendment on the theory that it is permissible to allow the court to select an award figure that reduces a jury award, since the jury award at least establishes the outer limits of the award. Since judicial increase to a jury award is theoretically boundless, however, it is held to compromise the right to jury trial, even though the party faced with additur may opt for the new trial. *See Dimick v. Schiedt,* 293 U.S. 474 (1935). The different approaches to increasing and diminishing a jury's verdict do not appear to have a solid foundation in logic, but despite the Supreme Court's longstanding, if somewhat tortured, pronouncement that additur is not permitted under the Seventh Amendment, it is the current law. Some states permit additur, and this has never been held to violate the U.S. Constitution.

Remittitur is not a proper tool to address verdicts resulting from passion or prejudice, since the passion or prejudice that produced the inflated jury award may have also caused the decision on liability. In that circumstance, a court, having found a verdict resulting from passion or prejudice, must grant a new trial without the remittitur option. *See Minneapolis, St. P. & S.S.M. R.R. v. Moquin,* 283 U.S. 520 (1931).

IN PRACTICE

If the court orders a remittitur, the verdict winner has a choice: accept the lower amount or proceed with a new trial. If the victor prevails in the second trial, it may accept this verdict or appeal the judgment, contending that the court erred in granting the new trial and remittitur in the first place or that the remittitur offered was unreasonably low. If the remittitur is accepted, the verdict winner must file a statement accepting the remittitur and consenting to a reduction in the jury award with the clerk of court within the time provided by the court's remitter order.

H. Motions to Amend Findings

Rule 52(b) permits a party to move the court to amend findings of fact and conclusions of law made in a bench trial. The rule specifically provides that the motion may be coupled with a Rule 59 new trial motion. At the outset, one should differentiate between these various motions. As previously discussed, a Rule 59 new trial motion may be made after either a jury or a bench trial. A Rule 59(e) motion to alter or amend a judgment can also be made after either a jury or a bench trial. A Rule 52(b) motion to alter or amend findings of fact can be made only after a bench trial and is similar to a Rule 59(e) motion.

These motions must be served and filed within 28 days of the entry of judgment in federal court, and in a similarly short time period in most state court proceedings. A motion made under Rule 52(b) must, in fact, seek alteration of the judgment or amendment of the findings of fact and cannot properly seek a new trial or the functional equivalent of a new trial under the guise of seeking amendment of the court's findings of fact. An appellate court reviews the Rule 52 initial or amended findings of fact under the clearly erroneous standard and reviews Rule 52 initial or amended conclusions of law under the de novo standard.

So what does Rule 52(b) offer? The candid answer is not that much, at least as far as the basic verdict is concerned. If counsel is dissatisfied with the decision or the merits of the judgment in a bench trial, he or she should seek a new trial rather than amendment of the findings. However, if the court's findings contain factual errors that prejudice the verdict loser on appeal or in subsequent litigation, the Rule 52(b) motion can be very helpful and should be promptly made because most courts do not treat these types of mistakes as justifying relief pursuant to Rule 60(b).

EXAMPLES & ANALYSIS

EXAMPLE: In a patent infringement case tried to the court, the court may render a decision finding infringement and then applying an improper method of computing damages and performing the accounting due the verdict winner.

Analysis: Since the method used by the court is challenged as wrong, the findings should be challenged immediately by a Rule 52(b) or 59(e) motion (or by both, in the alternative) rather than a later Rule 60(a) motion to correct clerical mistakes. In a variant of this example, the court might have correctly calculated the arithmetic of damages but might have begun its calculation six months too early (or too late), resulting in an erroneous damages figure.

IN PRACTICE

A victor may also want to use a Rule 52(b) motion to correct erroneous or problematic findings. For example, findings might include gratuitous conclusions adverse to a party but not material to the adjudication of the dispute. A timely motion to delete or amend the objectionable material should be made even in cases where no motion for a new trial is made. Ordinarily an appellate court will not be interested enough to rule on such extraneous negative commentary unless the aggrieved party was sufficiently upset to have made a timely motion to amend findings. However, if counsel wishes to point to the court's gratuitous remarks on appeal as indicating prejudice by the court, forgoing the Rule 52 motion may not be wise.

I. Relief from Final Judgments and Orders

Rule 60 provides a mechanism for obtain relief from certain orders or judgments. Motions under this rule differ from other post-verdict motions because they are not so routinely brought and are not required to obtain appellate review. More important, they serve a broader purpose and are not subject to the same strict time limits applied to the motions discussed above. They allow relief from orders as well as judgments.

Trial courts have authority to provide relief from their own judgments and orders. Rule 60 provides two important categories of the relief available. Rule 60(a) allows relief from clerical errors, while Rule 60(b) allows the court to correct a much broader range of errors or defects. Importantly, both rules may be available even after the time to appeal from the order or judgment has passed.

A motion for relief from a judgment or order is most often used in three broad classes of situations: (1) when a clerical error has been made in the final order or judgment, (2) when default or a default judgment has been entered, or (3) when post-judgment events have occurred or are learned of.

Fed. R. Civ. P. 60 lists many of the grounds that may permit the court to vacate an order or judgment-clerical error, mistake, inadvertence, surprise, and excusable neglect, newly discovered evidence, fraud, misrepresentation, or other misconduct of a party, void, satisfied, or in some other way invalid judgment; or any other reason justifying relief. In addition, Fed. R. Civ. P. 55(e) provides grounds for relief from a default judgment.

1. Clerical Errors

Courts readily allow relief from clerical errors. Fed. R. Civ. P. 60(a) permits the court to correct clerical errors at any time and allows this action to be taken upon the motion of a party or on the court's own initiative.

> Courts often refer to actions taken without prodding from the parties as being taken "**sua sponte.**" "On the court's own initiative" seems just as clear, even though written in plain English rather than Latin. "On the court's own motion" is sometimes used, but it seems a bit less precise, as the court doesn't really bring a motion to itself.

If the district court elects to make a correction on its own initiative, it is not required to give notice to the parties or hold a hearing, though most courts would give notice to all parties of any correction, especially if it is based on matters outside the record.

THE RULE — Rule 60(a)

Relief from a Judgment or Order

(a) **Corrections Based on Clerical Mistakes; Oversights and Omissions.** The court may correct a clerical mistake or a mistake arising from oversight or omission whenever one is found in a judgment, order, or other part of the record. The court may do so on motion or on its own, with or without notice. But after an appeal has been docketed in the appellate court and while it is pending, such a mistake may be corrected only with the appellate court's leave.

Even if a notice of appeal has been filed, which would normally divest the court of jurisdiction, the court retains the authority to correct clerical errors until the appeal is docketed at the court of appeals (a date that varies among circuits but often can be one to two weeks after the filing of the notice of appeal). Thereafter, the parties or the trial court may seek, and usually readily obtain, leave of the court of appeals to have the district court correct the clerical error prior to decision on appeal.

Courts liberally correct clerical errors. The policy of liberality in correcting clerical error continues at the appellate level. Fed. R. App. P. 10(e) permits the court of appeals broad discretion to correct an error, to seek a stipulation of the parties to correct the error, or to remand for the limited purpose of correcting the error or determining if an error was made.

Disputes often arise as to what constitutes "clerical error." Having a clerk involved certainly militates in favor of that finding, but Rule 60(a) applies to more than mere arithmetic and typographical errors. It has been used to correct arithmetic mistakes, the misnaming of parties, errors in taxation of costs, the rate and period for recovery of interest, and the entitlement to attorney's fees. Clarification of an earlier ruling to implement the actual intent at the time of the ruling is also possible, even if the omission is not made by clerical staff. Motions under Fed. R. Civ. P. 60(a) may also be used to add evidence inadvertently omitted from the record on appeal and to amend a judgment or verdict to conform it to the jury's intent.

Rule 60(a) cannot be stretched to obtain reconsideration of matters or to make substantive changes in the final order. It may be used only to make the order reflect what was actually intended when it was rendered. If counsel seeks to change the substantive impact of the order or judgment, relief needs to be sought under Fed. R. Civ. P. 60(b) or, where appropriate, in a separate action.

Correction of clerical error is available under Rule 60(a) to correct error in any order or judgment, whether final or not. Relief from an order or a judgment on the other grounds permitted by Rule 60(b) is available only for final orders or judgments.

Fed. R. Civ. P. 60(b) sets forth six grounds for obtaining relief from a final order, judgment, or proceeding. These grounds cover a wide variety of circumstances, but all go to the validity of the judgment or order and that would have dictated a contrary result had they been known to the court before the judgment was entered or the order made.

THE RULE   Rule 60(b)

(b) Grounds for Relief from a Final Judgment, Order, or Proceeding.

On motion and just terms, the court may relieve a party or its legal representative from a final judgment, order, or proceeding for the following reasons:

(1) mistake, inadvertence, surprise, or excusable neglect;

(2) newly discovered evidence that, with reasonable diligence, could not have been discovered in time to move for a new trial under Rule 59(b);

(3) fraud (whether previously called intrinsic or extrinsic), misrepresentation, or misconduct by an opposing party;

(4) the judgment is void;

(5) the judgment has been satisfied, released, or discharged; it is based on an earlier judgment that has been reversed or vacated; or applying it prospectively is no longer equitable; or

(6) any other reason that justifies relief.

A motion based on any of these grounds is directed to the discretion of the court. Not surprisingly, the moving party has the burden to establish that these factors have established. In addition to showing the existence of one of these factors, in order to obtain relief from a final judgment or order the movant must make a showing of timeliness, a meritorious defense, lack of unfair prejudice to the opposing party, and exceptional circumstances. (These are additional requirements for a successful Rule 60 motion that have been created by court decisions and are not contained in the rule).

IN PRACTICE

A court may treat a motion labeled as something other than a Rule 60 motion as a Rule 60 motion. An untimely motion to amend a judgment, or for amended findings, may be considered a Rule 60 motion for relief from a judgment. This provides a useful option—if one with limited prospects—to seek relief when the time for anything else has passed.

2. Grounds for Motion

Because Rule 60(b) sets forth six different sets of grounds for relief, and because the time limits for bringing motions for each vary, it is important to understand at least the broad outlines of the six grounds. There are hundreds of reported decisions on these motions, so it is usually quite possible to find precedent that matches closely the facts of a particular case.

3. Mistake, Inadvertence, Surprise, and Excusable Neglect [Rule 60(b)(1)]

A party may avoid a judgment or final order on the grounds of mistake, inadvertence, surprise, or excusable neglect under Fed. R. Civ. P. 60(b)(1). To do so the movant must establish that the mistake was understandable or even excusable. Courts are particularly vigilant to deny relief from a party's tactical decisions. The court will not be interested in providing parties with relief from strategic decisions that prove, in retrospect, ill-advised. Although most Rule 60(b)(1) motions involve mistakes made by the losing litigant, mistakes by the court are also potential grounds for relief.

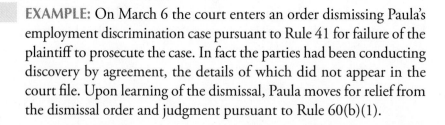

EXAMPLES & ANALYSIS

EXAMPLE: On March 6 the court enters an order dismissing Paula's employment discrimination case pursuant to Rule 41 for failure of the plaintiff to prosecute the case. In fact the parties had been conducting discovery by agreement, the details of which did not appear in the court file. Upon learning of the dismissal, Paula moves for relief from the dismissal order and judgment pursuant to Rule 60(b)(1).

Analysis: Because the order is predicted on a mistaken understanding of the status of the case on the part of the judge, it is likely this motion would be granted. If the parties had failed to follow direction from the court to advise it of the status of discovery, or had otherwise contributed to the court's misunderstanding, the result might well be different.

4. Newly Discovered Evidence [Rule 60(b)(2)]

Fed. R. Civ. P. 60(b)(2) permits the court to grant relief from a judgment or an order on the basis of newly discovered evidence, but only for evidence that "with reasonable diligence could not have been discovered in time to move for a new trial under Rule 59(b)." This may sound familiar from the discussion of the motion for a new trial. It should, as the standards governing relief because of newly discovered evidence are the same under Rule 59(b) and Rule 60(b)(1).

The moving party has an uphill fight under this section of the rule, and must show: (1) that there exists "new" evidence, not merely evidence that supplements that already in the record; (2) that the evidence, if it had been presented prior to judgment, would have likely affected the outcome of the case; and (3) that this new evidence could not have been discovered in time through due diligence. The new evidence need not be so compelling that it would certainly have changed the result, but a reasonable probability that the new evidence would have had effect is necessary. Courts stringently assess whether the moving party is raising an issue that would have been avoided with due diligence before or during trial. The courts do not view this as a free-pass for a "do-over" for the losing party, and certainly to not allow it to be a means for relief from ill-advised tactical decisions.

EXAMPLES & ANALYSIS

EXAMPLE: Debra is sued for negligence in causing a simple car accident. The lawyers for the parties agree to forgo discovery in order to obtain an early trial date. After lengthy deliberations, the jury returns a record verdict for the plaintiff. Because of the record verdict and the ensuing newspaper coverage of the otherwise-mundane case, an eyewitness to the accident stepped forward about two months later, and ultimately contacted Debra's lawyer. The eyewitness stated that she saw that Debra had had a green light, and that the plaintiff's light was red and had been red for several seconds before the accident. Debra moves for relief from the judgment pursuant to Rule 60(b)(2) on the basis of the newly-discovered witness.

Analysis: Most courts would find this evidence is new and would have had a sufficient likelihood of changing the outcome. This motion will turn on the factual support for the claim that the defense couldn't have located it with more effort. The key will be for Debra to establish that the new-found witness could not have been located—and preferably that there had been an effort to locate any eyewitnesses to the accident. The defense attorney's establishing that she was instructed by the insurer to keep costs down would not be helpful. The agreement to forgo discovery is a problem to overcome, but it is not clear that anyone knew of this witness, so that decision might have had no impact on the court because discovery would not have turned up the witness's name. It does suggest that the case was not vigorously prepared.

5. Fraud, Misrepresentation, and Other Misconduct [Rule 60(b)(3)]

> **Intrinsic fraud** is fraud perpetrated by the parties against each other that the litigation process should, at least theoretically, unearth; extrinsic fraud is fraud that prevents a party from raising a claim or defense, as when one is tricked into letting the statute of limitations expire.

Rule 60(b)(3) permits the court to relieve a party of the burden of an order or a judgment where fraud, misrepresentation, or other misconduct exists. The rule rejects any distinction between intrinsic and extrinsic fraud, a basis for distinguishing fraud that historically generated many cases and little certainty.

Courts have historically recognized the inherent power of the courts to vacate judgments procured through fraud. *See Hazel-Atlas Glass Co. v. Hartford–Empire Co.*, 322 U.S. 238 (1944). This inherent power of the courts is restated in Rule 60(b)(3), but is not limited by the rule. Thus, even if relief is not available under the rule, the court may entertain a separate action for relief on the grounds of the fraud. A motion for relief from a judgment based on fraud may be made anytime if the alleged fraud is on the court, but must be made within one year after the judgment becomes final if the alleged fraud is fraud on the opposing party.

Fraud under this rule must be shown by clear and convincing evidence. Although misrepresentation and misconduct would normally have to be proved merely by a preponderance of the evidence, the respect for finality of judgments requires their proof by clear and convincing evidence in an attack on the judgment. As with any Rule 60 motion, the court may exercise its discretion to determine both whether the bad conduct has been adequately proven and whether the wrongful conduct is sufficient to invalidate the judgment attacked.

6. Void Judgment [Rule 60(b)(4)]

Rule 60(b)(4) allows a party to obtain relief from a void judgment. A void judgment is one entered by the court without authority or jurisdiction. Since subject matter jurisdiction cannot be waived, this rule is available to attack a federal judgment which is void. Constitutional infirmity of any court's decision regarding personal jurisdiction is difficult to establish if the court takes any reasonable steps to provide notice and a hearing. A merely erroneous judgment, no matter how ignorant a view of the law it may embody, is not void.

If jurisdictional questions are submitted to the court and decided, even erroneously, or if the party attacking the judgment had an opportunity to contest jurisdiction but failed to do so, the court's determination of jurisdiction is either res judicata or law of the case and cannot be set aside. *See Durfee v. Duke*, 375 U.S. 106 (1963).

Motions for relief from void judgments are different from other Rule 60 motions in two significant ways. First, the rule is completely nondiscretionary. If the judgment is void, it must be vacated. Second, there is no time limit for this motion. Although the rule appears to require the motion to be brought within a "reasonable time," the motion should be granted whenever brought, again provided that vacating the judgment does not disturb substantial and legitimate reliance interests.

7. Satisfaction or Release of Judgment or Change of Underlying Judgment [Rule 60(b)(5)]

Fed. R. Civ. P. 60(b)(5) permits the court to vacate judgments when the judgment attacked has been satisfied, released, or discharged or when the prospective application of the judgment is no longer equitable. This ground would exist if a judgment were entered in one district and docketed in another. If the first judgment were modified by the court in any way or if it were paid or released, then the judgment derived from it would be subject to vacation or similar modification.

These provisions relate to "prior judgments" in the case or related cases and not to legal precedent in unrelated cases that has been reversed or modified since the judgment attacked was rendered. However, a change in mandatory precedent that is given retrospective application may constitute grounds for relief pursuant to Rule 60(b)(6) (other grounds when justice requires). Although retroactivity normally accompanies a judicial change in the law, courts are unlikely to race to disturb judgments more than one year old.

The most frequent ground for motions under Rule 60(b)(5) is a change in circumstances that makes continued prospective application of the judgment unfair. New legislation, change in case law, and change in the underlying facts are the most frequently successful bases for obtaining Rule 60(b)(5) relief. An example would be the destruction by fire of a prison for which the state was under court order to maintain minimum staff ratios. The historical basis for the rule is the court's inherent equitable power to modify judgments so that they will not become unfair, superfluous, or wasteful due to changed circumstances. However, once again, the interest in finality requires that the party attacking the judgment demonstrate by a "strong showing" (presumably by clear and convincing evidence) that the changed circumstances justify relief from prospective application of the judgment. The mere passage of time is not enough.

Consent decrees are judgments that may need to be modified or vacated after a period of time elapses. On a motion to modify a consent decree, the court must determine: (1) whether the provision sought to be modified is central to the basic purpose of the decree and thus forbidden; and (2) if not, whether significant changes in the circumstances warrant revision of the decree; and (3) if so, whether the proposed modification is suitably tailored to address the changed circumstances. Consent decrees typically have a reasonable life span depending on these factors.

8. Any Other Reason [Rule 60(b)(6)]

Operating as the last resort of the truly desperate, the Rule 60(b)(6) "catch-all provision" applies only if another section of Rule 60 does not provide relief. And it is often hard to find a reason that suffices. The rule gives courts the ability to grant post-judgment relief from a judgment or an order, without any time limitation. Although the rule seems boundless in its scope, courts have set strict limits on its use. The rule is there to provide justice in those unusual cases where substantial justice has been denied.

In order to use this section, the party must demonstrate a reason for failure to challenge the judgment on appeal or at an earlier time and must also establish inequity of the judgment attacked. As a general rule, a motion under Rule 60(b)(6) requires "something more" than a motion grounded on one of the other sections of Rule 60. Examples of successful motions under this section have involved misconduct by the court (certainly not the instant court), egregious blunders by counsel (always from another firm), incarceration (again, from another firm), incompetency (well, maybe down the hall), other factors preventing the party from taking earlier action (*e.g.*, long hunches), and retrospective changes to the applicable law. A court may also review a motion to dismiss based on a settlement agreement under this subsection of Rule 60.

9. Timing of Rule 60 Motions

The timing rules for Rule 60 motions are one of the things that makes the motion invaluable-relief under the rule may be available even after the time for other post-trial motions has passed and also after the time to appeal has passed. (The other distinguishing feature is the potential breadth of the motion, as discussed above.)

THE RULE   Rule 60(c) & (d)

(c) Timing and Effect of the Motion.

    (1) Timing. A motion under **Rule 60(b)** must be made within a reasonable time—and for reasons (1), (2), and (3) no more than a year after the entry of the judgment or order or the date of the proceeding.

    (2) Effect on Finality. The motion does not affect the judgment's finality or suspend its operation.

(d) Other Powers to Grant Relief. This rule does not limit a court's power to:

   (1) entertain an independent action to relieve a party from a judgment, order, or proceeding;

   (2) grant relief under **28 U.S.C. § 1655** to a defendant who was not personally notified of the action; or

   (3) set aside a judgment for fraud on the court.

Rule 60(c) establishes two timing rules for Rule 60 motions. Motions based on subdivisions (1), (2), or (3) of Rule 60(b), must be brought within a reasonable time and in any event not more than one year after the date the judgment was entered. Rule 60(b)(1), (2), or (3) motion brought any time within one year will be generally be timely, but some motions made within a year have been found to be unreasonably late. As is true in many aspects of litigation, moving forward as soon as the grounds for doing so emerge is a good idea. There is no fixed time limit for motions based on sections (4), (5), and (6), but these too must be brought within a reasonable time after judgment. Because there is no fixed time limit, the "reasonable time" requirement is more carefully considered by the court. Moving promptly can only be good.

One crucial feature that distinguishes Rule 60 motions from other post-trial motions is that the filing of a Rule 60 motion does not increase or "toll" the time for taking an appeal. Additionally, a Rule 60(b) motion may be made during the pendency of an appeal, despite the fact that the trial court would normally be divested of further jurisdiction.

IN PRACTICE

Although the establishment of deadlines in Rule 60(c) seems clear, in practice, courts have sometimes used fairly fluid definitions, labeling the ground for relief as something other than the most obvious. Motions for relief from judgments that are subject to the one-year limitations period cannot be disguised as motions with more generous limitations periods, but courts do occasionally allow that tactic to work.

Although motions for relief are generally addressed to the court that made the original decision, disappointed litigants with proper cause satisfying the Rule 60(b) grounds may also file an independent action for relief. Courts have generally required that the judgment from which relief is sought in an independent action be "manifestly unconscionable" before the judgment will be reopened.

J. Setting Aside Defaults and Vacating Default Judgments

If a party fails to appear in an action, a default will be ordered and a default judgment entered. Defaults and default judgments frequently cause motions for relief from orders and judgments. Consequently, once the order is entered, the only recourse available to the defaulted party is a motion for relief pursuant to Rules 55(c) and 60(b).

Rule 55 and default are discussed extensively in Chapter 7, as is default judgment. Rule 60 comes in if default judgment has been entered, requiring that the party seeking to vacate a default judgment satisfy both Rule 55 and meet one of the Rule 60 grounds for vacating a judgment. Setting aside the entry of a default may be available if good cause is shown. Fed. R. Civ. P. 55(c). If a default judgment has been entered, the judgment may be set aside or "vacated" pursuant to Rule 60(b).

Although appeal is another available way to attack a default judgment, assuming the party learns of the judgment while it is appealable, it is not entirely satisfactory. Since the defaulted party was not a part of the trial court proceedings, the record on appeal is unlikely to urge reversal. Appellate courts are generally not receptive to appeals raising issues that have not been presented to the trial court. Thus, relief from the default should usually be sought in the trial court.

Default occurs when a party obtains a decision that an opposing party has failed to appear in the action. A default is obtained by submitting proof to the clerk that the opposing party has "failed to plead or otherwise defend." Upon such a showing, the clerk must enter default in favor of the moving party. This default settles the liability issues of the case on the merits but is not a judgment. The default is not an adjudication of damages or other relief issues, and a judgment cannot be rendered until damages are proved. Following a default, a **default judgment** may be obtained in either of two ways. If the claim is for a "sum certain or for a sum which can be by computation made certain," the clerk may enter a default judgment. Rule 55(b)(1). Where the sum due is uncertain, a hearing or other fact-finding process is required. If the party against whom default is sought has appeared in the action, the moving party must give written notice of the application for default judgment.

Where a party seeks relief from a default judgment, Rule 60 is applied equitably and liberally to achieve substantial justice. In deciding whether relief is warranted in a motion for relief from default judgment, the three relevant factors are considered,

1) Whether the party seeking relief is culpable. A party's conduct is culpable to warrant the denial of a motion for relief from a default judgment if it displays either an intent to thwart judicial proceedings or a reckless disregard for the effect of its conduct on those proceedings.

2) Whether the party opposing relief will be prejudiced. The prejudice must be significant and not harmless, and the mere fact that it would lose its judgment is not sufficient.

3) Whether the party seeking relief has a meritorious claim or defense. A claim or defense is meritorious if there is some possibility that the outcome of the suit after a full trial will be contrary to the result achieved by the default. The test of merit is not the likelihood of success, but merely whether the claim or defense is sufficient at law.

A court may deny a Rule 60 motion if any one of the three factors is not present.

Counsel may attack a default judgment in two ways. First, the substance of the default may be challenged, showing that it was not properly granted. Second, the order or judgment can be attacked using the grounds contained in Rule 60(a) and (b). For example, Rule 60(b)(1) provides for setting aside a judgment on grounds of mistake. The first option is not normally available because it is not often that the opposing party fails to follow the rules concerning defaults (the rules are not complex, most lawyers manage to comply with them). If a claimant fails to give the three-day notice required by Fed. R. Civ. P. 55(c) when the defendant has appeared, the motion for relief will be granted.

IN PRACTICE

Although "appearance" normally requires the filing of an answer or a motion, for the purpose of attacking default judgments courts also require the three-day notice to be given to parties who have contacted the claimant, concluding that this constituted a constructive appearance, one at least sufficient to require notice. This is partly a rule of practicality—the court isn't really interested in entering a judgment by default only to have to decide a motion to vacate from a person who was in contact about the case and just hadn't formally appeared.

If the default judgment is properly entered, the movant must show the applicability of Rule 60(a) or (b) to obtain relief from the judgment. Defaults are disfavored, and a trial on the merits is strongly preferred by the courts. Thus, denial of a motion to set aside a default after the movant has established one of the grounds of Rule 60 is likely to be viewed as an abuse of discretion.

In addition to establishing that Rule 60 applies, the party seeking to set aside a default or default judgment must establish that there is a valid defense on the merits and that the claimant will not be substantially prejudiced by vacation of the default. The requirement of establishing a meritorious defense is obvious and may be accomplished by submitting a proposed answer with the motion. Some courts require that a proposed answer be submitted with the motion papers. Courts have little interest in permitting a party to avoid or even delay the inevitable result if it is, in fact, inevitable. The fact that the claimant will have to try the case on the merits, a burden inherent in vacating any default, is clearly, standing alone, insufficient prejudice to prevent vacating the default.

Additionally, if there are means to ameliorate the prejudice, the court will consider using them. For example, if the claimant incurred significant expense in obtaining the default, the court can require the payment of those expenses as a condition of vacating the default.

ADDITIONAL EXERCISES

1. Prickly sues Direct alleging defamation because Direct, when asked for Direct's opinion of Prickly by a potential employer, stated that Prickley "was a nice guy and very hard-working—but dumb as a brick." In his case-in-chief, Prickley calls Employer as a witness, who relates the conversation with Direct. On cross-examination, Employer admits that in spite of Direct's statement, Prickly was hired and that the "dumb as a brick" comment had no impact on the salary or benefits offered Prickly because the compensation package was set by corporate policy from the company's far-away home office. Direct moves for a Rule 50(a) JAML in his favor. **What result?**

2. Penny Widow sues Demon Trucking for the wrongful death of her late husband, who was mowed down by a Demon Truck while crossing the street to retrieve a whiffle ball hit out of the yard by their young son. Both the boy and Penny witnessed the collision, which killed the husband on impact. At trial, a Rob Lowe-lookalike spectator sits in the front row behind plaintiff counsel table every day and makes a point of exchanging pleasantries with Penny whenever possible, often while the jurors are still in the courtroom. Overcome by the weirdness of it all, plaintiff counsel conducts and investigation and discovers that the dashingly handsome spectator was hired by Demon Trucking's counsel. Plaintiff moves for a mistrial, which the judge denies because "the jury might render an award that will make plaintiff plenty happy" based on the facts of the collision and death. The jury returns with an award of $500,000. Penny's late husband was a 40-year-old doctor with average annual income of $250,000 per year. Penny moves for a new trial, contending that Demon's skullduggery impermissibly tainted the jury by trying to give the impression that Penny already had a handsome new beau and was not a particularly grieving widow. **What result?**

   (a) **What if Penny's counsel did not find out about the true nature of the courtroom spectator until after judgment had been entered?**

   (b) **What if Penny's counsel did not find out about the true nature of the courtroom spectator until two years after judgment was entered?**

3. Priest Paul Populist is an anti-war activist attempting to organize opposition to possible U.S. intervention in a country in the Middle East that is racked by civil war. District Attorney Dan Danger is concerned that Priest Paul may have potential terrorists in his organization and secretly tapes the group's meetings and taps the parish phone lines as well as Priest Paul's mobile phone. When this is discovered, Priest sues Dan, alleging a violation of the civil rights of all upon whom the DA eavesdropped. Dan moves for dismissal pursuant to Rule 12(b)(6) alleging absolute immunity as a prosecutor, which is denied. He then moves for summary judgment, again on the absolute immunity defense and also arguing that he is entitled to qualified immunity because the limits of wiretapping for national security purposes are not well-defined. Dan argues that even if the court ultimately rules the surveillance was constitutionally invalid that the law was nonetheless not clearly established at the time the surveillance was conducted. The court denies the summary judgment motion.

(a) After Priest Paul's case-in-chief, DA Dan moves for Rule 50(a), again asserting both immunity defenses. **What result?**

(b) Assume (rightly or wrongly) that the prior motion is denied. During his case-in-chief, Dan testifies that he thoroughly researched this area of law prior to approving the surveillance and found no controlling precedent forbidding such action. He concedes on cross-examination, however, that he was aware of precedent from other jurisdictions holding such surveillance to violate the Fourth Amendment right to be free of unreasonable warrantless searches and seizures. In addition, Dan proffers Professor Cornell Karnak, the country's leading authority on the electronic surveillance and the Constitution. He testifies that precedent in this area of the law is "a mess" and that the boundaries of proper investigatory conduct for prosecutors are hopelessly unclear. DA Dan makes a Rule 50(a) JAML motion. **What result?**

(c) Assume (rightly or wrongly) that the Priest Paul's case goes to the jury, which renders a verdict for DA Dan. Three days later, one of the church parishioners overhears Dan discussing the case with one of his assistants in which Dan states that he "can't believe they bought that line about my researching all the cases. I haven't cracked a law book in 20 years. And even if the law had been clear, I would do it all over again. We just can't take the risk of these do-gooder religious types being infiltrated by terrorists." Based on the parishioner's affidavit attesting to overhearing the conversation, Priest Paul moves for a new trial. **What result?**

(d) Assume that the parishioner overheard this conversation thirteen months after trial rather than three days after trial. **What result?**

(e) Assume instead that the jury verdict was for Priest Paul in the amount of $1 million and that DA Dan moves for a new trial. **What result?**

(f) **What if the jury verdict had been for $20,000? $100,000? $3 million?**

(g) Reconsider questions 3(e) and 3(f) above after assuming that instead of simply seeking damages based on deprivation of his constitutional rights, Priest Paul was so upset about the surveillance that he developed ulcers and other health problems and continues to have trouble sleeping at night, often awaking with nightmares in which he is being chased by a SWAT team seeking to beat him senseless.

Quick Summary

• Post-decision motions give the court a chance to change its mind, correct errors, or fine-tune how it decided a case.

• Post-trial motions may be necessary to obtain meaningful appellate review.

• Some cases are finally decided on post-trial motions, obviating the expense and delay that an appeal would entail.

• Key motions are: for judgment as a matter of law; for amended findings; for a new trial; or for relief from an order or judgment.

• Prevailing parties also may want to bring post-trial motions, either to modify the relief ordered or to seek additional relief in the form of costs and disbursements or, where allowed by contract or statute, attorneys' fees.

19

Appeals

Key Concepts

- Role of appeals in civil cases
- The rarity of appeals—most cases settle or are decided without an appeal
- Unitary appeal rule—one appeal at the end of the case
- Review limited to matters raised and decided on the record
- Jurisdictional statutes and rules
- Appealabilty and reviewability
- Standards of review

Introduction

Law students spend years reading appellate decisions, or at least pithy portions of them, and learn that trial courts decide very little of real moment. In a common law school narrative, until the United States Supreme Court speaks, every issue is open for debate. In the real world of litigation, appellate decisions rarely play the role one might imagine. For the mass of cases, the litigation process proceeds much like Napoleon's infamous 1812 march on Moscow, where he started to Moscow with a large army, and returned home only with a very small fraction of his troops. The attrition at the side of the road faced by litigants may be different in nature from that faced by Napoleon's army, but the effect is similar—many disputes arise, but precious few are litigated to conclusion in the appellate courts. Disputes begin in the context of life and interactions of the parties, but the vast majority are resolved either before suit is filed or during the course of litigation in the trial court. Some more are resolved during the appellate process without a decision.

A "typical" or "average" case may have a high probability of being settled, but averages can be a bit misleading. For some disputes, it is clear to the parties and onlookers that it will take a trial court decision and appellate review of it before the dispute will possibly be resolved. Others present no conceivable "staying power" that would warrant even a trial, let alone an appeal. And of course knowing that a vast majority of cases settle before trial does not provide very useful information about what should or will be done in any one particular case. Any particular case may very well be headed to the appellate courts, and the client's rights are only represented adequately if the lawyer knows how the appellate process works. The purpose of this chapter is to provide an overview of this important part of the civil litigation process.

The mere potential availability of appellate review also has some impact on the parties and probably the trial judge. Indeed, this impact is one of the justifications for having appellate review in the first place. Appellate decisions in prior litigation operate as both binding legal precedent and practical guideposts that can have a clear and profound impact on later cases.

A. Appellate Review and Systems

Appellate review is available in the federal courts and every state's courts in most cases. Most often, this right to appeal is a right to a single appeal at the conclusion of the case. Appeals to higher levels of appellate courts are almost universally only discretionary appeals. Interlocutory appeals, taken before the final judgment, are discretionary and similarly the rare exception rather than the rule.

The procedures and rules in the appellate courts are at once marked by great commonality as well as tremendous variation in the details. Every appellate court requires the filing of some written brief, but there is probably no single form of brief that would comply with the rules of every appellate court. That, of course, is never necessary—it is only necessary that it comply with the rules of the appellate court where the appeal is filed. It is thus necessary to know and follow the applicable rules for the particular court in which an appeal is pending.

Most appeals are heard by multi-judge panels that review the case as a joint, collaborative effort by the three judges. Many appeals include an oral argument from the parties, though the majority of the courts allow argument only in some cases; many appeals are decided without argument. Appeals typically, but again, certainly not universally, result in the issuance of a written decision. In some cases, that written decision contains only the caption of the appeal and the decision—"Affirmed" or "Appeal dismissed." More often, a more robust opinion, of the type you have read so many times, will be issued.

1. The Unitary Appeal Rule

The nearly universal rule in the United States is that a party is entitled to one—and only one—appeal in any case. In the federal courts, the unitary appeal rule is implemented by what is known as the "final judgment rule." Thus, a party must raise all claims of error in a single appeal following a final judgment on the merits. *See, e.g., Richardson-Merrell, Inc. v. Koller,* 472 U.S. 424, 429-30 (1985) ("The statutory requirement of a final decision" [under 28 U.S.C. § 1291] means that "a party must ordinarily raise all claims of error in a single appeal following final judgment on the merits.") (internal quotations omitted). This requirement is a fundamental part of federal appellate jurisdiction by statute.

THE STATUTE   28 U.S.C. § 1291

Final Decisions of District Courts

The courts of appeals . . . shall have jurisdiction of appeals from all final decisions of the district courts of the United States . . . .

A final decision is one that terminates the litigation and leaves nothing for the trial court to do but execute the judgment. For example, an order pursuant to Fed. R. Civ. P. 37 that imposes sanctions on an attorney for discovery abuse is not a final, appealable order since the matter may be reviewed after final judgment on the merits. This rule creates one of the most important questions at the outset of every appeal: appealability.

> **Appealability** is the requirement that this case is ready for appeal now and, more specifically, that this particular order or judgment is appealable now.

EXAMPLE: Phred sues his employer for breach of contract and failure to pay wages due within 10 days of the last day of work as required by statute. The court grants the employer summary judgment on the statutory wage claim on the grounds a required timely demand was not required, but grants Phred summary judgment finding that the employer did breach the employment contract. The trial court orders entry of judgment on the summary judgment. Because the damages trial will require expert testimony, both sides appeal the summary judgment decision.

Analysis: Both appeals are premature—taken from a non-final order. The trial court still has to resolve the amount of damages, a major part of the contract claim. The fact that judgment is entered does not affect the finality analysis—it may be a judgment, but it is not a final judgment.

2. Exceptions to the Final Judgment Rule

Only a final order or judgment is automatically appealable. If an order or judgment is not final it cannot be appealed as a matter of right, but may be reviewed in an appeal from a final order or judgment. As is true for so many rules, however, there are exceptions to the "final judgment rule." These exceptions generally fit into one of four categories:

- Statutes or rules allowing appeal as of right, without regard to finality;

- Statutes or rules providing for discretionary interlocutory appellate review;

- Common-law based exceptions; and

- The authority of the appellate courts to issue extraordinary writs.

1. Statutes or Rules Allowing Appeal as of Right, Without Regard to Finality. In federal court, 28 U.S.C. § 1292 allows that interlocutory orders granting, continuing, modifying, refusing, or dissolving injunctions or refusing to dissolve or modify injunctions are immediately appealable. This section does not permit interlocutory review of **temporary restraining orders** but does apply to preliminary injunctions and, of course, permanent injunctions. Section 1292(a) also permits the immediate appeal of certain receivership orders and of interlocutory decrees determining the rights and liabilities of parties to admiralty cases.

State court practice is quite varied on the grounds allowing an appeal as a matter of right, so it is important to look at the applicable statutes and rules.

A hybrid rule that is important in more complex cases is contained in the rules of civil procedure. Rule 54(b) permits the court to enter a judgment on one, but not, all of the claims for or against a party and render that judgment final and appealable.

THE RULE   Rule 54(b)

Judgment; Costs

* * *

(b) Judgment on Multiple Claims or Involving Multiple Parties. When an action presents more than one claim for relief—whether as a claim, counter-claim, crossclaim, or third-party claim—or when multiple parties are involved, the court may direct entry of a final judgment as to one or more, but fewer than all, claims or parties only if the court expressly determines that there is no just reason for delay. Otherwise, any order or other decision, however designated, that adjudicates fewer than all the claims or the rights and liabilities of fewer than all the parties does not end the action as to any of the claims or parties and may be revised at any time before the entry of a judgment adjudicating all the claims and all the parties' rights and liabilities.

IN PRACTICE

Rule 54(b) converts what would otherwise not be appealable at all—a partial judgment that leaves other claims still to be litigated—into an appealable partial judgment. It is important that a party aggrieved by the judgment knows that the 54(b) certification has the effect of making the order appealable now, on pain of it becoming final if not appealed within the normal period after its entry. The party has the right to appeal, but must do so at that stage in the proceedings, and will not be allowed to do so later.

EXAMPLES & ANALYSIS

EXAMPLE: (*Note: this is only a slight variation of the previous Example.*) Phred sues his employer for breach of contract and failure to pay wages due within 10 days of the last day of work as required by statute. The court grants the employer summary judgment on the statutory wage claim on the grounds a required timely demand was not required, but grants Pat summary judgment finding that the employer did breach the employment contract. The trial court orders entry of judgment on the summary judgment order, and includes the "magic language" of Rule 54(b) that there is no just reason for delay in entry of judgment. Phred appeals the summary judgment dismissing his statutory wage claim.

Analysis: The inclusion of the Rule 54(b) language makes this summary judgment appear to be appealable. It relates to the decision of the entirety of one of the two claims in the case, and completely decides that claim. In reality, the appellate court might well examine the reasons supporting the trial court's certification that there is no just reason for delay in entry of judgment—it is not clear what harm would flow from resolving the remaining claim and having a single appeal.

Another hybrid rule is also contained in the Rules of Civil Procedure. Rule 23(f) grants the appellate court jurisdiction to entertain an appeal from an order granting or denying class certification.

THE RULE   Rule 23(f)

Class Actions

* * *

(f) Appeals. A court of appeals may permit an appeal from an order granting or denying class-action certification under this rule if a petition for permission to appeal is filed with the circuit clerk within 14 days after the order is entered. An appeal does not stay proceedings in the district court unless the district judge or the court of appeals so orders.

Under this rule, orders regarding class certification can be appealed without any further action or certification by the district court judge, but they remain discretionary with the appellate court. In practice, most of the federal circuits have allowed these appeals sparingly, requiring any appeal to be taken at the conclusion of the case.

2. Discretionary Interlocutory Appeals. Section 1292(b) permits a judge to certify an interlocutory appeal for immediate review. There is a significant limitation in this basis for appeal—before an appeal can be perfected on this basis the trial judge must certify to the court of appeals that the order (1) involves a controlling question of law (2) as to which there is substantial ground for difference of opinion and (3) immediate appeal may materially advance the ultimate termination of the litigation. Moreover, the appellate court has discretion regarding whether to accept the certification. Even where an interlocutory order is certified and accepted for immediate appeal, the district court proceedings are not stayed unless the trial judge orders a stay pending appeal of the certified order.

3. The Collateral Order Doctrine. An important common law exception to the finality requirement is the **collateral order doctrine.** This doctrine is not a creature of federal rule or statute but is a judge-made exception to the seemingly ironclad finality rule of 28 U.S.C. § 1291. The doctrine, first authoritatively announced in *Cohen v. Beneficial Industrial Loan Corp.*, 337 U.S. 541 (1949), (and followed in *Mohawk Industries, Inc. v. Carpenter,*

558 U.S. 100 (2009)), requires that (1) the order appealed be separate from and collateral to the merits of the litigation, (2) the order determine an important issue that must be accorded effective appellate review, and (3) effective review of the order be in doubt if interlocutory review is not permitted. This third factor is viewed as a requirement that the order be effectively unreviewable on appeal from a final judgment. In practice, the three-point test has been a weighted one. The more collateral the matter, the more important the matter, and the more fruitless appeal after termination of the entire action, the more likely the appellate court to consider the order immediately appealable.

Since the 1970s, the Supreme Court has taken a generally strict view of the final judgment rule and a restrictive view of its exceptions. For example, the Court in 1987 held that a trial court's denial of intervention as of right to a citizens' group was neither a final order nor an appealable collateral order. In 1988, the Court abolished the *Enelow-Ettelson* doctrine (adopted in *Enelow v. New York Life Ins. Co.*, 293 U.S. 379 (1935), and *Ettelson v. Metropolitan Life Ins. Co.*, 317 U.S. 188 (1942)), which had previously treated as immediately appealable a denial of a stay requested on equitable grounds as part of an action at law. *See Gulfstream Aerospace Corp. v. Mayacamas Corp.*, 485 U.S. 271 (1988). In 1989, the Court definitively answered an open question in the circuits by holding that a trial court's refusal to enforce a forum selection clause did not meet the *Cohen* collateral order doctrine criteria for interlocutory review. *See Lauro Lines S.R.L. v. Chasser*, 490 U.S. 495 (1989).

Similarly, in *Mohawk Industries, Inc. v. Carpenter*, 558 U.S. 100 (2009), the Court reaffirmed the collateral order doctrine, but found that an order requiring disclosure of documents over an assertion of the attorney-client privilege did not meet the third requirement of the doctrine.

Examples of matters frequently found to satisfy the collateral order doctrine are filings on attorney disqualification, discovery rulings concerning allegedly privileged information (although this category is probably now foreclosed by *Mohawk*), contempt citations, and gag orders placed on the press. A few states have explicitly recognized their own collateral order exceptions. Many states, however, merely permit discretionary interlocutory review on petition, and the criteria they use in exercising discretion for accepting or rejecting immediate appeal suspiciously resemble the collateral order doctrine.

Many of the motions previously discussed in this text could conceivably fit the collateral order doctrine or be suitable for immediate certification for appeal in a manner similar to 28 U.S.C. § 1292(b). When counsel loses a motion in the trial court, it pays to be alert to the possibility of successful interlocutory appeal. The area is complicated and limited only by the imagination of counsel and the governor's or President's supreme court appointments. To some extent, a policy of strict finality places the judicial system's interest in efficiency ahead of individual interests in swift justice. Counsel can use this ever-present tension to craft compelling arguments for and against interlocutory review in particular cases.

The thirty-day time period for filing a notice of appeal under Fed. R. App. P. ("FRAP") 4(a)(1)(A) is normally the type of "jurisdictional" deadline that once missed is gone forever. However, FRAP 4(a) also provides a grace period of an additional thirty days in which a lawyer that misses the appeal deadline can ask the trial court for an extension of time to appeal. This extension can be granted only if the neglect of the attorney was "excusable." Although such requests for additional time are thought to be both rare and rarely granted, it does happen. Most often, the movant is only half successful—establishing the "neglect" part of the test without difficulty, but not establishing that the neglect was excusable.

4. Extraordinary Writs. Appellate courts have retained their authority to issue a wide variety of extraordinary writs. Four of these created jurisdiction in exceptional circumstances and are issued with some frequency by appellate courts. As for all prayers, prayers for extraordinary writs are frequently made, but not so frequently answered.

Writs of mandamus, prohibition, certiorari, and quo warranto are those most commonly encountered. These writs afford a petitioner an opportunity to obtain the review of otherwise unappealable orders. Some states, while abolishing these common law writs in name, provide similar remedies by rules or statutes permitting review of interlocutory orders. These remedies created by rules or statutes mimic the common law writs but attempt to eliminate any historical and technical restrictions on their use. These modern proceedings have been variously entitled applications for extraordinary appeal, requests for discretionary review, and special actions. By whatever name, these remedies provide a party with emergency relief that may look and feel like an appeal, but a writ proceeding is not technically an appeal, but rather, is an original proceeding in the appellate court. It is commenced by petition rather than notice of appeal. *See* FRAP 21. Mandamus is a traditional writ for an affirmative order compelling a lower court or inferior official to perform a duty or to exercise lawful authority. Prohibition is a traditional writ restraining a lower court or judicial official. Certiorari is a common law writ ordering a lower court to certify a matter for review to a higher court. This writ of certiorari differs from petitions for certiorari submitted to a supreme court to obtain discretionary review of a final order or judgment. **Quo warranto** is a more focused writ, and is used in election law to obtain appellate court review of the authority of someone to hold a public office.

> **Quo warranto** is a writ directed to someone claiming a public office to establish by what authority he or she claims that office. It may question the eligibility for the office or the validity of an appointment or election.

The most frequent occasions justifying the use of an appellate court writ include:

- Jurisdictional errors.

- Denial of a fundamental right, such as trial by jury.

- Action in excess of the trial court's power.

- Absence of other adequate remedies regarding a substantial issue.

Relief by extraordinary writ is generally allowed only in exceptional cases or to prevent a clear miscarriage of justice. *See, e.g., Dairy Queen, Inc. v. Wood,* 369 U.S. 469 (1962)(use of writ approved to compel constitutionally-protected right to jury trial); *cf. World-Wide Volkswagen Corp. v. Woodson,* 444 U.S. 286 (1980)(personal jurisdiction of state court before Court on writ of prohibition)(case included in Chapter 2). Writs are issued only in truly exigent or emergency circumstances. *Will v. Calvert Fire Ins. Co.,* 437 U.S. 655 (1978). Courts are very reluctant to grant these writs because the fair administration of justice discourages piecemeal litigation and premature appeals. A petitioner seeking emergency remedies has a heavy burden to show that it is "clear and indisputable" that an emergency writ should issue. Generally, this means that a court under challenge must have acted outside its jurisdiction or clearly abused its discretion in a manner causing immediate harm requiring expedited review.

EXAMPLES & ANALYSIS

EXAMPLE: Paula sues Diverse Pharmaceuticals for injuries she sustained after taking its new sleeping drug Euphorphil. Her case was consolidated with those of other plaintiffs, and during discovery Diverse made a number of decisions in discovery that might be called "hardball tactics." The district judge determined that these tactics warranted the imposition of monetary sanctions of $1 million and the further sanction of requiring Diverse's German scientists to appear in the United States for their depositions. Diverse seeks a writ of mandamus from the court of appeals, arguing that the court exceeded its authority in ordering a massive fine and in requiring foreign employees to travel to the United States to be deposed.

Analysis: There is little question about the trial court's power to order a sanction in response to discovery misconduct, so that issue would not make a promising one for review by writ. That discretionary authority is not unbounded, however, and the $1 million fine is a severe sanction that might or might not warrant issuance of a writ. Requiring foreign employees to be produced in the United States is not a sanction explicitly authorized by Rule 37, and that might itself support issuance of a writ (although Rule 37 doesn't provide a laundry list of the only authorized sanctions). The sanction here did not meet the requirements of 28 U.S.C.A. § 1783(a), which allows a court to compel attendance of a foreign witness in the United States, but only where the testimony cannot otherwise be obtained. Because it was not clear that was so, the order could be held to exceed the court's jurisdiction, thus justifying issuance of a writ.

3. Appealability and Reviewability

Appealability defines whether an appeal can be taken from a particular order or judgment. But an important part of the unitary appeal rule is that although an appeal can only be *taken from* the final order or judgment, when a proper appeal is taken (from an appealable order or judgment) the appellant can then obtain *review* of earlier decisions.

EXAMPLE: Pat sues for injuries from an accident, claiming that the brakes on the car failed shortly after they were repaired by Dan O's repairs. In that case, the trial court allowed the defendant to amend the complaint to add a new count for consumer fraud and entered an order refusing Dan's request that plaintiff submit to a medical examination, denied a motion for summary judgment on statute of limitations grounds, and granted the plaintiff's motion to exclude Dan's expert witnesses on the grounds they were not disclosed in a timely manner. Following trial in which a jury found liability and awarded substantial damages, the trial court entered judgment on that award. From which of these decision may Dan obtain appellate review, and how?

Analysis: Although the trial court's decisions allowing amendment of the complaint, denying the motion to require Pat to submit to a medical examination, denying summary judgment, and granting a motion *in limine* would not be *appealable* because they don't end the litigation, once the trial is held and a final judgment entered, they would all be *reviewable* on a timely appeal from that final judgment. They key would be to make sure that appeal was taken in a timely manner and, in many courts, that Dan makes it clear in the notice of appeal that it is seeking review of each of those earlier decisions.

A party may only obtain review of decisions by which it is aggrieved. This rule prevents a party who has ultimately prevailed on the issue or in the case from seeking review of every interlocutory order the court entered. The Supreme Court recently cast doubt on just how devoted it is to the time-honored requirement, in holding that a party could appeal a ruling on constitutionality of conduct despite having prevailed on the grounds of qualified immunity from liability. *See Camreta v. Greene*, 563 U.S. ___, 131 S. Ct. 2020 (2011).

4. Standards of Review

Probably the single most important part of appellate review, and the most important key to understanding how appellate courts view cases is the standard of review. Courts review issues by applying very specific standards that guide how the court reviews each issue raised. These standards have been termed the "lens" though which the appellate courts view the cases.

You might wonder, if standards of review are so important, why haven't you heard too much about them. You've read enough appellate decisions by now, right? The best explanation for this is that many of the cases in many casebooks omit the discussion of standards of review, because they do not illuminate principles of tort or contract law. But to understand what an appellate court is really doing, you must understand the standard of review, and if you are going to advocate for a party to an appeal, you must know these standards.

Standards of review are a set of rules that specify how much deference the appellate court must give to trial court rulings. Viewed another way, they constrain how much latitude the appellate court has to reverse or modify the trial court decision.

The three most important standards of review are "de novo," "abuse of discretion," and "clearly erroneous." These three are progressively more deferential to the trial court decision. They cover the majority of appellate issues. (The substantial evidence standard applies to some administrative agency review and is essentially an enhanced version of the clearly erroneous standard.) These standards are covered in the table below:

Standard of Review	Definition and common use
Clearly erroneous	Used to review findings of fact. Fed. R. Civ. P. 52(a). Requires "definite and firm conviction that a mistake has been committed." *United States v. U.S. Gypsum Co.*, 333 U.S. 364, 395 (1948). **[High level of deference to trial court]**
Abuse of discretion	Used to review discretionary decisions of trial court. Appellate court defers to trial court to high degree. **[Extent of deference may depend on how "broad" trial court discretion is]**
De novo	Used to review questions of law or mixed questions of fact and law. Appellate court decides issue anew. **[No deference to trial court decision]**

De novo review allows the appellate court to review the trial court decision without any deference to how the trial court decided the issue. De novo review is applied to the trial court's decisions on matters of law. Appellants are eager to have the de novo standard applied because it offers the broadest review—with no deference to the trial court's decisions of law.

Abuse of discretion is a deferential standard, and probably a variable one since it is predicated on the extent to which the trial court has discretion to rule on a question. The broader that discretion, the more deferential the appellate court must be in reviewing the discretionary ruling. Put perhaps more memorably, "[a]buse of discretion must be eye-popping, neck-snapping, jaw-dropping egregious error." Roger W. Badeker, *Wide As a Church Door, Deep as a Well: A Survey of Judicial Discretion, The Journal*, Mar./Apr. 1992, at 33.

The clearly-erroneous standard is used to review fact-finding by the trial judge or jury. It is the most deferential of all—it requires clear error to overturn the trial court, and it is mandated by the rules of civil procedure.

THE RULE	Rule 52(a)(6)

Setting Aside the Findings

(6) Findings of fact, whether based on oral or other evidence, must not be set aside unless clearly erroneous, and the reviewing court must give due regard to the trial court's opportunity to judge the witnesses' credibility.

It is exceedingly deferential to the conclusions of the fact-finder. A good (and aromatic) measure of this standard is: "To be clearly erroneous, a decision must strike us as more than just maybe or probably wrong; it must strike us as wrong with the force of a five-week old, unrefrigerated dead fish." *Fisher v. Roe*, 263 F.3d 906, 912 (9th Cir. 2001), quoting *Parts & Elec. Motors, Inc. v. Sterling Elec., Inc.*, 866 F.2d 228, 233 (7th Cir. 1988).

EXAMPLES & ANALYSIS

EXAMPLE: Preston sues his former employer, DC Publications, for breach of their employment agreement, following his termination. During the pre-trial proceedings the court granted DC's motion to dismiss Preston's claim for front-pay, concluding that the applicable state law did not allow that remedy. Although Preston demanded a jury trial, the court held that because Preston sought equitable relief, the case would be tried to the court without a jury. The court also ordered the trial bifurcated, with liability tried first, followed by damages. At the conclusion of the liability trial, the jury returned a verdict for DC. The judge adopted those findings in denying equitable relief as well as damages. Preston brought all required post-trial motions, which the court denied, and Preston appeals, challenging the dismissal, the denial of a jury trial, and the birfucation of the trial. What standards of review will apply?

Analysis: The court's review of these appellate issues will not be at all identical from issue to issue. The question of whether the law allows a terminated employee a front-pay remedy is a legal question—the law either allows the remedy or it doesn't, and because it was decided on a motion to dismiss, factual issues did not play a role. The court would therefore analyze the dismissal through the lens of de novo review, giving no deference to the trial court's decision. The order denying a jury trial is similar. The law recognizes a party's right to a jury trial, or it doesn't, and it is not a fact-based decision. In this case, the court's ruling was based on a ruling that the fact Preston sought equitable relief as well as legal precluded a jury trial of right. The court would also review that decision de novo. The bifurcation decision is fundamentally different. Trial courts have discretion over how cases will be tried, and there is no legal entitlement to a one-phase trial (or to a bifurcated one). The consequence of this is that the appellate court will review the decision for abuse of discretion.

EXAMPLE: In Preston's suit, assume all the same history, but the jury returns a verdict for Preston in the liability trial on each of his claims. In the damages trial, the jury awards him every item of damages. As to the equitable relief he sought—reinstatement—the court adopts the jury's verdict and grants reinstatement based on the verdict. This time DC brings post-trial motions, which are denied, and DC appeals. DC argues that the jury verdict and the court's findings in support of its reinstatement order are contrary to law and unsupported by the evidence. DC also argues that the damages are excessive, reflecting passion and prejudice on the part of the judge. Now what standards of review will apply?

Analysis: The appellate court will address these issues in a similar way, reviewing each issue through the lens of a standard of review. Because the issues are different, the standards of review may be (and will be) different here. DC's main complaint relates to its disagreement with the factual determinations embodied in the jury's verdict and the court's findings in support of its reinstatement judgment. The challenge to the factual findings will be decided under the extremely deferential clearly-erroneous standard of review. These findings are not immune to review, but the court will not disturb the findings unless there is no evidence in the record to support them. The claim of excessiveness is similarly subject to a very deferential standard, but deference to the fact-finder is limited to the range of the proof of damages, bounded only by the "maximum amount" rule that would limit any award to the maximum amount a reasonable fact-finder could award. If a greater award is made, the court can order a reduction to that maximum amount.

5. Review on the Record

Appellate courts review trial court decisions "on the record." This has important ramifications for the litigants: issues to be raised on appeal must be raised in the lower court or agency and they must be decided there. Both the raising of the issue and the decision must appear **on the record**. Normally this means they must be raised in writing and filed with the record or raised in open court with a court reporter present. The appellate court will not consider, with very few exceptions, material outside the record.

The "on the record" requirement is not hard to meet, but it is easy to ignore the details that are very important. Matters should be raised by motion, not by letter or phone call. Motion responses should actually be filed with the court, not merely delivered to judge's chambers. Objections, offers of proof, requests for relief should all be made on the record with a court reporter present; if it isn't said on the record, it essentially "didn't happen" to the appellate court.

IN PRACTICE

The requirement that issues be raised and decided "on the record" can be an unfortunate trap even for lawyers who are prepared, capable, and experienced. Many important trial court proceedings ordinarily take place in chambers or at the "sidebar" where the court report is not recording the proceedings. This is perfectly normal, and necessary to the efficient conduct of the trial. What the lawyer must do, however, is place on the record the important requests made in the off-the-record discussion and any rulings by the court that may be relevant.

These days email may pose another trap—a judge may be happy to treat an emailed request as a motion, and may even decide it by return email. If more is not done to file these exchanges, the record will reveal nothing about the "motion" or the "order" deciding it.

6. Appellate Court Jurisdiction

Appellate courts have jurisdiction allowed by a constitution and usually, amplified by statutory provisions. These definitions of jurisdiction for appellate courts parallel the jurisdictional authorities for the trial courts.

Jurisdiction in a particular appeal is established, certainly in federal court, by filing a notice of appeal to the appropriate appellate court. This step, if done correctly, transfers jurisdiction over the subject matter of the appeal to the appellate court.

What is necessary to do it correctly? First and foremost, it requires careful attention to the specific requirements of the court. In no area of appellate practice is it more important to master the details, and there is probably no area where broad-brush procedures are similar, but the details are different.

  a. **Time is crucial!** Because perfection of an appeal is a matter of jurisdiction, the time limits are strictly enforced. *See, e.g., Bowles v. Russell,* 551 U.S. 205, 214 (2007)("[t]oday we make clear that the timely filing of a notice of appeal in a civil case is a jurisdictional requirement."). For this reason, it is a wise practice to appeal early in the appeal period, and not wait for the last day. A mistake made with 15 days left—say the notice of appeal is filed in the wrong court—quite likely it can be corrected; if made on the last day, the client may be out of luck.

b. Do everything right. If you are only going to get something right, make sure you complete the jurisdictional parts. Typically these are:

· Filing a proper notice of appeal with the proper court or courts (in federal court this means filing in the district court, not the court of appeals).

· Service of the notice of appeal (or directing the service if the court serves it rather than the parties—this is the federal court procedure) on all the parties in the action, and not just the party or parties known to be adverse on the issue appealed from.

· Payment of a required filing fee (this may or may not be viewed as jurisdictional, but is universally required, so why overlook it?).

Additional steps that may be required, but are generally viewed as non-jurisdictional, are providing a cost bond (no longer required at all in federal appeals) and completion of court information forms to allow docketing of the appeal.

c. Draft a complete notice of appeal. This is a simple form to draft, but one that requires careful attention. There are several ways to draft one that is legally insufficient and hard to explain to a client who no longer has a right to appeal. The requirements are easy to state, and should result in a sufficient form for all jurisdictions, but the local rules should still be consulted.

· Caption. Include the complete caption of the trial court action. Even if the trial court has reverted to a shorthand caption, the appellate caption should be the complete, proper caption for the case; if the court has entered an order directing that a shorter caption be used, use of that shorter caption should be sufficient, but otherwise it should be the full caption developed in the substantive pleading stage.

· Specify by full name the party or parties appealing. It is tempting to say "the above-named plaintiffs appeal . . . ." That temptation should be resisted. That shortcut will be fatal if there are plaintiffs "above-named" who are included as a group under "et al." or some other label and may be fatal even for those named. The better practice, by far, is to list each appellant in the body of the notice of appeal, by complete name.

· Specify the specific judgments and orders appealed from. This should be the title of the document and the date filed. The bare minimum here should be the final judgment in the case. If review is sought of any earlier rulings not encompassed in the final judgment, they should be listed as well. Failure to do so may result in their being unreviewable on appeal.

· Specify the name of the court (or agency) **from which** the appeal is being taken.

· Specify the appellate court **to which** the appeal is taken. Make sure it is actually the court that has appellate jurisdiction. An appeal taken from a federal court to a state appellate court is doomed to failure, even if your word processed form does remember that the appeal was taken to that court last time (from a state court order).

IN PRACTICE

A good practice is to check with the court and make sure everything is in order as far as commencing the appeal. Many courts will send a notice to the parties either confirming that everything is complete or noting deficiencies. There is nothing to prevent a careful lawyer from seeking out this information. Obviously, this is useless information if you have filed (or only attempted to file) on the last day.

7. Effect of Appeal on Trial Court Jurisdiction

Quick question: does filing an appeal halt or suspend the decisions appealed from? Should it?

There is no question that a proper appeal divests the trial court of jurisdiction over the matters appealed from. If there are undecided matters that are related to the matters appealed from, say a motion to reconsider, the trial court is without jurisdiction to act on them unless authorized by the appellate court.

Enforcement of the judgment, as opposed to modification of it, is a different matter. The mere filing of an appeal generally does not stop the enforcement of a trial court judgment. In federal court a judgment is only stayed briefly after entry; once that automatic stay ends, the judgment can be enforced. A party appealing from a money judgment may obtain a stay of enforcement, but this is generally conditioned on the posting of a special form of surety bond called a "supersedeas bond."

> A **supersedeas bond** is a surety bond whereby a surety (typically, an insurance company) agrees to step in and satisfy (pay off) the judgment in the event the appeal is not successful. It has the effect of making the prevailing party secure in knowing that it is not suffering increased risk of uncollectability because of the appeal. Indeed, in many cases the appellee is better off if a bond is posted—collecting on the surety bond is a lot easier than collecting the judgment regardless of when collection efforts begin.

IN PRACTICE

The cost of a supersedeas bond can be significant. The surety will charge a premium of several percent of the amount of the bond, and will require that the appellant also post security with the surety in the amount of the bond—a letter of credit, a mortgage of real estate having substantial equity, or a pledge of stock. This total cost is often substantial, and may offer a significant deterrent to an appeal.

In most appeals, however, the trial court proceedings will not be stayed without the posting of security, typically a supersedeas bond. (The most consistent exception relates to governmental entities—they are often exempted from any requirement to post security in order to obtain a stay.)

The amount of the bond is set in the first instance in the trial court, subject to possible review by the appellate court. As a rule of thumb, however, the bond is likely to be in the amount of the judgment plus interest for the likely appeal period plus the likely amount of costs if the appeal is lost. Sometimes, the bond will be set in an amount that makes it impossible for the appellant to post the bond.

Even if a supersedeas bond cannot be posted, it may be possible to obtain a stay by filing a motion with the trial court, although a stay without bond is both discretionary and available only in limited circumstances.

Courts increasingly recognize that the imposition of an onerous supersedeas bond requirement may effectively interfere with a party's right to appeal.

8. Importance of Rules

The Rules of Civil Procedure we discussed throughout this course are important to trial practice. But they pale in comparison to the importance of the Rules of Appellate Procedure and local rules in the appellate courts. The appellate court rules are detailed and vary quite a bit from court to court. Even within the federal court system, each circuit has detailed local rules that impose requirements that supplement the federal rules of appellate procedure in important ways. There are many requirements that would make a brief containing elements required in one circuit would not be acceptable for filing in another.

The reason the rules are so important is that the ease the court's consideration of each appeal in an expeditious way. The court can find what it is looking in a brief because the rules specify where it should be. The imposition of time limits for the various steps leading up to argument ensures that the court has everything in place to permit it to be prepared for argument and for issuance of a decision when the argument is completed. Compliance with the rules allows the court to function with less effort and greater efficiency, and may also help it ensure that it bases its decision on the best information available.

9. Briefing and Argument

Appeals are decided upon briefs and, in some cases, oral argument. Of these, every appellate judge and lawyer would say the brief is most important. Oral argument is exciting, fun for those to do it enough to be comfortable, and may even change the course of the appeal. But the vast majority of the cases the winner is chosen based on the briefs. The discussion in the past few pages should suggest to you what makes for an effective brief.

An effective brief:

- Clearly states the issues upon which relief is sought;

- Analyzes the issues in terms of the applicable standard of review; and

- Omits the issues that are effectively unreviewable because of a very deferential standard of review.

Briefing is a one-way outgoing transmission of your argument, with no immediate feedback as to whether the message is being received by the court. But **oral argument** is fundamentally different—the oral advocate gets an opportunity to respond to questions from the court and to understand if her arguments are generating flashes of understanding from the court (or signs of derision). This is the whole point of oral argument, and it is very important that counsel take advantage of it to accomplish that purpose.

Appellate oral argument may be the marquee feature of the appellate process, and it is important to many appeals. In one study, judges kept records of months of arguments and the impact they believed in had on their decisions. The study suggests that oral argument changes appellate judges' minds between 13 and 31 percent of the time. *See* Hon. Myron Bright, *The Power of the Spoken Word: In Defense of Oral Argument*, 72 Iowa L. Rev. 35, 40 nn.32 & 33 (1986).

Even good trial lawyers make serious mistakes at the appellate lectern. There are many instances of theses gaffes, and others. Common mistakes arise from a fundamental misunderstanding of the importance and role of argument. *See* David F. Herr & Cynthia F. Gilbertson, *Improving the Odds on Appeal*, 60 Bench & Bar of Minn., Aug. 2003, at 17, 21 (enumerating common errors). Among the common mistakes:

a. **Not preparing.** The advocate needs to know the record and needs to know the law. And know it cold. Anticipate every question that may be asked.

b. Wasting time on background, chaff, and other drivel.

c. Viewing questions as interruptions. They aren't—they are the essence of appellate argument, and counsel should welcome the chance to talk about something at least one judge is interested in.

d. Sticking to the outline. Yes, this is a vice! Questions only "interrupt" the rigid lawyer who has a plan that is not flexible. Having an outline may be useful; slavish adherence to it is not.

e. Promising to answer questions later. Even if this promise is kept, it is a problem. Promising to answer later and then not answering may be worse, but only a little worse.

f. Declining (or failing) to answer questions. Answer the question! Answer first, and provide an explanation if necessary. It drives judges crazy to hear a long answer and only have to speculate as to what answer may be trying to fight its way out through the verbiage.

g. Refusing to deal with the case's problems. Every case has some negative facts, a difficult issue, or an unhelpful precedent. Oral argument is not a place to ignore them or wish them away—it is the place to confront them, wrestle with them, explain them, and possibly even minimize them. The goal is to help the court understand why you win despite these problems, not to hope the court won't know about them. Even if the problems don't come up at argument, they are likely to come up later.

h. Refusing to concede. Sometimes concession is necessary. Every case might present some question where any rationale advocate would have to concede loss under some hypothetical set of facts. You should be prepared to explain where the line is, but if the court is pressing for discussion on a set of facts "over the line," concede.

i. Recognize a "softball." Not all questions are hostile. Recognize when the court is asking you a "softball question"—a question that you should be elated to get to answer—the court may be feeding you a question so you can make a point for one of the other judges.

j. Sitting down without telling the court what specific relief you want. Tell the court specifically what relief is appropriate—appellate courts are particularly interested in knowing if a decision can decide the case, or if a remand is necessary for further proceedings.

10. Decision and Mandate

Following argument, most appellate courts meet and discuss the appeal and effectively "decide it." The exact procedure varies from court to court, and even somewhat from case to case within the same court, but generally the judges express their views about the case in order of seniority (or reverse seniority), a vote is taken, and the case is assigned to one of the judges to prepare a draft opinion. That draft is prepared and circulated to the judges for comment and possibly, correction. If judges do not agree with the result itself, they may elect to prepare a dissenting opinion; if they agree with the result but not the language of the majority opinion, they may decide to prepare a concurrence. These diverging views of the case may cause an additional conference of the judges, or may result in judges changing their views of the case.

In rare circumstances the change in votes may make what was to be the opinion of the court into a dissent, and a dissent would become the opinion of the court. This requires revision of the opinions and sometimes explains a longer lapse of time from argument to decision.

The appellate court retains jurisdiction over the appeal even after decision. The device by which jurisdiction in the appellate court is terminated is the mandate. The mandate usually sends the case back to the lower court with directions to implement the appellate court's decision.

11. Rehearing and Further Review

Most, but certainly not all, appellate courts permit the parties to seek rehearing following decision. You are familiar with the most common—by far the most common—result of this process: the designation "reh. denied" following the citation. Rehearing occurs, but it rarely results in a different result. It the federal courts a party seeking rehearing can also suggest to the

> **Rehearing en banc** allows the entire court, composed of the members of the panel deciding the case plus all members of the court in regular service (not those sitting in some special capacity, such as "Senior Status") to decide the cases. Due to the size of some appellate courts, "en banc" cases are heard by some smaller subset of the entire court.

court that the motion for rehearing should be taken up not by the panel, but by the **en banc** court.

A sharply divided panel decision might favor the filing of a request for en banc consideration, but there should also be some good faith argument that the issue is more important than merely that the panel "got it wrong."

Appellate review in the federal system, and in most state courts, is provided by an appeal to a court of appeals (that may or may not be an appeal of right) and then by a discretionary appeal to a supreme court (or the Supreme Court in the federal system). That review is always a discretionary, and in most instances review is limited to a fraction of the cases decided by the intermediate appellate court.

A party seeking review in the United States Supreme Court must petition for a writ of certiorari. Fewer than three percent of cert petitions are granted even among this self-selected group of cases. Lawyers seldom recommend and clients seldom want to pay for efforts to obtain Supreme Court review unless the case is one that might realistically gain such review.

The U.S. Supreme Court does not sit as a court of error correction (although the Justices are probably more likely to be interested if they think a decision below was wrong or unfair) but instead has a mission of deciding important constitutional matters and resolving disagreements about federal law among lower courts. (Remember per Chapter 4 on *Erie* that the Supreme Court does not make state law nor should it be interested in state law except to the extent there is a conflict with federal law). Consequently, the types of cases obtaining Supreme Court review tend to be big constitutional matters or questions of interpretation of federal statutes of broad application on which the circuits have reached conflicting results.

For guidance on the intricacies of the certiorari process and on practice before the Supreme Court generally, see Stephen M. Shapiro, et al., *Supreme Court Practice* (10th ed. 2013) (still known fondly to some as "Stern Gressman," after the long-time authors of earlier editions).

Quick Summary

- Appeal of trial court decisions is a widely-accepted, part of American civil procedure.

- The fundamental rule is that a losing party is entitled to one appeal, at the end of the case.

- Unitary appeal at end of case translates into the "final judgment rule"—appeal is normally taken from a final judgment.

- Exceptions to the finality requirement include statutes allowing specified decisions to be appealed, provisions for discretionary interlocutory appeal, the collateral order doctrine, and review by extraordinary writ.

- On appeal from a final order or judgment, the appellant can obtain review of earlier decisions.

- Appellate process is a blend of jurisdictional law and rule-based procedures.

- Appellate courts review issues under specified standards of review that define how much deference trial court decisions are entitled to—these range from great deference to fact-finding under the clearly erroneous standard to no deference to legal determinations under the de novo standard.

- Appeals provide a means of correcting errors that deny a party a fair trial—they are not a routine means of revisiting all the trial court's decisions.

- Appellate court jurisdiction is limited, and time limits are crucial to the definition of that jurisdiction. An appeal filed a day after the deadline is a lost cause.

20

Remedies, Judgments and Preclusion

Key Concepts

- The Three Primary Types of Potential Litigation Remedies: Monetary Damages; Injunctive Relief; and Declaratory Relief
- Temporary and Preliminary Injunctive Relief
- Judgments and their Enforcement
- Preclusion doctrine, including Claim Preclusion and Issue Preclusion

Introduction

This chapter addresses remedies including interim remedies such as temporary restraining orders and preliminary injunctions) and judgments in general (including judgment collection) and then concentrates on "preclusion"—the degree to which a prior judgment is conclusive in a later action. Finality and preclusion are important concepts with which lawyers must be familiar.

A. Remedies

1. A Word About Remedies

In deciding whether to sue and upon what terms to settle, counsel needs to be aware of the realistic range of remedies that a party might obtain through litigation. By "remedies," we mean the types of relief that a litigant may obtain through litigation. In variance with most civil procedures casebooks, we are not treating remedies as a separate category but instead discuss aspects of remedial relief in the context of other chapters in the book. For now, the following discussion must serve as your introduction and guide to remedies. Remedies can be a complex topic and in most law schools rates its own stand-alone law school course. It also is often a separate topic on state bar examinations.

As noted in Chapter 1 on subject matter jurisdiction and Chapter 15 on jury trial, remedies are classified as **legal** and **equitable**. The term "legal" remedy means something more specialized than merely a remedy provided under the law. In this context, if means a remedy that is historically classified as legal on the basis of the historical categories that arose under Anglo-American law as result of England's long separation of courts of law and courts of equity. The former courts could accord only "legal" relief while the latter courts could award "equitable" relief. (Note that in this context, "equitable" does not have its normal meaning of "fair" but instead refers to the classification of the type of relief.)

For the most part, legal relief means monetary relief and a money judgment (see below regarding the precise meaning of "judgment") in favor of a party. Some other remedies are classified as "legal" for historical reasons (*see* Ch. 16). But in 90 percent of the circumstances, we are talking about a money judgment when we speak of legal relief.

Equitable relief generally means an injunction—which is a court order commanding the losing party. The command may be positive (*e.g.*, get off plaintiff's land) or negative (*e.g.*, do not begin building a wall on plaintiff's land). The important point is that by issuing the injunction, the court is attempting to coerce the losing party's behavior and in doing so to vindicate the winning party's legal rights.

Another key category of relief is **"declaratory"** relief, which (at the risk of sounding tautological) declares the rights and responsibilities of the litigants. Declaratory relief can be considered its own category or a subset of equitable relief because it is the type of relief that was granted by the Courts of Chancery in England prior to the American Revolution—and these were courts of equity rather than courts of law. The better view is probably that declaratory relief is its own category because the American system generally has juries making factual determinations in cases seeking a "declaratory judgment."

As noted in Chapter 16, whether a claim is considered legal (in which case you get a jury trial) or equitable (in which case you get a bench trial) for purposes of the Seventh Amendment right to jury trial is largely determined by historical analogy and examination of the remedy sought. As a general matter, courts must structure the trial process so that jury consideration of a factual dispute is not precluded by a prior judge-made determination of the facts in the same case. However, if a prior bench trial results in a judgment, it may foreclose a second trial on the matter even if this has the practical impact of preventing jury consideration of the issue.

Examples and Answers: What is the proper classification for the following types of relief? Can you explain the rational for the answers?

- Determination that plaintiff is the rightful beneficiary under a will.
    This is declaratory relief.

- Determination that an insurance policy does not cover a fire loss because the policyholder intentionally set the fire.
    This is declaratory relief.

- A legal order ending a marriage and awarding custody of the children to the mother.
    This is declaratory relief.

- A judgment that defendant owes plaintiff $100,000 in unpaid commissions.
    This is legal relief.

- An order that defendant must remove his pink flamingos from plaintiff's front lawn.
    This is equitable relief of the type that will typically be embodied in an injunction. If the defendant fails to get rid of the flamingos, the court may hold defendant in contempt for violating the terms of the injunction.

- An order forbidding defendant from coming within 100 feet of plaintiff's warehouse.

    This is also equitable, injunctive relief.

Counsel must consider which of these broad categories of remedies and their specific subsets may be available to a client as part of the process of determining whether to commence civil litigation or whether to pursue different particular avenues of ADR.

2. Enforcing Injunctions

Equitable relief often involves some form of an injunction either requiring a party to perform certain acts or to refrain from specified conduct. A permanent injunction is the equitable relief that is granted at the conclusion of trial. When a permanent injunction is granted, it must identify the persons or entities subject to the injunction and detail the required conduct or restrictions of the injunction. It must also be properly served upon those subject to the injunction, and ordinarily the party obtaining the injunction must post a bond or provide other security for compensating the opposing party should it turn out that the injunction was improperly issued and caused injury to the opposing party.

Defects in these aspects of injunctions can result in a party or its agents disobeying the injunction and not suffering a penalty. But if the injunction is properly crafted and served, it binds those subject to it. Violation of the injunction then constitutes contempt of court that may subject the violator to civil or criminal penalties.

EXAMPLES & ANALYSIS

EXAMPLE: **Civil and Criminal Contempt.** Civil contempt is the imposition of a penalty designed to coerce compliance with a court order. It remains in effect until the party in contempt complies with the order. For example, a landlord may be ordered, pursuant to a lease breached by the landlord, to provide air conditioning to an office building but refuse or drag its feet. The court imposes a civil contempt fine of $10,000 per day for each day the building remains without air conditioning. After 10 days, the landlord relents and turns on the AC. The $100,000 fine belongs to the court and may be used for valid judicial purposes. If the landlord keeps the AC off, the fines continue to mount up.

EXAMPLE: Could the court order the money split pro-rata among the tenants? Given to charity? Given to the government to reduce debt? Given to the local university or school district for a scholarship fund? Isn't it crazy to have all this money paid to the court while the tenants remain without air conditioning?

Analysis: Courts have broad equitable power over accumulated contempt fines. But rather than give the money away (which probably exceeds even this broad power), the court is more likely to use the funds to remedy the problem that the party in contempt has failed to remedy. For example, when enough fines have accumulated, the court might order the money used to fix or install air conditioning sufficient to comply with the order. *Caveat:* Some would find this use of the money controversial but we think it well within the court's power under the facts of the hypothetical, assuming that the landlord is accorded due process before the air conditioning company arrives on site.

If the landlord fails to pay accumulated fines or if the landlord remains recalcitrant and continues to leave the building without AC despite the fines, the court may charge the landlord with criminal contempt, which requires a more involved evidentiary hearing and higher standard of proof (beyond a reasonable doubt rather than preponderance of evidence). If the landlord is found in contempt, the court can impose criminal penalties, including incarceration, upon the landlord.

B. The Law and Practice of Preliminary Injunctions

A **preliminary injunction** is an injunction issued to constrain a litigant's behavior while the trial is pending. When the trial is over, whatever relief the court orders replaces the preliminary injunction. A **temporary restraining order** (commonly called a **TRO** but sometimes called a temporary injunction) is an order restricting litigant behavior for a shorter time until the court can decide on the preliminary injunction.

Preliminary injunctions and TROs are governed by Fed. R. Civ. P. 65 and state counterparts. In order to seek either, there must be an actual case, which (as discussed in more detail below) is commenced by a complaint filed with the court. Although a party to an existing case may seek temporary injunctive relief after the case is underway, there usually is no lawsuit pending at the time client and lawyer decided to seek injunctive relief. This means that counsel must draft and file a complaint and usually must serve it on defendant as well. Rule 65(a)(1) requires "notice to the adverse party" as a prerequisite to a preliminary injunction.

A preliminary injunction hearing may be treated as the trial of the matter if the court so orders, a process known as "advancing" trial on the merits to the time of the preliminary injunction. *See* Rule 65(a)(2). "Even when consolidation is not ordered, evidence that is received on the motion and that would be admissible at trial becomes part of the trial record and need not be repeated at trial. But the court must preserve any party's right to a jury trial." *See* Rule 65(a)(2).

TROs may be granted **"ex parte"** or without notice to the other side if the court is convinced that notice would be inconsistent with providing effective temporary relief. Case law construing Rule 65 provides more detail on these standards. Rule 65 also provides that a TRO cannot last for more than 14 days unless extended by the court for another 14 days. *See* Rule 65(b)(2). In addition, plaintiff and defendant can agree or "stipulate" to extend the TRO until the time for conducting a preliminary injunction hearing or even until the conclusion of trial. *See* Rule 65(b)(1).

THE RULE   Rule 65(b)

Temporary Restraining Order

(1) **Issuing Without Notice.** The court may issue a temporary restraining order without written or oral notice to the adverse party or its attorney only if:

   (A) specific facts in an affidavit or a verified complaint clearly show that immediate and irreparable injury, loss, or damage will result to the movant before the adverse party can be heard in opposition; and

   (B) the movant's attorney certifies in writing any efforts made to give notice and the reasons why it should not be required.

Rule 65(b)(2) addresses the contents of the TRO as well as the time limits discussed above.

In addition to issues of timing and notice, the major procedural distinction between a TRO and a preliminary injunction is that the latter cannot be issued until there has been an evidentiary hearing on the matter. Consequently, there is usually witness testimony, introduction of relevant documents, cross-examination, and argument about whether the requested preliminary injunction is justified under the law.

1. The Four Preliminary Injunction Considerations

Rule 65 provides a good deal of information about TROs and preliminary injunctions but does not actually set forth the criteria by which courts are to decide how to determine whether to grant the requested relief. Case law over the years has generally required consideration of four factors when assessing the request for injunctive relief. But as discussed below, there can be some variation among the courts regarding their weighting of these factors and whether all four factors must auger in favor of the movant in order to support relief.

- The **degree of harm** the movant will suffer if the relief is not granted and the ability of the court to rectify the harm as part of final relief granted after trial;

In order to get preliminary injunctive relief, the movant must be able to show that it will be badly injured if something is not done and that this cannot wait until the conclusion of the litigation; this prong of the test used to require that the movant's injury be "irreparable" but over the years it has become sufficient for most judges if the harm is merely serious and very hard to rectify after it has taken place. For example, it may be difficult to calculate the amount of business the movant will lose if a competitor is wrongfully allowed to operate next door in violation of the shopping center lease.

- The **balance of harms** between movant and respondent if the relief is granted or denied;

The court will generally not grant a preliminary injunction if by doing so the court saves the movant from serious harm only to subject the defendant to more serious harm. For example, a court would not likely grant a school's motion to prevent a student from taking final exams because of a controversy over the value of shares of stock that had been used to pay the student's tuition (assuming that the law school otherwise permits tuition to be paid in stock). Barring the student from finals after a semester of work will be very disruptive and hard to fix later. By contrast, if the stock is not sufficiently valuable to cover the tuition, the court can order additional tuition payments.

- The movant's **likelihood of success** on the merits of the case itself;

No matter how sympathetic the court may be to a claim of serious harm incurred during the pendency of litigation, the court will not grant preliminary relief if the movant's case looks like a sure loser. Courts are adjudicators, not charitable agencies.

EXAMPLES & ANALYSIS

EXAMPLE: The movant may correctly claim that being evicted from an apartment will be a serious hardship but if the movant admits that it has not paid rent for six months simply because the landlord has failed to repaint the second bedroom as promised, a preliminary injunction is unlikely.

Analysis: As you will learn in contracts, only "material" breaches of a contract (and a lease is a contract) justify complete nonpayment so the movant will almost certainly lose at trial. Most likely, even if the movant is right about the failure to paint the bedroom, this does not justify judicial intervention to recover something as small as a new coat of paint and does not justify a total stoppage of rental payments. The landlord presumably remains entitled to rent minus the cost of what it should have spent to paint the bedroom. Many states have "repair and deduct" laws that permit tenants to fix a problem and then subtract the cost from the next month's rent. In these states, the tenant's claim is even weaker because it can remedy the situation at little or no cost or risk.
Note that in a case like this, the balance of harms probably weighs against the movant as well. The landlord probably suffers more from being completely stiffed on months of rent than the tenant suffers from lack of new paint in the bedroom.

And (finally) the fourth factor

- The **public interest.**

In general, courts prefer not to be involved in controlling the daily activities of litigants. As a result, the typical/preferred/default remedy in most cases is entry of a money judgment in favor of the winning party. If all goes well, the losing party simply pays the judgment and everyone goes on with their lives. As discussed below, some losing litigants may resist payment, forcing the winners to pursue judgment creditors' remedies to collect the judgment. But, ordinarily, entry of a money judgment does not impose nearly the burden on courts that is imposed by the entry and enforcement of an injunction (preliminary or permanent) requiring certain conduct or restraint.

For example, in some famous cases involving school desegregation and rectification of inhumane conditions in mental health facilities or prisons, courts have properly provided injunctive relief—but as a result, courts have been involved in policing compliance with the injunctions for years or even decades. Unless the case for injunctive relief is sufficiently compelling or the relief requested is particularly simple and easy to enforce, courts ordinarily favor monetary relief over injunctive relief if the monetary relief is not obviously insufficient. In addition, the public interest may come into play based on specialized circumstances of the case.

EXAMPLES & ANALYSIS

EXAMPLE: A vendor alleging breach of contract to work on a ski jump for the Winter Olympics may seek an injunction requiring that it be permitted to perform the work. The Olympic organizers take the position that the vendor is incorrect and that the job properly belongs to another vendor who is already at work and in whom the organizers have more confidence as to the competence of the work.

Analysis: Even if the vendor seeking the preliminary injunction scored high on the serious harm, balance of harms, and likelihood of success on the merits prongs of the four-factor test, a court might well decide that the public interest counsels in favor of letting the organizers complete the ski jump with their preferred vendor so that the event takes place as planned (and without Sven Henrik Olsten ending up thrown into the crowd due to a defect in the ski jump). The movant vendor can be compensated with a money judgment in the amount of lost revenue if it prevails in proving that the ski jump job was supposed to be his.

2. Variant Application of the Four-Factor Test

Not only may states diverge somewhat in their consideration and application of the four-factor test, but even within the federal court system, the various Courts of Appeals vary in their enunciation of the preliminary injunction standard and application of the four considerations. For example, some courts find a possibility of irreparable harm to be sufficient while others require a likelihood or probability of such harm. Similarly, some courts find the likelihood of success on the merits factor satisfied if plaintiff's complaint is not an obvious loser while most insist that the claim appear to be quite compelling, with something of a range of views on what constitutes a sufficient likelihood of success.

Some courts require that every one of the four factors weigh in favor of the movant (the so-called "sequential" test) while most appear to find it sufficient if the four factors on balance support the requested preliminary relief. Some have endorsed the sequential test and argue that this is mandated by Supreme Court precedent. *See, e.g., Winter v. Natural Resources Defense Council, Inc.*, 555 U.S. 7, 21-22 (2008) (denying request for preliminary injunction to suspend military shelling of uninhabited island for target practice due to purported environmental damage). Most commentators, including your course book authors, prefer the sliding scale or "gestalt" approach (our term), which provides greater flexibility to the court to "do equity" (*see* Ch. 16 re law and equity) and reflects what most courts appear to be doing empirically.

One important study published two decades ago found that courts had substantially eliminated the traditional requirement that there be a showing of irreparable injury in order to obtain a preliminary injunction and were instead merely considering and balancing harms with a view to determining whether an injunction made sense under the circumstances. *See* Douglas Laycock, *The Death of the Irreparable Injury Rule*, 103 Harv. L. Rev. 668 (1990). *See also Walgreen Co. v. Sara Creek Property Co.*, 966 F.2d 273 (7th Cir. 1992)(in opinion by noted Judge Richard Posner, court discusses use of injunctions to provide more efficient means of awarding relief with minimized transaction costs and social waste while de-emphasizing purported irreparable nature of injuries; although the decision involved final relief, its exploration of factors has clear implications for preliminary injunction decisions as well).

C. Declaratory Relief and the Limits of Adjudication

Courts have a relatively wide array of remedies that can be brought to bear on behalf of a winning litigant—but it is not an infinite array of remedies. Indeed, one of the attractions of negotiated or mediated settlement is the ability of the disputants to craft a more customized solution to their problems rather than being forced to choose from the limited menu of litigation remedies.

THE RULE	Rule 57

Declaratory Judgment

These rules govern the procedure for obtaining a declaratory judgment under 28 U.S.C. § 2201. Rules 38 and 39 govern demand for a jury trial [see Ch. 15]. The existence of another adequate remedy does not preclude a declaratory judgment that is otherwise appropriate. The court may order a speedy hearing of a declaratory-judgment action.

THE STATUTE	28 U.S.C. § 2201

Creation of remedy

(a) In a case of actual controversy within its jurisdiction, except with respect to Federal taxes [and certain other regulatory matters such as tariffs and trade regulation] any court of the United States, upon the filing of an appropriate pleading, may declare the rights and other legal relations of any interested party seeking such declaration, whether or not further relief is or could be sought. Any such declaration shall have the force and effect of a final judgment or decree and shall be reviewable as such.

As you may remember from Chapter 16, the establishment of the declaratory judgment remedy created some issues. Some opposed it on the ground that such actions were too close to advisory opinions, but this view has been rejected because the statute requires "a case of actual controversy." A request to answer a hypothetical question does not suffice. Declaratory judgments are now a common form of litigation remedy but cannot be used as a means of negating or avoiding jury trial rights a litigant would have in the absence of the declaratory judgment procedure. *See* Chapter 15.

EXAMPLES & ANALYSIS

EXAMPLE: Phineas Phogg files a declaratory judgment action against his neighbor, Donna Dragherfeet, seeking a declaration that a "Wally Wizard Castle Trampoline" (one of those air-filled staples of suburban birthday parties) used for her child's birthday celebration is wrongfully trespassing on his lawn. He also seeks a preliminary injunction to have the Castle moved and a permanent injunction that the Castle never darken his lawn again. And Phineas also wants damages, alleging that the Castle (in place for two weeks) killed his prize floral garden and parts of his lawn. He does not demand trial by jury but Donna does.

Can the judge proceed to adjudicate:

• The preliminary injunction motion?

• The declaratory judgment action?

What if Phineas sought a TRO?

Analysis: The judge does not need to impanel a jury to hear and decide a preliminary injunction motion because it is (1) a motion, and motions are ordinarily for the judge to decide absent other factors and (2) is "preliminary" and thus not a final judgment. Deciding the motion does not make a definitive decision about the neighbors' boundary lines, rights, or responsibilities because there remains—at least in theory—an upcoming trial at which a jury can be impaneled.

But in practice, what is the effect if the preliminary injunction is granted? Remember, the "preliminary" relief sought is removal of the Castle, which was probably rented unless Donna has considerable wealth, a large family, and a consistent preference for balloon castle trampoline party activities.

Once the Castle is removed from the Phineas property, it is unlikely to be put back. Now you know why litigants often contest preliminary injunction motions as zealously as trial. In many cases, the decision to grant or deny a preliminary injunction effectively determines the bulk of the case.

Because (per Chapter 16), a permanent injunction is an equitable remedy, the judge may grant it without the specific advice of a jury. But under *Beacon Theatres* and its progeny, the judge must first present to the jury (assuming summary judgment or other pretrial disposition is not apt) common factual issues implicated in any "legal" claims in the action. The Phineas claim for monetary damages is a legal claim. Even if he does not want a jury (jurors with kids in this apparently upper middle class town might view Phineas as a Phuddy Duddy who doesn't like kids), Donna has a right to insist on it.

The elements of the legal claim are: (1) trespass (2) causing (3) damage to flowers and grass. In order to prevail on the equitable claim (seeking to eject the Castle from his property), Phineas must at a minimum prove trespass. There is a common issue of fact that must be tried to a jury before the judge can enter the requested permanent injunctive relief. He would also have to prove causation (a factual issue) and damages (a factual issue).

It is hard to imagine a TRO applying to this case because these orders typically attempt to simply preserve the status quo. Phineas wants the Castle off his property, which sounds more in the nature of an injunction. A court would be highly unlikely to require removal of the Castle without an evidentiary hearing—and conducting such a hearing makes the resulting order a preliminary injunction rather than a TRO. A TRO might be apt if Phineas was attempting to prevent Donna's family and friends from continuing to use the Castle while a preliminary injunction motion is pending and inflicting further damage on his flowers and lawn.

By its terms, 28 U.S.C. § 2201 eliminates the declaratory judgment remedy for certain actions such as determination of the charitable status of organizations for tax purposes (26 U.S.C. § 7428), determination of eligibility for military commissary and exchange benefits, (11 U.S.C. § 1146), anti-dumping rules related to tariffs (19 U.S.C. § 1516(a)(f)(10)) and approval of new drugs (21 U.S.C. §§ 355, 360b). Can you see why Congress might want to exempt these types of actions from general federal trial court jurisdiction?

D. Judgments and Collection

IN PRACTICE

The Importance of Obtaining and Collecting a Judgment

As you have now undoubtedly discerned, the object and result of most civil litigation is a money judgment, *i.e.*, an order that the losing party pay the winner a certain amount of money. As you learned in Chapter18, the winning party is also usually entitled to prejudgment interest on the damages it has been awarded as well as the "costs" incurred in pursuing the litigation (but not usually the counsel fees expended; attorney's fees are recoverable for the prevailing party only under special circumstances discussed in Chapter 18).

The term "judgment" is one of technical art in litigation. Although we have described a judgment as an order to pay or do something (and this is accurate so far as it goes), an "order" is not a "judgment" unless the order provides that the court is entering judgment on the matter. As established by Rules 54 and 58, excerpted below, a judgment is a separate document filed in the court record that states that judgment is entered in a matter and sets for the terms of the judgment. The terms may include payment of damages (plus interest, costs, or attorney fees if warranted), an affirmative injunction that the losing party do something or a negative injunction that the losing party refrain from doing something. In order to be valid, a judgment must be rendered by a court that has power over the subject matter of the action (*see* Ch. 1) as well as power over the defendants *(see* Ch. 2 regarding personal jurisdiction), and proper venue, with the parties given due process (adequate notice and opportunity to be heard by a sufficiently unbiased judge and factfinder) prior to entry of the judgment. *See* AMERICAN LAW INSTITUTE, RESTATEMENT (SECOND) OF JUDGMENTS § 1 (1982).

The formal entry of judgment in a matter is a particularly important event of the civil litigation process. It generally means that the matter is concluded although there may be entry of "partial" judgments pursuant to Fed. R. Civ. P. 54. When there is entry of "final" judgment for the case as a whole, the case may then be appealed by the losing party or even by the winning litigant as to some aspect of the case on which it thinks it should have won more (*see* Ch. 19 regarding Appeals). The entry of judgment is important for establishing a number of important timelines affecting post-trial motions such as motions for a new trial, which do not begin to run until judgment is entered.

Rule 54 defines a judgment as a "decree or any order from which an appeal lies" and provides that judgment may be entered separately on individual claims or on behalf of an individual party even if portions of the case remain to be adjudicated. Rule 58 establishes the technical requirements of a judgment (*e.g.*, that it be on a separate document) and by defining when judgment is formally entered, governs the running of deadlines based on entry of judgment. Note particularly that several important types of judicial decisions are not subject to the separate document rule and are treated as judgments even if the court's ruling is not embodied on a separate document filed with the Clerk of Court.

To qualify as a separate document entering judgment, the judgment form must be self-contained and apart from the underlying opinion or order reflecting the court's reasoning. *See LeBoon v. Lancaster Jewish Community Center Ass'n*, 503 F.3d 217, 224 (3d Cir. 2007), *cert. denied*, 553 U.S. 1004 (2008). This typically requires that the order: be self-contained and separate from the opinion; state the relief granted; and not address the reasoning behind the decision, which is in a separate memorandum or perhaps even via a ruling from the bench (which is transcribed by the judge's court reporter).

1. Collecting Judgments

Once a judgment is entered, the winning litigant can collect the judgment if the losing party does not pay. Federal Rules 64 and 69 provide that in seeking to collect a judgment, the winning litigant may take advantage of any of the creditors' remedies available under the state law of the forum state in which the federal court trial took place and judgment was entered. A judgment is a debt just as funds due under a contract are a debt. The holder of a judgment is often referred to as a "judgment creditor" in seeking to collect a judgment that is not voluntarily paid by the losing party. The entry of judgment may create a lien on real property of the judgment debtor located in the judicial district where the judgment was entered. Applicable statutes usually codify the lien and procedures to follow to secure it against a debtor.

2. Types of Collection Actions

Among the types of collection remedies available to winning litigants are:

Execution—the process of enforcing a judgment by having the sheriff or another authorized officer seize and sell the judgment debtor's property.

Attachment or Seizure—the process of gaining legal control over debtor property prior to execution. After property is attached, judgment debtors often pay the judgment in order to get the judgment creditor to refrain from execution. A related process is sequestration or providing notice of a judicial lien on the property in order to discourage potential buyers and thus encourage the judgment debtor to satisfy the debt in order to have the lien or a sequestration order removed.

Garnishment—a form of collection in which a third person holding property of the debtor is ordered to pay the property or a portion of the property to a judgment creditor. For example, you as a judgment creditor may serve a writ of garnishment on a bank which has a savings or checking account of the debtor and the bank will be required to pay funds from the account up to the amount of the debt. Or you may serve a writ of garnishment on the debtor's employer—but under most state laws, no more than a certain percentage of the debtor's wages can be garnished at one time. With a wage-earning debtor, the judgment creditor can get paid, but it may take awhile unless the judgment is small.

Replevin—an order that property be returned. In federal court, the replevin remedy tends to be subsumed by any permanent injunction awarded to the winner of the case which may, as part of the injunctive relief, order return of property. But a writ of replevin is still a common remedy, particularly in state court and particularly as a preliminary remedy.

Example and Analysis: A vendor who has sold a refrigerator where the customer stops making required monthly payments may seek a writ of replevin rather than awaiting the outcome of full litigation of the matter. As a practical matter, the dispute may end when the vendor gets the refrigerator back because obtaining a money judgment against someone too poor to make monthly payments on the fridge will not be of much use. But vendors nonetheless may press ahead, if nothing else but to show that they will not be trifled with when it comes to getting paid when selling goods on credit.

Sequestration—This is similar to attachment in that property is brought under the control of the judicial system but differs in that with sequestration the property is in essence immobilized and held by the system whereas attachment is generally a precursor to a judicial sale of the attached property.

Arrest—Imprisonment as a means of debt collection has fallen out of favor but a debtor can be held in contempt and imprisoned. In the wake of the economic downturn of 2008, there have been in some states reports of creditors pursuing debtors in this manner although technically the debtor is not arrested for debt but instead is arrested for some other infraction (*e.g.*, speeding) and then is forced to pay outstanding judgments in order to avoid a night in jail before the matter can be heard in court. Although we like creditors as well as the next guys, serious constitutional and ethical issues surround this type of debt collection.

Of course, the same judgment debtor who is refusing to pay is also unlikely to lay out his financial records. But pursuant to Fed. R. Civ. P. 69, the creditor may depose the debtor and conduct other discovery in aid of collecting the judgment. If the debtor refuses to cooperate without a valid objection, the debtor may be held in contempt.

E. Preclusion: *Res judicata* and Collateral Estoppel

Introduction. Preclusion doctrine exits to further the legal system's policy of finality and to avoid duplicative, wasteful, or inconsistent litigation results. The basic idea underlying preclusion is that a litigant is entitled to a "day in court" or (more practically) full, complete and fair litigation (which may of course terminate during the pretrial stage). But a litigant is not entitled to multiple bites of the apple. Determining whether a case includes the same claims, parties, or issues as an earlier case is not always easy, particularly when the legal system is also concerned that the outcome of the first case not be read so broadly as to deny a litigant its rights in bringing a subsequent case. Preclusion doctrine is heavily informed both by the legal system's desires for finality and efficiency and by the system's commitment to fairness and due process.

As you have noted throughout this book, the law of Civil Procedure is created by a mixture of the Constitution, statutes, the Federal Rules, and case law. Some areas such as pleadings, joinder, and summary judgment are extensively discussed in the Rules. Venue is subject to an extensive statutory scheme. Other aspects of civil litigation are determined less by the rules (either because the rules do not say much about the area or are textually indeterminate) than by case law doctrine. For example, the *Erie* Doctrine construing the statute in light of constitutional considerations of equal protection has been developed largely through case law. Preclusion doctrine is similar. Most of the "law" in this area is case law rather than statutory or rule-based law.

Although there is not an extensive federal statute regarding preclusion, there exists particularly authoritative secondary authority in the form of the *Restatement of Judgments*, promulgated by the American Law Institute.

1. The Concept of Claim Preclusion/*Res Judicata*

The concept and doctrine of *res judicata* (Latin for "the thing decided") has existed for some time. The notion is that once a claim has been adjudicated, it cannot be re-litigated. The preferred modern term is "claim preclusion" not only because fewer lawyers know Latin than a century ago but also because it more accurately describes the concept and its impact. Once you litigate a claim to conclusion, you are precluded from re-litigating the claim. If this were not the rule, dissatisfied litigants (especially those with money), could keep suing and suing, in forum after forum, causing waste, inconsistency, and what most of the legal profession regards as injustice.

Although the first outcome may have been wrong (*e.g.*, incorrect law was applied, the jury was misled or rendered an atypical or even bizarre verdict), the law assumes there is a better than equal chance that it was correct and that a second, different decision is likely to be "wrong." In addition, the prevailing presumption of the legal system is that it conducts correct adjudications most of the time. Consequently, the conventional wisdom in law is that justice is better served over the long run by sticking with the first decision and precluding re-litigation of the same case.

But the system is also aware that claim preclusion has a potential for injustice if construed so broadly that litigants are deprived of their right to a "day in court" simply because the first case has some similarities with the second. As a result, courts apply claim preclusion (and its cousin collateral estoppel/issue preclusion) with considerable care.

2. The Elements of Claim Preclusion

To obtain the benefit of claim preclusion and foreclose further litigation, a party in a subsequent action must show the existence of:

a. A prior claim that was fully adjudicated on the merits.

The claim must have resulted in a final judgment on the substantive claims at issue. Dismissals based on procedural defects such as improper venue or lack of personal jurisdiction do not constitute adjudication on the merits (*see* Chapters 2 & 3). Informal resolution of claims does not count as adjudication. Regulatory decisions are sometimes treated as adjudications but often not because they do not result in a judgment or other exhaustion of legal remedies.

b. That the current subsequent action arises out of the same claim as the earlier action.

The claims need not have the same nomenclature. For example, in Case One, the claim could have been styled as "conversion" under the preferred language of that jurisdiction while in Case Two, the claim could have been styled as "wrongful appropriation of the property of another." What matters is whether the two cases involve claims that are substantively the same even if they do not formally have the same name or classification

c. That the parties in the subsequent action are the same as in the earlier action—or that parties in the subsequent action are "in privity" with a party in the first case.

"Privity" means sharing the legal identity or a similarly close tie. This is perhaps the most commonly disputed issue in claim preclusion matters. Where the parties are exactly the same, application of the doctrine is relatively straightforward. But the second case may involve persons or entities (*e.g.*, affiliated corporations, business collaborators) presenting difficult issues of whether the litigants in Case Two are sufficiently in privity with those of Case One.

Unless all three elements of claim preclusion are satisfied, the first judgment is not *res judicata* and the second claim is not precluded.

3. The Concept of Issue Preclusion/Collateral Estoppel

Like the term res judicata, "collateral estoppel" has a lengthy history and has been replaced in more refined legal circles with the term "issue preclusion" because the latter is more accurate and reduces the confusion that tends to surround the word "estoppel" which is used in so many legal contexts (*e.g.*, promissory estoppel in Contracts, equitable estoppel, judicial estoppel, and common assertions that an opponent is estopped from doing something because it is inconsistent with prior conduct).

The concept is similar to that of claim preclusion but is broader in that it can reach not only claims made in prior cases but issues addressed in prior cases. But the concept of issue preclusion or collateral estoppel is also narrower than res judicata/claim preclusion. A court's earlier decision in Case One may make a determination of an issue that is binding in Case Two— but all of Case Two is not determined by the outcome of Case One.

4. The Elements of Issue Preclusion/Collateral Estoppel

To have issue preclusion, the following elements apply.

a. The issue (of law or fact) in a subsequent case must be the same as in the prior case that resulted in a final judgment on the merits.

b. The litigant against whom issue preclusion is sought must have been a party to the earlier action or be in privity with a party to that action who had adequate incentive to contest the issue.

c. The issue must have been actually litigated and decided.

It is not sufficient if an issue is raised but not adjudicated or if a pending issue is removed from the case by stipulation of the parties or by failure to press the issue in the earlier trial.

d. The determination of the issue in the earlier case must have been essential to the judgment in that case.

Elements 3 & 4 together mean that a prior issue must have been "necessarily decided" in Case One to have preclusive effect in Case Two. This can be a sticking point of issue preclusion practice. The prior decision may address and decide an issue that is present in the subsequent case—but if the prior decision on the issue was gratuitous and not necessary for resolving the prior lawsuit, there can be no issue preclusion. There can be substantial debate over whether the issue needed to be decided in order to adjudicate the earlier action. As a general rule, the test for determining necessity will be whether the issue had to be resolved in order to address an essential element of the prior action.

Unless all prongs of this test are satisfied, there cannot be issue preclusion. *See also* ALI RESTATEMENT (SECOND) OF JUDGMENTS §§ 17, 24.

Preclusion (as contrasted with something like tort liability) tends to be a relatively apolitical area on which the ALI, like the profession generally, is rather united. Everyone is against needlessly repetitive litigation and inconsistent results and in favor of giving litigants fair access to a "day in court." But even in a non-partisan atmosphere, balancing these goals may be difficult. As you consider the rules of preclusion and their application, consistently ask yourself whether the current system is excessively protective or insufficiently protective of litigant access to the courts and whether the rules of preclusion go overboard seeking efficiency and finality or whether they give disputants too many "bites at the apple."

5. Illustrating Claim and Issue Preclusion

EXAMPLES & ANALYSIS

EXAMPLE: Phats Hatfield sues Domino McCoy in both West Virginia state court and Kentucky state court, contending in each case that Domino has encroached on his property by building a fence and grazing cattle on his land. On April 1, 2012, the West Virginia court enters judgment for Hatfield. On May 1, 2012, the Kentucky court enters judgment for McCoy. On June 1, the State of Kentucky begins proceedings to acquire the area where McCoy's cattle were grazing as part of a road construction project. Who should the State treat as the owner of the land for purposes of compensation for the taking of private property?

Analysis: The State must of course compensate the owner of the land—but there are two different decisions identifying two different owners. Rather than analyzing the relative persuasiveness of the respective decisions, the court deciding the third case will consider the later judgment authoritative and treat McCoy as owner of the land at issue. *See* RESTATEMENT (SECOND) OF JUDGMENTS § 15.

A VARIANT OF THIS EXAMPLE: Now, assume that Phats has appealed the Kentucky decision declaring Domino to own the land and that two years later, the Kentucky Supreme Court reverses and rules the land indeed belongs to Phats rather than Domino. But during these two years, another trial judge in Kentucky has permitted the State to condemn the land and pay Domino for it based on the Kentucky decision that found Domino to own the land. But that decision has been reversed and Phats is now the legal owner of the land. Can Phats force Domino to give up the money paid by the state for an involuntary taking what was once legally "his" property? Can Phats force the State to compensate him in addition to Domino?

Analysis: The short answer is no. Even when a judgment (*e.g.*, the eminent domain takings payment by the State to Domino) is reversed on appeal, prior decisions that accorded preclusive effect based on the earlier judgment are not automatically nullified. However, the earlier judgment regarding title to the land could be attacked in a Fed. R. Civ. P. 60 motion to correct the (now seen as "mistaken") finding of land ownership by Domino. *See* Chapter 18 regarding Rule 60 motions seeking modification or vacation of judgments.

EXAMPLE: Pau buys land from Dov but Dov refused to honor the contract and convey the land to Pau. Pau sues and wins. The court orders Dov to convey the land as per the contract and judgment is entered, with the land becoming Pau's property. Then Pau sues Dov for monetary damages. Dov moves for summary judgment to throw the second case out. What result?

Analysis: Because all of Pau's claims are merged into the first action against Dov, Pau cannot later attempt to obtain additional or greater relief than that obtained in Case One. By seeking more and different relief in Case Two, Pau is "splitting the cause of action" against Dov, which is not permitted. Pau continues to keep the land but cannot continue the suit against Dov.

EXAMPLE: Pam is injured when hit by a car driven by Dave. She sues Dave's insurer to recover for the injuries. The court dismisses the case on the ground that a tortfeasor's insurer cannot be sued until the plaintiff has obtained a judgment against the tortfeasor. Is Pam precluded from bringing the suit in the future?

Analysis: No. The decision dismissing the claim against the insurer as premature was not a decision on the substantive merits of the lawsuit. In particular, Case One did not make a determination regarding duty, breach, negligence, causation, or damages. If Pam's case against Dave is successful, Dave's insurer can then be sued and neither claim or issue preclusion will prevent the action.

EXAMPLE: Pete sues Dana in small claims court (where the maximum amount of a judgment is limited to $2,000 by state law) for $1,000 for failing to pay for 1,000 "One Dollar Widgets." Dana counterclaims alleging that the widgets are defective and effectively worthless, which not only eliminates the need to pay but also results in a $5,000 verdict for Dana rather than Pete because of damages the widgets did to Dana's factory when used. What can Dana collect? What should Dana do next and what preclusion question arises.

Analysis: Dana can collect as much as $2000 in the Case One action, as this is the total limit of the Court's jurisdiction. Dana can also take the judgment to any court with jurisdiction over Pete and seek to collect up to $3,000, depending on the Case Two court's limit.

6. Relatedness: The Concept of a "Series" and the "Same Transaction or Occurrence"

For claim preclusion to obtain, Case One and Case Two must involve the same claim, which in turn means that the two cases must both arise out of the same "transaction or occurrence," including any series of connected transactions out of which the action arose." According to § 24 of the *Restatement (Second) of Judgments* the factual grouping that constitutes a "transaction" or that constitutes a "series" is to be determined "pragmatically, giving weight to such considerations as whether the facts are related in time, space, origin, or motivation" and "whether they form a convenient trial unit, and whether their treatment as a unit conforms to the parties' expectations or business understanding or usage."

Recall that when determining whether a counterclaim is permissive or compulsory (*see* Ch. 7), the test is whether the counterclaim arises out of the same transaction or occurrence as the initial claim. Remember as well (*see* Ch. 10) that an amended complaint relates back to the date of the original complaint when it involves the same transaction or occurrence. In making these inquiries, courts have used the **"same facts and law," "same evidence"** and **"logical relationship"** tests, with the logical relationship being most popular.

7. Preclusion: Sword or Shield?

Preclusion doctrine is ordinarily viewed as a shield that protects against repetitive litigation, particularly multiple suits by stubborn opponents engaging in a vendetta but lacking a very good case. However, preclusion can also be used as a sword in order to establish a fact in order to win a claim and establish liability or obtain relief. The following case—*Parklane Hosiery v. Shore*—illustrates how issue preclusion may be used as a sword.

The *Parklane* case excerpted below presents the question of whether civil litigation plaintiffs can also use the outcome of a bench trial against the defendant to establish an element of liability and save plaintiff the trouble of introducing information altogether as well as taking the risk that a jury in the second civil trial might find a statement not to be false or misleading.

Traditionally, one could not get the benefit of issue preclusion from a prior decision unless one was also subject to that same decision's issue preclusion. This is the rule of **"mutuality"** that held sway for decades. However, in 1972 the Supreme Court held that a litigant could invoke **"defensive"**

issue preclusion even when not itself bound by the judgment in which the issue had previously been adjudicated. But there remained the question of whether a litigant could make **"offensive" use of issue preclusion** in the absence of being bound by the prior judgment. The Shore plaintiffs sought to make offensive use of Parklane's loss in a bench trial in an SEC enforcement action in order to establish an element of liability in their civil action seeking damages from Parklane.

FROM THE COURT

Parklane Hosiery Co., Inc. v. Shore

439 U.S. 322 (1979)

Supreme Court of the United States

JUSTICE STEWART delivered the opinion of the Court.

This case presents the question whether a party who has had issues of fact adjudicated adversely to it in an equitable action may be collaterally estopped from relitigating the same issues before a jury in a subsequent legal action brought against it by a new party. The respondent brought this stockholder's class action against the petitioners in a Federal District Court. The complaint alleged that [Parklane] and 13 of its officers, directors, and stockholders, had issued a materially false and misleading proxy statement in connection with a merger.

The amended complaint alleged that the proxy statement that had been issued to the stockholders was false and misleading because it failed to disclose: (1) that the president of Parklane would financially benefit as a result of the company's going private; (2) certain ongoing negotiations that could have resulted in financial benefit to Parklane; and (3) that the appraisal of the fair value of Parklane stock was based on insufficient information to be accurate. The proxy statement, according to the complaint, had violated the Securities Exchange Act of 1934, 15 U. S. C. §§ 78n(a), 78j (b), and 78t (a), as well as various rules and regulations promulgated by the Securities and Exchange Commission (SEC). The complaint sought damages, rescission of the merger, and recovery of costs.

Before this action came to trial, the SEC filed suit against the same defendants in the Federal District Court, alleging that the proxy statement that had been issued by Parklane was materially false and misleading in essentially the same respects as those that had been alleged in the respondent's complaint. Injunctive relief was requested. After a 4-day trial, the District Court found that the proxy statement was materially false and misleading in the respects alleged, and entered a declaratory judgment to that effect. The Court of Appeals for the Second Circuit affirmed this judgment.

The respondent in the present case then moved for partial summary judgment against the petitioners, asserting that the petitioners were collaterally estopped from relitigating the issues that had been resolved against them in the action brought by the SEC. A private plaintiff in an action under the proxy rules is not entitled to relief simply by demonstrating that the proxy solicitation was materially false and misleading. The plaintiff must also show that he was injured and prove damages.

Since the SEC action was limited to a determination of whether the proxy statement contained materially false and misleading information, the respondent conceded that he would still have to prove these other elements of his prima facie case in the private action. The petitioners' right to a jury trial on those remaining issues is not contested.

The District Court denied the motion on the ground that such an application of collateral estoppel would deny the petitioners their Seventh Amendment right to a jury trial. The Court of Appeals for the Second Circuit reversed, holding that a party who has had issues of fact determined against him after a full and fair opportunity to litigate in a nonjury trial is collaterally estopped from obtaining a subsequent jury trial of these same issues of fact. The appellate court concluded that "the Seventh Amendment preserves the right to jury trial only with respect to issues of fact, [and] once those issues have been fully and fairly adjudicated in a prior proceeding, nothing remains for trial, either with or without a jury." Because of an intercircuit conflict, we granted certiorari.

I

The threshold question to be considered is whether, quite apart from the right to a jury trial under the Seventh Amendment, the petitioners can be precluded from relitigating facts resolved adversely to them in a prior equitable proceeding with another party under the general law of collateral estoppel. Specifically, we must determine whether a litigant who was not a party to a prior judgment may nevertheless use that judgment "offensively" to prevent a defendant from relitigating issues resolved in the earlier proceeding. In this context, offensive use of collateral estoppel occurs when the plaintiff seeks to foreclose the defendant from litigating an issue the defendant has previously litigated unsuccessfully in an action with another party. Defensive use occurs when a defendant seeks to prevent a plaintiff from asserting a claim the plaintiff has previously litigated and lost against another defendant.

A

Collateral estoppel, like the related doctrine of res judicata, has the dual purpose of protecting litigants from the burden of relitigating an identical issue with the same party or his privy and of promoting judicial economy by preventing needless litigation. *Blonder-Tongue Laboratories, Inc.* v. *University of Illinois Foundation*, 402 U.S. 313, 328-329 (1972). Under the doctrine of res judicata, a judgment on the merits in a prior suit bars a second suit involving the same parties or their privies based on the same cause of action. Under the doctrine of collateral estoppel, on the other hand, the second action is upon a different cause of action and the judgment in the prior suit precludes relitigation of issues actually litigated and necessary to the outcome of the first action.

Until relatively recently, however, the scope of collateral estoppel was limited by the doctrine of mutuality of parties. Under this mutuality doctrine, neither party could use a prior judgment as an estoppel against the other unless both parties were bound by the judgment. Based on the premise that it is somehow unfair to allow a party to use a prior judgment when he himself would not be so bound, the mutuality requirement provided a party who had litigated and lost in a previous action an opportunity to relitigate identical issues with new parties.

By failing to recognize the obvious difference in position between a party who has never litigated an issue and one who has fully litigated and lost, the mutuality requirement was criticized almost from its inception. This criticism was summarized in the Court's opinion in *Blonder-Tongue Laboratories, Inc.* v. *University of Illinois Foundation, supra.* The opinion of Justice Traynor for a unanimous California Supreme Court in *Bernhard* v. *Bank of America Nat. Trust & Savings Assn.*, 122 P. 2d

892, 895 (Cal. 1948), made the point succinctly: "No satisfactory rationalization has been advanced for the requirement of mutuality. Just why a party who was not bound by a previous action should be precluded from asserting it as *res judicata* against a party who was bound by it is difficult to comprehend."

Recognizing the validity of this criticism, the Court in *Blonder-Tongue* abandoned the mutuality requirement, at least in cases where a patentee seeks to relitigate the validity of a patent after a federal court in a previous lawsuit has already declared it invalid. . . . The Court also emphasized that relitigation of issues previously adjudicated is particularly wasteful in patent cases because of their staggering expense and typical length. Under the doctrine of mutuality of parties an alleged infringer might find it cheaper to pay royalties than to challenge a patent that had been declared invalid in a prior suit, since the holder of the patent is entitled to a statutory presumption of validity.

B

The *Blonder-Tongue* case involved defensive use of collateral estoppel—a plaintiff was estopped from asserting a claim that the plaintiff had previously litigated and lost against another defendant. The present case, by contrast, involves offensive use of collateral estoppel—a plaintiff is seeking to estop a defendant from relitigating the issues which the defendant previously litigated and lost against another plaintiff. In both the offensive and defensive use situations, the party against whom estoppel is asserted has litigated and lost in an earlier action. Nevertheless, several reasons have been advanced why the two situations should be treated differently. Various commentators have expressed reservations regarding the application of offensive collateral estoppel.

First, offensive use of collateral estoppel does not promote judicial economy in the same manner as defensive use does. Defensive use of collateral estoppel precludes a plaintiff from relitigating identical issues by merely "switching adversaries." Under the mutuality requirement, a plaintiff could accomplish this result since he would not have been bound by the judgment had the original defendant won. Thus defensive collateral estoppel gives a plaintiff a strong incentive to join all potential defendants in the first action if possible.

Offensive use of collateral estoppel, on the other hand, creates precisely the opposite incentive. Since a plaintiff will be able to rely on a previous judgment against a defendant but will not be bound by that judgment if the defendant wins, the plaintiff has every incentive to adopt a "wait and see" attitude, in the hope that the first action by another plaintiff will result in a favorable judgment. Thus offensive use of collateral estoppel will likely increase rather than decrease the total amount of litigation, since potential plaintiffs will have everything to gain and nothing to lose by not intervening in the first action. [A]pplication of collateral estoppel may be denied if the party asserting it "could have effected joinder in the first action between himself and his present adversary."

A second argument against offensive use of collateral estoppel is that it may be unfair to a defendant. If a defendant in the first action is sued for small or nominal damages, he may have little incentive to defend vigorously, particularly if future suits are not foreseeable. Allowing offensive collateral estoppel may also be unfair to a defendant if the judgment relied upon as a basis for the estoppel is itself inconsistent with one or more previous judgments in favor of the defendant. In Professor Currie's familiar example, a railroad collision injures 50 passengers all of whom bring separate actions against the railroad. After the railroad wins the first 25 suits, a plaintiff wins in suit 26. Professor Currie argues that offensive use of collateral estoppel should not be applied so as to allow plaintiffs 27 through 50 automatically to recover. [*citing* Brainerd Currie, *Mutuality of Collateral Estoppel: Limits of the Bernhard Doctrine*, 9 Stan. L. Rev. 281 (1957) and Restatement of Judgments § 88].

Still another situation where it might be unfair to apply offensive estoppel is where the second action affords the defendant procedural opportunities unavailable in the first action that could readily cause a different result. If, for example, the defendant in the first action was forced to defend in an inconvenient forum and therefore was unable to engage in full scale discovery or call witnesses, application of offensive collateral estoppel may be unwarranted. Indeed, differences in available procedures may sometimes justify not allowing a prior judgment to have estoppel effect in a subsequent action even between the same parties, or where defensive estoppel is asserted against a plaintiff who has litigated and lost. The problem of unfairness is particularly acute in cases of offensive estoppel, however, because the defendant against whom estoppel is asserted typically will not have chosen the forum in the first action. [*citing* Restatement § 88 (2)].

C

We have concluded that the preferable approach for dealing with these problems in the federal courts is not to preclude the use of offensive collateral estoppel, but to grant trial courts broad discretion to determine when it should be applied. This is essentially the approach of [RESTATEMENT] § 88, which recognizes that "the distinct trend if not the clear weight of recent authority is to the effect that there is no intrinsic difference between 'offensive' as distinct from 'defensive' issue preclusion, although a stronger showing that the prior opportunity to litigate was adequate may be required in the former situation than the latter." The general rule should be that in cases where a plaintiff could easily have joined in the earlier action or where, either for the reasons discussed above or for other reasons, the application of offensive estoppel would be unfair to a defendant, a trial judge should not allow the use of offensive collateral estoppel.

In the present case, however, none of the circumstances that might justify reluctance to allow the offensive use of collateral estoppel is present. The application of offensive collateral estoppel will not here reward a private plaintiff who could have joined in the previous action, since the respondent probably could not have joined in the injunctive action brought by the SEC even had he so desired. Moreover, consolidation of a private action with one brought by the SEC without its consent is prohibited by statute. 15 U. S. C. § 78u(g).

Similarly, there is no unfairness to the petitioners in applying offensive collateral estoppel in this case. First, in light of the serious allegations made in the SEC's complaint against the petitioners, as well as the foreseeability of subsequent private suits that typically follow a successful Government judgment, the petitioners had every incentive to litigate the SEC lawsuit fully and vigorously. Second, the judgment in the SEC action was not inconsistent with any previous decision. Finally, there will in the respondent's action be no procedural opportunities available to the petitioners that were unavailable in the first action of a kind that might be likely to cause a different result.

After a 4-day trial in which the petitioners had every opportunity to present evidence and call witnesses, the District Court held for the SEC. The petitioners then appealed to the Court of Appeals for the Second Circuit, which affirmed the judgment against them. Moreover, the petitioners were already aware of the action brought by the respondent, since it had commenced before the filing of the SEC action. It is true, of course, that the petitioners in the present action would be entitled to a jury trial of the issues bearing on whether the proxy statement was materially false and misleading had the SEC action never been brought—a matter to be discussed in Part II of this opinion. But the presence or absence of a jury as factfinder is basically neutral, quite unlike, for example, the necessity of defending the first lawsuit in an inconvenient forum.

We conclude, therefore, that none of the considerations that would justify a refusal to allow the use of offensive collateral estoppel is present in this case. Since the petitioners received a "full and fair" opportunity to litigate their claims in the SEC action, the contemporary law of collateral estoppel leads inescapably to the conclusion that the petitioners are collaterally estopped from relitigating the question of whether the proxy statement was materially false and misleading.

II

The question that remains is whether, notwithstanding the law of collateral estoppel, the use of offensive collateral estoppel in this case would violate the petitioners' Seventh Amendment right to a jury trial. . . . The petitioners contend that since the scope of the Amendment must be determined by reference to the common law as it existed in 1791, and since the common law permitted collateral estoppel only where there was mutuality of parties, collateral estoppel cannot constitutionally be applied when such mutuality is absent.

The petitioners have advanced no persuasive reason, however, why the meaning of the Seventh Amendment should depend on whether or not mutuality of parties is present. A litigant who has lost because of adverse factual findings in an equity action is equally deprived of a jury trial whether he is estopped from relitigating the factual issues against the same party or a new party. In either case, the party against whom estoppel is asserted has litigated questions of fact, and has had the facts determined against him in an earlier proceeding. In either case there is no further factfinding function for the jury to perform, since the common factual issues have been resolved in the previous action.

The law of collateral estoppel, like the law in other procedural areas defining the scope of the jury's function, has evolved since 1791. [T]hese developments are not repugnant to the Seventh Amendment simply for the reason that they did not exist in 1791. Thus if, as we have held, the law of collateral estoppel forecloses the petitioners from relitigating the factual issues determined against them in the SEC action, nothing in the Seventh Amendment dictates a different result, even though because of lack of mutuality there would have been no collateral estoppel in 1791.

JUSTICE REHNQUIST, dissenting.

It is admittedly difficult to be outraged about the treatment accorded by the federal judiciary to petitioners' demand for a jury trial in this lawsuit. Outrage is an emotion all but impossible to generate with respect to a corporate defendant in a securities fraud action, and this case is no exception. But the nagging sense of unfairness as to the way petitioners have been treated, engendered by the *imprimatur* placed by the Court of Appeals on respondent's "heads I win, tails you lose" theory of this litigation, is not dispelled by this Court's antiseptic analysis of the issues in the case.

* * *

I think it is clear that petitioners were denied their Seventh Amendment right to a jury trial in this case. Neither respondent nor the Court doubts that at common law as it existed in 1791, petitioners would have been entitled in the private action to have a jury determine whether the proxy statement was false and misleading in the respects alleged. The reason is that at common law in 1791, collateral estoppel was permitted only where the parties in the first action were identical to, or in privity with, the parties to the subsequent action. It was not until 1971 that the doctrine of mutuality was abrogated by this Court in certain limited circumstances.

Abandonment of mutuality is a recent development. The case of *Bernhard* v. *Bank of America Nat. Trust & Sav. Assn.*, 19 Cal. 2d 807, 122 P.2d 892, generally considered the seminal case adopting the new approach, was not decided until 1942. But developments in the judge-made doctrine of collateral estoppel, however salutary, cannot, consistent with the Seventh Amendment, contract in any material fashion the right to a jury trial that a defendant would have enjoyed in 1791. In the instant case, resort to the doctrine of collateral estoppel does more than merely contract the right to a jury trial: It eliminates the right entirely and therefore contravenes the Seventh Amendment.

The procedural devices of summary judgment and directed verdict are direct descendants of their common-law antecedents. They accomplish nothing more than could have been done at common law, albeit by a more cumbersome procedure. By contrast, the development of nonmutual estoppel is a substantial departure from the common law and its use in this case completely deprives petitioners of their right to have a jury determine contested issues of fact. I am simply unwilling to accept the Court's presumption that the complete extinguishment of petitioners' right to trial by jury can be justified as a mere change in "procedural incident or detail."

II

In my view, it is "unfair" to apply offensive collateral estoppel where the party who is sought to be estopped has not had an opportunity to have the facts of his case determined by a jury. Since in this case petitioners were not entitled to a jury trial in the Securities and Exchange Commission (SEC) lawsuit, I would not estop them from relitigating the issues determined in the SEC suit before a jury in the private action. I believe that several factors militate in favor of this result.

First, the use of offensive collateral estoppel in this case runs counter to the strong federal policy favoring jury trials, even if it does not, as the majority holds, violate the Seventh Amendment. . . . Second, I believe that the opportunity for a jury trial in the second action could easily lead to a different result from that obtained in the first action before the court and therefore that it is unfair to estop petitioners from relitigating the issues before a jury.

The ultimate irony of today's decision is that its potential for significantly conserving the resources of either the litigants or the judiciary is doubtful at best. That being the case, I see absolutely no reason to frustrate so cavalierly the important federal policy favoring jury decisions of disputed fact questions. The instant case is an apt example of the minimal savings that will be accomplished by the Court's decision. As the Court admits, even if petitioners are collaterally estopped from relitigating whether the proxy was materially false and misleading, they are still entitled to have a jury determine whether respondent was injured by the alleged misstatements and the amount of damages, if any, sustained by respondent. Thus, a jury must be impaneled in this case in any event. The time saved by not trying the issue of whether the proxy was materially false and misleading before the jury is likely to be insubstantial. Much of the delay in jury trials is attributed to the jury selection, *voir dire*, and the charge. None of these delaying factors will be avoided by today's decision.

It is just as probable that today's decision will have the result of coercing defendants to agree to consent orders or settlements in agency enforcement actions in order to preserve their right to jury trial in the private actions. In that event, the Court, for no compelling reason, will have simply added a powerful club to the administrative agencies' arsenals that even Congress was unwilling to provide them.

CASE ANALYSIS & QUESTIONS

The Shore plaintiffs efforts to invoke issue preclusion from an earlier bench trial also raised the concern that this might be depriving the defendant of its right to a jury trial in the second action.

- Do the courts (trial, appellate, and Supreme) let them?

- Why or why not?

- Is offensive use of issue preclusion too good a deal for plaintiffs in such a case?

- Or is it (like the class action device itself) just another way of leveling the playing field in conflicts involving individual investors and commercial businesses?

Note that all this is largely academic if the government is not bringing enforcement actions such as the one against Parklane—but perhaps not if there are multiple civil actions against commercial defendants. But remember that a defense judgment in a class action binds the class members and prevents a second suit by an individual class member even if mutuality is required.

- Why (in the absence of issue preclusion) would Parklane have been entitled to a jury trial in the second action?

- Why (you really have to know this by now) is the name of the Supreme Court case *Parklane v. Shore* rather than *Shore v. Parklane*?

- Why did the Supreme Court exercise its certiorari discretion to grant review?

- Is then-Justice Rehnquist (he became Chief Justice in 1986, replacing the retiring Warren Burger) protesting too much?

- Is Parklane really getting railroaded by the legal system like some poor teenager from the wrong side of the tracks?

- Didn't Parklane have its "day in court" with the first trial?

- Or does the bench trial aspect of the first trial essentially gut the principle of saving fact disputes for the jury as expressed in *Beacon Theatres v. Westover* (*see* Chapter 16 regarding the Seventh Amendment Jury Trial right)?

- What aspect of the Justice Potter Stewart's majority opinion arguably provides a safety net to prevent the realization of Justice Rehnquist's fears?

- Are you satisfied that it is enough of a safety net?

F. The Opportunity—and the Problem— of Virtual Representation

Notwithstanding cases like *Parklane v. Shore*, obtaining issue preclusion is not as easy as that case may make it seem. Remember: Parklane was a litigant that had no shot at successfully interposing a lack-of-privity defense. The same Parklane that was found to have issued a misleading statement in Case One was the very same Parklane being sued over the same statement in Case Two.

If Case Two had involved a lawsuit against an investment advisor or attorney who had authored or contributed to the statement, the issue would have been much closer because the defendant in Case Two was a different entity or person than the defendant in Case One. However, it can be argued with some force that legal or financial professionals working with a retail client are sufficiently "in privity" to permit the application of issue preclusion.

If Case Two had involved a lawsuit against an investment newsletter that carelessly reprinted the misleading statement, the newsletter would almost certainly be immune from issue preclusion because the newsletter's publisher, editor, and reporters were almost certainly not affiliated with the retailer. Where the defendant in Case One is legally distinct from the defendant in Case Two, issue preclusion is almost impossible to attain.

If 30 other investment newsletters also recklessly reprinted the misleading statement, issue preclusion would remain hard to attain, even if in case after case the factfinder consistently continued to find the statement false and misleading. The classic example of this reluctance was a hypothetical train wreck made famous in an article by University of Chicago Law Professor Brainerd Currie in which 50 injured passengers sued the railroad for negligence in 50 separate lawsuits. Applying prevailing preclusion doctrine of the time, it appeared that there could be no issue preclusion even if each trial kept reaching the same verdict on negligence time after time after time—a result Currie criticized. *See* Brainerd Currie, *Mutuality of Estoppel: Limits of the* Bernhard *Doctrine*, 9 STAN. L. REV. 281 (1957).

In the years since Currie wrote, preclusion doctrine has expanded. We know now that if the first ten passenger lawsuits resulting in findings of negligence by the railroad, that Passenger No. 11 would probably be able to obtain a finding of negligence via issue preclusion. How do we "know" that courts will now permit issue preclusion in this type of case? If Passenger No. 11 could obtain issue preclusion against the railroad, why not Passenger No. 8—or Passenger No. 5? Or Passenger No. 2? But if the railroad wins ten straight lawsuits, it will probably be unable to obtain issue preclusion (and summary judgment in its favor) against Passenger No. 11—the same result as when Professor Currie wrote. Why? Because each passenger is a new plaintiff unaffiliated with the prior plaintiffs that lost on the issue of negligence.

Many observers undoubtedly wonder why the legal system seems (despite occasional cases like *Parklane*) so often to require seemingly needless litigation. Presenting a layperson with the train hypothetical and its long line (no pun intended) of defense verdicts but trial after trial after trial on the issue of negligence would probably generate considerable criticism of the wasteful and costly practices of courts. Over time, many lawyers, scholars, and judges began to have doubts as well. *See, e.g.,* Robert Bone, *Rethinking the Day in Court Ideal and Nonparty Preclusion,* 67 N.Y.U. L. REV. 193 (1992)(urging broader application of issue preclusion and less adherence to the traditional requirement of privity or its near-equivalent).

This position has made some inroads but the status quo of preclusion doctrine remained conservative when the following case reached the U.S. Supreme Court. In *Taylor v. Sturgell*, the Supreme Court addressed the issues of "virtual representation" and was unanimously unwilling to extend the concept to the case before the Court (and implicitly to the degree advocated by some scholars). Justice Ginsburg's opinion provides a wonderful summary of current doctrine which, although retaining the traditional rules set forth in the *Restatement of Judgments*, does not close the door to some modest expansions of the doctrine under apt circumstances.

Commenting on the evolution of preclusion doctrine, one well-regarded treatise observed:

> As the rules of litigation have changed in the evolution of modern procedure, so have the rules of *res judicata*. The changes in the joinder and discovery rules have come about through statutes and rules of court. The corresponding changes in the rules of *res judicata* have been developed almost entirely through decisional law that evolved in the wake of these legislative reforms. The basic proposition of res judicata, however, has

Courts and commentators often speak of conserving "judicial" resources and appear to be focusing primarily on the time, money, and energy that must be expended by judicial personnel in order to resolve a matter. But be aware that for every hour a judge or law clerk spends on a case, there are probably several hours invested by counsel and the litigants. The citizenry will also be "taxed" in the form of participation as witnesses or jurors as well as taxpayers funding the judiciary. Instead of using the potentially misleadingly underinclusive term "judicial" resources, it might be more accurate to talk about "legal" resources or "social" resources being consumed by litigation.

remained essentially the same: A party should not be allowed to relitigate a matter that it already had opportunity to litigate. As the rules of procedure have expanded the scope of the initial opportunity to litigate, they have invited a corresponding expansion of the extent to which that opportunity forecloses a subsequent opportunity. [T]his is the clear tendency of the modern law of res judicata.

Fleming James, Jr., Geoffrey C. Hazard, Jr. & John Leubsdorf, *Civil Procedure* § 11.2 at 674-75 (5th ed. 2001).

But, as reflected in *Taylor v. Sturgell*, a broad approach to preclusion is not a boundaryless approach to preclusion.

FROM THE COURT

Taylor v. Sturgell

553 U.S. 880 (2008)

Supreme Court of the United States

JUSTICE GINSBURG delivered the opinion of the Court.

"It is a principle of general application in Anglo-American jurisprudence that one is not bound by a judgment in personam in a litigation in which he is not designated as a party or to which he has not been made a party by service of process." *Hansberry v. Lee*, 311 U.S. 32, 40 (1940). Several exceptions, recognized in this Court's decisions, temper this basic rule. In a class action, for example, a person not named as a party may be bound by a judgment on the merits of the action, if she was adequately represented by a party who actively participated in the litigation. In this case, we consider for the first time whether there is a "virtual representation" exception to the general rule against precluding nonparties. Adopted by a number of courts, including the courts below in the case now before us, the exception so styled is broader than any we have so far approved.

The virtual representation question we examine in this opinion arises in the following context. Petitioner Brent Taylor filed a lawsuit under the Freedom of Information Act seeking certain documents from the Federal Aviation Administration. Greg Herrick, Taylor's friend, had previously brought an unsuccessful suit seeking the same records. The two men have no legal relationship, and there is no evidence that Taylor controlled, financed, participated in, or even had notice of Herrick's earlier suit. Nevertheless, the D.C. Circuit held Taylor's suit precluded by the judgment against Herrick because, in that court's assessment, Herrick qualified as Taylor's "virtual representative."

We disapprove the doctrine of preclusion by "virtual representation," and hold, based on the record as it now stands, that the judgment against Herrick does not bar Taylor from maintaining this suit.

II

The preclusive effect of a federal-court judgment is determined by federal common law. *See Semtek Int'l Inc. v. Lockheed Martin Corp.*, 531 U.S. 497, 507-508 (2001)[*see* Chapter 4 regarding the *Erie* doctrine and applicable law]. For judgments in federal-question cases—for xample, Herrick's FOIA suit— federal courts participate in developing "uniform federal rule[s]" of res judicata, which this Court has ultimate authority to determine and declare. For judgments in diversity cases, federal law incorporates the rules of preclusion applied by the State in which the rendering court sits. The federal common law of preclusion is, of course, subject to due process limitations.

Taylor's case presents an issue of first impression in this sense: Until now, we have never addressed the doctrine of "virtual representation" adopted (in varying forms) by several Circuits and relied upon by the courts below. Our inquiry, however, is guided by well-established precedent regarding the propriety of nonparty preclusion. We review that precedent before taking up directly the issue of virtual representation.

A

The preclusive effect of a judgment is defined by claim preclusion and issue preclusion, which are collectively referred to as "res judicata." These terms have replaced a more confusing lexicon. Claim preclusion describes the rules formerly known as "merger" and "bar," while issue preclusion encompasses the doctrines once known as "collateral estoppel" and "direct estoppel." *See Migra v. Warren City School Dist. Bd. of Ed.*, 465 U.S. 75, 77, n.1 (1984).

Under the doctrine of claim preclusion, a final judgment forecloses "successive litigation of the very same claim, whether or not relitigation of the claim raises the same issues as the earlier suit." *New Hampshire v. Maine,* 532 U.S. 742, 748 (2001). Issue preclusion, in contrast, bars "successive litigation of an issue of fact or law actually litigated and resolved in a valid court determination essential to the prior judgment," even if the issue recurs in the context of a different claim. By "preclud[ing] parties from contesting matters that they have had a full and fair opportunity to litigate," these two doctrines protect against "the expense and vexation attending multiple lawsuits, conserv[e] judicial resources, and foste[r] reliance on judicial action by minimizing the possibility of inconsistent decisions." *Montana v. United States*, 440 U.S. 147, 153-154 (1979).

A person who was not a party to a suit generally has not had a "full and fair opportunity to litigate" the claims and issues settled in that suit. The application of claim and issue preclusion to nonparties thus runs up against the "deep-rooted historic tradition that everyone should have his own day in court." Indicating the strength of that tradition, we have often repeated the general rule that "one is not bound by a judgment in personam in a litigation in which he is not designated as a party or to which he has not been made a party by service of process."

Though hardly in doubt, the rule against nonparty preclusion is subject to exceptions. For present purposes, the recognized exceptions can be grouped into six categories. The established grounds for nonparty preclusion could be organized differently. The list that follows is meant only to provide a framework for our consideration of virtual representation, not to establish a definitive taxonomy.

First, "[a] person who agrees to be bound by the determination of issues in an action between others is bound in accordance with the terms of his agreement." For example, "if separate actions involving the same transaction are brought by different plaintiffs against the same defendant, all the parties to all the actions may agree that the question of the defendant's liability will be definitely determined, one way or the other, in a 'test case.'" The RESTATEMENT [§ 62] observes that a nonparty may be bound not only by express or implied agreement, but also through conduct inducing reliance by others. We have never had occasion to consider this ground for nonparty preclusion, and we express no view on it here.

Second, nonparty preclusion may be justified based on a variety of pre-existing "substantive legal relationship[s]" between the person to be bound and a party to the judgment. Qualifying relationships include, but are not limited to, preceding and succeeding owners of property, bailee and bailor, and assignee and assignor. [RESTATEMENT §§ 43-44, 52, 55]. These exceptions originated "as much from the needs of property law as from the values of preclusion by judgment."

The substantive legal relationships justifying preclusion are sometimes collectively referred to as "privity." The term "privity," however, has also come to be used more broadly, as a way to express the conclusion that nonparty preclusion is appropriate on any ground. To ward off confusion, we avoid using the term "privity" in this opinion.

Third, we have confirmed that, "in certain limited circumstances," a nonparty may be bound by a judgment because she was "adequately represented by someone with the same interests who [wa]s a party" to the suit. Representative suits with preclusive effect on nonparties include properly conducted class actions, and suits brought by trustees, guardians, and other fiduciaries [RESTATEMENT § 41].

Fourth, a nonparty is bound by a judgment if she "assume[d] control" over the litigation in which that judgment was rendered. [RESTATEMENT § 39]. Because such a person has had "the opportunity to present proofs and argument," he has already "had his day in court" even though he was not a formal party to the litigation.

Fifth, a party bound by a judgment may not avoid its preclusive force by relitigating through a proxy. Preclusion is thus in order when a person who did not participate in a litigation later brings suit as the designated representative of a person who was a party to the prior adjudication. And although our decisions have not addressed the issue directly, it also seems clear that preclusion is appropriate when a nonparty later brings suit as an agent for a party who is bound by a judgment.

Sixth, in certain circumstances a special statutory scheme may "expressly foreclos[e] successive litigation by nonlitigants . . . if the scheme is otherwise consistent with due process." Examples of such schemes include bankruptcy and probate proceedings and quo warranto actions or other suits that, "under [the governing] law, [may] be brought only on behalf of the public at large."

III

Reaching beyond these six established categories, some lower courts have recognized a "virtual representation" exception to the rule against nonparty preclusion. Decisions of these courts, however, have been far from consistent. Some Circuits use the label, but define "virtual representation" so that it is no broader than the recognized exception for adequate representation. But other courts, including the Eighth, Ninth, and D.C. Circuits, apply multifactor tests for virtual representation that permit nonparty preclusion in cases that do not fit within any of the established exceptions. The D.C. Circuit, the FAA, and Fairchild have presented three arguments in support of an expansive doctrine of virtual representation. We find none of them persuasive.

C

The FAA argues that "the threat of vexatious litigation is heightened" in public-law cases because "the number of plaintiffs with standing is potentially limitless." FOIA does allow "any person" whose request is denied to resort to federal court for review of the agency's determination. 5 U.S.C. § 552(a)(3)(A), (4)(B) (2006 ed.). Thus it is theoretically possible that several persons could coordinate to mount a series of repetitive lawsuits.

But we are not convinced that this risk justifies departure from the usual rules governing nonparty preclusion. First, stare decisis will allow courts swiftly to dispose of repetitive suits brought in the same circuit. Second, even when stare decisis is not dispositive, "the human tendency not to waste money will deter the bringing of suits based on claims or issues that have already been adversely determined against others." This intuition seems to be borne out by experience: The FAA has not called our attention to any instances of abusive FOIA suits in the Circuits that reject the virtual representation term theory respondents advocate here.

IV

For the foregoing reasons, we disapprove the theory of virtual representation on which the decision below rested. The preclusive effects of a judgment in a federal-question case decided by a federal court should instead be determined according to the established grounds for non-party preclusion described in this opinion.

Although references to "virtual representation" have proliferated in the lower courts, our decision is unlikely to occasion any great shift in actual practice. Many opinions use the term "virtual representation" in reaching results at least arguably defensible on established grounds. See 18A Wright & Miller § 4457, pp 535-539, and n.38 (collecting cases). In these cases, dropping the "virtual representation" label would lead to clearer analysis with little, if any, change in outcomes. "[T]he term 'virtual representation' has cast more shadows than light on the problem [of nonparty preclusion]."

> **Stare decisis** and **preclusion**, despite their similarities, are different concepts. Stare decisis refers to the judiciary's inclination to follow precedent and leave legal doctrine unchanged unless convinced the doctrine was wrong all along or has become outmoded or unwise because of changed or unanticipated circumstances. Preclusion means that a previously adjudicated case or issue cannot be relitigated. Preclusion does not sweep as wide as stare decisis in that the preclusion of a party from further litigation on a particular issue or claim will usually not affect others as might a legal precedent that applies to many lawsuits. But within its more confined sphere, preclusion is all-powerful. It ends any further disputing of the parties themselves even if it does not provide influential legal analysis. Conversely, stare decisis sweeps broader (e.g., a leading precedent may apply to hundreds of thousands of cases) but need not be followed forever (e.g., the court may overturn the precedent) or found applicable to the instant case (because the court differentiates it from the types of cases subject to the legal precedent in question).

A

It is uncontested that four of the six grounds for nonparty preclusion have no application here: There is no indication that Taylor agreed to be bound by Herrick's litigation, that Taylor and Herrick have any legal relationship, that Taylor exercised any control over Herrick's suit, or that this suit implicates any special statutory scheme limiting relitigation. Neither the FAA nor Fairchild contends otherwise.

It is equally clear that preclusion cannot be justified on the theory that Taylor was adequately represented in Herrick's suit. Nothing in the record indicates that Herrick understood himself to be suing on Taylor's behalf, that Taylor even knew of Herrick's suit, or that the Wyoming District Court took special care to protect Taylor's interests. Herrick's representation was not "adequate."

That leaves only the fifth category: preclusion because a nonparty to an earlier litigation has brought suit as a representative or agent of a party who is bound by the prior adjudication. Taylor is not Herrick's legal representative and he has not purported to sue in a representative capacity. He concedes, however, that preclusion would be appropriate if respondents could demonstrate that he is acting as Herrick's "undisclosed agen[t]."

Respondents argue here, as they did below, that Taylor's suit is a collusive attempt to relitigate Herrick's action. The D.C. Circuit considered a similar question in addressing the "tactical maneuvering" prong of its virtual representation test. The Court of Appeals did not, however, treat the issue as one of agency, and it expressly declined to reach any definitive conclusions due to "the ambiguity of the facts." We therefore remand to give the courts below an opportunity to determine whether Taylor, in pursuing the instant FOIA suit, is acting as Herrick's agent. Taylor concedes that such a remand is appropriate.

We have never defined the showing required to establish that a nonparty to a prior adjudication has become a litigating agent for a party to the earlier case. Because the issue has not been briefed in any detail, we do not discuss the matter elaborately here. We note, however, that courts should be cautious about finding preclusion on this basis. A mere whiff of "tactical maneuvering" will not suffice; instead, principles of agency law are suggestive. They indicate that preclusion is appropriate only if the putative agent's conduct of the suit is subject to the control of the party who is bound by the prior adjudication.

B

On remand, Fairchild suggests, Taylor should bear the burden of proving he is not acting as Herrick's agent. When a defendant points to evidence establishing a close relationship between successive litigants, Fairchild maintains, "the burden [should] shif[t] to the second litigant to submit evidence refuting the charge" of agency. Fairchild justifies this proposed burden-shift on the ground that "it is unlikely an opposing party will have access to direct evidence of collusion."

We reject Fairchild's suggestion. Claim preclusion, like issue preclusion, is an affirmative defense. *See* Fed. Rule Civ. Proc. 8(c). Ordinarily, it is incumbent on the defendant to plead and prove such a defense, and we have never recognized claim preclusion as an exception to that general rule. We acknowledge that direct evidence justifying nonparty preclusion is often in the hands of plaintiffs rather than defendants. But "[v]ery often one must plead and prove matters as to which his adversary has superior access to the proof." In these situations, targeted interrogatories or deposition questions can reduce the information disparity. We see no greater cause here than in other matters of affirmative defense to disturb the traditional allocation of the proof burden.

For the reasons stated, the judgment of the United States Court of Appeals for the District of Columbia Circuit is vacated, and the case is remanded for further proceedings consistent with this opinion.

ADDITIONAL EXERCISES

1. Pia Peterson takes Numb-It to deal with her chronic joint pain. Commuting home from work one night, her car drifts over the center line and has a serious, close to head-on, collision with Donna Drinker, who is headed home after happy hour with a blood alcohol count above the legal limit. Both suffer substantial injuries and sue one another. Despite

being legally drunk, Donna, who was in her proper lane and driving the speed limit, obtains a defense verdict and a judgment of no liability. The verdict form asked the jurors the following questions.

> Do you find by a preponderance of the evidence that Donna Drinker was under the influence of alcohol or any other chemical substances at the time of the collision? Yes _X_ No ____

> Do you find by a preponderance of the evidence that Pia Peterson was under the influence of alcohol or any other chemical substances at the time of the collision? Yes ____ No _X_

In the months after the trial, both Pia and Donna read in the newspaper that Numb-It has been associated with an unusual number of adverse reactions, including momentary mini-blackouts as well as more serious seizures. Pia comes to believe that she drifted over the center line because she was in the throes of a mini-blackout, of which she has had several in the years since the accident. She discontinues use of Numb-It and sues its manufacturer DrugCo. Donna has also been having mini-blackouts and then suffers a tragically massive seizure leaving her almost totally disabled. She also sues DrugCo. Both Pia and Donna include in their damages claim injuries suffered in the car collision.

In both cases, DrugCo moves for summary judgment arguing that neither Pia nor Donna can prove an essential element required for recovery: use of Numb-It on the day of the accident. In Pia's case, DrugCo points to the jury verdict that Pia was not under the influence of alcohol or drugs.

In Donna's case, DrugCo notes that the record is replete with reference to Donna's inebriation on the day in question and that the jury's affirmative answer to the question must have referred to alcohol use rather than illegal or prescription drug use. In Donna's case, DrugCo also argues that the auto accident case also conclusively establishes that Donna's driving was not affected by any use of Numb-It on the day in question. Fighting back, Donna moves for partial summary judgment via offensive issue preclusion ala *Parklane Hosiery v. Shore*, arguing that it is now established as a matter of law that she had alcohol or drugs in her system on the day of the accident. **What results?**

2. Pam Pedestrian is hit crossing a Las Vegas street by an automobile driven by Dan Driver and owned by Deena Driver, Dan's estranged wife. Pam sues both in Nevada state court. Deena contests jurisdiction, contending that Dan (who still had car and house keys despite the impending dissolution of the marriage) took the car without her permission to go on a gambling spree.

Deena, a Californian, has never set foot in Nevada and has no business, real estate, or other ties to Nevada. Pam seeks exercise of personal jurisdiction over Deena on the theory that Dan was indeed using the car with her permission and is supported by Dan's testimony. The court holds a factual hearing regarding Deena's Rule 12(b)(1) motion to dismiss for lack of personal jurisdiction and finds Deena's testimony more credible than Dan's and thus no personal jurisdiction over Deena, who is dismissed as a defendant.

> Automobile liability insurance (or the posting of a bond) is necessary in all states as a condition of obtaining a license in order to demonstrate that a vehicle owner is sufficiently financially responsible for any losses that may be caused by the vehicle's operation. Unfortunately, the amount of insurance required is usually ridiculously low (e.g., policy limits of $30,000 per accident) in view of the injuries that can be caused by cars. Nonetheless, the insurance "on the vehicle" may be all that is realistically available to compensate accident victims in that many tortfeasors have few assets and earn only modest wages that can be garnished. That's why Pam wants to have Deena found liable—so that her insurance will apply. Ordinarily, someone who borrows a car is a "permissive" user and the car owner's insurance applies if there is an accident, at least for the statutory minimum required. But if the automobile use by a non-owner is unauthorized, the vehicle's insurance typically does not cover any accidents taking place during the time of unauthorized use.

Pam proceeds against Dan and obtains a $800,000 judgment at trial against Dan, who has returned—penniless—to California (where Deena has changed the locks on the house as well as regaining control of the car). Continuing to look for a way of accessing the automobile liability insurance on Deena's car, Pam sues Deena in California, where Deena cannot prevail on a lack-of-personal-jurisdiction defense. Deena moves for summary judgment, asserting claim preclusion in her favor based on the Nevada finding that Dan had taken the car without her permission. **Will Deena win? If she does not, can Pam obtain summary judgment based on the Nevada trial result finding negligent driving that caused** *injury to Pam? And if so, could Deena dispute the $800,000 damage award?*

3. Pat Lender brings an action against Donna Debtor to recover an installment of interest allegedly due on a promissory note purportedly executed by Donna with interest payable to Pat. Donna denies executing the promissory note. After trial, Pat prevails with a jury verdict and judgment. When the second interest payment is overdue, Pat sues again for this installment. Donna again denies making the note. **Can Pat obtain summary judgment?**

4. *Variant No. 1*—Per Curiam brings an action against Devin's Deep Dish Pizza, alleging national origin discrimination (Per is of Swedish extraction and contends that Devin, despite his own nomenclatural issues, is hiring only workers with Italian names to work in his "authentic" pizza shop). Per succeeds in his claim, is hired, and the court enters an order enjoining Devin from any further national origin discrimination.

Variant No. 2—Devin prevails in the litigation, with the court's opinion praising "the wide variety of ethnic diversity found in this melting pot of pizza."

Subsequently, Paula Curiam, Per's wife, who hails originally from Tanzania, brings suit against Devin alleging gender discrimination in hiring because of an asserted preference for male cooks, bartenders, and servers.

- *Would Paula be entitled to summary judgment under Variation No. 1 pursuant to a theory of offensive issue preclusion per Parklane Hosiery v. Shore?*

- *Would Devin be entitled to summary judgment under Variation No. 2 because of the court's finding of no discrimination in Per's case?*

5. Paula and Per eventually succeed in unionizing Devin's Pizza Parlor. Everything runs smoothly until the workers announce a strike during Super Bowl weekend. Devin sues to enjoin the strike as a breach of the collective bargaining agreement. The court dismisses the action based on a statute that deprives it of jurisdiction to issue this type of

relief. Later, this holding in *Devin v. The Per/Paula Union* is overruled in a case involving different parties. The rule of law is now that courts have jurisdiction to enjoin such strikes. On the basis of this development, Devin again sues to enjoin the strike, which has extended into the NCAA Basketball Tournament's "March Madness" period. ***Can Devin maintain this action, or is it barred by the earlier decision rejecting Devin's previous effort to enjoin the strike?***

6. Let's test the "incentive to litigate" and "expectations of the parties" aspect of preclusion. In Case One, a college student at Ivy University in Massachusetts graduates and returns to the family home in Los Angeles. Subsequently, he is sued by a former landlord for allegedly rewiring his campus apartment's electric system in an effort obtain free long distance phone calls. He allows the landlord to win by default and retain his $500 security deposit (*see* Ch. 15 rather than flying back to Massachusetts to defend the claim.

   A few months later, the current tenants of the apartment perish in an electrical fire. In wrongful death actions alleging defective wiring, the families of the victims sue the landlord (who failed to restore the wiring to its original condition), and the former tenant. They cannot (for what we hope are obvious reasons) seek to benefit from claim preclusion because the landlord's action to retain the security deposit is not the same claim as the wrongful death action. They do, however, seek to obtain partial summary judgment establishing as a fact that the wiring by the former tenant, put it in the defective condition resulting in the fire (*see* Ch. 15). ***Will the court grant the motion and impose issue preclusion upon the former tenant?***

7. Paige sues Dennis, alleging breach of a $100,000 contract (he simply refused to pay for several truckloads of perfectly good widgets) and wins a jury verdict in March 2010. Minutes after the jury returns its verdict, Judge Globetrotter is on an airplane to Ruritania, where he is scheduled to lecture the Ruritanian judiciary (a group of cronies appointed by the totalitarian dictator currently ruling the country) about the wonders of judicial independence. He returns a week later and gets caught up on other cases and excursions. In the meantime, Paige has attempted to cajole payment form Dennis, but he has refused. In March 2011, Paige finds out that Dennis has more than $100,000 cash in a storage locker.

She immediately presents a copy of the complaint and verdict form to the owner of the facility.

- *What will the owner do?*

- *What should Paige do?*

- *What should she have done?*

- *What if Dennis files for bankruptcy in June 2010? In June 2011?*

- *What can Dennis do to attack the verdict? When must he do it?*

Quick Summary

- There are three primary types of litigation remedies: Monetary Damages; Injunctive Relief; and Declaratory Relief.

- Courts may provide temporary or preliminary injunctive relief. In deciding whether to grant a request for such relief, courts consider the harm to the movant from not granting the relief balanced against the harm to the party enjoined as well as the movant's likelihood of success on the merits and the public interest.

- A "judgment" is a particular type of court order embodied in a separate document that grants final relief on a matter. Judgments are important for establishing various deadlines and for determining the rights of the parties.

- Once obtaining a judgment, the winning party must enforce it or collect it. In seeking to do so, the judgment winner may use a number of remedies provided by law.

- Preclusion doctrine provides that once certain things are decided in a judgment, they cannot be relitigated.

- Claim Preclusion (also known as Res Judicata) prevents the re-litigation of a previously adjudicated matter, at least between the same parties or those sufficiently closely associated with them (the "Privity" requirement).

- Issue Preclusion (also known as Collateral Estoppel) prevents the re-litigation of a fact determined in a prior action that was actually litigated and necessary to the prior judgment.

- The primary public policy underlying both types of preclusion is finality of decisions and the avoidance of wasteful repetition of litigation. However, in spite of the policy in favor of finality, preclusion of a claim due to a prior adjudication must be fair or the court will not permit preclusion.

- There is something of a modern trend toward broader application of the preclusion concept, but courts have stopped short of permitting "virtual" representation.

An Overview of Civil Litigation and Dispute Resolution

A. The Study of Civil Procedure

Civil Procedure is regarded by many as the most difficult course in law school. Notwithstanding some possible implicit bias toward this view, we think this perception is largely accurate. Civil Procedure is tough because it involves learning a new language of procedural jargon and an unfamiliar set of procedural rules as well as unfamiliar doctrinal rules and notions of public policy and jurisprudence. While all law school courses involve this to some degree, Civil Procedure seems to do more of this.

Civil Procedure, because it involves the litigation process, also often intertwines with questions of evidence, as well as touching on dispute resolution generally, which brings to bear another body of work regarding Alternative Dispute Resolution ("ADR") (discussed further below).

 Our goal in this coursebook is to demystify the material and to present it in the context of the rules that govern it and the practice context in which the issues arise. We believe this coverage allows a better and more practical understanding of litigation and the role civil procedure plays in the litigation process.

Although there may be moments in class or passages in the assigned reading that seem too "ivory tower," remember that you will be in the hurley-burly of law practice and the real world soon enough. Take this time in law school to learn not only the concepts, technicalities, and mechanics of civil litigation, but also to appreciate the larger historical, economic, social, political, and psychological context of disputing. In that vein, this book will occasionally cite to important secondary literature that you can consult for further reading either in this course or later in law school or in practice.

B. Procedural Rules and the Rulemaking Process

Rules of litigation procedure, such as the Federal Rules of Civil Procedure, also have the force of law and are in effect statutes governing a specialized field. The Federal Rules of Civil Procedure are the statute-like law of Civil Procedure. There are also Federal Rules of Appellate Procedure, Evidence, Bankruptcy, and Criminal Procedure. They should be read and applied in the manner in which you would read and apply statutes even though they generally come into being in a manner different than does a statute.

The Federal Rules are not usually enacted by Congress (although Congress can pass legislation to establish, alter, or abolish a procedural rule applicable in federal courts). Rather, they result from a process in which an Advisory Committee studies issues related to an aspect of procedure and drafts a new or amended rule. The Advisory Committee members are appointed by the Chief Justice.

The product of a particular Advisory Committee (*e.g.*, on the Civil Rules, the Appellate Rules, the Evidence Rules, etc.) is in turn reviewed by the Standing Committee on Practice and Procedure of the U.S. Judicial Conference. Then comes review by the entire Judicial Conference (a body composed of the Chief Judge of each Circuit Court and a selected District Judge from a district within each Circuit). The proposed Rule or Amendment is then reported to the Supreme Court, which in turn may promulgate the Rule or Amendment to Congress. If Congress does not act within 180 days to stop or alter the promulgated rule, it becomes law as a part of the Rules of Procedure. Ordinarily, it takes four to five years for a proposed Amendment to run the gauntlet of the vetting process and become part of the Rules.

This process is established by the Rules Enabling Act (28 U.S.C. § 2072), originally enacted in 1934. The concept of the Enabling Act was that the judiciary, as the group most familiar with court operations, should have primary authority for propounding the rules that would govern court operations. But to ensure that judicially-promulgated Rules were not too insular and did not favor judicial interests at the expense of other interests, the Enabling Act provided a mechanism by which Congress could step in and stop promulgation of a Rule or revise a promulgated Rule.

For the most part, Congress has not intervened and the rulemaking process has remained largely the province of the judiciary. Arguably, the rulemaking process has become more judge-centric over the years. Lawyers and law professors were heavily represented on the original Civil Rules Advisory Committee and its Reporter, Charles Clark, dean of the Yale Law School, along with University of Michigan Law Professor Edson Sunderland were highly influential, Clark regarding pleading, joinder, and motions while Sunderland was the "father" of the discovery rules.

Today, although the Reporters (persons charged with drafting the particulars of a Rule and accompanying Committee notes) of Advisory Committees continue usually to be law faculty, almost all current Committee members are judges, with only two or three practitioners or professors on what is usually a 15-member Committee. Some have criticized this development, which has held sway for 30 years or so. For the past 25 years, as a result of 1988 legislation, the rulemaking process itself has been very open, with mandated public hearings and records of the hearings and submissions by interested parties.

C. The Hierarchy of Construing the Federal Rules

Because the Federal Rules of Civil Procedure are essentially statutes governing litigation, interpreters (lawyers, judges, law professors, policymakers) generally approach them as if construing a statute. Those seeking to apply or understand a Civil Rule consider:

> **The Text of the Rule.** As with statutes, the language of the Rule is the primary source for determining its meaning. But as with statutes, language can be indeterminate, inconsistent, or ambiguous. For the most part, however, a careful reading of the text of the Rules will reward you with a good understanding of the Rules. For beginning law students, there will be some difficulties presented by technical language in the Rules that cannot be well understood until students become more familiar with the history and traditional application of a textual term in the Rules.

> **The "Legislative" History of the Rule.** Conveniently, each Rule of Civil Procedure is accompanied by notes of the Advisory Committee concerning the Rule, beginning with the notes accompanying the Rule's original promulgation and including notes accompanying all subsequent amendments. Sometimes, these notes are short and merely state

that an amendment made technical but non-substantive changes. But many of the Committee Notes provide an extensive explanation of the background of the Rule and its meaning. In addition, the records of public hearings and the commentary received by the rulemakers are also part of the history and background of the Rule but are less authoritative than the Committee notes.

The Purpose and Objective Underlying the Rule. In addition to the intent of the drafters reflected in the Committee Notes and official record of the Committee, other evidence of the purpose and intent of the rules that may be reflected by the context surrounding the drafting of a rule, in particular the perceived problem to which a Rule amendment was responding.

Caselaw Construing the Rule. To the extent that Rule text and drafting history does not provide a definitive construction of the Rules, caselaw interpreting the Rules takes on particular importance. Once established, the cases construing the Rules become, at least as a practical matter, almost as important as the text of the Rules, even more so for parts of the Rules that are not clear on their face. Now that the Civil Rules are more than 75 years old, there is so much interpretive caselaw that precedent has to a large extent supplanted the type of *de novo* analysis of text and drafting history that would normally be important when construing rules or statutes for which there is comparatively little caselaw.

Because some of the Civil Rules (*e.g.*, discovery rules) are not often the subject of appellate opinions, trial court decisions can take on particular importance. Where the bulk of caselaw is trial-based, this also has the effect of flattening hierarchy because of the manner in which district courts are not bound by the opinions of one another. But because there is not a formal hierarchy, the prominence of particular trial judges can take on additional importance in determining the impact of a district court decision construing a Rule. In addition, informal custom and practice in a given legal community may be particularly important in determining what a rule "means" and how it is applied in litigation.

Where an issue is new or novel and there is little existing precedent, early trial court decisions on the matter become especially influential. For example, in early 2012, a Magistrate Judge's decision on document production received substantial attention because it was the first opinion approving of the use of predictive coding for the review of electronically stored information that is the subject of a document request. *See Moore v. Publicis Groupe,* 287 F.R.D. 182 (S.D.N.Y. 2012).

For those interested in further examination of approaches to interpretation, leading statutory interpretation texts can be very helpful because the Federal Civil Rules are essentially statutes and because many important Civil Procedure issues such as jurisdiction and venue are governed by statute.

D. Federal Procedural Statutes

National statutes are found in the U.S. Code (which is the government's official publication) and in the U.S. Code Annotated, a West publication. Because the latter also includes citations to cases interpreting Code provisions and reference to drafting history, lawyers generally find this more helpful than merely reading the Code alone. The Code is organized into numbered "Titles" that deal with particular topics. Title 28 governs federal civil litigation procedure.

When you see a citation such as 28 U.S.C. § 1331 you know it is a procedural statute just as you will come to know that sections in Title 42 deal with civil rights and those in Title 29 deal with labor law. The rules and statutory supplement assigned for this course in conjunction with this textbook will almost certainly include selected provisions of Title 28.

There are many good sources of information regarding approaches to interpreting laws, rules, and other legal writings. *See, e.g.:*

- ANTONIN SCALIA & BRYAN A. GARNER, READING LAW: THE INTERPRETATION OF LEGAL TEXTS (2012);

- LINDA D. JELLUM & DAVID CHARLES HRCIK, MODERN STATUTORY INTERPRETATION: PROBLEMS, THEORIES, AND LAWYERING STRATEGIES (2d ed. 2009);

- WILLIAM D. POPKIN, MATERIALS ON LEGISLATION: POLITICAL LANGUAGE AND THE POLITICAL PROCESS (5th ed. 2009);

- WILLIAM N. ESKRIDGE, JR., PHILIP P. FRICKEY & ELIZABETH GARRETT, CASES AND MATERIALS ON LEGISLATION: STATUTES AND THE CREATION OF PUBLIC POLICY (4th ed. 2007) and

CASES AND MATERIALS ON STATUTORY INTERPRETATION (2012).

What you learn about contract interpretation can also be applied to construing the Federal Rules and procedural statutes. *See, e.g.*, JOSEPH M. PERILLO, CALAMARI & PERILLO ON CONTRACTS (6th ed. 2009); E. ALLAN FARNSWORTH, CONTRACTS (4th ed. 2004).

E. The Criminal-Civil Difference

This is a course in civil dispute resolution, not criminal law or procedure. Criminal cases not only involve the obvious difference of prosecution by the government but also involve different standards of proof (**"beyond a reasonable doubt"** rather than civil litigation's **"preponderance of the evidence"** standard) and potential implication of different constitutional issues (*e.g.*, right to counsel, against self-incrimination, and against unreasonable searches or seizures in criminal litigation vs. right to jury trial and due process in civil litigation, although due process is often an issue in criminal litigation as well).

F. Burdens of Proof and Standards of Proof

Before launching into the specifics of civil litigation, it helps to have a good grasp of some basic concepts that are often tossed around but also may be insufficiently explained, especially for those new to the field.

The **burden of proof** is an important concept in law and logic. Law generally is reluctant to depart from the status quo unless the party seeking the departure shoulders the burden of proof to justify the affirmative relief sought (*e.g.*, an injunction or money judgment). In most cases, it is pretty clear that the person bringing the lawsuit has the burden of proof because this litigant (the "plaintiff") is seeking something from the opposing party (the "defendant").

For example, if the defendant has breached a contract with the plaintiff, the status quo may be that the defendant has the money and the plaintiff is unpaid. The plaintiff may be entitled to payment for work done or goods supplied, but the plaintiff will need to prove that this is the case before a court will order the defendant to pay funds to the plaintiff. Similarly, the defendant may have negligently driven through a red light and hit the plaintiff in a crosswalk. But the plaintiff will have to prove this to the satisfaction of the legal system—and will have to prove up the amount of damages caused by the defendant's negligence—in order to gain a judgment in its favor.

More technically, burden of proof in law refers to two distinct concepts. One is the **burden of production**—of coming forward with information or evidence, or at least a response. For example, if a defendant makes a properly supported motion for summary judgment as described in Chapter 16, the plaintiff has a burden of production to respond to the motion. If it fails to do so, the motion may be granted.

The other sense in which the phrase is used means the **burden of persuasion**, which is usually what laypersons mean when they talk about the burden of proof. The party seeking a change from the status quo has the burden of persuasion. Unless it shoulders this burden, no change in the status quo will be ordered and hence no relief for the plaintiff. The burden of persuasion differs in law depending on the type of case or claim at issue. **Law recognizes three basic burdens of persuasion.**

- **Preponderance of the Evidence.** Under this standard, the burden of persuasion is met so long as the party bearing the burden has produced at least somewhat more evidence on the issue than the party that does not bear the burden.

The preponderance standard is often described as one in which the burden is satisfied if there is even a feather's worth more evidence on the side of the party with the burden. Imagine the metaphor of the scales of justice and that the evidence on each side of a question is in equipoise. The addition of a single feather on the scale of the party with the burden satisfies the preponderance standard. Using the yardstick of percentages, the preponderance standard is 50 percent plus a feather.

The preponderance standard is the one most widely used in civil litigation. It applies to tort claims based on negligence, breach of contract disputes, property disputes, and most statutory claims.

- **Clear and Convincing Evidence.** Under this standard, the party with the burden of persuasion must show by clear and convincing evidence that it is entitled to prevail.

The clear and convincing standard means that the party with the burden must have more than a slight advantage when comparing evidence for and against its position. Imagine once again the scales of justice. To satisfy the clear and convincing standard, the scales must not only be uneven but also must tilt distinctly in favor of the party with the burden of persuasion. Using the yardstick of percentages, the clear and convincing standard is usually expressed as 60-70 percent certainty, although there is no uniform agreement for using this measuring stick.

The clear and convincing standard is applied to civil claims where the legal system is more concerned than usual about wrongfully holding the defendant responsible and tends to be applied in claims that are either disfavored for public policy reasons (*e.g.*, defamation because it chills free speech or requests for punitive damages because this may blur the civil/criminal distinction) or has particularly bad consequences for a losing defendant (*e.g.*, fraud claims that can wreck a reputation as well as creating tort liability in what otherwise would have been a mere breach of contract suit).

- **Beyond a Reasonable Doubt.** This standard, used in criminal prosecutions, requires that the factfinder have no serious doubts about the guilt of defendant.

Juries in criminal cases are commonly instructed that a reasonable doubt is one that would make a person hesitate about an important decision. If you're not sure that a house has a sturdy roof and back out of buying for that reason, you have a reasonable doubt about the home's construction. A reasonable doubt does not require that there be no doubt at all, only that the doubt be sufficient to forgo or delay action.

Prosecutors typically have good conviction rates despite this heightened burden of persuasion. For example, it might be possible that the criminal defendant running from a murder scene holding a blood-soaked knife and showing signs of a scuffle was not the perpetrator but absent other evidence (*e.g.*, the defendant was seen scuffling with others trying to protect the victim), a juror would be unlikely to harbor reasonable doubt about this defendant's guilt. Expressed as a percentage, beyond a reasonable doubt connotes something like 90 percent or better certainty, although there is no universal agreement on this point.

G. Disparate Positions, Disparate Resources, and Their Impact on Litigation

An unfortunate aspect of litigation and law is the maldistribution of legal resources. As with most everything else, legal resources and advantage are disproportionately distributed in society. Certain legal devices such as the contingency fee may partially level the playing field, but the playing field remains fairly slanted in favor of society's "haves" (and "have mores") rather than the "have nots" (or those who have relatively less).

Nearly 40 years ago, a now-prominent law professor captured this concept well in a now-famous article.

He argued that even where there are legal rules favorable to have-not litigants (such as the minimal requirements for pleading a case provided by Federal Rule 8; but see Chapter 6 and note how this liberality has been constricted in the recent years), that "haves" would nonetheless do well in litigation because they tend to be "**repeat players**" who have substantial ongoing experience with litigation while the "have nots" tend to be "**one shot**" players who litigate perhaps as little as once in a life-time. As a result, the repeat players devel-

> See Marc Galanter, *Why the "Haves" Come Out Ahead: Speculations on the Limits of Legal Change*, 9 L. & Soc'y Rev. 95 (1974). This article has been cited in more than 800 scholarly articles; it's a true classic in that it has affected the thinking of many later writers and has been the subject of its own seminar.

op an expertise, economy of scale, and savvy that permits them to do better in litigation than one might expect judging solely from the merits of a case or the overall structure of the rules or the substance of the applicable law.

This insight, once novel, is now widely accepted. Different socioeconomic and political groups react differently to it, however. Repeat players see nothing amiss and point to potentially countervailing conditions such as sympathy for the underdog. One shot players and their allies find it a regrettable aspect of a status quo in which inequalities are not only the norm but are cumulative. That is, those with less money also tend to have less education, less political power, fewer options, etc.

While this coursebook is not intended to be a political screed, neither are we blind to the obvious realities of modern society. In assessing the utility of civil litigation and considering any reform or assessing case outcomes, one should always be cognizant of the distributional aspects of a law, rule, case, doctrine or system. We say this as group of authors with mixed political attitudes. As individuals, we may have our preferences about Democrat-vs.-Republican, regulation-vs.-markets, minimal government-vs.-comprehensive regulation. But as lawyers and teachers, we all agree that civil litigation should aspire to apply the substantive law accurately (even if it is substantive law that some of us might individually dislike), that litigation procedure should facilitate this, and that unequal litigant resources should not interfere with these goals. This concept is captured well in the very first Federal Rule of Civil Procedure.

THE RULE   Rule 1

Scope and Purpose

These rules . . . should be construed and administered to secure the just, speedy, and inexpensive determination of every action and proceeding.

Relatedly, students should realize that the Rules of Civil Procedure, like all legal rules of which we are aware, are **rules of reason**. They are not intended to be applied in isolation but as a whole. They are not to be read so hyper-literally as to bring about an absurd result. Neither should the Rules produce litigation activity and expense disproportionate to the dispute in question in light of the interests of the litigants and the justice system. A sense of **proportionality** is required when construing and applying the Rules. For example, as you will see in Chapter 12, the scope of discovery is broad, extending to anything relevant to any claim or defense in a case—but the courts have substantial power to control and to restrict discovery of even relevant matter in order to apply the rules in a way appropriate to the controversy at hand.

H. Assessing the Case and Mapping Out a Strategy

After prospective client intake, investigation, and research checks out, the prospective client becomes an actual client represented by counsel. Now it's time to strategize about the case and to determine how best to proceed. Initial strategic considerations are discussed below.

- **Figuring out what the case is about.** Every good lawyer thinks it is important to have a "**theory of the case**"—a view as to what really happened, what the law requires or permits under such circumstances, how best to explain the matter to judges and jurors (and perhaps to the outside world if the case is newsworthy), and what relief will be sought. A good theory of the case involves a good narrative.

A Note on Storytelling. Lawyers have to be able to tell a compelling story on behalf of their clients. We don't mean "story" in the negative sense sometimes associated with the term (as in "that's just a story," or a "storybook" description that defies reality). We mean a realistic account of the matter that makes narrative sense so that those unfamiliar with the matter (like judges, jurors, opponents, and insurance adjusters) can understand what happened, appreciate your client's position, and agree with it in spite of the adversarial opposition. A good theory of the case is not blindly one-sided or self-serving but should tell a compelling story that makes the judge or jury want your client to prevail. An effective narrative does not overstate the case but appreciates both the strengths and the weaknesses of the client's claim and adjusts the narrative and the planned proof accordingly to highlight the strong points of the claim or defense and attempts to defuse the weak points as much as possible.

- **Whether to sue.** This includes not only a comparison of civil litigation and its alternatives (see the discussion of alternative dispute resolution below) but also a determination of whether the matter is reasonably susceptible of a negotiated resolution without taking the step of suing. In addition to the tactical and logistical considerations of dispute resolution, counsel should evaluate the merits of the cases, available remedies and the degree to which they match client objectives, and the costs of litigation as comparted to alternatives. In calculating the cost, consider not only monetary expenditures but also the emotional toll on the client and affiliated persons as well as the time, disruption, and inconvenience of litigation.

Counsel may be able to resolve the matter with a phone call or a "demand letter" setting forth the client's situation and suggested resolution of the claim. There may even be insurance adjusters or other representatives of a prospective defendant already trying to achieve an informal settlement.

Part of the mark of a good lawyer is appreciating the degree of formality and detail required for each case or each stage of the case. One goal of effective law practice is to deliver the best outcome for the client in relation to the stakes involved and cost expended. It would not be good lawyering to spend days crafting and supporting a detailed demand letter and exhibits if the defendant was willing to offer the same settlement merely upon receiving a phone call.

• **What To Seek in Relief.** In taking a case, counsel must have at least a rough idea of what the client wants. Is it money? Changed behavior? Protection? A definitive statement as to fault? Usually a client is primarily interested in compensation. But the client may also be interested in an order removing the neighbor's swing set from his land or an affirmation that she is the owner of a green 2010 Toyota, or that the fired employee stay away from the workplace and not interfere with the ongoing work of others. Sometimes, the client may want something as simple as an apology—in which case informal action may be more successful than full dress litigation. Chapter 20 discusses **remedies** in more detail.

I. Stages of Dispute Resolution and the Litigation Process

Disputes sometimes lie dormant or unrecognized for a long while, perhaps so long that the applicable statute of limitations has expired and no claim can be made. But once a dispute is recognized, its processing and resolution generally follow a pattern beginning with investigation, informal negotiation, perhaps exploring ADR device (*e.g.*, arbitration, mediation), and then moving to litigation, although in many cases, commencement of litigation is what serves for prompt negotiation and use of ADR. **Litigation** generally follows a pattern and proceeds in the following stages.

Pleading— Litigation always involves the exchange of a **complaint** (Rule 8) and **answer** (also Rule 8) and often a **counterclaim** (Rule 13) and reply to the counterclaim. Where there are multiple plaintiffs or defendants, these co-parties may have **cross-claims** (Rule 13) against one another as well, with answers to the cross-claims. In addition, an existing defendant may implead a third-party defendant through a **third-party complaint** (Rule 14). Rule 11 places certain obligations on the pleadings as well as motions and other papers. Rule 10 governs the captions of pleadings while Rule 15 deals with amendments to pleadings.

"Early" Motion Practice. A motion is a request that the court enter an order. Motion practice is a substantial part of contemporary civil litigation. Rule 12 provides a list of common **motions to dismiss** or other motions attacking the pleadings. In addition, there are a variety of possible **discovery motions** such as for **protective orders** restricting discovery or **motions to compel** discovery.

Disclosure and Discovery of information by means other than informal investigation, review of the opposition's disclosures, or the conducting of one's own discovery. Discovery devices (addressed in Chapter 13) include **interrogatories**, **document requests**, **depositions**, and **requests for an admission**.

Additional post-discovery motion practice. After discovery concludes, another round of motion practice typically ensues. **Summary judgment** motions (governed by Rule 56) are a common feature of pretrial litigation. On the eve of trial, there may be **motions "in limine"** (Latin for at the threshold) for pretrial evidence rulings. A common variety aims at excluding the other side's experts. As trial approaches, there is typically a final pretrial conference with the judge and adoption of a final pretrial order to govern the proceedings.

Trial. At trial, there typically is **jury selection**, **opening statements**, **direct examination** of witnesses, **cross-examination** of the witnesses, **closing argument**, and **jury deliberation** prior to rendering a verdict. At trial, the rules of evidence and the custom and practice of trial conduct play an important role. In a jury trial, the jury renders a **verdict** after it concludes its deliberations. In a bench trial, the courtroom proceedings simply adjourn and the judge in the privacy of chambers authors **findings of fact and conclusions of law** pursuant to Rule 52.

At trial, there may be many motions regarding the evidence or trial procedure (certainly there will be **objections**). In addition, the parties may move for **judgment as a matter of law** (Rule 50(a)), for the adoption of particular jury instructions, and so on. After trial, common post-trial motions may seek a judgment as a matter of law (Rule 50(b)), imposition of costs (Rule 54 and 28 U.S.C. § 1920) and counsel fees (pursuant to various statutes or common law doctrine that do not apply in most cases where each side bears its own legal fees), or a **new trial** (Rule 59). Further after trial, a party may move to **vacate or modify a judgment** (Rule 60).

After trial and verdict or findings, a **judgment** is entered. Post-trial motions pursuant to Rules 50 or 59 make the judgment inoperative until the court has ruled on the motions. Once this is done, a losing party may **appeal** but must do so within 30 days of the judgment in order to be timely. The judgment may be for either monetary relief or injunctive relief or some combination of the two. The winner may engage in the **judgment collection** efforts designed to force payment if payment is not made voluntarily. As discussed in Chapter 20, entry of final judgment operates to preclude repetitive subsequent litigation by the parties or those sufficiently aligned with the parties.

J. Litigation Planning—At the Beginning, Consider the End

Once focused on litigation, counsel needs to address a number of concerns. In mapping out a strategy, counsel should determine what the client wants at the end of the process (*e.g.*, monetary compensation, return to work, the end of an infringing practice, etc.). Counsel should also consider how the client's requested relief will be implemented. Should it be a judgment for a certain amount of money? An injunction ejecting someone from the client's property? A determination that a debt is not owed? Once envisioning the goals and form of a final judgment, counsel can think "backward" as well as "forward" by making sure that there is a plan to achieve each step necessary to obtain the required result.

For example, if the goal is a large money judgment to compensate for breach of a contract, counsel should consider:

- what the judgment will look like *and*

- what the jury verdict form and answers will look like *and*

- what closing arguments should be made *and*

- what jury instructions should be given *and*

- what evidence should be in the record *and*

- what discovery is necessary to obtain that evidence and avoid pretrial dismissal *and*

- how the pleadings should be crafted to facilitate that discovery *and*

- what informal investigation is necessary to craft those pleadings satisfactorily.

While doing this, counsel should also have in mind potentially effective means of settling the dispute, including "win-win" situations in which the defendant can provide satisfactory recompense to the client in a relatively painless manner. For example, if the breach of contract was shrinkage of the client's sales territory, perhaps the client would be better off with a re-instated, redrawn or expanded territory, something the defendant is willing to provide because this allows it to avoid having to immediately pay cash to your client. Or perhaps a tort plaintiff will accept a series of compensatory payments, which is easier for the defendant to afford, rather than insisting on lump sum compensation.

With these long-term perspectives, counsel then can better execute the following steps required for pursuing client goals through civil litigation.

1. Determining Who to Sue

This is often not as easy as it sounds. Sure, you know who generally wronged the client. But what is the legal entity that owns or operates the sandwich shop that engaged in discriminatory hiring or left the floor in a dangerous condition resulting in the client's fall and injury? Presumably, counsel has traced the relevant business records and identified relevant individuals or organizations at fault. But there may be gaps in knowledge that can only be closed, if at all, with the aid the litigation process and discovery. Some defendants may need to be named as "John Doe" or "Jane Doe" parties until you get enough information to identify them (*see* Chapter 5 regarding complaints and pleading).

Even when you know who everyone is, you still might not want to sue everyone. For example, some arguably culpable people might be impor-tant witnesses that can incriminate more culpable people. Why sue the bar patron who simply failed to shout "duck" and risk making him defensive when what you really want is for him to finger the goon who hit the client with a beer bottle? Likewise, you might wish to concentrate on parties with insurance or sufficient wealth to compensate the client. For example, in a barroom brawl case, your best target financially is often the bar that failed to provide adequate security or served liquor to obviously drunk patrons. The bar ordinarily has more liability insurance and more money than the physical perpetrator of the assault.

Conversely, you may in some cases make a special effort to sue some parties not because they are especially culpable or wealthy but because their presence in the case confers certain procedural advantages. For example, as you will see in Chapter 1, in a state court action naming a defendant from the same state as the plaintiff can prevent out-of-state defendants from removing the lawsuit from state court to federal court. Plaintiffs who prefer state court to federal court frequently do this—and it is perfectly ethical as long as your decision to name the in-state defendant comports with Fed. R. Civ. P. 11 (*see* Chapter 5) even if the in-state defendant is not your primary target on the merits.

2. Determining Where to Sue

Forum selection (often discussed under the pejorative of "**forum shopping**") is a significant part of lawyering. In many cases, a prospective plaintiff may sue in more than one jurisdiction (*e.g.*, state or federal, New York or New Jersey). In choosing between different states, counsel needs to consider the degree to which certain possible forums lack sufficient contact with certain defendants (Chapter 2 on personal jurisdiction fleshes this out). Assuming that several different states would all be permissible locations for the lawsuit, counsel must then consider practical factors such as the composition of the bench and jury pool as well as the venue within the state that would obtain (*e.g.*, rural v. urban). Some places are more plaintiff-friendly and others tend to be more supportive of defendants. Some jury pools are known for high awards and others are stingy.

Considering State Court vs. Federal Court. State Courts tend to be organized on a county basis. Urban state court districts are usually one county, but some state court districts in rural areas can encompass several counties. But even the largest state court districts are usually not as large as federal court districts. This means that the federal jury will usually, but not always, be drawn from a larger geographic area. Because state court districts are usually smaller and more compact, you have a better idea of the demographic characteristics of the jury pool and whether they match up with the demography you would prefer for a jury that hears your client's case.

Federal court judges are appointed. District court trial judges and appellate court judges are appointed for life and can only be removed for misbehavior such as conviction of a crime. Bankruptcy judges and magistrate judges (who often preside over discovery disputes and other pretrial matters) are appointed for a term of years rather than for life but otherwise enjoy similar job security. State court judicial selection varies. Although several states follow something close to the federal model, 80 percent of the states have judicial elections of some type and in perhaps 20 states judicial elections seem close to indistinguishable from the rock-em, sock-em world of electoral politics generally. State judges, having less insulation from electoral politics, may be less independent and lawyers always have concerns that a judge's rulings may be influenced by the power, prominence, and wealth of a litigant or counsel—particularly if the litigant has been a substantial contributor in the past or can retaliate against a disliked judge at the next election through campaign contributions, attack ads on television, and the like.

And, of course, there may be differences in the rules of procedure and their application. If, for example, state rules of civil procedure provide broader discovery and you are at an informational disadvantage relative to the defendant, you may prefer state court. Or the federal procedural rules may permit you to join more claims and defendants in one action than do the state rules. If you want to ensure that everyone connected with the dispute is brought into the action and that all claims are aired, this weighs in favor of selecting federal court—provided there are not other factors weighing more heavily in favor of state court. Or state law precedent may make it easier for a plaintiff to survive a Rule 12 dismissal motion or a summary judgment motion.

3. Judge vs. Jury

Once within a chosen forum, one needs to decide whether a bench trial with the judge not only presiding over case presentation but also making findings of fact is preferable to a jury trial, assuming that you otherwise have right to a jury trial (*see* Chapter 16). If one of the other parties to the case demands its right to jury trial, your desire for a bench trial is ineffective. In spite of bilateralism of the right to jury trial, there may be agreement on a bench trial (or at least a failure to make a timely demand for a jury trial). The conventional wisdom is that plaintiffs want juries while defendants are inclined more toward judges—but again, be careful of the conventional wisdom. Consider the type of case, the jury pool, and the characteristics of the bench. You may even know the identity of the specific judge assigned to the before the time for demanding jury trial has lapsed.

4. Considerations of Applicable Law

As you will learn in Chapter 4, courts do not ordinarily apply general legal principles but usually apply specific federal law or the law of a particular state. The applicable state law may not be that of the court's home state but in deciding what law to use, the court will use the "choice of law" approach of the state in which the court is located. In addition, the conventional wisdom is that if the issue is close, most judges opt for applying forum state law because it is the law with which they are more familiar and comfortable and because this creates less work and reduced risk of error (e.g, a good judge can learn a lot about a different state's law in a relatively short time but will almost certainly be more proficient in applying familiar law). In many cases, state-to-state differences in law are minimal. But where there are material differences in potentially applicable state law, counsel must think harder about which law will apply and whether the choice of law rules of one court are more likely to yield favorable law than those of another court.

5. Deciding What Claims to Bring

After having investigated and conducted a Rule 11 analysis, you know what claims you are permitted to bring. But do you want to bring all of them? Some may create side issues you don't want. Or they may be weaker, thus consuming your resources or detracting from your strong claims. On the other hand, as discussed in Chapter 12, the scope of discovery in federal court and many state courts is linked to the claims and defenses that have been pleaded. If you don't plead a claim, you may be denied discovery that is generally helpful to your case.

Realize as well that you are not required to give each claim the same attention. You can plead a claim and then leave it relatively undeveloped. For that reason, most lawyers plead all non-frivolous claims, at least at the outset. Later on, you might amend the complaint and delete some claims or stipulate to dismissal. But you do not want to unwittingly omit a claim and then later realize it was a strong basis for recovery. As noted in Chapter 20, if a claim is not brought, it often cannot be brought later after the conclusion of the matter.

6. Drafting the Complaint

Having thought through the matter in light of investigation and research, you are now ready to draft the complaint. In addition to determining the claims you will make, think about whether you want a bare bones document (as discussed in Chapter 6, relatively little detail is required in most cases) or one that provides more of a narrative or even a "settlement brochure" for opposing counsel. Or, if what you really want is a detailed document likely to prompt a settlement offer from the opponent, this might be more effectively done through a well-drafted (and not excessively bellicose) letter containing supporting documentation tabbed for easy reading.

7. Crafting Disclosures

As you will learn in Chapters 12 and 13, federal courts require each party to make basic disclosures at the outset of the case regarding information such as witnesses, documents, damages sought, and applicable insurance. One advantage of being plaintiff is that you know the lawsuit is coming and can begin preparation. By contrast, the defendant usually must wait until the complaint and then begin reacting to the claim.

Expected Disclosures From the Defendant. From pre-complaint investigation, you will know a good deal—but not everything. Be ready to examine defendants' initial disclosures (required under Fed. R. Civ. P. 26 as discussed in Chapter 12) for confirmation and study the new information provided by the disclosures.

8. Seeking Discovery

After assessing the disclosures on top of the information you acquired informally, you will know what information you still need and can craft a discovery plan for attaining it. More on this in Chapter 12. Will you need expert consultants or witnesses in order to prevail in the matter? This is part of the discovery you must provide but it helps to think about retention and deployment of experts in the context of the overall discovery plans (and battles) of the case.

Anticipating the Defendant's Discovery Efforts. In similar fashion, you can visualize the other side of the case and anticipate defendant's information requests and prepare to respond. Often the response will be simply to provide what is requested. But there are different means of providing requested information. Select the type that is most economical for your client and reflects positively on your client—but remember that you have ethical obligations. You cannot distort or destroy information that is validly subject to discovery.

Possible Limitations on Discovery. Along these lines, consider whether to seek protective orders limiting discovery as well as motions to compel discovery you wish to obtain. Think about which protective orders are likely to be necessary What types of protective orders? How do you support your position? Will additional research be required?

9. The Potential Utility of Pretrial Motions

As a plaintiff, the practical goal in most cases is to avoid pretrial dismissal or trimming of the case and to obtain a settlement or judgment after trial. Defendants typically hope for pretrial dismissal of at least some claims and thus will do more planning of Rule 12 motions to dismiss, Rule 56 motions for summary judgment, and the like, while plaintiffs will devote efforts to planning the defense of such motions. Remember, however, that not every case requires extensive motion practice. This may not be cost effective, particularly if a motion is not likely to succeed.

10. Assembling the Legal Team

Should you retain co-counsel for the case? On that note, should you prosecute the case yourself—or is this the type of case on which you should affiliate co-counsel or even refer the matter to other counsel. The Rules of Professional Conduct in most cases permit fee-sharing between referring counsel and trial counsel so it is less excusable than ever for a lawyer to take on a client if the lawyer is not competent to handle the matter. In the past when referral fee-sharing was banned, lawyers had a financial incentive to hold on to cases that might be outside their competence and resource level. But today, a lawyer can serve as an intake lawyer, refer matters to specialized counsel if necessary, and still be compensated provided the client consents and other conditions of ABA Model Rule of Professional Conduct 1.5 are satisfied.

11. Litigation as a Subset of Civil Dispute Resolution

Disputes often arise and are resolved without invocation of the courts. Although civil litigation remains an option when less formal methods fail, it is important to remember that most disputes are resolved through informal methods such as shrugging off small slights and injuries, **negotiated resolution**, **administrative tribunals**, **mediation**, **arbitration**, or another form of ADR.

"Alternative"? Dispute Resolution (ADR). Many in the legal profession (and laypersons involved in dispute resolution) may object to our labeling non-litigation outcomes as "alternative" dispute resolution and argue that the correct term is "dispute resolution" so as not to implicitly favor or promote litigation as the dispute resolution norm, which to some extent occurs whenever we label anything but litigation to be the "alternative."

Although we understand the sentiment and concede that most dispute resolution in the world does not involve complete adjudication, we continue to believe that ADR is the correct term both because of its historical roots (the non-adjudicatory dispute resolution movement arose as a proposed alternative promoted by critics of litigation) and because in most cases litigation is in fact the default method of resolving disputes when the disputants cannot agree on another method. Further, much successful ADR occurs "in the shadow of the law" to use a memorable phrase popularized by two early ADR scholars.

When upset with the conduct of another person or entity, the "victim" has a number of options ranging from simple endurance or forgiveness to full scale litigation. The most prevalent form of ADR is direct **negotiation** leading to compromise and resolution. Where the disputants are unable to reach an accommodation by themselves, they may invoke the aid of a neutral third-party for **mediation** of their disputes. Or they may submit the matter to arbitration, a less ritualized form of adjudication. **Arbitration** may also be agreed upon by contract prior to the arising of an actual dispute. In addition, there are several common variants or hybrids of these major ADR devices.

Negotiation is the most common form of dispute resolution. Just as the name implies, it involves disputants discussing means of resolving their dispute without resort to trial or trial substitutes. There is a substantial emerging literature regarding effective negotiation, mediation, arbitration, and other ADR methods that is well worth consulting for any lawyer.

The book inaugurating the modern negotiation discipline is Roger Fischer & William Ury's GETTING TO YES: NEGOTIATING AGREEMENT WITHOUT

GIVING IN (1981), a classic, with several subsequent or revised editions. Key insights of *Getting to Yes* are that people (not only disputants but prospective collaborators) should bargain over interests rather than positions and that more information and greater trust often improves the odds for successful negotiation.

The illustration they used was one of two persons fighting over the rights to an orange. If bargaining over positions, the likely outcome is splitting the orange down the middle, a result that gets each 50 percent of what they want. But what if it turns out that one wants the orange for the pulp to make juice while the other wants it for the rind to bake a pie? If the parties know this, they can each get 100 percent of what they want, a true win-win situation. But to develop this information, the parties will need enough trust and candor to produce this information that can lead to a better result.

Limits of class time will prevent most civil procedure instructors from doing anything more than touching on negotiation theory or particular ADR techniques. Excellent sources for further information include:

- STEPHEN J. WARE & DENNIS NOLAN, PRINCIPLES OF ARBITRATION LAW (2014);

- MAUREEN ARELLANO WESTON & STEPHEN K. HUBER, ARBITRATION: CASES AND MATERIALS (3d ed. 2011);

- CARRIE MENKEL-MEADOW, ET AL., DISPUTE RESOLUTION: BEYOND THE ADVERSARIAL MODEL (2d ed. 2012);

- LEONARD RISKIN, ET AL., DISPUTE RESOLUTION AND LAWYERS (5th ed. 2014);

- STEPHEN J. WARE, PRINCIPLES OF ALTERNATIVE DISPUTE RESOLUTION (2d ed. 2007);

- JAMES J. ALFINI, ET AL., MATERIAL ON MEDIATION THEORY AND PRACTICE (2d ed. 2006);

- ROBERT H. MNOOKIN, ET AL., BEYOND WINNING: NEGOTIATING TO CREATE VALUE IN DEALS AND DISPUTES (2004).

Important to negotiation is each respective party's **"BATNA" (best alternative to a negotiated agreement)**. For most disputants, this means the realistic range of likely outcomes if the matter is fully litigated. Determining this requires counsel to assess both the chances of winning, the likely damages awarded at trial, any proportional assignment of fault that may affect the award, and additional potential items of recovery such as prejudgment interest, costs, counsel fees, or possible punitive damages.

In addition, counsel must assess the realistic odds of collecting a judgment from the opponent. If the opponent is trending toward bankruptcy, a "bird in the hand" settlement now might be better than a larger award after trial that becomes uncollectible or reduced because of bankruptcy.

> But be aware: as you will learn in bankruptcy class, payments made too close to the filing of a bankruptcy petition or in an effort to defraud other creditors may be pulled back into the debtor's estate.

A common approach to evaluating a case is to calculate the likely amount of damages that can be proven at trial multiplied by the probability of winning on the merits regarding a negligence, contract breach, or statutory violation claim. For example, an unperformed contract may have cost plaintiff $100,000 in lost revenue but there is a 50-50 shot that defendant can persuade judge or jury that the nonperformance was excused by the **"force majeure"** events beyond its control. Assuming a 50-50 shot at winning at trial, the value of the claim is $50,000.

If, however, the breach of contract is clear and there is no defense with a possibility of succeeding and the contract contains a **liquidated damages** clause stipulating that in the event of breach, $100,000 will be paid, the plaintiff appears to have a claim with an almost ironclad value of $100,000. But even in such cases, the value of the claim may need to be discounted by the costs of pursuing the claim to even an almost certainly successful judgment, the possibility that collecting the judgment will be difficult (*e.g.*, if the defendant heads to a foreign country that refuses to honor U.S. legal claims or files bankruptcy), and the possibility, however miniscule, that even when the claim is very strong, things could go wrong at trial.

In a case this strong, plaintiff would ordinarily not take much of a discount—but as always, the totality of the circumstances is important.

Mediation involves use of a neutral third party to facilitate discussion between the parties and attempt to achieve a negotiated resolution through the aid of the mediator. Although it is controversial in some academic circles, most practitioners agree that it is permissible for the mediator to express views about the relative strength of various party positions and arguments so that they can better gauge the likely outcomes from litigation if the mediation is not fruitful.

Mediators add value by meeting separately with the parties to build trust and help develop information in order to improve the odds for settlement. They can also (unless it is prohibited as too evaluative) provide a useful, arms-length assessment of the claim in serving as a sounding board for the disputants.

> This divide over apt approaches to mediation is generally labeled a clash between **"facilitative"** mediation (the type most favored by most ADR scholars) and **"evaluative"** mediation, which appears to be common and perhaps even dominant in practice. Some have argued that the best mediation is inherently **"eclectic"** and should combine and alternate between the two styles as demanded by the needs of the case.

Early Neutral Evaluation involves an expressly evaluative process by a neutral third party, one who advises the parties as to the neutral's impressions of the case. This provides the parties with a dose of reality that can be useful in dialing down the expectations of the parties. For example, a plaintiff may not be impressed that defendant thinks the claim is worthless. But if former Judge Smith, serving as a neutral evaluator, tells the plaintiff that his damage estimate is too high, this is likely to bring the plaintiff's demands to a lower range that may in turn encourage a serious offer by the defendant.

Arbitration is a determination of the dispute conducted not by judge and jury but by an arbitrator or a panel of arbitrators. A single arbitrator must be **neutral**. Where there is a panel of arbitrators (usually three), all may be neutral or the procedure may call for each disputant to select a **"party-appointed"** arbitrator, with these arbitrators subsequently selecting a neutral **"umpire."** Arbitration operates in practice much like a bench trial but with relaxed evidentiary standards.

In addition, the Rules of Evidence do not as a technical matter apply to arbitrations although they may be used as a guide to admissibility. Also, arbitration providers such as the American Arbitration Association (AAA) and Judicial Arbitration & Mediation Services (JAMS) often have their own rules of procedure and evidence that differ from those applicable in court.

Pursuant to the Federal Arbitration Act, 9 U.S.C. §§ 1-16, arbitration awards can be turned into enforceable judgments upon proper presentation to the courts. An arbitration award may also be vacated or modified, but only according to the provisions of the Act, which provides for far narrower and more deferential review than one finds in an appeal from a district court trial. State versions of the Uniform Arbitration Act are to the same effect.

These Acts provide that agreements to arbitrate are specifically enforceable and that the parties to such agreement can be compelled to arbitrate. Since the 1980s, the U.S. Supreme Court has shown strong support for compelling arbitration even when the arbitration clause in question was contained in a standardized, complex contract that was not expressly negotiated or perhaps not understood by one or more of the parties to the contract.

Mixed Methods or Hybrids. A variety of combination methods of dispute resolution exist.

- **High-low arbitration** involves the parties stipulating to a range of acceptable awards and the arbitrators making a decision within that range. The type of arbitration used in Major League Baseball requires the arbitrators to chose either the player's proposed salary or that of the owner. The idea is that this should encourage both sides to be reasonable rather than taking extreme positions in an effort to anchor the arbitrator's thinking on one end or another of the continuum.

- Some courts have found success with a **summary jury trial** in which persons from the jury pool are brought in (and usually not told that their verdict will not be binding) and presented with opening arguments, a witness and key documents from each side, and then closing arguments. The jury's experimental verdict is then used in a manner similar to early neutral evaluation to attempt to make the parties reasonable in their negotiation positions.

- In **Med-Arb** (short for mediation combined with arbitration), the mediator attempts a facilitated negotiated settlement but in the event of disagreement is permitted to morph into an arbitrator and decide some or all of the dispute.

A Short List of Useful Resources for Learning and Researching Civil Procedure.

An introductory civil procedure text cannot comprehensively address the many nuances of civil litigation. Students wishing additional information will find the following sources particularly helpful:

- STEVEN BAICKER-MCKEE, WILLIAM M. JANSSEN & JOHN B. CORR, A STUDENT'S GUIDE TO THE FEDERAL RULES OF CIVIL PROCEDURE (2014);

- WILLIAM M. JANSSEN AND STEVEN BAICKER-MCKEE, MASTERING MULTIPLE CHOICE FOR FEDERAL CIVIL PROCEDURE MBE BAR PREP AND 1L EXAM PREP (2014)

- DAVID F. HERR, ROGER S. HAYDOCK & JEFFREY W. STEMPEL, FUNDAMENTALS OF LITIGATION PRACTICE (2014 ed.);

- ROGERS S. HAYDOCK, DAVID F. HERR & JEFFREY W. STEMPEL, FUNDAMENTALS OF PRETRIAL LITIGATION (9th ed. 2013);

- GEOFFREY C. HAZARD, ET AL., CIVIL PROCEDURE (6th ed. 2011);

- LARRY L. TEPLY & RALPH U. WHITTEN, CIVIL PROCEDURE (4th ed. 2009).

- Students interested in presentation of additional leading cases on a topic or the background stories of key cases can consult LINDA S. MULLENIX, LEADING CASES IN CIVIL PROCEDURE (2d ed. 2012) and KEVIN M. CLERMONT (ED.), CIVIL PROCEDURE STORIES (2d ed. 2008).

Appendix: United States Judicial Circuits

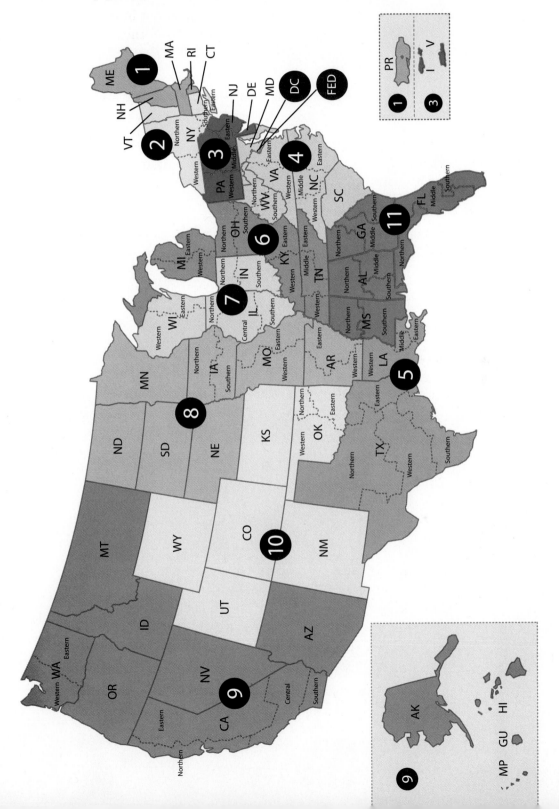

INDEX